Praise for *The Meanest Man in Congress*

"From his youth in a rough corner of Texas to his service in the Marines in World War II and on to Congress to help build Lyndon Johnson's Great Society, Jack Brooks's story is full of lessons for lawmakers, for voters, for Americans searching for meaning in confusing times. The McNultys have created a highly readable account of a fascinating, important man's life and times." — CHARLES MADIGAN, author, reporter, professor

"Tim and Brendan McNulty provide us with a much-needed biography of Congressman Jack Brooks, who was a leading figure among two generations of Lone Star political legends that included Sam Rayburn, Lyndon Johnson, and many others. Any student of national politics in the mid-twentieth century will relish looking again at those turbulent times through the squinting, purposeful eyes of Beaumont's Congressman Jack Brooks." — CAL JILLSON, professor of political science at Southern Methodist University, author of *The American Dream: In History, Politics, and Fiction*

"Right when we all seem to have forgotten what public service and political compromise ought to look like, along comes *The Meanest Man in Congress* to remind us. Jack Brooks—crusty, colorful, and yes, mean—leaps off the pages into our collective consciousness in this timely biography." — JAY ROOT, *Texas Tribune* investigative reporter and author of *Oops! A Diary from the 2012 Campaign Trail*

"Finely reported and illuminated by exquisite detail, Timothy and Brendan McNulty's work hurtles readers back through time to the challenges of a tumultuous twentieth century. This comprehensive work on the improbable life of Jack Brooks is a reminder of a time when our nation was not governed by a zero-sum, winner-take-all ethos that divides Americans and the world into us and them." — GEORGE DE LAMA, president of the Eisenhower Fellowships, former managing editor of the *Chicago Tribune*

"When I came to Congress, Jack Brooks proved a guide and friend. He was a master legislator, canny operator, and giant of the House, who brought a formidable mix of charm and intellect to the fight for liberty, equality and justice for the American people. His principled leadership, richly chronicled in this first biography, leaves an extraordinary legacy." — NANCY PELOSI, Speaker of the U.S. House of Representatives

"Cigar-chomping, irascible, and fiercely dedicated to his beliefs, Brooks shaped Texas and national politics for four decades. A fascinating window into the political history of the post-World War II era and a darn fun read." — **BRANDON ROTTINGHAUS, professor of political science, University of Houston**

"The McNultys do a superb job documenting Brooks's fascinating personality and career. But this father-and-son writing team goes beyond Brooks himself to chronicle how a villainous turn in our politics made us the divided nation we are today. A thorough account and enjoyable read." — **JAMES O'SHEA, author and former editor of the** *Los Angeles Times* **and managing editor of the** *Chicago Tribune*

"From the Great Society to Watergate to the Iran-Contra scandal to the Clinton crime bill, Congressman Jack Brooks was a larger-than-life figure in our nation's political history. His dedication to vigorous congressional oversight of the executive branch should stand as a role model for today's legislators. *The Meanest Man in Congress* tells his remarkable story." — **TERRY MCAULIFFE, former Virginia governor**

"An eminently readable biography of one of our nation's longest-serving Congress-men that also chronicles the era when the words 'bipartisan' and 'compromise' were not anathema. This book provides a reminder of how government can work when patriotism supersedes partisanship, and how a politician's relatives can use their status for greater good as opposed to personal enrichment." — **KERRY LUFT, former Washington bureau chief, Tribune Co., former news editor,** *Bloomberg Politics*

"I can't think of any member of Congress who did more for America's space program than Jack Brooks. As the book points out, Brooks strengthened NASA during its formative years and later saved the International Space Station (ISS) in the post-Cold War era when Congress sought to cancel Big Science program. Today, a quarter of a century later, the ISS still circles high above Earth as a symbol of America's ability to bring the nations of the world together in peaceful exploration of space." — **DANIEL S. GOLDIN, 9th NASA Administrator, 1992–2001**

"This is a book of nostalgia for the days of good governance represented by a crafty, persistent, and honorable congressman who put country above party to pass monumental legislation. Reading this biography—a Herculean task of research I much admired—can make you weep over the passing of those times, when skillful legislators could navigate through partisan politics to higher ground." — **DAVID K. SHIPLER, former** *New York Times* **correspondent and Pulitzer Prize-winning author**

THE MEANEST MAN
IN CONGRESS

Constructive change doesn't come just because you think something isn't right . . . it is tough, tedious work. . . . I've tried to change a thousand things in government and only managed a few.

— JACK BROOKS

THE
MEANEST MAN
IN CONGRESS

Jack Brooks and the

Making of an American Century

BRENDAN AND TIM MCNULTY

FOREWORD BY JIM WRIGHT

NEWSOUTH BOOKS

Montgomery

To Genevieve Anne McNulty, wife and mother

❧

NewSouth Books
105 S. Court Street
Montgomery, AL 36104

Library of Congress Cataloging-in-Publication Data

Names: McNulty, Brendan, author. | McNulty, Tim (Timothy John), 1947- author.
Title: The meanest man in Congress : Jack Brooks and the making of an American
    century / Brendan and Tim McNulty.
Description: Montgomery : NewSouth Books, [2019] | Includes bibliographical
    references and index.
Identifiers: LCCN 2018060111 (print) | LCCN 2019000857 (ebook) | ISBN
    9781603064118 (Ebook) | ISBN 9781588383211 (hardcover)
Subjects: LCSH: Brooks, Jack, 1922-2012. | United States. Congress. House—
    Biography. | Legislators—United States—Biography. | United States—Politics
and government—20th century. | Texas—Politics and government—20th century.
Classification: LCC E840.8.B765 (ebook) | LCC E840.8.B765 M36 2019 (print) |
    DDC 328.73/092 [B] —dc23
LC record available at https://lccn.loc.gov/2018060111)

Design by Randall Williams

Printed in the United States of America by the Maple Press

Contents

Foreword

JIM WRIGHT (1922–2015)

Jack Brooks was one of a kind. Everybody who really knew him recognized Jack as an original. He was a man of strong convictions and unambiguous loyalties, impelling likes and some dislikes, both of which he could express in remarkable clarity, force, and eloquence. Jack was no shrinking violet and was little given to pussyfooting or vague nuance.

Nor would he ever stoop to being part clown or publicity hound. Counting his forty-two enormously productive years in the U.S. Congress, his six in the Texas legislature, and his combat time spent overseas as a fighting Marine in World War II, Jack Brooks served our country professionally and with unique distinction for a full half century. It will surprise some to read in this book of the major national reforms quietly and efficiently sponsored by Brooks. He wasn't doing these things for bragging rights. He never tried to hog the spotlight. Jack was focused on results for Americans.

His approach to crafting legislation, of which ordinary millions of Americans are the unknowing beneficiaries, reflected one of his favorite hobbies—repairing and perfecting clocks and watches. In both pursuits, he was a perfectionist. He always brought the same patience and professionalism to working a major bill through Congress that he liked to spend making an errant clock resume running or stop losing five minutes a day.

There's an old saying that Congress is composed of two types—the show horses and the workhorses. Even when filling a leadership role which may require a bit of the former, Jack Brooks never lost sight of a need to be and to encourage the latter.

I learned a long time ago that it was hard to get ahead of Jack on anything. He was exactly four days older than I, and he never permitted me to forget it—nor to catch up—during the three-and-a-half decades we served together in the U.S. Congress, one of the few institutions in society where seniority is more valued than riches or royalty.

Returning from World War II, Jack and I managed to get ourselves elected to the Texas legislature in 1946. We were both twenty-three. On one cold January morning, I showed up for work at the storied state capitol wearing a new, gray Homburg hat. It had been a Christmas present. Jack, who preferred the five-gallon Texas western with a broad brim, shook his head ruefully. "Jim," he said, "my constituents wouldn't vote for me if they saw me wearing a hat like that!"

It was a clue to Jack's nature. Studiedly down-to-earth. Straightforward. Unpretentious. Plainspoken and plainly dressed. But unashamedly ambitious and clearly going somewhere, while never forgetting his roots and where he was from.

Life had not been easy for Jack. A child of the Great Depression, he suffered the agonizing death of his father and discovered prematurely the harsh disciplines of hard times and hard work. Undaunted, Jack struggled his way through college and journalism school at the University of Texas. He was, when I came to know him, studying and sweating through law school. Sharp needles of memory would prod him throughout a distinguished career in which he did great things to lighten the blows of adversity upon economically and culturally afflicted millions who've faced growing up in America unprotected by the soft and feathery cushions of financial fortune.

Jack and I both loved the Texas legislature in those days, but we both dreamed of going to Congress, where we believed we could do much more to promote equality of opportunity for those who, by cruel circumstance, were bereft of the chance to rise in fulfillment of that peculiarly American promise of upward mobility.

Jack, characteristically, got to Washington two years ahead of me; he was first elected in 1952 from Texas's most southeasterly district and I from the north-central region in 1954.

Mindful of my friend's earlier advice, I had not brought my Homburg, and Jack again gave me good advice: "Two things are above all important up here, Jim," he offered. "Without those two, you're born dead. The first is a superb staff, and the second is the right committee assignments. Staff can make or break you. You'll get blamed for any errors they commit, and you'll get credit for every miracle they perform. Pick them able and not afraid of long hours, and inspire their personal loyalty. You alone can do that.

"Then get yourself appointed to a committee that fits your convictions and your constituency's needs. In other words, one you can use to make national headway in what you stand for, and one whose good works can benefit the folks who elected you."

With the right mix of ideals and pragmatism, Jack had chosen one committee, Government Operations, which he reckoned might offer a more rapid rise on the seniority ladder. As a consequence of Jack's clock-like calculation, he became chairman of this committee with oversight jurisdiction into all the functions of American government when still a relatively young member, quite an accomplishment in those sometimes geriatric-dominated years of the U.S. House of Representatives.

Jack also aspired to serve on the prestigious Judiciary Committee, for which his legal training had prepared him. Thus, he'd combined one panel of early opportunity with another of wide, inherent power. No wonder he got a lot done in those forty-two years.

Jack's massive legislative accomplishments include such blockbuster laws as the Civil Rights Act of 1964 and the Voting Rights Act of 1965. In 1989, after fourteen years of serving as chairman of Government Operations, Jack advanced to the coveted chairmanship of the House Judiciary Committee. From this post, he crafted the Omnibus Crime Control Act of 1991 and other widely heralded pillars of our lawful society.

Throughout his tenure in Congress, Jack was known for insisting on open, competitive contracts for work on government projects, including those dealing with new technologies. His work is widely credited with saving many billions of taxpayer dollars and with improving the performance of private as well as government technology.

Jack Brooks's second imperative—to look after the needs of his home constituency—was attended to with fervor. In the state legislature he had demonstrated his gratitude to Lamar Junior College (which he had attended on a scholarship) by leading the effort to make it a four-year state institution. In Congress, he continued to attend to its needs.

Gulf Coast shipping owes greatly to Jack's legislative championing of ports and deep-water channels that serve the needs of that burgeoning region. No less attentive was he to the needs of public health and the creation of facilities greatly enhancing the University of Texas medical branch in Galveston.

Yet, in a very real sense, each of these legislative redwoods was rooted in soil generously watered and fertilized for years by thousands of small deeds performed individually for humble folk. Small indeed to the government, perhaps, but at the moment wondrously important to the individual involved.

A serviceman's father dies, and he desperately needs a weekend pass for the funeral, maybe even a possible reassignment to a base near his aging mother. An employer of a local company must request that her passport application be expedited, allowing her to make the company-assigned schedule. Bewildered, each entitled by law to enter a door the private citizen simply cannot locate in the maze of bureaucracy. In the average district, a congressman sympathetic to plain, average people and not deluded that he is too important to concern himself with their problems, with willing help from his staff can assist literally thousands of worthy people each year.

It has been argued that an assiduous concern for individual private citizens in the human crises of their lives provides the rock-solid foundation of mutual understanding and respect that enables a conscientious representative to be a national lawmaker to follow his sincere convictions and knowledge in the big, widely consequential, even if emotionally controversial subjects, like civil rights laws or war and peace.

Virtue, some say, is its own reward. I'll leave you to decide that one. I'll just tell you that Jack wound up with a splendidly beautiful family—his wife, Charlotte, and marvelously successful children—and more money from wise and patient investments that he made on his own than almost anyone could need.

His story is one to remember. Read this and enjoy. The next time somebody tries to tell you a decent, honorable, hardworking guy can't get anywhere in American politics, or in the U.S. Congress, remember Jack Brooks, and rejoice.

The late Jim Wright, Speaker of the House of Representatives from 1987 to 1989, wrote this foreword before his own passing in 2015 in anticipation of this manuscript's completion. The text has been edited for clarity.

Preface

It was Jack Brooks's wish that his story be preserved for future generations, and before he passed, he and his wife, Charlotte, his colleagues, and his staffers spent untold hours sharing their memories of his life. There are traces of Brooks sprinkled throughout our collective past, yet this book is the first time this extraordinary American's story has been told in full. The project would not have been possible without the support of the Brooks family and friends, his congressional papers carefully stored at the Dolph Briscoe Center for American History, and access to his personal effects.

He was a loving father and husband and a loyal friend, but this book specifically looks at his congressional career and the contributions he made to American life. Given the vast breadth and complexity of moments that he lived through and shaped, it cannot be a definitive account. Perspectives will differ, and the country is still struggling to understand the finer points of the social contracts and public responsibilities of that era. But it is our hope that this account pays tribute to his labors; reveals how good governance can be achieved through nonideological, principled work; and serves as a leaping-off point for future generations of students, politicians, and citizens interested in serving the common good.

T. McNulty, B. McNulty

Acknowledgments

Acknowledging all the individuals and institutions that helped bring a nonfiction work to fruition is a daunting task. While writing is solitary, the history, ideas, and inspiration that go into a biography of such a public man as Jack Brooks are contributed by those who knew him best, those who worked with (and sometimes opposed) him, and those who were touched by his character and distinct personality. The most intimate insights into his life came from, of course, his family. His wife, Charlotte Collins Brooks, cherished her husband of more than fifty years and remembered details of family life that Brooks himself may have been oblivious to, including the sight of Texas Governor Dolph Briscoe charging up in his dusty black Cadillac just in time for Brooks's wedding.

Brooks's eldest son, Jeb, was not only a champion of this work but also a driving force in focusing on how his father's career provides a striking example of good governance. Brooks's older daughter, Kate, who was painstaking in locating photographs, and younger daughter, Kim, who kept track of the writing progress, all provided a deep look at the private man who was the public politician. The late Marie Brooks Manry, his sister, recalled much of his early story and the family's genealogy back to before the Civil War. Erik North, a family friend, ably recalled many of the shared family stories over the years.

Brooks's office staff, in Beaumont and Washington, and Dorothea Lewis Wynn in Galveston, were invaluable in recalling their time with Brooks and in pointing the way to interview subjects and research documents. Dianna Coffey, who worked in both the Washington office and the district office in Beaumont, shared her astounding memory, contacts, and insights throughout. Gene Peters and Sharon Matts in Washington, D.C., recalled key moments in legislative history and the dynamics of Brooks's office life, along with his relationships with both colleagues and subordinates. Matts, who was one of only a dozen or so women who served as a congressional office manager at the time, recalled delicious anecdotes about Brooks's sly humor. Coffey, Matts, and Peters were exceedingly generous with their time discussing "the Chairman" and reading the early manuscript to correct errors or misunderstandings.

Former Speaker of the House Jim Wright happily recalled his long friendship with Brooks and the political intrigues they shared as seatmates in the Texas legislature and on the floor of the House of Representatives. Wright, whose congressional district included Fort Worth, was also with Brooks during the tragic assassination of John F. Kennedy in Dallas.

Many others in Beaumont were generous and absolutely key to remembering the life and times of Brooks. Federal District Judge Thad Heartfield spent hours going over important and delightful moments of his friendship with Brooks. So did Hubert Oxford III and Wayne Reaud, two of the most prominent lawyers in the region, who were important to Brooks's career.

Others in Beaumont who were instrumental in understanding Brooks's impact on his district and how he campaigned over the course of forty-two years include William "Bill" Lytle, who introduced Brooks in the predawn light to union members reporting for work at plant gates, and the late Cleve Nisby, who helped coordinate his appearances to the African American community in Beaumont and elsewhere. Lupe Flores shared his personal memories of working with Brooks, as did Representative Nick Lampson and state legislator Carl Parker.

Former staffers such as Jon Yarowsky contributed telling stories about their boss. Key committee staff, including Jim Lewin and his wife, Carol, generously sat for hours recalling the often complex negotiations over legislation. Harry McAdams was a fascinating lunch companion in Austin as he detailed the "sausage making" of critical legislation.

Sinclair and Shawn Oubre were diligent in their search for flaws in this manuscript, and any copy editing errors are the result of the authors overlooking their corrections.

Terri Davis at Lamar University discussed the politics of Brooks's portion of eastern Texas and the Louisiana border. Robert Robertson, a local historian, was extremely generous in sharing his own research into Brooks's life and career.

Before this writing began, the Brooks family organized a video project to record the memories of many friends and colleagues. Those videos shot by Jon Bassana proved invaluable, especially as some of the interviewees are now deceased. Former Texas Governor Dolph Briscoe, for instance, was a "bosom friend" of Brooks since their college days at the University of Texas. Hunting and fishing companions over the decades, they remained close until Briscoe's death.

Brooks's office records were quickly packaged after his stunning political loss in 1994. They first went to Lamar University, where his office furnishings are arranged in a special room in the library. Later, the boxes of hundreds of cubic feet of records were moved to the Dolph Briscoe Center for American History at the University of Texas. Staffers there and across the small sunlit courtyard at the Lyndon B. Johnson Presidential Library were gracious in fulfilling requests. The scholarship at both institutions is astounding. Another resource that is a hallmark of America's transparent freedom of information is the Library of Congress and the Congressional Research Service, which provides the political leadership with historic context and accurate accounts of every aspect of life in the United States.

To focus on specific years in Brooks's life—his military record during World War II, for instance—the U.S. Military Records Office in St. Louis is a startling repository of information on individual servicemen, from the training they received to the transport ships that carried them across the oceans. Brooks served in the South Pacific during the island-hopping phase of the war and then in China for a time after the Japanese surrender. Mustered out after the war, he then served in the Marine Corps Reserve until mandatory retirement at age sixty-five. The paper records of those four decades are also on file in St. Louis.

We also note the generosity and spirit of officers and historians at the

U.S. Marine Corps Historical Division at Quantico, Virginia. Their guidance and eagerness for accuracy is much appreciated.

The individuals at all of the institutions mentioned here display a dedication to historical truth, whether they shared footage from C-SPAN archives, Freedom of Information Act (FOIA) requests from the FBI, or clippings of articles from the *Beaumont Enterprise* newspaper.

Many others generously gave us their time, support and advice, including Charles Madigan, Carly Davis, Bryan McNulty, Peggy Roberson, Annie Hsieh, Josh and Anna Martin, Martin Cohn, Jola Kaczmarek, Mitch Morinec, and others who know who they are. Lastly, we want to thank all the staff at NewSouth Books, who did the Lord's work in diligently editing, assembling photos, and designing this book before publishing and promoting it. That team included Suzanne La Rosa, Randall Williams, Beth Marino, Matthew Byrne, Lisa Harrison, Lisa Emerson, Kelsie Kato, Lisa Emerson, and Coke Ellington.

T. McNulty, B. McNulty

A Note of Thanks from the Brooks Family

It is difficult for people to discuss politics these days. In truth, I think it has always been this way. As Jack Brooks's son, I grew up with one foot in a private, normal life, and the other foot on the floor of the U.S. House of Representatives.

For the first three decades of my life, I was fortunate to be able to observe debates over public policy simultaneously from two different vantage points: from the view of the actual decision-makers—the "workhorses" of Congress—and from how those actions were reported to the public through the media. It will come as no surprise when I tell you that politics is never like what people see on TV.

In the past, when the difficult topic of politics came up, the best thing I or my sisters could do was to tell people about our father, Jack Brooks. Of course, while we cannot be unbiased about our own dad, we truly believe that he was a great example of what a public servant should be.

Thanks to years of work and dedication from Tim and Brendan McNulty, this portrait of Jack Brooks's exemplary demonstration of public service is a gift that can be shared with everyone. If a poor boy born in Crowley, Louisiana, can accomplish so much good in one lifetime, then it is my sincere hope that long into the future other people of goodwill can be inspired by his example. Let us celebrate our government, our Constitution, and our great public servants like Jack Brooks. This biography is a wonderful guide towards that goal.

— JEB BROOKS

THE MEANEST MAN
IN CONGRESS

Introduction

All politicians, whether they deserve it or not, attract labels that are used over and over again. These labels are a form of shorthand, an easy way to make a point. Throughout Jack Brooks's forty-two years in the House, the wiry congressman came to be called by many names. Those who knew him well called him "the Chairman" because he headed two of the more powerful committees in the House. Others addressed him as Mr. Chairman or simply Congressman.

Corporate executives, federal officials, and cabinet members who testified before him and other committee members during hearings often called him an "S.O.B.," but only afterward and under their breath. What they really meant by it, Brooks would tell his staff as a sly smile broke across his face, was "Sweet Old Brooks."

Ten American presidents occupied the Oval Office during Brooks's time in Washington. Among them he found adversaries, allies, a crook, and a dear friend. Lyndon Johnson, with whom he would remain close for twenty years, told aides that he feared ever crossing Brooks. Gerald Ford, when trying to pass his own budget though Congress, called Brooks the "snake killer," echoing an old Texas adage. Jimmy Carter, who relied heavily on Brooks's support to see his own agenda enacted, referred to him as a "tough son of a bitch" and not one to be underestimated. Richard Nixon, in the throes of his own removal from office, referred to him as simply "the executioner."

To many, both Democrats and Republicans, the irascible Texan was known openly as "the meanest man in Congress." His colleagues in the House once even organized a roast for him under that banner. They meant it as a compliment, but not everyone who used it did. The moniker signified respect and yet betrayed a certain caution. No one wanted to be on the opposing side of Jack Brooks in a legislative fight. If you suspected a problem in your department or agency, you absolutely did not want to testify before his committee.

Much has been written in recent years about the "Greatest Generation," a term popularized by former television anchor Tom Brokaw. The term describes those men and women who lived through the sacrifices and hardships of World War II and recreated a society eager to look forward, to forget the deprivations of the Great Depression and the scars of a global conflict. In the latter half of the twentieth century, millions of American—men and women indelibly influenced by those events—entered a period of relative peace and enormous prosperity. Despite a hot conflict in Korea and a larger Cold War with the Soviet Union that was to last for decades, America was on the rise, and the politics of Washington created changes in the social contract for American citizens. Postwar prosperity was evident in jobs, in housing, and, perhaps most of all, in a sense of confidence and achievement.

The New Deal policies enacted during the 1930s and 1940s exemplified an ideal that the government could be an active instrument in creating a better and more prosperous world, and Jack Brooks was among those Americans who saw a seat in Congress as a means of exerting some influence over that process.

The United States House of Representatives, with 435 voting members, was designed to be the country's most immediately sensitive governing institution. The House's roiling and responsive nature is set by its two-year term of office, forcing each member to reaffirm himself, his party, and his work for the next election. Ever since the first session of Congress convened on March 4, 1789, thousands of men and women have left their homes to serve in the "People's House," the raucous assembly of lawmakers who come to Washington from districts each contoured—and increasingly contorted by gerrymandering or politicized redistricting—to now represent roughly 700,000 Americans. Based on the 1787 national population, each House member in the first federal Congress represented just 30,000 citizens.

The House is an unruly institution that operates under strict rules, and those who know them best almost always have the advantage. Since the beginning, the House has been an institution both combative and compromising, with the first characteristic invariably leading to the second. Many members serve only one or two terms. Most arrive with the best of intentions, eager to make change, establish themselves, and gain a foothold on a career of public service, only to leave with barely a trace, a fading mist of breath on a mirror.

Jack Brooks was good at his job. He learned it through experience and honed his skills during decades in the marbled corridors and wide meeting rooms of the Capitol. Brooks earned his place in Congress through select committee assignments that taught him how the nation was governed and how Washington politics really worked.

The power that a committee chairman wielded during Brooks's time was tremendous. To staffers and even junior congressman, the chairman of an important committee was like a minor god who held life-and-death sway over legislation before his own committee and could wield his influence on the heads of other committees. Chairmen did not take orders from their party leadership; within the bounds of their jurisdiction, they could investigate nearly whatever they felt required investigating.

In ferreting out waste, fraud, and abuse, the bounds of Brooks's jurisdiction on the Government Operations Committee spanned the entire executive branch, from the Department of Defense to the General Services Administration to White House staff and most everything in between.

Brooks believed, first and foremost, in the efficient and effective use of taxpayer dollars and, to that end, preached that the government should be run like a business, with each dollar accounted for and put to best use. Cushy contracts awarded through dubious procurement methods were anathema to him. Nor were incompetence or ignorance valid excuses when it came to executing the fiduciary duty of government officials dealing with the public's treasury. Despite the reluctance of executive agencies, especially the departments of Justice and Defense, Brooks single-handedly pushed the federal government to create independent inspector general offices in each department. On the Hill, his name became synonymous with government oversight.

Such was his reputation that nearly a quarter century after he left the chairmanship of the oversight committee, the editorial board of the *Washington Examiner*, a conservative Republican publication, recalled his crusade against waste, fraud, and abuse by government agencies, stating: "House Republicans would do well to study the Brooks approach if they are serious about getting control of federal spending."

Brooks's blunt manner and insistent questions only added to his cantankerous and crusty demeanor. Up on the dais in the chairman's seat, his visage was legendary: jut-jawed with a cigar in his mouth, peering over his glasses at recalcitrant witnesses and forgetful cabinet members who, despite any power they may have held outside the hearing room, were subject to his questioning inside of it. He had a proclivity for grilling witnesses on not only the technical minutiae of their work or proposal, but also the fundamental rightness of their actions.

Another guiding principle of his work was the notion of congressional prerogative and independence. He was no doubt a proud partisan, but he firmly withstood assaults from both Republican and Democratic administrations against congressional prerogative. Congress is an equal partner in governing, and he was not going to allow that to slip away out of convenience or politics or simple inattention. Being a fellow Democrat did not allow someone to change Brooks's view of what was constitutionally proper.

At the highest levels of government, the true art, the essence of politics, is getting compromise, not as the goal but a way of achieving goals. Brooks enjoyed the wrangling, the step-by-step plays for compromise and achieving his own legislative goals. One of the truest lessons of democratic government comes from understanding what your opponent needs to help win him over on what you care about. He did not always agree with his fellow Democrats, but they often came to see the potentially ruinous distinction between Brooks not voting for your bill and Brooks actively opposing it. Even President Carter learned to never take Brooks's acquiescence for granted just because of their common party affiliation. Brooks was not one to sheathe his political teeth. People knew him not only as a fighter but also as someone who enjoyed the fight. His favorite stories of overcoming opposition from colleagues or rivals almost always ended with a well-worn phrase, "Well, he's for me now," which meant that Brooks, through either charm or coercion, had made the person see things his way.

During Brooks's time, compromise was understood to be what girded lawmaking; it was a constitutional function that not only greased the wheels of government but was also essential to the long-term health of the Congress. It made legislating palatable, softening the taste of defeat and sobering the pleasure of victory. In the marketplace of ideas and competing interests, bipartisan legislation was hammered out on the anvil of mutual concessions. Safeguarding the interests of constituents on issues both large and small, rather than hewing to a rigid ideology, was paramount.

As a result, relations between the parties were more cordial. Congress was not just a company town, it was also a family town. Members of both parties often socialized together after work; they knew each other's wives; their children went to the same schools.

Despite holding opposing positions, ascribing to the notion that your political opponent or adversary was actually your enemy would have made it impossible to find common ground, which would have made it impossible to legislate.

The ideological entrenchment and extreme polarization that would follow Brooks's era and sour congressional effectiveness from the mid-1990s into the foreseeable future was still years away when Brooks was first elected to serve in the House. Partisanship was evident on all sides, but zero-sum positions, winner-take-all politics, and declarations denouncing compromise were simply not in the thinking of that day.

The "revolution" that marked Brooks's exit from government delineated a clear line in which the modern era of America politics began. One era had come to an end in Congress, and a new, more politically polarized time was about to begin.

It started with the success of Newt Gingrich, a bombastic lecturer at an obscure college in northern Georgia turned congressman who then ran for thirty years on the jagged, implausible path that led him to become an ally of the New York City real estate broker and television barker who is now the forty-fifth president of the United States. Though both men are Republican, the confluence of anger and tribalism and celebrity they embody amplified the traditional partisanship of American politics into a rueful winner-take-all contest where no compromise is welcome or acceptable. That style of governance is the antithesis of Brooks's brand of governing and legislation.

Changes in culture, air travel, media consumption, political money, and thinking about the role of a legislator have calcified divisions, some fear irreparably. The lessening of collegiality between the parties might be best exemplified in the fact that many congressmen and women now leave their families behind in their districts while they spend only three or four days a week in Washington, sometimes sharing dorm-style apartments with like-minded members.

The House, and American politics in general, have taken other drastic turns. Partisanship is more vitriolic, personal destruction has become common, two generations of legislation have been largely overturned, and a new style of governing, one that relies more on sound bites for television cameras and posturing on wedge issues held dear by the most ardent of the political bases, has taken root.

The role of committees has waned too. In many cases, they have become little more than instruments for the majority party's leadership to be directed and leveraged in pursuit of larger national agendas. The prestige of the chairmen and their expertise on their given subjects have suffered as a consequence.

By the time he left Congress, Jack Brooks was one of the longest-serving members in the history of the House, present for 13,858 roll call votes on the House floor. Over the span of four decades, he became a power broker in government operations and an enforcer in government spending. He came to understand the political process so well that he could work through it, over it, and around it. If a Democratic president wanted a bill passed, House leadership pointed him to Brooks. If a junior congressman had a good idea but few legislative skills, he was instructed to seek out Brooks. If Republican members needed a no-nonsense, bipartisan solution, they knew to whom they must speak.

Considering all this, Brooks was primed for higher office. From his marine service to his legal background to the early patronage of renowned Speaker of the House and fellow East Texan, Sam Rayburn, Brooks could easily have run for Senate, the obvious progression for many ambitious House members. With his reputation and friendships, he also could have accepted a cabinet position, like a rumored nomination for attorney general in the mid-1960s. However, he never sought a different office, and his reasoning was simple: the best way he could serve his community and the country was by being an effective representative for southeast Texas.

Brooks's relentless inquisitions into corruption and inefficiency led to direct improvements in American life, from longer-lasting light bulbs to a safer commercial airline industry to a nationwide reconsideration of executive power and its abuse. His legislative accomplishments also saved the federal government untold billions of dollars. Indeed, his impact on events and government operations was so institutionally wide and deep that some have described him as one of the most influential men that most Americans have never heard of.

The Great Depression, World War II, the aftermath of the John F. Kennedy assassination, civil rights legislation, the birth of modern computing, the Watergate impeachment hearings, the Iran-Contra scandal—any eyewitness to such watershed moments in our nation's history might be worthy of a biography. Brooks, however, shaped these events, bending the arc of history through the force of his intellect, the stubborn nature of his will, and his compassion for the marginalized and disenfranchised.

PART I

Jack Brooks for Congress!

You ought to be interested in helping people. But you ought to be interested in helping everybody.

—JACK BROOKS

Dallas 1963

The Democrats had ruled Texas politics for as long as anyone could remember. Since the Reconstruction era ninety years earlier, there had really only been one political party in the state. As a candidate, if you could beat the field of other Democrats in the primary, you were all but assured victory in the general election. By 1963, the party controlled almost every one of the state's political offices. Of the state's twenty-three congressional districts, only two were represented by Republicans, and those men would not have their seats for long.

LOVE FIELD: Morning rain still puddled the tarmac, but the late November sunlight had burned through high clouds and glinted off the silver and blue markings of Air Force One, a new Boeing 707 that just moments before had touched down at Dallas's Love Field airport, bringing the thirty-fifth president of the United States back to Texas, a state he had just barely won three years earlier.

A gaggle of press and well-wishers had gathered on the tarmac to greet the assembly. Secret Service agents estimated two thousand people were waiting behind the waist-high barriers. The flight from nearby Fort Worth had only taken twelve minutes, but to keep the visit on schedule and perhaps create a more impressive entrance, they had decided to fly into town. The twin passenger jets certainly presented better than a caravan of limos and police cars clearing traffic while driving the thirty-six miles between cities.

Taxied up next to the president's Boeing 707 was Vice President Lyndon Johnson's plane, known as Air Force Two. The political power emerging that morning from the two aircraft was formidable. The latter carried Johnson, his staff, and a colorful entourage of thirteen Texas congressmen who had come along for the trip, shuttling from event to event in the tail cars of each motorcade and then from city to city in the vice president's plane. Having a popular president take a multi-day tour of your state was exciting, and no one wanted to miss out.

Among the youngest of those delegates was Jack Brooks, an energetic subcommittee chairman from the industrial southeast Gulf Coast of Texas. While only forty years old, Brooks was no political novice; he had commanded troops in World War II, served several terms in the Texas legislature, and had just a year earlier been reelected to his sixth term representing Texas's Second District in the U.S. House.

After ten years in Congress, Brooks was gaining a reputation for his no-nonsense chairmanship of an obscure yet important subcommittee on government activities. The young Texan's confidence had risen alongside his influence and seniority in both that subcommittee and on the powerful Judiciary Committee. Brooks's loyalty to Johnson and other Democrats earned him a place at the table. More to the point, during the 1960 election, Brooks had pledged his support to the Kennedy team and subsequently delivered his district.

The trip to Texas was barely a day old, and Kennedy had received an enthusiastic welcome in San Antonio and attended a dinner in Houston honoring Albert Thomas, a senior representative. The entourage overnighted in Fort Worth, where Kennedy and others had ridden in a motorcade downtown with Christmas decorations already festooning the streets and crowds of people standing five deep cheering as the limos and staff cars passed by.

The visit to Dallas amounted to a brief stopover—a motorcade through downtown and a quick speech to business and civic leaders—before heading to Austin, the state capital, for a black-tie fundraising dinner later that evening. Politicians and trip handlers were anxious about the reception Kennedy would receive from the public at this Dallas stop in particular. The city was a solidly Republican enclave in the state and had voted overwhelming for Richard Nixon in 1960. Recently, the political spirit had taken on an unsettling and hateful tone. Adlai Stevenson, a former Democratic presidential candidate, had been attacked during an appearance in Dallas just weeks prior. On the morning of Kennedy's Dallas trip, two large newspaper advertisements circulated, accusing him of various offenses, including appointing anti-Christians to federal office, supporting Communists, and treason. Kennedy reportedly told his wife and closest staffers, "We're heading into nut country today." It was not only the political rhetoric that alarmed some in his administration; the level of violence statewide was a concern. Texas led the country in homicides at that time, and among its large cities, the city of Dallas led the state.

But Kennedy needed Texas in the upcoming election. After winning by a mere 40,000 votes statewide, Kennedy decided to return to Texas three years later as an act of peacemaking and unity for the state's Democrats. Touching all the bases as he thought about the year of campaigning ahead, the president even made a morning call from his Fort Worth hotel room to former vice president and Speaker of the House John Nance Garner, wishing the ninety-five-year-old Democrat a happy birthday.

The factions within the party ran from staunchly conservative to zealously progressive, and tensions that had been simmering below the surface were now threatening to boil over. For Kennedy to navigate among the Texans was not going to be easy.

AUSTIN-BOSTON CONNECTION: There existed a strong, if unusual, political connection between the Texas and Massachusetts Democrats, the so-called Austin-Boston connection, which had ruled the House leadership ranks for decades, and which occupied both the presidency and vice presidency in 1963. Besides sharing common ground on social and labor issues, both constituencies shared a love for bare-knuckle politics.

The legendary former Speaker of the House Sam Rayburn, from the one-horse north Texas town of Bonham, had presided over the House Democrats for twenty-one years, with Bostonian John McCormack serving as his longtime majority leader and "lieutenant." As president, Kennedy enjoyed and respected Rayburn, who had passed away two years earlier. The two were even able to work together in the House, albeit briefly, before Kennedy left for the Senate as his political star rose. When the ambitious young president announced the Apollo space program to a joint session of Congress in May 1961, Rayburn, in his capacity as Speaker, sat behind him up on the dais.

With the calming and unifying influence of Rayburn gone, however, tensions amid the Democrats were becoming more evident. The Kennedy-Johnson alliance itself had met skepticism on both sides when Kennedy, after winning the nomination over Johnson at the 1960 Democratic National Convention in Los Angeles, asked the man to be his running mate in the general election. Putting a powerful and popular Southerner on his ticket would shore up many more votes than another East Coaster would. Johnson, after a long career in Congress, both as a rising representative in the House and then as majority leader in the Senate, had surprisingly put aside his own aspirations for the White House when he agreed to Kennedy's proposition.

At the time, the vice presidency was not seen as a stepping-stone for the Oval Office but rather as a career ender, a mostly ceremonial position that came with no real power. Franklin Roosevelt's vice president, Garner, had famously referred to the job as "not worth a bucket of warm piss," so for Johnson, who had seriously entertained a presidential run in 1956 as well, there were mixed feelings about this role, which mostly entailed standing around in the background.

There was a personal or cultural incongruity as well. Kennedy's brother and confidante, Attorney General Robert Kennedy, detested the Texan, considering him offensive, ambitious, and untrustworthy. Kennedy's staffers, nicknamed the "Brain Trust," as many hailed from Ivy League schools in the Northeast, had taken to deriding the Texan as "Uncle Cornpone" for his country speech and manner. Robert Kennedy had also, perhaps intentionally, bungled the nomination of one of Johnson's suggested candidates for a federal judgeship two years earlier, only to then reverse course and support her for the bench. The personal slight had stung Johnson, as had several other gestures from the president and his staff, including the vice president's relegation to a separate aircraft for all the president's travel. There were even rumors among aides that during Kennedy's planned stay at the Johnson Ranch he might inform the Texan that he was off the ticket for the 1964 election.

DELIVERING SECOND DISTRICT: Despite some shared values between voters in Massachusetts and the Lone Star State and the historic connection between Texas and Massachusetts Democrats, the Kennedy brand had never been truly popular in Texas. When Kennedy ran for the presidency, Brooks told Kennedy's campaign leaders that he personally would get out the vote for Kennedy in his district, but Brooks also insisted that Kennedy's people stay away from campaigning in Beaumont, Orange, and Port Arthur—really anywhere in Jefferson County and the surrounding area. He knew his own district, and though Kennedy was charming and an excellent campaigner, Brooks knew that the New England liberal's message would be better received coming from a Texan. Brooks recounted:

> One thing that Kennedy remembered was that when we started that campaign in 1960 I went and told Bobby [Kennedy] that I would run the campaign in my district if they would stay out of it and not send a bunch of hotshots down to try and run it, and if they did that they would be on their own. And he didn't take any time at all. He said, Sure, Jack, we'll do that.

Kennedy went on to win Texas, controversially and by the slimmest of margins. With Texas, he also won the Electoral College and therefore the presidency. Brooks remembered:

> Well, I did. I worked at it and opened it up with Rayburn at the farm, and I invited all the precinct leaders from all over the eleven counties I had then. Had a lot of people at the farm. I told them I didn't want to hear one word about Catholics and religion in this campaign. My daddy was a Mason, and I'm a Mason, and I'm for John Fitzgerald Kennedy, and I think he'll make a splendid president. And you know my district was primarily Protestant but had a lot of Catholics in it. We never had that issue come up in the district. [Kennedy] carried the state of Texas by 40,000 votes. And Johnson and Kennedy knew that; they were good on numbers, and they understood that my congressional district had delivered by the same margin they had won the entire state. And they didn't forget it. Bless their hearts. We got a lot of projects.

Brooks's effort was not forgotten.

JACKIE: Jacqueline Kennedy was one reason why the crowds had come out so eagerly on this Texas visit. And a treat for her, perhaps one reason she decided to make the trip, was planned for the third day: a morning of horseback riding at Johnson's ranch along the Pedernales River in Texas's central Hill Country. Kennedy had been to the ranch once before, just eight days after being elected president, and Johnson had taken him game hunting, a ritual among Texans. Jackie's interest, however, lay with the horses. She had grown up riding and because of her affinity for them, the couple had even purchased a modest home in northern Virginia's horse country an hour outside of Washington.

Jackie, dressed in a pink Chanel dress and matching pillbox hat, was first out of the plane and down the back steps in Dallas. The mood was electric as bystanders laid eyes on her for the first time. She was followed closely by her husband, who held carefully onto the side rail because of his persistent back pain. The handful of Texas political leaders in both planes waited their turn to exit and wave to the assembled local officials, cheering supporters, and photographers.

At the base of the stairs, the Kennedys greeted the reception committee and a throng of people, and as John Kennedy plowed into the group to shake hands, Jackie held onto the arm of the gentlemanly but ailing Representative Albert Thomas. She also accepted a bouquet of red roses, which later would rest alone in the back seat of a car parked outside Parkland Hospital. Bouquet in hand, Jackie made her way along the line of the eager crowd gathered on the tarmac, shaking hands with all the ones stretched out to reach hers.

The First Lady rarely traveled with President Kennedy and remained characteristically shy. To give Texans a chance to see her up close, newspapers had printed the motorcade route, along with maps and times, ensuring that thousands of families would be lining the roadways to wave at the couple and accompanying parade of officials.

MOTORCADE AND DISCORD: Once greetings had been made, the entourage sorted themselves into the awaiting motorcade, a twenty-vehicle snake replete with police motorcycles and follow-up press buses. A pilot car would set out first, about a quarter mile ahead of the other vehicles, followed by the lead car driven by Dallas Chief of Police Jesse Curry.

The logistics of shuttling the chief executive, his wife, senior White House staff, the governor, and a large collection of legislators through downtown Dallas were difficult, and all the more so because of several outsized egos and some quiet contempt that permeated the group.

There were severe crosscurrents in the state's politics between the conservatives, centrists, and liberals, all of whom were Democrats. Despite the unified power they had in Washington, the political rifts among them on social, economic, and fiscal issues were pulling the party apart at its seams.

Discord over the future direction of Texas was palpable, and it was no secret from the public either. Stories in the *Washington Post* leading up to the trip spoke of the "squabbles" and "brewing fights" among Texas Democrats. The *Dallas Morning News* that day ran this headline: "President's Visit Seen Widening State Democratic Split."

PRESIDENT'S CAR: The president's new limousine, a nine-passenger Lincoln that had been painted midnight blue at Kennedy's request, carried Kennedy, Governor John Connally, and their wives. Fastened to the front fenders were two small American flags, as is the custom with vehicles carrying the president. President Kennedy and Jackie sat in the back seat waving left and right to those gathered along the roadside. Governor Connally and his wife, Nellie, sat on jump seats in front of them facing forward. Connally had on his characteristic white cowboy hat, though he quickly placed it on the seat once the cars started moving.

Kennedy had been working with Connally, but others distrusted the governor's loyalty. Connally had climbed and charmed his way up from being an administrative aide to Johnson (then serving as a congressman) to secretary of the Navy and then to governor of Texas in just ten years. Connally now was powerful, but his personality and his politics were divisive, especially within the Democratic Party. Kennedy considered him a "Shivercrat," the derisive term for conservatives in the mold of former Texas governor Allan Shivers, who had broken party ranks with Democrats in the

1950s to support Eisenhower, the moderate Republican, for president. The "Shivercrat" moniker was just one of many in a long line of colorful terms that evolved for conservative Texas Democrats. There would be others in the years to follow. Liberal Democrats had reason for their unease with Connally; within a decade, he would leave the party to join the Republicans.

In the Dallas motorcade that morning, a Secret Service backup limousine, a 1955 Cadillac, trailed only a car length or two behind the president's car. Two agents stood on running boards on both sides of the backup limo, ready to hop off and manage crowds if the motorcade slowed down. The president's Lincoln also had running boards along its rear sides, but Kennedy had asked agents not to travel on them, wanting to avoid a distracting, uneasy buffer between him and the assembled crowd. Four motorcycle police riders flanked the limos.

YARBOROUGH AND CONNALLY: Slightly behind the lead cars followed the vice president's Lincoln convertible, where he rode with his wife, Lady Bird, and Senator Ralph Yarborough, or "Smilin' Ralph," an outspoken liberal firebrand. If Connally represented the conservative end of the Texas Democrat spectrum, Yarborough represented the other, so much so that he had even alienated some moderate Democrats in the Texas delegation and was facing a tough reelection campaign himself.

The animus between Yarborough and Connally was intense, so the seating in the first few cars had been carefully arranged and then rearranged. Yarborough refused to sit in the same vehicle or at the same table with Connally. President Kennedy himself had to finally step in and all but order Yarborough to take it easy and just ride with Johnson if he felt that cross about it. The *Dallas Morning News* had even speculated in a headline article about which table Yarborough would be seated at the upcoming luncheon that day.

Behind the vice president's vehicle, another Secret Service backup car and the remainder of the procession followed.

REPRESENTATIVES: The thirteen Texas congressmen divided themselves among three vehicles toward the rear of the procession. Brooks crammed into the twelfth car back, a white Ford Mercury Comet Caliente, a two-door convertible already packed with Albert Thomas, Jim Wright, and two other congressmen. Brooks rode in the front seat by the door, with Thomas squeezed between him and the driver.

Jim Wright had been born four days after Brooks and liked to tell people that he had been trying to catch up to him ever since. After World War II, Wright joined Brooks at the University of Texas at Austin, then in the Texas legislature, then in the U.S. House of Representatives, which he would eventually attain the speakership of some twenty-three years later.

The tall and genteel Albert Thomas was the eldest of the group at sixty-five. The appreciation dinner in Houston that Kennedy attended the night before was meant to dissuade Thomas from retirement. Since entering the House in the same 1937 freshman class as Johnson, Thomas had risen to become a powerful chairman on the Appropriations Committee and had succeeded in steering significant federal monies to the state, including a major victory two years earlier when he engineered the placement of NASA's Manned Spacecraft Center in his home district of Houston. The facility would create thousands of jobs and serve as a boon for the local and state economy for decades. Colleagues were loath to see him leave Congress, and his dinner had become a primary driver for the president's trip to Texas.

Including the other cars—carrying the Dallas mayor, the president's physician, telephone and Western Union technicians, and three carloads of press photographers and wire service reporters—the presidential entourage stretched over two city blocks in length. A police car brought up the rear, trailing the remaining buses for White House staffers and the rest of the press corps.

Despite the simmering tension, so far the Washington pols had behaved, either for the sake of appearances or a sense of comity. As they traveled between cities aboard Air Force One and Air Force Two, talk among them was convivial. That morning, a story in the *Washington Post* signaled an easing of the tension, or at least the appearance of such, with the headline, "Texans Hide Hatchet as Kennedy Arrives."

Just before noon, the motorcade departed Love Field and began its steady, seven-mile route to downtown Dallas, heading down West Mockingbird Lane before turning on Lemmon Avenue.

BROOKS AND KENNEDY: Jack Brooks respected Kennedy. The two men were products of wildly different circumstances. The Texan's own modest upbringing—being raised by his widowed mother in a series of rented houses and working his way through school—was distinctly different from Kennedy's privileged New England background. But there was humility and honor in Kennedy that Brooks could relate to in his own life, and neither man had much patience for those who were pompous.

During World War II, Kennedy could have avoided service for medical reasons but instead chose to actively seek it out. Brooks had done exactly the same. In early 1944, Kennedy was on his way back to the States to undergo treatment for injuries when a Japanese destroyer demolished the small torpedo boat he captained, PT-109. A few weeks later, Brooks was being shipped off from San Francisco to the same stretch of embattled islands northwest of the Coral Sea.

They shared ideological stances too. Both men were fervent in their support of worker unions. Kennedy had served on labor committees in both the House and Senate before championing worker rights as president. Brooks owed much of his political success to his ability to connect with and fight for the workers who manned the petroleum refineries in and around Beaumont. This shared commitment manifested itself in a desire to craft meaningful public policy that protected the rights of workers and in a dogged pursuit to see that social justice was done.

CIVIL RIGHTS: Kennedy's legislative priorities and civil rights agenda reflected his commitment to social justice and were part of the reason for his trouble in Texas. Civil rights was one of the most divisive issues of the day in Texas and throughout the country. Even Democrats, especially Southern Democrats, were divided.

Only two weeks before Kennedy's visit, Texas Democrats had rejected an effort to repeal the state's poll tax, which functioned as a vehicle for suppressing black and other minority voting. The fear was that these demographics would form new, uncertain voting blocs and ultimately exercise significant influence on Texas politics. The refusal of voters to repeal this tax, which Johnson had previously called "the shame of Texas," was a major political loss for liberal lawmakers. Despite their differences, even Connally, Yarborough, and some top Republicans had publicly supported the repeal of the racist poll tax.

Everyone knew where Kennedy stood. His election win had been by a razor-thin margin, but he took 70 percent of the African American vote. They had placed their trust well. Kennedy sent army and federalized National Guard troops to force the desegregation of the University of Mississippi and the University of Alabama after the universities ignored repeated court orders. After the shameful tactics of Eugene "Bull" Connor, Birmingham's Democratic commissioner of public safety, who ordered the use of fire hoses and attack dogs against peaceful protesters, the Kennedy administration accelerated efforts in drafting a comprehensive civil rights bill.

Though Brooks's district included some of the more racist towns in East Texas, he had already earned a reputation as a strong civil rights proponent, opposing demagoguery against the black community from his earliest election. He knew and respected too many people in the community to fall in line with the segregationists. As a result, Brooks's strongest support in the district was from the black community and from black and white oil workers and union members.

In 1956, the segregationist "Southern Manifesto" sought to unite politicians against the Supreme Court's ruling in *Brown v. Board of Education*, which ruled that segregated public schools were unconstitutional. A bloc of nineteen senators and eighty-two representatives from the eleven states of the old Confederacy signed onto a declaration condemning the court ruling. The pledge was effective, as even moderates felt politically compelled to endorse the cause.

Jack Brooks, a very junior representative at the time, was one of roughly a dozen white Southern congressmen who refused to sign the Southern Manifesto. Despite the political fallout they risked in their home districts, they knew that the segregationist cause was fundamentally wrong.

While Brooks was wary of Attorney General Robert Kennedy and some of the president's staffers, he recognized the Kennedy charm—the president's skill in navigating Washington and inspiring hope among many Americans, including Brooks himself. But for all his intellect, charm, and good intentions, Kennedy did not possess the congressional skills of Johnson or even of some of the junior congressmen riding in the car with Brooks that day in Texas. Kennedy's other policy priorities, collectively known as his New Frontier initiative, were languishing in various stages of development in assorted legislative committees. He had never mastered the art of navigating bills through the intricacies and banalities of Congress, including the complex committee system.

Brooks sat on the Judiciary Committee, where Kennedy's ambitious civil rights bill was still being debated. In fact, Brooks was the only young committee member to work with committee chairman Emanuel Celler in crafting that bill into something they felt could pass both chambers of Congress, a detail that Celler recounted aloud as he passed a celebratory scotch Brooks's way when they were done.

By November, Kennedy's bill was clear of several procedural hurdles and had won endorsement, not only among Democrats but also from several Republican lawmakers.

SECURITY: The presidential limo was equipped with a six-piece Plexiglas top stored in the trunk that could be assembled in different configurations. Kennedy often rode in the car standing up, and just the week before, during a visit to Tampa, he emphatically told his security detail that he did not want to use the Plexiglas top; it only protected him from rain, not bullets, and he wanted the people to get a good view of their leader.

On the outskirts of town, a group of people alongside the road held aloft a banner: "Please Mr. President, stop and shake our hands." Kennedy had the whole procession pull over and motioned the people to come toward him. He stayed in the car and shook each well-wisher's hand as the rest of the entourage watched the telegenic young president do what he did best.

Once more before entering downtown the president brought the entire procession to a halt to greet some nuns and schoolchildren. After three years in office, his enthusiasm for the campaign trail hadn't diminished.

SHOW HORSES AND WORKHORSES: Though Sam Rayburn, or "Mr. Sam," as he was affectionately referred to, had died two years earlier, his presence still loomed large in Washington. The quiet Texan who had deftly led the House from the World War II era to the space age had mentored Brooks, Johnson, and countless other congressmen along the way. Rayburn was known for his aphorisms, of which he had many. He had shared one with Brooks early on in his career—in Congress, Rayburn told Brooks, there were workhorses, and there were show horses. Given the way politicians clamored for attention, it usually was not difficult to tell which one was which, and all young representatives needed to determine which one they would be. It was a maxim that stuck with Brooks until old age.

Kennedy was a breed apart, both a workhorse and show horse. The son of a well-connected multimillionaire, he had dutifully served his country and become a bona fide war hero. In Washington, he shined on camera and also worked diligently after hours on complex policy improvements.

RAYBURN DAM: Just weeks before the Texas trip, Brooks introduced a special resolution to rename the McGee Bend Dam and Reservoir, a newly constructed dam in East Texas, the Sam Rayburn Dam and Reservoir in honor of his late mentor and friend, who had helped Brooks years earlier when he sought funding for an expanded construction project. The reservoir would become the largest lake wholly within the state of Texas.

Once it had passed through Congress, the special resolution was ready for the president's signature. Brooks had learned a valuable lesson after attending another signing in the Oval Office the previous year when Kennedy signed a joint resolution creating the Sam Rayburn medal. Twenty-seven witnesses stood behind the president's desk as he put his signature to the document, and the diminutive Brooks stood in the rear, all but invisible to the camera save a bit of his forehead. He would not make that same mistake twice.

At a private signing ceremony in the Oval Office, Brooks—the sole attendee other than the White House photographer—leaned over the president's desk and watched with glee as Kennedy signed his name to the bill. Kennedy, dressed in a dark suit and striped tie—flanked at his desk by models of clipper ships and a musket on the wall—handed Brooks the pen he used to sign the resolution and offered his congratulations.

It was a heady time for Jack Brooks. Three years earlier, a month before Kennedy's inauguration, Brooks had finally settled down and married Charlotte Collins, a Capitol Hill staffer who had caught the congressman's eye. As Kennedy's motorcade made its way through Dallas, Brooks's young wife was eagerly awaiting him in Austin, where the group was expected later that day.

DOWNTOWN: Once the motorcade reached Main Street downtown, the crowds along the sidewalks were up to five people deep, and some spilled out into the street. Folks waved from the open windows of buildings along the route. Some waved from light poles they had climbed. That Texans had come out in such droves for this trip pleasantly surprised both the Kennedys and the congressional delegation.

The scene as the motorcade rode through downtown felt like a special kind of victory for the feuding Democrats. Passing through what even the sulking Yarborough admitted was the largest crowd he had ever seen in Dallas, the president was in good spirits and filled with enthusiasm. It was then that Nellie Connally famously remarked to Kennedy, "Mr. President, you can't say Dallas doesn't love you."

As they neared the end of Main Street, Brooks and the other representatives were seventy-five yards behind the president's car, still amid the great mass of people, cheering and smiling at the press cameras. The feeling among the congressmen was simply "ebullient," as Jim Wright would say later.

The procession ahead of them had reached Dealey Plaza and had just done a scissor-cut right onto Houston Street and then a quick left onto Elm Street. Brooks looked all around at the high-rise office towers that rose hundreds of feet above the north Texas plain and the cheering crowds and then all of a sudden—*Crack! Crack! Crack!*

Three loud bursts rang out! It lasted only a matter of seconds. The passengers in Brooks's car flinched and then froze. The cheering spectators quieted and looked down the street. The sounds had come from up ahead of them, where Secret Service agents were now yelling for passengers to get down in the vehicles.

Some thought that a car had backfired. Yarborough and someone in Brooks's car thought a miscreant had set off a cherry bomb, but Brooks knew immediately that it was gunfire. He had spent enough time in combat to recognize the sharp cracking sound from a muzzle blast. The other hunters and military veterans in the motorcade also recognized the unmistakable sound of gunshots. Brooks remembered:

> I heard those couple of shots. I felt certain they were shots, and I knew something had gone wrong because the caravan speeded up. I went with the caravan, and we went right to the hospital.

Secret Service agents who had been walking jumped back on the cars. The drivers in the first cars speeded up and pulled away. The rest of the motorcade followed suit. The police motorcycles had turned on their sirens, and the string of vehicles swept under the overpass in Dealey Plaza and onto a stretch of road away from downtown.

After ambling along all the way from the airport, the vehicles in the motorcade now reached speeds up to sixty and seventy miles an hour, the roadside a blur as the six men held on inside Brooks's convertible. After two or three minutes, Brooks's car and those carrying the other congressmen lost sight of the cars ahead of them.

It had been ten minutes of frantic racing and confusion since the gunshots rang out. Secluded in the rear of the motorcade, nine cars back from Kennedy's, neither Brooks nor any of the other five men in the car had any further information on what had happened. There was no White House radio in the car, but Thomas knew there was something terribly wrong when the cars did not take an appointed turn but instead continued on toward the hospital. Even of those in the vice president's car, only one person had seen the bullet strike Kennedy's head. That man, a veteran Secret Service agent, immediately understood the implications and turned his undivided attention to protecting Johnson.

PARKLAND HOSPITAL: The car with Brooks and the other congressmen pulled up outside the emergency room entrance of Parkland Memorial

Hospital, a drab thirteen-story yellow-brick Dallas County hospital. A flurry of activity and confusion buzzed outside the hospital trauma entrance underneath its two neon signs. Carloads of officials were arriving, and onlookers had gathered around the driveway while security attempted to keep order. Someone had seen Johnson rub his arm upon exiting his vehicle—he had been lying underneath the bodies of multiple agents since the first shot rang out—and that became the basis for rumors that he had been injured as well.

Brooks exited the car and made for the door. He saw his friend Larry O'Brien, Kennedy's campaign director and congressional liaison, looking bewildered. O'Brien was in shock and trying to reach the president's side, but local police and hospital staff would not allow him in. Brooks explained that O'Brien was a close presidential adviser and that he needed to be admitted, so Brooks, Albert Thomas, and O'Brien entered the hospital. None of them knew for sure the severity of the situation, but Brooks recalled:

> I had seen the look on people's face, and I just had that feeling that the president had been shot and was hurt badly. I just had that premonition right then, though I had no hard evidence, of course.

The hospital was a warren of sterile hallways leading in every direction and small rooms—for administration, examinations, and trauma—tucked throughout. After entering the emergency receiving room, Brooks was directed to turn a quick corner and then another and then another before he found Johnson and Lady Bird in the corner of a large, secured room with five Secret Service agents posted nearby.

Brooks approached but remained quiet and was soon joined by Homer Thornberry, another strong liberal voice, who had just resigned his House seat but had accompanied the group because Kennedy had recently offered him a federal judgeship. Brooks remembered:

> [Johnson] asked me to stay there, and I did. There wasn't much to do. You couldn't hear much information.

The anxious delegation waited for news. At 12:39 p.m. the first news bulletin was transmitted across the UPI wire service carrying the news: "JFK shot."

The president's limo and the first cars in the motorcade had arrived at the hospital within four minutes of when the shots had rung out. At that point, Kennedy had still been breathing, albeit in short, irregular breaths. With his body slumped on her lap, Mrs. Kennedy had at first refused to let go of her husband. The agents coaxed her to release him, and then gently took hold of the president and carried him on a stretcher into a trauma room, one of two small rooms in the interior of the building hastily set up for the entourage. The back seat of the limo was later described as containing an "abundant amount of blood," brain matter, and a bouquet of red roses.

Although the severity of the president's wounds suggested they would be fatal, no one in the president's party wanted to acknowledge it aloud, at least not until doctors could attend to him. Doctors examined him and worked to clear his breathing and sustain any vital signs of life while those outside the room waited quietly in the hallways and small rooms of the emergency department.

In the room with Johnson and Lady Bird, where the shades had been drawn and entrances guarded, Brooks asked Secret Service agent Clifton Carter, "How's Lyndon?" Carter replied, "He's OK, but the president's pretty bad." Someone else nearby—Brooks never knew exactly who—said quietly, "He's dead, Jack."

Brooks made his way back over to Johnson. Lady Bird had just been told that she and her husband were to leave the hospital immediately. So little was known about the attack that there was concern there could be more assailants. With the multiple injuries and all the commotion, many believed this to be an orchestrated attack.

Rufus Youngblood, the Secret Service agent who had flung himself into the back seat to cover Johnson at the first sound of gunfire, said, "We don't know the scope of this thing. We should get away from here immediately."

Johnson, believing "international Communism" was responsible, felt apprehensive. Not wanting to appear as if he were abandoning Kennedy, he resisted leaving the hospital, especially without the express consent of

Kennedy's staff. For the past three years, Johnson had cleared every move he made with the president's men first, especially Ken O'Donnell, Kennedy's primary aide. Johnson was not assuming anything yet.

Lady Bird absolutely did not want to go; of the three first wives in the presidential cars that morning, her world was the only one that had not been turned upside down. She wanted to be with Jackie and Nellie, both of whom were elsewhere in the hospital with or without their husbands. Since the agents would not let the vice president leave his guarded area, Johnson asked Brooks to escort Lady Bird to be with the other spouses. Brooks remembered walking with her into the trauma room where Jackie stood distraught.

> So I went with Bird to the room there. Not a big room, but a middle-size room where Jackie was staying. And right off that room was a room with Jack Kennedy laid out there with a sheet over his head, and he was obviously deceased.

Lady Bird later recalled she had never "seen anyone so much alone in all her life" as Jackie, standing there "quiet as a shadow" beside her husband's body. Lady Bird walked up and put her arms around the young widow and offered some consoling words. Brooks remembered: "Bird visited with Jackie for a little bit, and we left and went upstairs to a room where they had Nellie."

Nellie was crying as doctors attended her husband's wounds. When Brooks arrived with Lady Bird, he gave Nellie his handkerchief and reassured her, "Oh, he'll be out deer hunting at ninety." She wiped her eyes. Brooks later recalled thinking:

> I thought [Connally] was going to be all right. He had been shot and was not killed; he was right there in that hospital, a good hospital, and my theory is if they shoot you in the hospital you can pretty near get well unless they tear up your heart, your head. I just had that feeling.

Brooks and Lady Bird returned to the room where Johnson was waiting.

A priest arrived, and Kennedy received his last rites for the second time. He had received them once before in the Pacific during the war.

At 1 p.m. Kennedy was officially pronounced dead. His deputy press secretary, Malcolm "Mac" Kilduff, walked up to Johnson and addressed him for the first time as "Mr. President." Johnson later recalled feeling chills roll up his spine when he heard those words. Kilduff wanted Johnson to make a statement as president, but Johnson replied, "Well, we want to get the official report on that . . . we'll just wait until then."

Remaining in the hospital left Johnson and others exposed to unknown risks, and the Secret Service wanted to get Johnson away immediately, but he insisted on staying until Kennedy's death was officially confirmed. Elsewhere in the hospital, a quiet quarrel with the Secret Service erupted briefly when the coroner's office tried to claim possession of the president's body. Assassinating the president was not yet a federal crime, and a state statute stipulated that a body had to be autopsied in the county in which the death had occurred; local officials aimed to treat the investigation as a Dallas homicide. Still, there was little question the presidential detail would prevail in that argument.

The Associated Press quoted two priests saying at 1:32 p.m. that Kennedy had died. Still, Johnson did not want to leave without Jackie, and she refused to leave without her husband's body.

In the meantime, the security agents anxiously arranged a new, smaller motorcade to drive back to the airport. They readied to lead the small group out to two unmarked police cars.

BROOKS'S ADVICE: In its brief history, the United States of America had seen four of its presidents shot while serving in office. There in the Parkland Hospital trauma room beside Kennedy's deceased body, and later in the crowded fuselage of Air Force One, Brooks found himself giving counsel to a new president with an assassin still on the loose.

Wright recalled Brooks advising Johnson, "You need to get out and get back to Washington." Then, before they left the hospital, Brooks also advised Johnson to take the oath of office at the airport before leaving for Washington.

Years later, in a televised interview, Johnson said that while he accepted the Warren Commission report that the Kennedy assassination was the work of a lone gunman, he still could not say with absolute certainty that the assassination was not part of a larger conspiracy.

Brooks stood beside Johnson when the coroner finally came in and declared that John F. Kennedy was deceased. Brooks described Johnson's reaction:

> He was very sober during all of this period, very straight-faced, very cautious, thinking, planning, thinking about what needed to be done and what had to be done. There are a lot of changes, you understand, a lot of problems involved, and he was thinking about them. And the Secret Service wanted him to leave, get him out of there. We just stood there and waited for a minute, and he said, "Well, Jack, you go in the car with Bird and take Bird in this second car, and I'll take this first car, and we'll have two cars meet us at that side entrance there."

Along with three agents, Brooks and Lady Bird jumped in an unmarked vehicle, and the new president was stuffed into the backseat of another unmarked car with Police Chief Curry at the wheel and Thornberry sitting in the front. Johnson lay in the back seat below the window line with Agent Youngblood sprawled on top him for protection. Albert Thomas emerged late from the hospital and yelled for the cars to stop. Against his agents' advice, Johnson ordered them to stop and pick up Thomas, and then the elder—and taller—representative took the more visible space in front from Thornberry, who climbed in the back and sandwiched Johnson between himself and the agent.

Johnson instructed the accompanying motorcade police vehicles to leave their sirens off. The two unmarked cars and their police escorts raced back to Love Field, a distance of over three miles through central Dallas that they covered in just seven minutes. "We took off like a stripe-assed ape," Brooks recalled years later, adding it was fastest ride he ever experienced. Historian William Manchester later wrote that no one in the car spoke or moved as they slid past red light after red light through town. Lady Bird would later recall that it was upon seeing a flag already flying at half-mast that "the enormity of what had happened first struck me."

With the Johnsons gone, Kilduff went outside the hospital and made the official announcement:

> *President John F. Kennedy died at approximately 1 CST today here in Dallas. He died of a gunshot wound to the brain. I have no other details regarding the assassination of the president.*

BACK AT LOVE FIELD: Arriving back at Love Field, now enclosed by a much-increased security bubble, Johnson, Lady Bird, Brooks, and the other congressmen ran up the steps into the main cabin of Air Force One. They would fly back on the president's plane, which had better communication equipment than Johnson's plane, at the request of the Secret Service. Nothing was said, but later some remarked that even the presence of the vice president's aides on Air Force One added to the grief among Kennedy's staffers. The relationship between the two camps had never been an easy one.

A cacophony of television news from the stateroom, hurried activity to fuel and prepare the plane, and weeping resonated throughout the cabin. Brooks again spoke up and repeated to Johnson he thought he should take the oath of office right there, there was no reason to wait.

Just months after the Cuban missile crisis and still at the height of the Cold War and the ever-present threat of a first strike, it would have been grossly irresponsible to leave the nation and the world without a U.S. president and the command and leadership vested in that position. The flight time to Washington was several hours, far too long to leave the free world without a head of state, but other congressmen aboard lobbied that Johnson wait to take the oath until they were back in Washington. Brooks recalled:

> *My position was he ought to be sworn in right away, right then, not wait one minute; that the country was too important to wait for a big ceremony in Washington or do it there on the steps of the Capitol or something or other like that. No, sir, I wanted it done then! We have national and international commitments and problems that can arise at any second, and it's not like a corpora-*

tion which can have an acting manager for a month. This country is too big for that. We have too many international commitments. And any bobbling in that power is dangerous for the machinery.

Privately, Brooks also admitted that he did not trust Robert Kennedy. Brooks worried that the younger Kennedy, who had been at odds with Johnson from the beginning, would come up with some reason to delay or attempt to manage the transition himself. Homer Thornberry advised that it would be best to wait until Washington, but Albert Thomas sided with Brooks. The congressman's advice fell on willing ears; Johnson had previously expressed that, as vice president, he had felt continually undermined by the younger Kennedy. Indeed, the smoldering animosity between the two politicians became the subject of tomes.

Brooks said:

[Johnson] was indecisive about that. I said, well, I'll tell you what, Bobby Kennedy, who doesn't like you one bit, and you don't care too much for him, is going to be there, and he will distort the ceremony in some way or delay it.

Once situated aboard Air Force One, Johnson was faced with the first predicament of his administration. It was not sufficient to have a consensus among themselves; the Justice Department would have to sign off as well. He telephoned Robert Kennedy from the president's stateroom. It was Johnson's task to convince the attorney general, this man who loathed him and had just lost his brother, that it was in the best interest of the country that Johnson recite the oath of office right then and there without delay.

Succession is automatic upon the death of a president, and the reality was that Johnson had technically been president since he arrived at Parkland Hospital. Nevertheless, the attorney general was reportedly stunned at Johnson's request, yet reluctantly agreed that it would be best for the continuity of the government.

In another section of the plane, the congressmen and staff spoke quietly to one another about the uncertain events swirling around them as agents hustled about. Security at the airport and onboard was disorganized.

Brooks's young wife Charlotte had been at her parents' home in Cameron, Texas; all three were planning to attend the dinner in Austin that night. In the early afternoon, at the time of the assassination, she and her parents drove to Austin. Her stepfather had a new car, one with a tape deck in it, so they listened to tapes all the way, not the radio. Her parents dropped her off at the Driscoll Hotel, and they saw all the people in the lobby milling around. The wife of a lobbyist that both Brookses liked spotted Charlotte; the other woman could tell that Charlotte had not yet heard the news. At that time they only knew that the president was shot and that Jack had been in the motorcade with him.

JUDGE HUGHES: Typically, it was the role of the chief justice of the Supreme Court to administer the oath of office, but any judge would do. When President Warren Harding died of a heart attack forty years prior, it was Vice President Calvin Coolidge's own father, John Calvin Coolidge Sr., a judge and notary public, who administered the oath to his son. A historian might have noted that Chester A. Arthur had been sworn in by a New York state judge upon hearing of President James A. Garfield's death in 1881, but days later, the chief justice of the Supreme Court re-administered the oath because of doubts about the validity of the original oath.

Brooks suggested to Johnson that he bring in Judge Sarah Hughes, a federal judge who had been appointed by Kennedy just two years earlier. Brooks knew that she also happened to live nearby. Johnson made a call to another adviser in Dallas, Barefoot Sanders, who had recently been appointed by Kennedy as U.S. attorney for the Northern District of Texas. Sanders also recommended Judge Hughes.

Yet even the presence of Judge Hughes referenced the tension between Robert Kennedy and Johnson. Johnson had suggested in the spring of 1961 that Kennedy nominate her, but the Justice Department turned the idea down because, at sixty-four, she was considered too old for a judgeship. Johnson, feeling undermined, expressed his dismay to the president, who laughed off the vice president's concerns as paranoia. Hughes was connected to Speaker Rayburn as well. Weeks later, Robert Kennedy then reversed his decision on Hughes's nomination because Rayburn was holding up some unrelated pending legislation. No one spoke of how exactly it was all engineered, but the reversal did little to calm Johnson's suspicion of the attorney general.

There was confusion on board Air Force One as the assembled men and women waited; no one knew the exact wording of the oath, whether Judge Hughes was available, or when Jackie would arrive back at the airport. She had repeatedly refused to leave her husband's body behind. Then, only minutes before it was decided that Johnson would take the oath on the plane, Jackie left the hospital riding in a white hearse that carried the casket with her husband's body. At 2:14 p.m., the hearse arrived at Love Field and pulled onto the tarmac where the group had been so eagerly greeted hours earlier. Many hands came forward to lift the casket up the back steps of the plane. Jackie stepped up the staircase alone behind the casket. To make room for it, the flight crew had removed four seats in the rear compartment of the plane.

As it turned out, Judge Hughes had been waiting at the Dallas Trade Mart for the motorcade to arrive and then left for her home in nearby Highland Park when she heard of the shooting. After receiving the call from Air Force One and the directive to find Hughes, Barefoot Sanders recalled:

> I reached her at home and said, "They need you to swear in the vice president at Love Field. Please get out there." She said, "Is there an oath?" I said, "Yes, but we haven't found it yet." She said, "Don't worry about it; I'll make one up." She was very resourceful, you know. By the time she got to the airplane, someone had already called it into the plane. We quickly realized that it is in the Constitution.

She drove to Love Field in her own car and waited until a White House aide found her at one of the tarmac gates and talked her through the increased security. She boarded the plane at 2:30 p.m.

Johnson again called the attorney general, this time to tell him that within minutes he would be taking the oath aboard Air Force One.

THE OATH: Secret Service and the president's staffers were eager to have the swearing-in done quickly to get the plane in the air. As more people packed into the cabin, the temperature soared, and people became more anxious to begin. Judge Hughes asked if they should begin, and Johnson told her, "Mrs. Kennedy wants to be here. We'll wait for her."

After spending some moments in the rear stateroom, Mrs. Kennedy finally came forward into the presidential cabin. She had removed her bloodied gloves, but despite multiple entreaties for her to change into different clothes for the short ceremony, she still wore the bloodstained dress and nylons from the motorcade. After Johnson and his wife greeted her, they asked for her to stand with them as Hughes administered the oath of office. Larry O'Brien retrieved Kennedy's personal Catholic prayer missal from his private cabin and slipped it to the judge.

To get an official record of the event, White House photographer Cecil Stoughton placed himself behind Hughes and stood on a seat to take shots over her shoulder of Johnson and the rest of the crowd. All eyes were fixed on Hughes and Johnson. Stoughton, perspiring heavily, started framing the photo with the wide-angle lens on his Hasselblad camera as even more aides gathered in the space behind the Johnsons and Mrs. Kennedy.

The forward cabin was so packed with bodies that several aides and agents could only crane their necks from behind the compartment door to get a view. Stoughton called out individually to the participants and witnesses, instructing them where to stand so he could compose a proper shot. Among those crammed into the small cabin were: "Mac" Kilduff, who held a Dictaphone to record the oath; Jack Valenti, Johnson's media adviser; Representatives Thomas, Thornberry, and Brooks; Police Chief Jesse Curry; Evelyn Lincoln, Kennedy's personal secretary; Secret Service agents Roy Kellerman and Lem Johns; Pamela Turnure, Mrs. Kennedy's press aide; and Bill Moyers, the Peace Corps deputy director.

Johnson stood facing Judge Hughes with his right hand raised and his left resting on Kennedy's prayer missal. Lady Bird flanked him to his right and a dazed Jacqueline Kennedy stood to his left. Jackie's eyes were cast down. Johnson nodded to Hughes to begin, and at 2:38 p.m., Johnson recited the oath:

I do solemnly swear that I will faithfully execute the Office of President of

*the United States, and will to the best of my ability, preserve, protect and defend
the Constitution of the United States.*

Judge Hughes added "so help me God," which Johnson repeated, though
his words were all but lost as the pilot revved the jet's engines. The recitation
had taken twenty-three seconds. Less than two hours after the shooting,
the nation had a new president. Johnson's only public words immediately
afterward were: "Let's get this plane back to Washington."

Judge Hughes, Chief Curry, and the photographer disembarked, the
aircraft doors were closed, and the pilots taxied out to the runway. At 2:47
p.m., three hours and ten minutes after touching down in Dallas, Air Force
One lifted off for the trip back to Washington. Throughout the somber
flight, Kennedy aides stayed generally in the back of the plane, near Mrs.
Kennedy and the casket. A Secret Service agent sat alongside the casket the
entire trip. Johnson remained up front with the Texas group and some of
his personal aides.

Shortly after Air Force One was in the air, Brooks asked if the pilot or
someone in the cockpit could call his wife. Johnson relayed the message
to Agent Youngblood, who called Charlotte Brooks and told her that her
husband was on his way to Washington. Charlotte's parents dropped her off
at the Austin airport, and she began a five-hour trip with three large bags,
including Brooks's tuxedo and ranch clothes, arriving at their Washington
home later that night.

On board Air Force One, Johnson and several of his staffers worked on
the statement that he would give to the American people in Washington.
Brooks gave a brief account of the day's events to administrative assistant
Marie Fehmer, who took dictation from him and several others while the
plane was en route. Her notes from Brooks read:

> *Shooting was approximately 12:30 . . . heard three shots . . . turned around
> and hurried to hospital . . . knew immediately they were shots . . . saw two people
> on grass near freeway . . . man and child lying flat on ground . . . dodging shots.*

ANDREWS AIR FORCE BASE: Just after 6 p.m. eastern time, Air Force

One landed at Andrews Air Force Base. Robert Kennedy, who had been waiting, bounded up the mobile steps and rushed past Johnson to find Jackie. Brooks recalled:

> *I was a little disappointed in the attitude when we landed. Bobby Kennedy came on the back of the plane there, and they brought the coffin off, and they went off, kind of shoving, a little bit of a bad deal. I thought it was very poor taste on their part, and they shouldn't have been doing it that way.*

A crane vehicle was brought to the rear of the aircraft, and Jackie, still clad in her blood-soaked skirt and stockings, appeared to direct the logistics of lowering the casket. Once it had descended, a crew of eight serviceman carried the 400-pound coffin into the back of a gray navy hearse replete with a driver, nurse, and corpsman. Bobby Kennedy told Jackie a helicopter was waiting to take her back to the White House, but she demurred. She intended to stay with her husband. Once the casket was secured, she climbed in a side door to sit in the rear with his body. The car's original three occupants exited, the attorney general and five of Kennedy's staff took their place inside, and then the hearse and three follow-up vehicles left for the forty-minute drive to Bethesda Naval Hospital.

Only then did Johnson and Lady Bird exit the plane and walk over to a nearby podium where he would make his first public statement. Johnson had insisted that their arrival be televised live, to show the American public that the new administration was not in a panic. The president spoke to the assembled cameras as Brooks, Thomas, and Lady Bird stood nearby in the immediate background:

> *This is a sad time for all people. We have suffered a loss that cannot be weighed. For me, it is a deep personal tragedy. I know that the world shares the sorrow that Mrs. Kennedy and her family bear. I will do my best. That is all I can do. I ask for your help—and God's.*

Johnson then turned, shook hands with a few of the assembled foreign diplomats, and boarded the presidential helicopter, Marine One, sitting a few yards away, which would shuttle him to the south grounds of the White House.

A journalist approached Brooks, Thomas, and Thornberry for statements. The three members spoke with uncharacteristic restraint. Thomas, of whom the late president had spoken so kindly at the appreciation dinner in Houston the night before, spoke first. "It was awful, terrible." He continued, saying the first thing he thought of was Puerto Rico. In 1954, Thomas had been on the House floor with the entire Texas delegation when a group of Puerto Rican nationalists in the gallery above fired shots down at the assembled members. Referring to that morning in the motorcade, Thomas said, "I heard boom, boom, then later, another boom. I shall never forget that sound." The journalist wrote in her notes: "None of the three wanted to say much more. Words did not come easily." Thornberry's sole quote of record to the woman was "this was a horrible crime."

The journalist asked Brooks if he had been close to Kennedy when he was shot. All Brooks could say was "pretty close." The journalist jotted down that the young congressman's lips grimaced in the agony of recalling the moment.

A NEW HEAD OF STATE: Once Marine One landed at the White House, Johnson rejected the advice of several aides and Secret Service agents that he work immediately from the Oval Office and instead went directly through the Rose Garden and on to his vice-presidential office next door in the Executive Office Building (EOB), an ornate, post-Civil War edifice that overlooks the White House's West Wing. Just as Johnson had not wanted to appear grasping for taking the oath of office so quickly in Dallas, he also wanted to be sensitive to Mrs. Kennedy and her children by waiting until they were ready to move out of the White House residence.

Johnson got to work immediately. He conferred with Defense Secretary McNamara and Kennedy's national security adviser McGeorge Bundy as he walked to his office; he spoke by telephone to Presidents Truman and Eisenhower; he met with congressional leaders who had gathered at the EOB at his request. During all this, he also blocked off a few quiet moments to write notes to Kennedy's two young children, Caroline, then six years old and John Junior, who was only three. The letters were brief and very kind.

Charlotte arrived back in Washington several hours after Air Force One had landed, and Brooks went to meet her at the airport. She was understandably upset. The two of them drove to the EOB and picked up the new president, as well as his security detail. Brooks recalled:

> *The security was a little looser then, and my wife and I went and picked him up, came in our car. We drove him out there and the security went along with us.*

That night, Johnson and his family ate dinner with the Brookses, Jack Valenti, Bill Moyers, and a handful of others at the Elms, the Johnsons' large gated home in the expensive Spring Valley neighborhood in northwest Washington. The group stayed until 1 a.m., when the President retired to his room, changed into pajamas, and then sat up in bed watching news with three of his personal aides until 3 a.m. He continued running over what had happened that day, wondered how the press and public would interpret his administration, and mused about several proposals. Valenti remembered the president saying:

> *I'm going to pass that civil rights bill that's been tied up too damn long in the Senate. I'm going to get that bill passed by Congress, and I'm gonna do it before next year is done. And then I'm going to get a bill through that's gonna make sure that everybody has a right to vote. You give people a vote, and they damn sure have power to change their life for the better.*

Valenti remembered Johnson making similar comments about providing medical insurance and education to all Americans.

FIRST DAYS: Once-private tape recordings from those first few days, published and annotated years later by presidential historian Michael Beschloss, revealed a phone call Johnson made in the late afternoon, only two days after the assassination, to Brooks, who had been at his side for much of the time since their return from Dallas. Earlier in the day, Lee Harvey Oswald had been shot and killed in Dallas, and Kennedy's body was still lying in state in the Capitol rotunda. On the call, Brooks seemed to be bucking up the president, who was perhaps starting to feel the loneliness of the Oval Office. The official transcript of the White House recording went:

> *Brooks: It's not going to be an easy job, but there isn't anybody better pre-pared to do it than you. I told them on ABC Television yesterday that you're the best prepared vice president we ever had in the history of the country by training, temperament . . .*
>
> *Johnson: Well, good.*
>
> *Brooks: We've got to start being—not to be cold-blooded, but I mean to be realistic. We ought to be pointing out that we've got a fine president that can do the job because it's good for the . . . continuity of the country.*

Then they talked about having dinner, the president offered to send a car to bring Brooks back to the Elms "to have a drink, a sandwich. Pot-luck." He said Charlotte was welcome too. The two men would continue to speak regularly over the telephone, sometimes only for a minute or two, and usually around 6:30 p.m., to make arrangements for any plans they might have for that night. Brooks ended every call by telling the president, "Bless your heart."

That traumatic day in Texas and the return to Washington kept tens of millions of Americans glued to their television sets and radios night and day over a long period of national mourning. Throughout American history, certain tragedies have shaped the life of the nation. For Jack Brooks and millions of others in his generation, the events of December 7, 1941, altered whatever life they previously had imagined for themselves. For younger generations of Americans, the events of September 11, 2001, have had a similar social and cultural impact, though the full impact of that national tragedy is not yet entirely clear.

The Kennedy assassination was a tragedy of a different scale, involving not the deaths of thousands but the passing of only one man, and yet the president's death touched every aspect of American life, especially its social consciousness, through legislation that would mark a tremendous change in American politics.

The first days after the assassination also cemented a new kind of relationship between the new president and his congressional colleagues, ties that would have an impact not only on Texas, but also on the entire country for many years to come.

The economic and political priorities for the remaining year of Kennedy's first term would be enacted far beyond what he could have hoped for if he had lived. His New Frontier agenda shaped the next decade of legislation because, as Brooks recalled, Johnson was able to get "anything that was worthwhile" passed through Congress. Johnson, who had spent years in both the House and Senate, was a clever and resourceful politician, and he came to be regarded as one of the most successful presidents in terms of passing legislation.

THE PHOTO: The day following the assassination, newspapers across the country shared as much of the unfolding news as they could. Many ran a photograph that the White House had released the day before of Johnson being sworn into office on Air Force One. The new administration hoped to reassure a restive public that the transfer of power at this highest level of government had been executed swiftly and calmly. Lest anyone question the legitimacy of the new administration, the photo was proof of a constitutional transfer of power.

After leaving Air Force One, photographer Stoughton had rushed to the *Dallas Morning News* to develop his film and release an image over the Associated Press wire. In all, he had taken twenty black and white images of the moments before, during, and immediately after the short ceremony, but one photograph in particular captured the scene and mood with utmost clarity.

Flanked by Lady Bird and Jackie, Johnson, with his outstretched right hand, was the focal point. Stoughton had angled his camera to avoid the bloodstains on Jackie's clothes, but the look on her face and the wing of hair dropping across the side of her head showed a woman absolutely stunned by tragedy.

The image would become testimony not only to the tragedy of Kennedy's assassination but also to the democratic ideal of a peaceful transition from one leader to another. Knowing this, Johnson would have wanted the photograph to portray the orderliness of the proceeding, to pay respect for Kennedy and his widow, and to include a selection of men he could trust as he assumed the role he had been thrust into.

Among the twenty-six or more people packed into the small cabin, almost every single face is obscured in Stoughton's photograph. Behind Johnson, Lady Bird, and Jackie, and amid the mass of bodies, shoulders, arms, and hats, only three men are clearly visible. One is Jack Valenti, who quickly became the president's go-to personal aide. Another is Albert Thomas, stately and stoic, a representative of the Washington establishment.

And just behind Jackie and her forlorn face is the young congressman from Beaumont, Jack Brooks. Lacking any discernible expression beyond a grave seriousness, Brooks, a former marine, stands resolutely at attention as if bracing for the uncertainties and troubles that undoubtedly lay ahead.

Four weeks later, once ensconced in the presidency, Johnson would reveal to Thomas, "I sent for Thomas and Brooks and Valenti when I took the oath, and I plan to stay with you until we go to the graveyard together."

2

The Early Years

The southeast Texas coastal plain runs wide to the south past Galveston and deep inland from the Gulf of Mexico right up to the remains of the old forest, so abundant with growth they named it Big Thicket. In the nineteenth century, the lumber from the red and white oaks and cottonwoods of the bottomland forest provided the economic lifeblood for the region. Lumberjacks and other migrant workers moved to young Jefferson County in large numbers to cut and haul timber, first to trains and sawmills and then onto awaiting boats docked at the makeshift ports.

Whatever natural beauty exists in Jefferson County and its surroundings is mainly at eye level or below with the water in the bayous and coulees intersecting the sandy tidal flats that wave with tall switchgrass. The entire region is subtropical and operates under a powerful, oppressive humidity for most of the year. It leads the state in annual rainfall, which paved the way for another local industry; in the expanse of marshy grassland between the water's edge to the south and dense forest to the north lies one of the few areas in the country suitable for growing rice.

With the abundant rainfall, though, comes calamity. Despite the twenty-five miles to the Gulf shore, the county is highly susceptible to hurricanes. Storm surges move straight up the flats and waterways, and severe flooding has been common, if not predictable, for ages. At the advent of the twentieth century, a hurricane all but decimated the nearby coastal city of Galveston. The boomtown had promised to become one of the Texas's largest cities, even outpacing the then-fledgling sister city of

Houston. Galveston's sudden demise revealed the dangers of commerce along the state's Gulf Coast.

SPINDLETOP: The following year, however, this part of Texas, and the future of the country, changed dramatically again. In the preceding decades, when oil had been used primarily for kerosene lamps and John D. Rockefeller became the wealthiest man in the world, the country's known oilfields were in the northeast. Oilmen had drilled modest wells in Texas, and some early explorers noticed seeping ground oil, but in the 1890s, drilling in the area became serious.

In Jefferson County there was a twelve-foot high protuberance in an otherwise flat prairie that had been known to locals as "Big Hill." Oilmen decided to drill it in early 1901, and a salt dome gusher sprang forth, shooting oil over one hundred feet into the air and running for more than a week before it could be capped.

The Lucas Gusher, or Spindletop, as the well became known, represented the possibility of enormous riches hiding beneath the dry Texas grasslands. Spindletop peaked the following year at 17.5 million gallons of oil, and gradually over the next two decades, the well tapped out. However, the discovery set off a frenzy to find comparable wells farther west. Exploration continued farther into West Texas and up into the panhandle.

Spindletop did more than enrich its owners; it created notoriety across the entire country and prompted an oil rush that marked the beginning of the Texas oil boom. It represented not only new economic hope for Texas but the advent of the modern oil industry, a new industry for the nation, one that would transform the nascent country into a world power and revitalize the flagging industrial age.

CITY OF BEAUMONT: The new lifeblood of the region ran black and thick. Men looking for work all over the South and beyond began arriving in droves, hoping to find a job doing the backbreaking labor needed to produce and refine the oil. Built on the backs of poor, transient oilmen, the small prairie town of Beaumont—*beau* and *mont* in French meaning "beautiful hill"—sprang up alongside the well to feed and house the men. Beaumont became a get rich quick destination in less than a decade, its population doubling to more than twenty thousand citizens. Wildcatters, roughnecks, and oil speculators were among those flooding the once-placid river town.

Life in Texas was changing rapidly: to the west and south, the Houston Ship Channel was completed in 1912, and during the First World War, oil, along with farming and ranching, came to dominate most Texas business interests. A second strike at Spindletop in 1925 recreated a new oil rage in Beaumont and attracted another influx of entrepreneurs, businessmen, and expanding oil companies. Some of these companies would become names familiar to all Americans: the Texas Fuel Oil Company (Texaco) and Gulf Oil (now both Chevron), Standard Oil and the Humble Oil and Refining Company (Exxon). Those companies and others have represented the oil industry for most of the last century; they created a thriving industrial base for oil refining and petrochemicals in Beaumont, Jefferson, and the neighboring counties. They prodded early on to deepen the shipping channels up to Port Arthur, Orange, and Beaumont. Fresh water also was essential for their refining and petrochemical operations, so they looked farther upstream as well.

Cajuns: But equally important to the business interests of the growing community was having a plentiful supply of workers. Many of the oil workers were "coon ass" Cajuns, from Acadia and other parishes in southwest Louisiana, looking for better-paying jobs. The expanding economy created a gritty industrial zone and also attracted the moonshiners, gamblers, and those oil and gas workers who would support Beaumont's thriving downtown brothels well into the 1960s.

Truth be told, Jefferson and the surrounding counties have more in common with the loam prairie of Louisiana's Cajun country, with its groundwater and heavy humidity, than they do with the open and dry spaces most people associate with Texas.

But even before those oil settlements, there were cattle ranches and rice fields. The center of rice country is sixty miles east in a town called Crowley, Louisiana, where Jack Brooks was born and where his story begins.

One set of ancestors could be traced back before the American Revolution, another sided with the Confederacy a century later; some relatives were admired professionals, while others served jail time. In short, it was the fortunes and misfortunes of generations that ultimately brought the Brooks family to Beaumont.

Just as all family histories can be prone to embellishment, what is known of the Brooks family history includes possible nobility but also ancestors appropriately, if gently, referred to as rapscallions. Brooks's great-great-grandfather was thought to be a general in the French army and a cousin of a king of France. A few generations later, a first cousin was thought to have shot and killed three people in one day, supposedly in self-defense, and there was even some talk of horse thievery at the time. Family lore has it that whatever the motivation for the crime and the punishment, the cousin spent only two years in prison, and his main duty was to chauffeur the warden in his car. When Brooks last heard news of that relative, back in 1959, the cousin had married five or six times and was in charge of the valet service in the Rice Hotel parking garage.

One of the earliest known Brooks ancestors is Charlotte Geurry, who came from a French Huguenot family that embraced the Calvinist religion and was forced to flee France. As with many refugees at the time, they fled first to Ireland and then to the British colony of America, where they eventually settled in South Carolina. There Charlotte married a middle-aged man in 1835.

They produced several children, but perhaps the most formidable was their daughter, Clementine. She married William Frank Brooks and, just before the turn of the twentieth century, she gave birth to Brooks's father, Edward, in the small rural town of Crowley, Louisiana.

Brooks's family on his mother's side is known back to and beyond W. D. White, a doctor who practiced in Abbeville, Louisiana, into the mid-1800s. White's mother also had an ancestor from the Carolinas, a captain in the North Carolina battalion during the Revolutionary War. When the war between North and South began, White enlisted as an engineer in the Confederate forces. How he fared in the early days of the war isn't known, but he was present during the siege of Vicksburg in May and June of 1863, when Union forces under the command of General Ulysses S. Grant surrounded the Mississippi River town. Sometime before Lieutenant General John Pemberton's surrender on July 4, Dr. White took what Confederates commonly called "French leave," that is, he lit out for home rather than be captured by Union forces. Family legend has it that he got away holding onto a log and swam down the Mississippi River to safety, eventually making his way back to Abbeville and to his wife, Lucinda Reaves Lyons, who was reputed to be the prettiest girl around the Vermillion Bayou in southwest Louisiana.

White and his wife had a baby girl they named Carrie, whose childhood rocking chair Brooks kept. Carrie grew into adulthood and met Oscar Pipes, a newspaperman in Shreveport and later New Orleans. They raised several children, including a young girl they named Grace.

EARLY YEARS: Grace Pipes, then of Abbeville, Louisiana, was only sixteen years old when she married Edward Brooks, a man ten years her senior. The couple moved to Acadia Parish, to Edward's home on a dusty street near the center of Crowley. Their firstborn was named for his father, and their second child, Douglas, died when he was two years old.

On December 18, 1922, a third boy, whom they named Jack, was born in the parlor of their home. Though a bantamweight for most of his young life, Jack weighed slightly more than ten pounds at birth. Grace and Edward's only daughter, Marie, was born thirteen months after Jack, so close together that the children were teasingly referred to as "Irish twins."

Brooks's father prospered in those early years. The head of a young family, he became an up-and-coming dealer who worked for the rice millers of Louisiana. About a year after Marie was born, Edward moved the family to New York City to be close to the markets. Those were heady times for the family; business was good, and the athletic father took his youngest children, dressed smartly in snowcaps, boots, and identical navy blue coats, for long weekend walks in the park. They would often visit the Morris-Jumel Mansion in Washington Heights, a Georgian-style frame home where George Washington stayed when he was in residence in New York.

Grace Brooks, still in her twenties and living a life she had never expected, sang as she walked through their house. It would be a habit that her children embraced, even through the halls of Congress. Edward employed a Russian music teacher to help Grace develop her mezzo-soprano voice. Grace sang at churches around the city. She even considered a scholarship to attend Juilliard School, but thought that would take too much time away from her children.

The children remembered pillow fights on their beds, the bedroom coated in white feathers. Exuberant youngsters, they loved playing in the snow during their New York winters, but Brooks's blue eyes were sensitive to sunlight and to flashbulbs; he didn't like having his photo taken, something that the future politician had to overcome.

Edward had been a track star and played football in high school; Brooks recalled how he would run and show off by kicking his legs higher than his head. He once described his father as "a tall, courteous, pleasant man." But at some point in his early life, the elder Brooks had suffered a bout with pneumonia that the family believes hastened the heart condition that eventually killed him when he was only thirty-seven. High kicks aside, certainly Edward was not as physically strong or as fast as he had been in his school years. In New York, he blew a whistle to stop the children if they ran too far ahead. Once, a pair of Newfoundland-size dogs ran up to little curly-haired Jack and knocked him down; he was unhurt, but his wariness of dogs remained.

After three years in New York, the family fortunes changed drastically. In 1927, the rice market suffered severe blows, including the flooding of the Mississippi River, which ruined hundreds of square miles of rice fields in Louisiana. Among the many perilous realities of life along the Gulf Coast, including the 1901 hurricane that had decimated Galveston, this flood was yet another benchmark disaster that residents would even recall more than seventy-five years later, when Hurricane Katrina destroyed parts of New Orleans.

Brooks believed that his father had taken a risky "strong position" in the rice market, and after the market's dramatic downturn in 1927, the Brooks family, then living among New York's financiers and their brownstones in upper Manhattan, playing in Central Park and walking the gilded streets of urban wealth, lost not only their place in the city, but also their family home back in Crowley and the small farm outside of town.

After the rice market bust, the Brooks family traveled by ship back to New Orleans. Brooks remembered:

> It wasn't just happening to us, it was happening to everyone. No one complained. There wasn't anyone to complain to, but, no, my dad took it harder. My dad was born with a silver spoon in his mouth. And he still had the spoon, but no money.
>
> That's a training you get, and it's hard to give it up, so it was very hard on my dad, I think. But he was not a quitter. He would go and hunt for a job, go to the post office and anything. Finally, he got a job paving the streets of a city, Cleveland, Texas.

Many others would experience the Brooks family's sudden poverty during the coming Great Depression. One of Jack Brooks's great-uncles on his mother's side was said to have lost a multi-million dollar fortune and responded by jumping from a downtown building to his death. Brooks had more family in Louisiana: one uncle was a doctor, another a U.S. marshal, and another a big rice miller. Brooks particularly remembered Skeet, an uncle who was gassed in World War I and suffered from Parkinson's disease. Brooks remembered Skeet's having a car and driver and taking his young nephew around Crowley.

Indeed, Brooks's early life in Louisiana, before the New York years, had been privileged. In the home of Edward's mother, Clementine Brooks, there were rituals to be observed. The back door was left unlocked, and their African American cook arrived at 5 a.m. to brew the coffee. No one stirred until she passed around little demitasse cups of strong black coffee; Clementine was always served first. "She called the shots," recalled Brooks's sister, Marie. "She was the boss." Brooks described Clementine as "a matriarch and an old Cajun lady. She was tough as a boot, but she loved me, and I'd go spend two or three weeks with her in the summertime."

In the early 1930s, in the depths of the Depression, Brooks's father and mother worked part-time jobs to support the family. Brooks kept the mementos of his early life—his father's track medals and the scissors Edward used to cut the children's hair. Brooks said: "He would trim my hair with these scissors. We'd save going to a barbershop. We didn't have any money."

His father, still devastated by the loss in the rice market, first got a job as a timekeeper for the Works Progress Administration and later worked with his brother-in-law delivering cars for the Jackson Motor Company, driving them from Detroit to New Orleans. "That was hard on him," Marie said. "That was very unlike his background. That was hard work."

In their new, impoverished state, and with little work to be had in Crowley or anywhere nearby, the Brooks family went to Beaumont, where Grace's mother (who had been widowed at twenty-four) and two brothers were living.

Moving to a series of rented apartments and homes left childhood impressions—vivid memories not only of the houses but also of the owners: Leah Greenberg's daddy, who was a "soft goods" man downtown; Mrs. Wizner, who ran a gardening business across from a grade school classmate; Frank King, whose father managed the Magnolia Cemetery.

Brooks and his sister Marie could list the names of the streets they'd briefly called home, from First and McFaddin near the train tracks to Grand Avenue and elsewhere. After years of hearing this litany, Brooks's wife Charlotte jokingly called it the "parade of misery." However, Marie recalled, "I was never hungry, ever. I got cold now and then. Those houses were like paper, you know. And one heater."

The siblings remembered the early morning clicking high heels of the woman upstairs in a duplex on North Street, then the single-family frame home on Linson Street with the red-tiled roof. More than sixty years later, Brooks recalled:

When it rained that roof leaked like a sieve, and in the front room the wallpaper would sag in five or six places, and at that drip line we'd put some of the kitchen utensils, pots and pans, and we'd have funny-looking pots and pans all over that front room as that paper was sagging from the weight of the water that was seeping through. You did learn something, though; you never punched a hole in the paper to let the water out faster. Let it drip . . . if you punch a hole, the paper tears. If you just let it drip and move it quietly toward the center of the

drip line with a broom, the paper will then re-adhere to the ceiling, and when
it all dries out it looks pretty good. So much for that.

After the family moved to Beaumont, Grace's mother came to live with them. When Brooks and his brother Edward went off to war, his mother, grandmother, and Marie moved into a nicer house on Prairie in the South Park area of Beaumont; over the years some of their homes were better than others, but there was never a place to call their own.

They worked when they could, and they depended on help from others.

Some of Brooks's congressional staff and family were aghast when he publicly thanked the man who had given him a suit to wear when he was down and out. His sister recalled:

> *People during the Depression would give us clothes. I wore the cutest things,*
> *and I was scared to death that I would run into the person that gave them to*
> *me. Somebody gave Jack a suit, a very wealthy family that had a son about Jack's*
> *size. Jack was making a speech years later, and he said, "Well, there's Herbert.*
> *You know, Herbert gave me a suit." He told it right then, used all the names of*
> *the family and everything.*

Brooks was not embarrassed about having lived in poverty and shrugged off anyone thinking it awkward for a congressman to talk about receiving charity. "I didn't think anything of it, except that he was kind to me when I needed it." However, he became determined never to return to poverty.

GRACE BROOKS: When her husband died, Grace was a thirty-seven-year-old widow with three children to raise. She went to work even before her husband's death, trying to hold together the family in their very reduced circumstances. Eventually, the Christian Science church in Beaumont hired her as a soloist, and she sang there every Sunday for the next seventeen years.

Grace found another job at Gulf States Utilities. Then the largest power company in the region, Gulf States Utilities was just beginning to introduce potential consumers to cooking with electricity. Grace visited homes to explain modern techniques in the kitchen, and before long she even appeared on a regular program on local television. She became a spokeswoman for the new technology, weaning homemakers from their old gas ranges, teaching them how to cook on their new electric stovetops.

Enterprising in so many ways, once Brooks decided on a political career, Grace used her client contacts from Gulf States Utilities to campaign for him at a very grassroots level. One particularly clever move was when she had "Jack Brooks for Congress" stitched onto oven mitts.

Grace dressed as a woman of her time, practical in housecoats and patterned dresses, and she enjoyed playing dominoes and card games. "Breast your cards, dear," she used to tell Brooks when he would get lackadaisical while playing. "I can see your cards." Brooks would heed her advice to keep his hand close to his chest throughout his political career.

In the backyard of her house, Grace kept neat flower beds, with day lilies, azaleas, and hydrangeas. She was outspoken and possessed a droll sense of humor, another legacy her children shared. One evening years later, Brooks was back for a family dinner at Grace's home on East Drive. The telephone rang, and when she went to answer it, Brooks grumpily complained that she should let it ring. He said: "I wouldn't answer it if Jesus Christ himself was calling."

His mother sweetly replied: "Don't worry, dear. If he called, it wouldn't be for you."

Grace loved singing her gospel and country songs, a habit that echoed through the years as Brooks walked with congressional staffers down the Capitol's long marble corridors, humming an old tune. One of his gospel favorites was "Higher Ground." Later, Brooks owned a little jukebox that played more popular songs from the 1940s—"Put your Sweet Lips a Little Closer to the Phone," by the velvet-voiced Jim Reeves, and "Walking the Floor Over You," a honky-tonk classic written by Ernest Tubb, known as the "Texas Troubadour." Brooks also loved later hits, like Patsy Cline's "Crazy."

Brooks adored and deeply respected his mother and grandmother. Because of Grace's influence, for his time, Brooks was uncommonly reflective about women and their perspective. As early as 1966, he would hire women for leading staff roles when few other colleagues in Congress would.

I had the highest respect for [women], always loved and respected them.
Now, I found that women have a peculiar perspective for people and situations.
And if you know them fairly well and they tell you about some man or woman,
they understand them very well, maybe better than you do. Legislative problems,
personal problems—women have an excellent perspective.

POVERTY: While the local rich could enjoy a Southern languor and build new-money mansions, like the beaux arts McFaddin-Ward house, in the more genteel parts of town, most of Beaumont's citizens lived without much pretension and labored long hours, building up a hard edge common to industrial port cities around the globe.

Despite the poverty, there was an idyllic aspect to growing up in a town where people knew their neighbors and families stayed for generations, where Brooks could ride his friend Frank King on the handlebars of his bicycle, wait until the streetcar slowed at a turn so Frank would catch onto the back, then let the trolley pull them through town.

Among the memories of his early years in Beaumont—playing quietly under a house set up on short stilts; collecting small bags of cement from the Gulf Lumber Company yard and fashioning concrete roads and bridges; putting pennies on the train tracks; building a boat from roofing tin and then from wooden boards, taking it down behind Magnolia Cemetery to the bayou and drifting along, sometimes seeing gar fish or noticing a water moccasin in the bushes above his head.

Too young to understand the financial devastation of his family—the change in circumstances from a privileged life of snowy walks with his father and sister through Central Park to playing under the floorboards of a rented duplex in Beaumont—Brooks nevertheless shouldered whatever burdens fell his way. Brooks's older brother, Edward, was known as kind and affable, but without the same drive and tenacity that were evident in the younger brother from an early age. There was something different about Jack Brooks.

Brooks accepted responsibility without complaint—a thread that ran through his life. He opened a lemonade stand at old Firehouse No. 7, across the street from one of the family's rented apartments, and showed early signs of devilment when an alarm came in and he sneaked upstairs to slide down the brass pole from the second floor. In coming years, he also began to see opportunity and understand in the most fundamental way what other people needed and what they would be willing to take in return for whatever he and his family needed. They were lessons that prepared him not only for his wartime experiences but even more for the political life he led for nearly half a century. Brooks's life was an ever-expanding circle of responsibility.

In the Beaumont of Brooks's youth, rich and poor lived near each other. Brooks remembered getting occasional rides in the chauffeured car of one classmate, Aubrey Dixon, and playing with others who were uncertain where the next day's meals were coming from. When Thelma Plowden, the young daughter of the woman who did their washing, came to the door asking for a cup of rice, Grace Brooks told her, "We don't have much, but you can have half of what we've got." The notion of neighbors helping the less fortunate has become idealized in movies about the period, but Brooks remembered a genuine sense of unity and responsibility to help those who had even less.

One of Brooks's neighbors owned a small grocery store two blocks from their home on Magnolia Avenue and allowed Brooks to work there on Saturdays, sacking grocery bags and stocking the store. Brooks recalled Mr. Lumpkin's "good heart"—on Saturday nights the grocery would have a drawing; the winner took home two bags of food. "On more than one occasion I won, and I would come home with two big sacks and I could hardly carry them," Brooks said. "Mother would be delighted." She was a cook known for her gumbo and crawfish stews, with some crab legs thrown in for good measure.

JOBS: Brooks sold magazines before he was even a teenager. He sold street copies of the *Beaumont Enterprise* and on his bicycle delivered the *Literary Digest* to the homes of more affluent or literary Beaumont residents. As a grown man, Brooks was happy to display a gift pen that describes the eight-year-old boy as an "agent" for the *Digest* in 1930. Brooks also sold *The Saturday Evening Post* (a nickel an issue), *Ladies' Home Journal,* and *Country Gentleman,* which did not sell as well because it cost a full dime. Many years later, on the 125th anniversary of the *Enterprise,* Brooks recalled that his first exposure to the paper was selling Extra copies reporting the

Lindbergh baby kidnapping on March 1, 1932. That night, he earned an amazing sum of nearly five dollars.

One part-time job he did not get, however, had an outsized impact. Perhaps the best-paying job for any young man in town was caddying at the Beaumont Country Club. The tips were usually generous, and it was a chance to spend time among Beaumont's elite. But the club rejected Brooks's application, ostensibly because the directors thought he was too small and scrawny to tote around a bag of golf clubs. That rejection meant that Brooks had to look elsewhere for work, which eventually led to his interest in more career-oriented jobs in journalism and politics. Even more, the country club rejection made Brooks determined to never be held back or underestimated because of his size.

The rejection also cemented his suspicions about anyone rich and haughty. Though he had many wealthy friends throughout his life and, indeed, became wealthy in his own right, Brooks never swung a golf club, and in subsequent years, despite numerous invitations to the Beaumont Country Club and exclusive country clubs around Washington, he never joined any of them. As his mentor Sam Rayburn would say, "Forgive, but never forget."

ELEMENTARY AND HIGH SCHOOL: As early as grade school, it became clear that Brooks was exceptional. In 1933, at age ten, he won first place out of 2,670 submissions in a national contest for the *National Humane Review*. He also earned a scholarship sponsored by a wealthy local woman, Mrs. W. D. Gordon, affiliated with the Daughters of the American Revolution.

The peer relationships Brooks established during those formative years would last decades, for both personal and professional reasons. Even sixty years after graduating, some of his high school friends would still meet in Beaumont for informal lunches. First as a state legislator and then in Congress, Brooks lived away but returned constantly to his roots in Beaumont to campaign and maintain contact with his supporters and old friends—the key to political longevity.

Indeed, Brooks traced his first thoughts of Congress back to when he decided to support a friend's candidacy for "mayor" at Dick Dowling Junior High School. He eventually became his friend's campaign manager. The young man won and appointed Brooks as "city manager," a role he wanted because then he could appoint all the other members of the administration. He recalled appointments for Connor Baldwin and Gerry Green, Ellis Burgess and Dick Cason, Marilyn Ramsey and Marilyn Tillery. Many decades later Brooks remembered:

> *I appointed a lot of wonderful people who are still my friends. One of them lives right down the street here, been a friend of mine since we were in the eighth grade. And that made a difference in this old world.*

The Enterprise: In the summers of 1936, 1937, and 1938, Brooks took a job as a carhop for the Dairy Maid Ice Cream Company. He worked ten hours a day, from 1 p.m. to 11 p.m., seven days a week, for ten cents an hour, making some ninety dollars for the summer. He would also bring home a pint of vanilla ice cream for his mother. Constantly on the lookout for part-time work, Brooks almost took a job at the public library that paid twenty-five cents an hour.

In September of 1938 he found a more enterprising—and lucrative—job working as a cub reporter at the *Beaumont Enterprise*, routinely making 150 dollars a month. His brother had also worked at the *Enterprise,* and Brooks was able to attend high school even as he worked full-time on the afternoon shift. It was a blessing, Brooks recalled, because the pay was fifteen cents per column inch. Each page of a broadsheet newspaper was eight columns wide, and Brooks, because of his school schedule during the week, was assigned to cover schools and churches. He quickly learned that a routine photo of a preacher would bring in forty-five cents. "I'll never forget, one of those preachers sent me a postcard that said, 'God bless you for running my picture, please run it again.'"

It was a tremendous insight for Brooks then, an insight that would serve him later in life. People love to see their names, and especially photographs, in print, so he included the names of dozens of students and teachers in the newspaper. Other reporters who knew that Brooks was being paid on piece-work slipped him small stories that would increase his column inch count.

I also learned to work smart, and one school graduation, I ran a list of every graduate and their program. Now R. W. Akers would edit copy without mercy, and he used small Agate type for long lists, but he would never cut a name from the paper. He understood his constituents and what they valued.

It was a good lesson for a future politician, that it was people and not events that really mattered. Though perhaps at one point he took the practice too far, as the editor became upset when he learned that Brooks had earned more than $250 for one month, more than every other full-time journalist and more than Akers himself.

LAMAR COLLEGE: After Brooks graduated from high school, he attended a local two-year college that comprised a small collection of classroom buildings near the site of the old Spindletop oil well, which had since dried up, several miles from downtown. The school started out as the South Park Junior College in 1923 with 125 students and fourteen faculty members. The students met on the third floor of the new high school building. That same year, the name was changed to Lamar College, in honor of Mirabeau Buonaparte Lamar, a cavalry commander in the battle of San Jacinto in 1836 and the first vice president and then second president of the Republic of Texas. Within the next decade, buildings were added on the Lamar grounds, and an expansion located several blocks away on the Port Arthur highway included new classrooms and dormitories.

For Brooks and many of his high school classmates, friends, and neighbors, there was no other place in Beaumont for higher education. If they wanted a full college degree, they had to leave their homes, farms, or family businesses to enroll in school elsewhere. Brooks's life at Lamar was essentially an extension of his life in high school.

UNIVERSITY OF TEXAS: Brooks soon went away to the University of Texas, or "UT," in Austin, where he found more independence. He also discovered friends and classmates who helped expand his world, taught him some things about politics and—perhaps just as important to a young college freshman from a small town—helped him meet girls.

He moved to Austin with a few friends from Beaumont, but once there he rented a room in a two-story yellow frame boarding house, where he met Fred Neuman, who became president of the student body, and another boy, Whiskey Harper, who put out a monthly magazine.

College life in Austin was a joy for the young man who had never been much out of Jefferson County. Brooks recalled that much of his time, perhaps too much, was spent partying with male classmates, sharing kegs of beer, and chasing "coeds."

After his first year at UT, Brooks met Davis Carter and a boy he called "Big Jones." Later, they decided to move out of the men-only dorm and into their own apartment, conveniently located on the street right behind the Scottish Rite Dormitory, known locally as the SRD, a traditional women's dormitory since the 1920s.

Brooks was an A and B student in most courses—English, economics, zoology, and mathematics—though he suffered through more than one semester in classes like Beginning French. According to an instructor at Lamar who remembered Brooks's time at the school, the only class he ever received a C in was Public Speaking, interestingly enough.

PART-TIME JOBS: Brooks had a benefactor his first year in Austin. Mrs. W. D. Gordon wrote him a series of fifteen-dollar checks dated by the months of the school year. It was much-needed money. The family back in Beaumont was still struggling, his mother still working and living in rented homes, and his sister Marie needing help with various expenses. To help his family and cover the rest of his own tuition and living expenses, Brooks cobbled together different part-time jobs.

After a while he had moved into the Oak Grove co-op dormitory, where all students had to contribute to their room and board; he worked washing dishes after breakfast. Brooks recalled a lesson he learned on that job:

> *What I did was the best job, I thought, washing dishes for the breakfast meal. Weren't quite as many dishes and you could get it done pretty promptly. Everybody was hustling their bustle to get ready to go to school and so forth, and that's what I did. I did learn in the regular washing of dishes you could never*

wash more than four glasses with one hand. You can't handle five; you can only handle four. I could only handle four glasses at a time, dipping them in the water and so forth. That worked out pretty well.

Perhaps it reflects his own political modesty, but it also may suggest that Brooks understood limitations. He rarely set his sights on something that he could not accomplish. The glasses could have been a metaphor for his future ambitions. Politics is the art of the possible, and Brooks would only commit himself to what was possible.

In another part-time job working as a carhop, he displayed another trait that he maintained throughout his political career. He never forgot a slight. At the drive-in restaurant where he worked, if a customer ordered a milkshake but was nasty or said something unkind to the hard-working student, Brooks would not just ignore the insult. Before he delivered the milkshake to their car, Brooks took out the straw, folded it at the bottom, and put it back in the glass. No matter how much sucking power the customer applied, he would not get the milkshake to flow. After walking away, he would look back and watch the customer's consternation with no small satisfaction.

Brooks, described by one friend as having the energy of three people, continued to find other part-time work, including two jobs at the *Daily Texan*, the university's student newspaper. In addition to becoming a reporter and editor, he began making deliveries. He bought a Model A Ford from a cousin for $100 and named it "Henry." Each morning at 6 a.m. he cranked it to deliver thousands of copies of the *Daily Texan* to apartment buildings, dormitories, and offices around campus; he was paid the handsome sum of thirty dollars a month.

I parked in the back, and it was a Model A, and on a cold winter morning when you started that Model A it would pop like a cannon and wake up people for blocks, I suspect.

He declared journalism as his major area of study around the time that he had joined the *Daily Texan*. He brought his teenage experience and enthusiasm from his time at the *Beaumont Enterprise*, but he was also undoubtedly attracted to the newspaper's traditional independent streak.

Life in Austin suited Brooks. Through chance and his various pursuits, he had found himself immersed in a close group of interesting and ambitious friends. He would soon earn membership in the Friars Club, an exclusive honor society for students who had made significant contributions to the university. Only eight new members were selected each year.

BRISCOE: Among his fellow "friars" and numerous other friends that he would meet and remain close to for decades, there was one in particular who would have a profound impact on his life and career.

Dolph Briscoe came from a very wealthy family near Uvalde and had a deep Texas pedigree. His father was a self-made cattle rancher, owner of vast properties, and a direct descendant of Andrew Briscoe, who fought against the Mexicans during the Texas Revolution and was one of the original signers of the Texas Declaration of Independence. There is a county in the Texas panhandle named after him. Briscoe's father was also a business partner of former Texas governor Ross Sterling and on speaking terms with Harry Truman and Texas heavyweights like Sam Rayburn and Lyndon Johnson.

At school, Dolph was heavily involved with his fraternity and student politics, and he and Brooks started out as political rivals on campus in 1940. Their introduction to each other did not bode well for a friendship. Briscoe recalled many years later:

> There were two major groups there on the campus at UT at that time, and each group tried to dominate the campus politics, one being the independents, and the so-called frat people, who belonged to a fraternity.
>
> Of course, the independents outnumbered the frats, oh, I don't know, two to one, three to one, considerably. But those in the fraternity probably took more interest in campus politics and worked a little harder at it. And that's when I first got to meet Jack. He was a leader of the independents, lived over at the little campus, and he was a real leader . . . a really effective politician.
>
> Jack wrote for the Daily Texan, and he wrote one of the meanest articles about me—and I've had quite a few mean articles written through the years—but I'll tell you, it was the meanest article that I've ever had written about me.

I remember he called me the "Golden Boy of Chi Phi." I mean, in a very, very derogatory way, and went on in this article. And, it was enough to infuriate anybody. And it certainly had that effect on me.†

Briscoe recalled that during his sophomore year, he knew he needed a college degree but did not know what he wanted to do with it. His father repeatedly warned him against flunking out, but Briscoe would later insist that his future changed not out of fear of failing but through a romance with a local girl named Betty Jane "Janey" Slaughter, who changed his way of thinking about school and about Brooks. It was Janey's fondness for Brooks that would begin the two men's friendship.

After I met Janey, I had a different goal in mind, and that was to talk her into marrying me. Janey somehow saw a lot in Jack that I didn't see.

Briscoe and Janey married in 1942, and though fate would separate Jack Brooks from the couple, Janey was determined that the three of them would stay friends. Briscoe recalled:

She was determined that we ought to become good friends, because she saw in Jack somebody who was going to have a great future, and had the makings of a real friend. She had extremely good judgment about people, much better than I ever have had . . . You know, I thought, well, this so and so. He and I are gonna never get along. But, of course, it didn't turn out that way.

Briscoe had his own great future ahead; he would go on to become governor of Texas thirty years later, and his family's ranches would make him the largest landowner in the state. He owned such great swaths of land, 640,000 acres, that combined they represented almost the area of Rhode Island. Throughout the years, Brooks recognized that he could have contentious relationships with congressional leaders and government officials, but he was fond of saying that he could win over those opponents by

---

† This quotation is taken verbatim from a video interview that can be viewed at www.jackbrooksfoundation.org.

persuasion and sheer willpower. When he told stories about some of those battles, invariably Brooks would end the anecdote by saying, "Well, he's for me now." That meant that the person had come around and now saw things Brooks's way. After a rocky start, Briscoe was for Brooks now. After UT, he and Brooks would go on to be desk mates in the Texas legislature, then hunting partners through the years, and eventually, lifelong friends.

But like millions of other Americans, the lives they were expecting to live would soon be put on hold. The immense shadow of the war in Europe already darkened their early college years, and after one Sunday morning in early December of 1941, thoughts of the future changed radically for all Americans.

3

War!

The night of December 7, 1941, First Lady Eleanor Roosevelt chose to keep to her regularly scheduled evening radio address. After calmly explaining what immediate actions the president, his cabinet, and military officials were taking, she spoke words of comfort to the countless families who would be impacted by the challenges that lay ahead. She spoke of her faith in the country and reassured listeners that "whatever is asked of us I'm sure we can accomplish it. We are the free and unconquerable people of the United States of America."

The following day, at five minutes after noon, Speaker of the House Sam Rayburn banged down his heavy gavel to start a special joint session of Congress. House members were already in their places as members of the Senate, the Supreme Court, and the cabinet filed into the House Chamber and sat in their assigned seats. Finally, the large doors opened again and everyone stood at the announcement of the president of the United States.

Franklin Roosevelt, holding the arm of his son, James, who was in his dress blue Marine Corps uniform, slowly made his way to the lectern and gave a short but detailed account of how the bombing of a Hawaiian naval port and airfields, a place few Americans had ever heard of, was part of a coordinated Japanese attack to defeat the United States and its allied nations.

The Japanese torpedo planes that attacked Pearl Harbor that Sunday morning had an immediate impact beyond the crippling of much of the U.S. Pacific fleet; they galvanized the American public and made what had been a European war and distant Japanese threat come crashing home.

Isolationist groups had grown in number and political sway over the preceding years. The largest isolationist group, the America First Committee, had over eight hundred thousand members nationwide. Several rallies against America's entry into the war had been previously scheduled for the days that followed Pearl Harbor, including one in Boston, with Charles Lindbergh as the featured speaker. As the details of the Japanese attack became known, however, those rallies were quietly cancelled; regional chapters of the America First Committee disbanded, and the isolationist movement seemed to dissolve overnight.

In Congress that day, Roosevelt declared that the nation's "righteous might" would prevail. The country's transformation to a war footing was almost immediate. In small, mid-American towns like Beaumont, wartime strengthened the resolve and courage of citizens to band together for the common good.

Military recruitment numbers rose and public sentiment, solidified by anger and fear, now supported an aggressive entry into the war. Admiral William F. Halsey captured the collective feeling of the moment when he said, "Before we're through with them, the Japanese language will only be spoken in hell."

Young men, newly enlisted, appeared in crisp military uniforms at railroad and port towns such as Beaumont and Port Arthur. Men who had been unemployed in the Midwest and the South, along with more and more women, found jobs opening up in munitions and vehicle factories across the country. Farmers from the Northeast to California changed their crops, as more staples were needed for the war effort. Within months, rationing began for normal consumer items, including gasoline, tires, sugar, meat, milk, shoes, and nylons.

Pearl Harbor changed the college routine for Jack Brooks and millions of others around the country. He became aware of a larger world, though for all the dreams and musings a young man may have, he could not have understood the part he would play in it. Nor, as he and the rest of the country listened to Roosevelt's impassioned speech in Congress that day in the early winter of 1941, could he imagine that in just over a decade he would not only forge a deep friendship with Speaker Rayburn but also begin a long career in that same chamber.

ENLISTMENT: Brooks's military service was not really ordained until his friend and fellow editor, Bob Owens, left the school newspaper to enlist in the marines. Not much later, a marine recruiter came to the Texas campus to interview and sign up potential recruits. That is when Brooks had to use what he called "a little blackmail" to join. The recruiter declared there was no way that Brooks, who was five foot nine and just shy of 120 pounds, was going to be a marine; he was just "too slight and scrawny."

"He ended up recruiting a bunch of athletes, you know, big, bustlin' strong guys," Brooks recalled many decades later. The recruiter suggested that he look into the army, which was enlisting soldiers as fast as it could process them through boot camps.

But the pride of being a leatherneck, the traditional nickname for the marines, was already established and Brooks was determined to be part of it. He told the recruiter that he didn't want to go to "no damn army," that he wanted to be a marine, and if the recruiter wanted to get a story in the student newspaper now that Brooks was the acting editor, well, it may take several months before such a story might be possible. The recruiter quickly saw the sense of that, and that's how he came to sign up Brooks to be a Marine Corps reservist.

Though Brooks still had to wait for a call-up, he was already making a full-court press for an appointment to officer candidate school, getting the editor of the *Sunday Enterprise* in Beaumont, the head of Lamar College, and the dean of UT's School of Arts and Sciences to write letters of recommendation.

To accelerate his studies, Brooks took classes in summer school. He also enlisted school officials to write that he had fulfilled all the requirements for a degree in journalism. In the spring he campaigned to get early credit for his last class. He wrote to the Eighth Naval District headquarters in New Orleans:

With students leaving every day for the army, it makes me realize how little I am contributing to the war effort as a student. Is there any way I can be assigned to immediate active duty?

Though he would have to wait a little longer, his timing was right. The marines, anticipating the need for second lieutenants (who, as leaders of the small units, are the most visible, vulnerable, and high-casualty jobs in ground warfare) in a protracted war effort, wanted many of the enlisting college students to finish their degrees. Now nineteen years old and armed with a consent form signed by his mother, Jack Brooks formally enlisted in the Marine Corps Reserve as a private in November of 1942.

Halfway around the world, the first amphibious offensive operation by the U.S. Navy and Marine Corps was already underway in the British Solomon Islands east of Australia. Around the island of Guadalcanal, the Japanese Imperial Navy was being repelled for the first time by a strengthened American air and naval force. After an initial loss to a marine assault, the Japanese made repeated attempts to retake the island. The ferocity would last for six months and ultimately cause nearly five thousand American casualties from fighting, malaria, and other tropical diseases, while an estimated twenty-eight thousand Japanese were killed or wounded. Each side would lose dozens of ships and hundreds of planes. And Jack Brooks was on the slow route straight there.

TRAINING: Months passed as he finished school and waited for his call-up notice. Finally, he was ordered to travel by rail to the Marine Corps recruit depot at Parris Island, South Carolina, to begin training and active service. Brooks remembered:

> *The physical part was pretty tough for me. Push-ups were never my great strength. But I shot "expert" on the rifle range. And so all those athletes knew that at five-hundred yards, I could blow their brains out with live ammunition, and perhaps I would if they were not civil with me.*

Once a marine, Brooks went to the Marine Corps Officer Candidate School (OCS) in Quantico, Virginia, to join the 35th Reserve Officer Class. He said:

> *I did fine there because that was a lot of bookwork, and I didn't have a bit*

of trouble with that. The athletics part was a little tough for me, still, of course.

Recognizing his particular talents, his commanding officers offered Brooks a job as a trainer at Quantico. He could stay and help prepare other recruits for the war. It was a prestigious offer for someone who had enlisted as a private, and it would have been a safe and relatively comfortable alternative to the front lines. The country was now fighting on two fronts, and tales of the action dominated the news every day. Brooks wanted to be part of it. He loved a good fight and none would ever be as good as this. He turned down the job offer and continued to prepare himself for duty overseas.

FORT BENNING: However, instead of a combat unit, the Corps assigned him to an eight-week officer communications course at the Infantry School at Fort Benning, Georgia, a sprawling army complex along the Alabama border. There he applied to be in a machine gun outfit, but his test scores were too high. Although he would also receive infantry training, as a communications specialist he would be part of the rear echelon of troops supporting those on the front lines once, and if, he was ever sent into a combat area. He was confined to the 13th Company, 1st Student Training Regiment, an army unit, a bitter pill after years of anticipating being directly in the fight. He wrote his mother:

Dearest Mom,

All's well here at Benning . . . I'm beginning to like Ft. Benning much better, the course much better too. My but I hated it for a while. Communications was not exactly what I joined the marines for and I've been pretty bitter about having to go to this damned school at the Army post, . . . Was lucky to get this typewriter. It is the company machine and the First Sergeant let me use it and gave me the corporal's key to the office. Tonight I'm Charge of Quarters and will be on call all night. Sleep right here in the next room. Privacy for a change. It will probably make me feel strange to sleep in a room (small) by myself without 20 or 30 other men in the room. But it is warmer over here and quiet. I'll sleep like a baby.

After Fort Benning he was sent to Philadelphia for further training in communications and signals, and for a while, he thought he would even be sent to Boston for nine weeks to take Signal Corps courses at Harvard, a prospect he did not relish. There he would take courses on maintenance and operations of field radio equipment, code practice, radio procedure, and message center operation. But Brooks wanted to do more than just study, and so far, he was spending the war going from one training to another.

Service records show he had bulked up to 137 pounds, just heavy enough now to be a lightweight boxer. He said it was the first time he had received three square meals a day, and it was also the first time he would see a doctor regularly.

He was napping when a sergeant came into his barracks room in Philadelphia and called out his name and new officer service number: 0-2-9-1-7-0. It was a number he could immediately remember nearly seventy years later. The first zero meant that he was an officer, and the two stood for B, for his last name. The sergeant said his new assignment was with the I Marine Amphibious Corps, to an island in the South Pacific he had never heard of. Brooks finally was getting his wish to contribute at the front lines. "I told them next to me, I don't know where it is, but I'm going."

Brooks with a friend drove nonstop from the East Coast to Beaumont, a route he would take many more times in his life. On the way, he stopped in at the small cottage in Crowley to kiss his grandmother goodbye. She said, "Well, son, you won't see me anymore, but I love you, and take care of yourself." Mama Brooks, as she was called, was correct; she died before Brooks returned from the war.

In Beaumont he spent a preciously short time with his mother, sister, and close friends before taking the train all the way to San Francisco, where he was to await his next orders. For two and a half weeks Brooks was housed in the St. Francis Hotel with other soldiers. Whiling away his days practicing Morse code and map reading, he also lived it up as much as a twenty-one-year-old could. He went shopping for his sister in Chinatown, saw the San Francisco Symphony, and went on a couple of dates with an FBI employee and an airline stewardess, though he admitted in his letters that he did not really care for either. But there was a major's daughter! He wrote his mother:

Met a peach of a girl last night. Very pretty, smart & with a personality, smile & wit that is tops. Have a date with her Monday. Can't keep a good man down—I finally found a fine girl to date. This place has a lot of the other kind. Better stop now—

DEPLOYMENT: At 9 a.m. on March 18, Brooks reported to the port of San Francisco and found that he was to leave immediately aboard the USS *General J. R. Brooke*, a five hundred-foot long man-of-war troop transport vessel with twenty-eight guns that was loading up for the long haul across the Pacific Ocean.

That day, Brooks was assigned "officer of the guard" duty and oversaw a contingent of army privates as 3,600 troops and officers from the marines, navy, and army and weeks' worth of provisions came aboard all day and night. The task of overseeing the privates was simple but enjoyable, Brooks said, and because of it he met and made friends with some of the ship's officers, a wise move as, he recalled, their "friendship was to prove very valuable on the trip over."

The ship left port the next day on its cruise to the South Pacific where it would ultimately dock outside the city of Noumea on New Caledonia, a French territory where the U.S. Pacific fleet had set up a large base. The III Marine Amphibious Corps, to which Brooks was now assigned, had recently stationed there as well.

On board, Brooks was billeted with seventeen other officers on the top deck. Since he had come aboard first and had a friend who was familiar with the ship's layout, Brooks scored a top bunk with pipes overhead so both he and his gear would be situated nicely during the trip.

The vessel was part of a newly commissioned class of transport vessels, and it was very fast, according to his letters home. Exactly how fast he could not repeat for security reasons, but at the ship's since-reported top speed of seventeen knots, the crew needed two full weeks to traverse the 5,500-some nautical miles to their destination.

Life aboard the ship was active, with a disciplined schedule. A typical day included:

0545—REVEILLE—Call all hands

0602—General Quarters

0702—Sunrise

0715—Breakfast

0725—Church Call

0730—Catholic Mass on No. 4 Hatch if weather permits

0800—Turn to. Pipe sweepers, clean sweep down, fore and aft, all decks and ladders. Scrub upper decks. All Divisions police cleaning stations

1200—DINNER

1300—Turn to. All Divisions police cleaning stations as necessary

1400—Working party

1700—SUPPER

Sunset—General Quarters

2100—TAPS

There was also time to sit around the barracks rooms, talk, and play cards. Brooks wrote home that "shipboard life was one end of hearts and poker games." A new friend taught him to play chess. Men shared "the dope"—the latest news and rumors—with one another, which inevitably centered on where they might be going and how bad the conditions were there. Veterans aboard the ship would be pestered by newer soldiers about what the front was like, while those who had been at the front or confined to a boat for months would ask for updates from home.

Soldiers could not purchase airmail stamps on the ship, but Brooks made friends with a lieutenant who pulled some strings to get Brooks fifty stamps. After more than a week at sea, Brooks wrote home for the first time from somewhere deep in the middle of the Pacific. In a letter written on his own personal Marine Corps letterhead, his excitement was palpable.

27 MARCH AT SEA

Dearest Mom + All—

Left a few hours early + was rushed. But got a fine bunk to sleep in + all's very comfortable aboard. Eating like a king + enjoying the trip very, very much. You know, I like water + this ocean has got plenty of it. You can look for 20 miles or more in every direction on a clear day + not see anything but waves . . . I've met a lot of army + navy + a few marine officers. It's pleasant to talk with them. Get good gossip about this + that.

I'm going to the island I first thought I would go to. From there I expect to go where B. Deuster was located. At that place I'll get an assignment. This first stop should be interesting. Been brushing up on my French + I plan to use some of it . . .

Will write again on board. They'll probably mail them all when we land. I'm hoping we see a ship going back to the States that could pick up our mail

Food is excellent.—And did you know I weighed 155 with my uniform on in Frisco! I must weigh 145 stripped. Guess I'll work that up to 150 in time.

Morale among the men was high, and the commanding officers tried to reinforce that. A public letter went out to the ship's captain from King Neptune, or "Neptunus Rex, Ruler of the Raging Main." The humorous rite of passage read:

A Hearty and salty Welcome to my Domain . . . Information has also been received by the Royal Secretary, Shellback Davy Jones, that you have on board a sizeable contingent of landlubbers, beach-combers, dog-faces, sea lawyers, lounge lizards, parlor dunnigans, plow deserters, park bench warmers, chicken chasers, chit signers, shack men, liberty hounds, gyrenes, and other denizens of the mainland falsely masquerading as seamen.

Brooks kept a copy of the letter with the rest of his correspondence. The next day, Brooks and a majority of the others aboard crossed the equator for the first time, another rite of passage among sailors, one that often involved some goofy activity on deck initiating the men into the "Ancient Order of the Deep."

Life aboard the ship felt secure to Brooks, but the routine could be grueling. Brooks recalled that his first memorable assignment on the ocean voyage was to keep a despondent lieutenant who was returning to the front from committing suicide. Brooks found him climbing over the rail once, but Brooks grabbed him by the belt and pulled him back to the deck. He recalled years later:

If I had known then what I know now, I think I would have just pushed him overboard or let him go.

NOUMEA: On April 3, the USS *General Brooke* arrived off the coast of Noumea, a French outpost well below the Solomon Islands archipelago. The men had seen nothing but open water the entire trip, except for the last two days, when sightings of other military transports became frequent, and then again outside the harbor, where U.S. sub chasers abounded. Since the U.S. had turned the colony into its military headquarters for the entire Pacific theater, the sheer magnitude of the hardware and activity must have been an awe-inspiring sight for the greenhorn marines who had only heard about the front since enlisting.

Once on dry land again, Brooks bought fifty seashells from a "Ghuk," one of the native islanders, to have them strung onto a necklace for his sister. He also bought himself a stainless steel watchband made by the Seabees for five dollars. Word was that normal cloth or leather bands developed a nasty sweat smell in the heat.

Brooks and some other officers drove fifteen miles inland to a designated marine housing area of small huts. They shared one with screens on the windows (most of the huts did not have screens) and a latrine for eight. He wrote home:

I drew an officers' clothing roll today, an officers' pack, bedding roll, carbine magazines, carbine, field glasses, poncho, and some other gear. So you see there are some advantages to traveling as light as possible.

With no specific assignment and lots of time on their hands, the officers lounged together outside the hut on some inventive furniture that previous marines had put together with found wood scraps. Brooks wrote that the "mosquitoes are fierce but nothing worse than those Sabine marsh bombers" back home. He played a lot of hearts and learned acey-deucy, which was played with dice and a checkerboard.

The island of New Caledonia was a strategic location for the Pacific fleet, as it sat around a thousand miles from the allied shore of Australia and below the farthest extent of the Imperial Japanese Army's reach into the South Pacific. All of the front line combat areas were north of the island, so when soldiers sat around their barracks and shared the dope, they also speculated about "going north," which meant going into battle, and where they each individually might land.

There were myriad stories about which islands were the worst, which landings had decimated infantry troops, and what command's strategy might be for future operations. At Brooks's level, however, talk of where anyone would go was all just speculation. No one knew a thing about what would happen next. Secrecy was paramount. Even in their letters back home, marines could not tell loved ones where they were with any precision, nor could they divulge exactly what they were doing. Everyone understood that was the way it had to be.

Within any marine task force there would be units for infantry, engineers, and artillery, along with several other more specialized ones. Brooks knew he would be assigned to a signal battalion, as that was what he had been trained for, but as to where or with whom, he had no idea.

He submitted a request to be assigned to the 1st Marine Division, which he considered the best. It was the oldest and largest division, respectfully nicknamed "the Old Breed" by the rest of the Corps. The division had made the first amphibious landing of the Pacific War when it landed at Guadalcanal two years earlier. During the ensuing five months of battles, the troops had made a name for themselves, and Brooks wanted to be a part of it. He wrote home:

> Things are quiet here but I heard that I might get to go on the next operation. Exactly when that will be of course is something I have no idea of. Maybe two weeks, maybe six months. There is absolutely no way to tell since all orders pertaining to the operation are kept secret. Extreme caution and secrecy is essential even on islands like this. The "word" on such operations get around too well, and, so, to stop that, officials just do not give anyone any inkling of where or when.

While still stateside, Brooks had at one point instructed his mother to pay attention to the first letter of every paragraph of his letters. It was through this simple code that he would relay information to her about his whereabouts, information like names and directions that would otherwise be physically snipped out of his letters by the marine correspondence censors, a duty that Brooks himself had to perform for an hour most mornings. He must have forgotten to keep up with his code—the first letters from each paragraph in most of his correspondence amount only to gibberish—but his mother certainly did not. For the length of his deployment, over two years, she underlined the first letter of every single one of his paragraphs in hopes of parsing together a secret message.

Within two weeks, Brooks received notice that he would be an assistant platoon commander and coding officer with the headquarters staff of the III Marine Amphibious Corps on Guadalcanal, which had been retaken from the Japanese. The island was now a staging and resupply area for Allied assaults. By April 18, Brooks was back on a transport cargo ship steaming north for the Solomon Islands.

He would spend the next few months island-hopping, his life divided between island travel and weeks aboard various ships. For Brooks, assignment to the signal battalion meant being an "officer messenger" and carrying communiqués from headquarter units on the beachheads up to frontline troops. Roads were either hastily constructed or bombed out, and he often rode a hundred miles a day over them in a jeep, an activity he described simply as "tiresome." He used the travel to his advantage, though, trading this and that with his new contacts to secure sought-after goods such as: nail clippers, shaving lotion, good face soap, doggie truck driver caps ("which everyone wears around here"), limited quantities of chocolate, cigars, and leather shoe laces. He sent home knickknacks and collectibles—a Japanese pen, a rifle, a wristwatch, and a little silver plate.

Brooks developed heat rash, a skin condition he described as "worse than poison oak." It would rain once or twice every day, and the air was very damp. He tried to dry out the rash by sunning it, and he built a small platform to keep his cot off the wet ground. He also swam in the ocean water at the end of some days and was eating so much that he must have weighed 145 to 150 pounds. Life was not exactly comfortable, but

Brooks reported being generally happy and healthy. He wrote his sister:

> *Beaumont maybe somewhat slow but this rock I'm near right now is the end of the world. Not a palm tree with fronds on it . . . just a few stumps not over 10 feet above sea level and topped with white coral and sand . . .*

At night, soldiers watched movies below deck. For fear of being spotted by the Japanese, they often sailed with the lights out and the hatch doors sealed. Temperatures below deck would be stifling, so Brooks preferred to stay on deck and read.

Though attached to infantry, Brooks and his unit only came ashore after the fighting had ceased. As he got closer to the war itself, he witnessed the remains of some horrific scenes and wrote that some men were already getting the "1,000-yard stare" in their eyes. On June 11, his ship landed on a long, concrete jetty that the Japanese had built months earlier on a small atoll that had just been recaptured. Once ashore, he stopped and stared at a marker that read "E.D. 200." The initials "E.D." stood for "enemy dead," which meant there were two hundred Japanese soldiers buried there. Brooks surmised that they had probably been buried under a few feet of coral sand by a bulldozer. He saw Japanese concrete-reinforced pillboxes that had been cracked up badly by naval gunfire, and he hoped they would do "as well with those big naval guns on this operation." The Japanese resistance was gaining intensity with each Allied advance. Brooks again made a request for transfer, this time to the 4th Marines, an infantry regiment that his battalion was attached to. His friend's brother was with them and had just won the Distinguished Service Cross for heroism after dragging his sergeant out of enemy fire. That request from Brooks was also denied, as command had other plans for him.

After Brooks's arrival on Guadalcanal, he was put in charge of the officers' mess and assigned to the communications staff of Major General Roy Geiger, a legendary officer who commanded the entire III Amphibious Corps forces. He was also known as someone who operated outside the normal bounds of protocol when necessary. Geiger, a World War I veteran who had been the fifth marine to become a naval aviator, on at least two occasions personally "appropriated" light observation planes to do his own reconnaissance over battlefields, a highly technical and risky maneuver that less senior officers would not dare attempt.

Brooks was asked to become an aide to the general. To serve directly for the man would have been an honor, but Brooks turned the offer down. Despite the general's reputation and the opportunity this presented, Brooks did not want to spend his war protected and removed from the action. He recalled:

> *The general was a fine and distinguished general, Roy Geiger, wonderful man from all reports that I knew about him, but I didn't much want to be a general's aide. I thought I had not trained to do that and so I told them no. I thanked them but I didn't want to do that; I would rather be assigned to one of the company's in the communication section.*

NEWS FROM HOME: The logistics of war at times seem incomprehensible to combatants as well as civilians. Hundreds of thousands of men await orders on sea and on land, some preparing for the next battle, others held back as reinforcements in case of heavy casualties. From the time decisions were made or shipments were sent, it could take weeks for them to ripple along the chain and finally affect those near the action. Anxiety built along with the tedium, so basic activities like writing letters and cleaning mercifully filled in some of the time.

From the moment he left for boot camp, in addition to writing his mother every two or three days, Brooks also kept a long list of pen pals with whom he stayed in regular correspondence, whether penning letters on the stationery of hotels he was temporarily quartered in or typing out lengthy posts on thin rice paper he found while ashore on various islands. He told his family that the air mail service was very good on Tuesdays and Saturdays. A letter would take thirty-six hours to arrive in San Francisco and then probably another day and a half to reach Texas. Brooks mailed home all of the letters he received while he was overseas and gave his sister—who for a time preferred to go by the name "Cheré"—strict orders to file away all his correspondence, including the letters he received from family, friends, and a few amorous former classmates. Like a true politician, even in personal matters he put people to work for him right away.

> *Dearest Cheré,*
>
> *[Or?] is it still Cheré? Am hoping you're filing my letters promptly. It might not work out so well if Mother started reading them. And you too must be broadminded about these things. Esp. letters from Corrick & the Alabama queen. Or from Marie for that matter . . .*

He told his sister that he was having a fine time and would continue to do so unless a "fish" (torpedo) hit the small boat that transported him around the islands, which he believed was "loaded to the gills with bombs." In an attempt to allay her fears and probably his own, he added, "Anyhow I've got a life jacket and the odds are good, the water is warm, and the sharks are probably already well fed . . . "

He informed her and his mother about almost every aspect of his life and inquired all about theirs. His sister attended Lamar, but with only a year left, she had no desire to continue. Though already abroad when he learned of this, Brooks entreated her to stick it out until graduation, even offering to pay for her studies himself and pull whatever strings he could with the administration. He had always been very protective of his younger sister. She remembered years later:

> *One time at a high school dance, I was dancing with a boy who was not part of our group. He was visiting his aunt in Beaumont, and she got him to go to our dance . . . and I was dancing with this boy from Dallas. And I didn't notice anything different, but Jack was up there and tapped him on the shoulder and said "don't dance like that with my sister."' And I was so humiliated. It had something to do with a hand in the back, I don't know. He was kind of a creep, anyway. He went back to Dallas . . . Exactly where he belonged.*

In 1944 Cheré was single, and Brooks, despite all the distractions, told her he was keeping an eye out for eligible marines who might be passing through Beaumont once the war was over. Always playing the big brother, he also sent her detailed instructions on how to retrieve his deposited military salary to pay bills and purchase war bonds for her and their mother. If someone special had a birthday coming up, Brooks would include a note about how much his sister should spend to pick up something nice.

Among Brooks's correspondents were a network of journalists and former journalists that he had worked with at the *Daily Texan* at UT. In the years they had all reported and edited at the *Texan*, the publication clashed several times with the UT administration, including by encouraging equal admission of Negroes, a stance most remarkable at the time. During the war years, the old friends continued to apprise each other regularly about the goings-on in the state's House of Representatives and at the university. They addressed Brooks with a slew of nicknames from his college days and even before. Among them were: Jackie, Brooksie, Brooks lad, Jackson, Bascom, Bastom, and "Rah," among others. "Rah" stemmed from his partying days at school.

One of Brooks's journalist correspondents was Ann Corrick, or Corky as she was called, who had since moved from Austin to Washington to cover national politics and had even received an offer to work for the Associated Press. She regaled Brooks with her colorful prose and with stories like covering a press conference for President Franklin Roosevelt and seeing his little black Scottish terrier, Gala, sitting right in the middle of the lobby greeting everyone. Among the local political gossip was news that the Beaumont-area congressman, Representative Martin Dies, would not be seeking reelection to the U.S. House.

Brooks had a personal dislike of Dies that would only grow in the coming years. Publicly, Dies blamed a throat ailment for his decision not to run again, but Brooks and others understood it as tacit admission that he would not be able to beat a judge that the labor unions had backed to enter the race. The judge, Marty Combs, was a total stranger to Brooks then, but he would later play a central part in Brooks's career path. When news of Dies's decision broke, Brooks wrote his sister:

> . . . *In a few months I'm going to want you to send me the overseas edition of* Newsweek, *a magazine similar to* Time *magazine but not so damned conser-*

vative. I heard that my favorite character (to shoot), Martin Dies, was not going to run for Congress this time. Probably afraid he would get beat by someone. I only wish I could run against him.

Always with a mind on politics, Brooks frequently expressed his views to his family on a number of issues, including not having a ballot to cast in the 1944 presidential election while he was deployed.

9 June 44

The texas legislature may cheat me out of my vote this year but when I get back I'm going to do my best to make them rue the day they did it. Every congressman who because of racial and political fears voted against a national service man's vote strangled democracy.

29 August 44

About the election. Just tell them your brother is fighting for Roosevelt and not for Dewey. I went overseas after joining the Corps to fight for the principles I believe Roosevelt has. That he has made mistakes and errors I do not deny. But he can do more in 6 weeks then the pipsqueak can do in 6 years.

30 August 44

Remember, while I'm thinking of it, to vote for Roosevelt. And remind mother of the same thing. The Democrats are putting up an experienced and capable president and a brilliant vice president (Truman) against Republicans that can not stand against them in any way. So be sure and vote for the Democrats.

5 September 44

Undoubtedly the peace will be fouled up to a large extent but if Dewey is president at the peace conferences, I have no hope. He would not even try to stand up for the things I hold important.

There was other news too. In February, Ann Corrick included a snippet she had received in a letter from a mutual friend who was deployed in the Mediterranean Sea. She had found it too funny to keep to herself.

Oh. I think I said I thought jack the beast adkins is in north Africa? Well I know is now—I had a letter from his saturday. Apparently his fox hole is rather

well equipped—he wrote of champagne and a moustache, for which he claims
he is growing a goatee to match. The old rascal, I bet he is, too.

I'm going to quote a bit from his letter:

"When they speak of side arms in this country they mean a 3-inch gun. No
scotch here, no bourbon, no gin and particularly no rum. And also no tonk (the
VD rate is about 95 per cent here.) I don't know about chinese women, but it's
a g.d. lie about french women. I've lost my 20-20 vision looking for one of those
petit cocquettes they're always talking about."

Less than two weeks later, Adkins and three other officers failed to return to base in their boat. Two were reported killed, and two were reported
missing in action (MIA), yet there was no word on which were which. A
concerned Corrick called the office of Lyndon Johnson, who had a seat in the
U.S. House at the time. If any civilian might have advance news concerning
local soldiers on the front lines, it would have been Johnson. Johnson was
a familiar face around the state legislature, where Corrick, Brooks, and the
other young political journalists had worked; his district included Austin.
But he told Corrick that all he knew was that Adkins's boat had sunk, approximately at the same time as the "Anzio beachhead," which referred to
an Allied amphibious assault on the Italian mainland. Adkins had been a
dear friend to both Brooks and Corrick. A saddened Brooks wrote home
with the news.

Around the same time, Brooks's friend Elliot Katz wrote him while
recuperating on a hospital bed in England. Katz had broken his leg during
an "incident with a Jerry machine gun" while crossing the Soar River in
December. He subsequently had taken an involuntary bath in the river,
though it was the first "wash" he had been afforded in months. Katz and
Brooks had trained together at Fort Benning. Katz closed his letter by
giving updates on their friends from the unit who had since been killed
in action.

The next month, news came that Brooks's friends Bill Hart and Caesar
Martine were both listed as MIA. A few days later, a pen pal stationed in
Samoa relayed news that their mutual friend Powell Compere had been killed
in Europe. The friend added, "He had one of the most brilliant oratorical

and public speaking gifts I've ever seen. He could have had a very good political future."

GUAM: Brooks insisted he wanted to be assigned to a company in the communications section, and so he was transferred to Company B on the small island known as Bougainville, an Australian territory where Japanese forces still fought for small pockets of territory. From there, he spent long weeks at sea with the offshore reserves for the expected assault on the island of Saipan.

But the fortunes of war were still shifting from one battle to another. Troop movements were quick, and within a month Brooks received new orders to move with the forward echelon of the headquarters staff in an assault of the Marianas Islands. The targets were a key port and airfields on Guam.

The island had been a strategic, if vulnerable, American outpost since the end of the Spanish-American War. In the first few days after Pearl Harbor, the Japanese had captured the island and begun fortifying it against future assault. Guam was close enough to the Japanese mainland that if retaken, American B-29 bombers would be able to make bombing runs from Guam to Japan. It also provided a deep-water port, which would provide anchorage for American ships. By mid-1944, the island had become heavily defended against any Allied offensive.

The liberation of Guam had begun with harassing aerial attacks. Amid an enormous armada of battleships, cruisers, and destroyers, Brooks watched from his ship for days as around-the-clock aerial and naval bombardments softened up the Japanese defenses. Then on July 21, with Major General Geiger commanding the marines' assault, the first troops established a beachhead and began pushing inland. Brooks, the signal battalion, and over fifty thousand Americans followed suit shortly thereafter.

Eager to see more action, Brooks tried to transfer into the 22nd Marines, who were trying to capture the fiercely contested Orote Peninsula, where the Japanese were still deeply entrenched. But another lieutenant who was more senior in rank had also applied and got the appointment. The fighting was brutal, and many of the Japanese took extreme measures when faced with the advancing marines and their accompanying artillery and tank support. Cyril J. O'Brien's definitive account of the battle noted "suicides were many and random. Soldiers jumped off cliffs, hugged exploding grenades, even cut their own throats."

In taking the peninsula, the marines suffered almost one thousand casualties, including the lieutenant who had taken Brooks's spot. Brooks later learned that one night during a banzai charge, an enemy soldier had killed that lieutenant in his foxhole. Brooks said:

It was really tragic. I didn't try to get transferred there anymore.

Two weeks after the first landings, bombing and mortar shelling continued as a full third of the island had yet to be secured. By some local Guamanian accounts, there were still as many as six thousand Japanese troops fighting or waiting to fight on the island.

Brooks wrote home that he had arrived safely onshore but that conditions on the island were "hot, hot, hot, sandy, crowded and inadequate in many respects." It would be another nine days before Geiger declared that organized Japanese resistance was over and the "mop-up" effort began. In the twenty-one days of fighting for Guam, the marines lost 1,500 men with an additional 5,000 wounded. The signal battalion lost three men and thirteen were wounded.

After another month onshore, Brooks wrote again:

The climate here is nasty . . . wears you out. You can tell the difference in men who have been out here 30 months. Combat conditions are just bad. War is bad, dangerous, unhealthy and unpleasant . . . and the less you have to do with it, the better off you are.

By September, the mop-up of the island continued, and Brooks was moved to a pole construction company within his battalion. His unit was now responsible for putting in poles and cables right behind tactical or combat wire. Brooks wrote that he was "tickled to death" with his new job. The new company only had one man killed, so he was going to be fairly safe, he wrote his mother.

Brooks had a propensity for risk-taking throughout his life, but his actions were never reckless. His communication work, which frequently meant delivering messages in and around the fighting, was risky too. To deliver a message to the commanding general of the 77th Army Division, Brooks rode across and around the peninsula in a "DUKW," a small amphibious troop carrier built on the chassis of an army truck that could make short journeys through the surf. It was the first model of the odd boat now used for sightseeing on commercial "Duck Tours." "I wasn't worried about getting shot," Brooks recalled, "I was worried about the Duck! The pump wasn't working very well."

He delivered the message and returned to his unit safely that night. The next day a Japanese sniper who had tied himself high up in the branches of a tree shot and killed an army colonel at the same spot Brooks had been only hours earlier. One decision had proven fateful—the shiny eagle wings of the colonel's insignia were prominently displayed on his shoulders. Brooks usually kept his lieutenant bars underneath his dungaree jacket. "He didn't shoot me because I didn't look important." Many other Americans learned the lesson of keeping symbols of authority covered on the battlefield. Blending in with other soldiers near the front lines would become common.

Within a few months, life on the island for Brooks and his fellow marines returned to a certain civility and routine. Near his new temporary barracks, a departing army unit bequeathed a fifteen-acre parcel of arable land to Brooks and his tent mates. Before long, they had planted cucumbers, radishes, lettuce, cantaloupe, watermelon, and tomatoes.

Using both his position of moderate authority and his ability to negotiate, Brooks organized an informal "social club" for his platoon and friends, replete with plenty of cards, acey-deucy, and regular volleyball games among the officers. Even their lieutenant colonel played. Brooks later remembered:

> We played volleyball at night sometimes. One time we had a major from, think he was from Hallettsville [Texas], in transportation department, and he occasionally came over to our club to have a drink and visit, and we were friends. So one night he got the trucks out and lighted up a volleyball court over by his quarters, and we played volleyball for a little while by the lights in the evening, and it was not very wise because it became obvious that we were just a

few feet from the general's quarters, and so we closed it down pretty quick. We didn't get into any trouble, but they didn't like it.

Brooks was, in his own estimation, not a great player, but competent. In November, though, he broke his right thumb during a game. Considering all the trauma and death, however, it was not seen as much of an injury. Nor did it interfere with his work in communications. Nevertheless, in much of his correspondence with friends and family back home, many asked how his hand was recovering.

Seeing as how a social club needed space to convene, on October 23, Brooks and his men started out—with great gusto—building a primitive, sixty-foot by thirty-foot log cabin that would serve as a combined mess hall and officers' club. They installed "a beautiful bar," small tables for acey-deucy and cards, and even an attached latrine with running water. Of the entire endeavor, Brooks seemed most proud of the engineering that went into building the latrine.

He was so proud of their new officers' club, in fact, that he had one of his men sketch a detailed picture of it and then another man make prints of it on stationery so Brooks and others could send the image home. In it, the handsome, long single-story cabin sits between flowering palm trees and scenic South Pacific sky, marked with hints of clouds. Brooks wrote home:

> *I was elected to the board of governors at the last election and am entertainment chairman. . . . planning a big dance 10 november and hope to have 25 nurses there. It will be a lovely party. I hope.*

He did not get the full twenty-five nurses, but he did succeed in bringing fifteen to the officers' first big dance. He also brought his own colonel and several of that officer's visiting colonel friends for the buffet dinner and a seven-piece orchestra with a piano player and an Irish tenor. They polished off some six-year-old brandy and were all feeling a little ragged the next day. Shortly after the bender, he wrote his sister proudly detailing the soiree, adding a note of caution toward the end: " . . . Don't show this to Mom since I'll get a religious letter about it."

GUADALCANAL: After nearly five months on Guam, Brooks had orders to return to Guadalcanal. Days before leaving, though, he came down with dysentery and dengue fever, a tropical disease usually transmitted by mosquitoes that causes fever and terrible weakness. While dengue fever had been known in isolated areas, war in the Pacific spread various strains of the virus, including a deadly version. With high fever and the worst kind of other flu symptoms, there is no reliable treatment except rest and pain relievers. Eventually, after more time on the beach and aboard ship, Brooks recovered and returned to Guadalcanal by early January 1945.

His thumb had healed almost completely, and he had been given a new position leading the pole construction company. He wrote home:

> *I have a new assignment. Was in a light platoon. Now have a heavy construction (telephone pole line) platoon with about 88 men. That is a big platoon. It is the best in this battalion. The men know their jobs from a to z and do not mind working. They can do more work than you can imagine . . . even in this heat. In addition to that they do not complain seriously. Of course they crab a little about this and that, but when the word comes out to get hot and do something, they move out on the double. It makes it nice to not to find it necessary to be hard about things. I look forward to going on a "push" with them.*

Because of his background in journalism, Brooks was also called upon to become an official recorder of the summary court-martial used to keep discipline in a fighting force. These were quick judgments made by a senior officer to penalize, by loss of privileges or pay, those guilty of minor infractions. Brooks's role was, in essence, that of a prosecutor. He had to formulate and deliver closing arguments against the men standing accused of whatever offense. Brooks enjoyed the exercise but cited his own lack of legal experience as a frustration. He himself was reprimanded once for dereliction of duty when he did not properly authenticate a letter during a summary court-martial. Although the officer in charge declared a mistrial in the case, the record suggests the "discrepancies" charged to Brooks were technicalities.

In any event, that did not keep him from being promoted to first lieutenant and platoon leader on the first of February 1945. He wrote his mother with obvious glee:

> *FLASH....... young jack brooks, son of mrs. Grace books, was promoted to the rank of first lieutenant, united states marine corps reserve, on the 20th of February to rank from the 31st of January 1945. I'm happy about it and only wish Edward could make captain.*

His older brother Edward had joined the army and was stationed at an air base in Dallas. Edward was also eagerly awaiting a promotion to captain. Though Brooks was happy with his own advancement, he wrote his mother a measured assessment at the same time.

> *I'll never make captain . . . and I certainly hope the war does not last long enough to even put me near it. I feel sure that it won't.*

By February 1945 the situation in Europe was improving, and the sense among Brooks and his fellow marines was that Germany should just quit already rather than dragging out the inevitable. He wrote home:

> *. . . [Edward] better hurry if he is going to the European theatre. That business will be over in a few short months. I predict the Russians will take berlin by May 15. And when they do the war will be just about over over there . . . This one looks better daily but we still have a long ways to go.*

KITTY: On Guadalcanal Brooks began courting an attractive Red Cross nurse named Kitty. Dates were unique given their situation; he would sometimes requisition military vehicles to drive her around the island, which by now had become a sprawling U.S. supply base. One thing that charmed her was the way Brooks managed to skirt trouble. On one date he got the truck stuck in sand but was able to flag down and talk two passing military policemen into giving him and Kitty a lift back to his quarters. The men in his unit looked on as the MP jeep arrived, smirks all around as Brooks and his date sat silently in the backseat, the usual place for perps of all stripes. What kind of trouble had these two gotten themselves into?

The jeep pulled up outside Brooks's door, and he and Kitty stepped out and thanked their escorts. Jaws dropped as the men in Brooks's unit realized the MPs were not arresting the amorous young couple but chauffeuring them home. Kitty wrote Brooks a letter about it shortly after:

March 10th
Hi Jackson!

The next time you get stuck in the sand I hope it won't be on such a great day! I'm not sure whether your men were cheering you on or not?

When we rode into the area at such a great speed I hardly saw a head, but on the way out it looked like the Yanks being received in Berlin—Cheers, waves and lots of people! Next time when you have to hitch a ride don't stop MP's even if it happens to be only noon.

They were really swell, weren't they? In fact, if you still remember their names drop them a word of thanks. They too were wondering how you made out? The Sgt in charge of transportation simply howled (God damn him! as you say) and sent a jeep out to get you. I'm really sorry you were five minutes late and I hope the Captain is too.

Brooks's ability to cajole others was evident again when his unit received orders to set sail back to Saipan and Guam and were relocated aboard their ship, awaiting its departure. For several days, Brooks had been making it a practice to sneak off the vessel, a seriously punishable act, by riding to shore on the small laundry skiff. He would drive over to the nurses' quarters each night to spend time with Kitty and then return to his own billet in the morning. He reported to a Captain Glacier, who gave him friendly warnings to stop, otherwise both of them were going to get in trouble. But Brooks was pretty confident, especially about having the transportation officers on his side; at Christmastime he had provided them with more than a case of rum to smooth over any of his questionable movements. The only condition he required of the transportation officers was that they bury their empty bottles to hide all evidence.

And it worked out. As the ship transports prepared to leave Guadalcanal, Glacier agreed to drive Brooks and Kitty to the harbor. Two colonels standing on the deck of what was supposed to be the last shuttle off the island were looking back as the ship pulled away from the dock. They must have paused to watch the scene—a lone lieutenant on the beach giving a long kiss to a pretty nurse. Then the young man hopped into another launch and was motored out to the transport as it moved away. He leapt from the smaller boat and latched onto the ship's cargo netting like a buccaneer; a misstep would have landed him in the water and perhaps gotten him crushed between the launch and the ship. Once he had secured his footing, he began to climb up toward the gunwale. As his head appeared over the side, his platoon burst into laughter. He gave them a nod and a smile and made his way to the ship's officer quarters.

The USS *Barnett* had been built as a passenger steamer, but once the war began, the navy purchased and reconfigured it first for troop transport and then as an attack transport. The USS *Barnett* began the war in the Pacific, was reassigned to bring troops to the D-Day landings at Normandy, and then returned to Pacific operations after a stint in the Mediterranean. For two weeks, Brooks lived in the cramped quarters of the makeshift, converted transport.

Kitty, alone again on Guadalcanal, wrote him one last letter. On the upper margin she drew a tweeting red-breasted robin on a tree branch. She wrote "Second Day of Spring but we'd never know it here. Not a robin in sight." The rest of the letter read:

Guadawfulcanal
March 22nd
Dear Jack,

   Guess you departed at the right time. It's rained practically every day since and if it continues I'll begin to look mildewed myself. Everything else is. Imagine how I'd look green and fuzzy?
   . . . Someplace along the way I hope this letter reaches you, Jack, my dear. I do wish you lots of luck. All of it you need and after things have quieted down again we'll probably meet somewhere out here. I don't expect to stay here either

very long and may go up but that something I won't be sure about until it hap-
pens. But if it does we'll have some more brews together.
  Take care of the Brooks's favorite son, meaning yourself!

OKINAWA: Brooks was not headed to Guam; the ship was en route to
Okinawa. Since the U.S. had entered the war two years earlier, the push
toward Japan had been relentless. Bit by bit, U.S. command had reclaimed
the outer stretches of islands recently conquered by the Japanese. Now,
along with British and Australian troops, American forces were moving into
Japanese territory and cutting off their access to shipping routes to the rest
of their empire. The island of Okinawa lay only 325 miles from the south-
ernmost Japanese island of Kyushu. Some have likened Okinawa's strategic
importance in winning the war in the Pacific to that of the Allied staging in
England before the D-Day invasion. Japanese military leaders recognized
that American control of Okinawa would make it a dangerous staging area
for a future assault on Japan, as capturing the island would provide Allied
forces with not only multiple airstrips from which to execute a bombing
campaign against Japan's main islands but also a fleet anchorage and staging
area to assemble ground troops for the eventual assault.

Brooks's ship arrived off the coast of Okinawa on April 1, 1945, and he
went ashore the next day in what would be the largest amphibious assault
of the Pacific war, with troops being shuttled to shore amid small arms and
machine-gun fire from the entrenched Japanese. He wrote his sister:

> *I spent a pleasant day watching the troops go ashore and hearing with great*
> *glee the good news of the easy landing. I knew it meant a better deal for me the*
> *next morning. Almost went in that afternoon.*

During previous beach invasions, a number of marines and soldiers
drowned before ever getting ashore. They would charge out of the "Higgins
boats," as the landing craft were called, and fall into the water under the
weight of their weapons, ammunition, and heavy backpacks. Coral reefs
presented one obstacle, but others thought it might have had a little to do
with the drivers of those crafts being reluctant to get close to the shooting

and artillery fire, which led them to drop the bow ramps early and exposed troops to deeper waters and heavy surf, as well as Japanese gunfire. Hubert Oxford, a lifelong friend of Brooks, recalled his telling a story about one such landing:

> *Those guys, that first marine landing, I think it was on Tarawa, were drowned, and the first landing Brooks made he took his first sergeant back to the boat driver and told him to unleash his pistol. . . . He says, "Sergeant, if I get my feet wet, shoot the son of a bitch."*

The coxswain of Brooks's landing craft did not want to attempt to call Brooks's bluff, so he drove over the first sandbar and right up to the beach, so far up that Brooks remembered hearing the "rrrum, rrruum, rrrrumm" of the landing craft struggling to reverse off the sand. "My men got off with dry feet," Brooks said. "None of them drowned."

"We had a pretty good landing" on Okinawa, Brooks recalled, and indeed, after a prolonged bombardment with tons of explosives hitting the beaches and crackling the coral offshore, the Japanese unexpectedly ceded large tracts of beachhead to the invading forces.

At the end of the month, Brooks wrote home about the experience for the first time. He had not removed his clothes during his first ten days ashore, and after that, showers were only taken every two to three days. Brooks then spent two weeks of detached duty away from the main company "in a bad spot the [Japanese] bombed more than once. I've seen quite a few [of their] planes get shot down." He elaborated to his sister:

> *As you can see by the papers the Marine Corps did its job on the pleasant isle of Okinawa without too much trouble . . . although there were plenty of [Japanese] in our area. Quite enough in rear areas to keep me on the lookout. I was lucky for the first 10 days and careful after that. I have a beautiful shoulder holster for my .45 now. Morbid note: an mp officer gave it to me after I watched him take it off of a dead army first lt. killed along a road I had been over 50 times. My famous last words will probably be . . . "why worry?"*

But Americans forces quickly discovered that the Japanese, lacking their former manpower and naval strength, had changed tactics again, moving from a strategy of seeking an outright victory to one of trying to force the Allies into a negotiated truce. So instead of expending resources combatting the initial Allied landing, the roughly one hundred thousand Japanese soldiers dug in to the terrain further inland and intended to delay the U.S. movement as much as possible.

In this regard, the Japanese succeeded. They had accurately predicted the size and timing of the Allied invasion, and they had prepared creatively. A post-action Marine Corps report explained their defensive arrangements within the rugged terrain:

> *The main zone of defense was planned as a series of concentric positions adapted to the contours of the area. Caves, emplacements, blockhouses, and pillboxes were built into the hills and escarpments, connected by elaborate underground tunnels, and skillfully camouflaged; many of the burial tombs were fortified. The Japanese took full advantage of the terrain to organize defensive areas and strong points that were mutually supporting, and they fortified the reverse as well as the forward slopes of hills.*

After a relatively tepid beginning, the battle would go on to last eighty-two insufferable days, much of it in heat reaching 115 degrees, and made even more wretched by weeks of soaking rain that turned the shell-pocked landscape into a series of muddy bogs that swallowed howitzers and thirty-ton M4 Sherman tanks. Stories of how bombed-out, inaccessible muddy slopes became inundated with the putrefied remains of fallen soldiers became lore in combat history.

The marines' strategy was to push forward as fast as possible across the island, isolating the Japanese resistance and cutting them off from possible reinforcement. This fast-paced offensive, however, often left scores of isolated Japanese soldiers hiding in the brush or waiting in yet-undiscovered caves, ready to kill American troops that followed behind in support of the first assault battalions.

The Japanese conscripted as many as twenty thousand native Okinawans into a home guard they called the Boeitai. While their contributions as combat troops was limited, they assisted in other ways, like helping the soldiers build fortifications into the island's hillsides and engaging in guerrilla warfare against Allied forces' supply installations, telephone lines, hospitals, etc. These attacks deviled Brooks and his men, forcing them to return each day for repairs of the communication wires, putting themselves in direct line of sight for enemy sniper fire.

Brooks and his communications platoon moved into recently captured areas to install telephone poles and string communication wires that would connect command posts to the front. They also bore responsibility for delivering messages by hand. All of this exposed Brooks and his platoon to gunfire from snipers. Once, while he was standing atop a truck and reeling off cables, a sniper bullet creased his finger. Brooks recalled with a laugh:

> I jumped off that damn thing like a rabbit . . . And the men all hollered and laughed. Not that they were mean, they—it was funny. You gotta enjoy life as you go.

Some of the bitterest fighting came toward the end of the campaign. Brooks recalled the Japanese counteroffensive, during which they regrouped in areas such as Dakeshi Ridge. He recounted:

> It was a very nasty ridge that caused the marines lots and lots of trouble. We had lots of casualties in a very well-defended area.

Brooks spent four months on Okinawa, moving more than a dozen times across the hilly terrain. Operation Iceberg, as the Battle of Okinawa was code-named, would become the costliest single battle of the Pacific. The U.S. suffered more than 50,000 casualties, including some 12,500 soldiers and sailors killed or missing. Estimates of dead Japanese troops surpassed 100,000, while that of native Okinawans were as high as 150,000, a significant portion of the island's total population.

For a time, Brooks was quartered with an artillery unit. He later attributed some of his lasting hearing loss to this period. There were kamikaze attacks, and navy gunners were trying to shoot down the planes, but the Japanese were coming in low and firing their machine guns at the troops on the shore.

> *Everybody was in their foxholes, and I was walking around being sure they were and had their helmets on. They'd get lower and lower and lower and sometimes they'd be shooting right at us. And you'd have lots of shellfire in there.*
>
> *I was walking around, and some boy who was younger than I was, maybe some seventeen-year-old recruit, was in there and told his sergeant, "I wish I was brave like that Lieutenant Brooks." And the sergeant said: "if you drank as much whiskey as that son of a bitch, you'd be brave too." I did not say a word and didn't stop walking around checking them. That's the way it went, and that was part of my life. I did my job, and I got good marks.*

As the days and weeks Brooks spent at war began to blend together in his memory, Brooks downplayed the danger when he recounted stories from the front years later. But he vividly recalled how he learned to use the system. His instinct to make deals had only sharpened during his deployment.

Brooks and his men spent weeks under canvas tents, slopping through mud and wearing wet boots and deteriorating cotton socks. For troops in that tropical climate, where no one dared to take off boots for any length of time, certainly never long enough for them to dry, the very real danger was a painful condition known as "immersion foot," often called "trench foot" because of its prevalence during the trench warfare of World War I. Affected feet grow numb, blister, and eventually develop necrosis and gangrene if not treated. By then the only option is amputation.

So it was more than just a nice surprise when Brooks decided to go to the Army depot and find boots to re-outfit his waterlogged platoon. He signed up for fifty pairs of boots with the officer in change. Brooks also gave the man a gift, a .45-caliber handgun he had picked up. The officer handed him a requisition order. Brooks signed it with a name he made up on the spot and then went out to the depot to pick up the boots. On his way there, he slyly added a "2" in front of the "50" before he handed the paper to a supply sergeant. For goodwill, Brooks gave the sergeant a quart of whiskey as they loaded up the jeep with 250 pairs of boots hanging every which way. Brooks had pulled off one of his subtle coups of the war. He rode back to the barracks victorious, gave new boots to his friends, other officers, and the entire platoon.

On April 29 he wrote his mother with pride:

> *Have a nice pair of army boots. Got a pair for every man in my platoon and also enough for half of the other platoon in the company. They are regular top field shoes with a six inch leather top that buckles. Very tidy. Does away with leggings.*

Flush with success in the outfitting department, he looked at how little protection the pup tents gave his marines under the punishing days and nights of rain and swirling mud. Later, he "discovered" a bunch of large tarpaulin tents and passed them out to his platoon.

No matter the situation, efficiency and utility were always on Brooks's mind. Decades after the war, he recalled watching the trucks bringing back loads of dead marines from the front lines and remembered thinking at the time that "maybe those boots could be useful to someone else."

Brooks showed loyalty to his men, whether it was acting as a buffer between them and their critical and demanding captain, or the time he rushed into the mess sergeant's quarters and demanded the chow line be kept open because his marines were out working and returning too late for dinner. That sense of camaraderie had an impact; Brooks's loyalty inspired loyalty in others, creating bonds that lasted through the war and beyond. Though he was barely out of his teens, his experiences as a young man working at the newspaper and now trading and leveraging were providing valuable lessons and practice for his future endeavors.

Perhaps most importantly, Brooks learned to build constituencies everywhere he went.

After the fighting was over on Okinawa, Brooks discovered that officers could actually order liquor from the navy depot in San Francisco. He put up his own money, collected a hundred dollars from most of the other officers, kicked in another hundred for those who didn't have enough, and ordered cases to be sent to him on Okinawa. When the ship arrived, Brooks sent six men armed with submachine guns to pick up the cases.

Brooks set up a system in which men could buy a bottle of Three Feathers whiskey at cost, $1.03 a quart. He also had rum, which he called "Desperado." Brooks instructed his bartender that if he didn't like the person who wanted to buy, he could just tell them he could not sell without a chit or voucher from the marine in charge, a "tough-as-boots" colonel named "Snake" Peterson, who later made general. That deflection worked well because Brooks knew the colonel did not give out chits, ever, even if the men seeking them were brave enough to ask.

JAPANESE ASSAULT: The war was drawing to some inevitable and violent conclusion. Germany had formally surrendered on May 8, and now with Okinawa taken, preparations for an all-out invasion of Japan were underway. Brooks and his men were to be sent back to Guam to train for a final assault on the Tokyo Plain.

Everyone dreaded the coming fight. Unlike the Germans and Italians, Japanese soldiers rarely surrendered. The Americans expected them to be even fiercer when fighting for their home territory. Japanese civilians received training on how to fight with lethality, and though hopelessly outgunned, would likely have fought tooth and nail against any foreign soldiers on their homeland. The government propaganda of the day had them believe that American GIs ate babies and tortured captives. Brooks said:

> *When cornered they would fight like dogs. And on their homeland you could have expected them to be fighting from every hole and making our lives miserable and as short as possible.*

The marines expected to land the first troops with the army serving as backup for the initial invasion. There was talk among the headquarters staff of a possible 60 percent casualty rate. Earlier battles had seen rates as high as 20 percent. Brooks had seen the requisition order for the body bags to be held in reserve in China as the first marines made their assault. It was a memory that stuck with him. He wanted his unit to face facts:

I told my men exactly what they had said, and they said, "Well, we'll go."

So Brooks and his men boarded LST-567 and sailed away from Okinawa. LST stood for "Landing Ship Tank." It was a craft specifically designed to carry up to a dozen tanks, two dozen vehicles, and two hundred men. While on board, though, word suddenly came though that the U.S. had dropped something called an "atomic bomb" on Hiroshima. A second bomb was dropped on Nagasaki three days later. The destruction was absolute and at a scale never before seen.

By the time Brooks arrived back at Guam on August 12, there was talk that the Japanese were asking to surrender. Japan did, three days later.

We were prepared to go to Japan and then Truman dropped the atomic bombs, and I will be forever grateful to him because regrettably it killed an awful lot of Japanese civilians but it saved our lives.

The war was over, at least officially, and for Brooks and the other marines the relief was enormous. Their sense of personal disaster and possible death averted would last a lifetime. Decades later Brooks would stir up some controversy expressing how grateful so many were for the dropping of those bombs that ended the war. Marines and soldiers who had island-hopped for nearly two years, some even longer, could hardly believe that life had changed so radically in just a few short days. But only days after the formal end of the war, another surprise was in store for Brooks.

In advance of the surrender, troops understood there would be a point system that included time overseas, campaigns served in, and military needs to calculate in what order the marines and soldiers and sailors would return to the States for discharge, a massive undertaking called "Operation Magic Carpet." But when the new orders arrived, orders that should have detailed his route back home, Brooks instead read that he was being sent back to Okinawa and from there on to China. His war was not over yet.

CHINA: Well before the attack at Pearl Harbor, Japan had aggressively taken over parts of China and established military dominance in Korea and other regions of Asia and the Pacific islands. Japan ruled many of China's major cities, setting up puppet governments and police while at the same time a Communist revolutionary force was doing battle with the Chinese Nationalist (Kuomintang) government.

At the end of the war, there were more than 630,000 Japanese nationals, both occupying troops and civilians, to be repatriated from China. The U.S. also was helping to prop up the Nationalist forces and move them back into power. Added to that mix were armed groups of roving bandits and warlord gangs.

Several thousand marines were sent to Shanghai and to China's capital, Peiping, later known as Beijing. Brooks and others in the 1st Marine Division were assigned to the large river port city of Tientsin, now Tianjin, which at that time was China's third largest city.

After nearly two years abroad, Brooks understood wartime currency, so just the day before setting off for China, he and his platoon managed to commandeer a panel station wagon from the army. That night they painted it dark green, wrote "radio spare parts" on it, and welded a big lock on the back.

They then proceeded to load all the cases of whiskey they had. Brooks went to the chief enlisted man and the junior officer in charge of loading and a more senior man in charge of the deck. He said he would give each of them a half case of whiskey if they would save a spot on deck and batten down the station wagon in a place where Brooks and his platoon could watch over it. He figured if it had been stowed below deck, curious sailors or even other marines might have cut into it with torches and discovered the treasure inside.

But that was not their only concern. A typhoon had risen suddenly in the region, and all the ships had to leave port and ride out the storm on the open sea. Brooks said:

> *There was a lot of damage; it was a terrible typhoon. And I ran out of whiskey, and the men were all sick. It was a miserable trip. I prayed for those lady welders who had put those ships together 'cause here was yawl and buck. It*

was a real storm.

Two Liberty class cargo ships were lost, and a transport was badly damaged by the typhoon, which raged for three full days. As the seas calmed, Brooks and his shipmates rode aboard the USS *Cullman*, an attack transport that could carry up to eight hundred men along with their beach landing craft, and, after ten days of sailing, they anchored at a place called Taku Bar in an icy estuary of the Hai River Basin off the Yellow Sea. The railhead was several miles away in the small town of Tanku, China. Before disembarking, Brooks recalled, "my blood was thin as water having been in Guam and Guadalcanal for more than a year, and it was cold." He had befriended a navy officer with an alpaca wool pea coat and traded him a quart of whiskey for it. It was October 3, 1945, the beginning of winter in the hilly brown fields of North China.

The safe repatriation of Japanese soldiers and civilians was one part of the marines' mission in China; they were also needed to keep watch over the railways and bridges as the Communist and Nationalist troops returned to their own internal fight.

Brooks was in the last group to be ferried off the ship and travel on the hard wooden seats of the train up to Tientsin. He was billeted in the old Scottish Highlanders quarters, a brick barracks compound that dated back a full century to the First Opium War in 1840–42.

Keeping communications up between there and Peiping, seventy miles away, meant frequent trips to repair the long telephone lines. One of the most important communications links was in another foreign legation area known as the "French Arsenal" where the marines had established a big radio antenna with large spliced telephone poles supported by long strings of tensioned guy wires to keep them in place. There was a guard there from the former puppet government, but the Japanese, or perhaps the Communists, would get through in the middle of the night and cut the wires. Brooks and his team would then have to go back out to repair the lines.

Despite its proximity, he never did go to Peiping. He said:

> *Every time we went out there we got shot at. And that jeep would go as fast*

as it would go, and they would ricochet those bullets through the jeep but I never did get hit and my driver never did get hit. We were very fortunate. China was good, but it was cold as a frog. The Communists occupied all the outside of the cities, and they would shoot at that train occasionally, and I felt it would be just my bad luck to get shot sitting there on the train.

Brooks had Class 2 priority on all military flights, and one day he was dispatched to deliver a message to a general down in Shanghai. He had never seen the city, of course, and the boy from Beaumont marveled at the European flair in the wide streets of office buildings and apartments in the foreign legation areas. He was mesmerized by Shanghai's dual life, how the poor and hungry lingered outside the most sophisticated and expensive restaurants. He especially marveled at the bright lights of the riverfront district, known as the Bund, after he had spent so many months in the nighttime darkness of the islands.

He lingered in Shanghai for several days and then hitched a ride back by way of Tsingtao, another port city where the Germans had established a famous brewery, still operating today, and he stayed there another day. On his return flight to Tientsin, the pilots, who were used to flying in the tropics, not in the frigid air of North China, nearly crashed the plane because they let the wings get iced up. Everyone left the plane shaken, especially Brooks, who was mad as hell that they had so carelessly endangered his life.

Brooks's boss, a captain, was even madder, though, because Brooks had lingered in Shanghai. Already angry at some of Brooks's marines, who had been racing rickshaws down the narrow hutongs or alleyways, the captain now wanted Brooks court-martialed and reported him to the colonel, "Whispering Joe" Kaiser. The colonel asked Brooks what had happened, and Brooks replied honestly that he was twenty-two years old, had never been to such a place, and wanted to see more. The colonel told Brooks to get out of his office, which Brooks did without looking back. He learned later that Kaiser had first served in China decades earlier while about the same age as Brooks. He obviously understood. Years down the line, Brooks would be in a position to cut his junior colleagues some slack in similar fashion. You did not just go after people, even if they were junior, unless you had good reason.

Colonel Kaiser also may have been aware that Brooks had set up a domestic life with a "white Russian" girl outside the barracks, though the colonel never mentioned it to anyone. After fleeing the Bolshevik revolution in 1917, tens of thousands of Russians fled to China—including port cities like Shanghai and Tientsin—where they remained stateless and often in poverty but hoping to acquire a passport and a way out.

Because Brooks was in charge of communications equipment, he had strung his own telephone line from the battalion officers' quarters to the private apartment he shared with his girlfriend just in case he was needed in the middle of the night. The colonel once mentioned seeing Brooks early in the morning as he arrived for work and Brooks was just getting back from his girlfriend's apartment. Five or six of the junior officers knew of the arrangements and almost choked at the colonel's remark, but none dared say anything, either out of camaraderie or fear of interrupting the whiskey supply.

Brooks would not forget the captain's threat of court-martial, and he enjoyed, at least indirectly, a bit of retribution. He was at a bar with his girlfriend and several other officers when the captain leaned in and said something to her, something that must have been unpleasant because she wound up and slapped him in the face. Brooks recalled:

> *Not just a little slap, but a roundhouse slug that almost knocked him down. I was standing a little ways off and laughed, and that didn't please him much, but there was nothing he could do about it.*

He and the captain tangled other times over minor complaints, but Brooks was in line for his discharge, and in mid-January he finally got orders to transfer back home.

Brooks boarded the USS *Wakefield*, a pre-war luxury ocean liner named the SS *Manhattan* that had been completely transformed into a troop transport for wartime service. After nearly two weeks at sea, the USS *Wakefield* arrived at the naval base on Terminal Island in the San Pedro section of Los Angeles on February 1, 1946, and Brooks stepped back onto American soil.

His war service was essentially finished.

He visited with cousins in Los Angeles, but even the welcome parties were too much of a change after being away for nearly two years. The marines had wanted him to stay in the regulars, but Brooks felt he was behind the curve in a military career; many other officers around his age had already reached captain or major. He was still just a senior first lieutenant, and he did not see chasing others up the chain of command as a good way to spend the rest of his life. He was released from active duty in April.

Brooks never suggested any heroics on his part, but he did occasionally refer to times when he was shot at and, whether by luck or providence, barely avoided becoming one of the hundreds of thousands of U.S. troops killed in action. Decades later, the closest Brooks would come to acknowledging the emotions of that time was this:

> *The war was well underway and as most anyone will tell you, war is a god-awful combination of tedium, fear, and excitement. You become accustomed to sights and sounds and smells that are incomprehensible in civilian life, and you never want to get used to it . . . War changes everybody when they're in it. I had some friends killed; I had some close shots.*

For their efforts, Brooks and his fellow marines in the signal battalion jointly shared in a Navy Unit Commendation for their actions on Guam, Okinawa, and several other islands. It was the second highest award that a unit could receive, behind only the Presidential Unit Citation. The secretary of the navy's letter followed:

> *. . . The first American Signal Battalion to engage in amphibious landings in the Pacific Ocean Areas, the III Amphibious Corps Signal Battalion pioneered and developed techniques and procedures without benefit of established precedent, operating with limited and inadequate equipment, particularly in the earlier phase of these offensive actions, and providing its own security while participating in jungle fighting, atoll invasions and occupation of large island masses.*
>
> *Becoming rapidly experienced in guerrilla warfare and the handling of*

swiftly changing situations, this valiant group of men successfully surmounted the most difficult conditions of terrain and weather as well as unfamiliar technical problems and, working tirelessly without consideration for safety, comfort or convenience, provided the Corps with uninterrupted ship-shore and bivouac communication service continuously throughout this period.

Brooks would remain in the Marine Corps Reserve and rise to the rank of colonel before his retirement in 1972. But at this moment, Brooks had had enough of active duty. He still intended to go to law school. His path was not certain, but after two years in the Pacific and a few weeks on the West Coast with thousands of other former fighters, Brooks had a rough plan.

I was going to go home and run for Congress.

4

Legislature and Lamar

In late 1946, millions of young veterans began returning to civilian life, equipped now with the experience of two, three, and even four years of war and military duty. Many wanted to resume their former jobs, and others were eager to complete or begin anew their schooling. Brooks was among the latter.

After attending Lamar and then finishing his degree in journalism at the University of Texas, Brooks now had the idea that a law degree would help a future career in politics. This time, however, Brooks had more security than a fifteen-dollar-a-month check from a benefactor to sustain him; the education of millions of veterans, including Brooks, now had the support of a new and controversial government program.

GI Bill: The GI Bill of Rights—formally known as the Servicemen's Readjustment Act of 1944—was aimed at helping the nation's military veterans return to civilian life. At the time the bill was conceived, however, the then-radical idea of helping pay for the education of any veteran who wanted to go to college caused a contentious debate in the House and Senate. College was still considered by many a level of education reserved for only the most ambitious and wealthy, and detractors derided the concept as a step toward socialism.

Another provision, one guaranteeing a home loan, also worried some in Congress; considering how many had served in the military in the past few years, it would put an enormous financial burden on the country. But the most fractious debate of all centered on giving unemployed veterans twenty dollars a week in unemployment benefits. Critics argued that such a generous allowance guaranteed that unemployed vets would never look for work.

The entire bill, of course, was a tremendous success. By the end of the twentieth century, the legislation would become enshrined in American society and embraced by both parties, a form of social welfare that benefitted millions then and ever since, and one that has been renewed and expanded over the intervening years. Early fears of lazy, unemployed veterans were unfounded; less than 20 percent of the money allocated for those unemployment benefits was ever used.

In 1947, students using the GI Bill represented half of all college enrollments. In addition, the first children of the Baby Boom generation were being born, and the housing market could barely keep up with the demand from all those new families.

The sustained growth of those postwar years was a blessing to many, including the young Beaumont veteran who had vowed years earlier that someday he would buy a home for his mother to call her own. He did not use the GI Bill home guarantee; he wanted the house in his mother's name alone. Once he began working and making money, he found a neat brick cottage in Beaumont on a shady side street called East Drive.

HOUSE FOR MOTHER: Lack of permanence played an important role in Brooks's young adult life, and, just as it did for many millions of Americans, the war intervened, and future plans were put on hold. As soon as Brooks returned from service in the South Pacific, he was intent on going to law school and equally insistent that his widowed mother would have a house of her own, a small home with sturdy brick walls—one of the few in a neighborhood of frame houses—on East Drive; a brick mason who owned the lot had built the house for himself in 1938.

Grace Brooks finally had her own home, in her own name, for the first time in her life. Her mother lived with her, and the house became the center of Brooks's family life. When Brooks went off to serve in the Texas legislature, he would return to Beaumont and stay not in the house but in the garage, where he put in a bathroom and two closets, converting it to a small apartment and office. Even after he went off to Congress and returned home with his new wife, they stayed in the garage apartment. Grace left the house to Brooks, but long after his mother's death the house remained in her name. A small ceramic plate with the inscription "Good Morning, Gracie" continued to hang over the stove for years after her death.

After his return from China and a few weeks spent with relatives in California, Brooks returned to Beaumont to visit his mother, sister, and friends. Not unlike other veterans, it took months for Brooks to adjust to civilian life; for a while he even slept with a .45-caliber pistol under his pillow, a dangerous practice that nearly ended it for Eddie McFarland, one of his law school roommates. "Jack, don't shoot, it's me, Eddie!" his friend yelled when he stumbled into the apartment in the middle of the night.

Now that the war was over, Brooks felt a tremendous eagerness to restart his life and work and to do it in a hurry. He had been thinking and planning his future while stationed on the South Pacific islands and during the seemingly interminable time spent waiting aboard ships. He wanted to get back to Austin and even got a job for several months working at the state insurance regulatory agency. He enrolled in law school, but in 1946, impatient as ever, he also decided to run for a seat in the Texas legislature and won.

The 150 members of the Texas House of Representatives are part-time, mandated to meet less than half the year. But then Brooks did not expect to make a career of it, especially when the pay scale was still set at 1930 rates of ten dollars a day for the first 120 days in session and five dollars for each of the remaining days.

He was also a twenty-six-year-old bachelor who had spent the last two years in frequent danger and in the company of other men. Now, Brooks was stretched between school, work, and his social life, but in his mid-twenties he had the energy and enthusiasm to do it all. Brooks's law school grades were not stellar, and over the years he rarely referred to the brief time he spent actually practicing law in Beaumont. He recalled years later:

> My priorities were, understandably, women and whiskey and the legislature, and then law school, a very bad, bad precedent for [attending] law school. That was not the best way to go. I don't recommend it, very tough going for me. I did fine in the first two, of course, and in the legislature. I was fascinated

with the challenge of the legislature, just loved it. I really did. More than I ever
thought I would. And met a lot of people that had served in the armed forces.

Scores of young veterans became new legislators in those first few years
after the war. Many came with idealism and a desire to participate in the
democracy they had spent years defending. Others had a pet project important to their districts. Brooks already had set his sights higher. He was on
five committees his first term in the state legislature, and in his second term,
he served on six committees and became chairman of the Banks committee. The legislature would be good training, and Brooks instinctively knew
he would make good political contacts and that the experience would be a
reasonable stepping stone for a future in national politics.

BRISCOE AND WRIGHT: After the war, Dolph Briscoe had gone back to
school in Austin, but he was homesick for the family ranch in Uvalde, and
eventually he took Janey back to his home to make a life together. Though
he was more interested in ranching at the time, Briscoe was certainly familiar
with Texas politics; one of his neighbors in Uvalde was "Cactus Jack" Garner,
the fiery-tempered Democratic icon in Texas politics who was nicknamed for
both for the barren terrain of his hometown and for his prickly demeanor.

During one of what would be many hunting trips to Briscoe's ranch,
Brooks told him he had won a seat in the legislature. Janey was already eager
to get back to Austin. A nudge from Brooks may have persuaded Briscoe
to run for a seat in his own district and rejoin his friend.

The two had grown close and shared a deep respect for each other's
opinions. These were often shared while hunting together, though the topic
of conversation was not always politics. After one particular hunt, Brooks
put a slain deer in the trunk of their car. As they drove home, they heard a
sudden thumping coming from the back. After swerving to the side of the
road, Brooks grabbed a rifle, jumped out, and pointed it at trunk. Briscoe,
already standing there ready with the key to open it, saw Brooks pointing
the gun toward him and leapt three feet in the air. "Relax, Dolph. I ain't
gonna shoot YOU," Brooks said.

After Briscoe was elected to serve in the Texas legislature, he moved back to Austin and, with Brooks now in his second term, the old friends became desk mates. Their political partnership was cemented in Austin as they sat together at their double-wide, polished oak desks and leaned back to talk in oversized brown leather chairs in the House chamber.

There was a unique energy in the country at the time, one that was felt in the Texas legislature as well. Those young veterans of the war who were in office for the first time "did not fit the old pattern of following the leadership, or following the Lobby, you know," recalled Briscoe.

Another lifelong friend who followed Brooks's path from UT to the Texas statehouse across the street was future U.S. House Speaker Jim Wright. Years later, Wright spoke of the "radical" liberalism that took hold of both men as they entered the Texas legislature after serving in World War II.

> *Oh, did we ever [have ideas.] I will tell you just how radical we were . . . We wanted to do such outlandish things as abolish the poll tax! We even wanted to let women serve on the juries, if you can believe that. We wanted to tax gas, natural gas, and oil, and pay schoolteachers more money. We wanted to build rural roads. We wanted to have an anti-lynching law, of all the outrageous. . . . We wanted to let black students attend the University of Texas Law School. It was just amazing the degree to which those things would create waves of apoplexy among the comfortable establishment in Texas.*

FIRST BILL FOR LAMAR: Brooks was very intent on doing something meaningful for his constituents, including helping pass a minimum wage bill—the first in the state—and fulfilling the one pledge he had made when he asked voters to send him to the state legislature. He vowed that once he was able, he would see that Lamar College was upgraded to a four-year state institution.

According to John E. Gray, who would become president of the school in later years, Beaumont was, at the time, the largest population center in Texas without either a private or state college or university. Gray said, "Because Texas had not created a new senior college for twenty-five years, people thought it would be impossible to get it through the legislature."

Brooks promised that he would change that.

The first bill he introduced to make Lamar a state-financed institution actually passed the house. The bill then passed the state senate as well. But the freshman legislator did not have the experience to see how a clear path could suddenly veer into a thicket of opaque rules. He was stunned when Comptroller Robert S. Calvert refused to certify the bill. Under the Texas Constitution, the Comptroller has the duty to reject any legislation with appropriations that exceed estimated revenues. Calvert declared there would not be enough income to sustain Lamar's ambitions and sent Brooks's bill back to the house.

Brooks cussed him up and down, using the especially colorful vocabulary he honed throughout his life.

> *They eliminated my first Lamar College bill. They cheated me out of it by underestimating the taxes and overestimating the expenses, and the things that fell in between.*

The young man told the powerful state official that he was "motivated evilly and that he was utterly stupid and incompetent." Brooks also argued the merits, that incoming taxes would be sufficient to meet the school's needs.

> *But they got me. I didn't like that. I had been had. I was livid. I called him everything you could call him . . . And I called him everything they'd print, and a lot more. But as the results showed, he was dead wrong, just dead wrong.*

"THE LOBBY": Ever since the beginning, the Texas legislature had been dominated by agriculture and large ranching interests; in 1950, Texas boasted more than 1.5 million dairy cattle of varying breeds. The political life of Austin was well known to anyone who wanted to be a player, and it was considered unwise to go against the vested interests whose influence was almost tangible under the vast dome of the state capitol. This consortium of interests was ominously known as the "Lobby," and they ran the show.

Briscoe recalled his first session in the House, when he joined Brooks and others in discovering how the system worked.

Where in the past, the Lobby had been extremely influential, and where if you wanted to get along, you sort of had to go along with the leadership . . . Well, that was not true in those sessions of the legislature because the members who had come back from serving in the military didn't feel obligated to follow anybody's leadership.

The membership was very independent, and wouldn't fall in line just because somebody said, "Fall in line." They had enough of that in the army, you know, in the military. And they wouldn't fall in line, so it was a fun time to be in the legislature. You never knew what you could do, or never knew what somebody would try to do.

There were no offices for legislators; if someone wanted to dictate a letter to a secretary, others could hear. They could hear conversations between members and their constituents, so they knew what motivated some votes and what kind of pressure others were under. Everyone seemed to know everyone else's business, including those who were asking for money. Briscoe said:

You knew what they were doing that they shouldn't have been doing, and it created a very close relationship between everyone, and so you could have a lot of fun with each other. And, that we did . . .

As still happens in state legislatures, when there was an anticipated close and controversial vote coming up, one that some members would rather duck, the leadership would order the chamber's doors to be locked and then send a sergeant-at-arms to round up other members to achieve or maintain a quorum for the vote.

During one such late-night session, Brooks realized he had a previously scheduled appointment at the UT library, but he was at his desk, and the chamber doors were locked. Brooks got along with Speaker of the House Thomas Durwood Manford and his wife, Joyce. Manford, from Smiley, Texas, had an interest in raising chickens, and his detractors called him the "Chickenshit Speaker," and why will become clear quickly. Though he was a freshman legislator, Brooks was desperate to get to the library before closing, so he quietly passed behind the House rostrum, through Manford's office, and then into the speaker's private apartment that was just behind the main chamber.

He picked his way through the apartment, calling out Joyce's name. She was already in bed, and he quietly explained that a call for all the House members was on, but he needed to get to the library before it closed at 10 p.m. He told her, "I've got to get a book out of there, it's important, and I'll come back [in time for the vote]. You know that my word is good." She said, "All right," and Brooks stepped out her bedroom window, scuttled along the ledge to the stairs, got to his car, and made it to the library in time. "I wouldn't mention the name of the book," he recalled, "but she was very nice." Later he returned to the capitol and banged on the front door for entrance. He was in time for the vote.

There were other shenanigans, too.

He once hand-wrote a note to another member that appeared to be from a comely schoolteacher, a young woman from the legislator's district who was sitting up in the gallery above the House floor. The note read that she would like the member to visit her and wondered if he would come up and say hello. It even told the legislator what seat she was in, right in the center gallery and in the second row. Brooks recalled:

> *Well, he went up there, and it wasn't anybody that knew him, and the hus-band didn't think he was funny at all, not at all. This was the legislator coming up there to visit with his wife.*

Another member fell for a similar trick when he received a note from an attractive woman who said she wanted to see him and would be in town for several days, so would he just wave to acknowledge her. According to Brooks:

> *The legislator turned and he waved, and nobody said a word, did a thing. And he waved again, waved like this, got his handkerchief out.*

Brooks, describing this in pantomime, would take a handkerchief out of his back pocket to demonstrate, making increasingly larger and more exaggerated gestures to capture attention.

Here, got his handkerchief, waving his handkerchief like this, standing up,
waving his handkerchief hard, trying to get some woman's attention up there.
And we laughed, laughed so hard, I thought my stomach was gonna hurt. It was
funny. He never did spot that woman.

If anyone described the House at that time seeming more like a frat house
than a legislative body, they would not be far off. The hijinks extended to
voting as well. Brooks said:

Sometime we had a tough bill coming up. You'd have had a voting machine
and you voted—You left your machine on, and many people never locked them,
just left them open all the time, because it was trouble to carry a key and unlock
it when you came running in to vote. So we'd stand at the back of the rows, and
when the vote came, we'd just walk down the row, checking the machines that
weren't occupied, and voting the hell out of them . . . I'll tell you! We were rascals!

Brooks was happy to joke about all the votes his friend Briscoe was able
to make under such a system. When the legislature was in session, Briscoe
often went back to his ranch to work on Thursday night and came back to
Austin on Tuesday morning. So on those Mondays and Fridays when he
was absent, Brooks recalled helping Briscoe maintain an excellent voting
record. Or, as Briscoe responded playfully, "A wonderful record if I was
from Beaumont, Texas, or Jefferson County, but not necessarily if you were
from Uvalde!"

A network television affiliate aired an expose of that practice in 2007,
though it had been the norm in the legislature for the previous sixty years
and as long as anyone remembered. Much like the police official in the movie
Casablanca, who expressed absolute "shock" that there was gambling in
Rick's Café before collecting his own winnings, the Texas legislative leaders
expressed their utter shock that such practices went on in the House; they
solemnly ordered the members to police themselves in the future.

LAMAR AS A UNIVERSITY: After Brooks ran unopposed for reelection in
1948, he quickly set out to redress his Lamar defeat from the previous session.

He reintroduced the Lamar bill with a new strategy. He built on the skill he had developed as a young man in school and as a young lieutenant in the marines—the ability to assess what others needed or wanted in exchange for what he was trying to achieve. That wisdom would also be critical in a few years when he began his first run for U.S. Congress.

While Brooks was intent on getting Lamar upgraded to a four-year college, Briscoe's main interest was in getting the farm-to-market road program passed to improve the roads in his largely rural district. Briscoe said that he had no interest in Lamar, and because the roads in more industrial Jefferson County were already much better than the roads in Briscoe's district, Jack had no interest in his project.

"So we sort of joined forces," said Briscoe.

Brooks had the Beaumont Chamber of Commerce behind him as well; the group sponsored an excursion for about 150 people—legislators, their wives and staff—to come to Beaumont by train and then take a cruise down the Neches River on a pleasure boat owned by the Texaco Company. Brooks would later comment, "Lamar went up the river a two-year college and came back a four-year university."

But even that kind of courting, plus the support of Briscoe and other allies in the legislature, was not going to be enough to pass the Lamar bill through the new session of the legislature. Smarting from his earlier defeat, Brooks made some other calculations to give himself a leg up, including a decision to introduce a new constitutional amendment to end the "rotten rule" that allowed the comptroller alone to nullify bills.

That surprised and did not sit well with the "Lobby," including the entrenched lobbyists, who were well served by that powerful rule over finances. "The lobbyists, they were against it. We were spending money, and they were against anything that spent money," said Brooks. Members of the Lobby began pressuring the young legislator to withdraw his proposed amendment. "The Lobby didn't care about education," Brooks remembers.

The lobbyists as a group were against spending money for anything, and certainly not for a new college that would be in existence for generations, would cost the state tax money for years, for all their lifetime. They were dead set against it.

Brooks resisted their argument but showed more political savvy than in the previous session. He told them that of the two bills, he was actually much more interested in Lamar and, if that passed, he might lose interest in the constitutional amendment. Brooks was learning; he had sent an unmistakable message, and it cleared a path with the entrenched opposition. The bill creating the Lamar State College of Technology, with a curriculum that would emphasize engineering, technology, and science, passed through the House subcommittee. Step one accomplished.

FIRST DEFEAT: Still more hurdles lay ahead. Brooks thought he had lined up enough support for the bill, but he was mistaken. A handful of Lamar College officials had traveled to Austin to witness passage of the bill. As they sat overlooking the action, the bill went to the floor and lost by four or five votes. Brooks told them he would try again.

Brooks had voted for Durwood Manford as the Speaker of the House, but Manford was reluctant to get on the wrong side of the lobbyists. Though he knew Brooks and had even visited at his mother's house in Beaumont, Manford asked the former speaker, William Odie Reed, to handle the session.

Brooks had cultivated Reed, as well, and voted for him to be Speaker in the previous House session. He also knew that Reed enjoyed a few drinks during the day, so Brooks asked for recognition to bring up the bill, the exact same bill, a second time. In his relaxed frame of mind, Reed allowed it. "I had changed a few votes, but I lost again by two votes, which was sort of heartbreaking," Brooks said.

> Odie was determined to pass the bill, I mean, he was willing to cooperate, and I still was short two votes. The people in the gallery got up and went back to the hotel to drink and party and commiserate on how Brooks didn't know what he was doing. But I went and got the other votes. I went and put my arm around one old man. He never did vote with me, and I said, "You know, you old son of a bitch, you never were for me! You never did vote together. But I need you now, bad." The man looked at his wife who always sat alongside him when the legislature was in session. She nodded, and he turned to me and said, "Well, I'll go with you."

And then, I was walking down the other side of the gallery, just trying to pick people who were against it who might change. And I looked at him and I must've looked pretty sick. And the guy stopped me and says, "Jack." His name was Cheatham, big upright man from central West Texas. He said, "You know, I'm not gonna let them do that to you. I'm gonna vote with you. 'Cause you served in the Marine Corps with my boy."

Brooks, many decades later, began to weep with the memory.

And I had the votes. I made the motion and passed it. Old Cheatham voted with me. So did that old man. I made the motion a third time, passed the bill. Got it on the floor and passed it with one vote. Then, I called the people at the hotel and told them. And that's the way it was. Really! Tough, tough, road.

And then it still had to pass in the Texas Senate.

I went over, I got a picture made with Allan [Shivers], who was looking a little uncomfortable. And what I was telling him was, I know you're for it, Allan, I know you're gonna support me.

Shivers was lieutenant governor at the time, a more powerful position in Texas than even the governor. Shivers came from the same area of Port Arthur and Beaumont as Brooks, so naturally the people down there wanted him to do his part to make Lamar a four-year institution. Shivers had known some of Brooks's uncles in Port Arthur; one had even been his campaign treasurer when Shivers first ran for the state senate. Brooks said: "We were old friends, but I said 'What I want to know, Allan, is when?' I'd tell the people, 'When are you going to do it?'"

Shrewdly, Brooks had gotten Shivers to promise early that if Brooks could pass the bill in the House, then as lieutenant governor, Shivers would see that it passed in the senate. But, as Briscoe reconstructed the struggle, Shivers never believed that Brooks could pass it in the House. Briscoe recalled:

So this was Allan's way out. From his point of view, a good way out, I mean, because he was able to promise to those people down there that were so strongly interested, and felt so strongly that they needed a four-year institution of higher learning, he could promise him that he'd do his part, but first, that new representative over there, he had to do his part, and get it through the House.

Well, that's where Allan made a mistake. He didn't recognize the tenacity and the hard work that Jack Brooks would put into a project. So, Jack took on his project, making Lamar a four-year university, and everything else was secondary, or really off the radar. Lamar was it.†

Brooks knew Shivers would have to overcome a lot of pressure from the Lobby. But Shivers kept his word and rallied the senate to a vote two months later. Brooks later recalled:

Well, I tell you what, he had a tough fight, but Allan was tough as a keg of nails. The lobbyists said that he'd never be governor if he got that bill out. Allan wouldn't let them ask for permission to go to the bathroom, I don't believe, unless they promised to vote for that bill in the senate. He really locked it up tight, boy. He got them, and they voted for it, under his tough rule.†

The senate passed the measure by a vote of sixteen to twelve. Yet there was still one last hurdle. Governor Beauford Jester had to sign the law to make it official, and there was a good deal of speculation that he would veto it because of the additional cost to the state. Jester had also been a member of the Friars Club, the same UT student organization Briscoe had joined. Brooks needed to enlist Briscoe one more time. According to Briscoe:

Well, Jack said to me, "Now, you've got to go in to talk to Governor Jester and tell him that he has to sign that bill." And I said, "Jack, I don't know him. How? I don't think I could even get an appointment with him." He said, "That doesn't make any difference, you gotta do it. That's it." He said, "That was our deal, I've done everything I can for the farm-to market road program, which

---

† This quotation is taken verbatim from a video interview that can be viewed at www.jackbrooksfoundation.org.

*I don't give a [expletive] hootie about that . . . " You know, he put it a little
stronger than that, and he said, "You've got to do it."*

And I say, "Well, I don't know how I'm even gonna get in."

*"Well," he said, "You just call over there and tell him that you want to see
him."*

*Anyway, he was adamant that I had to carry out my part of the original
bargain, because he was very concerned that Governor Jester would veto it.
Anyway, I said, "Well, all right."†*

Briscoe called and got an appointment. He had been in the governor's
mansion once as a child, even slept in Sam Houston's bed, but he had not
met the governor since being elected to the legislature. Briscoe continued:

*So I got in there, and I went on, and I talked about how important Lamar
was, and how it was badly needed, and he listened very patiently, and then he
said something like this to me, he said, "Dolph," he said, "that's four hundred
miles from your district."*

I said, "Yes, sir." He said, "How come you're so interested in Lamar?"

*I couldn't think of anything to say, except, it just popped into mind, and
I said, "Governor, I'm interested in better education everywhere in the state."*

*And Jester sort of chuckled. But, anyway that ended our interview . . . Any-
way, I had done my part for Jack, and I'm sure it had no effect on Governor
Jester and what he did. But anyway, he did sign the legislation. I think he got
concerned about if he didn't sign it, what the repercussions would be for him
with Jack working against him in the House. I mean that's what did it. But,
anyway, I had to carry out my part of our farm-to market/Lamar partnership.†*

FARM-TO-MARKET ROADS: In return, Brooks kept his part of the bargain,
and every single member from southeast Texas voted for the farm-to-market
program. Brooks remembered:

So I got on the good roads program with him. He had a program for the

---

† This quotation is taken verbatim from a video interview that can be viewed at
www.jackbrooksfoundation.org.

state of Texas, and that turned out to be very useful, 'cause contractors love roads
programs, cause they get rich out of them. And most politicians love them, if
they're going to get a road in their area. So, we got it passed. It wasn't that tough.
The Lobby wanted to be against it, but it's kind of hard to be against a program
like that 'cause it has a lot of support.

There were actually several competing bills to improve rural roads
throughout the state, but legislators voted for the bill that Briscoe sponsored.
Funding for the rural roads passed and was signed into law. The effort to bring
higher education to Beaumont affected several hundred thousand students
during six decades and changed the expectations of several generations of
people throughout the "golden triangle" of southeast Texas.

At the time, however, there was still one aspect of the school that wasn't
to Brooks's liking.

It was segregated then. Would you believe that? In 1949? It sure was. But I
told them that it will be open, it would just take a little time. If I had put that
in this bill, tried to do that in this bill, we wouldn't have passed it. And it's better
just to have it here available, then we can get it. But we'll be in there. And that
was true. They were. It wouldn't be long.

For him, this would be the first of many examples of achieving what was
possible, not what would have been ideal. It would take about nine years
and several lawsuits before Lamar would first become integrated.

THE IMMEDIATE OUTCOME OF these victories and defeats was that Brooks had
become fascinated with the process of making legislation and understanding
what it takes to move bills into law. Brooks recalled:

That law school was hard work for me. You know, you have to study law
every day, and work at it. And the other members did, but they didn't fight in
legislature quite as hard. And I really stayed with it 'cause I was fascinated with
the way it functioned and operated, and the committee system and who was on
what committee, and how it all worked.

As would become evident years later, much of Brooks's career was built on these early experiences. Some are considered a "natural" in their line of work, whether they play baseball, write music, or perform on stage. For Brooks, knowledge of the political process would jibe nicely with his character and with his early life and experiences. He was known to keep track of both promises and slights and to be willing to go all out once he committed himself to a colleague or a piece of legislation. He was also stubborn and hated being wrong. Once, when a law professor challenged him on a fact of law, Brooks conceded but then worked to have the law changed to reflect his position.

Recalling their friendship of some sixty years, Briscoe talked about Brooks's "very unusual personality."

> *I mean he could gut you and still make you love him. Now, that takes a lot of talent, a lot of ability. So, he could be, you might call it mean, or whatever, but at the same time he could make you like it and like him. He was well liked, not just well liked, but better than that. I mean, he was highly thought of, and just on a personal basis, one-to-one, extremely well liked by everybody. He'd get along with everybody, even though he might have to, you know, sort of, I don't know any other word to use, but just gut them every now and then. You know, with a nice swipe. You know, in a nice way that didn't—that really didn't leave too much blood, you know, just a slight trace, but enough to be effective.†*

Others in the legislature and later in the halls of Congress and even in the White House would come to both admire and count on that tenacity, whether he was opposing them or supporting their agendas. The trait made his reputation. Briscoe said:

> *When he took on a project, like he took on Lamar, he was gonna get it done. There's no two ways about that. Just like later when he took on building that dam. You know, the dam for Mr. Rayburn. He was gonna get that done against all odds . . . And he put in the time and the effort to do it. And I think that one*

---

† This quotation is taken verbatim from a video interview that can be viewed at www.jackbrooksfoundation.org.

of the great, what do you call it, not a secret to his success, but it was certainly a major part of his success, was when he had a goal set, he was gonna achieve that goal, regardless of time, effort that he had to put into it. Nothing was going to divert him from that goal.†

Many years later, as Texas developed and highways linked small towns and farms, the tiny community college Brooks had attended also expanded. Today, Lamar University has more than fourteen thousand students enrolled, has added doctoral programs, and has become established in the state university system.

All his life, Brooks considered getting Lamar upgraded to a four-year college one of his proudest achievements, one that for him eclipsed many honors and accolades received over the decades in Washington. Perhaps he felt that way because it was his first real legislative victory, or perhaps because it was such a lesson in perseverance, bargaining, and swaying votes, a battle he came so close to losing.

---

† This quotation is taken verbatim from a video interview that can be viewed at www.jackbrooksfoundation.org.

5

First Race for Congress

D emocratic politics in Texas traditionally ran the spectrum from conservative to progressive, and primary election fights were often the most bitter. The Democratic primary for Texas's Second Congressional District in 1952 was more than crowded. The race started with an even dozen candidates, and, except for a few early dropouts, everyone stayed in to win, or at least to make sure that it wasn't a cakewalk for either of the two favorites, attorney Joe Tonahill from Jasper and the business community's choice, Beaumont's Walter Casey. Besides, with so many candidates and no incumbent, who could say what might happen?

In Texas politics in those days, there was only one certainty—the Republican candidate, whomever it might be, would lose in the general election. That's the way it was in southeast Texas and everywhere across the state; the Democratic primary was the only real contest for public office.

TIDELANDS: The election in 1952 was a big roiling event, both nationally and in Texas, where internal party fights were legendary. One of the most inflammatory issues involved the tidelands controversy between Texas and the federal government over which body should profit from oil leases on the nearly 2.5 million acres of land between low tide and the official international waters boundary just over ten miles offshore. There were oil companies and other interests on both sides of the question, and other states, including Louisiana and California, were also involved in the legal battle over their tidelands.

Revenues from oil leases supported the state's public school system, and

Texas had controlled the oil leases ever since the time of the Republic of Texas, which legally transferred them to the newly formed state of Texas in 1845. But the answer was by no means cut and dried, and the politics behind it were complex. Democratic Party politics were terribly split in the Lone Star State, where there were almost as many different factions of the party as there were politicians. President Truman and the Democrat's national presidential nominee, Adlai Stevenson, favored national owner-ship of the tidelands. But a group of Democrats who called themselves the "Texas Loyalists" supported the state's official position and eventually even came to endorse that presidential election's Republican candidate, Dwight Eisenhower, because he agreed with them.

The leader of the "Loyalists" was Brooks's one-time ally in the state house, Governor Allan Shivers (liberal Democrats derided the Loyalists as "Shivercrats"). Politicians at every level were expected to take a stand, and the subject was more inflammatory than voters today might imagine. The politics became so contorted that the state's longtime attorney general, Price Daniels, who opposed federal control, was nominated not only by the state's official Democratic Party (the so-called Loyalists), but also by the Republican Party. He won election to the Senate without a challenger.

The tidelands controversy, the Texas Historical Association notes, ulti-mately led to "three Supreme Court decisions against the states, three acts of Congress in favor of the states, two presidential vetoes against the states, and a major issue in a presidential campaign, before the states finally won the victory."

LABOR AND RACE IN THE DISTRICT: Divisions over issues of race and labor or "unionism" were particularly rancorous and had been raging since President Roosevelt introduced his New Deal administration in the early 1930s. Many who supported New Deal programs to support economic recovery split with the administration over social programs. In 1941, for instance, when Roosevelt created a fair employment practices committee, which called for racial equality in hiring, he upset a good many Texas Demo-crats, even those who once considered themselves original New Dealers, including his first vice president, Jack Garner.

The years leading up to the 1952 election reflected all the social changes, the legislation, and court rulings that resulted from the war and its consequences, both domestic and foreign. With Truman running for president in 1948, the national Democrats had endorsed a strong civil rights platform. This prompted some conservatives to join another breakaway group that became known as the "Dixiecrat" faction, led by South Carolina Governor Strom Thurmond. Dixiecrats were a pickup political party of white, conservative Southerners who wanted to protect segregation, primarily by arguing that states' rights were paramount over any federal intervention in racial issues.

Texas's Second Congressional District was no exception to the political and racial divisions roiling the national party. Many of the northern counties in the district were known for their support of the Ku Klux Klan, while the two most industrial and heavily populated counties, Jefferson and Orange, had more diverse populations.

Racial tensions increased in the 1940s as Beaumont's shipping and war plants expanded, sending a mixed population competing for jobs and housing. World War II, with the increased shipbuilding and need for more oil production, brought more people to the county and also exposed many long suppressed social and racial issues.

Bracketed between Houston and New Orleans, Beaumont was a microcosm of those cities and divided by social classes, with wealthier professionals on the west side, farther from the port and downtown. In 1943, a race riot erupted in Beaumont after a black man was accused of accosting a white woman.

But for all that, Jefferson County also maintained a peculiar position in the world of racial politics. The racism that often comes from isolation was tempered by the natural integration that unionized laborers, black and white, skilled and unskilled, brought to the community. Growing companies needed that influx of workers, and they had to accept the union organizers that accompanied or followed them. The union workers, no matter their color, were needed to operate the machinery of the oil plants and refineries, to maintain the pipelines, and load the ships.

Labor rights issues came almost in tandem with racial tension and became a charged issue among state Democrats. Even as unions such as the

Oil Workers International Union (originally the Oil, Chemical and Atomic Workers Union) were gaining steam after the war, many of them in southeast Texas, much of the political establishment in the state was very anti-labor.

In 1943, the Manford Act—named for the man who would be the Texas House speaker six years later—was among the first in the nation to use the phrase "right to work" to undermine unions' power. It was a semantic coup for Republicans, among a string of many for the GOP.

SCURRILOUS CHARGES AS A TACTIC: Many partisans aim to label or tar their opponents with a single word or concept. In the current political climate, Republican and conservative candidates and activists cry against the so-called "socialist" policies of Democrats and liberals. Those allegations of an ideology outside of the American mainstream seem an echo of similar voices from the 1930s through the 1950s when some politicians were quick to claim their rivals were Communists, Communist sympathizers, or, at the very least, Communist dupes. Though these loud and scurrilous charges in Washington and throughout the country were largely false, at the time they had a serious impact on political races and on people's lives and employment.

While the Texas "Loyalists" split the Democratic Party in the 1952 election, a precedent for such division had been set in 1944, even before the war ended, when very conservative Democrats who called themselves the "Texas Regulars" revolted because they were upset at wartime restrictions and the expansion of the federal government under Roosevelt.

MARTIN DIES JR.: Among them was Brooks's notorious predecessor in the Second District, fellow Democrat Martin Dies Jr.

Dies, whose father had held the same congressional seat from 1909 to 1919, was at first supportive of New Deal programs, but he eventually turned against the administration and opposed unions, immigration, and minimum-wage legislation. He became infamous for his strident pursuit of alleged Communists both inside and out of government. He had raised Roosevelt's ire even before the war, and the president described Dies's publicity-seeking personal attacks and allegations as "flagrantly unfair and un-American."

That criticism was particularly pointed because Dies was the first chairman of the House Un-American Activities Committee. The panel was known first as the Dies Committee, though the media later referred to it simply as HUAC. It was a precursor to a Senate counterpart run by Senator Joseph McCarthy and used aggressively in his own anti-Communist witch hunts.

Beyond working against FDR's reelection for a fourth term, Dies and the "Regulars" called for a return of states' rights, which was understood as a dog whistle for people who opposed many aspects of the New Deal agenda.

Dies remained in office from 1931 to 1945, even when he ran unsuccessfully for an open Senate seat in 1941. Through the latter half of his service, despite criticism from the president and others, he was undeterred in his attacks against "Communists" and Communist patsies.

Indeed, he was among those who sought to oust Homer Rainey, the president of Brooks's alma mater, the University of Texas at Austin. In the same vein, Dies attacked members of Roosevelt's administration as Communists and named 280 organizers for the Congress of Industrial Organizations (later the AFL-CIO) as committed Communists. That very personal assault on its own employees prompted the group to organize more voter registration in the Second District and to support a rival candidate for Dies's congressional seat.

In 1944, Dies decided to retire from the House, and Marty Combs was elected to represent the Second District. Dies's political career was not finished, however. Because of reapportionment, Texas added a new "representative-at-large" congressional seat. Dies held that seat for three terms, until it was abolished. In the late fifties, Dies again ran for the Senate to fill a vacancy and again lost, this time to liberal warrior Ralph Yarborough.

BROOKS FIGHTS COMMUNIST CHARGE: Brooks himself was a victim of the Red Scare when an opponent in the 1952 primary began a whisper campaign to spread the rumor that Brooks was secretly a Communist. The spurious charge, especially if you were sympathetic to integration and unions, was a serious threat, so much so that one of Brooks's supporters who campaigned alongside him carried a gun for protection as they worked through the district's northern counties.

Shortly after he heard of the rumor, Brooks was at a lectern during a campaign event in front of a large audience of voters. The story has since entered the realm of lore, and accounts vary. According to longtime political pundit Chris Matthews, Brooks told the crowd:

> *I fought the fascists for five years in World War II; I own a shotgun back at home, and I'll shoot any man who calls me a Communist.*

According to others who were there, however, Brooks quietly brought out his .45-caliber pistol, the one he had brought back from the war, and placed it on the lectern within view of the audience. He told the crowd if he found out who was spreading such a rumor, he would shoot him. It was an appropriately Texan response to the situation.

That put a stop to the rumor that Brooks was a Communist.

Brooks never knew if Dies had started the rumor or not, but the disdain Brooks felt for Dies, both politically and personally, never subsided, in spite of the years they would end up working together in the Texas delegation. Brooks's history with Dies went back to long before that, when Brooks was still in high school.

Brooks had considered going to West Point after high school. At the time, a congressman's support was needed to be considered a candidate for West Point. Brooks had requested as much through the usual process, and Dies had flatly refused. Brooks, not one to be deterred, then drove with his mother the many country miles over uneven and dusty roads to Dies's home north of Beaumont to make his case in person.

As they arrived at the house, Dies, standing on the porch of his country house, told Brooks and his mother that there was no need to get out of the car; he would not support Brooks's application. Brooks conceded defeat but asked, because they had a long drive home, if his mother could use the facilities. Dies said no and told them to get on their way. "I didn't forget that," Brooks told friends many years later. There was no greater insult, and Brooks would remain a fierce opponent ever after.

STATE SENATE: There was a time when Brooks contemplated running for the state senate against Roy Boy Cousins, the sitting senator. Brooks thought he had a good chance to win but worried that if elected he'd be forever tarred by the perception that state senators were beholden to special interests. Brooks feared:

> I'd be the only senator in there who would vote his principles, and I wasn't going to pay a lick and promise to the lobbyists, and I would be almost ostracized by the other members, and the senate wouldn't be a warm, happy place for me. And besides that, the record as a senator might not be helpful in running for Congress, which was my ultimate aim.

That cold-eyed look at politics was evident even early in his career; getting to Congress had been his ambition all along, and he was determined to make careful choices on the way. After his second term in the Texas House, Brooks already had accomplished his primary goal—getting the Lamar University bill passed. Now he needed to make some money to fulfill his promise to buy his mother a house of her own and to prepare for a congressional race. He returned to practice law in Beaumont, but his real target for the next two years was Washington.

MARTY COMBS: In 1950, the incumbent Combs was in his fourth term and was a member of the important House Ways and Means Committee. Combs once was described as an "almost shy Texas judge," and he was a close friend of Sam Rayburn. By all accounts, he was also an effective congressman for his constituents.

In her recounting of the Second District election that year, a local journalist wrote that Combs's accomplishments in his four terms in Congress included "securing the first appropriations for the McGee Bend Dam Project. He had worked for the deepening and widening of the Neches River, had been instrumental in securing the causeway between Louisiana and Texas at Port Arthur, and had fought for the oil depletion allowance, a tax benefit for the owners of oil and timber resources, which he believed was vital to the Texas economy."

Brooks declined when several local party leaders suggested he run against

Combs in the 1950 election; he believed Combs was an honorable man. Instead, Brooks went directly to Combs and told him he was interested in holding that seat one day. Brooks even volunteered to help manage Combs's reelection campaign. Brooks asked, however, if Combs would tell him when he was going to quit. Combs pledged that he would tell Brooks if he ever planned to retire.

The time came sooner than expected. About eighteen months later, Combs called Brooks to come visit with him at his cabin, where Combs revealed to the young man that he was gravely ill with lung cancer and had decided not to seek reelection.

Congressional elections over the years have transformed into enormously expensive vote-capturing machines, but they always evolve from small and personal decisions. Lolita Ramos, later the Jefferson County clerk, remembered a family story from her childhood when both her father, Ralph Ramos, and Brooks were in the Marine Corps. When they both returned from the war, Brooks saw the Ramos family living in a "little bitty" garage apartment with a tiny and failing icebox. Ralph was supporting his wife and three daughters on the pittance a newspaper reporter received, so Brooks immediately called his mother Grace, and through her work at Gulf States Utilities, she was able to get them a small but modern refrigerator.

Later that year, Ramos came home to find Brooks sitting on his back steps. Brooks announced that he was going to run for a seat in the state House of Representatives and asked for Ramos's help, Lolita remembered. "So Daddy said, 'OK, Jack, here's the deal, I'll do the writing, and you do the speechmaking and let's go." Their friendship continued through the years, and Ramos moved from print journalism to television and began the first television news program in Beaumont. Lolita's allegiance to Brooks also remained as she grew up and ran for county clerk herself. Brooks advised her, and she became the first woman to run for and win a countywide office in Jefferson County.

But before that, Brooks needed to enlist help from everyone he could find—every former classmate in high school and even grade school. Brooks, unmarried and the youngest man in the race, began canvassing the district that hot and dry summer of 1952.

Brooks's friend were essential to his campaign effort—some "light-footed elderly" and supporters such as Ed Hughes, an attorney in Jasper who would help organize the rural East Texas counties, with some others helping in Liberty and Chambers counties. "Eddie McFarland's mother knew a lot of people in Jefferson County," Brooks recalled, and his mainstay supporter, Bill Lytle, a strong union man, knew his way around every refinery and shipping plant in Jefferson and Orange counties.

With the help of his mother, his maternal grandmother, Carrie "Mama" Pipes, his sister, Marie, and brother, Edward, Brooks had the core of a campaign staff. Marie Brooks Manry recalled that while campaigning, she and her mother would go to some rough-and-tumble meeting halls to hand out cards and encourage the oil workers to vote for Brooks.

At one gathering in Orangefield, located about twelve miles east of Beaumont, Marie recalled: "I was at a table, but after thirty minutes I went over to a man who had helped me and said to him that nobody would speak to me. Nobody had said one word. They smiled, and they were nice, but not a word. He explained they didn't speak English, only (Cajun) French."

With the seat open, twelve candidates filed for the July primary. Emmett Wilburn, an attorney from Center, was the first to drop out, and he later endorsed Joe Tonahill of Jasper. That left Brooks and G. W. Stephens, who owned a lumber business; Walter Casey, a hotel operator; Ben Harrison, an attorney and member of the Beaumont school board; Tom Combs, the City of Beaumont mayor pro tempore; Jack Neil, general manager of the local KTRM radio station; and the Reverend M. T. Banks, a retired building contractor and the only black candidate— all from Beaumont. DeWitt Kinard, a general contractor and former state legislator, and Hugh Wilson, a refinery employee of Port Arthur, also stayed in the race, as did Julian Greer, superintendent of the Vidor school district.

Each candidate came to the campaign from different fields, and their concerns showed how diverse their interests were. Some campaigned on foreign policy, especially the United States withdrawing from the Korean conflict; some were businessmen who campaigned for tougher fiscal measures; others represented agricultural and lumber interests. A few spoke about the need for education, and most everyone agreed on better treatment for veterans and improving the Veterans Administration.

OTHER CANDIDATES: Television was not a major factor yet in elections, but candidates advertised heavily on radio and in newspapers. The *Beaumont Enterprise* endorsed Casey for the primary and said he was nationally recognized as one of the top ten business speakers in the nation. While Casey gave stirring campaign speeches, others barnstormed around, holding rallies with hillbilly bands and loudspeakers on trucks. Jack Neil traveled the dusty country roads in a caravan of white Cadillacs. Ben Harrison wanted to be known as the "Howdy, Folks" candidate. Brooks and Kinard had been in the Texas legislature and were comfortable greeting potential voters and running on their record in Austin. Brooks remembered:

> *All of those opponents were pretty decent people. I liked—I didn't dislike any of them. Later on in my campaigns, I got some rather sleazy opponents that I really didn't have much respect for. But these were all pretty decent folks, which is kind of nice, makes for a better campaign, actually. Even the Republican, of course.*

Three weeks before the election, the *Beaumont Enterprise* published a straw poll that had Walter Casey in the lead, followed by Jack Neil and Jack Brooks.

TONAHILL: But Brooks and others recognized that the most formidable opponent of all was Joe Tonahill of Jasper. Despite Casey being a gifted speaker and getting the newspaper's endorsement—"Walter Casey is a man of integrity and honest conviction"—Casey would eventually come in a distant fourth in the contest. Tonahill was the one to beat.

Tonahill was a popular, colorful, and well-known attorney, and he had the support of the lumber industry, a powerful force in the upper nine counties of the district. A former wrestler in school, Tonahill towered over most men, with his three hundred pounds spread over a six-foot-four frame. He had served in the navy in the war and a few years earlier had co-founded the Texas Trial Lawyers Association. His campaign slogan was "Let's clean up Capitol Hill with Tonahill." If there was any irony in that promotion, it went unsaid: Tonahill also was the son-in-law of U.S. Representative Howard W. Smith, the powerful conservative Democrat from Virginia who led a coalition opposing integration, labor organizations, and women's rights. Later in his career, Brooks had his own run-in with Smith and gave President Johnson a tip on how to handle the cantankerous and elderly representative.

In another decade, Tonahill himself would come into considerable notoriety as a defense attorney for Jack Ruby, the man who shot and killed President Kennedy's assassin, Lee Harvey Oswald. That publicity only added to his outsized reputation.

In this election, Tonahill definitely won a plurality of the votes—there were 20,716 for Tonahill versus 15,837 for Brooks. Neil was farther behind with 12,504 and Casey received only 9,299. Brooks felt momentarily deflated. But with so many others sharing the votes, Tonahill did not have a majority, which prompted a runoff contest for the two highest vote-getters the next month.

On August 16, just before the runoff, *Beaumont Enterprise* editor Robert W. Akers decided to endorse Brooks, his former employee, in the runoff, writing:

> *My own impression of Brooks is that he is absolutely forthright, that he does not equivocate, that he would risk losing votes before he would try to straddle an issue to please both sides . . . "*
>
> *. . . He is a friendly person and one of the hardest working young men to be found anywhere, because he is honest, upright and sincere, and because he is qualified by legislative experience to represent the Second District, Jack Brooks deserves to be elected.*

GIFT FROM BRISCOE: Brooks was grateful, but he knew a newspaper endorsement was not going to be the deciding factor. The campaign cost more than Brooks ever imagined he'd have to spend, especially because of the printed handouts and photos and newspaper advertising. He recalled spending about $10,000, quite a sum for a young attorney who had only started his law practice and bought a house for his mother. He didn't have that kind of money. There were some donations, of course, but he would have fallen far short without some critical assistance. Dolph Briscoe, with his sprawling ranch out of Uvalde, sold $6,000 worth of goats and contributed the proceeds to Brooks's campaign. In a very close race, that amount could have make the difference.

Brooks's motto was "B for Brooks," and his strategy was simply to "out-campaign" the others. "I started that campaign, and I worked day and night, just from can to can't," he recalled.

Brooks handed out his campaign cards at every coffee, dinner, and meeting he could find. He went to the black churches and the black ministers' association, an influential group. Brooks's campaign headquarters was on the mezzanine level of the Edson Hotel, but the major work was out in Jefferson and Orange counties, where Lytle would take him around to plant gates to talk with the workers.

> It was a hot, hot July and August. We finished the campaign. I worked every plant gate in Jefferson County, Orange County. We'd get up in the morning before dawn and Bill Lytle, who was my bosom friend, who worked at the Magnolia refinery, would drive me. He knew where the gates were located; it was kind of tricky to find them. Some gates were gates but only executives drove in, none of the workmen walked in, so you couldn't shake hands with them and work them, give them a card or anything. So we would go to those employee gates and be there when they started at six o'clock a.m. in Port Arthur and Mid-County and Beaumont. And we would catch some in the afternoon, and then they would have a special workman's gate, where they had a gate when they were doing a bunch of contract work within the plant, construction work of some sort, they would have a special gate set up for them. Well, that was two or three hundred men sometimes. They didn't get much attention and they were pretty receptive, pretty nice. And all of the workmen were pretty kind to me as I did that campaign.

The issues in the runoff followed the saying that "all politics is local." Both men worked their base of support and traded barbs about who was really behind their respective campaigns. Tonahill charged that Brooks was in the pocket of the unions, especially the CIO, or Congress of Industrialized Organizations, and Brooks questioned how much money Tonahill's campaign was receiving from the lumber interests.

That was a legitimate issue, because while both men supported the McGee Dam project, there was a real division on how the federal government was going to compensate or trade the lumber companies for the large tracts of forest that were being submerged behind the dam.

There was also a concern that the district itself was going to be broken up by redistricting, and that exacerbated the already clear divisions between the more industrial and unionized counties in the "golden triangle" and the rural upper part of the district. Brooks claimed that division was actually Tonahill's strategy for winning the election. He told the *Beaumont Enterprise* that Tonahill was:

> *attempting one of the oldest political maneuvers in the history of this type of politics. It is my belief that during the first primary he sought favor by pitting one section of the district against the other. He based his chief appeal in the upper region on the locale of his residence and not on his qualifications or his willingness to serve all the people of the entire district.*

TONAHILL'S WEAKNESS: Brooks relied on his own energy, but he also sensed a weakness in Tonahill, who did not relish the hand-shaking and face-to-face retail politics that Brooks was to become known for throughout much of his career. Brooks thought that Tonahill was not as eager and relied more on his "good ol' boy" manner than on personal connections to potential voters. In many respects that was true; Tonahill worked his larger-than-life reputation at gatherings in rural towns and his gregarious "Hook 'em Horns" greetings to fellow UT alumni.

> *He liked to drink and party, and I encouraged that a whole lot. Did whatever I could to encourage his enjoying life. And I, in the meantime, was working every plant, gate in this county, hard . . . When it was over with I told my mother I just didn't know, I could make more money selling apples than I could*

running for Congress. It was just brutal work to get elected, and I beat him by a little over 400 votes in the runoff. . . The only reason we did that was because I worked day and night, day and night, and Tonahill had a slight propensity to enjoy sitting around in the hotel with a little toddy and friends, good-looking friends.

According to former state senator Carl Parker of Port Arthur:

Everybody thought Tonahill was going to run away with it because he only lacked a few percentage points for a win. Well, back in that time, in '52, as you might imagine, integration was the hot topic, and East Texas is really part of the Bible Belt. It was more so then; it was more like Alabama and Mississippi than Texas. I mean it was red dirt and rednecks. Tonahill needed one more little thing to get over the top, so he came down to Beaumont, and I'm pretty sure he bought some large ads and encouraged favor with the editor of a black newspaper, and the newspaper responded appropriately by having a picture of Tonahill and the editor and some black leaders on its front page and talked about what a progressive Tonahill was and how he was going to help get school integration and so on and so forth. It was a little newspaper they distributed by just putting it out at various places around town.

But my dad [Harvey Parker, president of the largest local oil workers union] and Lester Roberts ran around and gathered up every one of those newspapers they could find and then took a trip up to Center, and places like Jasper, Newton, Buna, Kirbyville, and left one in every damned country store between here and there.

Parker laughed at the memory.

I don't know if that did it, but the vote up there turned around, and Tonahill lost considerable numbers.

Parker was only seventeen when he volunteered for Brooks's first congressional campaign, and though Parker's political career remained in the Texas capital, he and Brooks shared many campaigns back in the district.

I can't see Brooks to start talking politics in a crowd without his saying, "Yeah, Harvey trained that boy. I said he could snatch a sign down from a telephone pole with one grab."

The runoff was indeed a squeaker and a surprising turnaround; the results were 29,017 votes for Brooks and 28,577 for Tonahill. Brooks was almost certainly going to Washington.

GENERAL ELECTION: W. L. "Bubba" Pate said years later:

I remember when Jack Brooks first got elected in 1952. And you're talking about a guy that's fighting an uphill battle. I mean he's running against Joe Tonahill, for cryin' out loud . . . Joe Tonahill, well-respected attorney, nationally known. And, at the time, here's old Jack Brooks running against Joe Tonahill. With name I.D., Joe was much bigger. But, as I recall, when election day rolled around, it seemed like they were in a runoff. Jack Brooks just sat and worked him. That's when you talk about what it takes to get people to vote for you. In this case it was, "Hi, I'm Jack Brooks; I'm running for Congress." He was always a heck of a campaigner.

The election worked out just fine, Brooks said. That November in the general election, he faced Randolph Reed, a businessman who was new to politics and had switched his party affiliation from Democrat to Republican. Brooks described him as "a very colorful character." Tying himself to the popularity of Eisenhower, Reed focused heavily on withdrawing American troops from Korea. Richard Nixon, the Republican nominee for vice president, came to Beaumont to campaign for him, as Speaker of the House Sam Rayburn did for Brooks. There was really no contest. Brooks said:

I told [Reed] very early in the campaign that it would be a clean campaign and that I wasn't going into any personalities at all so he could count on that, and he had a closet full of skeletons, but I didn't want to go into that. And I got 68,353 votes, and he got 22,230, so I was elected and on the way to Congress to be sworn in in January of '53."

Brooks's first campaign for Congress was embedded in his memory. Half a century later, he not only recalled every one of the candidates in the election but each of their vote totals. The victory was quite an achievement for the man who was just about to turn thirty.

DRIVE TO WASHINGTON: In December 1952 Brooks packed his bags in the old car he called the "Green Hornet." Several friends pitched in to fix the car and buy him a new suit, and he started off to Washington as a member of the eighty-third Congress of the United States. He was excited to start his new career, but it would take some days to drive there. Several years hence, Eisenhower would lead the development of the Interstate Highway System, but until then, the roads across the Southern states pushed through small towns and between dusty fields.

To keep the new congressman company during the arduous 1,400-mile journey from Beaumont to the nation's capital, his mother Grace sat beside him all the way.

6

First Term

House elections for the previous term had been ugly as more Republicans charged Democratic incumbents with being communist sympathizers and worse. Deeply unpopular through most of his full first term, President Harry S. Truman had decided against running again at the helm of his own ticket. Instead, he personally encouraged the liberal governor of Illinois, Adlai Stevenson II, to lead the party. Stevenson, who both Rayburn and Brooks had supported, lost in a landslide, carrying only nine states, most in the staunchly Democratic South.

After a generation dominated by FDR and the Democrats, Brooks came into office just as Washington was preparing to inaugurate Dwight D. Eisenhower and welcome a new Republican administration. A frustrated GOP had lost the previous five presidential elections but rallied behind a war-hero candidate, displaying its pent-up anger over New Deal social programs and the handling of foreign policy regarding the Soviet Union, China, and Korea.

In 1952, Republicans swept in with Ike and gained control of the House, and Speaker Rayburn's tenure ended, though that would prove only temporary. The GOP won a majority in the Senate, as well, where Senator Joseph McCarthy's rampage against so-called communists in government was in full swing.

Though it was only of regional interest at the time, that year's election of one man would eventually have an enormous impact on the nation and on Brooks: a young congressman from Massachusetts, John F. Kennedy, won a surprising victory for a Senate seat against the patrician incumbent, Henry Cabot Lodge.

BROOKS AND MAMA: Once Brooks and "Mama" Grace arrived in the capital after their long trek from Beaumont, they found a hotel room before the big day; the official House swearing-in ceremony for the new Congress was scheduled for January 3, a cold Saturday morning in Washington.

After the ceremony, Brooks's first days in office were consumed, as they are for every freshman legislator, by the mundane and the thrilling: assembling a staff, having photos taken and voting cards prepared, greeting constituents who drop by to meet their new congressman. Members quickly figured out how to navigate the corridors of the Capitol and the House office buildings and learned that the young House pages were even faster studies as they trained to connect the scores of names and faces of freshman members.

Truman was still president of the United States when Brooks was sworn in on January 3, 1953, though for only another two and a half weeks. Despite a slight recession at the beginning of the decade, there was a strong economic forecast for the coming year. Government and private spending plans were robust, and some were already predicting that Eisenhower would enjoy the prosperity of the postwar boom and, likely, a two-term presidency.

REPUBLICAN MAJORITY: Republicans held a narrow majority in the eighty-third Congress (221 to 213 with one independent), and they voted unanimously for Joseph Martin as House Speaker. He had been Speaker once before, when Democrats had previously lost control of the House six years earlier. In early 1953, however, Democratic Party leaders seemed even more disorganized than usual; *Time* magazine described it as "a party, which is looking for an excuse to fly to pieces."

At the time, Brooks's assessment of the challenge was downbeat because he understood Eisenhower's appeal both to the country and to the Hill.

Eisenhower had a smile, a wonderful smile and manner, and I beat him in the district in '52, but I said if he runs again in '56, we'll never beat him, he has too good a smile. And he was a nice president, and I don't think there was a mean bone in his body. He got along with Rayburn and Johnson well, and we all certainly appreciated the good service he rendered.

Eisenhower was a practical leader, not an ideological one, but he did still have an agenda. Within six months of taking office he had visited Korea, and, as he had promised in the campaign, an armistice was signed, one that continues to this day. A former Supreme Allied Commander, Eisenhower bridged the divisions of competing commands while in the military and then in political life.

However, Eisenhower did not have to face extreme partisan confrontations. Instead he often relied on cooperation from the Democrats as he pursued the global and economic interests of a growing nation, a country that was truly entering what would be called the "American Century."

COUNTRY ABOVE PARTY: The sense of shared responsibility, at least among the top leaders, was evident during a meeting a few years earlier when Truman had called Eisenhower to the Oval Office to talk about General Douglas MacArthur, a larger-than-life figure known for his ego, whom they both distrusted. MacArthur had overseen an occupied Japan since the end of the war and had millions of supporters and much political capital back home.

Truman had just fired MacArthur and suspected that MacArthur would return to the U.S. from Japan and campaign for the GOP presidential nomination in 1948. He proposed that Ike join him on the Democratic ticket and that Truman would even step down and run as vice president again so Ike could become the Democrat's presidential nominee. Though it obviously never came about—at the time, Eisenhower did not want to be involved in national politics and soon was appointed president of Columbia University—the idea that national interest was more important than politics or position is remarkable.

DEMOCRATIC MINORITY: Preparing to leave the speaker's chair, Rayburn had assured the new president of bipartisan support on international affairs and defense. That was the traditional attitude; political divisions stopped at the water's edge. Such cooperation also would be critical throughout Ike's term, particularly as Lyndon Johnson, already experienced now in both houses of Congress, rose to become the Senate minority leader. His influence over fellow senators would either help or hinder Eisenhower's programs.

Democrats were weakened in the 1952 election, but Rayburn warned the incoming administration that any attempt to undo the New Deal and Fair Deal legislation would be met with heavy resistance. The new president, however, did not seem interested in confrontation; rather he wanted to use the nation's prosperity not only to face the Cold War threat from the Soviet Union but also to continue the postwar boom. The Interstate Highway System that bears his name, for instance, was a vast and critical project to expand transportation and link the country's economic regions. Just as Texas aimed to expand its farm-to-market roads, the growth of interstate highways played a critical part in enlarging cities by creating accessible suburbs. Along with advances in communication, it altered the nation's consciousness of time and distance.

There was a sense in Congress that GOP control in the House was only temporary; their margin of control was thin and Democrats expected to be back in power after the mid-term election. That perception was correct beyond their own dreams: beginning with the 1954 contest, Democrats would control the House for the next forty years and create a climate for progressive legislation for another generation.

The new congressman from southeast Texas, the youngest of that year's freshman class at thirty years old, could not have known what his time in Congress would have in store for him. The fortunes of the Democratic Party and his personal achievements and challenges were unforeseeable in the fog and drizzle of that late December 1952.

BOARD OF EDUCATION: It was known as the "Board of Education," a delightful term for a small meeting room (H-128) on the first floor of the Capitol building that a succession of House speakers used as a private office. There, by invitation only, congressmen would meet to discuss events of the day and strategy for upcoming legislation.

Since about 1850, the room was assigned to the Committee on Territories and then to the Committee on Elections. After the turn of the century, the dictatorial Speaker of the House "Uncle Joe" Cannon took it as his personal turf, and in the 1920s, during Prohibition, Speaker Nicholas Longworth of Ohio kept it as his own getaway room where he could have a private drink with friends, including his colleague and successor, John Nance Garner, who also used the room to connive and entertain his cronies. In an oral history of Congress, Darrell St. Claire, an assistant secretary of the Senate, recalled that during this period, "The whiskey vapor would come flowing into the chamber from the formal office, along with the laughter."

These speakers had called their unofficial gatherings the "Bureau of Education," which dovetailed nicely with the official names given certain offices during the period. John McDuffie of Alabama, who had served as Democratic Whip during the 1930s, was credited with renaming it the "Board of Education," according to his biographer, Ralph Brannen.

Vice President Truman was in the room in 1945 when a call summoned him to the White House with the news that President Roosevelt had died in his six-room vacation cottage in Warm Springs, Georgia. Truman later talked to the press about that call: "I don't know whether you fellows ever had a load of hay fall on you, but when they told me yesterday what had happened, I felt like the moon, stars, and all the planets had fallen on me."

RAYBURN: No man had a greater influence on the brand-new congress-man from Beaumont than Samuel Taliaferro Rayburn, a fellow Texan from Bonham and the senior political leader of the House. Rayburn's extraordi-nary career in Washington spanned forty-eight years and eight months in Congress, and he was the longest serving Speaker in history, for seventeen years between the onset of World War II and the first year of the Kennedy presidency. To most, Rayburn was known as "Mr. Speaker," but to those who considered him most affectionately, he was "Mr. Sam."

If Rayburn was essentially a lonely man, he was most engaged in his work; he loved politics and hearing political stories. Indeed, he once described the House as "my life and my love." But, according to his biographers, he was also realistic about power and its shortcomings. As he told one: "I believe there is still some sanity in Washington, although it doesn't come to the surface as often as it used to."

Brooks remembered:

> *I got sworn in, and on the first day of Congress, first day, Sam Rayburn came and put his arm on my shoulder and said, "Son, Jack, I want you to come and have a drink with me tonight and every night as long as we are both here." Well, what Mr. Rayburn was saying was that "I'm going to give you a Ph.D. in how I run this Congress. And I'm going to award you that degree when you come and visit with me at night" . . . and that's what we did.*

From January 1953 until the end of Rayburn's life, Brooks was one of the few who had an open invitation to this inner sanctum.

Rayburn was a father figure to Brooks, who had lost his own father as a child. When both men were back in Texas, Brooks took Rayburn fishing and invited him up to his farm in Jasper. He was always proud of his association with Rayburn, and later, as Rayburn declined physically, Brooks was solicitous of his health and looked after him with almost filial devotion.

> *Rayburn, of course, was my mentor in Congress, and I respected him, and I really adored him. He was tough as could be, but he was very kind to me.*

The two did not always agree—once Rayburn's neck and bald head turned bright red because he was so mad at Brooks's stubbornness on not letting a bill out of a committee—but the youthful Brooks was more often deferential. In his early years in Washington he learned the ways of Congress during the day and then continued to learn well into the evening; Rayburn's invitation to have a drink meant Brooks was welcome into the inner circle of Democratic leaders.

Rayburn's Board of Education was an exclusive and rotating group that came to drink and strategize. Other regulars included Lewis Deschler, the House parliamentarian, committee chairmen such as Hale Boggs of Louisiana, and on occasion even friendly Republican colleagues such as former

Speaker Joe Martin of Massachusetts and Minority Leader Charles Halleck of Indiana. Lyndon Johnson, another Rayburn protégé, often came over from the Senate side of the Hill. Though there were eleven women serving in the House when Brooks was elected (there were 106 in 2019), it was still a man's world, and Rayburn's all-male inner circle reflected that.

Generally, there was minimal drama. Brooks described Rayburn's sessions as intimate, candid discussions of upcoming legislation. Usually there were only four or five men in the room, joshing with each other and telling stories, and Rayburn would just slide the bottle over for members to pour their own drink or, as he called it, "strike a blow for liberty." This is what they had said years earlier when flouting Prohibition. Rayburn and Brooks favored bourbon and water but later switched to scotch, believing its ill effects on them the next morning were less severe. Rayburn's temperament and character eased many of the partisan arguments that were routine on Capitol Hill. Brooks described the camaraderie of Rayburn's group, even when a strong opposition leader like Charles Halleck stopped by:

> [Halleck] must've started at three in the afternoon because he'd been pretty well loaded when he came in there at six thirty and had a big argument. But he started it with me, not with Speaker Rayburn or McCormack or a couple of the other people that came. I was the youngest person there by far, and he would jump all over me. Well, I would just give him fits and go right back after him about Democratic policy, et cetera, because I believed in them, and Rayburn would just sit and smile.

Another of the regular attendees at the "Board" was Boston's John W. McCormack, a tall, thin, silver-haired Bostonian who didn't drink at all. He was the second-ranking Democrat behind Rayburn for twenty-one years and succeeded him as Speaker for the decade after Rayburn's death. He was not as successful at keeping the House or even his own Democrats in order. Brooks said:

> McCormack used to say "John," he called me John; he thought all men who were named Jack were really named John. And he always called me John, wrote

me letters named John. I told him a dozen times my name was Jack! I was chris-
tened Jack, but that didn't bother him . . .

It was a nice place in the evening to go by and have a drink, or maybe
a couple in those days, and John W. would say, "Don't you think you've had
enough?" And I'd say, "No, I think I'll have one more, Mr. Leader." Rayburn
would just push the bottle over. He didn't care how much I drank. He liked to
drink . . . then sometimes we were about to leave, Rayburn would pick up the
phone, "Hey! Yep! Come over. We'll be right here." It'd be Lyndon Johnson call-
ing, and he wanted to come over and visit. And he did.

Johnson usually had some bit of Senate business up his sleeve to negotiate.
Despite his and Rayburn's up-and-down relationship in the past, Johnson
was the only other member of the cabal with his own key to the "Board"
room, and he also knew how to handle the gruff older speaker. He would,
to the surprise of other regulars, sometimes arrive late, walk over to Rayburn
sitting behind his mahogany desk, bend over and kiss the man on his bald
head. Shortly after Johnson's death, Lady Bird Johnson unveiled a bust of
Rayburn in the National Portrait Gallery and told the audience. "Lyndon
always loved to think of himself as one of the 'Speaker's boys.'"

Rayburn's "boys" knew the rules if they wanted to be invited back.
Brooks remembered:

There was one member of Congress, Wilbur Mills, who was a very im-
portant member of the Ways and Means Committee, and would be chair-
man when the Democrats were in, and smart as a whip, from Arkansas, but
everybody knew that Wilbur Mills talked to the press a little too much. He'd
talk about what went on in there, and that wasn't good, so we'd be a little
circumspect.

Brooks remained circumspect whenever in the presence of media. He
spoke only if he understood the ramifications of his message first, be it be-
nign or pointed. In the first months, there were events such as an overnight
stay in a Navy submarine and a trip to New York that included a friendly
competition among a few members to climb the 168 steps of the Statue of

Liberty. Brooks used homespun language to a *New York Times* reporter to explain why he did not participate:

> *No use getting a-way up there and looking down at people. I'm a Democrat with a small D. I like to look at 'em straight in the eye.*

In an era when Washington was a more familial town, when families got together for picnics, wives gathered for lunch at the Congressional Club, and congressmen socialized as well as butted heads over policy and political positions, Brooks found another benefit to joining Rayburn's little cabal; he learned the value of knowing your opponent personally and the nuance of political opposition.

Politics in this time was not seen as a zero-sum game, an I win-you lose or you win-I lose competition that allows for no cooperation or compromise. Brooks recalled:

> *Actually, after it's all said and done, in the years to come, when I had legislation on the floor that was troublesome to Republicans, Charlie Halleck wouldn't vote for it, but he would not organize the Republicans against the bill and against me, which is a big plus in a political battle, it's the consideration that your opponents give you. That makes a big difference. Political strength is measured by the people you have working for you and voting for you and the lack of organization of those who are against you.*

Throughout his career, Brooks was explicit with others about how he would vote on a bill whether a Democrat or Republican favored it, whether its sponsor was a congressman or president. But he also made a distinction about whether he would actively oppose the measure and rally others to join him in opposition or if he would just let others decide for themselves.

Rayburn maintained friendships with Republican leaders like Martin and Halleck. Rayburn understood the importance of consensus-building, even if his party had enough votes to pass laws without Republican help. Rayburn was a tremendously partisan Democrat, but he was not an ideologue. Though he could be brusque, his manner sprang from a desire to be efficient. He readily recognized Republicans when they rose to speak on the House floor.

Unlike many of the hyper-partisan politicans in the decades since, Rayburn and his protégés sought out compromises with the other party and especially with fellow Democrats whose views ranged widely from big-city liberal to southern rural conservative. The politicians of the day worked diligently, often across the aisle, eschewed the spotlight (mostly), and, despite their political differences, enjoyed each other's company. They were effective and respected.

By the time Brooks entered Congress, Rayburn's career had already encompassed the entire New Deal and a world war. His name was tied to the enormous changes in federal law and administration that were part of the New Deal, including the establishment of the Securities and Exchange Commission (SEC) and the Federal Communications Commission (FCC). However, he once remarked, "Of all the bills I have helped on, I think I am the proudest of being the author of the Rural Electrification Act as it has brought so much good to farm homes throughout our land."

There were many lessons to be learned from the elder legislator. His word was good to both Democrats and Republicans, an attribute later ascribed to Brooks as well, his manner was quiet and friendly, and he led with humor. "There's nothing I hate more than an old fogey," he'd say, "unless it's a young fogey."

Equally important was his keen understanding of House rules. Rayburn was a careful parliamentarian, as was Garner, who had preceded him as Speaker. To become an excellent legislator, Brooks needed to figure out this particular system and how it could be manipulated. This went beyond being adept as a dealmaker. In everything from school to the military to Congress, Brooks seemed to have known almost preternaturally how one could work within the system and achieve intended results. If he broke rules to be effective, whether trading cases of whiskey for new military boots, or voting on the machine of an absent legislator, it was important for Brooks to know which rules could be broken. Perhaps even more important, Brooks learned to figure out what other members needed for their own districts or image or to drum up reelection votes. This was the gossip they exchanged

FIRST TERM 147

at Rayburn's Board of Education. Knowing fellow legislators' needs and helping provide them made consensus possible.

RAYBURN & BROOKS: Brooks and Rayburn, though forty years different in age, were both bachelors. After having a drink or two or more, on many nights they would go to one of their favorite restaurants in Georgetown or along the Potomac River and have supper together. Most everyone else was married and drifted back home to their wives for dinner, but those two had few other commitments. The seventy-year-old Rayburn lived alone in a small apartment and was known for a rather austere lifestyle. He had been married once, in 1927, to Metze Jones, the sister of his friend and fellow congressman, John Marvin Jones, but the couple separated in less than three months and the marriage was dissolved. Rayburn did have a few lady friends, including a Washington journalist at one time, but he never remarried. Rumors abounded, but it was not the sort of thing that was discussed.

Brooks was regarded as a very eligible bachelor who at various times had girlfriends either on Capitol Hill or around the District. His evenings would change when he would serendipitously come across his future wife, but that was seven years down the road.

Rayburn and Brooks also shared a lineage of many Texas politicians who became political leaders, either in Texas or Washington. Both men attended the University of Texas Law School, even as they served in the state legislature, both made their way to Congress, and, though their districts were extremely different, both won reelection term after term. Indeed, after his first election, Rayburn had no Republican opponent during his entire congressional career. After his first victory, Brooks had no Republican challengers for the next three terms, and when he did, he still won reelection handily in the following three.

It was a similar path for many other Texans, including Albert Thomas, Homer Thornberry, J. J. Pickle, Price Daniel, Lyndon Johnson, and Dolph Briscoe. For more than two generations, Democrats controlled every important political job in Texas. By reelecting members to congressional seats where seniority was paramount, a half-dozen of the most important committees were chaired by Texans through the mid-part of the century.

There were other ties between Rayburn and Brooks: both came from poverty. Rayburn recognized that his life could have turned out very differently: "I just missed being a tenant farmer by a gnat's whisker." Just as Brooks worked to pay his way through school and help his widowed mother, Rayburn swept school buildings and later taught classes to raise enough money for his own schooling. Brooks was fatherless at twelve. Rayburn, though he was the eighth of eleven children, spoke of the loneliness and monotony of growing up on a farm, sitting on a fence. Bonham, Rayburn's hometown, sits astride a wide plain just south of the Red River that separates Texas and Oklahoma. "Jack, when I was a boy," he told Brooks, "it was an event if a white mule came down the road."

Rayburn was known for his honesty and rectitude. The one congressional junket Rayburn attended in forty-eight years, he paid for himself. The short, bull-chested Texan didn't take money from lobbyists and turned down travel expenses whenever he gave speeches. At National Portrait Gallery's unveiling of Rayburn's bust, Brooks repeated a bit of wisdom from his mentor, "He used to say, 'Just don't ever lie to anybody; tell the truth the first time, and you're set for life.'"

Rayburn was known for his loyalty. And giving your word or pledge was not to be taken lightly. Though it was not really necessary, in 1952 Rayburn had driven the three hundred miles from Bonham to campaign with Brooks in his successful race against the Republican candidate, Randolph Reed. Brooks defeated Reed by a count of more than three to one.

In politics, a calling where shifting alliances are common, where pressure can come from any direction—whether the White House, a particular interest group, or even the emergence of a new rival—the value of personal loyalty could not be overemphasized as far as Rayburn was concerned.

In his book *Balance of Power*, the soon-to-be Speaker of the House Jim Wright, one of Brooks's dear friends, recalled when he was nominated by fellow Democrats to be the majority leader. Of the twenty-one congressmen in the Texas delegation, only two said they could not support him—Brooks and Bob Eckhardt of Houston, the reason being that they had already committed to another candidate. "Some Texans began razzing the two, but I put a quick stop to that. Since a member's word among colleagues is his stock in trade, I told Jack and Bob I understood and honored them for sticking with their pledge."

Loyalty was a big theme in the 1952 election. Both Rayburn and Brooks supported Adlai Stevenson, the Democratic Party's nominee for president, while Texas Governor Allen Shivers led his conservative Democrats, also known as "Shivercrats," to back the Republican candidate Dwight Eisenhower. Lyndon Johnson, who was concerned about his own Senate reelection chances in two years, was conflicted and tried to avoid upsetting either Rayburn or Shivers. There were consequences for equivocating. The rogue Democrats under Shivers prevailed, and that year was only the second time since Reconstruction that the state of Texas voted for a Republican presidential candidate.

Rayburn had a wealth of experience before becoming Speaker. He had served when Democrats were out of power, a time he called "in the wilderness." Rayburn's immediate predecessor in the office of Speaker, William Bankhead of Alabama (the father of actress Tallulah Bankhead), was in ill health with a heart condition for the last several years of his tenure, so Rayburn essentially had the responsibility of the Speaker for three years before officially holding the office in 1940.

In 1944, party leaders pressured Rayburn to accept the nomination for vice president for Roosevelt's fourth presidential campaign, a reelection that was not in doubt during wartime. Rayburn declined, even though he understood that whomever took that role was almost certain to rise to the presidency, as Truman, then a senator from Missouri, did the following year. Rayburn's ambition was to be in Congress, and he never sought higher office. In front of one gathering of Democrats in Washington in 1951, Rayburn said:

> *I am one man in public life who's satisfied, who has achieved every ambition of his youth.*

COMMITTEE ASSIGNMENT: At the outset of his first term in 1913, Rayburn was appointed to the House Committee on Interstate and Foreign Commerce, and he focused on railroads, an area of particular interest for sprawling Texas. When Brooks arrived in Congress, he began to learn the nuances of committee assignments under Rayburn's tutelage, and he was able to see longer-term benefits not immediately obvious to a freshman congressman.

Brooks had hoped for a seat on the prestigious Ways and Means Committee because his predecessor, Marty Combs, had been on that panel. But Rayburn said there was not an opening for him and instead helped position a disappointed Brooks onto a more modest panel, the Government Operations Committee, a less familiar committee that investigated government activities and spending. Before it was renamed that session, its unexciting designation was the "Committee on Expenditure in Executive Departments." Rayburn knew what he was doing; he had learned from his own experience the importance of gaining a name and momentum on a lesser committee rather than stifling in the more competitive ones. "I know one thing; if a position changes a person, that person is not big enough for the position. Just mark that down," said Rayburn.

Even though Democrats had lost control of the Congress in 1952, Rayburn still had influence as the minority leader and goodwill from the Republicans who may have suspected their hold on the House was temporary. When Democrats regained control in the next session in January 1955, Brooks not only moved up a notch in seniority but also, because several of the more senior Democrats returned to their original committees, he made an astounding leap; in only his second term, Brooks became chairman of a subcommittee. Brooks recalled:

> *Rayburn knew Congress backwards and forwards. And he knew the people. And he had power with chairmen like you have not seen. He'd just call them and tell them he was interested in this bill or that bill or whatever, and they'd say, "Yes, sir, we'll sure try and get that done, Mr. Speaker." Because he had helped put them on that chairmanship . . . No, Rayburn was a power they haven't had since.*

The Government Operations assignment meant that Brooks would be working with William Levi Dawson, the first black chairman of a congressional committee and a former Chicago ward boss with deep experience in the city's Democratic political machine and with legendary Chicago Mayor Richard Daley. Brooks said:

> *I was moving up pretty far because there were six or seven ahead of me that had gone on at that time. When a few above me left, I moved up, and, lo and behold, I was a subcommittee chairman after only two years . . .*
>
> *[Bill] Dawson was very kind to me from the start. He let me appoint my own staff, and I appointed some smart lawyers, and he let me run my own agenda. That was kind of unheard of in a way, but I didn't go around telling people I was a subcommittee chairman because many members had been in Congress twenty years and didn't have their own subcommittee."*

Dawson, an Army first lieutenant during World War I, was very old school and was heavily criticized during his tenure because he saw his loyalty to the political process and to the institution of the House rather than to his few fellow black members, such as Adam Clayton Powell, or to more aggressive civil rights legislation.

Representative Dawson saw that Brooks had a future to be nurtured. Years later, as Dawson was ailing, Brooks returned that loyalty, helping Dawson pass legislation that would not otherwise have had a chance. Brooks also brought the old ward boss to tears when he gave Dawson a treat, a jar of mayhaw jelly from East Texas. Brooks said Dawson was tearful as he said, "You know, I haven't had any mayhaw jelly since I was a boy in Georgia, before I went to Chicago with a little pasteboard box, a handbag, and ten dollars."

Such sincere tokens were precious to people who were constantly under pressure from lobbyists and other politicians to sway their thinking.

Another gesture, one Brooks made perhaps upon Rayburn's suggestion, was an invitation to President Truman in January 1959 to attend a biennial congressional breakfast that Brooks had begun hosting for each class of incoming freshmen representatives. The president, six years out of office, was clearly tickled to be included. He attended, dined on veal and venison sausage (which Brooks harvested himself from a hunt in the district), and cheerfully posed with Brooks, Rayburn, Johnson, and McCormack for a photograph. He later wrote Brooks:

> *Dear Congressman Brooks:*
>
> *You do not know how much I appreciated your invitation to breakfast the other morning, or how much fun I had there. I think I enjoyed it just as much, if not more than any new congressman present. Sam and Lyndon really spread themselves at that breakfast, Sam by saying nothing, although I have an idea that he already had talked to all the boys individually, and Lyndon by telling them exactly what they ought to hear.*
>
> *Sincerely yours,*
>
> *Harry Truman*
>
> *[P.S.] That picture inscription did not turn out very well. Will try again.*

UNDERSTANDING SYSTEMS: Brooks would not only experience and learn the political culture of Capitol Hill during that first term in Congress, but he also would define himself on broader terms, using his mother's work ethic and his own determination to become a leader. In a sense, this education was just building on his earlier years, from his entrepreneurial days hawking magazines, writing for the local newspaper and working the part-time jobs in college to provide enough money for his own education. In his military years, he learned the systems that worked to provide for his unit. In the state legislature, he realized the importance of local politics and tradeoffs in accomplishing his own legislative goals. Those four years in the statehouse had been a good early experience, but that still was only Triple-A baseball compared to the U.S. Congress. Now he was moving into a much more complex system, working with other members and their staffs from around the country. He needed to understand the competing interests behind legislation and how to use the rules to his advantage.

His early experiences helped him understand not only the value of compromise but also its limits. He knew to ask for just enough to pass a bill and was rarely accused of over-reaching. He often said he knew his limits, like when he learned that one could, for example, while working as a server in his youth, safely wash only four glasses at once, but not five.

It was his version of the old saying that politics is the art of the possible.

Rayburn advised Brooks that it takes about ten years to learn your way around the Congress and another ten for voters to decide if you're any good at it. Brooks was paying his dues for his career in the early 1950s, and he made another down payment—on a small, four-apartment house where the frugal young congressman lived in the basement and rented the other units to save money.

During that first term, Brooks also began his acquaintance with many of the people who actually make Capitol Hill work. Those less wise may show little regard for the secretaries and elevator operators, the carpenters and electricians, the police and researchers who keep institutions functioning, but Brooks memorized the names of those workers, a group that was often unseen and unheard. He affectionately called them the "worms in the woodwork," and Brooks's recognition plus the small kindnesses he showed them would make a difference over the years. Whether capturing a more convenient parking spot or acquiring coveted office space by having a team of carpenters reconfigure a general storage area, Brooks understood that treating workers with respect was both proper and provided advantages. He called himself a member of the Personnel Committee in the House; in fact, he was the only member of that committee.

Brooks's early years in Washington would bring remarkable change in the country, with many postwar developments—prosperity, the baby boom generation, a Cold War—already well underway. The scope of the issues undertaken by Congress was national, but the interests of the 435 members and their districts varied as much as the geography they hailed from. Agrarian interests had ruled Texas politics to a large degree, and it would take five more years before urban politics made its mark in Austin. In Washington and other large cities, however, their strong Democratic base created competing concerns. Even more, attitudes toward race split the country, and every politician had to navigate his or her own constituents.

Rayburn counseled Brooks on the importance of understanding his fellow House members. It was an education that Rayburn had extended earlier to another Texan, Lyndon Johnson, and to other freshman congressmen. Rayburn was getting older, and while his influence remained strong, he undoubtedly could see that his impact on the future of the House he loved would be to train and install future leaders and chairmen of the committees.

Brooks's first term was exciting enough with all the heady rush of a new administration and the national political scene, and there were big events on the national stage, from political wrangling over communism and racial equality to televised sessions of rancorous congressional hearings and the pursuits of a society now seen as a world leader in foreign affairs.

PUERTO RICAN SHOOTING IN THE HOUSE: Then, on March 1, 1954, another form of excitement came to the House chambers. Brooks was standing on the House floor when four Puerto Rican nationalists unfurled a flag from the visitors' gallery, yelled "long live a free Puerto Rico" in Spanish, and began shooting semi-automatic pistols down into the chamber. The thirty rounds they fired randomly struck four representatives and injured one seriously. Brooks, with his marine training, reflexively dove for cover and was not hit.

The incident, especially with the hindsight of sixty years, suggests how slow and cyclical the issues are and what little resolution is possible for many of them. The nationalist attackers (they would be termed "terrorists" today) received life sentences for the attack, though President Jimmy Carter pardoned them in 1978. In late 2012, Puerto Rican voters, still divided by some who demand independence, went to the polls and overwhelmingly asked for statehood.

1954 MIDTERMS: Aside from some sniffing interest by fellow Democrats in the party primary in 1954, Brooks didn't really have opposition for the rest of the decade. For the next three terms, in fact, he was reelected without a single Republican opponent. No one challenged him until the 1960 contest between then-Vice President Richard Nixon and John F. Kennedy. Even in that year, Brooks beat his Republican opponent, Fred S. Neumann, by nearly 70 percent, 75,657 votes to Neumann's 32,473.

Despite Eisenhower's personal popularity during his first two years in office, Democrats did indeed retake the House in November 1954, and Brooks's friend, former classmate and state legislator Jim Wright, won his first election to Congress as well. Wright often joked that he was always a few steps behind Brooks, from school, to the state legislature, and now to Congress. Decades later Wright recalled:

Jack was the first guy I talked to after I was nominated in the Democratic primary in July. That was, in those days, tantamount, they said, to election. So, I knew I was going to Congress. They ran a Republican, but that didn't matter. He didn't get any votes. I went up there to look for a place to live and to get squared away with Mr. Rayburn. I had been working with him in 1952 on the campaign—as Jack had, when the Texas Regulars tried to pull the ground out from under us.

Jack was the first guy I went to see. . . . .that evening Jack and I went out to dinner, and he was single in those days, and I was without my wife. We had a good time together, and he told me two things. He said, "Jim, the two most important things for you to remember and do are, be careful in the selection of your staff; you're going to need them. You're going to have to have capable, loyal people there. Be sure you get the ones you want. Don't just jump and grab anybody. And the second thing is the committee you serve on. Think about that and get the committee that you want, if you can. And Mr. Rayburn will help you, and you'll find that the rest of the delegation will help you." Well, those were two absolute truths!

And then the next day, I saw Rayburn and he had a few of us up that night to the Board of Education, and that was my introduction to that famous room on the first floor of the Capitol building directly under the House chamber, and that's where we would strike a blow for liberty.

RAYBURN SPEAKER AGAIN: With the Democrats back in control of the House, Rayburn once again was named Speaker, and he supported Brooks as chairman of a subcommittee on Government Operations. The committee didn't propose new legislation, but it was responsible for overseeing government contracts and spending. Brooks later acknowledged, "It wasn't a very important committee at the time," but for any freshman congressman to become chairman of a subcommittee after only one term in office was extraordinary. It also sent a quiet and unmistakable message to others that Brooks was Rayburn's protégé, and that carried more political weight than any title would.

That year, Rayburn also named Brooks to the Judiciary Committee. The seat on that committee would play a huge part in his legacy.

Rayburn held a simple maxim about the body he served in for so many years: Congress is made up of workhorses and show horses. Rayburn was definitely the former; he worked doggedly behind the scenes, drafting legislation and building and enforcing consensus behind his agenda.

It was not only Rayburn's patronage that propelled Brooks's advance. Brooks came to Congress with Rayburn's workhorse ethic and maintained it throughout his career. While the show horses participated mostly to get public attention, their names mentioned in newspaper columns and attached to popular bills, the workhorses were known for moving the bills forward, ironing out differences and personal disputes. Their role was rarely as glamorous as those preening for television cameras and mentions in newspaper columns, but they, like Rayburn and Brooks, understood a fundamental truth—progress in legislation is often slow, steady, and incremental.

7

The Late 1950s

In January of 1956, Brooks oversaw an investigation into the contracts of the General Services Administration (GSA), which, as the purchasing agent and property manager for the entire U.S. government, constituted an arena ripe for investigation. The GSA was created in 1949 by combining offices and departments generated during the war and in the boom years afterward. "Inefficient" was the kindest description, and *Fortune* magazine in 1955 described the agency as a mess, where the main ingredients were favoritism, factionalism, sloppiness, and waste.

It is hard to overstate the reach of the GSA then or now. The agency is a procurement and management operation that is both corporate and industrial, touching all aspects of government spending outside of the Pentagon. Charges of mismanagement began shortly after its creation and have reappeared in every election since politicians have campaigned on cleaning up such messes in Washington.

The Brooks Committee, as it became known, focused on a specific one million dollar contract to establish leases and nickel construction contracts for a forty-three million dollar expansion of a government nickel mining project in Cuba. The allegations suggested much larger issues of mismanagement and cronyism among Republicans then in charge. After the first of two hearings, the appointed head of the GSA, an Illinois politician named Edmund Mansure, resigned. The second hearing focused on meetings Mansure had held with others, including the former Republican national chairman, Leonard W. Hall. Those meetings, the evidence suggested, were to establish a loyalty test to the GOP to win GSA contracts.

It was the first high profile case for the young congressman from Texas, and it showed that Brooks was willing to go after senior government officials to fulfill his duty. "All we are interested in is good business practices in government housekeeping," Brooks insisted. Despite his mild explanation, his vigorous investigation also established that Brooks could be a bulldog in overseeing government regulatory agencies and all levels of federal spending. When it became known that Eisenhower was later considering appointing Hall to another job, Brooks released to the Senate the full record of his committee's second hearing from the investigation. He recommended that senators view it as some "entertaining reading" should the president nominate Hall "to any job besides dog catcher."

RACE AND CIVIL RIGHTS: For all the prosperity and good times, the 1950s was also a period fraught with racial tension. The Montgomery bus boycott, sit-in demonstrations at lunch counters in Atlanta and other cities, and innumerable small-town conflicts and protests by black Americans and their sympathetic white allies against segregation erupted across Southern states.

In 1954 the United States Supreme Court handed down the controversial *Brown v. Board of Education* ruling and, as Jim Wright described it, "a hot mountain of lava of anger spread across the whole South land when they decreed that there would be no more segregated schools."

Deep South states passed some 450 laws aimed at circumventing integration in the two years following *Brown v. Board of Education*, and in March of 1956 a segregationist document called the "Declaration of Constitutional Principles" was introduced on the floor of Congress. The document echoed the declaration of states' rights championed by John C. Calhoun before the Civil War, noting that the Constitution did not mention education, claiming that the Supreme Court had abused its power in *Brown v. Board of Education,* and, finally, arguing that the ruling was "creating chaos and confusion in the States principally effected."

Race issues dominated many a domestic agenda. Even before *Brown*, another Supreme Court case, *Sweatt v. Painter*, in 1950 paved the way for the latter decision by ruling against the notion of "separate but equal," determining that the University of Texas could not bar a black student from attending its law school. But the tenor of the times was powerful. When Ralph Yarborough, a staunch Texas liberal, ran against Allan Shivers for governor, the Shivers campaign hired a black man to drive a Cadillac with a Yarborough campaign sign through East Texas.

Segregation was deeply entrenched throughout the South, including in Jim Wright's hometown of Weatherford and all over Texas. Wright remembered that in 1955 there were numerous efforts to circumvent the *Brown* decision.

> *My first year, Jack's second term, there were efforts to try to pass all kinds of legislation that would let schools off from this . . .*
>
> *In fact, in my hometown it was so bad that they only had a school for colored children—that was the polite word of reference then—up to the eighth grade. If they wanted any further education, they had to go to Fort Worth. Fort Worth schools were taking and accepting them, but how in the world are the kids going to get to Fort Worth? If the family had a car, the parents used it for work.*
>
> *When I was mayor [of Fort Worth], I said, Listen, fellas, we've got to provide some ways to get those students over there and give them a chance. Get a school, a couple of school buses, and leave every morning with these young people and give them a chance to finish high school. Because, I said, if they don't—and I knew this would sail—I said, If we don't do this, some of these radicals over in Fort Worth are going to come and make us open up our schools. I had no idea that that [busing program] was coming. I was just doing it to get the kids a chance to go to school. And it was that bad. Some of the Southern states were passing what they called "Resolutions of Interposition," which said they were interposing their power between the federal government and these schools. So I think, you know, we settled that in Shiloh.*

Shiloh was the site of a ferocious 1862 battle when General Ulysses Grant's Army of the Tennessee vanquished Confederate forces. Nonetheless, the resolutions passed by many Southern states called on Congress and the courts to move slowly on integration. Within two years, segregationists began signing the "Declaration of Constitutional Principles," which came to be known as "The Southern Manifesto."

The Manifesto was a document produced in 1956 by those in Congress who vehemently opposed the recent *Brown* decision. In Washington, eighty-two representatives and nineteen senators from the eleven states of the Old Confederacy signed the declaration condemning the court ruling. The entire congressional delegations of seven Southern states signed the Manifesto.

Despite the political peril, Brooks and a couple dozen other congressmen from the Deep South refused to sign. As chance would have it, the document's principal advocate, Strom Thurmond, would one day be Brooks's neighbor in a small cul-de-sac in McLean, Virginia. Though Brooks's congressional district included some of the more notoriously racist towns in that section of Texas, Brooks had always had strong support among the black community, especially in Beaumont and Port Arthur. His constituents among African Americans and in the labor community had responded to his personal appeal and voting record, and, if there were any doubters in the early years, his commitment to the civil rights movement and his opposition to the segregationist bills at the state and federal levels confirmed their support.

Wright said the argument for signing the Manifesto was: "We have our way of life down here in the South, and most of the Southern members—I'm talking about from Texas and the Southeast—signed that thing. Jack and I didn't sign it; and we came under criticism, but it wasn't enough to kill you."

Former U.S. Representative Martin Frost recalled that Brooks and Wright were two of the few white Southerners who refused to sign that letter and who refused to publicly denounce the Supreme Court for its decision.

> *That was a gutsy move for a young congressman, early in his career. To be willing to take that kind of position, I think, showed what this guy was made of.*
>
> *Jack understood that part of being a Democrat is standing for the rights of all people, and you can't really be a Democrat and not stand for equality. Those of us who grew up in the South and who witnessed segregation, and the problems that minorities have faced in our state, have a deep appreciation for how important the civil rights movement was. And nobody was going to push Jack Brooks around on that.†*

---

† This quotation is taken verbatim from a video interview that can be viewed at www.jackbrooksfoundation.org.

Former Texas legislator Babe Schwartz remembered:

> *I'm going to tell you, he had a district that runs up into East Texas, and you refuse to sign the Southern Manifesto, or the White Man's Manifesto, and we had those battles in Texas. We had eight or nine segregationist bills introduced at that time. We had the White Citizens Council beating on us, and we had the Ku Klux Klan making us honorary members of the Ku Klux Klan, which I denounced on the floor of the House. I said, you can't be an honorary member of a dishonorable organization. But, I admired Jack so much in those days. Jack was concerned about his people.†*

Brooks's district at the time included long stretches of piney woods; isolated towns such as Vidor, Evadale, and Orange; places with run-down trailer parks also spotted with vestiges of grand homes from the turn of the last century; in between were crossroads with small clapboard churches and diners offering meals of boiled shrimp and frog legs. As progressive as he and Brooks were on social issues, Rayburn understood that many voters in both of their East Texas districts leaned toward or were actively segregationist. But he believed that he and Brooks could overcome the hostility at the ballot box.

Change was not swift. More than a year passed after the Manifesto before Majority Leader Lyndon Johnson managed to get cloture, a procedure to end debate and force a vote on the Civil Rights Act in the Senate. It was 1957, and for the first time since Reconstruction there would be a vote on a civil rights bill. According to Wright:

> *Obviously that became the first civil rights bill to pass Congress since those post-Civil War moments, and Jack and I, and several of the delegation, voted for that. I remember how Rayburn put it. I remember exactly what he said. He told someone to get a House page and ask me if I would come up and talk with him a moment at the Speaker's chair. . . . Rayburn was a man of relatively few words, but he knew how to sum up an argument. He said, "Jim, I think you want to vote for this bill. I know you're getting a lot of letters, angry, mean, vituperative letters, threatening you with all manner of retribution if you do."*

"But," he said, "I think you're big enough to overcome that. And I know you'll be proud in future years that you did." How about that? He didn't threaten. He didn't say, "You'll never get a bill on the floor of this House as long as I'm Speaker of it." He didn't say that. He didn't say, "I'll be thinking about this when the next committee assignments."

No, nothing like that. He appealed to the better side of the election, and he was right. I did want to vote for it. I was getting mean letters. I, it turns out, was able to overcome it. It didn't bother me in reelection. Of course people brought it up, but we all became—Jack and I and the others—proud that we did.

THE RAYBURN BUILDING: While the country was engaged in adjusting to the reality of a Cold War and unparalleled growth, Brooks was also getting grounded in what makes an effective congressman. With Rayburn's guidance, he began looking at issues that are under the radar of most who study Congress but are critical for members.

"Some have called the Senate the last plantation," said Erik North, a longtime Brooks family friend. "Then the House is the last feudal state. It was all about land and soldiers. The way you showed your prominence was land, which was office space, and soldiers, which was staff . . . and also parking."

Another way of thinking about organizational structure is to consider the three Ps—payroll, paper flow, and parking. Toward the end of the fifties, the growth of the government created a need for more office space on the Hill. An immense new building was under construction, and Rayburn, who was getting weaker both physically and politically, appointed Brooks to the commission overseeing the structure, which would eventually be named the Rayburn Building. He even walked with Brooks through the building and asked Brooks to choose an office for himself, though the process of establishing office space is based on seniority within the congressional class.

Built in the shape of an uppercase H, the building was innovative in terms of safety and wiring, and its footprint on the Hill is mammoth. While many "major" committees reside in the Cannon or Longworth buildings, the Rayburn Building became home to other major committees such as Banking, Armed Services, and the Judiciary, on which Brooks served.

It was no coincidence that both the Judiciary and the "minor" committee of Government Operations came to occupy choice first-floor offices in the center of the building, just an elevator ride straight down from Brooks's congressional office and most convenient to assigned parking outside. Throughout the years, the carefully watched acquisition of space and perks has been a signal of who has achieved or lost political clout. Such concerns are also part of a long-term strategy that was even more important at the time than it is now, for then seniority played an absolutely critical role in political fortunes. And Brooks was planning on a long career in the House.

BACK IN THE DISTRICT: Mindful of his constituents, and also of his mother and grandmother living in their brick home on East Drive, Brooks returned to Beaumont twice a month or even more frequently. He attended charity events, participate in county fairs, and even appeared on local television to give a small appraisal of what was current in Washington politics, always ending his five-minute talk with his down-home signoff: "Have a good suppa!"

On these visits home, his mother always let him know what she thought was most important to him and his constituents. She would often start a conversation with a local problem she thought Brooks could help solve, "You know, Mrs. Smith's boy is having a problem . . . "

Even though flights on propeller planes back to Beaumont from Washington could take considerable time, especially connecting through larger cities like Atlanta and Houston, Brooks made a point of returning as frequently as possible. On many weekends throughout the years, Brooks flew out of the stubby little DCA airport terminal across the Potomac River from the National Mall. Washington National Airport would later be renamed Ronald Reagan National Airport in 1998, much to the consternation of Brooks and many other Democrats. Brooks would not allow his staff to use the name, always referring to it instead as "National."

From DCA, the first leg of Brooks's biweekly visits home was on Delta Airlines, connecting in Atlanta to another Delta or Eastern Airlines flight on to Beaumont. A popular saying throughout the South was that even if you were going to Hell, you had to connect through Atlanta. The connection from Atlanta straight to Beaumont no longer exists. With airline deregulation, many flights to smaller cities throughout the country ended, and for many years now the only scheduled flights from Washington to East Texas arrive in Houston.

CHARLOTTE: For Brooks the election year of 1960 was momentous—because of politics certainly but also because of a chance sighting on a Capitol Hill sidewalk.

Before I first met her I saw her coming down the stairs of the Longworth Building. And I knew the worms in the woodwork—you know, the electricians, the carpenters, and those people. So I called those boys and told them about that pretty black-headed girl that came out that entrance last night. And I wondered who she was and where she worked.

His contacts identified the pretty, black-headed girl as Charlotte Collins, a worker in the congressional office of Bob Casey from Houston. The next day, Brooks went to Casey's office under the pretense of needing to ask him a legislative question. He also stopped by the desk of one of the office assistants and chatted her up.

"He called later and invited me out to dinner that night," Charlotte Brooks recalled decades later. She was pleased with the invitation but not starstruck. When asked what she thought about the congressman asking her out, she provided one of her deadpan replies: "What did I think? Free dinner!"

Later she explained, "I had worked on the Hill, so I knew what he did. I knew how things operated up there, so I didn't have to go through that angst." She also knew that scheduling was always an issue when dealing with members of Congress. "Then I think he probably had to go to Beaumont that weekend. It was kind of spotty."

Still, one date led to another, and a few weeks later, Brooks took Charlotte to a Friday night dinner with several others, including Sam Rayburn, who was irritated with Brooks because he was late.

Then Rayburn saw Charlotte and was besotted.

He was not the only one. Later, Art Buchwald, a legendary humor columnist for the *Washington Post*, wrote an article for the *Post* Sunday magazine listing the ten most beautiful women in Washington; a portrait of Charlotte graced the cover.

"[Art] called Jack and asked him if that would be all right," Charlotte recalled with a lift of her eyebrow. "How's that?" Nonetheless, she was willing to forgive the chauvinism of the time.

Brooks dismissed the publicity. "I already knew she was one of the ten prettiest girls in Washington. I made that decision myself."

MARRIAGE: On December 15, 1960, Brooks married Charlotte Collins in the living room of her uncle's house in Cameron, Texas. Dolph Briscoe arrived just in time from Uvalde in his dust-covered black Cadillac and stood as Brooks's best man.

Charlotte knew that she wasn't marrying a boy but a man just a week shy of his thirty-eighth birthday, a man who had lived through the war and who came with his own friends and habits. When Brooks was in Texas, for instance, Briscoe occasionally would fly up to Beaumont to collect Brooks, and they would go for a weekend of deer hunting on Briscoe's 140,000-acre ranch in Catarina, along the Mexican border.

Brooks took his new bride to the ranch for their honeymoon. One of Charlotte's memories of that is on the second night of her honeymoon, Brooks and Briscoe were out in an old ranch truck that broke down. After walking miles across the ranch, their leg muscles were sore. "I don't think I'd ever smelled Ben-Gay before, but it still makes my eyes water thinking about it."

Charlotte recalled that after that honeymoon trip, she and Brooks went for a more private visit to their farm in Jasper.

As 1961 dawned, the newlyweds were just barely moved into their home on C Street on Capitol Hill when Brooks invited everyone from the district to come by for coffee before Kennedy's inauguration and the parade down Pennsylvania Avenue. Though the traffic and snow made it hard to move around the city, the first guest showed up at their door at 8:00 a.m. in his shirtsleeves despite the frigid January morning, offering to help set up tables or serve coffee.

"He was one of the constituents. We had a lot of constituents there," recalled Charlotte. "We lived close to the Capitol, so we invited them to come and have coffee and walk over there. It was cold. There was a big snowstorm. Everybody was happy and seemed to be very united and excited about it."

McGee Bend Dam: In the fall of 1959, Rayburn mentioned his fondness for fishing and Brooks got an idea. The young congressman was currently trying to shore up support for an expansion of an ongoing dam project in his district. Seeing an opportunity, he asked Briscoe to invite Rayburn to his ranch to go fishing, and the Speaker accepted. So in November, the three men flew to Uvalde and then took one of Briscoe's private planes another eighty miles to the ranch in Catarina. The trio spent three days fishing in the water tanks that Briscoe had recently stocked with bass. Subtly, Brooks worked on the old man with his dam expansion ideas and Briscoe peppered his talk with issues important to the Texas ranching community. On their last day, Rayburn caught a large, beautiful bass, and Brooks recalled it was one of the few times he saw the Speaker break into a wide, genuine smile.

> *Rayburn and I were there fishing. Rayburn couldn't see very well, and he caught a big fish and called me, "Hey, Jack, come help!" So I went over there, and we were winding his line, and it looked like he had got some old boot that have been tossed in there, it looked so big. When I went to get the fish, the line broke on the leader, but I had my thumb in the fish gills, and I pulled him out. That fish weighed ten pounds, and Rayburn was tickled to death. It was a beautiful, beautiful bass. He said it would have weighed more if it hadn't bounced around in that pickup on the way in.*

They also went to see Briscoe's neighbor, John Nance Garner. Despite their differences—Garner thought Rayburn was too kind and easy-going, for example—Garner and Rayburn remained friends. When they arrived, Brooks noted that the former speaker and vice president wore a belt made out of rope and lived in a small house behind the big house he had given to his son. His crustiness was legendary.

Garner, of course, was pretty tough. When he'd offer you a drink there, which he did, he had plenty of whiskey. Everybody would pour themselves a drink, stand around, and then he'd go around and pour you a little water. I was last. Finally he got to me, and I said, "You're pretty tight with that water, Mr. Vice President." And Garner said "Well, they give me the whiskey, but I have to pay for the water."

He was a character. He gave me a box of cigars one time, and I thought the locals would drop dead right then, because he never gave anybody anything. His wife, though, apparently was just lovely, and everybody liked her, and she was a very balancing influence in his life.

Brooks ended up with Rayburn's support for the dam expansion project. He reminisced:

[Rayburn] was a very impartial Speaker. Except when my bill came up, he went to the floor and spoke, but normally he didn't take part in the discussion on the bill.

One time I had a bill that was near and dear to my heart. It was then called the McGee Bend Dam, the biggest fresh water lake in Texas. I was passing it and doing pretty good but I had some opposition and Rayburn got concerned about it. He was Speaker and was chairing the procedure, and he put somebody else in the chair and came down and spoke for the bill. He said, "I want you all to vote for this boy's bill. He's a good man, and it's a good bill and we ought to be for it."

RAYBURN'S DEATH: Rayburn's political and personal strength waned in the last few years of his life. In Kennedy's first year as president, Drew Pearson, a well-known Washington political columnist at the time, wrote about the backstage maneuvering on a 186 to 185 vote that Kennedy lost even though Rayburn made a rare move to round up votes on the floor of the House. Pearson wrote:

Rayburn got down from the rostrum and led the Democrats through the teller line for Mr. Kennedy and the Minimum Wage Act. But very few of his fellow Texans followed him. Only loyalists Wright Patman of Texarkana, Jack

Brooks of Beaumont, Homer Thornberry of Austin, and Walter E. Rogers of
Pampa stood with Sam. The rest of the Texans, who come around to Sam's birth-
day parties and pat him on the back as a great statesman, ducked.

Rayburn died of cancer on November 16, 1961, in his small, white two-story house in Bonham, Texas. Brooks said it was one of the saddest days of his life.

Four past, present, and future presidents attended Rayburn's funeral at the Willow Wild Cemetery in Bonham—Truman, Eisenhower, Kennedy, and Johnson—along with twenty thousand mourners. Despite the overwhelming attendance, the service was as modest as Rayburn's own neat and conservative suits. Behind that modesty, however, was a true "man of the House" as they called him, who, even as he suffered from cancer (which he referred to in public as his "lumbago"), guided the effort to expand the Rules Committee in 1961. It was a move that would be critical for the Democrats in bringing about the large social legislation that followed Kennedy's death.

In eulogizing Rayburn, the *New York Times* called him a man "regarded almost with awe in the House," and added: "It is as though a part of the Capitol has fallen down." In a more cold-eyed view, Kennedy described Rayburn as "a strong defender of constitutional responsibilities of the Congress." Rayburn's insistence on the proper role of the legislative branch was a legacy that lived on in those he mentored. When others noted that Rayburn served under eight presidents, he always corrected them gruffly, "I served *with* eight presidents." More than a decade later, when presidents independently tried to steamroll Congress, they discovered that Brooks shared that same concern for the prerogatives of Congress and would not budge an inch when he felt a president was overstepping his authority.

Rayburn showed that he could be known as a stern leader in Washington but considered a welcome friend to many back in his home district. Upon Rayburn's death, a Bonham mailman, Joe Kincaid, talked about going fishing with the Speaker and remarked: "As a fisherman, I'd say he was pretty good. As a man he was as good as they come." Shortly after Rayburn's death, Brooks entered a letter from the son of a former colleague into the *Congressional Record*. The boy, named Sam Rayburn Worley, wrote that the Speaker was "the type of person who makes you feel glad you're alive whenever you are around him."

RAYBURN DAM: Just ten miles northwest of Jasper, the dam on the Angelina River, whose expansion Brooks supported, is enormously important to the piney woods area of southeast Texas because it provides hydroelectric power, water conservation, and flood control. After Rayburn's death, Brooks introduced a bill in the House to rename the McGee Bend Dam the Sam Rayburn Dam and Reservoir.

There is a committee of various agencies that oversees the naming of large government projects. The secretary of the committee, an official from the Army Corps of Engineers, called Brooks and objected to the proposed renaming. Brooks quietly pointed out the political facts to the official, and Brooks promised that he would personally take the legislation to the White House for the president's signature.

> *They said I was on the wrong foot, that they didn't name two projects after the same person. They'd make it the Rayburn Dam or the Rayburn Reservoir, either one but not both.*

By this time Brooks was not only a veteran lawmaker, but his years on the Government Operations Committee had made him familiar not only with Congress but also with the bureaucratic ways of Washington. More than that, he was adamant that both projects would show respect for Rayburn's extraordinary career and achievements. The bureaucrat's attitude also "got his back up," and that was something most bureaucrats never did twice.

> *I said, "Well, I'll tell you what I'm going to do to you, friend." I didn't hesitate. I said on the phone, "I'm going to introduce a bill in the morning. [Charles A.] Buckley, who's chairman of the [Public Works] committee will be in New York. He's a ward boss working up there a good bit.*
>
> *"George Fallon from Maryland is second. He'll be in charge. I'll go to that committee tomorrow morning, ask Fallon to recognize me, and I'll introduce an amendment to my bill. Instead of the Sam Rayburn Dam and Reservoir,*

it would be the Samuel Taliaferro Rayburn Dam and Reservoir, and it would specify that his name be in letters about five inches, six inches long, high and deep, and that the Corps of Engineers, and all the other people associated with it will be in letters about three-quarters of an inch long." And I said, *"We'll pass it in the committee in the morning, and John W. McCormack from Massachusetts, Rayburn's friend and now Speaker, will recognize me, and I'll pass the bill by twelve or fifteen votes, and then it will go to the Senate. And my friends over there will pass it for Mr. Rayburn in a minute. They'll pass it probably that afternoon. And then it'll take a couple of days for the document; the documents are about this big [stretching his hands out]. They're signed by the Speaker of the House and by the President of the Senate. Big document, goes up to the President. Takes a couple days to get all the parchment set up."* And I said, *"When that's done, John Fitzgerald Kennedy, who is my friend, will call and say, 'When do you want to sign the bill?' And they'll sign it, and then you'll sure do it. Do you understand me?"*

The official quickly got the message.

He said, "It'll be fine the way it is."

I said, "Well, you have that letter in here before nine o'clock in the morning, and that's the way it'll be."

And that's the way it was. And I did make the change, and now it's called Rayburn Dam normally around here, but on the plaque it says Sam Rayburn Dam and Reservoir, like I wanted it.

When one of Kennedy's aides readied the bill for a White House signing ceremony, he called Brooks to ask whom he wanted to invite. "Nobody," replied Brooks. The aide laughed and said, "That's what the president thought you'd say." Whereas photographs of most signing ceremony include a crowd of onlookers, this one was remarkable for its empty space, just Kennedy seated at his desk in the Oval Office, penning his name to the document with Brooks standing beside him, hands flat on the desk, proudly looking on.

8

Rising Texas Tide

The days and weeks after the young president's assassination were a tumultuous time for the country, which was trying to absorb how its government and leadership was changing. On the morning of November 24, two days after Kennedy's death, nightclub operator Jack Ruby shot and killed Lee Harvey Oswald as he was being escorted between holding areas by Dallas police. Kennedy's body was lying in state in the Capitol Rotunda, set for burial the next day.

Johnson had been president for barely forty-eight hours, but he had been busy, having already met with congressional leaders and most of Kennedy's cabinet members, including Attorney General Robert Kennedy, and spoken with Presidents Eisenhower and Truman. He accompanied the Kennedy procession as people walked from the White House to the Capitol, and then he returned to his office at the Executive Office Building and met for several hours with the secretary of state, secretary of defense, CIA director, and ambassador to South Vietnam.

Brooks's and Johnson's sober opinion of Robert Kennedy seemed to be confirmed as the attorney general quickly aimed to secure his late brother's legacy and reputation, sealing all private files and Oval Office recordings. Johnson felt compelled to make the transition as smooth as possible, even keeping Robert Kennedy and some of the other senior staff members around in his administration, but Brooks advised him against it. He later elaborated:

He couldn't get in the office. The Kennedys had that office and wouldn't clear it out . . . It was a real, real sticky operation of gracefully getting them out of

that office so they could get it redone, or get a rug in it and get a desk in it, you
know, some presentable office furniture equipment. He was officing over in the
old Executive Office Building there for a couple of days, which was a bad deal,
communication-wise. You know, the telephone systems weren't adequate.

Though it was custom for the new president to occupy the White House quarters quickly, these were not normal times, and Johnson made arrangements to allow Jackie and her children time to adjust and prepare to move. Both he and Lady Bird were quite fond of Jackie, and they each made efforts to see that her transition from First Lady to widow did not have the added pressure of a too-quick relocation.

EVENING COMPANIONS: Later that same day, November 24, Johnson picked up his office phone just before five and was connected to Brooks.

It was a Sunday and Johnson invited Brooks and his wife Charlotte to dine privately with him and Lady Bird that evening. Charlotte was with Brooks at the time, so he put her on the line with the president, and she offered some kind words for him and his family.

Johnson ended up sending a car over to pick up the Brookses from their home on Capitol Hill and deliver them to the house. During his vice presidency, the Johnsons lived in an estate called the Elms in the Spring Valley neighborhood of upper northwest Washington. It was a gracious gated manor that they bought from Perle Mesta, a well-known Washington hostess who threw lavish parties there with artists, entertainers, and political elite from both parties. The handover was appropriate because the Johnsons were an exceptionally hospitable couple, and over the years their homes in Washington and Texas served more as extensions of Lyndon's office rather than private family residences.

Johnson told Brooks they would "have a drink, a sandwich," a potluck-style dinner that Johnson was known for, and that Lady Bird was accustomed to preparing, however late it might be. The car picked up the Brookses as well as fellow Texas legislator Homer Thornberry that night and brought them to the Elms.

The next day, Monday, November 25, Johnson attended Kennedy's funeral at St. Matthew's Cathedral. He had declared it a national day of mourning as Kennedy was laid to rest in Arlington National Cemetery. Late that evening, Johnson called Martin Luther King Jr. and reassured him that he would do everything he could to push through the stalled civil rights and tax bills in the Congress, part of Kennedy's New Frontier agenda. Johnson invited King to come see him the next time he was in Washington and to bring any recommendations he might have on promoting the civil rights agenda, which King would take him up on ten days later.

RETURN TO NORMALCY: Less than three weeks after her husband's death, Mrs. Kennedy and her children moved out of the White House and into temporary quarters in a red brick Georgetown townhouse owned by then-Undersecretary of State Averill Harriman. On December 7, with little fanfare, the Johnsons moved in to the White House. For Johnson, the transition to president was wrenching in many ways, including the loss of a privacy that even vice presidents typically enjoyed. Johnson needed a small group of people to confide in and to treat and be treated as if he could still have a normal relationship.

Johnson knew Brooks was a man who would speak to him with unvarnished truth about politics in Texas and about the concerns of other members of the delegation and others in Congress without the risk of anything being leaked to the press or to other politicians. Their friendship was well established years earlier, and Brooks's political future now seemed assured by his own doing.

Brooks recalled:

> *The only way, I guess, that I got along with Johnson all these years was that I always told him just what I thought was right—period.*

Brooks was not one to be awed by the trappings of power. In fact, there was a period in the 1950s when he and Johnson were at odds with one another over a disagreement about a judicial appointment. That estrangement, however, was soon patched. Brooks enjoyed the camaraderie of friends, and he liked to exercise his growing influence in the House, but he did not tout his connections, nor feel the need to talk much with the media. He provided Johnson with a sounding board and the continuity of someone who knew and studied national as well as Texas politics. In addition, both had learned the ways of Congress from Rayburn. They did not have to pretend with each other.

Johnson and Brooks had first met in the Texas legislature in 1946, when Brooks was twenty-three. Johnson, who had been a U.S. congressman for a decade already, returned to Austin to visit with the legislature. Brooks was impressed, though the pair met only briefly. They would not meet again until January of 1953, when Brooks entered Congress and received a standing invitation to Rayburn's evening cabal of card-playing, whiskey-drinking congressmen. Johnson, then a senator, would come late to Rayburn's sessions and supply the Speaker with news of the Senate. In return, Johnson would frequently ask Rayburn for personal favors, such as keeping a particular "sticky bill" in the House for as long as possible until Johnson could sort out its route to passage in the Senate before it even hit the floor. Rayburn had liked Johnson ever since the young man came to Congress, and had brought him into the fold of leadership and offered his wisdom on the House, much the same way he would do some years later with Brooks. Johnson would often return Rayburn's generosity by having the old master over for dinner.

MENTORS: Before moving to the Elms, Johnson and Lady Bird had lived for twenty years in the nearby Forest Hills neighborhood, just off Rock Creek Park in northwest Washington. There, Rayburn had been a regular, as was FBI Director J. Edgar Hoover, who lived only a stone's throw away.

These regular guests, mostly older bachelors, needed family on Sunday mornings, Lady Bird would say. Richard B. Russell, the senior senator from Georgia for whom the Russell Senate Office Building is named, was considered the most powerful man in the Senate during the late 1940s and early 1950s. After a decade of tutelage from Rayburn in the House, Johnson, once elected to the Senate in 1950, fixed his eyes on Russell, who was the leader of the Senate's Southern bloc, those senators from the eleven former Confederate states that voted in united opposition to progressive legislation. Russell, like Rayburn and Hoover, was also a bachelor with no spouse waiting at home and few personal invitations after work. The dinner invitations, which often preceded the weekend brunch ones, were usually framed by Johnson as just a practical way for the men to finish up whatever they were working on, which made the idea of any imposition a little easier for the older gentlemen to accept.

Years later, Johnson said:

> On Sundays the House and Senate were empty, quiet, and still; the streets outside were bare. It's a tough day for a politician, especially if, like Russell, he's all alone. I knew how he felt for I, too, counted the hours till Monday would come again, and knowing that, I made sure to invite Russell over for breakfast, lunch, brunch, or just to read the Sunday papers.

The dinner groups, which now often included Thornberry and Kennedy's adviser Larry O'Brien, would also listen to records and chitchat about anything at all. For the men there was always storytelling, light-hearted banter, and strategizing over bills or possible candidates back in Texas or committee assignments on the Hill. Johnson was also fond of playing cards and dominoes, keeping close tabs on who had beaten whom and never failing to remind people of the score.

Sometimes the dinners were big events, with guests from all walks of life coming by the dozen. Johnson's cadre of speech writers and special assistants were also frequently around, sometimes their wives as well. Johnson had many other close Texas aides on staff, such as his confidante and de facto chief of staff, Walter Jenkins, and Horace Busby, Johnson's speechwriter and adviser. Bill Moyers, then a young journalist who had just arrived in D.C. from Texas, was another; he would later become Johnson's press secretary and a fixture around the White House.

The near-ubiquitous presence of Johnson's staffers was not just a way to keep the workday going but a savvy technique that Johnson would use to collect information on other pols. With his own men placed at various locations at social gatherings, Johnson could in essence be present at four tables at once. He even got his staffer George Reedy installed in the Democratic cloakroom, the room just outside the Senate floor where senators, in hushed tones, would confer on which way they were voting and the like.

LADY BIRD: The closest presidential adviser is often, of course, the president's spouse. Lady Bird Johnson was a formidable woman who looked not only after Johnson's political and personal health but also his emotional balance and interpersonal dealings. Though Johnson's powers of persuasion were legendary, his approach usually resembled something like a freight train. Lady Bird, on the other hand, would use the velvet glove approach, whether to avoid someone or to command someone's presence.

Joseph Califano, who was LBJ's chief domestic aide (and later secretary of Health, Education and Welfare in the Carter administration), wrote about one such experience. Califano recalled coming back exhausted from a long out-of-town trip and Bird asking him to come over for dinner in the family quarters that very night. He tried to beg off, but Lady Bird made it clear that she wanted to have him there, and she told him only the family and Lyndon's good friends, Charlotte and Jack Brooks, were going to be there.

Califano still demurred until Lady Bird, in her sweet Texas drawl, added the clincher, saying that it seemed Lyndon only saw Califano at meetings when things were not going well, and she sure did not want Lyndon to confuse the message with the messenger. Califano attended the dinner.

Lady Bird was always at the ready with a welcoming smile and a table set for all. As his former special aide Bill Moyers recalled years later, "Johnson would call home late at night and say, 'Bird, I'm bringing the Senate to dinner tonight.'"

THE BROOKSES: As often happened within that circle of Texans in Washington, the Johnsons and Brookses had hit it off and were soon not just work but evening companions. The Johnsons liked having Charlotte and Brooks over to their home for dinner frequently, a practice they continued for years. The couples were comfortable with each other. The husbands were friends and their wives companionable.

The regular invitations continued, though after the assassination in Dallas the get-togethers seemed to carry more weight and to be less carefree.

Charlotte and Brooks had been newlyweds in the exciting early days of the Kennedy administration. Once settled in the White House, Johnson invited Charlotte and Brooks two or three times a week. Sometimes it would be for a major event or reception where everyone would be in formal dress, but more often than not it was just to have dinner alone with the President and Lady Bird upstairs in the family dining room. The Johnsons' older daughter, Lynda, had left to attend the University of Texas by then, but teenage Luci was still at home. Sometimes the four would bowl in the Old Executive Office Building next door, but most of the time they spent together was in conversation at those informal dinners in the family quarters on the third floor of the White House.

It was those dinners that the Brookses remembered so fondly.

After his heart attack in 1955, Lyndon Johnson used to sneak smokes, not when Lady Bird was in the same room, but when Charlotte and Brooks were upstairs at the White House at dinner or just chatting after their meal. Brooks would light up his cigar and Charlotte her cigarette, then, whenever Lady Bird left the room, Lyndon would lean forward and grab Charlotte's cigarette, take a puff or two, and hand it back before his wife returned.

The talk among the group was mostly about politics. Charlotte remembered: "Sometimes someone would come to brief Lyndon on a national or international development and he and Jack would go away." But otherwise the couples were left to themselves, often with Charlotte and Johnson sitting at one end of the table and Brooks and Lady Bird at the other. The comfort level between them was high, and Brooks would often poke fun at Johnson, sometimes at the president's expense. He recalled years later that he would ask the women to raise their glasses and give a toast to Johnson, needling him for his behavior that might otherwise be intolerable if not for his position. Or he would toast Lady Bird, saying,

'Here's a toast to Lady Bird Johnson, she's a wonderful saint because she puts up with the President Lyndon Johnson.' And he would drink to it and give me a dirty look from the other end, but he did not say a word because that was the truth, and he knew it, and I was just deviling him.

Brooks may have been putting it lightly. Lady Bird's tolerance for her husband's brash and moody temperament was well known in D.C. She bore his legendary public outbursts with a grace and patience that often left onlookers confounded. In addition to his admirable qualities, it was no secret that Johnson was overbearing and unreasonably demanding of those closest to him. In the face of this, family friends described Lady Bird as a "triumph of civility." She had long acknowledged to others that the public service Johnson was doing for the country was the family's number one priority and that, for a man with a near singular focus on politics and advancement, made the two of them a compatible pair.

Lady Bird was an extraordinarily shy woman, often visibly uncomfortable while performing the day-to-day duties of a First Lady, such as standing at receiving lines and attending parties or fundraisers. So it was not surprising that she felt at ease in the company of the soft-spoken Charlotte Brooks. Lady Bird, ever the dutiful wife and model Southern hostess, did not feel the need or pressure to entertain Charlotte nor Charlotte her. When they were not in the company of their husbands, the two women would "just take a break," according to Charlotte. "Lady Bird and I watched—what was that Western show that was her very favorite? *Gunsmoke*. Or, you know, one of those kinds of shows." The pair felt at ease together, despite the fact that they had been born almost a generation apart.

Though their personal styles differed, they shared much in common. They had grown up in small towns in Texas, Lady Bird in Karnack in East Texas and Charlotte in Cameron in central Texas. They were obviously capable women in their own right and both were well-suited to their roles in Washington. Lady Bird had run LBJ's office while he was away in the Navy at the beginning of World War II. She also financed his first congressional campaign with $10,000 of her inheritance, and later she purchased the radio and television stations that made the Johnsons' fortune, estimated at $20 million in 1963. Charlotte, much younger than Lady Bird and her husband, had worked in a congressional office before meeting Brooks, and for several years after their marriage she managed his congressional office and later ran the local banks in Texas that would become the source of their personal wealth.

Both women were seasoned campaigners for their husbands. Lady Bird had even taken on additional responsibilities during the 1960 presidential campaign and served as proxy for Jackie Kennedy when she was ill after a miscarriage. Charlotte began campaigning for Brooks in 1962 and would continue to campaign every two years for nearly three decades.

TEXAS GANG: Just as Kennedy had brought his so-called "brain trust" with him to Washington, Johnson surrounded himself with his own group, mostly loyal Texans who were alternately referred to as his "Texas Gang" or "Little Band of Lone Stars." Many shared an education at the University of Texas in Austin and had come up the political ranks and back rooms with each other. But following the assassination, Johnson moved into another realm, a presidential isolation that could not be widely shared. As he recalled in his memoirs, Johnson first felt that separation just hours after Kennedy had been pronounced dead, when Johnson walked into a room of colleagues, all quietly looking at him, and someone first addressed him as "Mr. President." He recalled, "I knew it would never be the same from then on."

In the final weeks of 1963, all of Johnson's friends rallied behind the new president and acted as a protective family. Continuity was the theme after Kennedy's assassination and Johnson had asked all staff to continue in their current posts, but by March 1964, the Texas influence in the White House was already being felt by both insiders and outsiders alike. The Ivy Leaguers who had insulated Kennedy in the White House for the last three years and derided Johnson behind his back as "Uncle Cornpone" for his Southern drawl and manners were now in the awkward situation of serving at his discretion. Robert Kennedy, who disliked Johnson and reportedly had been trying to get him off his brother's reelection campaign ticket for 1964, now reported directly to him. Brooks thought that keeping Kennedy's staff around was a mistake. He told a researcher several years later:

> *They were pretty arrogant. Of course, it was my advice to President Johnson that the first thing he ought to do was fire Bobby Kennedy and [Secretary of the Interior] Stewart Udall. I personally got along with them. I had no difficulties with them particularly, but I knew that they hated Johnson and they could not*

work for him. . . . my theory is, if somebody hates you, don't have them on the payroll. They're not going to be constructive. I'm sorry that they hate me, you're sorry that they don't like you, but you just can't have them on the staff. They're not going to be helpful to you. And in a political appointment, when you appoint them and give them the job, I think you ought to be bored for the hollow horn if you give it to somebody who's just dedicated to your destruction.

Johnson did not think he ought to do that. He thought he could work with them and he wanted to be kind. After he got to be president, you see, he didn't want to be unkind to anybody. He was aware of what power was, he understands power, and he wanted to be reasonable, considerate, thoughtful of all the people that worked for him and that had worked for Kennedy.

That handpicked Kennedy staff, many of who had become household names, like Press Secretary Pierre Salinger, and were connected with the Camelot era in the minds of most Americans, began to be peeled away like a husk. Special Counsel Theodore Sorensen and special assistants Arthur Schlesinger Jr., Brooks Hayes, and Timothy Reardon were gone. Kenneth O'Donnell and McGeorge Bundy were still around, but in name only, as was Larry O'Brien, who found his particular skills as congressional liaison in far less demand with the new president, who needed little advice in that realm. In their place came Walter Jenkins, Bill Moyers, George Reedy, and Jack Valenti, all of whom shared one vital characteristic: they were Texans. The shift even garnered an article in the *Washington Post* titled, "Texas Crowd's Taken Over."

Almost without exception, the Kennedy staff men who remain have diminished power and influence in the White House even though they do approximately the same work they did in the past.

JACK VALENTI: The replacements were a colorful bunch. Valenti was a Houston political consultant who had been liaising with the media on the fateful Dallas trip. His wife worked for Johnson as a secretary and through that connection Valenti had been within the presidential "bubble" that day and was one of the few identifiable onlookers in the photo of Johnson's swearing-in on Air Force One. Moments later, Johnson asked him if he would come back to Washington with him, and Valenti, of course, said yes, flying off to a new life with literally just the clothes on his back. After joining Johnson's staff, Valenti became one of the most unflappable promoters of the administration and later went on to a thirty-eight-year career as head of the Motion Picture Association of America. Though Valenti's credentials as a presidential staffer were called into question by some and his role lacked clear definition, he had as much energy as Johnson and had such a habit of being everywhere that some other White House staffers took to calling him "the Spook."

Valenti was the epitome of a yes-man. His allegiance to the president was above reproach. In the ensuing years in Washington, the saying went that if Johnson was walking and ever stopped short, they would have to extract Jack Valenti from his ass.

THORNBERRY: There were several other men in the Texas power equation when Johnson had become vice president. One was William Homer Thornberry, who was known to his friends as Homer, or simply "Mo." He, too, had taken a familiar path to Washington and had actually replaced Johnson as the representative for the Tenth Congressional District when Johnson left for the Senate in 1948. Thornberry and his wife, Eloise, also were often present in the small dining room in which the Johnsons hosted weekday guests.

Thornberry was born in Austin and went to college and law school at the University of Texas. He became a lawyer and a state house representative in 1936 and then joined the Navy at the outbreak of World War II, just as Johnson had. Upon returning home, he became a member of the Austin City Council and acting mayor. He was socially liberal and had a squeaky-clean reputation, which helped him easily win Johnson's seat in the House in 1948 and for six following terms. In early 1963, President Kennedy had asked Thornberry if he wanted a federal judgeship and Thornberry agreed, though he delayed leaving the House for several months because Kennedy believed he needed every vote he could muster for his upcoming legislation. Because of that appointment delay, Thornberry was in the motorcade with

Kennedy, Johnson, and the others on the trip to Dallas in November 1963. He and Brooks were together a few cars back from Kennedy's.

Thornberry was another frequent guest of Johnson's, especially in the last few weeks before he left for his federal bench. Johnson was not subtle in trying to keep him close; he invited Thornberry along with the Brookses to dinner or "a swim" half a dozen times during his first weeks as president. Thornberry's wife Eloise was back in Austin, and he was eager to join her. Johnson employed all his persuasive skills, but to no avail. Thornberry said he was committed to the judgeship. He was sworn into office on December 20, just four weeks after the assassination. The next day, J. J. Pickle, another friend of the Texas gang, came in to fill his seat.

Thornberry served as a federal judge for the western district of Texas for two years until Johnson appointed him to the federal Fifth Circuit Court of Appeals in 1965. Some thought he was a Johnson crony, especially when Thornberry was briefly nominated to fill in for an expected vacancy on the U.S. Supreme Court when Johnson signaled that he wanted to appoint another close friend, Abe Fortas, to the chief justice position. That was derailed when questions came up in the Senate about Fortas's liberalism and ethics, and his name was withdrawn. Consequently, so was Thornberry's, and he returned to the appellate court, where he served for thirty years more until his death in 1995.

CONNALLY: Another member of the Texas gang was John Connally, who in early 1964 still suffered from injuries from the assassination attack. Connally's conservative brand of politics was still divisive among the group, and he was up for reelection as governor. In an effort to shore up support for him, Johnson decided to draft a resolution backing Connally for reelection. Except it was up to Brooks to get each one of twenty-five Texan politicians to actually sign it, which all of them did except for Ralph Yarborough, the outspoken liberal senator who was quite open about his visceral disdain for Connally. As Johnson and others had found out long before, when Yarborough made his mind up, right or wrong, there was little use in trying to persuade him. In contrast to Yarborough's staunch support of progressive ideas, Connally was a man with no loyalty to party or ideology, and it was discovered years later that Connally had actually been trying to help Yarborough's Republican opponent in that year's election, a young George H. W. Bush.

THOMAS AND JOHNSON FEUD: For Texans, political rivalries are constant, but a seasoned politician is expected to know how to negotiate through a maze of personal and political needs. One of Brooks's older friends was Albert Thomas, who entered the House in 1937, the same year as Johnson.

Like Rayburn, Johnson, Thornberry, and Brooks himself, Thomas had attended the University of Texas Law School before being elected to Congress. And because Johnson was from Austin and Thomas from Houston, the two of them shared many of the same fundraisers and were both members of the exclusive "Suite 8F group," an informal coalition of Texas politicians and businessmen who carried an outsized amount of weight in Washington. Johnson's principal benefactors, George and Herman Brown of the construction giant Brown & Root, were members as well. The group was named because they would hold their get-togethers in Brown's Suite 8F of the Lamar Hotel in Houston.

Thomas and Johnson had a running feud for a quarter-century, ever since both had vied for the "Texas seat" on the powerful Appropriations Committee in 1937. Thomas won the seat through suspicious means, Johnson contended privately, and the two politicians had never liked each other since. As young representatives, Thomas had bristled at Johnson's very presence, which was often loud and attention-seeking. Thomas would mutter comments to others in the Texas delegation, but none would openly attack Johnson, who had the blessing, or rather protection, of Rayburn, which made him all but untouchable.

Each man knew that Brooks kept company with the other, so they would each warn Brooks to be careful. "You better keep an eye on old Albert," Johnson would say. "You know why those Secret Service men were on the running boards when Roosevelt went to Houston and Thomas was there? They didn't want Thomas to steal his watch!" Brooks found the feuding harmless, but it became clear that a resolution was overdue.

They were not friendly, and over the years they needled each other and were not very cooperative with each other. So after Johnson became vice president in 1961—this is nearly twenty-five years of these long-standing hard feelings, I told Johnson maybe we should have dinner sometime with Albert and Lera Thomas.

Brooks ended up in the role of peacemaker between the two old bulls, but it was Charlotte's idea to get the two of them together at the Elms. As Brooks retold it, he and Charlotte, Albert and Lera, and Johnson and Lady Bird sat down and had a drink. And then they had another.

Brooks and Thomas had their own disagreement about the appointment of a federal judge and about land Rice University had donated to the federal government but wanted back after the government decided not to use it for the original purpose. Brooks said:

I wanted the government to sell it back; it was theirs. Thomas and I had a pretty good argument about that, and he won. Rice University was happy, he was happy, and we settled our arguments. That's the way it was.

But before long, Johnson and Thomas were regaling each other with stories of how they had needled each other in the past. Brooks recalled:

Well, we got there, and we all had a drink or two or three, and Johnson and Thomas and I were sitting in a room, and they got to telling some of the things they had done to each other. That was something, and they kept on, and they were not mad about it, just reciting what had happened. They both got along with George Brown [of Brown and Root], who was a big contributor to both of them. But they had some differences over the years, I guarantee you.

But finally Lady Bird insisted that we come in and have some supper, it was getting late. So we went in and had supper and decided that they obviously had resolved their differences and were going to be friends, 'cause we had a nice supper, dinner, whatever you call it. Charlotte was going to drive me home, and Lera was going to drive Albert home, and Johnson was going to stagger off to bed, and we left.

After that dinner conversation, Johnson and Thomas became much friendlier. Their conciliation was so solid that later in 1963 a frustrated Johnson recounted his strongest political assets to Brooks over the phone, listing Brooks and Thomas together, along with the Speaker of the House and Senate majority leader. Brooks remembered:

> *That was a very significant dinner to the Texas delegation and to a lot of people, and I was delighted to have a part in it. Whenever we had a major problem or trouble with the delegation, I would tell Albert, and sometimes he was in a position to reason with them, or not have their appropriations in the appropriation bill. He was a very tough operator. Or sometimes Johnson would call [to straighten out the problem]. But it meant that we had Johnson and Albert on the same team working together for the betterment of the country, and the Texas delegation went along very well under those circumstances, much better than they might have otherwise.*

NASA IN HOUSTON: Albert Thomas had represented Houston and all of Harris County for twenty years and was responsible for much of the growth there, including the location of the NASA manned space flight center in Houston. Thomas was born in Nacogdoches, and his nickname was "Big Foot," as in, "Big Foot Thomas." Though he was thirty-three years Brooks's senior, the pair became friends, perhaps in part because of similarities in their backgrounds. Thomas, a fellow Methodist, had run off from home and joined the Army during World War I. His father threatened to disown him and Thomas eventually came home, went to the University of Texas School of Law, and became the Harris County district attorney.

Locating the space center in Houston had been a tremendous coup for Texas, and Thomas also served on the Joint Committee on Atomic Energy, increasing his influence on legislation affecting the Texas economy.

Thomas was well-mannered, a real old-school gentleman, and he was chairman of the defense subcommittee on the Appropriations Committee. Congress holds the purse strings, but it was the Appropriations Committee and its chairman who had the power to loosen or tighten the strings. Bills could come out of other committees, and they could pass a full vote on the House floor, but if the Appropriations Committee did not assign it any funding, the bill might as well have not been written.

Thomas dominated many others on spending issues. Some members did not like him, and he did not care. Even more, he resented upstart members in the House who didn't show sufficient respect for seniority. Brooks recalled:

> *He was a very tough cookie. He was nice and pleasant to everybody, but he did not bow down to anybody. And walking with him in the aisles sometimes, in the corridors, somebody would be not very courteous to him in saying hello or something or just passing by, and Albert would lean over to me afterwards and say, "I think I'll just cut his appropriations out." And he was going to go back to his office and take a pencil and draw it right through those appropriations.*
>
> *He had almost absolute power on the independent offices. He was chairman of a subcommittee on the appropriation committee. And those jobs are so powerful; they are as powerful as or more so than many full committees in Congress because they had charge of the budget for those areas of the government.*
>
> *But Albert was the kind that ran them, he knew what was in them, and he could stop them or he could put it in if he wanted to. He was my bosom friend and was very helpful to me in getting appropriations. Even though they weren't directly on his jurisdiction, he had influence. He was a very nice guy. Tall, thin, had a good eye for ladies, and he liked to play paddleball.*

But time and illness were taking their toll. Rayburn, a contemporary of Thomas's, had died a year earlier, and in early 1963 Thomas was considering retirement. Brooks said:

> *The last few years when he had a bad kind of cancer and he had been in charge of financing appropriations for grants for some research people, I believe it was in Iowa, they were working on blood on that point. He used to tell me, "you know, they're working on it, and they're making progress, but I don't think they'll make it in time for me." Bless his heart, they didn't, and when he was ill and doctors recommended he take pain medication, his wife, Lera, told me he wasn't taking it.*
>
> *I had lunch with him generally then every day, and he wouldn't take it, and*

I told him, "Albert, you old blankety-blank, I know you're familiar with dope addicts and needle marks they have on their arm, but you're not taking that kind of medication, and you are not going to live long enough to be an addict and you damn sure better start taking it; there is no use in your being in pain and being uncomfortable." I don't know of anybody else that would talk to him like that 'cause he was tough as a boot, but he just nodded and said "Yes, I guess I ought to," and he did from then on.

The kickoff of Kennedy's ill-fated Texas trip had been an appreciation dinner for some 3,200 supporters to persuade Thomas to run again for reelection. President Kennedy had changed his travel plans to attend the Thomas dinner in Houston on November 21, and there he told the assembly that "our leadership in space could not have been achieved without Congressman Albert Thomas." With the president and vice president and scores of fellow congressmen pushing him to remain in office, Thomas finally decided to run again.

The next afternoon in Dallas, in the midst of the group's frantic response to the killing, Johnson asked the younger and more agile Brooks to ride with Mrs. Johnson in a separate car back to the airport in case there was a wider attack. Thomas and Thornberry rode with Johnson in the high-speed motorcade back to Air Force One.

It was Brooks who recommended that Johnson take the oath of office aboard Air Force One before leaving Dallas and Thomas who reinforced the idea. Both men helped shepherd Great Society legislation through the House. Thomas was appointed chairman of the House Democratic Caucus the next year and ran successfully for another term in 1964, but his cancer was progressing; he had to turn down many offers to join Brooks and Johnson at dinners in the White House, and he died in 1966. His wife served out his term in office. Brooks fondly recalled:

He didn't fool with the Texas delegation much. He didn't have too much use for any of them. But he was good to me.

I was a pallbearer for him, and I inherited from him three very wealthy individuals in Houston interested in politics, very wealthy. And those three men,

until they died or until I left Congress, sent me $1,000 for every campaign I had
from then on at the very beginning of the campaign, and they were my friends.
One of them still is, we're still buddies. Albert was one of a kind in Congress; I
don't know any others like him. He was fun.

State of the Union Address: As Brooks had told Johnson just after
the assassination, there had never been a vice president as ready for the
presidency as he was. The observation would soon prove to be prophetic.
Johnson settled into the presidency with a calmness and agility that surprised some who had known him personally for years. Within his first few
weeks in office, Johnson began to apply his political skills and congressional
knowledge to the presidency to a degree never before seen. Many presidential
historians argue that it has not been matched since.

On January 7, 1964, Brooks connected by phone with Johnson.

> *Johnson: Hello?*
> *Brooks: Mr. President.*
> *Johnson: Where in the hell did you run off to? I thought you said you were*
> *going to call or come by.*
> *Brooks: You are the busiest man I ever saw.*
> *Johnson: How in the hell did you know? You never did even inquire. I told*
> *them to let me know if they even heard of you, and they said you ran off with a*
> *freshman mother-in-law, or something.*
> *Brooks: You had visitors out there until the world looked level. Are you feel-*
> *ing all right?*
> *Johnson: Oh, I'm tired as hell. I've been working hard, and I'm—*
> *Brooks: I know you have.*
> *Johnson: I've got so many damn problems.*

Johnson then laid into Brooks for his and Albert Thomas's plan to move
some Internal Revenue job from Dallas to Houston, Beaumont, and Austin. It
was too close to an election, and the Democrats needed that support in Dallas
to keep their senator and governor in office, the president reasoned. Brooks
agreed he would work on it, quietly, without mentioning Johnson by name.

Brooks then apprised the president of an issue that had arisen within the Democratic leadership ranks in the House, one that could potentially do real harm to the party, and asked Johnson to have an aide with intimate knowledge of the politics involved look into the matter for him. Johnson agreed. Then the president's mind turned to some far-reaching social proposals he was about to deliver. He expected significant resistance, especially from conservatives in Congress.

Johnson: . . . some of this poverty stuff I'm talking about. And they sure ain't going to like my budget.

The next day, on January 8, 1964, Johnson delivered his first State of the Union address to a joint session of Congress. In his remarks, he identified lack of education as the root cause of poverty and laid out the case for legislation that would become known as his "War on Poverty." Though Johnson had always told colleagues that politicians had no business talking about ideals, he made it clear that he would fight for the ideals of Kennedy and Hubert Humphrey and all the other liberal orators who had at one point or another enchanted the country with their passion and visions for equity. But Johnson, the former congressional giant who knew how legislators might respond to such rhetoric, would not attempt to sell it in the same manner. Within just the first few minutes of his forty-minute speech, he approached the inequities of society as a budget issue. He wanted to receive the $40,000 of productive life from the unemployed youth whom it took only $1,000 to educate today. Very few senators, whether they were Democrats or Republicans, could have argued against that. He was full of conviction and shrewdness in a way that only he was capable of.

This budget, and this year's legislative program, are designed to help each and every American citizen fulfill his basic hopes—his hopes for a fair chance to make good; his hopes for fair play from the law; his hopes for a full-time job on full-time pay; his hopes for a decent home for his family in a decent community; his hopes for a good school for his children with good teachers; and his hopes for security when faced with sickness or unemployment or old age.

Unfortunately, many Americans live on the outskirts of hope—some because
of their poverty, and some because of their color, and all too many because of
both. Our task is to help replace their despair with opportunity.

This administration today, here and now, declares unconditional war on
poverty in America. I urge this Congress and all Americans to join with me in
that effort.

Johnson proposed radically taking on the breadth of America's shortcomings in education, health care, unemployment, and discrimination and
fundamentally changing the scope of the federal government while doing so.
"Poverty is a national problem," he said, and therefore requires "improved
national organization and support."

Less than two months after taking office, Johnson was offering an analysis
and set of proposals so ambitious that fifty years later his first State of the
Union address would still be considered one of the most significant and
memorable ever given. It thrust upon Congress and the courts the entire
progressive agenda that not only Kennedy but also Truman and Roosevelt
had been fighting for since the 1930s. If successful, that agenda would ir-
revocably change the course of American history.

Once he finished his speech, Johnson returned to the White House,
and he and Lady Bird invited Brooks and Charlotte over for dinner. It was
a Wednesday. It was tradition then that the State of the Union was delivered at midday, a tradition that Johnson would change the following year,
pushing it to the evening so more people could watch it at home on TV.

The following Wednesday, the foursome met again. This time the couples
went for a swim as well as a meal. Johnson was fond of asking guests to
come over for a swim, something he made a point of doing during his first
few months in office. Brooks asked if he had a phonograph that could play
78 rpm records so they could listen to an old record, a "Roosevelt one."
The conversations were not always about politics, but they usually did not
stray far.

VALUABLE ALLIANCE: Typically, once the working day was done, Brooks
and Johnson would speak over the phone or in the Oval Office, and Brooks

would provide updates about the goings on in the House and with the Texas delegation in particular. The delegation met for weekly lunches on Wednesdays but with legislation on the line, news could hardly wait that long.

After his first term in the House, a young Johnson had enjoyed similar access to President Roosevelt, frequently meeting with him at the White House, often sharing meals with him in the private residence and playing bridge. Though Johnson was then one of the newest members of the Texas delegation, or perhaps because of his junior status, he had served as Roosevelt's confidant and supplier of information on the Texas delegation, including Speaker Rayburn and Roosevelt's antagonistic vice president, John Nance Garner, especially once Garner announced his own candidacy for president in December 1939.

As often happened with older men with power in D.C., Roosevelt had taken a special liking to the young politician and quickly put the full weight of his office behind Johnson to ensure a good start to his career. The president called in a favor and had Johnson appointed to the House Naval Affairs Committee, and in 1941 he even let the young representative announce his first and ultimately unsuccessful bid for the U.S. Senate from the White House steps.

By 1963, however, Brooks had been in Congress for over a decade and had already chaired a congressional subcommittee for years. He was not the young starry-eyed congressman that Johnson had been twenty years earlier, but an established politician who had begun to develop a name for himself that stood for fairness and good governance.

Although Johnson was fourteen years his senior and infinitely more powerful, there was parity between the two men. Perhaps it was their shared history—poor childhoods, industrious fathers who went bankrupt, University of Texas educations. Or perhaps it was just that they were both from Texas. They were Southerners, but they were not from the South; Texas was frontier land and had never fully embraced the ideals that Georgia, Alabama, or even neighboring Louisiana had. It had a culture very much its own, and in Washington, being a Texan meant something, especially to other Texans.

The characters of the two men, while strikingly different in several regards, also made for a good match. Johnson, always with his eye on bigger and better things, had been trying to move beyond the House ever since he was first elected to it in 1937. With so many members and with such a rigid hierarchy of seniority, he felt anonymous and hopelessly unable to influence events in any meaningful way in that congressional body. For him, representing his rural Tenth District constituents was just one necessary step toward ultimately achieving statewide, and then nationwide, recognition. During his eleven years in the lower house, Johnson made few speeches from the floor and seldom even rose to make a point of order in either support of or opposition to a bill. To many of his colleagues, he seemed genuinely uninterested in the legislative work of that body.

The contradictions inherent in public officials savvy and capable enough to reach the national stage have perhaps never been displayed in such sharp relief as they were in Johnson. From a dirt-poor beginning on the dusty plains of the Tenth Congressional District outside Austin, his critics claimed Johnson lied and cheated his way through the House, and then to the leadership of the Senate before circumstance placed him in the presidency.

Johnson's life, perhaps more than that of any other American politician, could be defined by the constant tension between the ruthless seeking and attainment of office and the goal of providing meaningful public service to those he represented.

Johnson took to heart Rayburn's maxim about show horses and work-horses on Capitol Hill. While Johnson was a combination of both, Brooks was decidedly almost entirely the latter, eschewing the spotlight.

Brooks was straightforward. He had never wanted to be anything but a congressman from Beaumont, and a low-profile one at that. Colleagues from both sides of the aisle knew him as a man who said exactly what he wanted and meant what he said. In fact, this uncomplicated attitude and sincerity of purpose was often the first thing that many friends and staffers recalled about the congressman.

KEY CONFIDANT: For Brooks and his work in Washington, it was most important to do one thing and to do it well. It is reasonable to suspect that Johnson may have found in Brooks the uncomplicated version of the politician he could have been had the pursuit of greater and greater influence not been his main priority.

For his part, Brooks knew that having an ally in the White House could only help with legislation that both men wanted to pass. Rayburn died in 1961 and, while the number of influential Texans in Washington was growing, the number who had grown up in earlier times and fought political battles together was slowly shrinking.

Washington Post editorial writer Leslie Carpenter, who kept a regular political column called Washington Beat, dedicated a weekend piece to Brooks and his access to the president. Titled "Brooks Becomes Key LBJ Confidant," it ran April 4, 1964:

> *Remember this name: Jack Brooks.*
>
> *Bright and gregarious, Brooks, 41, is a Congressman from Beaumont, Tex., and currently spends more time in the White House than anyone except the people who work there.*
>
> *Quietly and with hardly anyone realizing it because he never discusses his association with President Johnson, Brooks has become one of the most influential men in Washington. Mr. Johnson likes Brooks's company and invites the Congressman and his wife to the White House several evenings a week to dinner or to see a movie or just to talk.*
>
> *Brooks never takes advantage of his access to the President's ear and doesn't throw his weight around the Capitol, either. In fact, there aren't many people in Congress who realize how important Brooks has become. He would be the last to say.*
>
> *A political liberal who has consistently supported Kennedy and Johnson programs, Brooks is a proved foe of Government waste. As chairman of a House investigating committee, he has dug deeply into the tangled intricacies of bureaucracy and forced actions by various Federal agencies which have saved many millions.*
>
> *Wise in the ways of politics, he served terms in the Texas legislature before coming to Congress 12 years ago.*
>
> *As the man from Capitol Hill closest to LBJ, Brooks has taken the place of another Texas Congressman. Homer Thornberry, who resigned from the U.S.*

House last December to become a Federal Judge in Texas, had rated at the top among Mr. Johnson's personal friends.

Thornberry had already been confirmed by the Senate as a judge when President Kennedy was assassinated. Mr. Johnson, thrust in the Presidency, wanted Thornberry to remain in Washington, offering him several appointments in place of the judgeship in Texas. But Thornberry felt an obligation to the judicial appointment and left.

Mr. Johnson now sees Brooks with the frequency he used to see Thornberry— and that's more frequently than he sees anyone else in Congress.

Brooks had undoubtedly gained the ear of the president, and during a time that would become known as the most prolific period of legislation of any presidency, save perhaps Franklin Roosevelt's. During the next nineteen months, Johnson and his allies in Congress would manage to pass legislation that would redefine life in America and fundamentally alter the role of the federal government.

PART II

The Art
of the Possible

*I think of myself as someone who tries to be constructive.
Someone who understands that politics is the art of
compromise, that it's a lot more important to get something
done than get into a lot of battles and get a lot of publicity.
All you do is make enemies that way, and who wants to
have enemies?*

— JACK BROOKS

9

Legislation: 1961–1965

The federal government has always been the single largest purchaser of goods in the country. From acquiring "bullets, beans, and bandages" for the military to securing vast amounts of raw materials like metals and cement for infrastructure projects, everything the government buys, it buys in large quantities. The question of how the government could and should make such purchases had been around since as early as 1792, when Congress enacted special powers for raising militias for national defense and obtaining raw materials for the newly founded mint. Competitive bidding for such government contracts has been in place since 1809.

Since the creation of the Government Activities Subcommittee in 1955 under the tutelage of Rayburn, Brooks, as its chairman, had spearheaded investigations into the integrity and fulfillment of such government contracts. He did not have to delve into each contract—that would have been impossible for the staff of such a small subcommittee—but he kept his ear to the rail and initiated probes when issues came to his attention.

THE BROOKS COMMITTEE: Though the subcommittee was entirely new in 1955, its role in congressional affairs was one that had been created years earlier. In early 1941, Harry Truman, then a lowly senator without much of a public name, had been concerned about reports of profiteering and waste in the massive military expansion leading up to the country's entrance into World War II. In April of 1941, he succeeded in persuading the Senate to establish a special committee that would investigate defense contracts and the use of funds allocated by Congress. The committee became known as the "Truman Committee" and even the "Truth Committee." It was marked by its openness and nonpartisan rigor in ferreting out the mismanagement of funds. The obscure senator even took to traveling around the country in his Dodge to see for himself what was happening in manufacturing plants. Truman, buoyed by the committee's tremendous success, earned a vice presidential appointment from Roosevelt three years later. Being a protector of American taxpayer dollars was an image that played very well to the public, so well that Johnson chose to emulate the same mission with his preparedness committee during the start of the Korean conflict ten years later.

Brooks's subcommittee was not attached to any particular event or possible engagement. It was a permanent subcommittee that would investigate any government agency, contractor, or supplier if committee members suspected that dollars were being spent poorly. Each standing committee had numerous subcommittees, and the Government Activities Subcommittee was chaired by the most junior member of the Texas delegation. By Brooks's own admission, when the subcommittee was first established, "It wasn't a very important committee at the time."

But over the first few years, that would begin to change. The inquiry into the assigning of contracts at a nickel mine in Cuba in 1956 introduced the seriousness with which Brooks would take his role as chairman of the subcommittee. That inquiry and its series of hearings over the course of several years would garner headlines across the nation and lead to the resignation of one of Eisenhower's cabinet members, Edmund Mansure, head of the General Services Administration, which was responsible for nearly all nondefense purchasing for the government.

The Government Activities Subcommittee soon became known as the "Brooks Committee," and before long it would become known as the "Brooks Efficiency Subcommittee." In 1962, there were six men on the subcommittee: four Democrats and two Republicans. Brooks said that saving money through the subcommittee was the single most important contribution he was making in Congress. Part and parcel with saving money was often seeing to it that government agencies conformed to certain standards when buying goods and services.

FAA: In regard to standards for official conduct and safety, the subcommittee's work would again come to national attention with the lackadaisical operations of the country's governing body for airlines, the Federal Aviation Administration (FAA). The FAA came into existence in 1959 to replace the Civil Aeronautics Administration following a series of midair collisions, including one in which two commercial jets collided over the Grand Canyon, resulting in 129 deaths.

Accidents and crashes still occur, of course, but the airline industry has greatly matured since then. Safety standards increased enormously even before the tragedies of September 11, 2001. But in agency's early years, the FAA had notoriously poor standards, according to Brooks. Amid widespread safety concerns, allegations of misconduct by flight crews, and the agency's general lack of sufficient oversight of the commercial airline industry, Brooks's subcommittee began investigating the internal operations of the agency in 1962. Officials of the Civil Aeronautics Board (CAB), which would later be absorbed by the FAA, were also called to present themselves at the hearings.

Commercial flight crew conduct had little oversight. Flight engineers were accused of not having any mechanical skills. Flight attendants were generally trained more rigorously in areas like charm than in passenger safety measures such as evacuation procedures. Some commercial pilots had earned a reputation for misbehavior and juvenile hijinks, and the atmosphere around cockpits sometimes verged on that of a frat party. Stories and pictures circulated of pilots sleeping during flights, playing cards in the cockpit, flight attendants flying planes, for forty minutes in one case, flight attendants sitting in pilots' laps during flights. In one bizarre instance, a donkey had been brought aboard after a raucous party and while the plane was in flight, it kept trying to force its head into the cockpit. In 1962, the subcommittee held at least six hearings to determine the degree of mismanagement and what could be done about it. Brooks commented:

> *Personally, I want a flight engineer in the cockpit who as a mechanic knows every wire and rivet in the airplane; I want a working navigator on any flights that I have to make overseas, and I want flight attendants who know emergency procedures backward and forward to help save lives if there is a crash. I believe*

fourteen million other Americans want the same maximum safety when they fly that I do.

At the closing of those hearings, Brooks remarked on how impressed he was with the leaders of CAB and their "open-minded reception of the subcommittee's suggestions." The subcommittee estimated that CAB would cut its annual budget in half to $40 million by 1972 if it moved to modernize airline subsidy procedures and encourage more efficiency in local air service operations.

Because of the subcommittee's safety investigation and a report it filed in June 1963 that cited significant sloppiness among crews, the FAA agreed to begin performing unannounced inspection checks on cockpits. Pilots complained that this amounted to babysitting, but enough congressmen found it to be a necessary measure. By 1970, flight inspections became standard across the industry.

Of greater concern to Brooks was that the nation's air traffic control system at that time lacked automation and comprised, according to a Department of Transportation report, "essentially a manually operated system employing radar, general purpose computers, radio communications, and air traffic controllers." In the collision over the Grand Canyon, both pilots had been in sporadic contact with air traffic controllers, but neither was flying in controller airspace or under radar surveillance. This, coupled with the ever-increasing numbers of commercial flights, was a recipe for disaster, according to Brooks.

SUPERSONIC TRANSPORT: However, the political priority at the FAA lay elsewhere. Tension between the United States and the Soviet Union was ratcheting up throughout this period; the failed Bay of Pigs invasion and then the Cuban missile crisis absorbed the nation's attention.

Both Russia and Europe had made serious advances in supersonic transport (SST) for commercial use. Russia was developing the Tupolev Tu-144, and England and France were working on the Concorde. Both planes were designed to cruise at Mach 2.0 with a cabin full of passengers. American efforts to come up with a version lagged behind. Brooks's committee had been reviewing the SST project since 1962, when Russia publicly unveiled the design of the Tu-144. Not to be outdone by Communists, Brooks became a vocal supporter of the project.

For the next several years, the SST program would remain a quiet priority of Kennedy's and Johnson's, often with frequent clashes about the overall objective rising between FAA Administrator Najeeb Halaby and Defense Secretary Robert McNamara, sometimes played out in front of the committee. But regardless of strategic direction, Congress continued to invest public money into making the program work, but ultimately, plans for fleets of American supersonic aircraft never materialized.

LIGHT BULBS: Indeed, there were more mundane matters that took up the Government Activities Subcommittee's attention. Light bulbs were not a sexy issue, certainly not like jet planes or pilot misbehavior. Most Americans paid little attention to the technical specifics of the household item or questioned why they burned out when they did.

In the mid-1960s, incandescent light bulbs were essentially identical to the first models built in the 1890s. A one hundred-watt bulb in 1912 lasted one thousand hours. As technology advanced, the light bulb's lifespan had steadily increased until 1933, when General Electric reduced the standard to 750 hours, where it remained for the next thirty years. Fifty-odd years later, the light bulb's life was 25 percent shorter.

Brooks had noted how frequently he and Charlotte had to change bulbs at home, but his real interest began memorably in 1964 when several House custodians were changing the lightbulbs in his office chandelier. When one of the bulbs exploded, Brooks barked over to his staffer, "Ernie [Baynard], find out why those cotton-pickin' bulbs burn out so fast." Brooks understood that anything the federal government needed required a purchasing scheme on a vast scale. In 1963 alone, the federal government spent $3.8 million (the equivalent of about $30 million in early twenty-first century dollars) to replace common light bulbs in federal facilities, and that meant that the lifespan of lightbulbs concerned the taxpayers, whether they knew it or not.

Baynard and the investigators on the subcommittee's staff made it a priority. It quickly became clear that the lifespan of a standard incandescent electric bulb could be increased, at little or no cost to either the manufacturers or consumers, by simply widening and lengthening the filament. What resulted was a preliminary report issued by the committee, which Brooks distributed widely around Washington. The report noted that in "the 87 years since Edison perfected the bulb, there have been countless improvements in bulb design and product efficiency. Yet not one improvement [has] ever made toward increasing bulb life." One year later, the subcommittee issued another report, titled "The Short Life of the Electric Light Bulb," which revealed that household variety bulbs were intentionally designed to burn out quickly. The report presented the feasibility of doubling the lifespan of bulbs at no extra cost. That one caught people's attention.

Brooks's targets were the four large companies that made bulbs—General Electric, Westinghouse, Sylvania, and Champion. Brooks essentially dared the manufacturers to present one good reason why they could not improve light bulb lifespan, and he even gave them one year to produce the reason. When they could not, Brooks began preparing for public hearings. He demanded that manufacturers extend the lives of standard bulbs to match the significant declines in the cost of power over the preceding decades and that they begin marking each bulb with its lumen value and lifespan in addition to voltage and wattage. What Brooks wanted, the express ultimate objective of his investigation, was simply, as he explained in a press release at the time, "to have the National Bureau of Standards, working in conjunction with bulb manufacturers, establish a new standard" for the life of everyday household bulbs.

Shedding some daylight worked. By 1966, the federal government saved $2 million annually on light bulbs as a result of the subcommittee's investigation, and Westinghouse had agreed to place more specifications on its consumer packages. A year later, rather than participating in the public hearings, General Electric announced, in a release that received little media coverage, that it would introduce a line of fifteen-, twenty-five-, and forty-watt bulbs with double the lifespan at no appreciable increase in cost to consumers. Prices for sixty- and one hundred-watt bulbs, whose lifespan would be increased by 50 percent, would only see an increase of four cents, from twenty-eight to thirty-two cents per bulb. Westinghouse and Sylvania indicated that they would follow suit.

The publication *U.S. Consumer*, calling the developments a "victory of the first magnitude" and an end to "one of the most costly charades ever perpetrated on the American public," estimated that households would now save a combined $100 million annually. The article praised Brooks's role in the new standards:

> *This was no cheerful, voluntary gesture by the industry, however. It was the result of a three-year battle by a persistent Texas Congressman named Jack Brooks. He refused to swallow industry arguments that it could not be done. . . and he vigorously disagreed with executives who said the public would not want it. . . .*

Brooks also received praise from fellow committee member Dante Fascell on the floor of the House. Fascell asked that the following be put in the *Congressional Record*:

> *This improvement in light bulb design is a significant achievement for which Jack Brooks deserves a large share of the credit. His subcommittee's investigation once again demonstrates the continued interest and concern the Congress takes in the welfare of the American consumer.*

AUTOMATIC DATA PROCESSING: Of growing relevance to taxpayers was the burgeoning use of computers in daily life. Few individual households could afford or have use for such massive and complex machines, but government paychecks, benefits, and regular operations had begun to rely heavily on what was widely known as Automatic Data Processing (ADP).

Computer hardware, or "firmware," consisted of machines designed to execute one task or a small set of tasks. Depending on the tasks at hand, agencies bought or leased equipment from many different sources, and these machines were built to perform dedicated and usually very narrow tasks. They could not be used for other purposes nor could they receive data from each other since there was no unified coding language for ADP. The proprietary coding languages that were being developed and marketed by various companies were beneficial for technology's sake and for the progress of the global market for computing, but they led to huge inefficiencies for a massive user such as the U.S. government. In essence, there was little to no interoperability between computers.

The government needed compatibility because of all the different agencies using computers that needed to share data. Also, while some systems were totally over capacity, others lay underutilized, which led to massive losses in productivity. One government report revealed an estimated "500,000 hours of computer time went unused because data and program incompatibility prevented workload transfer from overloaded machines to underutilized ones."

Small-scale consumers were more or less indifferent to this lack of industry standardization because their use of any particular provider's equipment or system was limited, and they could easily switch to another provider with little expense. The switching costs for the government, however, were enormous, and the cost due to lack of standardization was almost incalculably high.

In 1956, IBM dominated the computer industry in the United States, including software. The company had 75 percent of the market share, with four other providers competing for the remaining quarter. IBM also had an almost exclusive contract with the federal government for its hardware, most of which was leased (about 75 percent in 1963), which led to huge profits for the company. If the equipment could instead be purchased outright, the potential savings for the government was estimated at $105 million annually after the first five years.

Standardization was against IBM's business interests, just as it would be for Microsoft and Apple decades later. The uniformity of code and operability would level the playing field, allowing new firms to enter the market and smaller players to gain more market share. IBM had vigorously opposed calls for voluntary standardizations from the American Standards Association, now called the United States of America Standards Institute. There also existed few market mechanisms that would encourage such a convergence among hardware or software developers.

The General Accounting Office (GAO), under the direction of

Comptroller General Joseph Campbell, had issued almost fifty audit reports to Congress from 1958 to 1962 on the need for a better system for buying and managing IT equipment and processes. The GAO cited "flagrant wastes and fundamental inefficiencies in Government acquisition and utilization" of ADP equipment. The GAO backed this up with studies that showed the potential cost savings. Brooks, taking heed of this, began "efficiency" hearings in July 1962. In March of the next year, he introduced H.R. 5171, an act concerning the "economic and efficient purchase, lease, maintenance, operation, and utilization of electronic data processing equipment."

Hearings began two months later to discuss the legislation and decide whether to authorize the administrator of the General Services Administration, Bernard Boutin, to coordinate and manage the purchasing program, whose budget was already in the hundreds of millions of dollars. Campbell testified before the committee, and Boutin and others pleaded their case. They believed—and so would Brooks—that the potential cost savings of a more effective system would be "substantially more than $100 million every year." Boutin had his team conduct a study by running cost comparisons of sixteen different types of machines in use by various federal agencies, some of which were only leased. He argued that decisions about the financial advantages of purchasing should be made "from the standpoint of the government as a whole, and not primarily from the standpoint of individual using agencies."

It was not an easy case. An article in *Datamation* magazine described it seven years later as "one of the most hard-fought battles ever witnessed in Congress between Brooks and the federal departments and agencies who preferred continuation of their old and inefficient ways." Even a top computer scientist at the National Bureau of Standards had said incredulously to Brooks, "You want to freeze the state of the art!" But Brooks persisted. James Tozzi, an official at the Office of Management and Budget (OMB), remarked at the time:

> *To win an argument in Washington, there are two questions you have to answer. How good is someone's substantive position? And how much elbow grease can be put behind that position? Jack Brooks always scores in the 90s on both counts.*

It was compelling and controversial legislation, and the House would go on to pass H.R. 5171 that year. The Senate, however, would not.

In an echo of his setbacks with Lamar College in the Texas legislature, Brooks was not deterred and continued to press the ADP issue in 1964 and 1965, keeping industrial and political developments in the mind of the president and writing articles for any publications that were interested. Other federal agencies, the OMB in particular, had agreed with the GAO on the significance of the inefficiencies in ADP. They issued a follow-up report, which Johnson approved and sent to Congress in March 1965.

Later that year, amid a spate of transformational legislation like the Housing and Urban Development Act, the Immigration Act, and the Higher Education Act, the Automatic Data Processing Act was successfully voted through both chambers. On October 30, without much fanfare, Brooks traveled to the LBJ Ranch outside Austin while on his way back to Washington. According to the president's daily agenda, Johnson had seventeen pieces of legislation to sign that day, and a morning and afternoon full of meetings. At 12:30 p.m., the president changed into a "dressier" jacket and welcomed Brooks and photographer Don Stodderl into his home office for the private signing, and at 12:38 p.m. he signed the Brooks Automatic Data Processing Act, establishing Public Law 89-306. Twenty minutes later, he and Brooks and a handful of others sat down to have lunch—enchiladas, chili, and green salad.

Though the legislation was to be implemented over the next five years, and the savings and industry changes would take years to recognize, this was a major coup. The federal government was already spending 3 percent of the federal budget on computer equipment and services, and computer use multiplied almost exponentially each year.

In addition, the government's demand for "interconnectability," which required information technology vendors to adhere to certain technical standards (and for the National Bureau of Standards to create those standards) revolutionized the federal procurement system. The effect it had on the principal vendors then trickled down to subcontractors in their supply chains. Decades later, Carl Cargill, principal scientist at Adobe Systems, explained the importance this had:

This was significant, since the federal government was the largest single purchaser of information technology in the world. From NASA to the Social Security Administration, from the Department of Education (another Brooks accomplishment) to the National Weather Service, systems began to become "interconnectable."

Even for industry specialists, it would be difficult to imagine the shape of the computer industry, and of even the current hyper-connected world, had the Brooks Act not been enacted. At the point where the mature Industrial Revolution was evolving into the beginning of the Information Age, this vision for how government and private industry should function had immense consequences.

Brooks's work did not go unappreciated at the time. In 1966, an association of government internal auditors awarded him for his continued vigilance, and the next year, Brooks was awarded the Federal Government Accountants Distinguished Leadership Award "in recognition of sustained and preeminent leadership in efforts to improve financial management in the Federal Government."

When the Bureau of the Budget released an ADP management report in February 1967, Brooks's name was featured prominently in the beginning of the news release. Brooks, suspecting his friend had a hand in that, wrote a letter of thanks to Johnson.

This was a most thoughtful gesture which I very deeply appreciate—an action which so obviously reflects your generosity that I am confident you were responsible for it.

10

Power in the Presidency

B rooks's toughness and party loyalty enabled him to bring some cohesion to the Texas delegation once Johnson had moved from the vice-presidency to the White House. Although twenty-three of the twenty-five legislators from Texas were Democrats, other members were either too narrow in their operations or too divisive in their policies and personalities. Brooks was just the right combination of grit and charm to pull and ply the Texas delegation into shape, a role he had played as early as 1959 when Rayburn sent him a telegram stating that all the Democrats in the delegation were to get behind Johnson as the 1960 Democratic candidate for president. That particular task would prove to be a temporary problem for Brooks later.

Though he was not part of the Washington scene, then-Texas Governor John Connally could have been a convener of men if not for his personality and perceived lack of political principles. While Connally was still recovering from the bullet wounds he suffered in the Dallas attack and running for reelection to his second term as governor, the responsibility for corralling the unruly Texas delegation and organizing a letter of support for Connally in 1964 was entrusted to Brooks, who obtained signatures from all twenty-five Texas congressmen but one.

Liberal candidate Don Yarborough of Houston was determined to unseat Connally in that election, and with his public support of civil rights legislation he was driving a considerable wedge within the state party, including calling Connally the "worst governor Texas has ever had." Senator Ralph Yarborough (no relation) also remained an outspoken critic, so uniting the delegation in support of Connally was no small feat for Brooks. Many of the same tensions and divisions that had threatened to tear the Texas Democrats apart just two months before had not been settled. Instead, the party unity they exhibited was largely forced upon them by the circumstances of the assassination and the personal influence of Brooks and Johnson.

Harry McAdams was an advocate with a decades-long perspective of the two men and how Texas politics worked in the Capital.

> *I sensed that the president wanted to have a one-stop shopping circumstance—he could talk to someone who was loyal to him and who understood what his objective was and that person then could go be the honest broker and bring the herd in line behind what he wanted to do. So from the president's perspective he was using Brooks.*
>
> *From Chairman Brooks's perspective, he was certainly not unaware the additional role of power that was vested in him that he had access to the president any time he wanted it and he could express his advice and opinions to the president any time he wished.*
>
> *If you were a member of the delegation and you sought to deal directly with the president you would have pretty quickly during those days found out that you'd get a lot further a lot faster if you channeled your interests through Chairman Brooks. I think he became the bridge between the delegation and the president, and that both he and the president benefited mightily by that relationship.*

Brooks knew that there was no greater ally in Washington than the president. Although he had risen to considerable influence during his twelve years in Congress, he was still one of 435 representatives in the House, and not yet even in the upper echelon of them in terms of seniority or the most coveted chairmanships. The edge he possessed therefore in dining and speaking regularly with the president gave him tremendous leverage in being an effective legislator, leverage that would have been nearly impossible through other means. As Brooks recalled one incident:

> *Johnson one time, while we were eating, had a phone call come in, and he had a senator on the line calling him from the airport. Prior to that I had a*

bill to require all of the government agencies to have an auditor that reported to them and if they didn't do anything about it in a couple months they reported it to me, my committee. It was a useful thing, it would have helped all the agencies, but they were generally against it. Strongly against it, and they wrote letters that way until I had Mr. Johnson talk to them about it.

They would write back a letter a little more constrained, like somebody's holding their hand while they signed the letter. But anyhow we passed it, and it went to the Senate, and they had not acquiesced altogether. Somebody had ratted out and got some senator over there holding up the bill in the Senate. And I told President Johnson that and so later that week we were having supper at the White House and the phone rang. It was that senator who was calling from the airport to talk to President Johnson.

The president said, "You know I am very interested in your legislation. In your state it's important, and it seems to have some merit," and then he said, "I am also interested in that bill by Congressman Jack Brooks that is sitting over there that you are holding up. Now if you can quit holding up that bill I am going to think more kindly about your state's activities. And that senator was apparently saying, "Yes sir, Mr. Johnson, we'll get that done. Johnson came back to the table and said, "I believe he is taking the hold off that bill tonight." That's the kind of work Johnson would do for you. He was a real hands-on helper when you needed help.

Johnson understood all the machinations of Congress, both formal and informal, and he knew better than anyone how they could be manipulated. Garner, who had been a mentor to Rayburn the way Rayburn was to both Johnson and Brooks, was a shrewd congressman from Uvalde, Texas. He spent decades consolidating power in the House before becoming, under Roosevelt, what some would call the most powerful vice president in history. Garner had once said, "The only way to get anywhere in Congress is to stay there and let seniority take its course." Neither Johnson nor Brooks had taken heed of that message. Johnson had spent less than a decade in the House furiously pursuing power and leadership roles until finally moving on to the Senate. During his first term in the upper house, he leapt over his senior colleagues with deftness rarely seen in that chamber. At the first notice of conflict on the Korean Peninsula in 1951, for instance, Johnson jumped at the chance to form a committee on preparedness that would oversee government acquisition of goods and materials for the military. This was, in essence, the exact same committee that Harry Truman had led ten years earlier at the onset of U.S. involvement in World War II, a role that had catapulted him from junior senator to vice president to president, all in the matter of a few years. Johnson even found a way to have himself appointed chairman of this new committee, "The New Truman Committee," as newspapers were calling it, though there were more senior colleagues that would have been more obvious choices.

Brooks had similarly found his way to an early appointment as chairman of the subcommittee on government activities and used that position to exert an outsized influence on the federal government.

LBJ as VP nominee: One of Johnson's biographers, Robert Dalleck, wrote that the competition for the 1960 Democratic nomination for president began as soon as the 1958 off-year campaign ended. There were six front-runners, including Johnson and Kennedy, along with senators Hubert Humphrey, Stuart Symington, Adlai Stevenson (who had lost the previous two elections), and New York Governor Averell Harriman.

Johnson, as Senate majority leader, was considered the second most powerful official in the running. Still, he held his cards close to his chest while positioning himself as the one who could step in as the Democratic nominee. He even engineered Texas election law in 1959 to allow a candidate to run simultaneously for two national elections so he could retain his Senate seat while still running for the Oval Office, a lesson he had learned from having to risk it all during his Senate campaign in 1948.

Wayne Reaud, a Beaumont lawyer and one of the most successful attorneys in Texas, was not of the same generation as Brooks, but the two men became friends. Reaud (pronounced "Rio") recalled Brooks telling him how difficult it was to tell Johnson that his first vote at the 1960 Democratic convention would have to go to Kennedy and not Johnson, the man he had been close friends with for the last six years in Congress.

I did not know this probably until the middle to late 1980s. And of course, the more I was around Jack, I was always probing for information about different things. But in the middle to late 1980s, I discovered, for the first time, that in the 1960 presidential election, as close as he and Lyndon were, he didn't support Lyndon. He supported Jack Kennedy.

Well, it's a little-known fact. And, I mean, he and Lyndon were close. I mean, they really were close. I said, why did you do that? He said, I had to pay a debt. I never got the whole story, but I will share with you what I know. This is a quote. "Old man Joe Kennedy came to me and called in a favor, and I had to support Jack."

And I said, Well, how did Lyndon take that? He said, Well, I went to Lyndon and said, Lyndon, let me tell you what happened. Here's why I've got to do it. And Johnson said, Jack, I understand. I don't blame you. And he, Texas congressman, close friend of Lyndon's, and he did not support him in the Democratic ballot.

I tried and tried for years to find out what it was, the favor that Joe Kennedy had done for him, and he never would tell me. I have a vivid memory of certain things. Words are my business, and so when I say I quote somebody, I'm not missing it by much. But he said, "Old man Joe Kennedy called me and called in a favor—came to see me and called in a favor." Wouldn't you like to know what that was?

Johnson calculated political fortunes like a card player studies hands. Maybe it was his days of playing bridge with Roosevelt or his poker playing with McCormack and others at the Board of Education. He also understood that it was important to have someone watching your back. Johnson needed reliable friends, especially in those early years after the assassination. Brooks was able to be that for Lyndon, whether it was telling him what people were worried about, or simple things like sending a note to Johnson's trusted aide, Walter Jenkins, only a few weeks after the new president was sworn in, advising that Johnson should not attend a Sunday service at the National Christian Church. Brooks knew the congregation there was still segregated and figured it wouldn't square with Johnson's intentions on the civil rights bill he was about to propose.

Johnson rarely reached out to individual congressman or even chairmen. Some may have seen that as a gesture of deference to Senate Majority Leader Mike Mansfield and Speaker John McCormack, but it had the effect of keeping the rank and file in check. To receive a call from the president meant that you must have some power, and Johnson did not want any congressional hotshots thinking that they had any power. Brooks was one exception. Another was Johnson's old friend Warren Magnuson from Seattle. He had served in both the House and the Senate alongside Johnson. Magnuson also saw combat in the Navy during World War II until 1944, when Roosevelt ordered all serving congressmen back to D.C.

THE CONNECTIONS TO TEXAS politics range wide, and Brooks found that relations, both political and familial, with his old opponents in Texas could impact the fortunes of congressional bills.

Joe Tonahill, the favored candidate whom Brooks had bested for the Second District seat back in 1952, was the son-in-law of Representative Howard W. Smith of Virginia, who led a conservative coalition that favored retaining segregation in public places and opposed integration in schools. Smith was also anti-labor, and he personally led opposition to the National Labor Relations Board (NLRB) set up by the Wagner Act of 1935. He oversaw a special House committee to investigate the NLRB, successfully undermined public support for the New Deal, and instigated meetings that ultimately set up the union-restricting Taft-Hartley Bill in 1947. Brooks said:

> *[Tonahill's] father-in-law was Judge Smith, chairman of the Rules Committee in Congress and a very powerful man from Virginia. He didn't welcome me in Congress, I tell you. However, I'll tell you what I did to him. I became friends with his rival—the senior Republican on the Rules Committee. He was a man named [Clarence] Brown from Ohio, who had a son about my age, who later served in Congress, and we were friends. Brown would help me some with Judge Smith on getting legislation. I told him one time in a hearing that I was having trouble with Smith.*
>
> *'Brownie, you're not gonna let him do that to me, are you?' The crowd kind*

of chuckled, but Brownie didn't let him do that to me. There weren't but four
or five members of that committee, and Brown was very important and strong.
But Smith was difficult.

A couple of years later, when Johnson was president, he had trouble with
getting his bills scheduled properly. That's what the Rules Committee does, write
rules and so forth, hours and debate and what kind of debate and distribution
of the time. And I told President Johnson that the way to get Smith for us is for
you to invite him down. He's a pretty old man now, and the way you would get
him for us is to invite him down to the White House, have lunch with him, let
the press know about it, tell him how important he is, and so forth, and he'll
love that. And that's what Johnson did. And he knew how to do that well. And
from then on, Johnson didn't have any trouble with Howard Smith. I thought
that was appropriate.

THE CIVIL RIGHTS BILL OF '64: But Smith is mostly remembered for
another stand he made against Kennedy and later Johnson, the obstruction
of the nation's landmark civil rights legislation.

The slow burn of racial tensions, non-violent protests, and brutal police
crackdowns had continued throughout 1963. In the spring, attempts at
desegregation in Birmingham were met with vicious crowds, water can-
nons, and police dogs. In August, Martin Luther King Jr. and scores of
other civil rights leaders led two hundred thousand protesters in the March
on Washington.

Although Democrats controlled both the House and the Senate, the
issue of civil rights remained one of the principal wedges threatening to
split the party in half, especially in Texas.

Kennedy's civil rights bill, H.R. 7152, had been sent to the House Judiciary Committee, where Brooks was a member. The full House Judiciary
Committee comprised thirty-five men, twenty-one Democrats and fourteen Republicans, all of them lawyers. Since Southern opposition was all
but guaranteed, the trick that Brooks and the bill's other backers, like the
chairman, Emanuel "Manny" Celler, and ranking moderate Republican,
William McCullough, faced was in drafting something that could attract
enough moderate Republicans to join the ranks of Northern Democrats to

ensure its passage. Simultaneously, the coalition had to fend off Southern amendments intended to strip the measure of any effectiveness. Chairmen Celler had assigned the bill to a subcommittee on antitrust, which he also chaired. The subcommittee's membership had been groomed over the years to be favorable to civil rights legislation; it included none of the full committee's senior Southern members. Brooks was the rare Southerner on whom Celler could depend. Decades later, Brooks recounted:

> I was working on the legislation with Emanuel Celler, who was chairman of the Judiciary Committee from New York. A very wonderful erudite scholar. A lovable man. He was wonderful to me. And I'd helped Manny on that, worked on it with him pretty steady. I was on his subcommittee, which helps. That's the right one to be on [laughs] if you're gonna be on a subcommittee.
>
> Well, we got that passed, and Johnson was good about it. Always very supportive. I heard some people say Tip O'Neill had something to do with it. I didn't know what!
>
> The committee was made up of a lot of Southerners. They were difficult. And on the morning we were gonna have a markup on the civil rights bill, one of [Robert] Kennedy's stalwarts from the Justice Department called me and said, "I hope you can come down and see the chairman now. He's concerned about this bill."
>
> So I went down to the committee. Celler looked like he was a little perturbed. And I said, "Manny," I said, "you came to Congress the year I was born. You've been here for forty years. What do you care what those dissident members say or think about you? Or anything else? Nothing. We'll go in there, gavel that thing through, recognize the people we need to make the appropriate motions. Gavel it through, take the vote, and it'll pass. Go on away, don't worry about it, that's all there is to it."

Brooks leaned forward, pantomiming opening a desk drawer.

> [Celler] pulled the drawer open of his desk —old school! Pulled out a bottle of whiskey, said, "Let's have a drink on it, Jack." He had a little drink, hands it to me, I had a little drink. The two honchos from the Justice Department, the

big shots, he didn't offer them a drink or say another damn word to them. Put
the top on the bottle, put it back in the drawer, closed it, and got up and went
in and had the meeting.

In September, the bill was approved in subcommittee and went to the
full committee. After two months of hearings, a more ambitious and far-
reaching version of the bill than that which had initially been proposed by
the Kennedy administration emerged from the House Judiciary Committee.
Both Kennedy and his brother Robert had even traveled to Capitol Hill
during the hearings to temper the previous version of the bill for fear that
it would become unattractive to moderates. Nevertheless, the strengthened
version of the bill passed. Out of the nine Southerners on Judiciary, Brooks
was the only one who voted for it.

Then the bill passed to the House Rules Committee, where Howard
Smith had let it be known that he intended to keep it from going any farther. It was still sitting there when Kennedy was killed in November, and
many thought that it would never move beyond that. But proponents of
civil rights were determined that Kennedy's assassination would not change
the forward trajectory of their cause, which had been gaining traction and
popularity among the public for the last twenty years. For it to stall out
just as it was reaching a critical mass among the general population would
have been unthinkable.

LBJ AND CIVIL RIGHTS: Johnson had a peculiar record on civil rights
issues. For twenty years in Washington, he had opposed every single civil
rights measure that he'd encountered in Congress. In his first speech on the
Senate floor, he gave a ninety-minute impassioned plea in opposition to
Truman's 1948 civil rights bill. It was assumed that he was trying to ingrati-
ate himself with the "most powerful man in the Senate," Richard Russell,
who was the leader of the Senate's Southern bloc, a formidable group of
senators from the eleven states of the old Confederacy that had effectively
blocked every piece of civil rights legislation.

But his opposition was not that simple; Johnson appeared to shrewdly
dance around the civil rights issue. He had not signed the Southern Manifesto,

a feat he would later speak of with pride. "I am not a civil rights advocate," he said. "The solution of the problem cannot be found on the federal level. It's my hope that wise leaders on the local levels will work to resolve these differences." Some suspected that the real reason for his reluctance was because he had thought civil rights was a losing issue for Democrats.

In 1957, however, once he had reached the position of majority leader in the Senate, he used every ounce of power and persuasion that he possessed to ensure the passage of that year's civil rights bill, the first to pass through Congress since Reconstruction a century earlier. He and Yarborough, the staunch Texas liberal, were two of only five Southern senators who voted in favor of that bill.

In 1963, the day after Kennedy's assassination, top civil rights leaders talked of issuing a statement "of full confidence in the new president and to declare a moratorium on racial demonstrations during the transition period." That same day, Johnson spoke over the phone with Martin Luther King Jr. about the need to continue what Kennedy had been pursuing.

The time for sweeping action from Congress on civil rights had come. In his first address to a joint session of Congress as president just five days after the assassination, Johnson said "No memorial oration or eulogy could more eloquently honor President Kennedy's memory than the earliest possible passage of the civil rights bill for which he fought so long."

H.R. 7152 was hopelessly mired in the slow machinations of the Rules Committee, where Howard Smith was not likely to let it see the light of day on the floor of the House.

Because of Johnson's charm and Brooks's advice regarding the old chairman, the bill did move to the full House, and on February 10, an amended version of H.R. 7152 passed by a bipartisan majority of 290–130. Republicans favored it 138–34; Democrats favored it 152–96. Brooks and J. J. Pickle, Thornberry's replacement, were two of the Southern Democrats who voted for the bill. A total of eighty-seven of them voted against it. In attempts to water down the bill, there had been 122 amendments offered. Only twenty-eight mostly technical revisions were actually written into the bill. Not a single amendment that the bill's managers opposed was adopted into the final version.

Brooks was the first to notify LBJ that the civil rights bill had passed. He called the president that evening at his ranch in Texas and gave him the final vote count and an update on how the Texas delegation had voted.

Seven days later, the bill was delivered to the Senate, where it faced an even greater uphill battle. Despite the fact that the Republican Senate Minority Leader Everett Dirksen had been a supporter of the bill since early 1963, other Republican senators stood in near lockstep opposition, and Southern Democratic senators were not at all sympathetic to the cause.

It was Johnson's longtime mentor and friend Richard Russell who led the Southern bloc in filibustering the legislation in the Senate. For sixty full working days, including seven Saturdays, the group of eighteen Southern Democrats and one Republican fought tooth and nail to obstruct the bill from coming to a full vote before the Senate. As fierce as their opposition was, the bill's supporters were fiercer still. In mid-June, forty-six Democrats and twenty-seven Republicans joined forces to approve the Civil Rights Act of 1964; only twenty-seven senators opposed it. Ralph Yarborough was the only Southern senator to vote for the Senate version.

In reconciling the Senate and the House versions, the bill had to be somewhat watered down, but the final version passed on July 2 and was signed into law five hours later by Johnson, surrounded by a full crowd that included congressional leaders, Robert Kennedy, Martin Luther King Jr., and other black leaders. The president used nearly one hundred pens to put his signature to the bill. After signing, he handed out the pens to key supporters, giving one to Dirksen, one to King and at least six to RFK.

Throughout that spring and summer, Johnson was also planning his campaign for the coming election in November. It would be the third time he sought the presidency, but this time he was running as the incumbent. Not only that, but by late summer it was clear to voters that he was running as the heir to the legislative legacy that the Kennedy administration had promised. Since assuming office, Johnson had masterfully aligned himself with Kennedy's supporters, who had been keenly suspicious of him in 1960.

On August 27 at the Democratic National Convention, Johnson accepted the Democratic nomination. Brooks, among others, suggested that Johnson choose Hubert Humphrey to be his vice president.

I remember when Johnson was deciding who he was going to select as vice president and talking about it with a couple of people at the dining room table at the White House when we would go down there, just a couple of friends. I always recommended Hubert Humphrey because I thought he was bright and articulate. Hard-working, dedicated, a wonderful man.

The themes of Johnson's campaign touched many foreign and domestic issues from nuclear arms to taxes, but the one most salient with voters turned out to be his pursuit of Kennedy's full legislative agenda on social issues, an effort aptly captured in the campaign slogan "All the Way with LBJ."

LBJ REELECTED AND THE GREAT SOCIETY: Just a few weeks before the election, Walter Jenkins, Johnson's chief of staff, was caught with another man in the bathroom of a YMCA and arrested by D.C. police on a charge of disorderly conduct. Jenkins had been Johnson's primary aide for twenty-five years in Washington, through the House, Senate, vice presidency, and now the presidency. Aside from being professionally connected, the two were friends as well. Jenkins held Lady Bird's fifty-first birthday party at his home.

Editorial judgments about publicizing the incident and arrest were split among major newspapers around the country, but Republicans were only too pleased to promote the story. The news promised to become a scandal, even pressing Johnson into calling for an FBI investigation. Many of Jenkins's associates in Washington ran for cover. Brooks and a few other friends, however, went the other direction. Like many others who knew Jenkins, Brooks had always liked the man, and he offered to help him in any way that he could. He also sent a bouquet of flowers to Jenkins's home and words of encouragement for him and his wife.

Though publicized nationally, the Jenkins incident failed to capture much traction, and on November 3, Johnson won reelection in a landslide against the Republican senator from Arizona, Barry Goldwater. Johnson carried the state of Texas with 63 percent of the vote to Goldwater's 36 percent, about the same margin Johnson enjoyed nationwide. He was at home at the LBJ Ranch when the results came in and were announced to the nation. Brooks dialed him at 1:10 a.m. to offer his congratulations. The two spoke briefly, and Brooks provided the impressive numbers from his district, which had only gone for Kennedy by the narrowest of margins four years earlier.

Johnson's victory coincided with a much broader liberal victory across the country, with many progressive-minded pols landing seats in Washington. The incoming Congress was the most liberal of any in preceding decades. Without this expansion of his support base, what would come next might not have been possible.

Johnson, through his formidable powers of persuasion and congressional savvy, set off on one of the most ambitious and successful legislative periods of any American president. Brooks recalled what Johnson managed to achieve over the following twelve months:

> I must say that Johnson was much more effective than Kennedy in getting those programs adopted by Congress because Johnson was a creature of the Congress. He had come to Congress in 1937, and he served on committees, subcommittees some years before he ran for the Senate and was elected to the Senate, where he served on committees, ran committees, and then ran the Senate.
>
> Johnson knew the ins and outs of subcommittee work and members and how they functioned. And he was a past master of the mechanism and the custom and the procedures in both the House of Representatives and the Senate. With his leadership, they passed virtually everything in the Kennedy program that was worthwhile. He got it passed. It was Johnson. Johnson was something special.

In May of 1965, Drew Pearson from the *Washington Post and Times Herald* expressed that same sentiment, writing:

> The legislative record chalked up by the 89th Congress so far is nothing short of phenomenal. Major bill after bill is clicking through committee, going up for a full vote, being signed by the speaker and vice president and then being shipped to the White House for the President's signature into law. Not since the early New Deal days of FDR has Washington seen anything like it.
>
> During the first year LBJ was in office, he passed fifty-one of President Kennedy's remaining bills through the Senate and forty-seven through the

House. . . No man has sat in the White House. . . who has had greater finesse
and more know-how in dealing with Congress than Lyndon B. Johnson.

It was the height of liberalism across the U.S., with bills like the Civil
Rights, Food Stamp, and Wilderness Acts of 1964 signed into law. The
following year, under the careful orchestration of Johnson, Congress also
passed each of the following: the Elementary and Secondary Education Act,
legislation establishing Medicare and Medicaid, the Voting Rights Act, a
bill creating of the department of Housing and Urban Development, the
Water Quality Act, the Immigration Act, the Highway Beautification Act,
and the Higher Education Act. Public sentiment was in full swing to the
left of the political spectrum, and Johnson and his progressive friends in
Congress were able to capitalize on that in a way that would dramatically
redefine the scope of the federal government.

In late 1967 Johnson signed the Public Broadcasting Act, which led to
the creation of Public Broadcasting System (PBS) and National Public Radio
(NPR), entities which would have important effects on public discourse
for years to come and which Brooks would later leverage to help usher in
a new level of transparency in government.

But just as the atmosphere had changed since 1963, it was continuing to change. In Texas, the political landscape was literally shifting as the
Texas legislature began redistricting and the boundaries of Brooks's Second
Congressional District were moved farther south and west toward Galveston
and Houston. The liberal moment would not last long, and future struggles
were already beginning to emerge.

11

Legislation: 1965–1968

After the resounding defeat of hard-line conservative candidate Barry Goldwater in the 1964 presidential election, many believed the country had reached a liberal consensus on the ideals of governance. On the heels of Kennedy's assassination, Congress's next eighteen months were perhaps its most productive in history, with the passing of such broadband liberal legislation as the Immigration and Education acts, the new Medicare and Medicaid amendments to the Social Security Act, and a host of other "Great Society" legislation. The civil rights movement had finally spurred meaningful changes in the lives of Americans with the passage of the Civil Rights Act of 1964 and the Voting Rights Act of 1965.

There appeared a sense of national harmony and understanding of the role that the federal government should play in ensuring equal rights for all races and ethnic groups and creating a "safety net" for the sick and elderly.

The apparent tranquility was deceptive. Just five days after Johnson signed the Voting Rights Act, race riots broke out in the Watts district of Los Angeles and before long spread to the inner cities of other major metropolitan areas. Riots, looting, and clashes with police became almost an annual summer ritual across the country, graphically detailed each night through shaky handheld news cameras on the street.

The president, consumed with seeing his aggressive legislative agenda through and holding fast to his position on Vietnam, continued to be battered by protesters. Brooks, ever the loyal friend and true to his political principles, continued to publicly support Johnson whenever he could. Shortly after his promotion to the rank of colonel in the Marine Corps

Reserves, Brooks told media that Johnson "has the responsibility of dealing with a situation as it exists and not as we might wish it to be." Johnson, as usual, was ever grateful for the support. He wrote Brooks in March 1967:

> *It is hardly necessary for me to tell you once again how much I am inspired and sustained by your advice and friendship. But I do want to tell you how very much I appreciate your statement of last week concerning Vietnam. . . with God's help and the continued support of men like Jack Brooks, I believe we are going to deal with it successfully.*

Turmoil was rampant as the sixties came to an end, from the protests at the 1968 Democratic National Convention and the assassinations of Martin Luther King Jr. and Robert Kennedy to the isolated bombings of the radical Weathermen in 1970.

Due in part to the segregation of communities and, conversely, to the integration that organized labor brings, Texas had escaped the most vicious types of racial conflicts that tore across the rest of the South. East Texas in particular, where the largest black populations lived, had been insulated from the worst of it, with a few striking exceptions over the decades. For example, despite the integration of the work force in processing plants and oil fields, Beaumont was the last significant school district in the United States to be integrated.

In June of 1943, there was a day of violence in Beaumont after an un-identified black man was accused of raping a white woman. As the legend goes, after fifteen hours of rioting through the port city, Jefferson County Sheriff Bill Richardson halted a mob with his tommy gun and told the group to get back to work building ships for the war effort. The *Rocky Mountain News* reported him yelling to the crowd, gun in hand:

> *I'm damned tired of all of this. Fact is, I'll take you all on—one at a time. And let me tell you, I'm going to keep law and order in this county.*

But Beaumont and the rest of the country had been on the upswing in the postwar era. Integration seemed inevitable, the Kennedy election lifted spirits, and Johnson's Great Society programs produced more progressive legislation than at any time since Roosevelt's New Deal.

The country's liberal moment proved to be ephemeral, however; more than half of the forty-eight liberal House members who had been swept into office on Johnson's coattails in 1964 were voted out of office in the 1966 election. The GOP also made inroads in state legislative bodies, and nine of the country's ten new governors were Republican. The pendulum of public opinion was swinging back to the right.

The nature of the Democratic and Republican parties at both the national and state levels were changing and deteriorating, particularly in Texas. As the attitude of compromise and cooperation collapsed, so did the New Deal coalition upon which it had been structured. In the context of social disorder, a growing military humiliation in Vietnam, and the beginning of a large shift in population from Northern states to the South and Southwest, the political philosophies attached to the traditional liberal and conservative monikers were shifting, and with that began a partisan realignment in Texas. Political labels were being shed out of economic frustration and anxiety as well as cultural suspicion about new immigrants. The polarization of American politics that would develop in later years was just taking root.

In the decade to come, an increasing mistrust of the federal government and the people at its helm would further push generations of American voters away from the Democratic brand and its paternal image. There were politicians who would ride this groundswell to become the rising stars of the GOP. California Governor Ronald Reagan and Texas Representative George H. W. Bush first took office in January 1967. Both had succeeded by tapping into the fears that gripped the voters who were not demonstrating for or against the president, the Vietnam War, or any other movement. Instead, these were the voters who had been sitting in quiet anxiety, sensing that America was in the throes of violent transition and feeling powerless to do anything to about it. These people resented the privileged college kids who railed against the government. This great mass of voters did not garner headlines or TV specials. They were almost by definition unnewsworthy, and perhaps that was the reason the size of their cohort was at first underestimated.

One man who did understand their numbers and their core frustrations, however, was Richard Nixon, the former vice president who had lost the White House to Kennedy in 1960 and then suffered an embarrassing loss in the California gubernatorial race in 1962. Though he remained in the "political wilderness," Nixon was maneuvering behind closed doors and setting himself up to take advantage of the evolving political atmosphere in the country. The parties had begun to split even further apart and to calcify in their opposition to one another. The discourse was not the same as it had been in earlier years. The polarization that was emerging would lead to a radically different political landscape in Congress and the electorate for decades to come and reduce the democratic process, many have argued, into dysfunction.

BROOKS AS ATTORNEY GENERAL: It was in this atmosphere that Johnson was considering naming Brooks as his candidate for U.S. attorney general. The position made sense; Brooks knew the law and enjoyed a good fight as much as any politician could. More importantly, Brooks had a certain vision for how the government should be operating and touching the daily lives of Americans, an area that would be of great interest in the coming years of Johnson's first full term. Brooks saw the role of government as protecting its citizens, not lording it over them. Johnson also knew Brooks to be fiercely loyal, and the congressman could defend a legal or congressional position as well as anyone. Though Brooks had always made it clear that he had no interest in serving the public as anything but a congressman from Beaumont, according to those who knew him well, he was interested in this appointment. His name was even floated in several national newspapers. For reasons only known to Johnson and Brooks, however, the nomination never came.

While the political foundations that had kept Democrats in the seat of Texas power since the 1920s had begun to fracture, the economic boom of the postwar era continued to buoy voter confidence. In Brooks's corner of Texas, business in petrochemicals and in the shipping ports was bustling. Unemployment in the district had fallen to an all-time low by 1966. In addition, water levels in the newly formed Sam Rayburn Reservoir had begun to rise as a result of the Rayburn Dam, and Brooks was in the midst of having his own legislation move through Congress toward passage. At the dedication of the Rayburn Dam, Johnson said Rayburn's creed, which he and Brooks shared, was "the greatest good for the greatest number." Brooks could not have been blamed for feeling some pride in the representation he had given his district during the preceding dozen years he had spent in Washington. Unfortunately, a surprise with major ramifications lurked around the corner.

REDISTRICTING: To more closely represent the "one person, one vote" principle established by the U.S. Supreme Court, in 1965 the Texas legislature passed a congressional redistricting process to ensure that all congressional districts contained a nearly equivalent number of citizens. Many people were upset with this and perhaps no one more than Brooks. In his Second District, the redistricted scheme would carve out Jefferson County, which held both Beaumont and Port Arthur, from the eight other counties that comprised southeastern Texas, including Orange, Tyler, Jasper, Shelby, and Harden counties. Or rather, the ranchland and the pinewood forests were to be snipped off from the two major economic engines they had always supported.

Culturally, the Second District had made sense. The river basin that stretched between the Sabine and Neches Rivers had always been identified as East Texas, the slim geographic and demographic margin between the Old South and the New Southwest. Those two rivers, which trailed down along the Louisiana border, were the only reason there was any industry in the area at all. People from Jefferson County had always had closer ties to the eastern Texas bloc of counties since pioneers had first settled in the Big Thicket area.

The proposed redistricting would separate Jefferson County from the rest of the Second District and combine it with parts of Harris and Galveston counties to the west, which were Gulf Coast areas and decidedly more conservative. The rest of the Second District would retain the name but absorb much of the Seventh District, which had been represented by Democrat John Dowdy since he had come to Congress the same year as Brooks. Dowdy, also a native Texan and a member of the House Judiciary, would see his career in Congress end years later when he would be indicted for bribery in 1972 and later serve jail time for perjury.

As Brooks's district was now being split in two, voters in the rural areas and along the dusty back roads, where his mother Grace and the entire Brooks family had campaigned for so many years, would no longer be his constituents. The area surrounding the Rayburn Dam, which Brooks had dedicated so much energy to fighting for, would no longer be in his district. Even Brooks's own family farm on 263 acres of land that he had bought in 1949 up in the pine tree forests of Jasper County would no longer be in the new district.

MARTIN DIES: Though the Texas legislative council contended that the move to redistrict was prompted by a 1963 federal court ruling, some editorialists at the time felt the effort was actually a thinly disguised power play by Governor John Connally and Martin Dies Jr. Connally, riding 60 percent approval ratings in Texas, was toying with the ideas of either running for the U.S. Senate against the Republican incumbent John Tower or seeking a third term as governor. He had also begun to reveal more and more publicly the ideological gap that existed between himself and the rest of the Texas Democrats, President Johnson included. Connally had personally requested that the state legislative council study the possibility of redistricting in Texas. The report and its recommendations were adopted by the council in January. The consequences would reverberate through Texas for a half-century.

As for Dies, he and Brooks had a long and unpleasant history. The Dies family was well known in East Texas, and Martin Dies Sr. had also represented the Second District, from 1909 to 1919, and had been a county judge and district attorney up in Tyler, Texas, before that. After Congress, he went on to become counsel for Gulf Oil, the company Brooks's mother had also worked for, albeit at a much lower level. The Dies family had long kept a ranch in Jasper as well. Brooks would later buy the ranch across the road. Martin Dies Jr., following in his father's footsteps, had represented the Second District from 1931 to the beginning of 1945, during which time he was the first chairman of the House Un-American Activities Committee, leading anti-communist charges against institutions and people like the University of Texas and, most notoriously, little Shirley Temple. When he decided not to seek reelection in 1945, he was succeeded by Marty Combs. Dies ran twice for the Senate, losing to Texas political giant Pappy O'Daniel in 1941 and then to Ralph Yarborough in the 1948 primary. Though the conservative, anti-communist Dies had considered running again for the Second District seat in 1952, the year Brooks won his first House race, Dies instead ran for and was then reelected as a "representative at-large" serving the entire state of Texas.

Years before World War II and before he left for college, a young Brooks had gone to see Dies Jr., "hat in hand," and ask for an appointment to the Naval Academy in Annapolis. Dies was already a congressman then, and he could pull strings for local boys if he wanted. Brooks's mother Grace called Dies's office and made an appointment. As Brooks recalled it, his mother drove him up the seventy miles of dusty country roads from Beaumont, and, without any facilities along the way, she was parched by the time they arrived at the Dies ranch. Dies came out to his front porch and said, "No need to get out of the car. I've looked at it, and I'm not going to appoint you." Dies said that Brooks "didn't have the wherewithal to make it at Annapolis," which ended the discussion before it even began. A dejected Brooks asked if his mother could at least come in and have some water and use the bathroom. Dies said no. The event left a significant impression on Brooks. He would go on to enlist in the marines instead, and he would still be able to keenly recall the snub some seventy years later. Brooks's friends all knew about his long memory, and many fondly recalled one of his favorite sayings, "forgive and never forget."

Redistricting brought serious political complications for Brooks. He had already built a name for himself in the region, but this switch meant that he would need to establish new relationships. One booster offered to "raise a few bucks from some stoggy [sic] conservative Wall Street tycoons," to which Brooks replied that since the new district would include areas covered by media from Houston, he was counting on having a "more costly campaign." Hundreds of his constituents wrote him personally to show how upset they were to lose him, but local leaders and editorialists in the new counties were mostly excited about getting Brooks's representation.

Brooks's reelection chances after redistricting seemed favorable. The complication was that the Ninth District, the area around Galveston County, was already represented by Representative Clark W. Thompson, another friend of Johnson's and a veteran who had served in Congress for thirty-two years. A December 1965 assessment in the *Wall Street Journal* stated, "House redistricting pits two key Johnson backers, Congressmen Brooks and Thompson, against each other." Thompson, also a former marine, had served with Rayburn, who was a great fan of Thompson's integrity and courage as a politician. Even Brooks and Charlotte were fond of and enjoyed the company of Thompson and his wife Libby. Fortunately for Brooks, however, the conflict never materialized, because Thompson, twenty-six years Brooks's senior, chose to retire from Congress instead of running for another term. The issue was settled without anyone having to pick sides.

Though the redistricting would have been an existential crisis for many politicians, Brooks's reputation reduced the event to more of a speed bump, which he approached with his typical pragmatism. He would write to constituents in early 1966 that though the district was to be altered, "the strong ties that have developed over the years will not be changed nor will the recognition of our need to work together."

SUCCESS OF ADP ACT: For Brooks there was little time to rest, despite winning several legislative and political victories. Most of the matters that came before Brooks's committee required continued vigilance, which often meant follow-up hearings. For instance, the issue of intentionally short-lived light bulbs persisted, mainly because the manufacturers resisted any and all changes, prompting the committee to hold more hearings and issue a second report in 1966. Fortunately, the implementation of the Automatic Data Processing Act, or "Brooks Act," as many called it, began reaping rewards quickly. A preliminary report in February 1967 from the Bureau of the Budget to President Johnson revealed that the federal government had already saved more than $100 million through operational efficiencies and improved purchasing.

However, there were continual efforts, both well-intentioned and not, to mitigate the law's effects, and the committee held further hearings to root out more problems with the government's usage of and spending on ADP, which already surpassed $1.1 billion annually.

One follow-up piece of legislation proposed allowing software companies and engineers to patent their own proprietary coding languages. Some saw this move as protecting, and thereby promoting, innovation in the field. Brooks, however, saw it as stifling the industry with further obstacles.

There had already been so few market conditions to encourage competition, leaving only the industry giants to reap real profits, and this development would only further entrench the largest players. Additionally, Brooks took issue with what he perceived as a reluctance from many managers within the federal government to learn more about ADP, now referred to as EDP, or "electronic data processing."

> *Despite the advances in the development of EDP and the miracles achieved through the use of these new techniques, we must constantly remind ourselves that electronic data processing is still in a relatively crude, initial stage of development, considering its potential. In terms of what data processing can do for man in his quest for a full and meaningful life, we have taken only a few initial steps in what will be a long and eventful journey. We have only entered the Neolithic age of computer utilization. We now have the most rudimentary of tools and are just learning their capabilities.*

Seeing that further prodding and direction was needed, Brooks later introduced a supporting bill in July 1969 obliging the comptroller general to coordinate with the Bureau of the Budget in developing "a standard data processing system to serve certain data needs of the federal government." The bill also called on the General Accounting Office to create guidelines for existing data processing systems. Brooks had a vision for how the GAO could take a larger role in overseeing government efficiency, and he would continue to incorporate them in a number of ways in the coming years.

FAA: One of the agencies that continued to vex Brooks and the committee at large, however, was the FAA. To Brooks, the FAA, which had responsibility for so many American lives, remained an example of utter mismanagement. In November 1965, an aircraft fire from ruptured fuel lines in a passenger plane near Salt Lake City resulted in forty-three fatalities. Like so many other accidents, the cause was found to be entirely due to pilot error. A Civil Aeronautics Board investigation further revealed that the pilot had previously failed several training and proficiency checks. A lack of sufficient safety standards continued to plague the industry and result in fatal crashes around the country.

Political priorities were a significant obstacle. In 1965, Kennedy's appointed FAA administrator, Najeeb Halaby, who had been an accomplished test pilot in World War II, stepped down. As his replacement, Johnson nominated retired air force general William McKee, a four-star general who had never flown a plane or obtained a pilot's license. Johnson required a waiver from Congress so a non-civilian could run the agency; one was granted and McKee was easily confirmed. McKee, a technician at heart who had just previously taken a position with NASA, later recalled that after his confirmation Johnson told him to find a good deputy to run the FAA; McKee's job would be to see the supersonic transport project through.

Sometime after McKee took office, Brooks's subcommittee had arranged for hearings to be held concerning the problems with the air traffic control programs. It had been almost five years since the FAA's Project Beacon report had been released, and Brooks was keen to see what progress had been made, though he and his staff already knew that there had been almost none. They had prepared a case to present, and according to Brooks's longtime staffer Gene Peters, "McKee was set up to get annihilated" at the hearings.

Then on the day before they were scheduled to begin, McKee paid Brooks a visit to introduce himself and say hello. According to Peters, the thrust of the conversation was that McKee was actually well aware that the FAA was a "disaster." McKee had attended West Point and held numerous command positions at military outposts around the world. He had enough time in the new position to recognize that systemic flaws pervaded the agency and that something needed to be done about it. The general's sincerity and approach resonated with Brooks, and so he called off the next day's hearings. Brooks reasoned that there was no point in making a fool of someone who understood what the problems were and was trying to do right. Brooks gave McKee some time to clean up and get situated as the new head of the agency. The areas for improvement, though, were many.

One particular source of embarrassment for both FAA officials and the congressmen questioning them was the agency's overuse of acronyms for technical terms. One such severely muddled comment during the 1966 hearings went, "The procedural AFTS safeguards on the OLR guarantee maximum TPFL." Officials at the FAA were so acronym crazy that some committee members grew reluctant to call them on specific points and thereby risk looking stupid during the hearings. Brooks would describe the encounters during those hearings in terms of "annoyance and disgust," but according to one contemporary account by political activist Ralph Nader, Brooks may also have felt foolishly uninformed because of the widespread use of acronyms and industry jargon. Brooks's concern received partial validation when it was revealed that even some of the FAA officials themselves did not fully understand some of the terms they were using.

Then the subcommittee's gloves came off. When the 1966 hearings wrapped up, Brooks ordered Ernest Baynard, the head of the subcommittee's staff of roughly five, to "find out all you can. . . get at the essentials of air traffic control." He also instructed Baynard to do it quietly and outside of the hearing process. The GAO offered support, and there were even some competent FAA employees temporarily assigned to the subcommittee during their inquiry. As an instruction to his own staff, Baynard had written on a green chalkboard in the office:

DON'T TALK TO:
1. FAA
2. DOT
3. GAO

The Department of Transportation (DOT) was the FAA's parent agency. The subcommittee staff were directed never to call, simply because "phone calls to those agencies are useless." Baynard explained that "no matter what they say they will do, they seldom do it. . . so we write letters and make them respond in writing. . . it does not save any time to phone those agencies."

So the investigations continued, and because of further delays in developing an automated air traffic control system, the subcommittee would resume public hearings again in 1968. In describing those hearings and more that followed the next year, Brooks publicly commented:

> *The overuse of acronyms and other abbreviations by FAA to describe units of the new system has created confusion and made it difficult for interested individuals to obtain a clear understanding of the new air traffic control system and the problems FAA faces in implementing it.*

CONGRESSIONAL OPERATIONS: Though it was frustrating work, this doggedness only improved Brooks's stature in the House. He had become, in effect, the whip for the Texas House delegation. He served on the House Select Committee on Standards and Conduct (for congressional behavior) that was established in 1965 to make recommendations to the House on how it should proceed in regulating itself. That committee issued a report in December 1966, in which Brooks compiled all existing laws and regulations relating to ethical conduct.

The report also suggested a standing committee be established to "modernize the operations of the Congress"; Brooks was one of only six House members selected to serve on that committee, the Joint Committee on the Organization of Congress, which held forty days of hearings and issued fifteen volumes of testimony and findings before issuing a report to Congress.

The next year, the Senate would pass its own reorganization bill. Brooks and fellow committee member Ray Madden then revised their original bill at least seven times to create something similar in the House. Since Brooks had been a part of that first joint committee, he had testified in front of the House Rules Committee, and in April 1967, the Rules Committee endorsed a law finally establishing a standing committee on Standards and Official Conduct. It was to be composed of six Democrats and six Republicans and would establish and enforce codes of conduct for representatives and their staff. With a note of satisfaction, Brooks released a statement of support for the committee's actions: "I am especially pleased that [the proposal] is identical to one which I submitted a year ago to the Joint Committee on the Organization of Congress." It took until 1971, but eventually both houses of Congress would pass the Reorganization Act, which was based almost entirely on that first joint committee's report in 1966.

CHARLOTTE AND JEB: Brooks's longtime friend and colleague Albert Thomas died on February 15, 1966. As per congressional tradition, his wife Lera carried out the rest of his term. Johnson, who had been at odds with Thomas until Brooks had brokered a connection between the men years prior, wrote the widow, "No man did more for Houston than Albert Thomas." Brooks's own wife began to take on more visible roles in Washington and back home. While remaining a member of his office staff, she helped coordinate Johnson and Humphrey's inaugural ball in 1965, helped coordinate several women's groups on Capitol Hill, such as the Women's National Democratic Forum and the Congressional Club, and was director of the Friendship House, an anti-poverty agency. She also usually attended campaign events with her husband, spending as many as twenty-five weekends a year back in the district during election years. The *Houston Chronicle's Texas Sunday Magazine* featured her on its cover in July 1967 and ran a complimentary four-page spread on her many activities. The story also noted that "the Brooks are among the most socially active couples in Congress, though they avoid the ostentatious soirees that frequently attract nationwide attention."

The following month, the couple welcomed an addition to the family, their first son, Jack Edward Brooks, or Jeb. The couple hitched a ride with Vice President Humphrey aboard his plane to Dallas, where the two politicians were addressing the state convention of the AFL-CIO. After first meeting Jeb at the Gladney Center for Adoption in Fort Worth, the Brookses brought him back to Washington on the same vice presidential airplane. They announced to the reporters who met them at Andrews Air Force Base that the child had seemed "unimpressed" with the fancy transportation and that he had in fact slept most of the trip.

The new father appeared to pursue the mystery of parenthood with the same no-nonsense approach he used with investigative hearings. A large photo of Brooks ran in the Sunday *Washington Star*. The congress-man, clad in shirtsleeves and thick-rimmed reading glasses and chomping on a big cigar, sat at his desk seemingly engrossed in the book he held up in front of his face, *Baby and Child Care*, featuring a cherubic boy on the cover. Brooks looked as out of place as could be, but that, of course, was the point. Brooks always had a wry sense of humor, and with this, he was signaling that though he had once been known around Capitol Hill as one of the more eligible bachelors, he had now finally and utterly settled down.

GOP DRIFTS RIGHT: The following year would prove to be as conse-quential as any in Brooks's time in Congress. At the end of January, the Tet Offensive began in Vietnam; a few days later, Nixon announced his intention to run, and within two months Johnson made his own surprise announcement that he would not run. In early April, Martin Luther King Jr. was assassinated and Robert Kennedy was killed just two months later. The tumultuous Democratic National Convention consumed the news in August, and with it came the rumblings of future political conflicts.

In 1964, the Republican Party, rather than drifting back to the cen-ter to remain relevant, had chosen to go the other way, embracing their fringe with the nomination of presidential candidate Barry Goldwater, an extremely conservative senator from Arizona, who was not only proud of his extreme conservatism, but also confident that it was the only way to defeat Communism.

This was part and parcel of the white backlash that pundits feared would develop after the progress of the civil rights movement. Hippies versus the fascists. Militants versus the squares. The left and the right shifted farther apart and began to denounce one another. Opponents were no longer just wrong on issues, they were traitorous, dangerous, and to be fought by any means necessary.

The man who so deftly stepped into this growing breach was Richard Nixon, Eisenhower's vice president, who had lost to Kennedy in 1960 and then failed to win the governorship of California in 1962, a politician that most people had all but buried in their minds. Nixon had been quietly campaigning for the job all along, supporting Goldwater's ticket when other national figures had abandoned him, because Nixon knew he would need those same delegates to get elected the next time around.

Historian Rick Perlstein, borrowing a term coined by Adlai Stevenson, referred to the nation of which Nixon took the helm as Nixonland, "the America where two separate and irreconcilable sets of apocalyptic fears coexist in the minds of two separate and irreconcilable groups of Americans. . . An amazingly large segment of the population disliked and mistrusted Richard Nixon instinctively. What [the DNC] did not acknowledge was that an amazingly large segment of the population also trusted him as their savior."

12

All the Way with LBJ

For Brooks, the president was a dear friend as well as a political ally. Even in the midst of his hectic schedule in the Senate, the Executive Office Building, and finally the White House, Johnson had managed to send Brooks a personal letter for his birthday almost every year since 1953. Brooks often said that the thing people did not know about Johnson was how thoughtful he was. When Charlotte's father, Vernon Collins, fell ill and was admitted to St. Luke's Episcopal Hospital in Houston, Johnson sent a personal note.

Dear Mr. Collins, Charlotte and Jack came by last night and told me that you were ill and in the hospital. Lady Bird and I are both so sorry but feel that any-one close to a wonderful girl like Charlotte is close to us. We just wanted you to know that we're thinking of you and pulling for you.

Early in 1968, when Jeb was just an infant, Brooks and his little family were in a car accident. The president responded immediately with a telegram:

We just heard that you were involved in an accident but were so very re-lieved to learn that no one was seriously hurt. Please take care of yourselves, and of Jeb, because we'll be depending upon him someday to take care of us.

Brooks responded in the same way during Johnson's hospitalizations. In 1965, Brooks sent the president a note telling him he would be glad "to come over and win a few hands" of cards. In February the next year

Johnson was again in the hospital, and Brooks, along with friends, J. J. Pickle, Willard "Bill" Deason, and two Supreme Court justices, Abe Fortas and Tom Clark, volunteered to visit the hospital and play dominoes with the president on any Saturday. As he knew Johnson enjoyed smoking and would have plenty of leisure time, Brooks sent him a cigarette holder as a get well present. Johnson responded:

That beautiful cigarette holder cheered my recovery from the operation considerably. It is just the right thing to use—in between smokes—as a bean blower for disciplining recalcitrant members of the Senate. Right now, I am deep in the heart of my favorite state and hope to be back soon with all of my good friends— a list headed especially by Jack Brooks.

Lady Bird could also be tremendously gracious. The Brookses gave her earrings one year, and she sent a note to Jack and Charlotte at the house on Capitol Hill.

The earrings are an absolute joy—I was enchanted with them and I don't have anything like them at all. The story behind how they came to me will also add greatly to the warmth and pride with which I shall wear them. You are so thoughtful to do this for me.
Always fondly,
Lady Bird

The mementos and notes are legion. There is a photo of Johnson with Brooks's mother, Grace, at the Brookses farm in Jasper. Brooks frequently visited the Johnsons at their ranch. Brooks recalled:

We went to his ranch many times and we would ride around in those big convertibles and look at his deer. But he never did want me to hunt them because he knew I would kill several of his big bucks, and he didn't want anybody killing those big animals, so I never did. But when I would land at the ranch in a plane, he'd meet me at the plane with one of those pretty girls who worked for him and hand me a scotch and water. And that was kind of nice, kind of a warm greeting from a president of the United States. That's the way we operated.

He came to see me one time. We lived up on the Hill, and I remember one Sunday morning I woke up, and I could hear him walking up the stairs, and I could hear Bird saying, "Lyndon, you should have called him." And it's Johnson and his wife and Secret Service men just coming to knock, say hello, and have coffee on a Sunday morning.

Charlotte and I were still in bed, we got up quickly and came down and visited with them and had coffee and had his picture made with him holding our baby son, Jeb, and looking in a big mirror we had on the wall down stairs.

They were wonderful people. Bird was a sweetheart; she's a thoughtful person. She had on a nice wool sweater with flowers embroidered on it that looked wonderful on her, and Charlotte had given her that a couple of years ago because we liked them and we loved them and we wanted to do things that they appreciated because they had been so kind to us.

One of the nice things was sailing on the Honey Fitz and Sequoia—yachts they kept on the Potomac River—and we would go out on the large one for the evening and have drinks and dinner on the ship. Go down the river and turn around and come back and everybody then go home. When you went out there you were supposed to get there early and wait and never drink or do anything, I guess, just stand around and wait for the president. When I got on board ship I would get the waiters to get me a drink while I was waiting. I didn't want to just sit around there for thirty minutes maybe, I wanted to have a drink then, and so I did. And when he would come in I would have a toast and say here's to our president and he would just look at me, he didn't say anything. But he understood, and he was very kind. He was something else, something else.

There was even a non-political connection between the two couples. Charlotte's mother went to San Marcos College, now part of the Texas State University system, a few years behind Johnson.

The president's warmth and hospitality extended to Brooks's mother. Brooks recalled:

He'd always ask about her, and that was very nice. And that weekend he said, "What do you think your mother's doing?" And I said, "I don't know."

Then he said, "Call 'em. I'm going to send the plane to come and get 'em." Which they did, sent that little plane to Cameron, Texas, and brought them back out to the ranch. And he wanted mother to be able to sleep in the room where Jackie Kennedy had slept. He thought that was a nice thing for my mother. And it was.

Screwworm: Screwworms are fly larvae that eat living flesh and cause havoc in cattle. Early programs to eradicate them in Florida and in some Caribbean herds were promising. After decades of research, the U.S. Department of Agriculture developed a program in the 1950s to sterilize the male fly and break the reproductive cycle by spreading the sterilized males into the native fly population.

For people not directly involved in the livestock business, there would be no reason to be aware of the screwworm or the devastating damages it had on the livestock industry in Texas, which Dolph Briscoe—classmate and UT, lifelong friend to Brooks, one of the richest landowners in Texas, and governor of Texas from 1973 to 1979—estimated to be in the hundreds of millions of dollars a year. He recalled, "It seemed we were going to have to do something about it, or we just couldn't stay in the livestock business."

In the late 1950s, Briscoe, who was then head of the state's Cattle Raisers Association, teamed his organization with similar ones representing sheep and goat farmers and other wildlife interests to raise more than $3 million to boost eradication efforts. In 1958, Briscoe buttonholed Johnson, who was then Senate majority leader, when they both were visiting Jack Garner in Texas for his ninetieth birthday. Johnson didn't have much interest in the issue when Briscoe brought it up.

He didn't say it, but he looked at me like I had mighta just gone off my rocker. The USDA insisted the [sterilization] program wouldn't work in Texas because herds could become re-infected easily from Mexico, but one of the two scientists who helped develop the program, Dr. [Raymond] Bushland, didn't agree with the agency, and he was vociferous. [However,] the agency would not start a screwworm eradication program in Texas.

Several years later, the problem had only intensified. Orville Freeman was secretary of agriculture at the time, Briscoe recalled, "and he was from a North-

western state where they never had a screwworm. So, I appealed to Jack for help, 'cause obviously we needed help. He called me and said, "OK, come on up to Washington, and then we'll work on it."†

Briscoe said the USDA had summoned Bushland to Washington for disciplinary action. "So, I got him into a real jam. I mean that was part of it." Brooks told Briscoe he would set up a meeting with the president:

Jack was on very good terms with President Johnson at that time. They admitted that years earlier they had not been on that good of terms, but they had gotten to where they were extremely close. In fact, there was no member of the Texas delegation or any other delegation in Washington that was as close, personally, to President Johnson as Jack Brooks.

So, Jack said, "I'll set it up, and we'll go over to the White House." And, of course, that, to me, was great. Just going to the White House for a country boy like me, now that was big enough, you know. I mean, boy, that was something. We drove over in Jack's car. They had a space reserved for Jack right next to the entrance to the West Wing, the west entrance. I thought, well, this is a pretty good start. The gate just flew open, and nobody questioned anything. They knew Jack's car, and of course, I was just riding along with him.

Anyway, we went in. We went into the Oval Office. And anytime you go into the Oval Office, it's a thrill. And there was the president, sitting at his desk, working. And, he said something like, "Sit down." And he was busy, so we sat down. And then there's a little private office that the president has next to the Oval Office. And when he got through, he said, "OK, let's go in here." So, we went into the private office, just the three of us. And, of course, I'd never been there. Never expected to go there. And we went in there, and it was time to strike a blow for liberty or whatever you want to call it.

Anyway, we had a drink, and talked, and I got carried away. You know, it was a tremendous experience just to be there. And then the president said, "OK, well, it's time to go up, and we'll have dinner." Well, that sounded good. So we went up to the private quarters, and that in itself was quite a thrill. Then Mrs.

---

† This quotation is taken verbatim from a video interview that can be viewed at www.jackbrooksfoundation.org.

Johnson joined us, and we went into the private dining room and had a wonderful dinner. And, of course, with President Johnson, you never had to worry about conversation. 'Cause he literally talked all the time, never ever stopped. And he liked to have, or had to have, people around. He had to have somebody to listen. And, anyway, we had a very nice dinner, and then he said, "OK, we've got some movie," I forgot what movie it was, "down in the projection room." And, the four of us went down into the basement of the White House, where there's one room set aside to show movies.

When the movie was over, say, I don't know whether it was ten-thirty, eleven o'clock or something, of course, I'd had the time of my life, you know, and I'd forgotten all about the screwworm program. Hadn't even thought about it. And then we were walking down the hall, and the president and Mrs. Johnson were going to the elevator, and Jack and I were going to go out to where his car was, and walking down the hall, Jack stopped, and he said, "Now listen, Briscoe, you dumb so-and-so," I mean, and so forth. Jack always had colorful language, and for all occasions. And he said, "We've been here now for five hours, and you haven't said one blankety-blank word about what you came over here to talk about, and we're about to leave, and you've not gotten one blankety-blank thing done that you needed to do." I mean, he gave me a lecture there. And he said, "You've got to talk to the president before he gets in the elevator."

Well, President Johnson stopped, and he leaned over on the wall, you know, and said that he was tired. And he could always put on a good show. And, so I realized then that I was about to have blown my opportunity. So, I talked to him about the screwworm program, and again, fortunately, he knew what it was, I mean, he knew what the screwworm program was for. He had doctored cattle when he was a kid, so he knew what we were talking about. And he said, "OK," something like this, "I'm tired, and I'm going to bed. But," he said, "I'll tell you what." One thing about President Johnson, he never forgot a friend. And if anybody had been his friend, he'd try to help you. And that night he said something to this effect, "I'll tell you what I'll do in the morning. The first thing, I'll call Orville Freeman."

I said, "I thank you, Mr. President." And that was it. I heard in the next few days what their plans were and how they were going to handle legislation and so forth. It was fascinating. But, you know, it wasn't my position to give

him any advice. Jack could, of course, but not for me. Anyway, it was a great
experience. And it was all because of Jack.†

VIETNAM: In the later years of Johnson's presidency, Vietnam was a painful subject that could not be ignored. It was the war that Johnson inherited, enlarged, and passed on, to his everlasting regret. The war protests began in earnest shortly after Johnson's response to the violence in Selma with his speech in March 1965 that laid out the framework for the Voting Rights Act. With that stirring talk, Johnson responded to the ever-present protesters outside the White House who thought he was moving too slowly on civil rights.

Within a month, however, more protesters were back outside the White House, railing against the war. Johnson became the object of these protests They met him at every public event he attended and chanted outside his home every night for the duration of his presidency.

> *"War Criminal!"*
> *"Hitler is Alive—in the White House!"*
> *"Hey! Hey! LBJ! How many kids did you kill today?"*

Over the course of his five years in the presidency, tens of thousands of American lives were lost in the jungles and rice paddies, many more Vietnamese from both the North and South died, and billions of dollars were spent in a conflict that would come to a tragic, drawn-out end under Johnson's successor, Richard Nixon.

For all the hope and vigor of the first two years of Johnson's presidency, including his landslide election against Goldwater in 1964, Johnson's full term in office was beset by ever-increasing casualty figures, misguided advice from his generals, and a loud anti-war movement that created division across the country, separating fathers from sons, setting students against their college administrations, and pitting draft resisters and protesters against the military. The military blamed the media for its waning support

---

† This quotation is taken verbatim from a video interview that can be viewed at
   www.jackbrooksfoundation.org.

among civilians. The uncertain goals of the intense fighting and bloodshed generated a political divide not only between Republicans and Democrats but also within the Democratic Party.

Brooks supported Johnson on the war and on most foreign policy questions, as he did with presidents Eisenhower and Kennedy before him. He attended weekly briefings at the White House on the "Vietnam situation" in 1964 and 1965, while Johnson was escalating the number of U.S. troops in combat.

As opposition to the war grew and the progressive cohesion of the mid-1960s transitioned into the charged and tumultuous divisions of the late-1960s, there were small but perceptible signs that all the personal attacks on Johnson, often vicious, were taking their toll on the man, who was quickly approaching his sixtieth birthday. Charlotte Brooks could see the president becoming increasingly weary from the onslaught.

> We'd sit up there and have supper and they were chanting outside, "Hey Hey, L-B-J, how many kids did you kill today?" He was hearing that. I think it just finally got to him. He talked about the war a lot. But you know, you just kind of listened. He just had to get it off his chest. His son-in-law [daughter Lynda's husband, Charles Robb] was over there in Southeast Asia. It was hard for him.

Brooks later recalled the effect that the war and its protesters had on Johnson:

> That was painful. Very painful for Johnson, who did not like to do things that offended or hurt anybody. He was very careful. When he became president and was running things I told him one time, "You know you are a little easygoing every now and then in some areas," that he didn't really crack down on a few folks and I thought maybe he should. He said, "You know, Jack, when you're president you have to be careful you don't hurt somebody you don't really want to hurt." Johnson all in all was a magnificent president. If it hadn't been for the war, which he didn't start originally, but he couldn't get rid of it. Those people didn't want to make peace. They had plenty of people to get killed. That didn't worry them at all—they just didn't want to quit.

1968 ELECTION: Eugene McCarthy and then Bobby Kennedy challenged Johnson in the Democratic primary, and Johnson, discouraged by so much division and pained by a subpar performance in the New Hampshire primary, decided to withdraw from the race.

Johnson had never given Brooks or any of his other confidants any indication that he would not seek reelection, a decision that stunned many in the nation when he made the announcement on March 31.

Brooks was riding in a car and listening to the radio when he first heard the news. He later recalled:

> It was a real shock. . . but, you know, I never chided him about it. I didn't think it was bad. These people say he shouldn't have done it, or he should have. I figure it's his own business.
>
> I thought he was entitled, if he didn't feel he was well enough to do it and wanted to survive, to quit. He'd worked his heart out, done a great job. There was another overriding consideration. I felt, and he never did tell me this, but I always felt that he thought that if he said he wasn't going to run that he might go on and work out an accord in Vietnam without being accused of political motivations. Plus the fact that I'm sure he'd served long and ably and kind of wanted to get back home. It's not so bad out on the ranch, you know.

Four days after Johnson's announcement, Martin Luther King Jr. was shot and killed outside his motel room in Memphis, an event that sparked race riots across the nation and reduced swaths of major cities to rubble. Two months later, Robert Kennedy was shot and killed moments after winning the California Democratic primary over McCarthy.

Prodded in part by those assassinations, Congress moved for the first time since the Depression to enact new laws surrounding the purchase of guns. On October 22, 1968, Johnson signed into law the Gun Control Act, which banned most interstate shipments of long guns to individuals, sales to individuals except in their own state (with some exceptions), the sale of long guns to persons under the age of 18 and handguns to those under 21, and the importation of military surplus weapons from abroad. It was the last piece of legislation Johnson would sign as president and a bittersweet victory for his administration. Just five years prior, Lee Harvey Oswald had used an alias to purchase an Italian 6.5 Mannlicher-Carcano rifle from a retailer in Illinois after seeing an advertisement in the National Rifle Association's magazine *American Rifleman*. Mail order purchases across state lines would no longer be possible.

In October, Johnson also halted all bombing of North Vietnam in advance of the planned peace talks in Paris. Two weeks later, Nixon won the presidential election on the promise of "peace with honor" in Vietnam.

LBJ's FINAL YEARS: In January, just a few weeks before Nixon's inauguration, the city of Nederland, Texas, passed a resolution thanking President Johnson for his service. Though Nederland only had a few thousand citizens and the gesture was hardly newsworthy, Brooks felt that the act actually meant a great deal. He sent Johnson a copy of the resolution and wrote a message to his friend about what it represented:

> *As you are preparing to leave the Presidency, I think this is an appropriate and honest expression of the respect and esteem you enjoy in the Ninth District of Texas and throughout our country. I know that as you review your years of service to our country you will feel a very great deal of justifiable pride. You also can be certain that this feeling is shared by the vast majority of Texans and Americans.*

Above all else, Johnson valued the loyalty of others. In interactions with his chief aides and speech writers, this manifested itself in the complete breakdown of any barriers between the president and his staff, which resulted in aides taking dictation as Johnson sat on the toilet or his chief, "Buzz" Busby, remaining at his bedside until Johnson was entirely asleep. Working with Johnson meant completely unobstructed intimacy.

Johnson was less demanding of his allies, but only in terms of the manner of loyalty that he required. He was a vote-counter in every regard, and for him it was not enough that his side win, the win had to be unanimous. One errant vote was a failure. He had to know that his colleagues were with him all the way, and if they were not, he would wear them down until they were.

For Brooks, what Johnson held most dear was his counsel, which was objective, and his support, which was unfailingly reliable.

> November 20, 1968
> Dear Jack:
> Lady Bird and I are delighted by the news of your reelection to Congress. It just would not be the same body without you.
> You have served your people—and your president—ably and well, and I want you to know that I will always be deeply grateful.
> Sincerely,
> Lyndon Johnson
> [Handwritten] See all of you at lunch tomorrow.

Inscribed photos line the desk, credenzas, and walls of the Brooks home. One reads:

> To Charlotte and Jack Brooks, whose fidelity and friendship have given me strength and purpose. Lyndon B. Johnson.

In January of 1969, the Johnsons left the White House and returned to their ranch, which had been their refuge, secondary office, and hosting facility since they had purchased it twenty years prior. The ranch, which had always been bustling and full of important guests, was now best characterized by its solitude. Johnson's own sense of mortality may have cast a dour atmosphere as well. He had told friends that he would not live much past sixty. His father had died of a heart attack around then, as had Johnson's uncle. He made it publicly known that he did not expect to last long either. He resumed smoking cigarettes, a vice he had not permitted himself to indulge in openly since his first heart attack in 1955. Though his daughters objected, on this issue he was not to be moved. "I've been president! And now it's my time."

13

Legislation: 1969–1972

After nearly two decades in the House, Brooks's influence and impact on Congress was palpable. Outside a relatively small circle of Washington politicos, he was still not as widely known as some of his colleagues. However, through his agenda for a better government and the dogged nature of his subcommittee, he continued to solidify his role as not just as an influential legislator and government watchdog but also as a congressional leader. Whereas he had spent the better part of the 1950s and 1960s learning and mastering Capitol Hill, he now understood Congress as well as anyone, including its role in defending the public good and its ability to safeguard its prerogatives from the other federal branches. His colleagues had long since noted how he would fight for such principles, and the leadership would soon tap him to not only take part in a plan to update Congress and its operations, but to lead the effort.

Still, Brooks had to win elections at home to have an role in Washington. In a mass mailing to constituents leading up to the 1968 elections, Brooks wrote:

> *This past year has seen our way of life challenged by those who disrupt and destroy through crime and violence... They compromise the continuing struggle of the American people toward progress and a better life for everyone... Meanwhile, the struggle against ignorance, and disease, major causes of social unrest in our nation, continues. Under a series of programs Congress has established in recent years, these just grievances will be remedied.*

He went on to tout the accomplishments of his "efficiency subcommittee," which had examined all programs of the twelve departments and agencies within its jurisdiction in the preceding two years. Additionally, due to a strong economy, Brooks's direction, and a lack of the racial strife that had torn apart other cities, his home base had fared well during 1968. That year, $39 million in federal funds found its way to the Ninth District to make improvements to the Galveston Harbor, the Intracoastal Waterway, the Sabine-Neches Waterway, and other coastal reserves. Millions of dollars also went to Lamar Tech and other local colleges.

NEW YORK TIMES ENDORSEMENT: Remarkably, even The *New York Times* came out with an endorsement for Brooks in his reelection primary bid against a Democratic newcomer. Why one of the largest and most respected East Coast newspapers had chosen to take a position on a small congressional election in rural Texas, Brooks could not understand at the time.

> *I was surprised about that. I guess they just liked my record; maybe they'd been interested in my record in favor of housing, my record in favor of Medicare—medical treatment for people, or my record in favor of veterans' benefits, or my work on computers. Maybe they were interested in that.*

Brooks won reelection comfortably with 61 percent of the vote, although it was his smallest margin of victory yet.

Nationally, Republicans picked up an additional five seats in the House after their historic gains in 1966, though Democrats retained firm majorities in the House and the Senate. The Texas delegation, which had been almost entirely Democratic for years, now included three Republicans, including a young George H. W. Bush, who had just won his second term.

NIXON WHITE HOUSE: Though many facets of Congress remained constant, the political and social upheavals of recent years ensured that Washington would be a different environment than it had been. Brooks no longer had insider access to the White House. To the incoming president, he was just another congressman, albeit a senior one, from the opposition party. His direct line to the Oval Office was now gone, and the new president had little use for a Democrat from coastal Texas with contrary views about the role of government, and more specifically, the role of individual government officials. For the first time since Brooks came to Washington, the man running the executive branch would be more ideological than the mainstream of his own party. For Brooks, this would make agreeing with the commander-in-chief, even on matters of national security, more problematic.

In early December 1968, Brooks received what may have been his first correspondence from President-elect Nixon. He made a polite appeal for staff recommendations for his incoming administration. But it was a form letter that Nixon's office had presumably sent to many congressional leaders. Nixon was no foreigner to Washington and had likely known for some time his administration picks. Shortly after the election, *Newsweek* featured the known advisers the president-elect was bringing with him. Some, such as H. R. "Bob" Haldeman, Robert Finch, and Herb Klein, were coming to be known as his "California Mafia," a slightly less flattering name than the "Brain Trust" or "Texas Gang" that had preceded it. There were brief profiles of eight men and one woman. In Brooks's copy of the magazine, two of the names were circled, Bryce Harlow and Robert Ellsworth.

Ellsworth was a liberal former representative from Kansas. He had spearheaded some of the GOP's unity efforts after that year's convention in Miami. Harlow was a career Hill staffer from Oklahoma who had been an aide and spokesman for Eisenhower. Harlow had remained loyal to Nixon while the former vice president was in the wilderness after losing the 1960 presidential election and the 1962 California gubernatorial election. The *Newsweek* piece called Harlow potentially the most important man on Nixon's team during the transition, citing his thirty years of experience in the Capitol as a congressional liaison. Brooks may have already known these two men, or perhaps he just saw them as his best chance for establishing new channels of contact with the White House.

In January, just before the inauguration, Brooks conducted some final work with longtime Johnson ally Barefoot Sanders to amend the Presidential Transition Act, which provided the aid of support staff and other services to Johnson and future outgoing presidents. Though the presidential transition services had been established for a six-month period, Brooks and Sanders saw it extended to a full year.

White House staff still recognized the importance of collegial relations with Democrats like Brooks, and the Nixons had begun several outreach practices, many of which were spearheaded by First Lady Pat Nixon, that served to open up the White House, which she thought had become accessible only to the elite of Republican political and business circles. One such practice was inviting different families each week to attend a nondenominational religious service in the East Room of the White House. On July 19, Brooks released an announcement to five radio stations in his district that upon Nixon's personal invitation, Brooks and Charlotte would leave Beaumont and return to Washington to attend church services with Nixon and his wife in the White House. The release stated that although Brooks was "a longtime political adversary of the president," Nixon nevertheless respected him "for his constructive legislative record." That same day, *Apollo 11*, the ship carrying astronauts Michael Collins, Buzz Aldrin, and Neil Armstrong, entered the moon's orbit in preparation for landing. The next day, the lunar module, carrying only Aldrin and Armstrong, would land successfully in the Sea of Tranquility while Collins would remain in orbit to bring them back home. In the same news release, Brooks said:

> *Although we have our political differences, I am pleased to join with our president in prayer during these most eventful days in our nation's history.*

There were other invitations as well. Before Christmas in 1969, Brooks brought Charlotte and Jeb with him to a Christmas service at White House.

Though the parties disagreed, a desire for cordiality remained. Just as many Democrats had gotten along with Eisenhower and respected Republican leaders like Senator Everett Dirksen had supported portions of Johnson's agenda, Brooks saw no reason to oppose or obstruct just for the sake of it.

VIETNAM: One opportunity for Brooks to support this new president was the ongoing war in Vietnam, which would soon spread to Cambodia and Laos. Ever since Johnson had called for a troop build-up in 1965, the issue of Vietnam had been splitting the Democratic Party in two, though there was no easy delineation between the halves. People disagreed on how to fight the war tactically, what efforts were required to win, and whether winning would be worthwhile. There was also disagreement on whether withdrawal, either upon mutual understanding with the North Vietnamese or unilaterally, would constitute failure. Perhaps most importantly, what would that failure mean for the United States' role in the world?

Brooks had a way of cutting through all of that. Since Eisenhower, he had supported every president and his respective policies in Southeast Asia. For Brooks, foreign policy was a singular area of governance where he deferred without exception to the commander-in-chief, especially when it involved the military. This was a rarity for the man who had not even supported all of Johnson's Great Society legislation. Brooks's time in the South Pacific and then in China before the Japanese surrender surely shaped his thinking. He had known firsthand how difficult and opaque foreign conflicts could become and what little value second-guessing provided.

Brooks's longtime administrative assistant and chief of staff Gene Peters remembered that the question of Vietnam was not an easy one for his boss, who had seen up close how nasty and unforgiving war could be. It was not something that Brooks just glossed over with ideological simplicity.

> In Vietnam. . . [Brooks's] problem. . . was that he was really concerned about these guys getting killed. That meant something to him. It was not just somebody else's kids. It was a real thing. But I do think that basically, deep down, he felt that this was something that we shouldn't have gotten into to start with. But now we're in it, let's defend it and see what we can do.

Brooks's support on Vietnam put him in line with nearly four-fifths of Americans who agreed with the president's policies after he addressed the nation on November 3, 1969, in what became known as his "Silent Majority" speech. Nixon laid out a path forward in Vietnam, even if historians would later question his truthfulness. Nixon called for the "Vietnamization" of the war, which meant a slow disengagement rather than speedy withdrawal, and one that would shift the burden of security to the South Vietnamese. He explained that the military had already begun to "expand, equip, and train South Vietnam's forces and assign to them an ever-increasing combat role, at the same time steadily reducing the number of U.S. combat troops." An estimated seventy million Americans had tuned in to watch this speech. Though drab in tone, it was groundbreaking in measure. He had referred to the war as a potential failure, which no previous president had.

A number of congressmen had previously filed a resolution of support for Nixon in his dealings in Vietnam. Perhaps amid some confusion or out of an instinct to maintain a good relationship with the president, Brooks wrote Bryce Harlow the following day to clarify that he had not withdrawn his name from the resolution, an act which he said took some forbearance after Nixon had tried "to make political gains out of our peace efforts" and cast an ugly light on Johnson's legacy. Brooks included an article from the *Evening Star* in the letter and copied Johnson.

Harlow had been quickly promoted to counselor to the president. He wrote a detailed response to Brooks three days later, reiterating Nixon's and his own "deep affection and admiration for LBJ." He included a news release citing a survey showing that 77 percent of Americans supported the policies regarding Vietnam that Nixon had outlined in the speech.

But the president's positions became increasingly difficult to defend. In April 1970, Nixon announced that his Vietnamization program was going so well that he was withdrawing 150,000 U.S. troops. Ten days later he announced that American troops, in cooperation with South Vietnamese armed forces, would be attacking "major enemy sanctuaries on the Cambodian-Vietnamese border" because of increased enemy activity there and in Laos.

As the months and years of Nixon's first term began to pass with few results, fissures appeared in Brooks's support for Nixon and his decision-making. Brooks toured Vietnam in early 1971 and met with marines who were "dug-in" against daily onslaughts of artillery fire and anti-personnel mines. During an interview later that year with a colleague conducting an oral history project for the Lyndon Johnson Presidential Library, Brooks said:

> *I say I'd like to see the war ended, but Johnson wanted the war ended. Johnson wanted the war ended, tried to end it, worked on it. Started the pacification*

program. I see Nixon now says it's a new program. Of course, Nixon had that plan in 1968 to end the war; that plan we haven't heard about. It's the best-kept secret in history because nobody has heard about that plan. . . I don't know how long he's going to wait. But I'm a little bitter about that. . . I really think it's unfair. I think it was raw demagoguery, and anybody that had a plan that was worth a damn should have given it to the country then—that day. There have been a lot of people killed since October '68, a lot of people wounded.

By 1972, Brooks's skepticism had worsened. In an interview with political activist Ralph Nader, Brooks was quoted as saying:

I give [presidents] the benefit of the doubt that they are doing their dead level best. Some have met with varying success. . . I don't defend Nixon, however. . . in fact, I think if by October 15 [1972] the election looks close, he'll have everything out. . . even the planes if he thought it necessary for his reelection.

Nader, in his own accompanying commentary in the publication that followed, made an even more forceful statement, writing "Jack Brooks believes Richard Nixon will do almost anything if he thinks it will give him another four years in the White House."

If Brooks in fact believed that, plenty of others agreed. The simultaneous loosening and expanding of the bounds of the Vietnam engagement had clouded an already murky war and defined a new kind of opposition to it.

THE PENTAGON PAPERS: The most defiant and brazen act of protest would be the June 1971 leak of a forty-seven-volume study that the Pentagon had carried out to understand how, over the previous three decades, the United States had become involved in Vietnam. Thousands of pages of classified documents, a tome of American decision-making from 1945 to 1968, which would come to be known as the "Pentagon Papers," were photocopied by Daniel Ellsberg, a former marine, Pentagon adviser, and think-tank analyst. Ellsberg, who had become progressively disillusioned by the war the closer he got to it, gave copies of the Pentagon Papers to the *New York Times* and the *Washington Post* and then seventeen other newspapers.

The documents elucidated how four consecutive presidential administrations had withheld basic truths about the reasons for fighting in Vietnam and the realities of the South Vietnamese partnership. The release implicated Nixon as much as anyone else. It had been he who stated as vice president in 1954, shortly before the fall of the French military outpost Dien Bien Phu, that "the Vietnamese lack the ability to conduct a war or govern themselves. . . [I]f the government cannot avoid it, the administration must face up to the situation and dispatch forces." Incidentally, it had been Johnson, then Senate majority leader, who had persuaded Eisenhower against unilateral U.S. engagement without participation from the British.

Nixon had been almost excited about the leak at first because it would reveal the Kennedy administration's alleged involvement in the assassination of South Vietnamese President Ngo Dinh Diem in 1963, and Ted Kennedy was a potential presidential frontrunner in the upcoming 1972 elections

However, Nixon's initial reaction soon gave way to a general anxiety over the effect that such leaks might have on his own administration. In taped conversations with aides Haldeman and Ehrlichman shortly after the release of the Pentagon Papers, Nixon recalled the 1948 controversy surrounding Alger Hiss, who was investigated by the House Committee on Un-American Activities on which the young Representative Nixon sat.

> We won the Hiss case in the papers. We did. I had to leak stuff all over the place. . . It was won in the papers. . . But what I mean is we have to develop now a program, a program for leaking out information. We're destroying these people in the papers. . . This is a game. It's got to be played in the press.

Thus was born a small operative unit within the Nixon administration that had the dual role of both uncovering the sources of leaked classified information and then leaking damaging information on those people to discredit them. An operation to steal files from Ellsberg's psychoanalyst would be one of the unit's first tasks, and a break-in at the Democratic National Committee's office in the Watergate Hotel in Washington less than one year later would be their last.

14

Congressional Operations

With all the major legislation and domestic policy changes since Johnson first took office, some of which redefined the social contract Americans had with their government, it was an opportune time for Congress to look inward and modernize its practices and structures. The Legislative Reorganization Act of 1970 established a permanent joint committee of Congress that would comprise ten members, half from the House and half from the Senate. The stated impetus for the committee was that American life was changing, and Congress would need to keep pace. Rapid advances in transportation and communication had made it necessary to ensure that Congress still resembled the society it served.

At the dawn of the twentieth century, being a congressman was essentially a half-time endeavor. Many legislators returned to their home states to private law practices when a session adjourned. Not only had it become a full-time job, the scope of matters addressed by legislators and the accompanying administrative burden signified a real change in the role of Congress over the preceding decades, and each individual congressman now required a large staff. Since 1950, the number of committees, including ad hoc and special-purpose subcommittees, had mushroomed from 100 to roughly 250. In addition, larger constituencies with more diverse needs and points of contact with government had increased the workloads of individual members of Congress. With a steadily increasing number of days that Congress met per annual session, the Reorganization Act forecast the workload only becoming even more onerous, calling for a more comprehensive review of ongoing programs and "strengthening control over Federal expenditures."

A second, and equally significant, reason for this reorganization effort was to keep the Congress strong and shore up its constitutional weight and jurisdiction against what some might have feared were an encroaching executive and judicial branches. Perhaps the previous years had seen too many landmark advances and decisions by Johnson and the Warren Supreme Court. Congress may have felt compelled to act before it lost any ground, either formally or informally, to the other two branches.

Like many meaningful changes in Congress, passing the act to establish the committee had already been a years-long uphill slog. The groundwork had been laid in 1965 when a temporary joint committee on which Brooks had been placed heard the testimonies of 199 witnesses over forty days of hearings, ultimately delivering a 2,322-page report the following year. One of the report's recommendations was the formation of a permanent Joint Committee on Congressional Operations, with a mandate to "review any aspect of congressional organization and operation." In addition the committee would be: "empowered to recommend changes designed to strengthen Congress, to simplify its operation, to improve its relations with other branches of the Federal Government, and to enable it better to meet its constitutional responsibilities."

This proposed committee would also aim to make recommendations that would include provisions to protect the minority party's interests in committee, alter the seniority tradition, and deal with ethical problems, where matters of conduct and conflicts of interests were concerned. Part of this effort was a new requirement in both the House and the Senate that members disclose their financial interests, an issue that would bring Brooks unwanted and undeserved attention before the decade was through.

There were numerous starts and stops, including the Senate's passage of a version of the bill in early 1967, but only after adopting forty amendments. The House, however, did not act, and the bill stalled.

All of this may have seemed very boring even to Capitol Hill insiders, and Brooks knew this matter was one that constituents likely could not have cared less about. Few residents of Beaumont and Port Arthur thought about the machinations of a legislative body a thousand miles away. Attention-grabbing news from Congress was typically limited to leadership struggles or individual "falls from grace." However, just as with procurement procedures and wasteful spending habits, Brooks knew that a government with antiquated operations was an affront to American citizens. Over the course of several years he and a colleague revised the language of the original joint committee's recommendations again and again to create something that could pass both houses, and Brooks testified repeatedly in front of the House Rules Committee, which still bore full responsibility for considering the reorganization bill before it could be passed on to the House for a vote. According to Brooks:

> *We couldn't get it adopted, couldn't get a rule on it, couldn't get Speaker [John] McCormack too strongly for it. I don't think that the parliamentarian Mr. [Lewis] Deschler was ever for it. Then they adopted another committee leader. It failed and they turned it all over to the Rules Committee; the Rules Committee then brought out this bill. . . It was loaded with things that are problems. They're going to change the whole system of what congressmen do.*

During the next session of Congress, the House Rules Committee stripped out the language calling for a Joint Committee on Congressional Operations; however, it did call for a joint committee devoted to one thing in particular: continuing study of congressional automatic data processing and information retrieval systems. That proposed committee would also supervise usage and make policy for the acquisition of computers in Congress. For Brooks, embracing the vast potential of computing was part and parcel with updating Congress.

COMPUTERS IN CONGRESS: In January 1969, the House again failed to enact an updated version of the Reorganization Bill, so Brooks introduced his own legislation, the Computers in Congress Bill. His argument, delivered on the House floor, called for a "coordinated, business-like approach to the introduction and use of computers in the Congress."

> *The time has come to use advanced electronic data processing techniques in the legislative process of the Congress. The state of the art in data processing*

and information handling has reached the point of development that these techniques can be of material assistance to Congress in coping with the constantly increased complexity and volume of data inherent in the legislative process.

Based on sound experience in business, industry, and government, a significant increase in operational efficiency can be expected through the efficient and effective use of electronic data processing techniques. It is clearly evident that application of these techniques to the budget and appropriation process as well as other aspects of our legislative responsibility can mean billions in savings annually to the taxpayers. Use of computers in Congress will bring increased efficiency and effectiveness to all operations and give the American people better service and more responsive government.

Optimum exploitation of computer techniques in the Congress will not be an easy task. It will be time-consuming and will involve a considerable outlay of public funds. However, the potential savings far outweigh the cost of such a system. And, in a more fundamental sense, we have no choice but to apply these techniques to the legislative process if the Congress is to continue to fulfill its obligation to the people.

Brooks's claim that introducing the effective usage of computers to the legislative process could save billions every year may have sounded outlandish to naysayers. By 1969, however, he had solid evidence to show the scale of possible savings. Each year the Bureau of the Budget produced an estimate on how much had changed under the new computer management system set up by the Brooks Bill in 1965. In 1969 alone, the total amount saved by the government was estimated at half a billion dollars.

DARPA: By 1967, the Department of Defense already constituted 63 percent of the federal government's annual computer usage budget of $1.1 billion. As often is the case with technological advancements, private industry needed some encouragement from the military. This phenomenon was so steeped in history that the Pentagon had actually created a division for it, the Defense Advanced Research Projects Agency, or DARPA.

By the middle of the 1960s, several of the largest research universities around the country had room-sized supercomputers that were designed to work on different tasks. Most were made by the computer giants IBM, DEC (Digital Equipment Corporation), Xerox, and General Electric, and they often had a discrete focus, such as database management, simulations, or graphics.

A single computer system could maintain separate accounts for as many as a few hundred individual users, many of whom could communicate with one another from terminals of the same system, exchanging messages or files. Different computer systems, however, remained unconnected. "Each of those little communities was an island, isolated from others," according to technology historian Marc Weber. The machines frequently used different coding schemes for representing information. The IBM System 360, for example, used EBCDIC (Extended Binary Coded Decimal Interchange Code) while some of the others used ASCII (American Standard Code for Information Interchange). These were binary languages representing text, numbers, or characters with sequences of zeros and ones. This was the next generation of data processing from the punch-card machines that were developed in the 1950s. With those machines, the binary options were determined by the presence or absence of holes at predefined points on a card, i.e., had the paper been punched through or not. These cards, often called Hollerith cards, had evolved from textile looms and automated machines like organ players from the century before. Inventor Herman Hollerith had chosen to use punched cards to store and process information in his tabulating machines, which were first widely used in the 1890 U.S. census. In computing, a lowercase "j" in ASCII, for example, would become "1101010," while a question mark would be rendered as "0111111," but in another coding scheme, they would be altogether different.

The lack of connectedness meant that if researchers from Boston wanted to access information from a university in California, they had to physically travel to that university. Research was the core business of these institutions, which naturally bred reluctance to then share their proprietary systems with others.

The tremendous inefficiencies this created, however, were not acceptable at the Pentagon, and data technology would not move forward if such lags were allowed to continue. DARPA made firm demands and corralled several top universities into a consortium called ARPANET, a private data network that connected computers from the University of California at Los Angeles (UCLA), the University of Utah, the University of California at Santa Barbara, and Stanford Research Institute (SRI).

Each of these institutions possessed complex computers with esoteric names like Sigma7, SDS940, and PDP10. The researchers at these different institutions could not force the computers to be compatible with one another, but they could control the way information would be sent and received. Using theoretical protocols, computer scientists in the U.K. and the U.S. were simultaneously discovering how to send "packets" of data over existing telephone lines. The original host computer would push the information to a local router, or IMP (Interface Message Processor) machine, which would break the message down into packets and send it over existing telephone lines to another IMP, which would then unpack or decipher the message and deliver it to its host computer, where the message would be seen by a person.

FIRST WEB MESSAGE: On October 29, 1969, almost four years to the day after Johnson signed the Automatic Data Processing Act into law in the study on his ranch, the first data message was transmitted between two of the ARPANET computers. Using a teletype terminal at UCLA, a graduate student sent a message to a professor and data programmer at the Stanford Research Institute, located 350 miles north. The student was attempting to log in to the SRI system. Hence, the first message to be sent through what would become the foundation of the Internet was simply an "L" and then an "O." The SRI system crashed before it could receive the "G."

The computers were rebooted, and about thirty minutes later, around 10:30 p.m., the message went through successfully. The objective had not been to establish a network. The network was a means to an end. The researchers needed a manner in which they could send and receive each other's data. Bill Duvall, the data architect and software implementer at Stanford, later spoke about the significance of that small success during an interview to celebrate the fortieth anniversary of the Internet.

The ability to basically break down the language barrier if you will. To have two really dissimilar computers talking to one another. That was huge because until then if you say "my file is in 'ASCII'" and somebody else would say "well, our machine is 'EBCDIC,'" you'd go [laughs], "Bummer!" They would never get translated. There were really some barriers that couldn't be crossed. I thought the idea of being able to, basically, cross that barrier so you could have different machines talking to one another was huge.

This achievement was precisely what Brooks had been fighting for as early as 1962. It did not garner headlines, and its significance did not fully register, even on those who were involved. A sea change was underway in the manner in which information was organized and exchanged. Like many great leaps forward in human progress, this advancement and others in computing technology developed in spurts and sometimes simultaneously around the developed world. Over the next five years, the first few experimental computer networks successfully transmitted electronic data between remote locations through a variety of different computing protocols. Brooks's contributions came from his being one of the few government leaders to take a long-term comprehensive look at what this would mean for the world ahead, both at the individual level and for government.

REORGANIZATION DEBATE: Three weeks after the first data communication was transmitted over ARPANET, Brooks appeared in front of the full House Rules Committee and argued against the current version of the congressional reorganization plan they were considering. This was at least his second testimony before the committee that year. He stated:

Although congressional reorganization is not an issue that generates wide constituent interest, the effective functioning of Congress is of primary importance to the American people. If Congress is poorly organized and inefficiently run, it will hurt not just ourselves but all of our citizens.

He went on to disagree with the minutiae of the current version of the reorganization plan, namely the process for hiring minority staff members, the clearance of committee procedures before the House floor, and the proposal that the Appropriations Committee would take on responsibility for reviewing multi-agency programs, an area that had long been within the jurisdiction of his own subcommittee.

Brooks then spent the second half of his testimony before the chairman and committee speaking about two provisions in the proposed legislation regarding the introduction and use of computers in Congress, which he argued were the real meat of the bill.

Congress must move forward in the use of computer techniques if we are to do an effective and efficient legislative job. But, the introduction of computers is difficult. They cost large sums and considerable time is needed to develop the data systems.

For almost ten years, the Government Activities Subcommittee, which I serve as chairman, has been actively involved in the study and investigation of computer acquisition and use in the federal government. As a result of these studies, an entirely new coordinated, business-like approach to the management of computers was adopted in 1965. As a direct result of the subcommittee's work, more than a billion and a half dollars has been saved. Furthermore, additional savings are accruing at the rate of between four and five hundred million dollars annually . . .

The fundamental concept that underlies this significant increase in efficiency in federal computer use and is responsible for these formidable savings in tax funds is a unified, coordinated approach in the acquisition and use of computers in any organization.

From a unified approach, we achieve compatibility. This means that data processed in one computer system can be processed by another. In other words, compatibility means that computers can talk to each other and that the data they collect can be merged and intermingled. This ability will be of immense importance in the use of computers in the Congress.

A unified approach also means the avoidance of duplications and voids in computer systems design. With some computers costing millions of dollars, or renting for hundreds of thousands of dollars a month, we cannot afford unnecessary duplications of computer capability in the Congress. Nor can we afford voids in our computer systems so that the reasonable demands for data that Congress needs will go unanswered because computer technicians failed to discuss systems design and coordinate their efforts at the earliest stage of computer implementation.

He also foresaw that the introduction of computers to both houses of Congress would require some coordination and oversight, a task that he recommended be left to the comptroller general.

Eventually, the reorganization bill passed and the permanent Joint Committee on Congressional Operations committee was created. This "permanent successor" to the earlier committee Brooks had sat on would seek to maintain "Congress's strength and vitality—through continuing review and, as the need arises, recommendation of necessary changes to its organization and operation." The committee was also charged with anticipating the "institutional requirements" necessary for decision-making, holding hearings that examined the branch's functioning, and making recommendations that assisted the "People's Branch to maintain its vitality in the American system."

The introduction of the publication outlining the Joint Committee's purpose and jurisdiction stated:

Congress mirrors the society which it serves and of which it is a part. Changing American lifestyles, increasing social and economic complexity, ever more rapid transportation and pervasive communications, more people who are more directly affected by governmental activity—all are reflected in the national legislature.

As a joint committee, it would be composed of ten legislators, five from the House and five from the Senate, with the chairmanship alternating between the houses every two years. The concept of "even committees" with equal numbers of Democrats and Republicans were a terrible idea in Brooks's mind. The structure kept anyone from taking control, and therefore also kept anyone from taking responsibility. When questioned about this committee in 1971, Brooks said:

The way to run something is to have control. If you've got responsibility, you ought to have control. I'm not for even committees. If the Republicans are responsible for something, I want them to have the control on it; let them do it. We'll file a minority report if we don't agree. But when you have even committees you have very bad compromises. . . Joint committees that are equal—I've got three years' experience to prove that they don't work well. That's a serious mistake.

The following year, once the permanent committee was established, Brooks was selected to become the committee's chairman. Senator Lee Metcalf, a former Democratic representative and Montana State Supreme Court justice, would serve as his vice chairman. The rest of the committee consisted of four senators and four representatives.

The vision for what Congress needed to modernize underwent several revisions before passage. One of those that made it closest to passage was a recommendation from the Rules Committee to establish a committee committed exclusively to studying congressional automatic data processing and information retrieval systems "to determine the feasibility of utilizing these in the operations of Congress." This committee would also have had authority to design policy for the acquisition and use of computers in Congress. The proposed committee did not appear in the ultimate version of the bill that passed. This suited Brooks just fine; since he was now chair of the joint committee, he would use the body for the purpose anyway. He did not guard his intentions; there was even an article in *Business Week* in August 1972 that confirmed he was using the joint committee to "advance computer applications for the benefit of Congress itself."

In the joint committee's formal commission, a significant concern was the Congress's standing in balance with the executive and judicial branches. As political and administrative changes would occur, a body was needed to determine if those changes would "strengthen or weaken Congress's hand in dealing with" the two other branches of government. Brooks's outspoken thoughts about the role of Congress and constitutional bounds of its jurisdiction made him a natural selection as chairman. Congressional leaders, Republican and Democrat alike, would have wanted a tough-as-nails advocate in that position.

Still, the assumed responsibility was awesome. Brooks had chaired his subcommittee since his early days in Congress. Rayburn had seen to it that he would have that experience. This committee was a full standing committee, though, and one shared with the Senate, the House's veritable older brother. This was also a committee that was concerned with the very existence of Congress. The fact that Brooks was entrusted with this terrific amount of responsibility showed, without a doubt, that he had become a leader in Congress.

Senators were understood to be experts in virtually every major legislative matter, foreign and domestic, whereas representatives were usually just expert in one or two areas, such as education or the armed forces. Because of this, senators were known to look down their noses at the representatives at times. Joint committees like the one on congressional operations were prime opportunities for some of this tension to rise, but the senators on the committee were deferential to Brooks. His expertise in government efficiency was widely known and respected. He knew how administrative agencies were to be run.

According to Gene Peters, who served as his top aide on the committee, the staff was non-partisan and came recommended by both the Democrats and Republicans on the committee. The majority did not keep secrets from the minority, a practice that would become more commonplace in the House in the coming decades.

15

Waste

Bill Dawson, Brooks's longtime friend and the chairman of the Government Operations Committee, passed away in November 1970. Dawson had served as an officer in the Army during World War I and then become the first African-American chairman of a standing committee. In addition to helping with Brooks's subcommittee assignment when the young congressman had first come to Washington, Dawson had always been a mentor and an ally. Brooks remembered him fondly as "a very friendly, pleasant, amiable chairman, who was good to me."

Chet Holifield, a Democrat from California whom Brooks also liked, then assumed chairmanship of the Government Operations Committee. Holifield had come to Congress ten years before Brooks and would hold the chairmanship until his resignation in December 1974. Holifield's ascension impacted Brooks by moving him up the ladder in seniority. Brooks was now the second ranking member of the full Government Operations Committee, which continually evaluated government activities and spending.

C-5A GALAXY: Cost overruns for weapons systems no longer surprised most congressmen. A study conducted in 1962 of twelve major programs revealed that they averaged 220 percent of their original total cost. The C-5A Galaxy aircraft from Lockheed was one of the largest aircraft ever built. It was one of the American responses to the increasingly worrying new planes being developed by the Soviet Union. With the possibility of conflict arising in virtually any corner of the world, the ability to move troops and supplies around the globe on short notice became critical.

The C-5A was a feat of engineering. The plane could airlift eighty-one troops to almost anywhere in the world, along with enough pallets of supplies to keep them stocked for weeks. The fuselage was so large and long that the Wright brothers' entire first flight could have been accomplished inside it.

Even larger than the airplane's outsized dimensions and capabilities, however, were the ballooning costs involved in its development and production. Almost as soon as Lockheed won the contract and began production in its Marietta, Georgia, factory, there was such dysfunction with labor and the aircraft's design specifications that the already enormous projected costs had doubled after the first few years.

After the 1962 study on cost overruns, Secretary of Defense Robert McNamara had consequently created the Total Package Procurement procedure, or TPP, which required contractors to submit all stages of costs in their initial bid for the Department of Defense to eliminate overruns. Lockheed had won the bid with an estimated cost of $16.5 million per plane for the first batch produced. Lockheed calculated that it would produce the first run of planes at a loss and then recoup those losses in subsequent orders so that by early 1969 when the second batch was produced, the actual figure had grown to $40 million per plane. This prompted both the House and Senate to take notice and earned newspaper headlines across the country.

Congress had in 1951 directed the Renegotiation Board to ensure that private firms in space and defense contracts were not making excessive profits. The board had been effective initially, according to Brooks. By renegotiating contracts, it had recovered $167 million in 1955 alone. By the early 1970s, however, the board had become, in Brooks's estimation, "almost totally ineffective in guarding the public's interest." He even lambasted the board's operations and results on the floor of the House in 1971. The purchasers did not help the situation much, though Brooks admitted that the Defense Department's wasteful spending habits had good intentions.

I never did feel that they were particularly venal. You know, not a lot of bribery or stealing. It's just mismanagement. They were just careless about it. They're concerned about exotic weapon schemes, primarily, and that's what they

concentrate on. And all of the other material is just kind of set aside. They don't
worry about those things. And yet, they amount to millions of dollars.

WHISTLEBLOWER: A. Ernest Fitzgerald was a mid-level civilian "cost expert"
working for the Pentagon in financial management who in January 1966
discovered cost overruns during a visit to Lockheed's factory in Georgia,
where the C-5A aircraft were being produced. When he alerted Lockheed
to these overruns and asked for further details, the company stonewalled
him. Further snubs only redoubled his efforts, and he developed something
of "religious mission" about getting to the bottom of the overruns. After
almost three years of pressing the issue, Fitzgerald was called in late 1968
by Senator William Proxmire to testify before the Joint Economic Committee, which also had jurisdiction to oversee defense spending. Proxmire
was another congressman who would make his name as a protector against
waste and abuse. Proxmire would, for the following twenty years, present
his "Golden Fleece Award" to whichever federal agencies or offices deserved
it for fleecing taxpayers.

Fitzgerald testified, giving detailed, but not classified, information
about the cost overruns in the C-5A's production. The next year, Air Force
Colonel Kenneth N. Beckman testified in front of Brooks's subcommittee
that two of his civilian bosses had authorized suppressing the cost overruns
by doctoring documents. The reason was that disclosure of the documents
"might put Lockheed's position in the common stock market in jeopardy."

One year after testifying, Fitzgerald was fired. He reported having spent
his last year isolated at work and relegated to meaningless tasks. The osten-
sible reason for his dismissal was a "reorganization and reduction in force,"
and even Nixon took responsibility for the action.

Brooks wrote an open letter to Attorney General John Mitchell three
days after the firing, asking him to initiate an investigation by a federal
grand jury. Brooks's rationale was not that Fitzgerald had been wrongfully
terminated—Brooks even said that he did not know the reason for the
firing—but rather the adverse effect that such firings would have on the
process of congressional oversight. His letter read:

If witnesses are to be fired for cooperating with congressional committees in-vestigating waste and inefficiency in Government operations, the ability of Con-gress to carry out its constitutional responsibilities will be compromised. . . If knowledgeable individuals in the Executive are to be subject to recriminations, to loss of their jobs, and other abuse, then the growing problem of maintaining legislative control over Federal expenditures will become even more intense.

Brooks could also have called Fitzgerald in before the subcommittee to testify, given the body's jurisdiction. Brooks had reportedly considered doing it, though he ultimately chose not to. Jim Lewin, Brooks's chief investigator on the subcommittee, said:

Brooks was very careful not to create the un-American Activities Commit-tee kind of an atmosphere. . . He didn't want to get anywhere close to that. So, it was his view that if you let the contractor put his hand in your pocket, he would go after the agency person who let him do that, rather than the contrac-tor. . . Did not want to get in a situation where his role is to put contractors under oath and try to put them out of business. That's not our role. Our role is to go after the systemic problems. And, we used those as examples, but it's the agency's management that allowed it, or the agency's corruption that nurtured it. That's what needed to be changed. Doing it a case at a time, we'd never get there. You keep just going after the individual contracts without solving the whole problem. That's not our role.

Fitzgerald eventually got his job back, but only after testifying further to the Subcommittee on Economy in Government and lodging a formal com-plaint against Nixon and two of his aides to the Civil Service Commission.

SUPERSONIC TRANSPORT: Around this time, Lockheed's ultra-secretive SR-71 Blackbird spy plane quietly slipped into the U.S. Air Force's arsenal. As a reconnaissance plane designed to fly over heavily defended airspace, its defensive strategy when it detected missiles was to simply outrun them. The aircraft could fly in excess of Mach 3.3 and cruise at an altitude of up to 85,000 feet, high enough that its pilots were required to wear spacesuits.

The plane was remarkable and employed some of the first modern stealth technology. However, it could not take any passengers. Building a commercially viable aircraft with the capacity to travel at that speed was something else altogether.

Competing with other nations to develop supersonic transport (SST) remained the priority, and Russia and Europe continued to make great strides while the U.S. fought to catch up. The Russian Tupolev Tu-144 entered the arena first, in December 1968, and the collaborative Anglo-French Concorde followed suit a few months later.

FAA Administrator McKee was a true believer in the next generation of weapons and technology and spearheaded the effort with aplomb. To encourage the endeavor, the federal government already made an investment of more than $1 billion into the project, which was being executed primarily by Boeing. Brooks had two primary concerns, the first of which was that, under the particular contract the government had with Boeing to develop these planes, the wording of which he described as a "trial lawyer's nightmare," the money was given as an investment and not a grant or subsidy. Boeing was to pay back the full amount once it had successfully produced the aircraft. However, the language in the contract made no mention of taxpayers being able to recoup their investment through royalties if the company ultimately manufactured SST planes that flew at a cruising speed below Mach 2.2. Brooks pointed out that Boeing could very easily decide to cut back on the plane's final speed as a result of operational feasibility or manufacturing costs. If that happened, the "obvious contract deficiencies" meant the public would only receive 13 percent of the original investment, and even that would be predicated on Boeing producing at least 300 planes.

This gap in the contract language was too vague for Brooks to bear. In writing to Secretary of Transportation John Volpe, he characterized the language of that section of the government's contract with Boeing as a mistake that could prove to haunt the government for years.

A few weeks later, Brooks made yet another speech on the House floor and addressed the speaker and other representatives just before they were to vote on an additional $290 million investment into the project. Brooks said:

This is an investment of public monies, not a subsidy nor a gift to the Boeing Company and the airlines. The public has been told that if the SST program is successful, all of the government's $1.3 billion investment will be returned through royalties.

Mr. Speaker, I have studied the contractual arrangement closely, and it is clear that the public's investment will be recouped only if the supersonic transport meets certain specific criteria, such as titanium construction, and [is] designed to cruise at least Mach 2.2. Any other design will not qualify for the much-publicized royalties.

The airlines and Boeing may ultimately agree to a production aircraft that does not meet these criteria. Obviously, much of the technology resulting from our investment in the SST could be used in the manufacture of a slower aircraft. In my opinion, the public should still be entitled to its share of the partnership.

Brooks then submitted into that day's *Congressional Record* a detailed explanation of all the loopholes through which the public could lose its entire investment. This mattered because Boeing and the FAA were still only beginning to grasp how costly it would be to fly at Mach 2.2; there were rumors that because of the costs, each party was quietly looking for ways to kill off the project. General Electric had already proposed a low-speed engine that was being seriously considered.

Brooks's second concern was whether there were adequate economic benefits from having an aircraft that could reach a cruising speed of Mach 2.7 (2,055 mph) rather than one that only flew at Mach 2.2 or even Mach 2.0, which would still be twice the speed of sound. Brooks questioned what there was to be gained in the performance and time saved and, perhaps most importantly, whether there would be enough passengers willing to pay the additional cost. In March, he wrote Volpe:

On at least three occasions over the past several years, the Subcommittee has requested the FAA, and then the Department of Transportation, to provide authoritative data indicating the relationship between the incremental increase in the cost of constructing an SST with a cruising speed of Mach 2.7, as contrasted to the incremental increase in revenues that would be realized from operations at this higher cruising speed.

It was a valid question, and one that others should have been voicing more publicly. In the race to build aircraft continually faster and more impressive than those from rival nations, many officials and technical experts were consumed by questions such as "can it be done" and if so then "how." There were fewer in leadership positions who were asking whether or not faster was worth it or what exactly was the optimal speed. On a sliding scale of cost analysis there was the point where one unit faster no longer represented one more unit of value to the government or to civilian passengers.

Time would show that Brooks had been correct. The various SST programs were short-lived. The Russian Tupolev flew only 102 flights in the 1970s before leaving commercial service, and only fifty-five of those flights included any passengers. A number of in-flight failures, crashes, and structural design flaws rendered it too unreliable almost as soon as it had entered service. The Concorde had a much safer record, flying for twenty-seven years, but was eventually grounded with no follow-up plans for a replacement SST.

FAA HEARINGS: Beyond the very cutting edge of aviation, however, the FAA also continued to bedevil the subcommittee in other ways. According to Brooks, the agency was run by "well-intentioned but not too competent people." Ten years after the FAA had issued its 1961 Project Beacon report on the state of air traffic safety, along with a list of recommendations to be made, there had been no significant upgrades to the country's air traffic control system. The changes would require an expensive, multi-year operation and Brooks suspected that the FAA had issues with making such a large request, especially since just conducting the research to figure out how to spend the money would be expensive in itself. Also holding up the implementation, according to Brooks, were countless problems, from technological limitations to poor management. To determine the specific reasons for the delays, Brooks announced in January 1970 that new hearings would be held on aircraft collision avoidance systems.

Prior to the hearings he declared, "The nation's air traffic control system is on a collision course with disaster." There were already millions of Americans flying around the country every day, yet the safety measures employed by air traffic controllers varied from region to region. One element that particularly concerned Brooks involved the usage of automated collision-avoidance systems. "Bad management, lack of money, and poor contractor performance have severely crippled the nation's air traffic control improvement program," he said.

Adding fuel to the fire were other advances in the commercial airline industry. Planes were getting larger and faster and yet the regulations governing their use remained the same, and were inadequate at that. Just as Brooks announced the additional hearings, Boeing rolled out its new behemoth 747 at Dulles Airport outside Washington, D.C. The 747 dwarfed all other passenger jets. It had two and half times the passenger capacity of the 707, which meant the potential catastrophe from accidents would be that much greater. First Lady Pat Nixon and former FAA Administrator Najeeb Halaby, now chairman of Pan Am Airlines, both took part in the christening of the gigantic aircraft.

After the hearings, the subcommittee presented its findings and conclusions on the state of affairs in air traffic safety in a report to the House. Among the serious problems outlined, it highlighted "a number of complex, interrelated causes for the multi-year delay in providing the Nation's air traffic controllers with the new, advanced, automated control equipment they need to handle the increasing traffic load." To realize implementation of the new automated system, the FAA would require $450–500 million a year from Congress. Brooks reiterated that the FAA was "plagued by poor management and administration," largely ignoring the "reasonable, constructive, business-like recommendations of the Subcommittee and the Comptroller General."

Within the realms of aviation costs and safety, Brooks's concern, like his congressional jurisdiction, did not stop at the Pentagon and airlines. Ever the watchdog for taxpayer money, his attention to detail brought him to the White House in what would be his initial, and least consequential, run-in with the Nixon administration. It had been reported that while he was traveling in Colorado, Nixon had flown his dog, and just his dog, on Air Force One from Washington to have the canine at his side. Every trip and flight hour of Air Force One came with significant costs, both in dollars and in time. Presidential discretion broadly determined when and how those planes were used, but it was understood that the aircraft was to be used for the needs and protection of the president and his family.

Brooks, through his committee, began demanding to see the flight manifests for Air Force One. The president's staff did not appreciate having to do this, but given the subcommittee's broad jurisdiction, they had no choice but to comply. This practice of sending the flight manifests with all passenger and trip details for Air Force One to Brooks's subcommittee became a routine activity that would last into the next administrations, both Republican and Democratic. For Brooks, the matter of oversight had little to do with politics.

By the fall of 1972, Brooks, by his own admission, had failed to effectively exact any changes at the FAA.

In a 1973 hearing, Congress questioned the arrangements between the airline industry and the FAA. Brooks said, " . . . it appears the regulated are regulating themselves. Such a procedure is most unique and requires exceptionally critical oversight." At the same hearing the administrator suggested the current system "recognized the practical necessity of utilizing the technical capabilities of the private sector in administering the many complex certification programs required by law." Brooks had been embarrassed in some of the FAA hearings, as had other members of the subcommittee, when presented with witness testimony that no one but an expert could decipher. But he was vocal about the inability of congressmen to become experts on everything. This limitation, however, did not mean they could not effectively manage taxpayer dollars. In describing his role as a public servant, Brooks often repeated a line from his friend and former Comptroller Joseph Campbell, "It doesn't take a hen to smell a rotten egg."

The advancement of the electric lightbulb was a clear example of that. Brooks had begun the investigation not with any technical background in electricity or manufacturing, only with his frustration as a regular consumer. Though it required grueling work, several years of hearings, and two separate congressional reports, the subcommittee's investigation eventually bore fruit, representing "a victory of the first magnitude," according to *U.S. Consumer* magazine. In January 1970, all lightbulb manufacturers were required to disclose life and output details on the bulb packaging. Max Kampelman, moderator of the weekly TV show *Washington Week in Review,* said:

> *For Congressman Brooks, the victory brought no headlines. For the consumer, it will mean a saving of millions of dollars. For the political scientist, it is another piece of evidence as to why the Congress of the United States, with all its limitations, survives as the oldest and most effective representative body in the world.*

16

Procurement

In early 1972, Brooks was invited to speak at the Watergate Hotel in Washington before an audience of procurement specialists from the American Bar Association and the National Contracts Management Association. His talk encapsulated the essence of all he had fought for in Congress and his philosophy on the duties of congressmen, their civilian counterparts, and oversight bodies in protecting the American people.

Because of the virtually unlimited scope of our responsibilities, members of Congress for the most part must, through necessity, be "generalists." In many instances, we simply do not have the time to acquire and maintain a detailed, intimate knowledge of every facet of the complex subjects that pass through the legislative process. Fortunately, however, that is not fatal. . . As you are well aware, just staying on top of the federal government's vast array of procurement regulation is a full-time job. Divorcing yourselves from the day-to-day application of the regulations to analyze their deficiencies and identify possible improvements is an even more difficult and time-consuming task, but occasionally we should make that effort.

The federal government is a unique animal when it comes to buying the goods and services it needs. We buy items no one else buys; we buy in quantities most people never dream of; we deal in figures the average person can't even comprehend. Over the years, it is interesting to see what we have done to the relatively simple contract principles of common law in an effort to protect the public and, at the same time, to afford fair and equal competition among those interested in providing for the government's needs.

In the last year or so, the term "contract overrun" has become an ugly word throughout the nation. "Contract overrun" is really nothing new. It is just a new term applied to an old problem. Deficiencies in federal procurement practices, particularly in the defense area or during war or national emergency, date back to the founding of the nation. The manifestation of these deficiencies, however, constantly change. At times there have been solutions, and, on occasion, we have settled for "apparent" solutions. For example, we soon learned that "cost plus percentage-of-cost" contracts weren't necessarily the most economical way to buy.

Regardless of what we might do, the procurement problem—to some degree—will probably always be with us. As the nation's population increases beyond 200 million, the size of our government will increase accordingly. Furthermore, we are in the midst of a worldwide technological advance and priority realignment in which our defense and social programs will demand an increasing participation by government at all levels.

The complexity of what the government procures and the unit cost of the items will continue to increase as we strive to keep pace with hostile nations abroad and meet social needs at home. The procurement of these goods and services from the private sector is and will continue to be an essential element in government operations. The federal government's procurement concept must, like the gyroscope, maintain stability while in motion. To come to rest would cause stagnation and a serious disruption in the nation's private enterprise system as well as in the effectiveness of the government.

Since the beginning of the military buildup before World War II, the Defense Department and other agencies of government have sought to solve procurement problems by a constant proliferation of regulations. On occasion, there have been daring innovations, some of which have been successful and others have failed. Responsible officials in the executive branch must continue to explore new procurement procedures, and I do not believe that the Congress or the public generally should react in a wholly negative manner when some of these improvisations or attempted improvements do not succeed. I would caution, however, that it might be ill-advised to improvise in multibillion dollar programs such as the C-5A where the cost of failure to the public would be so pronounced.

It is axiomatic that those most acutely familiar with the facts and closest to the problem area have a definite advantage in identifying problems and the optimum solution to them. For this reason, continued improvement in the Government's procurement system depends largely upon procurement officials in the Executive Branch and, to a significant but lesser extent, their counterparts in industry. (I say "to a lesser extent" because I don't want those contractors improving the government's procurement system all the way to the bank.) It is largely on the knowledge and understanding of these procurement officials that the president and Congress must rely in formulating new policies and procedures to meet constantly changing requirements.

During the next decade, I foresee an increase of legislative interest in procurement and a more decisive participation in achieving a solution to the procurement problem. Although Congress may have to adopt some statutory changes such as those dealing with the procurement of architects and engineers to overcome the recommendations of the comptroller general, the basic procurement statutes are generally sound. Both the Air Force Procurement Act of 1947, as amended, and the Federal Property Act of 1949, as amended, are clean, well-drafted statutes. Within the context of these statutes, the executive can structure many improvements in the procurement system in keeping with present legislative intent. As I see the problem, it isn't that our procurement statutes are deficient. The problem lies in establishing efficiency and effectiveness in carrying out those statutory directives. This is primarily the responsibility of the executive branch. For this reason, the principal impact on procurement so far as Congress is concerned will come from legislative oversight of executive operations.

As you know, Congress has approved a Commission on Federal Procurement, the recommendations of which will receive closest scrutiny and consideration when the commission's work is completed. In addition, Congress has authorized the study and development of uniform cost accounting standards, the application of which will have a significant impact on federal procurement and on congressional review of procurement activities. The Government Activities Subcommittee, which I serve as chairman, only recently completed a study of the Renegotiation Board which shows that its operations are little more than a façade and that virtually all of the one hundred largest corporations in America—doing 70 percent of defense work—totally escape renegotiation year after year. The committee recommended that the board be given the tools it needs to effectively carry out its functions and that it then be expected to do just that.

The most fundamental element of change in the congressional role with regard to procurement will be found in efforts now underway to improve the flow of data and information to the Congress and its committees. This will be primarily through the application of advanced computer techniques. The increase in the quality as well as the quantity of information Congress will have at its fingertips will make it possible for Congress to spot deficiencies in the procurement cycle at about the same time they should be apparent to officials in the executive branch.

Within three or four years, capability of this kind will begin to give Congress the information it needs for full participation in efforts to improve the federal government's procurement system. Using this capability, the problems that we can identify today, such as the understatement of project program costs, contract overruns, and excessive profits on defense contracts, should come within analytical control. We will also be able to identify much more quickly erratic and extraordinary jumps in expenditures for the procurement of common items. We will also be able to make much more accurate and timely comparisons with previous expenditures and predicted future outlays.

Hopefully, this increase in data and information will give both the executive and legislative branches a stronger position in dealing with problem areas we have been unable to effectively reach in the past. We hear a lot these days about bad quality and poor service. The federal government is the biggest consumer in the nation. It undoubtedly faces these same problems. The federal government, however, has more clout in the marketplace. It can, and should, demand not only that the initial costs be the lowest possible but that the item received be reasonably capable of performing its intended function. That is the job of you procurement specialists.

The American consumer is looking to the federal government for help. You have a direct role in extending that help. As the procurement of goods and services for the government becomes increasingly complex, it will become more difficult but certainly not impossible to assure that the government makes the best buy. With vastly better, more timely data from new information systems, we in Congress will be watch-dogging the procurement process as never before. We will be working to help make the system meet the highest standards of efficiency and effectiveness that the public justifiably demands.

Brooks and the other members of the Government Activities Subcommittee had held countless hearings and investigated cases from all across the government. There were, however, by 1972, a few cases that stood out in Brooks's mind—the GSA's awarding of contracts in the Cuba nickel plant, the advances in ADP policy, transportation safety—and the next would be focused on procurement policy. This topic, again, did not capture the imaginations or hearts of constituents, but for Brooks it was part and parcel with his congressional duty.

Over the years, I have utilized the subcommittee as a means of carrying out my strong philosophy favoring efficient and effective government that cares about the taxpayer's dollar and gets the most service to the public from each dollar the government spends.

GAO: The General Accounting Office (GAO), an independent agency, was charged with providing audit, evaluation, and investigative services to the president and Congress for the purposes of achieving greater efficiency in public expenditures. According to Ernest Baynard, Brooks's lead staffer, the GAO was also one of three executive agencies not worth speaking to. They rarely kept their word. Instead, staffers were instructed to carry out all communication in writing so there would be an actual record of what was asked and answered.

Brooks also put pressure on the office in his role as chairman of the Joint Committee on Congressional Operations, requesting by letter to the new Comptroller General Elmer Staats that he prepare a statement of his plans for upgrading their services according to the specifications of the 1970 Reorganization Act. Brooks was not picking on the GAO; he made identical requests to other offices such as the Congressional Research Service. Brooks's efforts focused on the "standardization of executive information systems as a means of improving the quality of fiscal, budgetary, and program data and information available to Congress." He insisted that the entities that provided Congress with valuable audit information be as organized and efficient as possible to ensure adequate review.

Chairman Holifield of the Government Operations Committee had held hearings on GAO audits of defense spending and had issued a report that was critical of their practices and found that the GAO had been unfairly aggressive in its auditing of defense contracts. Brooks disagreed. He felt the office's audits under former Comptroller Joe Campbell had been "hard-hitting and had meaning." Brooks took issue with Holifield's approach in reining in the GAO, though there was little he could do about it. Holifield's district was not heavily dependent on defense industry work, though there were others in the California delegation whose districts were. Some suspected at the time that Holifield had felt pressure from his colleagues to use his position as chairman to muzzle the GAO, an outcome that in Brooks's eyes diminished Congress's ability to oversee contracting.

ARCHITECTS & ENGINEERS BILL: Brooks had mentioned in his speech to the procurement specialists that one area of contracting that required prompt congressional action was the process for selecting architects and engineers. Though some good practices were employed, the process lacked the statutory rigor that Brooks felt should guide all federal spending. Architect and engineer (A/E) firms were defined as "those professional services of an architectural or engineering nature as well as incidental services that members of these professions and those in their employ may logically or justifiably perform." Since 1939, the selection of A/E firms for working on public buildings and spaces had been loosely guided by budgetary legislation, but that system lacked standardization, was racked with inefficiencies, and instituted a cap on fees of 6 percent of estimated construction costs, a limit that A/E firms found innovative ways to circumvent. Prior to that, government employees, instead of private firms, had been responsible for the construction of public works projects.

With the Federal Property and Administrative Services Act of 1949, which had established the General Services Administration, nearly all government procurement now came under the new agency's jurisdiction. For public projects, a federal agency would publicly announce the work and then receive bids from competing firms with their proposed scope of work, competencies, and estimated cost for the job. Often, the selection process would suffer from the agency's outsized preference for whichever firm or individual came in with the lowest bid. This process was poor practice for several reasons. First, it required the firms submitting bids to quantify the costs for their creative process before an adequate consultation with the purchasing agency about what they would like from the project. Second, and more consequentially, simply selecting whichever firm had provided the lowest bid led to the selection of lower-quality firms that were less qualified to perform the work.

There were other selection processes, including Qualification-Based Selection (QBS), in which providers of architect and engineering service would compete for a contract almost entirely based on their "qualifications and demonstrated competence." The issues of price and cost would only be considered during the negotiation phase with the leading bidder, after the selection period but before the contracting period. After an agency publicly announced work through a request for quotation, a selection committee would create a shortlist of the top firms and issue them with a request for proposal, in which the firms would outline more specifically their vision for the work.

The selection committee would evaluate the proposals and rank them in order of quality without seeing the attached costs proposed. Once ranked, they would reach out to the top firm to begin negotiating on specifics and cost. If an accord could not be reached, the selection committee would then move on to the second-ranked firm, and so on. This method was useful in ensuring that the top-quality service providers would be selected rather than the cheapest. Though it was commonly employed, it was not the law of the land for executive agencies.

After a lengthy investigation, the GAO submitted a report to Congress in April 1967, in which Comptroller General Staats requested it "clarify by legislation whether this traditional [QBS] selection system is authorized under appropriate federal procurement statutes" in selecting architect and engineering services under federal procurement statutes. QBS had been widely practiced for years, but it required formalization by statute. Most A/E firms and organizations enthusiastically welcomed this change. In anticipation of the report, several of the largest industry associations had organized the year before to establish the Council on Federal Procurement of Architectural & Engineering Services, or COFPAES, which served as "the unified voice of the architectural, engineering (A/E) and related services profession on issues related to federal contracting."

In May 1970, Brooks introduced his Architects and Engineers Selection Bill, which also would come to be known as "The Brooks A/E Act" or simply "The Brooks Act." The purpose of the bill, as stated in the legislation text, was to

> *place in statutory form the traditional system Government agencies have used for more than 30 years in the procurement of architect/engineer services. The bill would amend the Federal Property and Administrative Services Act of 1949 to establish a Federal policy for the selection of qualified architects and engineers to design and provide consultant services in carrying out Federal construction and related programs. The bill expressly declares it to be the policy of the Federal Government to negotiate contracts for such professional services on the basis of demonstrated competence and qualifications for the type of professional service required at fair and reasonable prices.*

Brooks understood that, within the bureaucratic context of the federal government, by allowing the fee to be even one of the determining factors in awarding contracts, it would inevitably become a primary factor, and thereby downgrade the qualifications and experience of the firms in the selection process. For the sake of spurring further competition, Brooks also argued that under the selection processes his bill sought to codify, A/E firms would be required to essentially compete twice for government work: first on the basis of their qualifications and second on the reasonableness of their fee.

There were plenty of parties who opposed this legislation, many of whom favored continuing with the "loosely constructed, open-ended contracts" that had been part of the status quo. Quite obviously, standardizing such procedures would redefine the way these firms sought and earned money from the federal government, and excess profits would become much more difficult to reap.

The GAO also feared that the Brooks Bill might actually reduce competition and increase costs to the purchasing agencies. Even the comptroller general disagreed with some of the provisions in the bill, namely that the fee would not be a factor in determining the relative qualifications.

For greater clarity, Congress established a Procurement Commission to review procurement laws and policies. After careful study of issues with the process and the details of Brooks's legislation, that commission submitted recommendations in favor of Brooks's approach. However, that same commission then created another panel, under the leadership of one of the comptroller's deputies, which came out in full support of the comptroller's positions. Given Brooks's respect for Staats, the congressman revisited his legislation and even adapted some of the language to address the comptroller's concerns.

The 1970 version of the bill passed in the House but then died in Senate, so during the following Congress, on February 1, 1972, Brooks reintroduced it. The most surprising fact was that the bill had passed through committee to receive a full vote in the first place. It had been considered and debated within the Government Operations Committee, in which Brooks now ranked more senior than all but one member. However it was that one member, Chairman Holifield, who was the most vocal critic of the legislation and its strongest opponent. Holifield, who was thought to be hostile to architects and engineers, had thrown his weight against it, twice. Despite bearing the brunt of Holifield's opposition, the bill passed through the committee for a full vote.

Prevailing over the direct wishes of a committee chairman within his own committee was a difficult thing to do. Doing it in back-to-back Congresses spoke to Brooks's increasing clout as a legislator. It also pointed to the ideological rift between Brooks and the chairman, twenty years his senior. They butted heads repeatedly on numerous issues, and Brooks would not retreat. William Jones, a Brooks staffer, said at the time, "the way they talk sometimes I think they will never speak to each other again. . . but they do the next day."

The bill eventually passed the House again, and the Senate finally approved it on October 14, 1972. It was formally signed as Public Law 92-582 two weeks later.

Remarkably, the law remained fully enacted and virtually unscathed from legislative attacks or regulations intended to weaken its provisions.

Government officials estimated that the A/E Act saved the government "billions in administrative and program costs" over the course of the following four decades. Staffer Jim Lewin remembered, "Through the oversight of the GSA, we looked at all GSA central procurements for other agencies under the Brooks Act. Every year they reported to him how much competition had saved the government, and it was always billions of dollars every year."

Some thirty years later, the American Council of Engineering Companies (ACEC) would even honor Brooks with its 2003 Distinguished Award of Merit. According to Jeff Potter, president of the American Institute of Architects, the Brooks Act "set the standard for better and more cost-effective design of federal buildings." The chairman of COFPAES, Christopher Stone, would later say:

> A further testament to Mr. Brooks's legacy is the fact that almost every state has enacted its own state law, known as a "mini-Brooks Act," and the process is included in the American Bar Association's Model Procurement Code for State and Local Government. The United States is a better place for Jack Brooks's service in Congress. The American people enjoy and benefit from the wise investment of public dollars in architecture, engineering and related services that has enhanced our quality of life, saved tax dollars, and placed an emphasis on competition in procurement based on demonstrated competence and qualifications.

An additional effect of the legislation, according to Potter, was that it "in turn, ushered in a new era of open and fair competitive bidding that ensured that the most qualified designers were selected for federal design contracts." What that led to was a "new generation of better-designed, more sustainable, and higher-performing federal facilities that last longer and are more cost-effective."

The act had further implications outside of the A/E realm. Many federal procurement procedures needed to be reviewed and updated to save costs and increase competition, those at the Department of Defense most notably. Before long, Brooks would leverage statutes from the Brooks Act to spearhead legislation to completely rewrite the government's procurement laws.

17

Family Life

In private, Brooks found himself relishing the comforts and joy of family life. He and Charlotte continued to settle down and establish roots in the Washington area. As young Jeb turned three years old, they adopted another child, a daughter, Kate. Three years later, their second daughter, Kimberly, would be born. Charlotte had stopped working, and the family moved across the Potomac River into a house with a one-car garage in the quiet suburb of McLean, Virginia. Brooks still worked long days, but he enjoyed being able to come home and spend evenings with the family. If he worked too late, he would warm up the dinner Charlotte left for him in the countertop microwave oven they had recently bought.

Brooks felt most comfortable when busy, though. He spent many weekend days working in the backyard. His former intern Nick Lampson fondly remembered Brooks inviting him and another intern over for dinner one weekend. Brooks had told them they would be having chicken and to come early in the afternoon. When the two young men arrived, Brooks met them at the door and said, "Well, boys. Come in, and we're gonna have dinner. But first we're gonna take a tree down in the backyard."

McLean was a comfortable area, popular with politicians, and a short drive down the George Washington Parkway to the National Mall. Senator Strom Thurmond lived two houses away, and former Virginia governor Linwood Holton lived two houses down on the other side.

LBJ's Friendship: Brooks remained in close touch with Johnson, who now spent almost all of his time at the ranch outside of Austin. The two couples stayed in touch after Johnson left Washington. No birthdays or major holidays went by without some notice of the high regard in which they held each other. One time that Brooks made the trip to see Johnson, the two went for a ride in Johnson's new Bell helicopter. When Brooks later recounted this to a new FAA director, the director was aghast. There had recently been serious complications with that type of helicopter, so Brooks asked the director to draft a memo, which Brooks then forwarded to Johnson, who replied, "The Bell people have been here and thoroughly checked out my helicopter, but, I want to thank you for your precautions and, most of all, for your concern. It was good to visit with you and I'll make sure it won't be too long before we do it again."

The former president relished the attention Brooks and Charlotte still paid to him and Lady Bird. Though he could not attend one joint birthday party they had invited him to in August 1970, he replied, "The best part of having a birthday is hearing from old and beloved friends and you are among the most beloved I possess." A short while later, Johnson did attend an appreciation dinner for Brooks at Beaumont's Red Lion Inn before the 1970 election, just as he had done once as president in 1968. Both times Johnson appeared without public notice, but the second appearance surprised even Brooks.

I had invited him, and I thought he might be able to come, slip off. By God, he did, just slipped off there in his own plane, flew in there and brought Luci and Pat. Came at the last minute. Didn't make a speech. . . if he makes a speech that's serious, they say he's running for president, trying to tell everybody how to run the world. If he makes a speech that's just friendly and quiet, they say, "That's all he had to say." But we did have a wonderful visit after that party, sat around and talked and visited.

Brooks also kept his older friend up to date, sending him news clippings when relevant, such as when Johnson and Lady Bird had announced they would turn over their 201-acre ranch to the public for preservation, and the *Houston Post* ran an article titled, "Bonanza on the Pedernales."

Brooks recalled one visit to the ranch in 1971:

We went out there and took Jeb and Kate. Before Kim was born. Jeb was about four. He invited the whole University of Texas football team, 'cause he thought that would please Jeb. Now Jeb didn't know one end of the football from the other, but that was a nice gesture. Then he gave the children rides in the bubble-front helicopter. Very, very thoughtful. Fun things.

LBJ's DEATH: Those few years were a special time for both men, but unfortunately Johnson died on January 22, 1973, at age sixty-four. The next day on the floor of the House, Brooks delivered these remarks:

> *Mr. Speaker, America has lost a great leader and I have lost a longtime personal friend.*
>
> *Lyndon Johnson was a man of rare capability, compassion and understanding, who wanted to be remembered as the President who did the most for the well-being and dignity of our citizens. History will reflect he was a great President and, as time passes, America will become increasingly grateful for all he did. I have known President Johnson and his lovely wife, Lady Bird, throughout my years in public office. We served together in the Congress and I worked with him to get his programs enacted when he was in the White House.*
>
> *Some of America's greatest moments in history occurred because Lyndon Johnson was President. All Americans live better because of his concern for people, for equality, for health care for the elderly, for opportunity for the poor, for the sanctity of the American Democratic system.*
>
> *I shall be forever grateful that he was my friend. Although he had the greatest power that man had ever known, he never lost his humanity. He could be abrupt and overbearing when he needed to get things done in a hurry, but he was never petty or mean. He somehow always found time to think of his family, his friends and those who needed his help.*
>
> *Just this month I visited with him in New Orleans and a few weeks before, he had Charlotte, my children and me as his guests at the Ranch. He seemed to be enjoying the chance he finally had to visit with his family and his friends. He took Jeb and Kate to see his ranch, the cattle and some of the game he kept there. He thoroughly enjoyed himself and the children returned his warm affection.*
>
> *I regret that he did not live longer to enjoy this leisure and time to indulge*

himself in some of the pleasures we take as common but that duty denied him—
a quiet family life—undisturbed visits with his wife, children and grandchil-
dren—time to relax and reflect on his accomplishments.

I had hoped that he would live another thirty years. Although this could not
be, I am grateful that I knew him, I am grateful for his advice and counsel—I
am grateful that we had him as our President. Time will honor this man in a
way that no amount of public acclaim ever could during his lifetime.

Former Texas governor John Connally delivered the eulogy at Johnson's graveside services. By then Connally had switched to the Republican Party and he and Brooks had developed a contentious relationship. In a short but conciliatory note, Brooks thanked him for his kind words "about the accomplishments and humanity of this most remarkable man." Brooks also wrote Nixon and thanked him for the kindness he had extended to Lady Bird and the rest of the Johnson family. He concluded that letter:

Being a former President is not the leisurely retirement that many envision.
I have heard President Johnson speak many times of how considerate and help-
ful you have been in helping him with transportation, security, use of the Blair
House, and numerous other arrangements. He always commented that you did
this willingly and without difficulty or fanfare.

A few months after Johnson's death, Lady Bird reached out to Brooks one more time:

Dear Jack, Lyndon always valued your support and friendship on the floor of
the House and I know he would have been grateful that you stood by him one
last time in the rotunda. Thank you for that final honor, and know that we are
still remembering your tribute with warmth and appreciation. Sincerely and
[handwritten] Affectionately, Bird

With the passing of political giants like Rayburn, Johnson, Thomas, and Dawson, Brooks lost most of those bosom friends whom he could also call mentors. Under their tutelage, Brooks had gained a deep understanding of congressional politics during his first twenty years in the House and had risen steadily through the ranks.

Along with Brooks, a number of his contemporaries also began to assume leadership roles with serious weight.

CARL ALBERT: Carl Albert, or the "Little Giant," as the diminutive statesman from Oklahoma was known, had entered Congress six years before Brooks and had been brought into Rayburn's inner circle just as quickly. Albert represented a district right across the Red River from Rayburn's, and Rayburn had said he liked the dirt under Albert's nails. Albert was tapped by the Speaker to become House majority whip because of the Oklahoman's work ethic and decency. Albert then rose to majority leader in 1962 and finally to Speaker in 1971.

Besides sharing whiskeys with Brooks at the Board of Education, Albert was also Brooks's friend and a regular guest of the Johnsons at the White House. Johnson and Albert had been close, and Albert's support had been vital to the passage of several Great Society programs, notably the Social Security Act of 1965, which had established Medicare. Brooks knew Johnson was influential in Albert's selection as Speaker, but another congressman, who at the time of Albert's appointment spoke to the *Washington Post* on the condition of anonymity, was even more frank about the nature of congressional succession. "The leaders of the House are chosen by the dead hand of the past. Carl will be speaker because Sam Rayburn picked him to be Whip in 1954. No one can beat someone who is on the ladder. The people here today don't really choose him. He was chosen in 1954."

As speaker from 1971 to 1977, Albert would be at the center of national events and a strong ally for Brooks in the coming years.

There were other friends rising in the ranks. In the fall of 1972, Dolph Briscoe was elected governor of Texas. Hale Boggs from New Orleans had just become majority leader, and Jim Wright from Fort Worth was on a path that would end at the House speakership.

Other changes were underway as well. Manny Celler had been chairman of the House Judiciary since 1949, save Brooks's first two years when Republicans were briefly in the majority. Celler had been chairman of the

Judiciary when it passed civil rights legislation in 1964 and 1965; he had also been chairman of the Judiciary subcommittee, of which Brooks was a member, where the legislation had originated. Celler, a Democrat from Brooklyn, had no qualms about going after those in his own party when the situation warranted it. He did not bow to Democratic presidents and never lost sight of the role he, as an individual, played in government. If Brooks, thirty-four years his junior, had been looking for a chairman to emulate, he could not have found a better one than Celler.

In June of 1972, Celler lost the Democratic primary election after forty-nine years in the House, making him the most senior congressman to do so. He was defeated by the young Elizabeth Holtzman, a liberal from Harvard who would later win the general election and be one of the freshmen sitting on the House Judiciary Committee during the impeachment inquiry.

That an almost completely unknown candidate had come in and defeated the sitting chairman of the House Judiciary Committee, one of the highest ranking positions in Congress, was a tremendous shock, and it would not happen again until 1994, though Jack Brooks could not have foreseen that yet.

PART III

The Meanest Man in Congress

I just tried to be fair. And when you're fair, that generally screws the Republicans.

— JACK BROOKS

18

The Executioner

The 1968 election significantly altered the political landscape in ways that would become increasingly evident years later. Nixon won five Southern states, even with George Wallace drawing off many like-minded voters. The Democratic candidate, Hubert Humphrey, squeaked out a win in Texas, the House remained in Democratic hands, and Brooks was reelected handily with a solid 60 percent of the vote. However, the conservative Republican "Southern Strategy" that began in 1964 with Barry Goldwater now gathered steam with Nixon's coded appeals to voters using slogans such as "states' rights" and "law and order." The shift away from the dominance of the Democratic Party in the South was starting to take hold and would eventually usher Ronald Reagan into the White House and change the complexion of Texas—and the nation's politics.

While those cultural, political, and demographic changes were underway, suspicions about Nixon's personal politics and practices arose not long after he took office. In 1970, the president persuaded Congress to give him the power to impose controls in wages, prices, and rents. Most economists and public officials knew that instituting such controls amounted to trying to micromanage the U.S. economy, an unimaginably vast and dynamic system, and most doubted that anyone would be foolish enough to try. While there was no consensus on the effectiveness of using wage and price controls, the nation was concerned about rising inflation and wanted action.

As president, historians have noted, Nixon was generally unenthusiastic about domestic policy, preferring to delegate his administration's policy design to a few trusted advisers rather than trudging through the weeds himself.

Foreign policy was what concerned him day and night. To him, that was the only thing really worth a commander-in-chief's attention.

ECONOMIC AND DOMESTIC POLICY: Nixon, however, also believed in political expediency; one year after receiving the legislative authority to alter the economy, he announced a package of sweeping changes dubbed the New Economic Policy, which he expected would stabilize the economy, halt inflation, and reduce unemployment. Politicians and policy experts still argue over many of those decisions, including one to end the gold standard, the arrangement that backed every American dollar by actual gold stores. He also ordered surcharges on imports and mandatory caps on all wages, prices, rents, and salaries.

As fortune would have it, Nixon was spurred into this decision by the prodding of his newly appointed treasury secretary, the now-Republican John Connally, who had advised him that no power should ever go unused. It was a bold move by the administration, and, as Nixon had correctly calculated, the initial public response was very positive. Both liberals and conservatives in the press emphatically applauded the move, citing it as an act of courage and decisiveness.

The 1972 elections were coming up, rising inflation was putting pressure on the economy, and voters were growing increasingly resentful of the foreign producers and currency speculators they blamed for the decline at home. Nixon's plan had a comforting sense of nationalism and would serve as an immediate stopgap measure to ease some of the economic pain voters were feeling until after the polls.

Politically, the move was brilliant. Economically, it was ill-advised, shortsighted, and would contribute significantly to woes that would reverberate throughout the rest of the 1970s. But that did not matter yet. In early discussions about his reelection campaign with his chief of staff Bob Haldeman, Nixon revealed his top priority, "I really want the economy to boom beginning in July 1972."

BROOKS'S DISTRUST OF NIXON: Brooks saw no consistency in the president's economic policies and characterized them as "increasingly confusing

and questionable." By the start of 1972, concerns over the economy dominated the letters and wires Brooks received from constituents back home.
The congressman wondered why Nixon had waited for the economy to
slip for two years before taking action. As Brooks wrote one constituent:

> *The program would have been much more effective if it had been initiated
> sooner, before the trend toward price and wage increases became a nationally
> established pattern.*

By early 1973, Nixon also had begun encroaching on Congress's authority
by halting funds to new construction projects. One of these hit the Ninth
District directly, a $1.9 million project to enhance a forty-foot channel in
Galveston, a project that had significant impact on the area. Brooks told
the *Galveston News*:

> *This delay is another example of the president's determination to ignore the
> will of Congress by refusing to carry out projects and programs the Congress has
> authorized by law.*

Brooks also began to frequently note that Nixon's economic program
was failing to halt inflation or create jobs.

Though the nation lauded Nixon's breakthrough on China, the administration's contradictory policies and actions in Southeast Asia did not help the
president's standing. Public opposition to the continued fighting in Vietnam
had reached a fever pitch and "OUT NOW!" placards were ubiquitous in
cities across the country. For Brooks, who had continued to back Nixon on
Vietnam through years of ebbing support (as he had Johnson and Kennedy
before him), the last straw came with the White House decision to begin
bombing operations in Cambodia. Brooks released a statement regarding
Nixon's bombing of Cambodia and his veto of a congressional mandate to
cut off funding for the program.

REELECTED!: Nixon won a landslide election in 1972, but the seeds of his
undoing were planted earlier. In June the year before, on the heels of the

release of the Pentagon Papers, Nixon authorized the creation of a secret special investigations unit, composed of key staff and former intelligence officers, which would operate behind the scenes, at his discretion. David Young, who served as an aide to Henry Kissinger, supervised several of the unit's operators. The story goes that when an older relative of Young's learned that he was working to fix leaks in the White House, she told him, "Your grandfather would be proud of you. . . he was a plumber." Young and his cohort later laughed at the misunderstanding, but after that, the covert unit simply referred to themselves as "the Plumbers."

Their work began with a few "black-bag operations" to discredit Ellsberg and others and then soon branched out into a complex operation of domestic surveillance, burglary, and corruption that included operatives from the FBI and the CIA.

WATERGATE BREAK-IN: Despite his abilities and political successes, intense suspicion and paranoia dominated Nixon's private life. A belief that almost every journalist was out to get him and that his enemies and critics would destroy him unless he could destroy them first were what drove the creation of this covert group, whose activities culminated one night, June 17, 1972, when six men broke into the Democratic National Headquarters in the Watergate Hotel in Washington, D.C. The break-in had been amateurish, and the men were caught. Eventually, two *Washington Post* reporters, working from tips from an anonymous source dubbed "Deep Throat," thirty years later revealed to be Mark Felt, an assistant director of the FBI, connected one of burglars to the White House through a large lump-sum payment by an organization working for Nixon's reelection campaign.

In January 1973, the two masterminds of the Plumbers, presidential aides James McCord and G. Gordon Liddy, were convicted of burglary, conspiracy, and wiretapping in the Watergate break-in. They had been watching the burglars' night raid from across the street and communicating with them through handheld radios. The following month, the Senate established the Select Committee on Presidential Campaign Activities to investigate the connection between the burglary and Nixon's reelection campaign. Closed-door testimony before what became known as the Senate

Watergate Committee validated rumors that corruption reached deep into the White House, and within weeks Nixon accepted the resignations of his closest advisers, Haldeman and Ehrlichman, as well as that of Attorney General Richard Kleindienst. Nixon also fired his chief counsel, John Dean, who had begun to cooperate with investigators.

In May, the Senate authorized the appointment of a special prosecutor for the Watergate inquiry, and the new Attorney General Elliot Richardson tapped Archibald Cox, a liberal Harvard Law School professor. The Watergate Committee held its hearings in the open and even permitted television cameras. The curtain had been drawn back.

Nixon's credibility with the public had been at an all-time high months earlier after he won a huge victory against George McGovern with 61 percent of the popular vote. That credibility was now in a rapid decline. For the last year, the public had been slowly introduced to the idea that in private Nixon displayed a pattern of abusing the office of the presidency and using public agencies and resources for private and political gain. Whether they chose to believe it was another thing. The Watergate scandal divided the public into two main camps, those who responded with utter disgust or supportive indifference. Either way, the administration had begun crumbling.

SAN CLEMENTE INVESTIGATION: Although Brooks found Nixon a competent administrator and respected the generosity the president had extended to the Johnsons after they left Washington, he did not particularly like Nixon, even decades earlier when Nixon had served as Eisenhower's vice president. Brooks felt the man was mean and dishonest and found his ambitions more than outsized. Shortly after taking the Oval Office, Nixon purchased two homes in Key Biscayne, a high-class resort locale outside of Miami, Florida. Then, in a remarkable move, he accepted a generous loan from a wealthy supporter for the down payment on a cliffside mansion in San Clemente in Orange County, California, all of which suggested that Nixon still yearned to have more luxurious accommodations, despite already having a presidential fleet of Boeing 707s, helicopters, and a yacht at his disposal.

To understand Brooks's attitude about government, one only need look at his role on the Government Operations Committee, which was dedicated to rooting out waste, fraud, and abuse, and Nixon's sense of entitlement simply offended Brooks personally. Whether it was because of his own humble beginnings or the contrast with Johnson, Nixon's grasping fomented a feeling in Brooks that this man was not fit to be president. Brooks recalled years later:

> *Nixon was a smart president. . . He just had one little flaw, thinking he ought to be rich, I guess like Johnson and Kennedy.*

Soon Brooks began to speak publicly about his concern over the president's behavior. Brooks also noted the increased costs Nixon required for his leisure, including Camp David, the mountain retreat two hours north of Washington, where presidents were able to unwind with their family and guests. Johnson had brought Brooks and Charlotte there often during his presidency. The furnishings and amenities under Johnson had appeared comfortable to the congressman, though after Nixon took office, a second swimming pool was constructed at a cost of $150,000, and the estate's annual operating expenses ballooned from just over $100,000 to $640,000 as Nixon had more security and technology installed, including forty new telephones. This last detail perplexed Brooks, who explained to others, "LBJ was always able to be reached."

There was not much officials would say publicly about all of that. Congress had always granted the Secret Service great latitude in providing for the safety and travel of the president. Much was left to their discretion, with Congress only cutting the checks. The Secret Service under Nixon, though, followed no apparent guidelines for the expenditures and began to unload its budget on other government agencies such as the General Services Administration, including bills for installing new heating systems, sewer lines for the pool, furniture for the president's den, and a $65,000 replica of the White House fence at his San Clemente residence, or the "Western White House" as it had come to be called.

The GSA was part of the executive branch, and consequently its actions and spending fell under the jurisdiction of the House Committee on Government Operations. More specifically, it fell to the subcommittee on government activities, Brooks's subcommittee. The concerns about Nixon's spending soon arrived at Brooks's doorstep in the form of a review of federal expenditures on Nixon's homes in San Clemente and Key Biscayne.

Brooks and Government Operations Committee Chairman Chet Holifield formally announced on July 12 that an investigation would be conducted into "the use of Federal Funds for improvements on [Nixon's] privately owned property." Four days later, in sworn testimony in front of the Senate Watergate Committee, former White House aide and the current administrator of the FAA, Alexander Butterfield, revealed that Nixon had installed a recording system in the White House upon taking office. Nixon ordered an end to the secret taping two days later, but the damage had already been done. Suggesting that those taped conversations contained information that would likely incriminate Nixon's aides, and possibly even the president himself, both Cox and Ervin immediately filed subpoenas in court to require they be released. Yet Nixon refused, citing the concept of executive privilege, and set in motion a constitutional battle that would roil the nation.

When asked by reporters two weeks later how the White House's stonewalling might also affect his subcommittee's investigation, Brooks appeared concerned but self-assured. GSA Administrator Arthur Sampson had initially agreed to turn materials over to the subcommittee but then reversed himself after speaking with two of Nixon's close aides. They had cited concerns about the materials leading to "news leaks and misconstrued figures." When asked about whether he would be issuing subpoenas, Brooks explained that the subpoenas would be directed at the GSA and the Secret Service, not the White House. When pressed about whether Brooks would be willing to pursue a "court test" if the subpoenas were refused by the GSA or anyone else, Brooks replied that he would be "pleased and honored."

Brooks slated hearings on the presidential properties to begin in late August, after the summer recess.

What the subcommittee learned was surprising. Nixon had made substantial improvements to his residences, all on the taxpayers' dime. Roughly $400,000 had been spent on landscaping work. A compound adjacent to the San Clemente home was acquired for the purposes of "presidential storage."

LEFT: *Ca. 1926, Brooks (far right), with older brother Edward and parents Edward and Grace Brooks, in New York City, during the good times. The family's fortunes changed the next year when the rice market crashed. They would soon return to the Gulf Coast.* BELOW RIGHT: *1925, Brooks age 3 at his birthplace in Crowley, Louisiana.*
BELOW LEFT: *Ca. 1938, Brooks went by "Jackie" through adolescence. His father died when he was 12. His mother's guidance and support were central to his political and personal success. (Brooks Family Photos)*

Brooks enlisted in the Marine Corps in 1942 at age 19. After training in infantry and field communications at Parris Island, Quantico, and Fort Benning, he was deployed to the South Pacific in March 1944. He served overseas for 22 months and participated in the Battles of Guam and Okinawa. He spent five months on Guam after the Marines and Army retook it from the Japanese. During downtime, he and his fellow officers built an officers' club, set up volleyball courts, and hosted parties, inviting musicians, Red Cross nurses, and visiting officers and guests. (USMC and family photos.)

ABOVE: *As a Texas state legislator, Brooks, third from left, tirelessly pushed a bill making Lamar College a four-year university. Here Governor Beauford Jester signs the bill into law in 1949. Giving students in his district the opportunity to stay home while earning a college degree remained one of the proudest achievements of his long career. (Lamar University)*

BELOW: *Brooks's family, including mother Grace and brother Edward, worked tirelessly during his first U.S. House campaign in 1952 to represent the 2nd District in southeast Texas. He defeated a popular local attorney by only 448 votes. (Brooks family photo)*

Top: *Brooks entered the U.S. House in 1953, when he was 31 and a bachelor; his mother drove with him from Beaumont to Washington the first time.* Middle: *Grace Brooks wrote popular cooking and hosting columns in the* Beaumont Enterprise. *She also made home visits and ran seminars for local housewives as a home service advisor for Gulf States Utilities.* Bottom: *The House Democrats were led for decades by "Mr. Sam" Rayburn. On Brooks's first day in Congress, Rayburn invited him to his office hideaway, the so-called "Board of Education," where a bipartisan inner circle of both houses of Congress would discuss politics over whiskey at the close of every workday. Rayburn said Brooks would be welcome for as long as he was in Congress. It turned out to be 42 years.*

Brooks hosted a biennial breakfast to welcome new Democratic congressmen; guests feasted on venison sausage and quail from Brooks's own hunting trips in his district. Among the 1959 guests were House Majority Leader John McCormack, President Harry Truman, Brooks, Speaker Sam Rayburn and Senate Majority Leader Lyndon Johnson.

LEFT: *Brooks relaxing.* RIGHT: *Brooks arranged a 1959 fishing trip with Rayburn to future Governor Dolph Briscoe's ranch. Brooks later said it was the most relaxed he had ever seen "Mr. Sam." Brooks holds a 10-pounder caught by the Speaker—Briscoe had made sure beforehand that the pond was well-stocked with hungry bass. (Dolph Briscoe Center for American History)*

Jack and Charlotte Collins Brooks after their wedding, December 1960.

Brooks was all-in for the JFK-LBJ ticket in 1960. He campaigned in his district with House Speaker Sam Rayburn (left) and to oil refinery workers near Beaumont, Texas (right). Brooks told Kennedy's people that he would deliver his district for the Democratic ticket as long as they did not come down to try to help. Brooks's ability to connect with working-class constituents—"look 'em in the eye"—helped him win election to 21 consecutive terms.

ABOVE LEFT: *Brooks with the vice president and president, 1961.*
ABOVE RIGHT: *Accepting a signing pen in the Oval Office in September 1963 after President Kennedy signed into law a Brooks-sponsored bill.*

BELOW: *In one of the most iconic photographic images in U.S. history, Brooks is just over Jackie Kennedy's shoulder on Air Force One on November 22, 1963, as Vice President Lyndon Johnson takes the presidential oath of office following the assassination in Dallas of President John F. Kennedy. The oath ceremony took 23 seconds. Mrs. Kennedy then sat beside her husband's body, while the others on board withdrew. Brooks remained by the new president's side on the long, somber flight back to Washington.*

The Brookses and Johnsons were close friends. When Johnson became President, he and Lady Bird invited the Brookses to the White House almost weekly to dine, watch TV, and relax.

Johnson signed Brooks's Automatic Data Processing Act into law during a quiet moment in October 1965, at the President's ranch outside Austin. It was a humble beginning for the law that would foster the rise of the modern IT industry.

To Jack Brooks
from his longtime friend —
Lyndon B. Johnson

Johnson's presidency was one of the most productive legislative periods in American history, with dozens of new laws that fundamentally changed life in America. Brooks supported Johnson's Great Society agenda but not every part of it. He was no pushover, even when the President gave him the "Johnson treatment." Johnson once admitted to an aide that Brooks was the only congressman he was ever scared of. The two remained close confidantes and friends until Johnson's death in 1973.

This is a picture of a new father, down to his shirt sleeves and hard a
He is Beaumonter Jack Brooks, a member of the U.S. House of Represen
a brand new—and quite demanding—constituent to take care of. For pictures
Brooks, known as "Jeb," turn to Page 16-C.

CLOCKWISE FROM ABOVE: *The*
Beaumont Enterprise caught
Brooks in 1967 reading up on
how to be a father prior to Jeb's
adoption; LBJ with Charlotte
and son Jeb; the Brooks home
in McLean, Virginia; Brooks
and Jeb on the family tree
farm in Texas; Charlotte on
the cover of the Houston
Post's *Sunday magazine, for*
a profile of the "social worker,
secretary, socialite" who ran the
household, worked in Brooks's
Congressional office, and
promoted his campaign events.

Brooks's Government Activities Subcommittee was investigating questionable Nixon expenses in 1973 before the Juciary Committee begain impeachment hearings.

The President
The White House
Washington, D.C.

Dear Mr. President:

The Committee on the Judiciary has directed me to advise you that it finds that as of 10:00 A.M. April 30, you have failed to comply with the Committee's subpoena of April 11, 1974.

Sincerely,

Peter W. Rodino, Jr.
Chairman

ABOVE: *Brooks prodded Judiciary Chairman Peter Rodino to compel Nixon to comply with the special prosecutor's subpoena.* **LEFT:** *Rodino then drafted a formal letter stating the president's non-compliance. Always a vote-counter, as Rayburn and Johnson had been, Brooks scrawled on the letter his tally of likely committee member votes on the Articles of Impeachment. Nixon later famously called Brooks "The Executioner."*

Brooks gave Jimmy Carter a pair of cowboy boots when Air Force One landed at the Beaumont regional airport in June 1978. Carter was there to dedicate the Jack B. Brooks Federal Building, but he also sought Brooks's help in pushing his agenda through the House.

Brooks took his children Kate and Kim to meet the president on the South Lawn of the White House in July 1977.

Brooks got Speaker Tip O'Neill in 1977 to allow a closed-circuit feed of House floor proceedings for the sake of the historical record. But Brooks opposed televising Congress for the public, arguing that it would create a spectacle rather than benefit House members. He eventually lost that battle.

TOP: *Brooks with Vice President George Bush and President Ronald Reagan in the Oval Office in 1981. Brooks didn't care for Reagan but engaged him on bipartisan legislation.*

CENTER: *Lamar University, with money raised from private sources, erected a life-size bronze statue of Brooks in 1989 to honor his life's work and the decades of support he gave to the institution.*

BOTTOM: *Brooks walking on Capitol Hill with House Minority Leader Dick Gephardt and young Congresswoman Nancy Pelosi, about 1990, when she was in her first term.*

Top: *Brooks suffered a sudden near-fatal bout of pancreatitis during his 20th term in office. His staff, with cigars, eagerly welcomed him back from the hospital in 1989.* Center: *President George H.W. Bush served with Brooks briefly in the Texas congressional delegation during the late 1960s. Brooks, with him in 1991, called him a pretty good guy and a friend.* Bottom: *Brooks with Texas Governor Ann Richards in his Washington office in 1992.*

Top: *Brooks, here in 1990, sat on the Judiciary Committee from 1955, his second term, until he left office. He attained the chairmanship in 1989 and served for six years. Brooks loved a good fight. During those three terms, he introduced more than 70 bills that were then referred to his committee for debate, taking on the telecom, insurance and gunmaking industries, among many others.* Bottom left: *Brooks and President Clinton make a call to astronauts aboard the International Space Station in 1994.* Bottom right: *Brooks had a long interest in the space program. He is pictured here in 1961 at the Navy Nautical Test Center with a test pilot wearing a high altitude pressure suit of the type later used by the Gemini astronauts. NASA Administrator Dan Goldin credits Brooks with saving the ISS when its funding was about to be cut. Others credited Brooks with keeping Houston's Johnson Space Center active when NASA was consolidating. In 2001, the agency awarded him its highest civilian honor.*

ABOVE, FROM LEFT: *Representative Jake Pickle, former Speaker of the House Jim Wright, Brooks, and former Texas Governor Dolph Briscoe in 1994. The latter three had known each other since attending the University of Texas 50 years earlier. Each served in WWII and then got elected to the Texas legislature shortly afterwards.*

BELOW: *A favorite photo of the Brooks family, taken at Christmas 1987 shortly after Brooks's recovery from pancreatis. From left, Kim, Charlotte, Jack, Kate, and Jeb.*

A $400,000 helipad was constructed, and significant numbers of staff, both Secret Service and GSA, were permanently assigned to these residences year-round at a cost of approximately $1 million annually.

The subcommittee also discovered that more than $144,000 in improvements had been spent just that year on the home of Vice President Spiro Agnew. Though seven years earlier Congress had authorized the construction of a permanent home for the current vice president at the Naval Observatory in Northwest Washington, no funds had yet been appropriated for such a project.

The subcommittee finished its hearings in October and revealed that a total of $17 million in taxpayer dollars had been used to upgrade the president's homes. The purchases lacked any oversight, there were no guidelines for managing the expenditures, and in some cases non-government employees were making the procurements through oral requests to vendors.

The General Accounting Office concurred with Brooks's findings, stating that many of the government expenditures at the Key Biscayne compound and the San Clemente villa were not necessary for security reasons and had significantly improved the value of the properties for Nixon's personal gain. That was not the way Nixon saw it. At a press conference on September 5, the president responded to a volley of questions. "As a matter of fact," he said, "what the government did in San Clemente reduced the value of the property. If you see three Secret Service gazebos, and if you see some of the other fences that block out the rather beautiful view to the hills and the mountains that I like, you would realize that what I say is quite true," he assured. "It reduces its value as far as a residential property is concerned." At least one GSA official tried to substantiate the president's claim. Brooks retorted, with characteristic aplomb:

> Anytime you want to desecrate my property with all that money, you just come on down to Texas and do it.

Not content to merely remedy the current situation, by that fall Brooks had introduced legislation that would limit the expenditures made by any president in making security improvements or other measures at a privately owned home. Titled the Presidential Protection Assistance Act of 1973, it required advance written requests by the Secret Service to Congress for major expenditures and for reports to be submitted every six months.

The misuse of public money reflected what Brooks saw as an acute disregard for the power entrusted to presidents. Clearly Nixon felt there were no limits to the entitlements and powers he was due, even if they came at the expense of the public and despite the wishes of Congress. Brooks made a statement:

> *The lifestyle of the current president has reached a level totally alien to the average American working man and woman. The president has so removed himself from the ordinary, everyday cares and concerns of the American people that he has no understanding of our needs, our problems, and our goals.*

Adding fuel to the fire, just as the subcommittee's hearings were ending, Vice President Agnew resigned amid corruption charges stemming from when he was chief executive of Baltimore County. The offenses were unrelated to the presidency, but the consistent whiff of corruption now coming from this administration was unmistakable. Two days later, Nixon nominated House Minority Leader Gerald Ford to replace Agnew.

FORD NOMINATED AS VP: Brooks described Ford as "not the smartest character that came down the pike" but well-intentioned and decent. Ford's views were without a doubt conservative and partisan, but generally the long-term congressman from Grand Rapids, Michigan, was respected and well-liked by members of both parties in the House, where he had earned a reputation for being straightforward and fair. Confirmation for the nomination was thrown to the House Judiciary Committee.

Thomas "Tip" O'Neill, the colorful House majority leader, understood where the influence and thrust of that committee's authority lay. He wrote Brooks a short note a few weeks later: "With the nation in the turmoil it is, I believe it is highly imperative that quick action be taken by the Judiciary Committee." Brooks replied that he shared O'Neill's high opinion of Ford and that Judiciary Chairman Peter Rodino had already assured members that the committee would be moving forward with the matter, although in a manner that would likely not be as rigorous as Brooks would have liked.

Many expected Ford's nomination to sail through the committee. In rising to the position of House minority leader, he had clearly already been vetted by the public and shown that he was capable of leadership at the highest levels of government. As the confirmation hearings began, though, Brooks, on his own accord, submitted an exhaustive list of fifty-two questions to Ford, requesting that his responses be kept for the record. Given the recent behavior of the Nixon White House, Brooks's questions were highly relevant for a man who Congress was now considering putting one heartbeat away from the presidency. Most of the questions were general inquiries into the administration and role of government. He asked Ford for his views on withdrawal from Vietnam, Nixon's use of wage and price controls, protection for journalists, the independence of regulatory agencies, and grain sales to the Soviet Union, among other things. In the last dozen questions, however, Brooks wanted to gain some clarity for the battles he understood were brewing ahead.

47. If a president admits to or it is proved that he has committed a felony, should he be removed from office?

48. If a president knowingly orders actions that are illegal and/or violate the Constitution, should he be removed from office?

49. Is a president responsible for the official actions of his immediate staff and his personal representatives?

50. If a president lies to the Congress, should he be removed from office?

51. If a president lies to the American public, should he be removed from office?

52. If a president falsified documents to gain a personal tax advantage, should he be removed from office?

There was going to be some reckoning for the president's activities, and Brooks rightly understood that the new vice president would likely have a significant role in how that played out, either in Congress, the courts, or public opinion. He wanted Ford's opinion on the record, but perhaps he had already drafted charges against Nixon in his head and was testing the waters for how they might be received.

Ford replied that he had already answered many of the questions asked by Brooks in his testimony before the House Judiciary Committee and the Senate Committee on Rules and Administration. He then submitted written responses to the twenty-two remaining questions in a letter to Rodino.

> *Yes, the president was entitled to use the FBI in coordination with the Attorney General.*
> *No, the CIA should not be involved in domestic surveillance.*
> *Lying to Congress is abhorrent but in itself not justification enough for removal.*
> *Finally, yes, intentionally falsifying documents should lead to impeachment and conviction.*

Six days later, as the Senate voted 92 to 3 to confirm Ford, Brooks told a reporter from the *Houston Chronicle* that he expected the House Judiciary to recommend to the full House that they do the same, which they did on December 6 with a vote of 387 to 35. Ford took the vice-presidential oath of office an hour later. Then Brooks made a statement on the House floor that started out light but had a sharp message embedded. "[Ford] is a Republican and there is no way to make him a Democrat," said Brooks. He commented that he had come to know more about Ford than he ever wanted to know, and he offered that Ford was straightforward, honest, candid, capable, fully qualified. Then Brooks brought up the main issue for the country.

> *Should the office of the president be vacated within the next three years, Gerald Ford has shown that he has the capability of bringing much-needed personal honor and integrity to the highest office of the land.*

The next day, on vice-presidential letterhead, Ford, who was known to his friends as "Jerry," had letters prepared to the congressional leaders who had been instrumental in his confirmation. The messages were gracious and most likely identical for each of the congressmen. Ford expressed sadness at leaving the House and thanks for the confidence that Congress had entrusted in him. However, in his letter to Brooks, he wrote a personal note in pen at the bottom of the letter:

P.S.
You were tough but GREAT.
J

SATURDAY NIGHT MASSACRE: Murmurs of Nixon's possible impeachment began in July, when a Democratic congressman from Massachusetts introduced the first resolution calling for such an action. The idea continued making headlines through the fall, reaching a crescendo after October 20, following what became known as the Saturday Night Massacre.

Special Prosecutor Archibald Cox was adamant about receiving the full, unedited Oval Office tapes and had refused to accept summarized material in their stead, so Nixon told Attorney General Richardson to fire him. When he refused, Nixon accepted Richardson's resignation and then demanded that his second-in-command, Deputy Attorney General William Ruckelshaus, fire the special prosecutor. When he refused, Nixon accepted his resignation as well and called upon an even lower-ranking official, Solicitor General Robert Bork, suddenly promoted to acting attorney general, and Bork finally fired Cox and abolished the office of special prosecutor.

Such a reckless move had a profound impact around the country and shocked even White House insiders. Congresswoman Barbara Jordan, in office only since January and the only other member of the Texas delegation on the Judiciary Committee, told the *Houston Post* that Richardson and Ruckelshaus were "men of conscience" and "their resignations remind us that it has become difficult for men of conscience to serve President Nixon." Jerome Waldie, another Judiciary Committee member, said outright that he would bring forward impeachment resolutions once that body reconvened. Waldie added that by withholding the tapes and digging in, the president seemed determined to make the impeachment process a test of "the guts of the members of Congress, which [Nixon] considers a better bet." Within days, more than sixty congressmen had signed resolutions calling for impeachment. Many Republicans in Congress even admitted that impeachment proceedings were now very likely.

That was not necessarily a bad bet for the president to make. Although many in Congress did not like him, personally or politically, very few wanted to be responsible for removing a sitting president. The potential damage to the Constitution and the American political system, not to mention their own individual careers, appeared too great for many to bear. Judiciary Chairman Rodino was of that mindset.

But Nixon soon learned there was another member of that committee who was more than willing to jump headfirst into a brawl over the boundaries of the executive office. The fight might have been handled discreetly behind the closed doors of Congress during the preceding year and a half, but if it was to be a messy and public brawl, that suited Brooks all the same.

SURPRISED BY THE DEGREE of public outrage at the firings, Nixon announced a few days later that he would allow Judge John Sirica, the chief judge of the U.S. District Court in Washington, to listen to the Oval Office tapes and decide whether they be given to the federal grand jury.

Majority Leader O'Neill, who admitted that this did not change the course for an orderly investigation in the Judiciary, said that the president's acquiescence should "dampen the fires for impeachment." When asked if this changed his mind regarding the impeachment inquiry, Brooks told his aides, *"not one iota."* He released a statement to Texas media that same day saying:

> *The President's conduct indicates an apparent disregard for the rule of law. Unfortunately, it is imperative that the Congress immediately undertakes a thorough study of the President's actions and determine whether impeachment should be brought.*

Speaker Albert decided the twenty-two resolutions of impeachment introduced in the House would go to the Judiciary Committee, which had done a fair job with Ford's appointment hearings. Albert announced on national television on October 26 that the Judiciary Committee would receive all the charges against the president and would decide how to proceed from there. The committee would not conduct its own investigation as the Senate Watergate inquiry had, hauling witnesses in to testify before a grand jury and collecting new material that could be used to bring indictments against the co-defendants. Instead, the committee would review the findings of that ongoing inquiry, and several other related inquiries, to determine whether any of the president's actions constituted an impeachable offense.

Judiciary staffers would later admit that it was really O'Neill's idea to send the impeachment resolutions to the Judiciary. O'Neill, who would soon become Speaker of the House himself, had an outsized presence and influence on Capitol Hill. Judiciary Chairman Peter Rodino was an unknown entity, a Democratic machine politician from New Jersey who had not made much of an impact in his twenty-five years in the House. But O'Neill was a friend of Brooks, and Brooks was essentially next in line on the Judiciary.

On October 25, a Texas chapter of Common Cause, a nonprofit, nonpartisan government watchdog group, released a public letter to Brooks asking him to help restore a prosecutor to the Watergate inquiry, fearing that all the findings Cox had made would be for naught unless the post was filled with another truly independent attorney. Less than a week later, Nixon appointed Leon Jaworski, a Democratic lawyer from Houston, to replace Cox. Both Democrat and Republican congressmen praised the selection of Jaworski, calling him a man of "integrity and ability" who would not be intimidated, even by a president.

But Brooks still looked into the matter personally. His staff members assembled a profile and conducted a background check. They found no proof that Jaworski had ever made a political donation to Nixon, but they did discover that his law firm had a Mexican subsidiary, which raised some eyebrows. In the past, Mexican counterparts had made donations to American politicians and then been reimbursed by their American colleagues. Brooks's aides found no evidence that this was true in Jaworski's case, however, so Brooks released the following statement to the Houston newspapers:

> *Leon Jaworski is an able lawyer and a fine man. If he has full authority and, in fact, total access to Presidential memoranda such as notes, tapes, documents, and if his inquiry is not limited, I have confidence he can do the job.*

Jaworski was sworn in and testified before Brooks and a subcommittee of the Judiciary that the president had given him "the most solemn and substantial assurances of freedom" in his investigation of Watergate. He also immediately requested the same tapes Nixon had refused to hand over to Cox.

Nevertheless, outrage in Congress over the president's actions would not be squelched. Within a few weeks' time, a total of thirty-one representatives introduced resolutions calling for impeachment.

Congressional observers considered Rodino a good, well-intentioned man. He had served in Congress for twenty-five years but only rose to the Judiciary chairmanship in early 1973 after Manny Celler, who had dominated the committee for two decades, lost in the Democratic primary. Rodino acknowledged privately to his staffers that he felt he was still in the shadows of Celler, who remained one of Brooks's dear friends.

Rodino, like Brooks, had seen combat in World War II, and he was not an ambitious man, at least relative to many of his congressional peers. In fact, he was uncomfortable with the attention the impeachment hearings would bring. Even more, he did not want to be the arbiter of the president's guilt or innocence. Given the committee's task, this was a difficult position for any public servant, but especially for one from the opposition party. He thought there was a strong likelihood that the country would perceive him as, at best, partisan and at worst, corrupt.

Perhaps as a result, Rodino took an overly cautious tack in pursuing the case, and his timidity was palpable to the other members. Rodino held a Democratic caucus in early November so all the members on the committee could talk. When someone asked, "What next?" Brooks spoke up, "Well, our only choices are whether to shoot him or to hang him." Rodino almost choked. Unlike Brooks and many of the other Democrats on the committee, he lacked a visceral partisan disdain for Nixon.

At the end of that meeting, Rodino announced that he would be available on Tuesday and Thursday mornings for breakfast in the members' dining room of the Capitol for anyone who wanted to discuss the proceedings. He issued an internal memo to colleagues a week later expressing disappointment that no one had come.

Garner J. Cline, associate general counsel of the Judiciary Committee, wrote Rodino a list of suggestions for ways the committee could coordinate with the Senate committee, enlist the Library of Congress to assist with the use of computers, and assign roles to committee members. He wrote, "Many staff members are without specific instructions and, consequently, are nonproductive."

Whether Rodino's style reflected a lack of leadership ability or just a different approach is still open to debate. To Brooks, the tough-talking former marine who relished legislative fights, the chairman "wasn't worth a shit" in the impeachment process. He was certainly fair and experienced as a legislator, but Brooks thought Rodino "didn't have the guts a chairman needs to have." The next in line on the committee, technically, was Harold D. Donohue, a Democrat from Massachusetts who was not in good health and serving what would be his last year in Congress. Brooks, with twenty-one years in the House, was the next most senior, but many aides and House colleagues felt that he already ran the committee.

The Judiciary Committee was composed entirely of lawyers because of the legal complexity of the issues it handled. It had been notable during the 1960s for its role in writing landmark civil rights legislation, largely on a bipartisan basis, but its composition had changed drastically since then. Only five of its thirty-eight members in 1973 had served on the committee in 1964. Seventeen of the thirty-eight had been in Congress less than four years, and eleven of those had entered the House just ten months before. In keeping with the widening political divisions that were growing around the country, the committee was extremely divided. That November, Richard Lyons of the *Washington Post* noted: "the Democrat side has become more liberal and the Republican side more conservative in the past decade and that in brain power Democrats have made the greater gain."

To further avoid any criticism that the committee's work was partisan, in December Rodino decided to create a select panel of the committee's most senior members that would conduct the preliminary investigative phase of the proceedings by reviewing, in secret session, evidence gathered from earlier investigations into Watergate and other activities. He first envisioned this select subcommittee as comprising the five most senior Democrats plus the four most senior Republicans. After several weeks, he changed his mind and decided it would be made up of each of the seven chairmen of the Judiciary's standing subcommittees and Jack Brooks.

The idea was that most of the younger and more vocal Democratic members of the committee, such as Barbara Jordan of Texas and Robert Drinan of California, would be excluded from the panel. Many of them had already spoken publicly of their belief in the president's guilt. For example, John Conyers, an outspoken "bomb thrower" from Detroit, was already on Nixon's secret "enemies list" of eighty-odd politicians, journalists, and celebrities that the president did not trust. Larry O'Brien, then head of the Democratic National Committee, was also listed, along with the entire Congressional Black Caucus, entertainers and actors such as Barbra Streisand and Paul Newman, and even football quarterback Joe Namath. Dozens of newspaper and television reporters and businessmen who supported Democrats also made the list.

On November 14, the *Washington Post* ran the profiles of each of the impeachment subcommittee members. It described Brooks, then fifty years old, as:

> *A tough-talking, partisan, liberal Democrat in the Lyndon Johnson tradition, and the congressman closest to LBJ during his presidency. He sat with Celler and Rodino on the civil rights subcommittee, but recently has concentrated more on Government Operations Committee work, where he investigated federal spending on President Nixon's private properties and was critical of it.*

The committee had to decide whether it would appoint a prosecutor to head the investigation, as Cox had led the Senate's. Brooks's name was thrown around as one possible option, but although he was senior and highly respected, many still considered him too critical and partisan to act as a prosecutor.

Three days later, at a conference of newspaper editors at Disney World in Florida, Nixon defended himself, saying, "I have earned every cent. And in all of my years of public life I have never obstructed justice."

Then he rather infamously declared: "People have got to know whether or not their president is a crook. Well, I'm not a crook. I've earned everything I've got."

Over the next several weeks, seemingly at a loss for how to proceed, Rodino decided to conduct a search for the right prosecutor in private. He had his chief of staff, Francis O'Brien, and O'Brien's brother, John, conduct the search. Rodino had promised the leadership he was putting together a staff, but three months into it he still had nothing.

JOHN DOAR: On December 20, after what some thought was an inexcusably long search for a task of such urgency, Rodino selected John Doar, a Republican from Wisconsin, because he liked the objective and nonpartisan approach that Doar laid out during his interview. It paralleled Rodino's own sentiments and would hopefully repair the damage done from the Senate's recently adjourned Watergate Committee, whose proceedings had been seen by the public as loose and questionable.

Doar had been in the civil rights division of the Justice Department from 1960 to 1967, working his way up to assistant attorney general. He accompanied James Meredith in 1962 as the young black man entered the University of Mississippi, where Doar and federal marshals remained by his side for the first several weeks of classes. At the Justice Department, Doar focused on civil rights abuses in the South, such as voter intimidation and vigilantism. Democrats and Republicans alike welcomed his appointment as special counsel to the committee. He had earned a reputation for fairness from his palliative presence among protesters at the Selma marches in 1965 and for quieting a crowd ready to riot in Jackson, Mississippi, after the funeral of Medgar Evers in 1963. In 2012, President Barack Obama would honor Doar with a Presidential Medal of Freedom.

He was also, in Brooks's recollection, completely useless in the impeachment process. He was an academic rather than an investigator. His humorlessness was a defining trait; he valued order and tidiness and fully expected it from those he worked with. To Brooks's chagrin, Rodino had found exactly the kind of man he wanted to work with. One of Doar's top priorities in beginning the inquiry, he told reporters, was to establish a "secure and elaborate filing system." Once the inquiry was formally underway, he instituted a hard and fast rule barring staff from speaking with the media, sharing inquiry documents, or even bringing papers home with them at the end of the day. When he learned that a staffer had broken protocol and brought some files home with him, he chastised the man for his carelessness and told him, "The greatest tribute to a man would be that if he died someone could come into his office the next day and pick up where he left off."

In an effort to keep the inquiry from appearing partisan, Doar switched the format of witness testimonies from sworn statements under oath to informal questioning, once he learned that committee members could attend. The incensed Brooks, who started referring to the unelected Doar as "the Chairman," also made clear his opinion of Rodino's leadership in this process.

The committee was charged not with conducting a new investigation but rather completing an analysis of all the findings of the previous investigations to see if articles of impeachment against Nixon should be recommended to the full House. Under Article II of the Constitution, a president can be impeached for "Treason, Bribery or other High Crimes and Misdemeanors." The term "high crimes and misdemeanors" was a very old one, lifted entirely from its use in English law and dating back as far as the fourteenth century. It was reportedly added to the impeachment clause in the Constitution by James Madison to "hold a president responsible for appointing unworthy subordinates."

Actual impeachment experience was scarce in Washington. The authorities and guidelines for an impeachment are loosely laid out in the Constitution, but there had not been an impeachment of a president for over one hundred years, since Andrew Johnson was impeached in 1867. Lawmakers who understood the practical implications of such archaic and vague terms as "high crimes and misdemeanors" were few and far between.

But Brooks was an exception.

DOUGLAS IMPEACHMENT: In 1970, at the urging of Ford from the floor of the House, twenty-five representatives submitted a resolution to the Rules Committee to impeach the staunchly liberal Supreme Court Justice William O. Douglas, on the grounds that he had engaged in misbehavior while on the court and had unduly accepted speaking fees from a private organization that had income from gambling casinos. Specifically, it accused Douglas of receiving $85,000 from the Parvin Foundation, an entity of lobbyist Albert Parvin, the same kind of financial dealing that led to Douglas's protégé, Abe Fortas, resigning from the bench. Ford also alleged that the jurist had written "revolutionary" articles for left-wing and pornographic magazines. The resolution charged Douglas with high crimes and misdemeanors and misbehavior in office.

Celler, then chairman of the Judiciary Committee, announced that a select subcommittee had been created to handle the matter in a more expeditious and expert manner than the full committee would have been able to. It had only five members, each with extensive legal experience: himself, Brooks, a Democrat from Colorado, and two Republicans from Michigan and Ohio.

The case, though politically motivated, exposed Brooks and the others on the special subcommittee to the murky distinctions of not fulfilling public duties versus criminal activity. What did it mean to impeach a federal judge? The special subcommittee entertained two different concepts of impeachable offenses, both of which were based on the idea that a federal judge could be impeached for either criminal conduct or serious dereliction of duty, but differed regarding non-criminal behavior where the actions had no connections with the performance of office.

In the subcommittee's first report in the investigation, several distinctions were presented that would later have significance in the proceedings on Nixon, all of which were highlighted in Brooks's copy of the report.

> *Impeachment resembles a regular criminal indictment and trial but it is not the same thing. It relates solely to the accused's right to hold civil office. . . the framers of the Constitution clearly established that impeachment is a unique political device; designed explicitly to dislodge from public office those who are patently unfit for it, but cannot otherwise be promptly removed. . . About the only thing authorities can agree upon. . . is that an offense need not be indictable to be impeachable. In other words, something less than a criminal act or criminal dereliction of duty may nevertheless be sufficient grounds for impeachment and removal from public office.*

Ford, who not only led the impeachment effort but also served as a witness against Douglas in the hearings, requested that a Detroit law firm study the "good behavior" provision as it pertained to federal judges. The firm produced a memo, furnished to the subcommittee, stating: "We conclude, that misbehavior by a federal judge may constitute an impeachable offense though the conduct may not be an indictable 'crime or misdemeanor.'"

Eight months after the resolution was introduced, the small committee stated it found "no creditable evidence that would warrant preparation of charges on any acceptable concept of impeachable offense." There was no long justification given, just a few paragraphs. Recalling that time, Brooks said there was simply no evidence against Douglas. In 1989, House leaders again appointed Brooks to manage impeachment proceedings against federal judge Walter Nixon (no relation to the president) of Mississippi. Nixon was impeached by the Senate for perjury and removed from office.

Just before the president's impeachment hearings, Celler was beaten in the Democratic primary. The victor, Elizabeth Holtzman, a thirty-two-year-old professor at Harvard Law School, took Celler's seat on the Judiciary Committee. She had just published a book titled *Impeachment: The Constitutional Problems*, which explored the nature of impeachable offenses. Holtzman referred to this tome as the committee members' "bible," and several of them, including Barbara Jordan, could be seen on television reading it. Holtzman came to understand an impeachable offense as a political crime, signifying an abuse of power or a series of abuses. However, as Brooks had explored with the case of Douglas, the waters were murky. Even if a public servant was found to have committed a felony criminal offense, it did not necessarily constitute a failure to carry out the duties of the office. On the other hand, politicians had been removed from office for activities that broke no state or federal laws.

Further complicating things was the fact that the official in question now was not just any public servant but the president, whose standing at the top of the executive branch made this case without precedent.

For example, if the president had misused the FBI or directed the CIA to act outside his authority as president, that would not have constituted a crime. However, in that it undermined his duty as president, Brooks and most Democrats were adamant that it should be an impeachable offense.

Nixon's defense attorney, James St. Clair, and Edward Hutchinson, the most senior Republican on the Judiciary, wanted the committee to define an impeachable offense as a felony, a strictly criminal offense. That would be the more severe charge and also harder to prove, especially given the wide berth of executive powers typically granted a president.

The White House and Republican members of the Judiciary also fought to have the investigation delineated very clearly around the Watergate cover-up. Anything further, they argued, was beyond the scope of what the House inquiry had been set up to investigate.

Brooks, most of the Democrats, and even some Republicans disagreed. They were concerned with what was described as a pattern of behavior that was unbecoming to the office of the presidency and perhaps criminal in nature. Brooks was fully aware of the rights granted to the House in an impeachment, and he would not have the inquiry proceedings encumbered by anyone.

HOUSE INQUIRY: Doar soon had thirty-five lawyers working for him, not investigating—because that was not the inquiry's purpose—but analyzing the investigations that had been conducted up to that point. As Brooks and his staff commented later, all the new hotshot attorneys and staffers seemed to do was make photocopies. Ever the monitor of wasteful government spending, Brooks referred to this troupe of mostly young Ivy League attorneys as the "Million Dollar Impeachment Staff."

Doar wanted to hire young lawyers whom he trusted, but who had also not taken a public stance on the president's innocence or guilt. One candidate was turned down when it came to light that he had signed a petition concerning the Watergate scandal. Doar demanded that the staff never refer to Nixon as anything but "the president." He was not to be called "Nixon" or anything else, certainly not anything derogatory. These staffers worked under tight security in a recently annexed House office building that used to be the Congressional Hotel, and there the staff quickly ballooned to seventy-four full-timers.

Doar envisioned that his staff would perform the first phase of the inquiry, which involved collating all the findings of previous investigations and then defining what constituted an impeachable offense. The staff was divided into four task forces, two of which were dedicated to the facts of Watergate, one to the activity of the Plumbers, and one to lesser items.

Doar's team also had to set forth the procedures that would be followed by the Congress in conducting the investigation and then potentially the trial. Doar said he and Rodino were not going to be satisfied with less than a two-thirds vote; they did not want a bare majority, with Democrats voting one way and Republicans the other.

Among Doar's staff was a bright and energetic young woman, Hillary Rodham, who had just completed law school the year before. Doar knew the Hillary and her soon-to-be husband Bill Clinton from when they had invited him to Yale to judge a contest. He had first asked Clinton to join his staff, but the young attorney declined; he was teaching law in Arkansas and had already decided on a run for Congress. Clinton suggested Rodham, who was working at the Children's Defense Fund and was underwhelmed with the prospect of moving to Arkansas.

Rodino's chief of staff, Francis O'Brien, also took on a lead role in selecting candidates, a role that would cause him to cross Brooks at least once. As O'Brien later recounted:

> *I remember one day I got called up from Congressman Brooks office and asked to come over. So I went over and Jack Brooks had a resume in front of him.*
>
> *Jack Brooks says, "Boy," he said this gentleman's name, I can't remember him. He was on the staff. He was a young lawyer from I think Yale or something. He said, "Do you know so-and-so?" "Yes, sir," I said. "The chairman assigned him. He's a member of staff."*
>
> *He said, "Boy, do you know where he's from?" I said, "I'm not sure what school he went to so, no, sir." "Do you know where he was born?" the congressman asked. I said, "No, sir." He said he was born in Beaumont, Texas. He said, "Does that mean anything to you?" "No, sir."*
>
> *I was dressed in a three-piece suit and fine tie. Jack Brooks reaches across the table and grabs my tie and starts pulling me across the desk, big desk, says,*

"Boy, that's my district. Don't you ever hire somebody from my district without getting my approval."

My necktie was very tight at that point around my neck, and he dropped me, and I go, "Yes, sir." I went back. Jack Brooks. I had approval.

Brooks's former staffer Gene Peters recalled how Brooks ran the committee:

Mr. Brooks didn't jump in on this; he basically was invited in by a reluctant chairman. Now, there was a member who was senior to Mr. Brooks on the committee—Mr. Donohue, Donohue of Massachusetts. Mr. Donohue. . . to put it politely, was past his prime. It was his last term, he was having some problems, so he really was not the man who could have handled it. Mr. Brooks then was the next man in line and he took over. And he did . . . he basically was the man who handled that operation. I'm not saying this because I was with him. I'm saying it because I saw it. I was part of this.

Mr. Rodino hired a fellow named John Doar, who the Democrats on the committee referred to [as] "Mr. Rodino's Republican council" who's going to handle it for us. And then Mr. Doar had this budget that was outside the control of the Members [of Congress]. I don't know, it was millions to hire people to do this. Now, if you get the impression I was not impressed with Mr. Doar, you're right. But it became very clear that it would be in the hands of this fellow.

It had a side effect that Mr. Rodino's staff on the Judiciary were very unhappy because they were shut out of the biggest act of their lives! Jerry Zeifman, the General Counsel, is livid to this day about it. And let me say we got a lot of help out of his staff, out of Rodino's staff, in what we did. Jerry Zeifman, Jim Cline, and the staff were very helpful.

But the way this operation was handled was that the Democratic members, basically the power row—the top row: Kastenmeier, Conyers—but the senior Democrats on the committee would meet, generally daily, in Jerry Zeifman's office in the Judiciary Committee and they would discuss what they were going to do, and how they were going to do it.

Mr. Brooks took his own staff, assigned responsibilities, and at this time we had quite a bit of staff, since he had. . . two committees he was chairing, so he did have good staff and we were assigned responsibilities to do certain areas of investigation and we did 'em.

The night that the committee impeachment hearings opened . . . Mr. Brooks had a fellow named Bill Jones who was head of his Government Operations [General Counsel], a gentleman named Doug Dibellos who was with the Legislative Counsel's Office . . . and I was involved in it. And we sat in a subcommittee office and drafted the Articles of Impeachment. We drafted 'em for what was available. No Member saw them, except Mr. Brooks, who approved them. Then we took them to. . . there were two members, James Mann of South Carolina and Mr. Flowers of Alabama. These were two Southern Democrats who were very close to the Republican Members. And their job was—they went over to the Republicans and they negotiated. So the Republicans' position was if Flowers and Mann will agree to it, you can go ahead and proceed on that basis.†

There were disagreements on many matters, but there were also difficult questions about the scope of what constituted an impeachable offense. Many claimed the language was far more inclusive that just criminal behavior. Hillary Rodham and several other staffers claimed that "to limit impeachable conduct to criminal offenses would be incompatible with the evidence concerning the constitutional meaning of the phrase ["high crimes and misdemeanors"] and would frustrate the purpose that the framers intended for impeachment."

At the same time as the impeachment hearings, Brooks's staff discovered that Ford had been paid by two separate entities for the same official trip. While they could have made it public and caused some embarrassment to the new vice president, Brooks realized it was a simple accounting mistake and chose to bury it. Knowledge of the error never made it beyond the committee aides.

In early December, Nixon requested that the Congress's Joint Committee on Internal Revenue Taxation review his tax filings and give their findings on their legality. Brooks wrote a detailed letter to Rodino, copying the rest of the congressional leadership, explaining how the committee had

---

† This quotation is taken verbatim from a video interview that can be viewed at www.jackbrooksfoundation.org.

not been created to determine the legality of any individual's returns. Such a matter should be decided in the courts. Further, in light of the impeachment inquiry, the Joint Committee agreeing to review the request would be impinging on the Judiciary Committee's jurisdiction and improperly sharing the responsibility for impeachment with the Senate. A few days later, Tip O'Neill, who had been copied, replied: "I have received the copy of the letter you sent to Peter. Personally, I think you are absolutely correct, but don't know what we can do about it."

Joseph Califano, formerly a chief aide to Johnson on domestic affairs and Secretary of Health, Education, and Welfare, who was at this time back in private practice, sent Brooks a copy of a speech Califano had given to the D.C. chapter of the Federal Bar Association that November titled "On the Impeachable Offenses of Richard Nixon." Brooks reviewed the speech and underlined one particular passage near the end regarding the rights of the House inquiry in conducting its work.

As opposed to the Senate inquiry, which was directed at aides, cabinet officers, and other officials, the House inquiry, Califano explained, with its sole focus on the president, "carries with it clear and unequivocal authority to obtain documents and materials that under other circumstances might be subject to claims of executive privilege."

This issue of how sacred executive privilege was would come to embroil Congress and the president in a bitter fight over materials (the Senate committee had subpoenaed more than five hundred tapes) for the next eight months, ultimately leading to the landmark Supreme Court decision in *United States v. Nixon*.

STASIS: By January one of Brooks's concerns was becoming a reality. There was a growing perception in Washington and the public at large that the inquiry was going nowhere. Rodino had taken too long to pick a prosecutor, the members were slow in getting together, and the whole operation seemed to lack direction. The special subcommittee for investigating had not directly questioned a single witness to build its case; they were still examining the findings of all the previous investigations.

A January 21 article in the *Washington Post* titled "Impeach Nixon Effort

Floundering" reported that nearly two dozen of Doar's staff of attorneys were dedicated to answering routine mail regarding the impeachment and that documents relating to the president's finances had to be turned away because the committee "was not ready for them yet."

For Brooks, there was no excuse for these kinds of delays. His subcommittee on government activities, the staff of which was doing double duty for the impeachment inquiry, was still investigating expenditures on the president's homes even while everything else swirled about.

Calls for action were mounting. Majority Leader Tip O'Neill, perhaps the highest official to do so thus far, had just called for Nixon to resign. His Republican counterpart, John Rhodes, gave a weak reply that such a request was premature. By March, however, he would agree.

O'Neill also reportedly gave Brooks and other senior committee members a signal to put the spurs to Doar and Rodino. As a function of Rodino and Doar's efforts to prevent leaks to the media, most of the members of the Judiciary had not seen any evidence in the case three months after it had been assigned to them. Rodino and the committee's most senior Republican, Edward Hutchinson of Michigan, said that the risk of files being shared with others outside the committee meant the members were "going to have to [wait] until some kind of report is made by the staff."

Brooks privately confided in O'Neill: "This thing is getting nowhere. It's falling apart. There isn't any movement."

That the committee members' ability to investigate the inquiry assigned to them would be contingent on the judgment and output of a gaggle of unelected lawyers was a proposition that Brooks found completely absurd. He relayed as much in a letter he had hand delivered to Rodino on January 30:

Dear Mr. Chairman,

In view of the fact that the members of the Judiciary Committee are being asked to rely on the information and opinions put forth by our staff, I request that we be supplied a resume of the qualifications of all staff assigned to the impeachment investigation.

It would be most helpful if the resumes include all previous employment and experience with legislative hearings and investigations. Additionally, I would appreciate knowing what titles they have been given and what salary they are receiving.

Then in pen at the bottom, Brooks deftly suggested that the issue might be brought up on the floor of the House, where the chairman's decision making and hesitation might attract ridicule from other members.

P.S. We'll need this detail for the House Administration Committee anyhow — + perhaps for questions you may get on the floor—
JB.

O'Brien, Rodino's chief of staff, was stuck in the middle of the situation. He recounted:

Brooks was a terror. . . Feelings could not have run higher. There was a lot of conflict between Brooks and Rodino. A lot of conflict. The press had no idea of the depths of animosity.

John Gardner, the founder of Common Cause, criticized the delays in the committee's inquiry:

Rodino has not functioned as a strong and decisive person. . . His performance to date has been very disturbing. . . We recognize it can't be speedy, but what we're talking about is a beginning. . . I don't know if it's his ineptness. . . Just looking at it, I can't understand why a thing of this importance just sits around.

To the criticism, Rodino replied that he was more interested in making history than headlines. He and Hutchinson wanted to have prepared the committee's case before asking the House for the power to subpoena documents from the president. However, Rodino had expressed several times already that he hoped the committee would have finished its inquiry and presented its findings to the full House by April 30.

Members understood that Nixon would claim executive privilege to deny any requests for more material, especially regarding private conversations between him and his aides. That would throw the conflict into the courts, further complicating the proceedings. However, some constitutional experts on the committee thought that if Nixon defied a subpoena from Congress, that in itself would become an impeachable offense. One way or another, it was becoming clear that a large constitutional battle was imminent.

The battle began January 31. The full Judiciary Committee met at 10 a.m. in Room 2141 of the Rayburn Congressional Office Building to consider passing a resolution requesting subpoena authority. Room 2141, the Judiciary Committee hearing room, was neither large enough nor adequately equipped to support the numbers of reporters, television cameras, and spectators that these hearings would bring, yet because of the historical gravity of the situation Rodino denied requests to relocate to a different venue.

According to newspaper reports, Doar drafted the resolution, which requested sweeping powers to investigate, subpoena evidence, and compel testimony, potentially from the president himself, in conducting the inquiry. The resolution further stipulated that these powers should allow the inquiry to work across traditional boundaries between the branches. The president had said in his State of the Union address the night before that he would fully cooperate with the inquiry, "in any way I consider consistent with my responsibilities" to the office of the presidency. That qualification was key. It meant Nixon would turn over what he wanted to and claim executive privilege for what he did not.

One week later, the full House voted, 410 to 4, to officially authorize the Judiciary to investigate "whether sufficient grounds exist to impeach President Nixon." In another three weeks, seven of Nixon's former staffers would be indicted by a grand jury for offenses related to the Watergate break-in and cover-up. In the indictment, Nixon is listed as an unindicted co-conspirator.

Before an audience of the Federal Executive Board of Arlington, Texas, in January, Brooks said:

> *It's a heavy price to pay, but if any good can come out of Watergate and all*
> *that travesty has come to symbolize, it must be the recognition throughout our*

federal government, the business community, and the public at large that every
individual is accountable for his or her own actions. The defense that "My boss
told me to do it" is not available to anyone.

Referring to Nixon's refusal to turn the tapes over, Brooks said, "The president's conduct indicates an apparent disregard for the rule of law."

Edited tapes of Nixon's conversations, or selected transcripts, had been trickling in, with great reluctance from the White House, since March. Each new installment of recordings raised as many questions as it answered, and each left the members feeling as if they were not receiving the full story.

The special prosecutor handed a satchel of tapes over to the committee in March. Simply demanding all the tapes from Nixon was tricky; if the committee sought a court-ordered subpoena, then they were submitting their entire purpose and power to impeach to judicial review. Doar and Rodino walked a fine line to persuade the president to turn the tapes over and to build public support that he do so.

On April 3, as a result of an investigation into his past tax filings, Nixon was forced to pay $432,787 in back taxes plus $33,000 in interest.

In April, Jaworski, still prosecuting the Watergate investigation in the Senate, obtained a subpoena requiring the president to hand over sixty-four additional tapes. They were believed to contain conversations in which the indicted men, and possibly the president himself, made incriminating statements.

Instead, two weeks later the president appealed directly to the American people in a televised announcement. He reported that the White House was releasing 1,200 pages of transcripts of conversations to the Judiciary, despite the fact that the committee wanted the actual tapes. He asserted that the language in the tapes themselves could be taken so out of context so as to support the allegations of any political hatchet man. What he was providing was the substance of those tapes, reassuring everyone that he had personally overseen the editing. It was a clever gamble; video clips on the nightly news showed White House staff delivering boxes of transcripts to the Judiciary by the carload. Surely that meant Nixon was complying with the spirit of the court orders, if not the letter.

However, Nixon's public support, which had been holding somewhat firm given the circumstances, began to evaporate. Through the transcripts, the public saw firsthand the lowbrow speech the president favored and how he conspired with his aides to seek revenge against their perceived enemies. The conversations were crude and petty. The language and tone of the president and his aides surprised even some of the lawmakers in the Judiciary. *Time* magazine said the transcripts "showed a President creating an environment of deceit and dishonesty, of evasion and cover-up." The conservative editorial board of the *Chicago Tribune*, which had backed the president in 1968 and again in 1972, reversed its position and called for Nixon to resign immediately. "We saw the public man in his first administration and we were impressed. Now, in about 300,000 words, we have seen the private, and we are appalled." The editorial went on to say the transcripts offered "a sickening exposure of the man" whom they said had been revealed as "devious," "profane," and "preoccupied with appearances." A majority of Americans now agreed that Nixon should either resign or face impeachment. Even a longtime supporter, Republican House Majority Leader John Rhodes, told reporters that Nixon ought to at least consider stepping down.

To the relief of Rodino, the release of the transcripts and subsequent public backlash lightened the psychological burden of the Judiciary Committee to some degree. The public could now see that Rodino and his committee were not conducting a witch hunt.

Once the documents were ready, Doar went to Judge Sirica and, without consulting the committee members, agreed with Nixon's lawyers' insistence that the members remain silent throughout the upcoming hearings. Under penalty of being held in contempt of court, committee members were not to speak to the media or engage in any public discussion of the hearings.

Brooks was enraged when he found out what Doar had done. That an unelected official had the gall to tie the hands of congressional committee members and impinge on their rights as public servants by agreeing to what was in essence a gag order was an absurdity. Brooks respected the prerogatives of Congress, perhaps more than anything else, and through his nature and approach he demanded that others respect them too, be they U.S. presidents or street cleaners.

Brooks yelled at his staffers, Gene Peters and William Jones, to bring Doar over. The special counsel arrived, and Peters remembered what his boss said next:

> Now you can tell [the judge] that we're not going to do this, or I'm going to down there and tell them. We will not, I will not be bound by that. We will do what we feel is right. And Sirica, the judge, will not decide what we release or don't release.

Peters recalled that Doar, the celebrated attorney from Boston, was almost in tears by the end of the conversation. Brooks even wrote the judge, copying every other member of the committee,

> Mr. Doar was not authorized to enter into such an Order by me, nor to my knowledge, by the Judiciary Committee, and, therefore, I am notifying you that I am not bound by provisions contained therein.
>
> I EXPRESSLY do not waive any Congressional immunity for actions on my part as a Member of Congress, and deny that I am in any way subjecting myself to the jurisdiction of the United States District Court for the District of Columbia as a result of said Consent Order.

The scuffle even made it into the newspaper. The members did not sign the agreement, and neither Judge Sirica nor anyone else expected them to limit their own capacity to examine and review the case that was about to be brought forth.

HEARINGS BEGIN: Open hearings began on May 9. Before the full Judiciary Committee and a gallery of reporters, Rodino said a few words about the gravity of the inquiry. Harold Donohue made a motion to expel the cameras and media and continue in executive session. The whole thing was over in twenty minutes.

Numerous staffers concluded that Doar intentionally ran these sessions in a way that was entirely boring to committee members and anyone else who might have been in the room. His recitations of these statements of information were so dry and mundane that after the first day, John Conyers commented that if the public had been privy to Doar's presentation of the evidence, they would have been "bored to death." Precisely the kind of reaction that Doar and Rodino wanted. No new information had arisen, just a rehashing of the previous investigations' findings. Each statement of information along with its supporting documentation was read aloud to the committee rather than just provided to each member to read. This was ostensibly done so that all members would have equal access and understanding of the case, despite the fact that it took nearly six weeks of private sessions to get through all the material.

Doar and Rodino wanted these proceedings to be, above all else, bipartisan, regardless of the final outcome. Brooks, on the other hand, thought the president was a criminal and had seen enough supporting evidence by then to feel confident about it. For Brooks, this was not about process, though process surely mattered. For him, this was about ridding the country of a corrupt president, one who had not upheld the oath he swore to the Constitution. Brooks was determined to right the wrong. He had said, in private and not-so-private conversations, "One of these days the Republicans are going to wake up and find they've got a bullet to eat for breakfast."

Though Doar had made clear to the inquiry staff that they were not to speak with the media during the course of the hearings, Brooks continued to make it clear that neither he nor other committee members would limit their congressional capacity for the sake of a more orderly process. On May 14, the same day the committee issued a second subpoena for Nixon to release the Oval Office tapes, Brooks spoke to reporters about the need for an article of impeachment concerning the use of government funds to improve Nixon's private properties, deftly managing to sneak in a jab at another Republican with obvious presidential ambitions. Brooks said:

> What if they elected somebody, I don't think he's running now but he's a Republican anyhow, and he won't get elected, a man like [Nelson] Rockefeller, who might have TEN homes around the country! I don't know how many houses he's got. We obviously cannot spend five or six million dollars at each of the homes

that the now-governor of New York, Rockefeller, has. He's a wealthy man, he wouldn't expect it. But neither could we leave this to chance.

Two weeks later, the committee wrote a letter to the president warning him that "continued withholding of subpoenaed evidence could result in a presumption of his guilt." In early July Nixon released actual tapes to the Judiciary. Members and some senior staff sat wearing headphones in the committee room and, for the first time, listened to the conversations between the president and his aides. Bernard Nussbaum, a senior staffer, had heard the tapes just prior and was not wearing headphones. "I wanted to just watch the committee. I'll never forget this. I saw this committee, especially the Republicans. . . I saw the faces of the members get flush, the Republicans. They acted very disturbed."

By late June, the inquiry seemed stuck again. Much of the blame, at least in Washington, was laid at Doar's feet. The committee continued to hear a drab recounting of the evidence in closed session. However, the evidence was building. It was becoming clear that corruption pervaded the White House, even to the Republican stalwarts who had promised to be the bulwark against a partisan inquiry. The damage to the president and his administration was overwhelming, and slowly, more and more Republicans began to admit that they would vote their conscience, an indirect way of saying that the president's actions were indefensible.

The president left shortly thereafter on an overseas trip to try to build some more political capital. He first stopped in the Middle East, where crowds still greeted him enthusiastically after his recent success in easing some of the tension between the Arab countries and Israel since the Yom Kippur War the year before.

He continued to Moscow, where he and Kissinger met with Soviet General Secretary Leonid Brezhnev for a summit aimed at improving relations between the U.S. and Soviet Russia. There was the typical pomp and ceremony, but the summit proved unproductive; some speculated that the Soviet leader was wary because of Nixon's declining power at home.

ARTICLES OF IMPEACHMENT: The list of potential charges had been winnowed down from fifty-six to thirty-seven. The nineteen lesser charges were dropped because they were either without basis or low priority, according to Doar. The remaining charges fell into the categories of domestic surveillance, illegal campaign practices, Watergate break-in and cover-up, Nixon's personal finances, and the use of government agencies for political purposes.

Rodino wanted the full committee to appear in front of the gallery and television cameras to begin the process of choosing which articles to pursue. His thinking was that the members would come up with the charges as the hearings proceeded, there in full view of the public. Doar agreed with him. It seemed the prudent thing to do, to let the public observe firsthand that there were no political axes being ground and that the entire affair was highly fair and being carried out in the most statesman-like and commendable fashion.

Again, Brooks differed. It irritated him to no end that his colleagues were more interested in avoiding criticism than in conducting an effective inquiry. Drawing up the allegations in public would not only be messy, it would cede some control over the committee's hearings, if only in the minds of committee members, knowing they were on camera.

Brooks decided he would be responsible for writing the articles of impeachment against the president. In early July, Brooks had combined what he saw were Nixon's ten most egregious offenses. He enlisted his own trusted staff, including Jones, Peters, the legislative draftsman, and his office manager, Sharon Matts, to work on the articles—formalizing language and drafting and collating misconduct that belonged in the same series. Matts, who worked for Brooks for nearly thirty years, explained that the congressman divided staff up into task forces:

> He had each of us in our own investigative teams, and we would draft up things that we would present to Congressman Brooks, and then he decided which articles were substantive enough to be thought of as an impeachable offense.

The congressman struggled over which were the most important, which should be combined, and how the terms should be spelled out before the committee. Congress had never formally indicted a president before so the wording had to be perfect. Brooks marked up and crossed out copies of the drafts for weeks. If Nixon was going to beat these charges, it was not going to be because of a technicality in the language. They would not state that the president "conspired" with close associates, rather that he acted "in concert" with them. Brooks deleted any adjectives that he thought might potentially confuse the issues. For example, the president did not withhold vital evidence; he just withheld evidence.

Once it was complete, Brooks distributed the working paper that proposed the seven articles of impeachment, first to the Democratic members of the committee privately. The Associated Press and the *New York Times* obtained a copy by July 18. The first three articles were the most significant, and even Doar admitted in private that the first charge, which pertained to the president's alleged actions concerning the Watergate investigation, mattered more than the others, both in the minds of the public and most likely in history.

Article I—Obstruction

". . . Richard M. Nixon, using the powers of his high office, engaged personally and through his close subordinates and agents, in a course of conduct or plan designed to delay, impede, and obstruct the investigation of such illegal entry; to cover up, conceal and protect those responsible; and to conceal the existence and scope of other unlawful covert activities."

Article II—Misuse of Presidential Power

". . . Richard M. Nixon, in violation of his constitutional oath faithfully to execute the office of President of the United States and, to the best of his ability, preserve, protect, and defend the Constitution of the United States, and in disregard of his constitutional duty to take care that the laws be faithfully executed, has repeatedly engaged in conduct violating the constitutional rights of citizens, impairing the due and proper administration of justice and the conduct of lawful inquiries, or contravening the laws governing agencies of the executive branch and the purposed of these agencies."

Article III—Disobeying Subpoenas from Congress

"Nixon. . . in violation of his constitutional duty to take care that the laws be faithfully executed, has failed without lawful cause or excuse to produce papers and things as directed by duly authorized subpoenas issued by the Committee on the Judiciary of the House of Representatives on April 11, 1974, May 15, 1974, May 30, 1974, and June 24, 1974, and willfully disobeyed such subpoenas."

At a Democratic caucus amid the hearings, someone asked about the theme of the second article concerning misuse of the FBI, CIA, and IRS, and complained that it was confusing and difficult to understand. Brooks, as one staffer remembered it, was leaning way back in his chair and smoking his cigar. Then he came down on the chair hard, took the cigar out of his mouth, and said, "The theme of this article is we're gonna get that sonofabitch out of there!"

The Supreme Court, including three justices appointed by Nixon himself, began hearings on *United States v. Nixon* on July 8. On July 19, Doar formally presented articles of impeachment to the full Judiciary Committee. When the time came for the committee to openly debate the articles, Rodino opened this new stage of the inquiry and, on filmed recordings, Brooks's voice is audible as Rodino gently uses the gavel to start the proceedings. "Hold it up high," Brooks says into Rodino's right ear.

In Rodino's opening statement, he referred to the Byzantine emperor Justinian, the English barons who compelled King John to accept the Magna Carta, and to the intentions of the Founding Fathers.

I as the chairman have been guided by a simple principle, the principle that the law must deal fairly with every man. For me, this is the oldest principle of democracy. It is this simple but great principle, which enables man to live justly and in decency in a free society.

It falls to the Judiciary Committee to understand even more precisely what "high crimes and misdemeanors" might mean in terms of the Constitution and the facts before us in our time.

Shortly before the hearing, Representative Paul Sarbanes, a Democrat from Maryland, was given the task of reading the articles aloud before the committee and cameras, a status-building move that some claimed made a name for him in the House and perhaps helped propel his later career in the Senate.

A curious fact, however, is that before laying these charges against the president, Sarbanes had never seen them before. The articles had just been drafted and Sarbanes was given a copy at the same time as the other committee members. Brooks and his staffers had carefully considered the staging of the reading. Rodino believed he was above reading the articles and Harold Donohue was too infirm. Brooks clearly was too partisan; Flowers of Alabama and Mann of South Carolina were both conservative Democrats and too politically vulnerable, and John Conyers was, basically, too black.

"We do not have a choice that, to me, represents anything desirable," Flowers said at the time. "I wake up nights—at least on those nights I've been able to go to sleep lately, wondering if this could not be some sordid dream. But, unfortunately this is no bad dream," he said. "It is the terrible truth that will be upon us here in this committee in the next few days."

Mann, whose district voted for Nixon four to one, was not in any leadership position but was able to bridge the ranks of Republicans with both conservative and liberal Democrats.

"We have built our country on the Constitution," he said on the first day of debate. "That system has been defended on battlefields and statesmen have ended their careers on behalf of the system and either passed into oblivion or immortality."

In a later debate, Mann delivered one of the most quoted lines of the hearings. "We would strive to strengthen and preserve the presidency," he said. "But if there be no accountability, another president will feel free to do as he chooses. The next time there may be no watchman in the night."

On July 24, the question of just how powerful and above judicial review an American president could be was laid to rest.

The Supreme Court justices, in a unanimous decision, ruled that Nixon must turn over the Oval Office tapes. Attention immediately turned to Room 2141, where the Judiciary Committee was set to begin ten hours of formal debate. Watching them intently were over a hundred reporters, seventy-five other spectators, and an entire nation glued to its televisions. Each member was given fifteen minutes to speak.

Brooks said:

> *If ever there was a time to put aside partisanship now is that time. There would be no Democratic gain from removing a Republican president and having him replaced by another Republican who. . . might well receive a great outflowing of support from our people. We must now report to the House of Representatives and the American people our conclusions as to whether there is sufficient evidence that Mr. Nixon, while serving as president, has violated his oath of office and thereby jeopardized our constitutional system of government.*
>
> *This is not a pleasant duty, but it is our constitutional duty. Its performance may mean ignoring personal and political relationships of long standing. But we as well as the president are on trial for how faithfully we fulfill our constitutional responsibility.*

The next day, newspapers across the country ran a photo of Brooks on the front page. The congressman was sitting in his committee chair, wearing his thick-rimmed reading glasses, an outstretched copy of the conservative *Washington Star News* in his hands. Across the front page ran the headline: "Key GOP Panelist: Case Strong." Brooks appeared to be reading it intently, with neither humor nor joy. But considering the situation, one could have suspected a pleasant, cantankerous grin on his face had it not been for a thick, lighted cigar clenched between his teeth. Whether staged or not, the image was more than a campy photo opportunity; it embodied a career in Congress.

Before the committee voted, even the cautious Rodino felt the case against the president had been made. There was little doubt that a simple majority of the committee would vote to impeach. The question was how many of the Republicans on the committee would join all twenty-one of the Democrats. Would it be token bipartisanship or would it be a resounding judgment. Brooks was not worried. He knew a woman who worked as a Republican aide and supplied him with updates on how the caucus was leaning. He was confident that it would be a solid indictment.

On the night of July 27, a Saturday, the committee convened to consider the first article of impeachment. A bomb threat was made and the room cleared, but no bomb was found. Then two young protesters in the hearing room began chanting for Nixon to be impeached for war crimes in Cambodia before being ushered away. As the call came to Rodino, the chairman cast a soft "aye," voice shaking just slightly, and looked down as a blitz of camera flashes went off all round the room. When the vote was finally cast, six Republicans joined all twenty-one Democrats to pass the obstruction charge, which contained nine categories of unlawful activities that the president allegedly engaged in to obstruct the Watergate investigation and cover up other activities. Eleven Republicans voted nay. Nixon later relayed that he was swimming at his home in San Clemente when the vote passed. When an aide called to relay the news, the president was standing barefoot in his beach trailer getting dressed, wearing old trousers and a blue windbreaker emblazoned with the presidential seal.

There were still other articles to consider, and during the next three days the committee would pass two more articles, Article II, regarding the misuse of power and violating the oath of office, and Article III, concerning the refusal to comply with court-ordered subpoenas in the investigation. Again, six Republicans voted to pass Article II. The third left more room for personal judgment; only two Republicans voted in favor, and two Democrats broke ranks and voted against, but all three articles passed with a clear majority.

But passage of the first alone was a monumental event. It took only the approval of a single article to send the issue to the full House, where a simple majority vote could impeach and send the matter to the Senate for trial and possible removal from office.

On July 31, the sixth and final day of open debate, Brooks made the following comments before the committee:

> No man in America can be above the law. It is our duty to establish now that evidence of specific statutory crimes and constitutional violations by the president of the United States will subject all presidents, now and in the future, to impeachment.

With respect to the president's taxes, I submit to the committee, that when Mr. Nixon personally signed his tax returns, he attested to false information with the purpose of defrauding the American people of approximately one half million dollars.

Under incredible pressure on all sides, even from the leadership of his own party, one week later Nixon released the transcripts of three conversations he had with Bob Haldeman one week after the Watergate break-in, in which the president demanded that the FBI stop investigating. This was the smoking gun, explicit proof that Nixon had been involved in Watergate and then knowingly obstructed the investigation.

The tape was brought into the Judiciary Committee room and played for some of the Republican members. Representative Charles Wiggins, who had led a passionate defense on the committee, reportedly broke down in tears. Several Republican members said that they would change their previous votes if they could. The front page of the *New York Times* the following day carried the headline, "Wiggins for Impeachment; Others in G.O.P. Join Him."

The tide had shifted. Even hardline supporters of Nixon who had fought every attack against him were now speaking publicly about their decisions to vote for impeachment. One of the most damning rebukes came from House Republican Leader John J. Rhodes. Two days later, after speaking privately with Rhodes and Ford, who advised him that there was no support in Congress to fight the charges, Nixon appeared on national television and announced that he would resign his office effective the following day.

Nixon stated that the entire focus of the presidency and Congress should be on ensuring peace abroad and prosperity without inflation at home, which he mentioned twice in his remarks, and he closed with a quote from Theodore Roosevelt. His resignation speech made no admission of culpability. Nixon said that he had tried his best, dared to pursue great things for the country he loved, and come up short. As with most of the seminal speeches he made in his career, from Checkers to civil rights to Vietnam, Nixon trod a fine line between ruin and salvation.

Rodino was relieved. Brooks was elated.

I felt, "That's wonderful! Get the son of a bitch out of there." Other mem-
bers liked him, some of them. But most of them didn't. He had a good reason
to resign.

Well, if I could, I'd 'a hung 'im! And everybody knew it. I didn't like him; he
wasn't any good. He was a pretty good administrator, to tell you the truth. But he
had some very bad qualities, and I worked him over pretty good.

One month to the day after Nixon's resignation, President Ford issued
the former president a full pardon, declaring that the national nightmare
was over and the healing process should begin. In the same televised address,
Ford also announced the launch of a program that would grant conditional
amnesty for some men who dodged the draft to avoid being sent to Vietnam.

Ten years after the momentous hearings and Nixon's dramatic resignation,
Brooks reflected on that time and on the president. He had not softened
his attitude toward the disgraced leader.

Today, former President Nixon is exactly the same man as he was then: He's
quite intelligent. . . has a good memory. . . is very articulate. . . but amoral in
his dealings with public money and constitutional obligations. . . ten years ago
the American people and their representatives in Congress proved that our system
of government works and that our Constitution is strong and capable of meeting
any challenge.

GAVELS: Brooks knew people around the Capitol, not just the congressional leadership, and not just staff members, but the people who worked
in elevators, hallways, and behind clerical desks. In his particular role as
chairman of the government activities subcommittee, he was involved in
the hiring of many of them. They mostly knew him, too, and appreciated
that he took the time to remember their names and those of their family
members. One of them was Harold Wills, a federal employee who worked
around the Capitol as a locksmith, carpenter, and jack-of-all-trades. Brooks,
with either a keen sense of irony or humor, asked Wills to make him several
sets of three gavels, the ceremonial wooden mallets used by speakers and

chairmen to begin and end legislative sessions. Each set was to contain three gavels, one for each day of hearings. He also made one special request: that Wills fashion the gavels out of the pinewood from the inaugural podium that Nixon had stood on while being sworn into office. Wills obliged and a short time later delivered the gavels to Brooks, who then fixed each set inside a glass frame, along with a small copy of Nixon's resignation letter, which had been addressed to Henry Kissinger. Brooks sent these impeachment mementos to several close friends, including a federal judge. Brooks kept one set of gavels for himself and hung it up on his wall.

19

Snake Killer

B y the end of 1974, the fifty-two-year-old Brooks was busy. He remained the ranking member of the House Judiciary Committee,
continued to alternate chairmanship of the Joint Committee on
Congressional Operations, and chaired the Commission on Information
and Facilities as well as a subcommittee of government operations on defense
and legislation. And his stature was continuing to rise.

Chet Holifield, who had taken over as chairman of the Government
Operations Committee from Bill Dawson, had decided to retire at the end
his sixteenth term in Congress. Holifield had risen from a poor Arkansas
farm to become known around Congress as "Mr. Atomic Energy" for his
work in the field and his reputation as an advocate for weapons testing and
a nationwide network of underground fallout shelters that would house
millions. Though Brooks and Holifield had bristled during hearings at times
and had spats over matters like auditing policy, Brooks had always liked
the man personally. However, the senior legislator's absence would move
Brooks into the chairmanship of the full permanent House committee, a
position he had never held before.

With Brooks at the helm, the committee would take on new meaning
for the government and how it operated. As chair of the Government Activities Subcommittee, he had already enjoyed broad discretion to oversee
expenditures and regulation throughout the government. With the full
standing committee, his reach and authority would be greatly magnified.

In his first year as chairman, the committee issued no fewer than fifteen
investigative reports. Brooks wielded incredible power, claiming, "We had

a Democratic proxy from every member of the Democratic side, sufficient votes to pass anything."

According to congressional historians, Brooks would take the committee from an era where it was "considered a congressional backwater" and turn it "into an aggressive investigatory arm that touched many federal agencies."

Still, though, this is not what Brooks had in mind for himself. What he wanted was the chairmanship of the Judiciary. That was where the real power lay. The power that he felt Rodino had employed too ineffectually during the last two years, the power that Manny Celler had used to push through some of the most progressive legislation since the New Deal and Reconstruction.

IN EARLY 1975, THE world was changing rapidly. The Vietnam War ended with the fall of Saigon in April, but a slew of new troubles had risen to take its place. Most prominently, oil shocks and inflation dominated the headlines. Oil prices had risen since the OPEC embargo in 1973. In 1974 alone, prices for petroleum had quadrupled, and they would keep rising through 1976. Prices on everything continued to rise, while domestic productivity sagged and unemployment abounded, giving rise to the term "stagflation."

Democrats had won large majorities again in both houses, perhaps in part because of Ford's preemptive full pardoning of Nixon, a pill that many throughout the country found hard to swallow. Yet the incoming Ford, declaring the "long national nightmare" over, entered the White House calling for solidarity among the populace and "a moratorium on partisanship" in Congress. The major concerns of the day were oil security and a continually rising rate of inflation. The economy was in recession and the country was headed toward a fiscal crisis.

That January, a humble Ford, just five months into his presidency, had given his first State of the Union address to the newly convened Ninety-Fourth Congress, and he did not parse his words:

> I want to speak very bluntly. I've got bad news, and I don't expect much,
> if any, applause. . . I must say to you that the state of the union is not good:
> Millions of Americans are out of work. Recession and inflation are eroding the

money of millions more. Prices are too high, and sales are too slow. This year's
federal deficit will be about $30 billion; next year's probably $45 billion. The
national debt will rise to over $500 billion. Our plant capacity and productiv-
ity are not increasing fast enough. We depend on others for essential energy.

To upend the deficit, and indirectly create more jobs, Ford proposed a
$16 billion tax cut. He said the country had been self-indulgent, increasing
the size of government benefits, Medicaid in particular, for years without
fully understanding how much they would cost or how they would be paid
for. He also predicted ten years of "energy difficulties" for the world.

He continued:

I have just concluded the process of preparing the budget submissions for
fiscal year 1976. In that budget, I will propose legislation to restrain the growth
of a number of existing programs. I have also concluded that no new spending
programs can be initiated this year, except for energy. Further, I will not hesitate
to veto any new spending programs adopted by the Congress.

A few weeks later, Congress would pass Ford's Tax Reduction Act of
1975, cutting $23 billion in taxes. Ford had dozens of proposals that he
wanted to see through Congress; he soon found that one of his main opponents would be Brooks.

Ford and Brooks had known each other for two decades at that point.
The two had exchanged letters, mostly cordial, since as early as 1956. Brooks
respected Ford for his decency—his most commonly attributed trait; he
found the former congressman to be "a good, honest straight-forward
[man]." There was a humility and humanity in Ford that had been deficient
in Nixon. Ford, who had been a star athlete at the University of Michigan,
had also come from blue-collar roots and made personal stands against the
entrenched racism around him when it was far from the popular thing to do.

Ford likewise respected Brooks, even amid the House's vice presidential
confirmation hearings in 1973 when the congressman had grilled the former
speaker on his views about executive power and the bounds of congressional
oversight. During meetings in 1973 in which Democratic members of the

House Judiciary were seeking to delay Ford's confirmation hearings until dirt could be uncovered, Brooks was often a lone voice of dissent. One member told the chief of the committee staff, "You should be chasing every nickel and dime in Ford's income tax records until you find something wrong. You know that 95 percent of Americans cannot survive an intense tax audit, and you have got to find something on Ford." Others raised questions about a condo Ford had recently bought in Vail, Colorado. The group confronted Brooks one morning and asked him to support their cause. As one firsthand account recalled it, Brooks, looking icily at his Democratic colleagues, said:

> *What you guys are trying to do is half-assed, candy-ass foolish politics. Let's do what's right by the Lord. We will confirm Ford. Now, as to Nixon: The son of a bitch committed high crimes and misdemeanors. Let's impeach the son of a bitch as soon as possible. But we will confirm Ford first. I've got to look my grandchildren in the eye and tell them I did what was right.*

Later, Brooks stated publicly at the confirmation hearings that if Ford were to be confirmed, he would be a "vast improvement over Mr. Nixon."

By 1975, Nixon had moved into near-exile in his San Clemente ranch, but his antics continued to bedevil Brooks and his committee. Congress had voted to extend a flat sum of $200,000 to assist Nixon in transitioning back to civilian life, but Nixon had already spent almost double that amount by January 1975 to maintain his two properties and a legion of staff. Papers reported that Brooks, "one of the toughest watchdogs in Congress . . . [was] keeping a sharp eye on the Nixon spending." Nixon had also previously vowed to repay the back taxes that he owed, a promise he would not keep, as Brooks reminded the public for years.

Three months after taking office with a looming deficit, federal spending was at the forefront of Ford's agenda. Ford introduced a detailed plan to cut expenditures and impose surtaxes "on all corporations and on individuals with well above-average incomes." He proposed an individual surtax, which he termed "very progressive," taking much more from high-bracket taxpayers than middle-income taxpayers. Low-bracket taxpayers would be exempt. Ford said inflation had pushed people into higher tax brackets and created distortions in the tax system. He argued for $30 billion in higher energy taxes to be refunded to taxpayers.

One central tenet of Ford's budget and tax reform package was continuation of a practice known as "revenue sharing," which meant returning federal tax dollars to states, which would have authority over how to spend the money. The country's governors enthusiastically supported the continuation of this arrangement, which had first passed in 1972. Ford saw the program, which had returned some $19 billion to states and local governments, as a "resounding success" and a perfect embodiment of the federalist ideal. He said the program "combines the efficiency of the federal revenue system with on-the-spot judgments of local government." The idea had champions from both parties, from Hubert Humphrey to Barry Goldwater, and it received key support from moderate Republican Nelson Rockefeller.

Ford met with members of the Government Operations Committee on November 6 to discuss continuing the practice, and the president learned that despite the popularity of the measure, it would not be an easy sell. What Brooks hated about the concept was that "revenue-sharing dollars kills the idea that public officials should be held accountable for the expenditure of public funds." By extension, why should the federal government be exacting these taxes if they did not know exactly what they were intended for? He also argued that often the monies "tend to prop up antiquated governmental structures rather than requiring them to reform."

Brooks's opposition garnered national attention. Ford's aide James Cannon, in his book, *Gerald Ford: An Honorable Life,* recalled:

> *Opposing us was one of the craftiest and most powerful members of the House, Jack Brooks of Texas. As chairman of the House Government Operations Committee, Brooks was the gatekeeper to the House legislative process. And he despised revenue sharing. The day we introduced a bill to extend the program, Brooks told the press: "We are going to do to revenue sharing what we do to rattlesnakes in Texas—kill 'em while they're young."*

Ford's aides continued to work on other congressional Democrats and had eventually lined up enough by early 1976 to approach Brooks again.

Ford invited him to the Oval Office for a meeting on the issue. He did not need Brooks to support the measure, only to allow it to come before the full House for a vote. Brooks, sharp as always, quipped to the president, "It's lonely here at the foot of the cross, Mr. President," receiving a round of laughter in the room. For an hour, the two went back and forth until finally, Brooks relented.

The revenue sharing extension bill took several months, but Brooks kept his promise. Speaking to reporters in March, he said, "I am going to do everything I can to convince the Congress that this program should be continued, but only long enough for all of us to find better solutions to the problems." The extension bill later passed the House with a vote of 233 to 172, and Brooks stayed determined to wean the federal government off the practice. In June at a White House press conference, a reporter asked the president what Brooks had said to him at a recent meeting; the microphones had cut out just before Brooks began speaking. Ford told the audience:

> *I think Congressman Brooks' views are well known. He has been against general revenue sharing; he was in 1972; he is opposed to it in 1976. So, I don't think you needed any amplification of Congressman Brooks's views. He holds them very strongly, and we respect them. We just think he is wrong.*

Brooks would continue to repeat that favorite Texas saying of his—"The best time to kill a snake is when it's young."—often enough that in due time, when remarking on Brooks's close examination of the budget process, President Ford referred to him as "a snake killer."

In May, *Texas Monthly*, the popular bible of Texas culture and goings-on, ran an article rating the best and worst members of the Texas congressional delegation. The authors described the delegation, which was wholly different from that of the Rayburn era, as likely in the process of breaking up. For seventeen years with Rayburn at the helm, the group had reliably delivered its votes en masse for the speaker's compromises and priorities. Nowadays, though, small fissures in ideology and temperament that had remained latent were coming to the fore. Younger members typically no longer came from the same rural backgrounds that the senior ones had, and they certainly had no intention of quietly ascending the ladder of seniority. The Texas bloc hinted at moving toward the heterogeneous profile of the delegations from other large states like New York and Pennsylvania, which showed little cohesion in their actions.

The Texas cabal still remained one of the most powerful on Capitol Hill, though. In ranking the members, the authors of the *Texas Monthly* piece wrote that in most cases there was broad consensus about the esteem with which each of the politicians was held. The one notable exception among the bunch, however, was Brooks. The only consensus on Brooks, according to them, was, "People either love Jack Brooks or they hate him. No one is neutral." They listed a slew of anonymous quotes by congressmen, journalists, and congressional insiders:

> *"He's tough and methodical. He holds people's feet to the fire. He doesn't really care if he's liked."*
>
> *"He abuses people. He'd rather make a foe than a friend. He likes to think he's outspoken, but in fact he's just rude."*
>
> *"He has great ability. He saved millions of dollars with the Brooks Act. He does play hard, but he has great integrity."*
>
> *"A weasel. Hated by many, feared by all. He is one of the most blindly partisan people I've ever known, and he completely dissipates his influence."*
>
> *"He's the House embodiment of LBJ, an extremely skillful legislator—not in the drafting sense, but in the leadership sense. He has both power and influence: he knows the rules, knows how to maneuver, knows how to get things done. He's well thought of."*
>
> *"He's very strange. He's shrewd and adroit, but unsubtle; he makes people mad when he need not do it. He's more feared than anything else. He has power but not influence."*
>
> *"He's smart, profane, candid, and cunning. I've known him for years, but when I go into his office, it's like I've walked into a buzz saw. Before I can sit down, he's hit me with two or three savage things about me or the clients I represent. He's too acerbic for his own good. But then, most of the interesting men in Congress are."*

"He's easily the most vengeful man on the Texas delegation. I perceive him as a crook."

The article's authors went on, "One thing is clear: Brooks has immense power."

WITH THE AMERICAN PUBLIC still reeling from the traumatic experience of Watergate, the fear of public corruption ran high in the country. Additionally, in 1976 Tongsun Park, a Korean lobbyist attached to the Washington embassy, was charged with funneling bribe money and expensive gifts from the Korean government to U.S. congressmen in exchange for favorable positions toward South Korea. The allegations implicated as many as one hundred congressmen, including Speaker Carl Albert, whose Korean American aide, Suzi Park Thomson, became a central figure in the investigations. The scandal, which spanned two years, involved hearings by the House Ethics Committee and further investigation by Special Counsel Leon Jaworski, who had worked on the Watergate investigations. Ultimately, it led to the resignations and indictments of only a few congressmen. Albert, further implicated through the questionable allegiances of Thomson, would choose not to seek another term.

It was within this context that both the House and Senate enacted new requirements from congressmen on disclosure of their financial interests and dealings. These new disclosures revealed that Brooks was one of the wealthiest men in Congress, a detail that aroused the suspicions of the media and others on Capitol Hill. The congressman had not come from a wealthy family, and his only work between the marines and Congress had been in the Texas legislature, not a place where one could accumulate much capital. However, Brooks had been investing in Beaumont area banks for some time. By the mid-1970s, Charlotte was chairman of the board of two banks, and she and Brooks were significant stockholders in three others.

That knowledge alone did not satisfy. One staffer within the Texas delegation was quoted as saying, "He's a self-made man. He made it all in banks while he was in Congress. He hates bigness and he hates wealth—except his own."

Paul West, a reporter from the *Dallas Times-Herald*, began an investigation into Brooks and the sources of his personal wealth toward the end of 1976. West's investigation, seeking to uncover one type of wrongdoing or another, would last for nearly a year and a half. When he finally submitted his report, replete with Brooks's filings to the Federal Election Commission (FEC), the story ran on the front page of the Dallas paper. The findings showed no instances of wrongdoing, and the FEC's own audits referred to Brooks's filings as some of the best they had ever seen.

The new disclosure requirements led to scrutiny for many members of Congress. The *Fort Worth Star-Telegram* began to examine the financial dealings of Jim Wright, who in January 1977 had just become House majority leader. Dave Montgomery, a reporter in the paper's two-person Washington bureau, would produce several stories that, while not conclusive of any improprieties, would come back to haunt Wright when a partisan-backed witch hunt arose later in the decade.

JIMMY CARTER: With the new Congress in 1977 came Jimmy Carter, the humble peanut farmer who had risen to the governorship of Georgia and then come from virtual obscurity to win the primaries in Iowa, New Hampshire, and five other states, eventually securing the Democratic nomination. Carter beat Ford by a thin margin in the general election. Ford had run for reelection without Nelson Rockefeller, who many people, including Brooks, really liked. Brooks was also coyly sorry to see Ford go: "*I hated to see Ford leave because he was a minority leader and we [Democrats] had a field day.*"

At the cornerstones of Carter's campaign had been a vow to drastically reduce the number of government agencies, thereby streamlining bureaucracies and improving efficiency, all for the end goal of making government more responsive to the needs of its citizens. As the Georgia governor in 1971, he had reduced the number of state agencies from three hundred to twenty-two to ferret out inefficiencies, bureaucracy, and duplication. He would cite this achievement as one of his major contributions as governor, and he was eager to make similar changes to the federal government. Carter said, "We now have nineteen hundred agencies and departments in the federal government that I know about. I intend to cut those down to no more than two hundred."

During his first trip to Washington just weeks after the election, Carter met with Brooks and Senator Abe Ribicoff from Connecticut. By this time, Brooks had as much know-how and sway in Congress as anyone in Washington. His staffers described that first meeting with Carter as Brooks "explaining the facts of life." Personally, the two Southerners hit it off very well. Both had come from poor rural roots and risen to prominence by their wits and determination. Carter had attended the U.S. Naval Academy during World War II, and after the war ended he became an officer in charge of a submarine crew. Each also had three children, though Carter's were older.

Carter explained to Brooks and Ribicoff in their first meeting that he intended to seek authority to reorganize the federal government to improve its efficiency. Carter recalled, "I met with [them] to explain how important I considered the authorization." Since the federal bureaucracy had become so onerous, duplicative, and intrusive, he proposed to combine agencies that conducted overlapping activities, reduce the number of civil servants, and change regulations in a number of policy areas. His advisers had warned him that the political costs would be great, while the potential payoff might not be, but Carter had already decided this was a top priority.

The request was not new; numerous presidents since Eisenhower had been granted such powers. Yet after the perceived efforts of Nixon to repeatedly sidestep Congress, they had not extended that authority since 1973. But Carter's entire campaign had been predicated on the idea of having a transparent and citizen-oriented administration in the White House. The proposal that the president laid out seemed fine to Ribicoff, but it failed to impress Brooks, who had just spent years leading the reorganization of Congress. The organization of government was the Congress's responsibility, not the president's, and the request could set a troubling precedent for future presidential meddling. Further, as governor, Carter may have had the ability to make such drastic changes in Georgia, but the federal government was too massive and interconnected for any one public servant to come in and dictate sudden shifts, even if he was a president.

Just two days after the New Year, Carter invited Brooks down to his family home in Plains, Georgia. Carter's director of the OMB, Bert Lance, who people had taken to calling the "deputy president," escorted Brooks and Brooks's longtime chief of staff, Bill Jones, down to the president-elect's home. Carter pressed his case for the reorganization authority again, recalling later that this time Brooks had come "well prepared for our argument. He had a grin on his face and a briefcase full of records of the Kennedy and Johnson years." Brooks, not hiding his frustration, told the president,

Governor, Lyndon Johnson was the greatest arm-twister Washington has ever seen, and he did not like to get beat on Capitol Hill. Look at this list! He was never successful in getting more than one-third of his proposed reorganization plans through Congress, even with this special procedure. If you win this argument on the legislation, you still won't have anything to show for it.

In particular, Brooks had concerns about a provision that would allow a single committee in the House to stop a measure. Also, Carter wanted to bypass the normal legislative procedure and pursue a "presumption of agreement" route, whereby if neither house vetoed his proposals within a sixty-day period, they would become effective automatically. Brooks preferred that ratification come through the existing legislative process. Carter later said, "I was as stubborn as he was." The conversation grew tense, so much so that Bill Jones tried to move the group onto a different topic. Carter remained adamant, though, telling Brooks, "Mister Chairman, this is something I have promised the American people. I've got to have it, and I need your help." The president left what he called the "stalemate" feeling both shocked and emboldened. It took a lot of gall for a single congressman, from the same party no less, to flatly disagree with the policy directives of the president. The meeting, though not the details, was covered by the *NBC Nightly News*.

Days later, Carter invited several other Senate and House leaders down for a series of meetings in his family's home. Incoming Speaker Tip O'Neill and Brooks's friend Jim Wright, now the House majority leader, were among the small group. During a break in one discussion, Carter told O'Neill and Wright that if Brooks or any other chairman interfered with his agenda, in particular his plans for reorganization, he would use the bully pulpit of the presidency to persuade them otherwise. Wright later recalled that O'Neill looked as if he had been handed "strychnine on the rocks."

"That would be the worst thing you could do, Mr. President," said the Speaker. "Particularly with a fellow like Brooks. Jack doesn't get mad; he gets even. You don't know your throat is cut until you try to turn your head."

At the start of the Ninety-Fifth Congress, Democrats retained a large majority in both houses. Getting major legislation passed by a final vote would not be as hard as getting the bills through committee hearings and Republican obstruction to the floor of the House.

When Carter entered the White House, he began a practice of holding Tuesday morning breakfasts with congressional leaders to deal with the most pressing legislative matters of the day. That first Tuesday morning when the congressmen entered the small dining room off the East Room, O'Neill, a large man, saw the humble spread of breakfast food laid out on the table and bellowed, "Jesus, Mr. President, I thought we won the election, for crying out loud!" Though Carter would have subsequent breakfasts more amply catered, the moment was representative of a larger disconnect between the president and how he thought things should be and the realities of Congress and Washington. Brooks would become a regular invitee to the Tuesday breakfasts and other meetings in the Oval Office.

Carter remained determined to charge ahead with fulfilling his campaign promises. Just one week after his inauguration, he requested that Congress pass a $31 billion proposal to stimulate the economy. To further his reorganization plan, he even approached Republicans to support the idea. Carter expected that a number of them might quickly give their support, as many always spoke of being in favor of reducing "big government." Their support might in turn pressure the Democrats to come around.

He also sought to isolate Brooks, twice inviting the members of his committee to the White House that February without extending an invitation to Brooks. According to one of Brooks's aides at the time, "Carter showed disrespect for congressional tradition by 'going around the chairman.'"

This tactic of going head-to-head with Brooks did not proceed as Carter planned. In his autobiography, Carter revealed:

In fact, because of Jack Brooks's opposition, as the new Congress prepared to convene, I could not get any Democratic member to introduce my proposed reorganization legislation!

So Carter changed his approach and began to engage with Brooks, meeting with him and Senator Ribicoff often. Both men eventually agreed to hold hearings in their respective committees on the reorganization legislation. Within weeks, Congress passed the measure in both the House and Senate. Brooks had held out his support until one minor concession had been made, and then even he voted for it. The magazine *Government Executive* featured Brooks on the cover of its April issue and ran a comprehensive article titled "Reorganization—Congress Has a Responsibility." Later that month, Brooks and Ribicoff stood behind Carter as he signed a bill granting him "special authority" to reorganize the federal government.

The partnership began to bear out other successes. Brooks introduced the Consumer Protection Act of 1977 that month along with Frank Horton, the ranking Republican representative on the Government Operations Committee. Carter supported that legislation. At the same time, in response to the national energy crisis, Brooks corralled twenty-four cosponsors and introduced the Department of Energy Organization Act to establish a cabinet-level agency that could "assure a coordinated national energy policy," among other things. Five months later the bill had passed through both the House and the Senate and was signed into law, creating the twelfth cabinet-level federal agency. In an extension of Carter's promise to reorganize the government, Brooks sponsored the Civil Service Reform Act of 1978, which gave the president direct control over civil service operations. Carter signed that bill into law on October 13.

With powerful champions like Brooks and Ribicoff pushing Carter's legislative agenda in both houses of Congress, the administration accomplished an impressive list of achievements in a relatively short amount of time.

SOME HISTORIANS CREDITED CARTER'S initial boost in the presidential primaries to one of the first campaign promises he had made: to create a federal Department of Education, replete with a cabinet-level secretary who would report directly to the president. In Georgia, he had pushed through the Adequate Program for Education in Georgia, a reform bill that had significantly enhanced government support for vocational and preschool education, among other things.

Teacher unions had thus far not made much of a foray into national politics, let alone presidential elections. Their efforts, much like the federal government's education policy, both stemmed from and focused on education at the local level. That would change. For Carter, the issue mattered enough that beginning after his campaign announcement in 1974 and continuing for the next two years, he met repeatedly with the leadership of the National Education Association (NEA), the largest teacher's union in the country, to discuss its priorities.

Once his administration was in full swing, though, there was growing suspicion that Carter would not make good on his promise to create a Department of Education. Just ten days after the signing of the Department of Energy bill, the *Washington Post* published an editorial: "Promises to Keep: Will Carter Really Create an Education Department?" With increasing pressure from his supporters, Carter soon felt compelled to act.

The majority of the federal government's education functions sat within the Department of Health, Education and Welfare (HEW), a behemoth of an agency that dwarfed every other one, including defense. HEW oversaw more than four hundred major government programs from national health insurance to Social Security to drug regulation and welfare. It also dominated federal expenditures, consuming over half of the government's annual budget. There were only two organizational budgets in the entire world that were higher, that of the overall U.S. federal government and that of the Soviet Union. The agency employed 145,000 federal workers among 800 different sub-agencies and operated throughout 5,200 buildings across the country. Social Security required three quarters of the budget. The new Medicare and Medicaid programs cost over $30 billion annually, and welfare required another $12 billion. Sandwiched in between all of these was education, constituting just 5 percent of the agency's budget, a modest $9.1 billion.

Many who were familiar with the agency knew full well that education got the short shrift in terms of priority and attention. Ribicoff, who had been a longtime friend of Kennedy, was appointed to run HEW in 1961. After a year and a half, Ribicoff left the agency, citing the "inertia of the bureaucracy." He thought the "E" was getting shortchanged between the "H" and "W," so immediately after he entered the Senate, he introduced legislation to separate education into its own department. He then continued to introduce the unsuccessful legislation in every Congress for the next twelve years.

By August 1977, the Senate version of the bill had earned a majority of the Senate as cosponsors, with Republican Strom Thurmond signing on as the fifty-first, and hearings began in October.

But the plan also had many groups who were diametrically opposed to it. In consolidating the government's education department, the legislation also called for the transfer of hundreds of education-related programs that were scattered outside of HEW, programs that ran the gamut from school lunch to military schools, representing an estimated $10 billion of the federal budget. As one young aide on Ribicoff's staff observed, "Each program served a special group, or constituency, and had its ever-present guardian friends in Congress. Moving one could create all kinds of controversy." This bill proposed moving quite a few.

The American Federation of Teachers, with 450,000 members, opposed the bill, as did numerous Indian tribes, supporters of the Head Start program, and groups fighting the transfer of student nutrition programs from the Department of Agriculture to the new agency. Even HEW's new secretary, Joe Califano, a former Johnson aide who Carter had uneasily appointed, rejected the idea of splitting off education.

On this issue, Brooks had little personal skin in the game. Beyond the expansion of Lamar University, education had never been one of his main political commitments. Staffers knew that Brooks would refuse to introduce or support an education department bill that included transferring the Head Start program, which was operating successfully just where it was. Carter had not yet explicitly asked Brooks for his assistance, and Brooks did not offer it.

Carter's leadership style, or lack thereof, according to some, continued to cause trouble for his agenda. The *Washington Post* ran an opinion piece on April 20, 1978, titled "How Much Has Carter Learned?" that questioned his political priorities and methods after "15 months of disillusionment and disappointment" since his taking office. While praising Carter's mental faculty, the authors lamented the fact that the man attempted to enact radical changes in areas in which he (or the topic) lacked a viable constituency. The piece included a quote from Oliver Wendell Holmes in reference to Franklin D. Roosevelt as "a second-class intellect but first-class temperament," adding that some officials within the Carter administration "think the description might well be reversed in the president's case." Brooks later privately criticized Carter for failing to understand how Congress really worked, although he admitted that the president would learn quickly.

The only problem with Carter is he was smart as a whip, and decent and honorable. But he thought he could do everything better than his assistants. And he could, but he couldn't do it all. . . I was fortunate to have an outstanding staff supporting me. That makes a difference. You can't do everything yourself. Nobody can. Carter proved that when he was president. He's smarter than all those people that worked for him. He was, but he tried to do everything, and he couldn't.

After failing to get any traction in the House on the Education Bill in 1977, Carter and his staff engineered a personal appeal to gain Brooks's support in 1978. In late June, Carter was scheduled to make a three-day trip to Texas to attend a Democratic fundraiser in Houston, review a military demonstration at Fort Hood, and visit a few major cities. Around the same time, in Beaumont, local officials were set to re-dedicate a forty-four-year-old administrative building as the Jack Brooks Federal Building.

Carter's schedule was amended to include Beaumont on his Texas tour. Carter saved seats aboard Air Force One for Brooks and four other Texas congressmen. Midway through the flight, Carter made a final review of a memo put together by one of his congressional liaisons. It detailed the virtues of creating the separate education department and illustrated how the legislation could benefit Brooks as well. Carter then invited the congressman into the plane's presidential cabin for a one-on-one meeting and asked for his help. Numerous associates contended that Brooks, when boarding the plane, had absolutely not made up his mind on whether to help advance this plan. Carter, already on shaky political ground, could not bear to lose such a central legislative battle.

The next morning, a Saturday, thousands of residents of the Ninth District turned out for the dedication ceremonies in Beaumont. The building, a stately three-story structure with Corinthian columns, sat squarely in downtown Beaumont just blocks from the Neches River. It housed Brooks's district office as well as representatives from ten major federal agencies. From the podium in front of the building, Carter delivered these remarks:

> *Twenty-five years ago, when I was leaving the Navy to come home to Plains, Georgia, to be a farmer, a young freshman congressman was leaving Beaumont to go to Washington. In that quarter of a century, the Ninth District has garnered more federal projects than ever before: the Intercoastal Canal, the nation's first strategic storage facility for oil, a whole host of federal works projects too numerous to name this morning, research grants for your district colleges and universities, and a wide variety of miscellaneous federal contracts and awards.*
>
> *I don't recall a single major federal program in Plains in the last twenty-five years. [Laughter] One reason I came here was to get Jack Brooks to help me in the future. If he brings down to Beaumont more than you can handle, I want Plains to be the first spillover point for things that you reject. . .*
>
> *I know that the name that we are placing over the door today will represent the commitment to lean, competent, efficient government that Jack Brooks has fought for throughout his career. . .*
>
> *The General Accounting Office, not given to compliments—much more inclined toward criticism—has said that this one man has been responsible for saving for the federal government billions of dollars—not millions, but billions of dollars—and I want to thank Jack Brooks, as president.*
>
> *I'm sure that you are thankful to have Jack in Washington, but you're no more thankful than I am to have him there. When I was first elected president, with your help, one of the things I promised was to reorganize the bureaucracy, to bring some order out of chaos, to institute reforms that would make the delivery of services to you, with your tax money, more efficient.*

I was told by many people that there was one man in the Congress with whom I would have to work closely, because he would be the key to improving those federal government organizations. It was Jack Brooks. And I asked Jack Brooks to come down to Plains to talk to me about it. He came down—he was the only congressman who came in that group—to tell me what he thought ought to be done. I told him what I thought ought to be done. We were mostly in agreement, but I have to confess to you that there were some differences. I knew that I was going to be the new president of the United States, and I was sure that in a showdown with just one congressman, that the president could win the argument.

I hear many of you laughing, because you know already that I'm going to tell you that I was mistaken. But I have to say that the changes that Jack Brooks recommended in the reorganization bill that did pass under his leadership were good.

In an act that would recur throughout his career, with widely varying consequences, Brooks reluctantly chose to deliver a key victory for the president. Five days after the dedication ceremony, Brooks introduced H.R. 13343, "A Bill to Establish a Department of Education." According to his staffers, Brooks still disliked the move to create the separate agency but chose to lead the effort in the House solely because Carter had requested his help. Though always his own man, Brooks's sense of loyalty to the sitting president won out. Brooks's version of the Education Bill did not include the transfer of the Head Start program, but otherwise reflected much of what Carter's and Ribicoff's staffs had proposed to Brooks. Emblematic of the lukewarm support the bill had in the House and the upward battle it would face, only two other representatives signed on to cosponsor it. The version the Senate passed ended up with nearly sixty cosponsors.

Adding urgency to the process was the upcoming congressional adjournment in October. O'Neill had set an August 11 deadline to committee chairmen for reporting bills to the House floor. Anything after that would not be considered for a vote in this Congress; the education bill would then need to be reintroduced in the next Congress, starting the process over completely in both Houses. It had taken the Senate eighteen months from the introduction to the passage of their version. Brooks had six weeks. Beyond that, the bill would first be sent to subcommittee, albeit one that Brooks chaired, the Subcommittee for Legislation and National Security. The subcommittee would have to hold hearings and then mark up the legislation before passing it on to the full committee, which would have to do the same before passing it on to the House. But before the House could consider it, the bill would need to obtain a "rule" by the Rules Committee, setting the terms for its consideration. Getting a rule for the bill was not a foregone conclusion. O'Neill had begun using that committee as a means of buffering himself from the demands of fellow Democrats and of fighting off minority amendments by placing complex and restrictive rules on major pieces of legislation. If it were not killed by the Rules Committee, as much legislation was, the bill would be placed on the Speaker's agenda. Only then would it receive a vote.

The subcommittee hearings began in July. Brooks had learned from his friend Manny Celler, the longtime chairman of the House Judiciary Committee, that if you wanted a bill to pass the House, you first sent it to your own subcommittee. Celler had used this practice to draft and then pass the Civil Rights Act of 1964 and the Voting Rights Act of 1965 before the bills proceeded on to the full Judiciary.

The reception in the subcommittee ranged from lukewarm ambivalence to total opposition. Supporting this meant taking a risk politically and financially. It was an election year, and congressmen already felt pressed by the onslaught of Carter's agenda.

For three weeks of hearings, Brooks pushed the subcommittee along, dodging and acquiescing to specific transfers to keep forward momentum. Special interests came to plead for their causes as well. The committee heard damning predictions from representatives of Indian tribe associations, science teachers, children's nutrition groups, and even the AFL-CIO. Representative Horton, the new OMB director, Jim McIntyre, and handicapped groups, among others, voiced supporting perspectives. Eventually a much-amended version passed to the full committee, but detractors kept it from passing until two days before the deadline.

In the committee, led by Representative John Erlenborn, dissenters fought the bill by employing a technique termed "filibuster by amendment," calling for entire passages to be read aloud for each minor amendment, introducing dozens of spurious riders and amendments, sometimes two or three times apiece, and insisting on repeated roll call votes just to tangle up the procedure. They were hoping that Brooks and his supporters would lose heart and tire of the cause. But Brooks, armed with his proxy votes, fended off dozens of measures introduced solely to sink the bill. Finally, Erlenborn found the one issue in which he could corral members of both parties around, an amendment prohibiting the transfer of authority over schools for children of military personnel, both domestic and abroad. Brooks was both a service member and a father of three. He implored the other members, "The Department of Defense spends $127 billion, and this is $350 million, a mere drop in the bucket. They are not vitally concerned with education. Everybody knows that." His plea swung two dissenters back to his side and the DOD amendment, designed to kill the bill, failed to pass by a single vote. The committee finally voted to pass the bill.

Once in the Rules Committee, the bill encountered another battery of amendments proposed by Erlenborn and Representative Dan Quayle. Brooks and Horton attended those hearings as witnesses to ensure that the bill did not flounder. Finally, in October, the Senate version sailed through to final passage. The following day, it failed to pass in the House and Congress adjourned for the year.

Brooks would have to do it all over again the next year.

One day before it was ready again for a final vote in July 1978, a senior aide to Carter sent the president a memo laying out in very clear terms what the president was to do to get this bill passed. The confirmed ayes and nays, coupled with those leaning one way or the other, meant that passage or defeat could come down to a single vote. The memo named the seven people Carter must contact and what the messages were to be for each. Majority Leader Wright might finally help if personally appealed to; Dan Rostenkowski needed to reaffirm his support, and Peter Rodino could influence others in his New Jersey delegation. Finally, the memo stated:

Your last call should be to Chairman Brooks and the message should be a

combination of (1) "Thanks for all your help so far"; (2) "I have talked to Tip,
Jim Wright, etc., and asked them to really get in and help"; and (3) "Is there
anything else I or my staff should do?"

The memo continued by instructing Carter to enlist his appointees throughout the federal government to pick up their phones and talk to their friends in the House.

The next day, lobbyists swarmed the Capitol Building, attempting to cajole members one way or the other. The bill just narrowly passed, 210 to 206.

That afternoon there were champagne bottles popping and revelry in the committee room to celebrate the slim victory. Brooks addressed the assembled crowd of supporters, pretended to wipe the sweat from his brow, and said, "I've seen some close votes in my time, but whew!" Vice President Mondale spoke with Brooks over the phone later that night to extend his congratulations. Carter, who was at Camp David, called Brooks "with his hearty thanks to the man who carried the heavy ball for him."

Just days after the House vote, Carter spoke to the nation about various criticisms that Washington and the public at large had been leveling at his presidency. The issue was a "crisis of confidence," he said. He began orchestrating the resignations of thirty-four of his top aides and secretaries, beginning with Califano at HEW.

There remained serious issues in aligning the Senate and House versions of the bill. Though the bill had passed in both houses, in undergoing this "conference" procedure, which would resolve the sixteen major differences between the bills, the legislation could be killed, as its sworn opponents still promised to do. Brooks would become chair of the special joint committee charged with resolving the differences since rumors swirled that Ribicoff would shortly be announcing his retirement. When he and Brooks and other members and staffers from the Senate and House first met to discuss the process, Brooks asked him point-blank in front of the galley if the rumors were true. Ribicoff said yes and, in polite jest, that he would sure miss working with Brooks on matters like this. Brooks fondly replied, "If I had as much hair as you do, I'd retire too," to the delight of those assembled in the room.

With Speaker O'Neill working members in the center of the House floor and Brooks and Horton working around the edges, the new joint version of the bill passed, again narrowly, 215 to 201. That evening Carter, clad in jeans, hosted Brooks, Mondale, and key House members at another celebration party in the Roosevelt Room of the White House. The following day, the front pages of newspapers around the country announced the win. The *New York Times* called it Carter's "first major domestic victory" and the *Washington Post* story announced that the House had just given him "one of the largest legislative victories of his presidency."

On October 17, TV cameras, photographers, and hundreds of people watched as Carter—flanked by Brooks, Horton, Mondale, Ribicoff, and OMB Director McIntyre—presided at the bill signing in the White House's East Room. After much applause and cheering from the audience Carter began to expound on the virtues of the bill. He said,

> *It's not going to be a panacea which can resolve every problem immediately. But I am determined to make it work. And I am very grateful to all of those who have been instrumental in reaching this goal after I don't know how many years of frustrated efforts.*
>
> *Today's signing fulfills a longstanding personal commitment on my part. My first public office was as a county school board member. As a state senator and governor I devoted much of my time to education issues. I remain convinced that education is one of the noblest enterprises a person or a society can undertake.*
>
> *I would like to thank the leadership of both houses of Congress for bringing this historic measure to final passage. I would like to pay particular tribute to the leadership role of Chairman Jack Brooks, Senator Abe Ribicoff, Senator Chuck Percy, and Congressman Frank Horton. Your relentless dedication to this legislation has earned you the gratitude of every citizen. . . .*
>
> *I would like to introduce now to speak for the House Jack Brooks, who is a formidable ally to have in a tough fight. [Laughter] He hates to lose and he rarely does. . . . Had it not been for him, we would not have prevailed. . . . I am deeply grateful to Jack.*

This was perhaps Carter's singular legislative victory. His presidency would have other highlights, like the Camp David peace accord he brokered while Brooks pushed the education bill through the Rules Committee in 1978, but none that so involved Congress. It was one of the few major pieces of legislation passed in 1979. Though both Democrats and Republicans had voted for it, and many had cosponsored the bill in the Senate, the victory would soon become a lightning rod for the GOP. The repeal of the legislation became the core of the party's 1980 platform, and the future Republican president would even talk about an all-out repeal for years to come.

Reminiscing on his struggle to win Brooks's favor, Carter later wrote in his memoir:

> *I learned one lasting lesson from this hair-raising experience: it was better to have Jack Brooks on my side than against me. I found him to be an excellent legislator, and went out of my way to work closely with him in the future. We soon became good friends and allies. I consulted with him on all my subsequent reorganization plans; largely because of his support, ten of the eleven bills submitted passed Congress.*

One time in private company back in Plains, Carter spoke in plainer language to dinner companions, including Curtis Wilkie, a well-known journalist for the *Boston Globe*. Carter recalled with admiration how Brooks had been "the best ally anyone could have on Capitol Hill. He is a tough son of a bitch," the president quipped. "And a mean in-fighter."

The following year, on December 20, 1980, on a sub-freezing Saturday afternoon, Brooks and Charlotte along with their three children and Charlotte's mother went to Camp David. Charlotte remembered, "It was a wonderful, relaxing place, and we used to go often with the Johnsons. We liked to bowl up there. It was just a nice spot to get away, and close by." Carter had recently lost his reelection bid to Ronald Reagan, and the president surprised the Brooks family by showing up unexpectedly with Rosalynn for the weekend.

The temperature at night was around fifteen degrees, and Brooks and Charlotte ate in the dining hall with some of the other adults staying for the weekend. Jeb and Kate were almost teenagers and spent much of the time "tearing around in the golf carts," but Kimberly was only five or six years old.

I remember it was bitter cold, and the kids, you know, used golf carts to get around. And we were all having dinner, and we went to go back to our little cabins, and the golf carts were all gone. The kids were out riding around on them at night. [They had] left us to walk from the dining hall all the way back . . . and I couldn't find Kimberly.

We found out they were over watching a movie, so we walked over there, and looked in the room, and there was the president sitting on the floor, cross-legged, and our little Kimberly sitting at his lap.

Charlotte called and motioned to the young girl to stop bothering the president and come along. But Kimberly shook her head and said, "No!" Charlotte remembered Carter looking up, smiling, and telling her, "It's OK."

CAMERAS IN CONGRESS: The 1970 Legislative Reorganization Act that set the stage for Brooks's work on the Joint Committee and Carter's reorganization agenda had also allowed for televised coverage of certain House committee hearings. Three years after its passage, members had voted to open all committee sessions to coverage unless a majority of the panel voted against it. There had been proposals on recording House proceedings going back as early as the 1940s, when Representative John Coffee proposed live audio broadcasts, citing "mounting public interest throughout the country" in the legislation being considered by Congress in the postwar era. When pundits argued that the American people would be bored by the tedious nature of Congress's proceedings, Coffee insisted that "the people are entitled to know what is going on in Congress, without editorial deletion and without expurgation at the hands of radio or other commentators. Why should not the people judge for themselves?" In the wake of the Watergate scandal, trust and transparency were again central issues in voters' minds.

Opinions in Congress differed, however. Some legislators thought that all congressional activities might as well be televised. There were no technological obstacles to doing so, and certain events like the annual State of the

Union address and speeches from foreign dignitaries had been televised for years. There had even been a short, limited broadcast of two hours from the House floor in January 1949, though it had only covered the opening day ceremony and was shut off before Congress tackled the business at hand.

Brooks, always a proponent of using technology more effectively to advance the performance and purposes of Congress, liked the idea of televising certain congressional activities. Much as television had been allowed to selectively cover the Judiciary Committee's Watergate dealings, there was value in creating a record of what happened at certain moments of import and decision-making.

For Brooks, there was an enormous difference, though, between Congress being televised and it being "on television." There was no reason to show every last moment of the House in session. If all activities were televised, legislators would be given a perverse incentive for showboating. When "gavel-to-gavel" coverage was proposed in 1974 during hearings of the Joint Committee on Congressional Operations, Brooks thought it would be "similar to continuous coverage of hospital operating rooms for the purpose of improving the image and understanding of the medical profession." Many other members of the committee agreed. That position would begin to change, however, later in the year when the Nixon impeachment hearings took place before the Judiciary Committee. There had been many, including lead prosecutor John Doar, who had advocated the idea of that committee writing the articles of impeachment before the television and public, a proposal quickly shot down by Brooks and others.

Speaker O'Neill, the dominant Democratic force in the Democratic House, privately hated the idea of television in Congress. He had adamantly opposed proposals of having television cameras in the House since they had begun to sprout up. Several of Brooks's staffers recalled that O'Neill's famous temper would come out when the concept was discussed.

O'Neill may have been the most powerful voice in the House, but Brooks, was chairman of the House Commission on Information and Facilities, a sub-unit of the Committee on Government Operations. This gave him wide access to the nuts and bolts of Congress's functioning. It also gave him access to the Capitol building's security cameras, which had been installed in the main House chamber and transmitted live feeds to congressional security offices for years. Peters remembered how Brooks had used his chairmanship to tilt the existing security cameras so that they covered the speakers and not the entry doors and seats. Thus began Brooks's television proposal, Peters recalled:

> What Brooks did was Brooks pushed [O'Neill] to the point where we do a pilot program. Now Brooks is smart enough to know if you've got a pilot that's good, it never ends. . . . We didn't have any money, didn't want to go get into that. So what happens? We brought in security cameras, set them up, fixed locations, said here. Now who could object to that?

The pitch worked on the speaker. He announced Brooks's pilot program—to begin on March 15, 1977—that would be a "ninety-day test of closed circuit broadcasting from the House floor to a few offices in the Capitol and the Rayburn Building." But if the initiative were to be successful, questions remained about how the feed would be distributed and to whom.

At the time, the "Big Three" television networks—ABC, NBC, and CBS—had immense power, the kind that even congressmen feared. The networks dominated television in the 1970s, while more Americans began to consume their news through television rather than print. At the time, there were only five cable networks, two of the first being the dedicated movie channels HBO and Showtime, and few of the cable channels expressed much interest in what was expected to be dull broadcasting.

There was a widely held fear that if the networks controlled the televisions in Congress, they would use the material for their own benefit and not necessarily for the benefit of the public or Congress. Members feared that footage would be edited to emphasize conflict or to show legislators in the worst possible light. O'Neill said, "We were disgusted with how the major networks covered the Republican and Democratic national conventions. If a guy was reading a newspaper, they'd always show a close-up of him. If a delegate was picking his nose or scratching his ass, that's what you would see." Some feared that if the networks were given control, it might not be long before their news coverage could have an effect on the functions of the legislative body itself.

On the other hand, there were vocal proponents of allowing the networks to take control, notably Trent Lott from Mississippi and John Anderson from Illinois, both of whom sat on the Rules Committee. During a committee hearing in which network control had been all but decided, Lott wrote a motion and presented it to the chairman, intending for it to end debate and relinquish control to the networks. However, the motion was so poorly and hastily written, Brooks observed, that all it called for was for Brooks's staff to deliver a report to the committee. It had been precisely what Brooks had wanted. Thirty days later, much to the surprise of Lott and his backers, Brooks's staff delivered a report to the committee recommending that the House control the system rather than the networks. Abiding by Lott's own motion, Brooks had won and Lott was irate.

C-SPAN: Simultaneous to this, a relative outsider was pushing for a slightly different vision. Brian Lamb ran the Washington bureau of a cable industry trade magazine called *Cablevision*. He lacked real political connections, but he shared a vision for televising Congress, though it differed from Brooks's. Lamb envisioned a "cable-industry financed nonprofit network" for televising not just committee hearings but entire sessions of Congress. The channel would also cover other public affairs events and policy discussions and, through its mission and fundraising, be neither beholden to Congress nor to any of the established networks. He called his idea the Cable-Satellite Public Affairs Network, or C-SPAN.

Lamb had a small team working with him. During the closed circuit pilot, they approached Brooks's staff, saying that they already the backing of a cable news outfit and asked if the congressman would allow them to broadcast the feed from his security cameras out through this new C-SPAN channel. In October, Lamb went with his camera to interview Representative Lionel Van Deerlin, himself a former broadcast journalist from California. When Lamb walked into Van Deerlin's office, the congressman was watching the floor proceedings on a small television through Brooks's pilot program. Lamb recalled:

I walked into his office, and he was sitting there. He had an old picture of himself looking at what was nothing more than a black and white television set and a security system, basically, that had been set up in the House of Representatives so they could test to see what it would look like if they were on television. No one in the outside world could see the feed. I'm interviewing him, and at the end of the interview—we didn't have cameras on; there was just like your tape recorder, audio—I said to Mr. Van Deerlin, "What would you think of the idea, if the House would go on television? That we could carry this to the satellite and into cable television homes for the whole day?"

Lamb so impressed Van Deerlin with his concept that the congressman walked over to the House floor, where members were debating the matter that same day, and gave an impromptu speech introducing Lamb's proposal. The House voted 325 to 40 to allow the televised coverage and delegated responsibility for the details to O'Neill. Within a year of the launch of Brooks's pilot program, the House passed measures approving televised proceedings and funding for the establishment of its own television system.

The pilot program continued after the six-month mark as Brooks had expected it to. Even colleagues were appreciative. The chairman of the Committee on House Administration, Representative Charlie Rose from North Carolina, wrote Brooks in March 1978 thanking him for his assistance in Rose's production of an instructional video "to inform members of Congress and their staffs about the wide variety of computer services available to congressional offices." Rose remarked: "Some viewers have told us that the live action scenes are the best part of the film. These scenes would not have been possible without your help."

Lamb recalled a one-on-one meeting with the Speaker several months later, to discuss the implementation of the proposal. One of O'Neill's stipulations left final control of the camera positions in the hands of legislative staff, under the direction of the Speaker, and not the new cable network. O'Neill also required a verbal agreement that C-SPAN would provide continuous coverage of all House sessions. O'Neill was of the mind that if Congress was going to go through with this idea, it might as well go all the way. The final concept grated on Brooks, who had supported the concept to serve as a tool for members rather than journalists.

With a total of four employees, including Lamb, C-SPAN first went live on March 19, 1979, broadcasting via satellite the feed to nearly three million homes. The session lasted two hours and twenty minutes, and numerous representatives spoke of the day's significance. A youthful Al Gore from Tennessee was the first to speak before the cameras: "Television will change this institution, Mr. Speaker, just as it has changed the executive branch, but the good will far outweigh the bad."

Gore, alluding to the increased transparency it would bring to the government in the post-Watergate era said, "It is a solution for the lack of confidence in government. . . . The marriage of this medium and of our open debate have the potential, Mr. Speaker, to revitalize representative democracy."

Both supporters and opponents knew that however modest this first step would be, it represented a historic change in how Congress would function and interact with the public. What most did not predict was the effect it would have on the relationship between politicians and their donors.

After the first day's broadcast, Lamb booked a room in one of the House office buildings and invited several congressmen and members of the cable industry to watch the first transmission with him. Given Brooks's integral part in the overall effort, Lamb invited him to speak to the group. Brooks took the microphone and said, "The House is on television today, no thanks to you god-damned folks."

The format that eventually took shape did not resemble the vision Brooks had for televising Congress. Within a few years, there would be instances of abuse, where the medium would be used for representatives to grandstand and push their own agendas. For example, because the cameras stood fixed on the middle of the House floor and narrowed in on the speaker's dais, some representatives, including, notably, a future Speaker of the House, would often give lengthy diatribes to completely empty chambers, and even pretend to respond to audience questions and attack as if they were engaged in a great debate with their colleagues.

This intentional misrepresentation—fooling viewers into thinking they were actually watching Congress at work—was precisely the type of gaming that Brooks had feared with the ultimate format chosen for recording.

IG ACT OF 1978: To extend the kind of centralized oversight achieved by the GAO, Brooks sponsored the Inspector General Act of 1978, a bill which sought to establish twelve independent auditor offices, one for almost every federal agency. The offices were charged with investigating instances of waste, fraud, and abuse within their own ranks by conducting audits and investigations. Brooks wanted to institutionalize watchdogs throughout the government.

Politically, the bill found broad support. Democrats and Republicans alike welcomed the idea of establishing a clear and standardized oversight mechanism within each of the executive agencies. Each of these offices would serve the same role as the GAO in keeping Congress regularly informed about problems and deficiencies within the agencies. The bill also called for whistleblower protections for those who might reveal wrongdoing or bad practices in their testimony.

Still, the bill encountered fierce challenges from the Department of Defense, which argued that numerous auditors had been established throughout the services for decades and that the forcing the military to abide by civilian oversight models was a mistake. The legislation had momentum, though, and was headed for approval. Ira Shapiro, a young staffer for the committee handling the Senate version, recalled one day during the frenzied last week of the Ninety-Fifth Congress when all the members were hurriedly seeing their work pushed through or defeated.

> *The inspectors general legislation appeared to be sailing through to enactment. I had worked out an agreement with the House committee staff; the Senate would pass the legislation with certain changes, and the House would accept the changed bill, eliminating the need for a conference. Still, in the frenzied closing days of a Congress, nothing is over until it's over.*
>
> *One morning, my assistant, Grace Allen, a gray-haired woman who always radiated calm, came into my office looking very worried.*
>
> *"Ira, Chairman Brooks is on the phone for you," Grace said.*

"You mean Brooks's staff?" I responded.

"No," she said, "it's the chairman himself."

I only knew Jack Brooks, the chairman of the House Government Operations Committee, by reputation. An experienced and savvy legislator, Brooks was a bald, beady-eyed Texan who had fought in the Pacific in World War II and was one of the few Southerners to support the Civil Rights Act and the Voting Rights Act. Brooks was legendarily tough; he probably flossed with barbed wire. His calling me could not be good news.

"Hello, Mr. Chairman," I said, trying to sound calm and upbeat.

"Shapiro, how are you, boy?" Brooks rasped.

"Good, Mr. Chairman," I responded. "How are you?"

"Not good, son." Brooks snapped. "The CIA amendment is screwing up the IG bill. You need to fix it." He hung up the phone.

I had been working on the IG bill continuously for months. I knew every word of it, and every contentious issue. I had no idea what Brooks was talking about.

The phone on my desk rang. It was [Senator Tom] Eagleton.

"Ira, I just got off with Jack Brooks," Eagleton boomed. "He's furious about the CIA amendment. Says it will sink the bill. You have to fix it."

I reached for courage to tell Eagleton that I had no idea what Brooks was talking about. But the phone line went dead as he hung up.

My Senate career, which had seemed so promising just a few minutes ago, flashed before my eyes. I didn't know what to do. Somewhat numb, I started flipping through my files, looking for a file labeled "CIA amendment," which I knew didn't exist. I went down the hall to the men's room to throw cold water on my face. When I returned a few minutes later, Grace seemed close to panic.

"Ira, it's Chairman Brooks again," she said, with an alarmed look. "He wanted to hold for you."

I picked up the phone. "Hello, Mr. Chairman."

"Shapiro, where you been, boy?" Brooks inquired.

"Just down the hall, Mr. Chairman, in the men's room," I stammered.

"Shapiro," Brooks continued, "The CIA amendment? Forget it, son. Wrong bill." And he hung up the phone.

The young staffer, scared witless but instantly relieved, went to find Eagleton on the Senate floor to tell him what had happened. The senator "literally fell over laughing. He crashed onto the Senate staff couch."

The bill did pass, and at its signing Carter called the offices of the new inspectors general "perhaps the most important new tools in the fight against fraud." In the following Congress, Brooks also introduced the General Accounting Office Act, which gave the executive's central auditing agency more force in overseeing federal expenditures. Carter signed the legislation into law on April 3 and gave Brooks one of the silver and green pens he had used to sign it.

Seven months later, in one of his last official acts as president, Carter penned his signature onto the Paperwork Reduction Act of 1980, a piece of legislation to eliminate unnecessary and costly information-collecting that Brooks had sponsored and then deftly and quietly moved through Congress. The groundwork for the bipartisan bill had been set in place five years prior, when Horton chaired a two-year commission to investigate how the government requested information from businesses and individuals. That commission then made recommendations to Congress in October 1977 on how to correct inefficiencies.

Carter signed the paperwork bill into law in the Cabinet Room of the White House on December 11, 1980, just one month after he lost his re-election bid. Brooks, Horton, and Senator Lawton Chiles of Florida stood behind him.

"We have addressed the bureaucrats, and we've won," Carter said, stating that the bill would tackle the 10 to 15 percent of the federal budget that was spent on information and paper processing. Carter cited the legislation as "one of the most important steps we have taken to eliminate wasteful and unnecessary federal paperwork and also to eliminate unnecessary federal regulations."

Senator Chiles remarked:

> *Mr. President, you mentioned that this was one of the first things that you talked about in your cabinet meeting. It was also one of the things that you talked about on the stump all over the country when you were campaigning. I*

think this is certainly a promise fulfilled, and I'm delighted to have had a chance
to participate in that. . . . I'm delighted to participate with Jack Brooks. When
you get him working on something, you know he's going to take care of his side.
You've just got to worry about your side.

Brooks went a step further, telling Carter:

In 1965, with the ADP proposition on computers that has saved the gov-
ernment billions of dollars, we had the same pressure from some of the same
bureaucrats fighting President Johnson—and they've fought you. But you had
the courage to do it. . . . It is the most important legislation that you have passed
and that we have been able to work on. It will help this government run the
information upon which decisions are made that cost billions of dollars a year.
Thank you, sir.

As usual, Brooks did not heap his highest praise upon headline-catching,
controversial victories like those he had won with the creation of the Departments of Energy and Education. He had saved it for simple, mundane
victories like this, which would lose the battle for headlines every time, but
would have vast ramifications on how the government would function for
the benefit of its citizenry.

20

Iran-Contra

By 1981, Brooks was considered an elder both in the Democratic Party and in the House. He was one of the "old oaks" according to Speaker O'Neill, referring to the Democratic wall that Brooks, Rodino, John Dingell, Claude Pepper, and Jamie Whitten could reliably provide in a good partisan fight. Together they also chaired some of the most influential committees in the House. Brooks had served in fourteen congressional terms, seen presidents come and go, even been intimately present for the final days of the Kennedy, Johnson, Nixon, and Carter administrations. There remained a few congressional colleagues who were either older or more senior than he, but there was arguably not a single legislator in all of Washington with more legislative accomplishments or breadth of experience in the internal workings of the House.

Brooks had already amassed an impressive lifetime's work for the citizens of Beaumont and for American taxpayers, but there remained something else still driving him. He never spoke openly to colleagues or staffers about his personal ambitions—representing the fine folks of southeast Texas was fulfillment enough, as the message likely went—but he did strive for more. It was not attorney general; it was not Speaker of the House or majority leader, positions that his friends and contemporaries had been filling for years now. For Brooks, the dedicated legislator, congressional watchdog, and attorney with one of the sharpest legal minds in Congress, there was one position in particular that represented the height of what he could achieve and how he could serve the nation: the chairmanship of the House Judiciary Committee.

There were all kinds of committees in Congress; Brooks had been in-volved with many, and he had chaired quite a few too—select committees that were assembled for specific and temporary issues, joint committees that comprised members from both houses; and permanent standing committees, which were the real deal in congressional power. But even within standing committees there were divisions, namely between the minor ones and the major ones. Brooks's Government Operations Committee, where he had served as chairman since 1975, was one of a few, full standing committees in the House, but it was still a minor one. Since Sam Rayburn had placed him as chair of one of its subcommittees in 1955, Brooks had greatly ex-panded the reach and import of that committee; however, it did not carry the same gravitas as the major committees—Appropriations, Rules, Foreign Affairs, and Judiciary. These committees did not just resolve matters, they decided fates.

There was no other single entity in the legislative branch so entrusted and frequently called upon to serve as arbiter of the U.S. Constitution and to inform the practical direction of the federal government during existential crises as the Judiciary Committee. In some regards, the House Judiciary Committee may have represented the most meaningful and direct link between the federal government and the voice of the people. When it came time to decide questions with ramifications for how the U.S. system should work and how its individual servants were to serve the public—and when that had to be done from deep within the trenches of the government machinations—the House Judiciary Committee was the body America looked to for clarity and guidance.

In 1964 and 1965, Brooks had been a new member of the committee and only played a partial role in helping to shape the landmark civil rights legislation that it drafted and passed onto the House floor. During Nixon's impeachment process ten years later, Brooks had gained seniority and experi-ence but was still only the third ranking member on the committee, though many said he effectively ran it. The fact that Brooks and his staff drafted the articles of impeachment against Nixon give further credibility to this idea. Still, even as its most influential member, Brooks could not determine what matters came before the committee or how investigations and hearings were to proceed. That power belonged solely to the committee chairman, which since 1955 had been either Emanuel Celler or Peter Rodino. For Brooks, the chairmanship, which he had stood next in line for since 1975, would be the pinnacle of his life in Congress and a capstone for his career.

Nevertheless, there remained unexplored areas of government that still interested Brooks. Several of them belonged in the realm of foreign policy, diplomacy, and trade. In 1980, O'Neill appointed Brooks to be one of Congress's representatives on the North Atlantic Parliamentary Assembly, which was a little-known group of legislators from member states of the North Atlantic Treaty Organization (NATO) military alliance. Both consortiums had sprung out of fear of the Soviet Union in the aftermath of World War II, and the Parliamentary Assembly members convened to inform their respective governments on defense and security issues, essentially serving as a forum for parliamentarians to come to an understanding about common threats and internal tensions.

Though Brooks had limited foreign policy experience and his war years accounted for most of the time he had spent outside the U.S., he was an experienced committee chairman and understood the art of negotiating. He was adept at determining the interests and overcoming the distrust of other nations. He also enjoyed dealing with issues that went beyond Congress's internal politics.

For their part, the other parliamentarians in this defense group looked to the U.S. delegation for its dominant role in the Cold War, and Brooks sat at the head of that delegation. On a personal level, many of the Europeans had a fondness for the plainspoken emissary out of Texas who regaled them with anecdotes and jokes. Once, Brooks was toasting the host of a formal dinner in an English mansion, and looking up at the ancestral portraits lining the walls, he raised his glass, saying, "And here's to your daddy, the Duke."

On trips abroad, Charlotte was his frequent travel companion. She fondly remembered:

I know how you would think he would not be the one that would be the diplomatic equivalent for these parliamentarians, but the Europeans especially liked his straightforward manner about many things. In fact, there was some dispute between the Greeks and the Turks and they asked specifically for him to mediate.

Brooks himself recalled:

We had the NATO parliamentarians. . . . and I was president for two years, two terms, and a member for a good many. They changed the rules, so I remained a member of the standing committee, which sets the policy, even after I was president, so long as I was a member. That seemed appropriate, I thought.

Note the peculiarity of a small-town boy from Texas causing this group of European parliamentarians to change their own rules to keep him.

While the parliamentarians and their meetings rarely garnered major headlines, they did travel in a rarified atmosphere. Just as some were pleasantly taken aback by Brooks's manner, he was also tickled by how down-to-earth his colleagues, even the Americans, could be away from cameras and microphones. He recalled running one of the programs and not being able to fit all the attendees inside an old legislative office in Williamsburg:

So we had a reception at one of the houses that the Rockefellers had restored that was part of the Williamsburg complex, and he picked up the tab for that meeting. Wonderful, big party. [Nelson Rockefeller] loaded them up with whiskey, and they drank and sang. They had a wonderful time.

Nelson and I were out back, out looking at the lawn in the back for a minute, quietly resting just a minute, talking to each other, and he was telling me he has a boy about Jeb's age. At that time, they were just little fellas, and he said, "You know? My son said, I don't know, Daddy, why you would even want to think about being president! They don't have a golf course! And not a very big pool."

Ooh! He was not bragging, he was just telling me this as just kind of a joke. And he wouldn't tell anybody else. He wasn't bragging about being rich. He just wanted to know how that little boy felt. I thought that was interesting.

GOP IDEOLOGY: The days when an unabashed Democrat and unabashed Republican could happily converse outside of work were coming to an end, however. There were cultural and economic drivers leading voters in Texas and all over the South to reimagine how they saw themselves politically.

Politics and rancorous partisanship often suffuse relations between the Congress and whoever is sitting in the White House. That antagonism had taken an even sharper and longer-lasting turn when President Nixon employed what came to be known as the "Southern Strategy," enticing white voters in the South and elsewhere to abandon the Democratic Party because of its pursuit of civil rights legislation.

Deep fissures between American voters had grown during the boom years of the postwar era, the tension of the Cold War, and tumultuous events of the civil rights movement. Nixon had been the first to successfully identify and exploit these differences as he created a broad base to win the presidency in 1968 and then again in 1972. The Republicans, learning from his success, were now codifying those same fissures into distinct new voting blocs that were to be courted by name, all with the intention of slowly gathering them under one political umbrella: the new GOP.

A broader constituency was sought, one in which all sorts of disparate communities and voting blocs could find themselves welcome. "There is room in our tent for many views," Reagan said. By measures deliberate and long-reaching, a patchwork of unrelated interests and positions—anti-abortion arguments, the call for more tax cuts, insistence on absolute gun rights, or opposing immigration—was artfully sewn together by the one major commonality that they did share: they had not yet been explicitly claimed by the Democrats.

Coalescing these voters into a unified identity would be one of the political masterstrokes of the century. Enjoying firearms would soon become an ideal that implicitly meant believing corporate tax rates were too high. If you found government operations to be too invasive and costly, you were also expected to be firmly anti-choice. Some low-income Americans would soon be coaxed into believing that a highly exclusionary political agenda given the cleverly deceptive moniker "trickle down economics" was in their best interests.

Aligning the party and its political goals with evangelical Christianity would prove to be the most fruitful political success for decades to come. The impact of this strategy on national elections continues to this day and was evident especially through the 1980 election and during each successful Republican presidential bid. Like Nixon, Ronald Reagan embraced disaffected white Democrats, and he also took advantage of the economic frustration of voters during Carter's administration. There was a political upheaval underway and Reagan, the former film actor and one-time Democrat, had transformed himself into a genial conservative and captured the spirit of that upheaval.

Before long the unthinkable began to happen: in the land of Sam Rayburn, Ralph Yarborough, and Lyndon Johnson, the Democrats began to lose elections. Republicans went from having two members in the Texas delegation in 1976 to having ten in 1984. Within a generation, Texas would go from having almost no Republicans in statewide elected offices to having no Democrats in those positions.

Texas and the entire South had begun to redefine itself politically, foreshadowing trends that would spread throughout the country, fundamentally change the tenor and rules of engagement between the two political parties, and set in motion a series of events that would lead to the most dysfunctional and vitriolic political stalemate in generations.

IF CARTER'S RISE TO the presidency seemed like an aberration, stemming from a surprise performance at the Iowa primaries, Reagan's had been anything but. He had been building a nationally focused political machine since before he set foot in the California governor's mansion. In 1976, he had narrowly lost the Republican nomination to Ford. In 1980, with a broad base of conservative support, he ran again and Americans overwhelmingly favored the affable former actor, who brought star power to the political scene, over Carter, the modest, former submarine commander who carried his own luggage to and from Air Force One.

Thus the decade began with a Democratic Congress wary of a very popular Republican president, and a South that was quickly changing from blue to red.

Reagan's style was to set the tone with a few overarching ideals and then let staffers wrestle out the details. His bid for the presidency had focused on just a few themes: lower taxes, smaller government, and a stronger military. This last one was pointed at stemming the scourge of Communism as it spread across the globe.

MILITARY SKIRMISHES: Brooks's front row seat to the escalation of the Vietnam War during the Johnson administration meant that he was well-versed on the intricacies of Cold War positions and negotiations. Now at the NATO Parliamentary Assembly, new conflicts in Afghanistan, Grenada, Honduras, and other spots around the world were keeping the delegates busy.

Western European member states had always taken some solace in the knowledge that while the Soviet Union certainly had conventional nuclear firepower, it lacked the tactical ability to fight a strategic nuclear war because its weapons were imprecise. Advancements in the accuracy of Soviet nuclear missiles changed that equation. A new ballistic missile with the NATO reporting name "SS-20 Saber" was a mobile, truck-mounted, fifty-foot-long intermediate-range weapon. It could be hidden anywhere in the vast Russian forest, launched at a moment's notice, and deliver a nuclear warhead to any military base or installation within three thousand miles with no warning. The shores of the U.S. were safely out of reach, but NATO members in Western Europe were understandably shaken.

In early 1983 Reagan announced his space-based and expensive Star Wars proposal. It was the beginning of a military spending decade that would ultimately force the Soviet Union to concede and lead to its dissolution.

Though Reagan has been lionized since his time in office, there was no love between the president and Brooks, who characterized the Californian as "not a bad president, but a so-so president" and "not particularly bright." Brooks was always blunt: "We didn't have any warm relationship."

In February of 1984, it came to light that the U.S. Information Agency, an executive agency under the State Department that aimed to "streamline the U.S. government's overseas information programs" had created a blacklist of people deemed unsuitable for speaking engagements abroad. The list contained eighty-four names, mostly outspoken liberals such as broadcasters

Walter Cronkite and David Brinkley, civil rights activist Coretta Scott King, and consumer advocate Ralph Nader. Brooks had been flagged for one reason or another, and he, like a lot of people on the list who had not known of the USIA's speaking program nor sought to participate in it, was delighted by the absurdity of the idea. He even had a letter hand-delivered to Ben Bradlee, the famed, longtime executive editor of the *Washington Post*: "Thought you might be interested in my comments on the Floor of the House of Representatives about our both being named to [USIA Director Charles] Wick's 'black list.'"

On the floor of the house, Brooks had said:

> *This action on the part of the Reagan administration's self-confessed electronic Peeping Tom—Charles Z. Wick—is something that we've come to associate with Republican administrations ever since Watergate, and President Nixon used his infamous hit list to single out American citizens for special treatment. . . . Such an action is a clear abuse of executive power, and it got President Nixon in deep trouble. Through the years we have developed procedures for dealing with such arrogant and outrageous abuses of executive power.*

Brooks had been on Nixon's hit list as well.

Reagan would dominate Washington politics for the next eight years. In the foreign sphere, his administration and other officials in Washington would find creative ways to influence global conflicts, with individual politicians and public servants playing surprisingly self-directed roles. This degree of autonomy, even for those in unelected roles, coincided with what would become a series of loose and disjointed military interventions.

Under the leadership of Brooks's Texas colleague and Second District successor in the House, Charlie Wilson, the CIA secretly supported the arming of the rebel Afghan Mujahideen fighting the Soviets. When the CIA refused to provide the rebels with field radios, Wilson, according to his *New York Times* obituary, sent one of his staffers to Virginia to buy "$12,000 worth of walkie-talkies from a Radio Shack outlet."

In October 1983, two days after a truck laden with explosives crashed into a U.S. Marine barracks in Beirut, killing 241 soldiers, Reagan ordered the curiously timed armed invasion of the tiny Caribbean island of Grenada, which had a leftist government with close ties to Communist Cuba and its charismatic leader Fidel Castro. Reagan sent more than seven thousand soldiers to the tiny island without so much as informing Margaret Thatcher or other leaders in the U.K., which still counted the tiny nation as one of its protectorates.

In 1986, after a naval incident in the Mediterranean and the bombing of a nightclub frequented by U.S. soldiers in Berlin, Reagan ordered precision airstrikes against two major cities in Libya, whose leader Muammar Gaddafi was aligned with the Soviets.

IRAN-CONTRA: In Nicaragua, the left-wing Sandinistas had risen to power and taken control of the government, establishing what many feared was a Soviet foothold right at America's doorstep. The right-wing rebels, or Contras, had taken to fighting the leftist regime from the jungle. Reagan and those in his administration wanted to fully support the Contras however they could, both financially and logistically.

After Congress learned that the Contras were selling drugs to help finance their fight against the Marxist Sandinista regime, it passed the Boland Amendment as part of an appropriations bill. The amendment, named after Representative Edward Boland from Massachusetts and signed into law by Reagan, banned official U.S. military aid to the Contras. Nevertheless, Reagan repeatedly entreated Congress to lend financial support to the "freedom fighters." The House routinely rejected these requests.

Just as the word "Watergate" had come to encompass years' worth of executive misdeeds and shadowy operations by leaders and staffers in Nixon's administration, a series of secret and illegal actions by federal officials under Reagan would soon become referred to as simply the "Iran-Contra Affair."

After Reagan and his staffers had tried the standard and constitutional approaches to providing military assistance to the Contras, only to be continually rebuffed by Congress, aides looked to find unconventional means to accomplish the president's goals in Nicaragua. The Boland Amendment had been aimed at curtailing the actions of the CIA and the Department of Defense. However, it did not explicitly mention the National Security

Council (NSC), a small advisory council that had been established by Truman to assist the president in national security and foreign policy matters. The NSC was led by Admiral John Poindexter and his deputy, Colonel Oliver North, a decorated U.S. Marine.

A plan was devised to achieve several of the administration's foreign policy goals: the U.S. would secretly sell arms to Iran, now in dire need of weapons for its ongoing trench war with Iraq. In return, Iran would use its influence to lobby for the release of Americans being held hostage by militants in Lebanon. The proceeds from the sale of those arms, which were priced artificially high, would then be covertly funneled through private American businesses to the Contras in Nicaragua to aid them in their fight against the Sandinistan government.

To Poindexter and North, the plan seemed like a win-win-win solution: American hostages would be released in Lebanon; what was perceived as an intransigent, nascent government would be thwarted by its own countrymen with no American boots on the ground; and, with untraceable private-sector profits, the executive branch would build a dedicated slush fund and covert foreign action capability outside the procedural checks of Congress that it could draw upon whenever necessary.

The plan also played into Reagan's hands-off managerial approach. The president was known for his inattention to detail and for delegating major responsibilities to his advisers once he had set the general course direction. What this scheme entailed at almost every level was unequivocally illegal and in violation of the Constitution, but the locus of decision making was sufficiently distant from the president to help insulate him from accountability.

It worked for a while, until a chance incident uncovered the entire operation. In October 1986, Eugene Hasenfus, a marine, and three American pilots were transporting an arms-laden cargo plane over the Nicaraguan jungle when they were shot down by a pro-Sandinista militia unit. The three pilots were killed in the crash, but Hasenfus parachuted to safety and was soon captured. As news traveled, a full-blown scandal had emerged. Reagan sought to squelch the matter quickly by ordering Senator John Tower to lead a fact-finding commission to investigate.

The following January, at the start of a new Congress, Jim Wright assumed the speakership of the House, replacing O'Neill. Wright had entered Congress two years after Brooks. Now, after thirty years, he again came looking to Brooks for leadership. If the rumors in the press were to be believed, this scandal was so egregious and embedded throughout the Reagan administration that the rookie Speaker could see it progressing down a path calling for impeachment. Wright recalled years later:

> *There had been laws violated. I mean, grossly violated. We had a law that said you can't spend any money promoting a war to overthrow the government in Nicaragua. We were doing it! We had another law saying we can't send any military equipment of any sort to Iran. And that was done. Violation! There was another law that said, any covert activity of the CIA, or other agencies, must be reported to the Intelligence Committee before it's done, and authorized . . . that was violated. All of those laws were violated.*

The alleged violations covered so many areas of government that the potential hearings could have spread throughout a dozen committees and subcommittees, each one of which would be vying for television coverage and media attention. So Wright and Senate Majority Leader Robert Byrd decided there would be just one joint committee with handpicked members to handle it all.

The Speaker asked Brooks if he would take the chairmanship of the House side of the joint committee, according to one of Brooks's aides who admitted to overhearing their quiet phone conversation. Brooks considered the role. There were obvious parallels to the Nixon administration's violations. If what the press was reporting was true, then this affair certainly warranted a careful look at whether Reagan was guilty of impeachable acts. But Brooks ultimately turned the Speaker down. He simply did not have the time, given all of his other responsibilities. Or, as later events would suggest, perhaps he did not have the energy for yet another drawn-out impeachment proceeding against a president. Or, he may have already read the tea leaves and realized that the country did not have the energy for another impeachment proceeding. There was a cyclical pattern to all of this executive overreach. Nixon had abused his power. Congress had muzzled Ford in response. Carter had persuaded the American people that the muzzle was not necessary, and now here they were again. Perhaps Brooks simply felt that leading the congressional charge against the White House once was enough for him.

Brooks instead recommended that the Speaker tap Representative Dante Fascell, who chaired the House Foreign Relations Committee. Fascell had a reputation for bipartisanship. But, ultimately, the majority consensus was for Lee Hamilton, ranking member of the Foreign Affairs Committee, to be the House chair, and Fascell ended up as vice chairman. Neither Brooks nor Wright thought Hamilton was the right man for the job, but, according to Wright, "Hamilton had a good reputation as a reasonable, calm, non-opposing guy, and most of the members wanted to go with Hamilton."

Brooks, Hamilton, and thirteen other representatives were placed on the House's Select Committee to Investigate Covert Arms Transactions with Iran. Together with the Senate's Select Committee on Secret Military Assistance to Iran and the Nicaraguan Opposition, chaired by Senator Daniel Inouye, the congressmen would begin hearings in May to try to understand the bizarre allegations, determine their merit, and ascertain who within the government bore responsibility or had even been aware of what had been going on. In his own defense, Reagan claimed that congressional restrictions on U.S. aid to Nicaraguan rebels did not apply to him, an assertion that Brooks and many others in Congress rejected as ridiculous.

The joint hearings were held over forty-one days between May and August. All of this played out in real-time coverage on C-SPAN, perhaps the first time the network coverage would garner prime-time numbers in its viewership. Senator Inouye, a Democrat from Hawaii, took the lead. Inouye had served in World War II, as had some of the other members of the committee. Inouye's contribution, however, had been remarkable. As a Japanese American living in Hawaii, he had served as a medical volunteer during the attack on Pearl Harbor. Once the ban on Americans of Japanese ancestry was lifted in 1943, he joined the army and was assigned to the 442nd Regimental Combat Team, composed almost entirely of Japanese

Americans. While Brooks had been in Guadalcanal and Okinawa, Chairman Inouye had been fighting the Germans in Italy.

Once the hearings were in full swing, it became apparent that those in the administration who were involved in the scheme were not penitent and would not go quietly. Brooks and others found the general arrogance of State Department officials and their propensity for misdirection to be an affront to Congress.

On June 3, the committee heard from Assistant Secretary of State Elliott Abrams, a thirty-nine-year-old de facto spokesman for the department and a specialist in Latin America. Abrams had previously spoken in private to members of the Intelligence Committee and vehemently denied having sought funds from foreign countries to aid the Contras. Abrams had also denied that the government was involved in any way with supplying arms to the Contras, claiming that the activities he was aware of were related to standard intelligence monitoring. Both of these statements were revealed to be outright fabrications. Abrams had himself solicited and received a $10 million contribution from the Sultan of Brunei after his boss had declined to make the request.

Abrams began his testimony with an apology for lying the previous year but quickly turned combative. Toward the end of Abrams's most open testimony, Brooks had heard enough, chastising the young assistant secretary in front of the television cameras.

> *I've been very troubled with the job that you did because you would have us believe that you just had no idea about private fundraising, about solicitation to foreign governments for a few million dollars, you had no idea about how the Contras were operating or where they were getting their supplies, you had no idea about a large number of people who were commuting almost daily between the United States and your area of surveillance. And yet, these missions went on for months while you were in office.*
>
> *You take more pride in not knowing anything than anybody I ever saw. . . . I can only conclude after this that you are either extremely incompetent or that you are still, as I say, deceiving us with semantics, or maybe the administration has intentionally kept you in the dark on all these matters so then you can come*

down and blatantly mislead us, the secretary of state, and the American people on all of these issues that we have been discussing. And I am deeply troubled by it and wonder if you can survive as an assistant secretary of state.

To which Abrams replied:

I don't work for you. I work for George Schultz, and he seems to be pretty satisfied with the job I've done for him. . . . The characterization that you have made of my testimony here yesterday and previous testimony, I think, is in too many ways to state in a brief answer, erroneous.

Brooks, without missing a beat, fired back:

I wouldn't think that you would agree with one bit of it because you have been very patiently telling us you don't know about this, you don't know about that, and you weren't informed, you were not authorized to tell the truth. That is the wildest story I ever heard. They were not authorized to tell the committee the truth about something. That is the most cockamamie idea I ever heard. Why do you have to be authorized to tell the truth to the appropriate committee in Congress?

Abrams began to reply: "Well . . . " but Brooks continued:

I don't want you to tell me. But you should have told the Intelligence Committee.

Perhaps sensing some blood in the water, Senator Sam Nunn then laid into the young official with the same fervor.

Now, how are we supposed to know that you are informed when you appear before the committee? How are we supposed to know whether you are authorized to tell the truth? In other words, before we ask you substantive questions each time you appear, do we need to precede that by asking you if you're authorized on this subject to tell the truth, the whole truth and nothing but the truth? Is that the way we begin our questioning of Elliott Abrams?

The tongue-lashing had an effect. The next day, the *Washington Post* featured an article titled "Elliott Abrams' Painful Lesson," citing the drubbing Brooks and Nunn had given him. Brooks called the assistant secretary a "lying son of bitch" to a *Los Angeles Times* journalist. Ten days after the appearance, 129 House Democrats sent a letter to Abrams's boss, Schultz, demanding Abrams's resignation for having "knowingly and deliberately misled Congress on several occasions."

Others who appeared before the committee received similar treatment. Ten days later, when private businessman Albert Hakim explained how he used traveler's checks and attempted to channel money to Oliver North, Brooks interrupted, "I think they'd shoot me in East Texas if I did business like that!" One reporter described the congressman as a "full-of-outrage, cigar-chomping shooting star."

As it would turn out, this all was simply prelude to what would become the lasting impression of that summer's hearings, testimony from Colonel North. As the committees prepared for the hearings, North had made clear that he had no intention of speaking before Congress again and was taking the Fifth under the advice of his counsel, Brendan Sullivan. The Senate committee proposed the idea of granting amnesty to North in exchange for his testimony.

Brooks disagreed with the idea entirely, and he was one of very few committee members who voted against it. Rodino and Dante Fascell joined Brooks in dissent. Several pundits, such as syndicated columnist Carl Rowan, lauded the congressmen for their opposition, though the majority opinion eventually won out.

In addition, the joint committee agreed, in spite of Brooks's protest, to allow North to skip the step of submitting lengthy testimony in private before the public testimony, as some others had been required to do. Like good trial attorneys, they never wanted to ask a witness a question that they did not already know the answer to. It ceded control of the testimony and invited chaos. As fortune would have it, that is precisely what happened when North testified, and the committee was wholly unprepared for the character they were about to introduce on prime time television to 240 million Americans.

During his first week of testimony, North, who cut a trim figure in a crisp military uniform, praised the popular president, unapologetically defended military action during the Vietnam War, and spoke of the pride he took in his own role in that conflict. Committee members all began by giving their gratitude to North for his military service to the country. They also increasingly spent time mentioning his eloquence and patriotism. Some committee members even appeared to undercut the seriousness of their own lines of questioning by their warm address of North's character and devotion to country. North delivered a pro-Contra speech and slideshow that he had given over one hundred times to members of Congress and private groups, at one time saying, "I still see no problem with taking the Ayatollah's money." North charmed many on the committee, and those watching at home, with his eloquence and earnestness.

One paper later characterized the testimony as a "public relations coup" handed to him by Congress on "an extraordinary platform on national television." In the wake of years of ugly memories of Vietnam, North appeared to something the country had been yearning for: a poised military figure with the thoughtful and measured speech of a humanist. Whereas previous witnesses had appeared as slick and impetuous bureaucrats caught in their own lies, North seemed to represent a traditional set of patriotic ideals. On his third day of testimony, he read a lengthy opening statement, even placing the blame at the feet of Congress for its fickle and vacillating nature while people were being oppressed and killed elsewhere in the world.

As televised congressional hearings and House floor speeches drew national politics closer and closer to live theater, North might as well have been a celebrity. He had charmed Congress and those watching at home through his earnestness, sense of duty, and courtesy to those grilling him on live television. The conservative columnist Michael Novak wrote, "Ollie North is the best movie star in the best movie we've seen in years."

Brooks had known better than the rest. "I would have sent [North] a subpoena," Brooks later said. "If he didn't come, I would have held him in contempt. He got a strategic advantage out of the special treatment, and that was foolish." Years later, the long-retired Wright reflected on the unexpected direction that Colonel North took the hearings, and the former speaker admitted that he wished he had taken Brooks's advice and steered Chairman Hamilton to deny immunity to North for his testimony.

As the days progressed, however, committee members began to scrutinize North's story more closely.

Brooks's turn to question did not come until North's fifth day of testimony, Monday, July 13. That morning the *New York Times* reported, "Republican presidential contenders, with the exception of Vice President Bush, are distancing themselves from Ronald Reagan and even criticizing the president for the first time in light of the Iran-Contra affair."

On a personal level, Brooks loathed the colonel and saw him as representing the same kind of arrogance and entitlement that had rightfully done in Nixon and his cronies. And, Brooks was never impressed by rank or uniform. Brooks was a marine, too, and a lieutenant colonel in the reserves, and he had stared down four-star generals during hearings about waste in the Pentagon. From his days of island-hopping in the Pacific, he understood the danger and complexity of war and the chain of command. The fact that "North took it upon himself to basically violate the laws, go against [Congress] . . . That's what pissed Brooks off," one of Brooks's longtime staffers said.

Brooks was one of the few committee members unafraid to speak plainly to North. Other committee members focused mostly on the facts. What Brooks wanted was for the colonel to explain how he understood his role in the executive branch and the role of the executive branch in government. He had no qualms with doing this publicly. Brooks zeroed in and first questioned North's decision to exercise his Fifth Amendment rights to remain silent until he had been granted immunity.

As you know, I didn't vote to grant you immunity from prosecution, because of the general principle. I think government officials should be fully accountable for their actions. You've stated numerous times during the past few days that you didn't think you'd broken any laws and you may not have. In any case, if you felt so strongly that you hadn't, I had a little difficulty understanding your reluctance to testify without immunity.

After the colonel's attorney interrupted that it was appalling that the congressman would assail his client's rights, Brooks then reassured the colonel that it was not his intent to accuse, though he then gave a not-so-subtle litany of what he considered North's offenses to be:

> At any rate, colonel, you did play a central role in the events that we're charged with investigating. And we're not here to prosecute anyone for accepting gratuities or diverting public funds, destroying government documents, lying to Congress, or any other conduct. We are here to determine only what did happen and the serious impact these activities may have had on the conduct of American foreign policy and, indeed, on our national security.

Brooks did not want a rehashing of the previous decade's impeachment hearings. He wanted to correct what was broken and move on. Brooks read aloud the statute that created the National Security Council, which stated that the council was to "advise the president with respect to the integration of domestic, foreign, and military policies." Brooks then asked:

> Now colonel, the National Security Council was never intended to be an operating agency of the federal government, was it?

The colonel replied, ambiguously, that it was the president's staff. Brooks wondered whether that meant that North believed its members were not bound by the functions of the NSC to "advise the president," to which North replied that he did not think they were. So Brooks asked:

> Well, notwithstanding your insistence on that, someone must have been pretty nervous because there was a lot of altering and shredding and removal, destruction of official documents. Now, colonel, are familiar with the Presidential Records Act of 1978? . . . Well, I'll tell you, then. That act was passed in an effort to prevent White House documents from being shredded or burned in fireplaces or removed from history in other creative ways as we have seen in the Watergate case a decade and a half ago. And it provided that documents generated by the president and his staff are the property of the United States govern-

ment and are not to be disposed of unless certain requirements are met. And that law was intended to prevent the very thing that you did, with the support of Admiral Poindexter, I concede, but certainly the loss of the documents that you shredded has altered our understanding of our nation's history, if not the course of history itself. And I would ask you, would you retrieve those documents from the shredder today if you could?

North responded that he had already given five-and-a-half days of testimony and did not see the point in answering hypotheticals. So, finally, Brooks cut straight at the heart of how far these quasi-governmental operations went and what role the NSC had been tasked with. It was an issue that had simmered on the fringe of media coverage since the domestic unrest of the late 1960s. Just one week earlier, the *Miami Herald* had run a cover story titled, "Reagan Advisers Ran 'Secret' Government." The lead ran:

Some of President Reagan's top advisers have operated a virtual parallel government outside the traditional cabinet departments and agencies almost from the day Reagan took office, congressional investigators and administration officials have concluded.

The article detailed alleged plans in which these advisers, operating without any formal directive but under the coordination of the National Security Council, prepared for the establishment of a "parallel government" in the case of an unspecified national emergency. The secret structure and contingency operations in question were referred to as Readiness Exercise 1984, or "Rex 84." The Federal Emergency Management Agency (FEMA) was reportedly given broad authority to acquire military and law enforcement assets across the country to respond to such threats, in effect instituting martial law. The article specifically stated that North, the NSC's liaison to FEMA, had "helped draw up a controversial plan to suspend the Constitution in the event of a national crisis, such as nuclear war, violent and widespread internal dissent or national opposition to a U.S. military invasion abroad." The parallel government it established, or the "secret government-within-a-government" as the lead counsel for the Senate Iran-Contra committee called it, bore responsibility for emergency preparedness functions. In the case of a civil disturbance, the plan allegedly called for the widespread detainment of subversive groups or dissenting individuals and the mass relocation of U.S. citizens to internment camps.

The parallel government comprised a loosely connected network of contacts throughout the federal, state, and local governments, with the upper echelon of players including a former national security adviser and CIA director. The *Herald* article explained that North's influence within this scheme was so great "that he was able to have the orbits of sophisticated surveillance satellites altered to follow Soviet ships around the world, call for the launching of high-flying spy aircraft on secret missions over Cuba and Nicaragua, and become involved in sensitive domestic activities."

Brooks asked directly:

> *Colonel North, in your work at the NSC were you not assigned, at one time, to work on plans for the continuity of government in the event of a major disaster?*

North pushed back from the table, looked uneasily to his attorney, and folded his arms. His attorney grabbed the microphone and addressed Inouye: "Mr. Chairman?"

Inouye smacked his gavel down and said to Brooks, "I believe that question touches upon a highly sensitive and classified area, so may I request that you not touch upon that?"

Holding public hearings regarding the machinations of government carried this risk. There were things that could not be talked about without raising larger questions that would not be easily answered. Brooks, with all his years of chairman experience, may have already known this. Just as North turned and whispered into his attorney's ear, Brooks continued undeterred:

> *I was particularly concerned, Mr. Chairman, because I read in Miami papers, and several others, that there had been a plan developed, by that same agency, a contingency plan in the event of emergency, that would suspend the American Constitution. And I was deeply concerned about it and wondered if*

that was an area in which he had worked. I believe that it was and I wanted to get his confirmation.

North and his attorney remained silent. Instead, Inouye again responded to Brooks, in a deferential tone for a committee chairman. "May I most respectfully request that that matter not be touched upon at this stage. If we wish to get into this, I'm certain arrangements can be made for an executive session."

Brooks responded that he might take it up in "another forum," likely alluding to his Government Operations Committee, but then let the matter drop. He spoke once more about the separation of powers and then read a quote from Reagan about operating within the law and how "noble ends can never be reason enough to justify improper actions."

That lofty principle appears to have gotten caught in somebody's shredder. Instead of operating within rules and law, we have been supplying lethal weapons to terrorist nations; trading arms for hostages; involving the U.S. government in military activities in direct contravention of the law; diverting public funds into private pockets and secret unofficial activities; selling access to the president for thousands of dollars; dispensing cash and foreign money orders out of a White House safe; accepting gifts and falsifying papers to cover it up; altering and shredding National Security documents; lying to the Congress. Now, I believe that the American people understand that democracy cannot survive that kind of abuse.

Brooks's brash questioning of North had a similar effect as his directness with Abrams. One commentator noted: "Many critics of North did not participate until they heard voices they agreed with." Many viewers at home apparently felt the same; Brooks received 15,876 letters and telegrams, many multiples of the numbers sent to more reserved members of the committees. That day was the also first day the Senate Select Committee received more anti-North phone calls than pro-North calls, twice the number, in fact. Brooks's own office began receiving hundreds of phone calls each day.

As one Brooks aide recalled later, Brooks had yet again been at the forefront of public opinion.

Senator Warren Rudman, a Republican from New Hampshire, speaking after Brooks, reminded committee members that North and Poindexter had shredded documents, lied to Congress and the attorney general, and withheld information from the president. "These actions are antithetical to a democratic government. They cannot be justified by passion, patriotism, or any other reason."

Inouye then postponed the hearings until the next day. The executive session proposed by Inouye happened behind closed doors that evening, though the content of what was discussed was never made public.

The following day, North's sixth and final day of testimony, the questioning by Inouye, Lee Hamilton, and Representative Louis Stokes took a decidedly more adversarial tone, prompting the *New York Times* to report that the committees were trying "to take back control of their hearings" from the colonel. Hamilton upbraided North, explaining that a "free government could not survive on lies and law-breaking by public officials."

Senator David Boren, chairman of the Senate Intelligence Committee, followed up on the "so-called Martial Law Plan," citing Brooks's line of questioning and coverage by the *Miami Herald*. Boren asked:

> [*The Herald article*] says, "Lieutenant Colonel Oliver North, for example, helped draw up a controversial plan to suspend the Constitution in the event of national crisis such as nuclear war, violent and widespread internal dissent, or national opposition to a U.S. military invasion abroad." And I would ask you; did you participate in or advocate any such plan to suspend the Constitution?

North fervently denied that he had or that the government had put such a plan in place. Bowen commented that the Intelligence Committee would need to be briefed separately. In the days following, the *Miami Herald's* reporter Alfonso Chardy, who had first reported on the Rex 84 plan, continued to dig and filed stories titled "North Denies Role in Plan to Suspend Constitution" and "North Helped Revise Wartime Plans." Both ran deep on the inside pages of the paper, though, and the story fizzled out shortly thereafter. Brooks told one reporter, "It's one of those things NSC does that it doesn't want people to know about."

As the hearings wrapped up, the aura that had once surrounded North dissipated. It was as if a temporary fever had worn off. Syndicated columnist Mike Royko wrote about how the colonel's pleasant appearance had seemed to transfix the country, despite its better judgment. "I'm just wondering what people would think if a guy who looked more like Woody Allen than like Clint Eastwood was telling them, 'Hey, sure, I shoved all those papers in the shredder because I didn't want anybody to know what we were doing?'" Carl Rowan, another popular Chicago-based syndicated columnist, wrote:

> What was once a halo around Colonel North's head looked more like a legal albatross around his neck as the hearings came to a close. . . . I liked the bull dog-gishness of Brooks, the Texas Democrat who knew a dangerous, lawless scheme, and cover-up, when he saw them. He didn't hurt himself by opposing grants of immunity and holding some big, important feet to the fire.

Chairman Inouye brought the hearings to a close, stating that there was a "junta" operating from the White House in this "chilly story of deceit and duplicity and an arrogant disregard for the rule of law." In his final remarks, Inouye said:

> [There exists] a shadowy government with its own Air Force, its own Navy, its own fundraising mechanism, and the ability to pursue its own ideas of the national interest, free from all checks and balances, and free from the law it-self. . . . Should we in the defense of democracy adopt and embrace one of the most important tenets of communism and Marxism: the ends justify the means? This is not one of the commandments of democracy. Our government is not a government of men; it is still a government of laws.

Nationally, the public response again revealed a clear divide among Americans, who, just as during the Watergate scandal, appeared evenly split on the issues: those who unfailingly supported the president and whichever actions he or his administration took, believing that the ends justify the means, and those who believed the government was to be ruled by laws and not by men. Michael Novak wrote that North's testimony had divided the country once again "between two antagonistic moral visions." The colonel openly admitted to the charges leveled against him, which detractors believed was enough to throw the book at the administration. However, North rebutted this conclusion by offering his own "moral framework" in which the actions he had taken were not only justified but also laudable.

Supporters did not care that unelected officials had secretly circumvented the law and conducted questionable and significant foreign policy actions on the president's behalf. They saw a telegenic man in uniform who loved his country and did whatever he needed to do in support of a Republican president, so the rest was merely details. These same advocates had been pro-engagement in Vietnam, overwhelmingly voted Nixon to power twice, and then defended his actions in office as the Watergate scandal broke. They now stood just as resolutely by North and the Reagan administration.

The volume of public outpouring on both sides was unprecedented, representing a change in the way Americans were engaging. A history professor at Indiana University later cited the half-million letters, telegrams, and phone calls from the public to committee members during the three months of hearings that summer as "perhaps the largest spontaneous popular response to a congressional activity in American legislative history."

There was little agreement on the effect the hearings had produced. Reagan doubled down and even appeared heartened by North's performance, telling reporters that further assistance to the "freedom fighters" was more likely now and that he would even "stand on the roof and yell" for more aid if needed. Senator Tower, who had led the first commission and filed a report in February, maintained that the hearings brought nothing new to light and would have been more appropriate if held in private. He suggested that some of his former colleagues had used the three months of public hearings to try to enhance their own reputations. "I would classify the whole thing as political theater. I think that some of the damage is to Congress. I don't think the Congress came out looking as good as they thought they might." Brooks, who only years earlier acerbically quipped that televising Congress for public consumption made as much sense as televising surgery for training young doctors, defended the panel, stating that it had been worth the effort to expose a "government within a government."

On November 18, the committee issued its report, stating, "If the president did not know what his national security advisers were doing, he should have." Brooks, along with Rodino, Boland, future Speaker Tom Foley, Fascell, and several other congressmen, submitted additional comments in the committee report, strongly agreeing with its bipartisan findings, yet taking issue with certain gaps in cooperation from the Reagan administration and their private counsel, most notably a collection of messages they believed Poindexter intentionally deleted. Because of "Reagan's personal commitment that the executive branch would fully cooperate with the committees, we did not issue subpoenas to any person or agency of the executive branch." In the report, they also agreed that Attorney General Edwin Meese had done such a poor job of analyzing the legal implications of the arms-sales scheme that he was likely either complicit with the cover-up or in total dereliction of his duty as the president's top legal adviser. The NSC had also obstructed investigations that were "perceived to be opposed to their activities."

Despite the seriousness of the accusations, Reagan never suffered much political damage from the ordeal. He had last fully addressed the scandal in March, praising the results of the Tower report and stating that while he fully accepted responsibility he also had not been fully aware of what was happening. It was for reasons like this that Reagan had earned the dubious nickname the "Teflon President." Nothing could stick to him. In this case, his hands-off style of governing had served him well.

Ultimately, eleven officials were convicted for their involvement in the scheme. North received a suspended sentence on three of twelve counts but had his conviction overturned after several years of appeals. In yet another echo of Watergate, Reagan's vice president, George H. W. Bush, commuted the rest of the sentences during his own last days as president.

For such an egregious series of actions, there had initially been a surprising reluctance to speak up and demand answers. Brooks's longtime friend Beryl Anthony found the moment typical of Brooks, though, and the role he often came to play in the political and public discourse:

If you go back and look at some of those transcripts or some of those tapes, he was one of the few people who actually had it right from day one. And he was out front before public opinion caught up. . . . Chairman Jack Brooks had it right, was in the minority, but history looking back would prove, that had [Brooks's] actions been followed, the course would have been a lot different. There are a lot of little stopping points along his career where you could take a very intense part, where the public was just all split, but you had a person who had the ability to sort through the chaos, find the kernels of truth, but then had the conviction and the courage, even when he was in the minority, to speak up, and then let the majority catch up with him. That's the mark of a confident, intellectually strong person. That's the kind of person I wish we had a lot more of in the Congress today.†

After almost forty years of giving the benefit of the doubt to the sitting president, Democrat or Republican, and his full support in matters of foreign policy and national security, Brooks had no choice but to break with tradition. The *New York Times* ran a short piece about Brooks:

Mr. Brooks said that affair showed, how "dangerously close the country came to seeing a few zealots subvert the entire Government process." "Political operatives in the White House and the Central Intelligence Agency took political matters into their own hands," he said as he skimmed over a briefing book highlighted with key points on the secret sale of American arms to Iran and the diversion of the proceeds to aid the contra rebels in Nicaragua. The congressional inquiry, while thorough, was not without personal disappointments. The major disappointment, he said, was "the continued refusal of the President and the Vice President to acknowledge the real facts."

Brooks later reflected on North and the role he had played in the affair. "He wasn't any good," Brooks said. When asked if he felt any kinship with a fellow marine who claimed to be fulfilling his duty, Brooks replied with a simple and unequivocal, "I didn't give a damn."

---

† This quotation is taken verbatim from a video interview that can be viewed at www.jackbrooksfoundation.org.

North would hold a grudge. Perhaps he considered his role and duty to the president to be above congressional oversight or maybe he just felt hurt by the congressman's words. Whatever the reason, the colonel would reappear several years later in Beaumont to play a small part in trying to see Brooks lose his seat in Congress.

21

Reaganomics and Runaway Spending

Reagan's 1980 presidential campaign had been built on a few simple positions: a strong stance toward the Soviet Union, increased spending on U.S. defense, lower income and capital gains taxes, a smaller federal government, and a balanced budget. He claimed the nation was in recession, though his advisers told him that, while inflation was high and growth stagnant, the recession claim was not exactly true. Reagan responded with a catchy one-liner: "Recession is when your neighbor loses his job. Depression is when you lose yours. And recovery is when Jimmy Carter loses his." Retorts like these and plans like his 1980 platform epitomized Reagan's appeal; he charmed people and that was enough.

Foremost among his domestic agendas were tax cuts. The mid- to late 1970s-era inflation and unemployment rates were being brought under control. Nevertheless, Reagan argued that cutting taxes for the wealthiest Americans would free up that capital for them to invest in their businesses, which would create jobs, spur growth, and ultimately expand the tax base through increased consumption. Meanwhile, decreasing the federal budget and money supply would keep inflation down as the economy grew. Reagan had settled on these concepts as the tonic for a lagging economy during his years as a spokesman for General Electric, where he gave presentations and rubbed elbows with GE's executives.

One of those execs, vice president and labor strategist Lemuel Boulware, would become his mentor in economic matters. Boulware's background, however, was in putting down labor strikes, and his theories were not economic theories but business management ideas. Reagan, a former Democrat, was drawn to their simple logic and formulated them into a platform. Cutting taxes, increasing military spending, and balancing the budget sounded like a winning plan.

In reality these contradictory campaign promises presented a dilemma—the government would bring in less money through tax revenue, spend a larger portion of that decreased revenue on the military, and somehow reduce the existing deficit, all at the same time. "Supply-side economics," "free market economics," "Reaganomics," "trickle-down economics"—the math did not add up, and there were many from both parties who criticized the approach as overly simplistic. Other Republican candidates, including John Anderson and former Texas governor John Connally, derided the proposals as fantastical. George H. W. Bush famously lambasted Reagan's proposals as "voodoo economics."

But there was a contingent of conservative officials who felt that a new economic model was needed to rein in excessive regulations and social programs that they held responsible for hampering growth. This movement of so-called "free marketers" preached that business owners and entrepreneurs would right the nation's growth trajectory if not for the "welfare bums" and lazy civil servants standing in their way. Reagan would also memorably say, "Government is not the solution to our problem; government *is* the problem."

1980 ELECTION: Days before the election, Brooks accompanied Carter on a campaign trip through the Gulf region. They made stops in Miami, New Orleans, and Texarkana, where young gubernatorial candidate Bill Clinton was among those waiting for the president. There was a building sense of dread amongst Carter and his supporters that the administration's accomplishments had not been successfully sold to the public. With the election only days away, the president and his proxies were still explaining his policies and trying to show that his record was a political asset rather than a liability. As the old maxim goes, in politics, if you are explaining, you are losing.

The group flew to Beaumont, where Brooks presented the president with a pair of handmade western dress boots onstage during a rally. He told the president: "We hope that you will wear them in good health and that you will have fond memories of the people of southeast Texas each time you put them on."

Carter spoke of several of his administration's major accomplishments: strengthening Social Security, stabilizing the oil supply, normalizing relations with the Chinese, protecting energy jobs domestically. Brooks later told reporters that Carter's tax cut also would allow low-income consumers to spend more for necessities. There was no unifying vision for Carter's agenda, though, it was just stuff that had been done.

Always cordial and appreciative, Carter wrote Brooks a thank-you once back aboard Air Force One and moving on to the next city:

> . . . *I was delighted by the exuberant, Texas-style welcome that I received. As always, your wit and humor added greatly to my enjoyment of the trip. As we enter the last few weeks of the campaign, I remain deeply grateful for your continued active support.*
>
> *With Best Wishes,*
>
> *Sincerely,*
>
> *Jimmy*
>
> *I especially enjoyed the new air conditioned climate you arranged (I'm wearing the stomping boots).*

On Election Day, Brooks's work helped Carter to carry Jefferson County. But even within Texas, it was a lone exception. Carter lost the state 41 percent to 55 percent, and he lost the country almost as badly. Republicans gained fifty-three seats in the House and twelve in the Senate, giving them a Senate majority for the first time in almost thirty years. Reagan, armed with the largest electoral college victory in generations, felt he had been given a mandate to see his policies enacted.

REAGAN'S BUDGET: When David Stockman, Reagan's chief fiscal proponent and the new thirty-four-year-old budget director, and his staff first entered the Office of Management and Budget in January 1981, they ran their numbers for the administration's fiscal plan through an OMB computer that was designed to model the nation's economic behavior. By their own accounts, the figures they received were "absolutely shocking." If enacted, Reagan's plan would create a deficit of $82 billion in 1982 and then $116 billion two years after that.

So, according to Stockman, his staff reprogrammed the computer and made the numbers work.

Two months later, Reagan—now armed with some new economic assumptions and favorable figures—presented his first budget proposal to Congress for fiscal year 1982. It called for $695 billion in federal spending and a $45 billion deficit, instead of a surplus. Defense spending saw the greatest increase. Reagan called for budget increases in each of the nine major Pentagon programs.

Procurement grew larger than any other category. In addition to the $49.1 billion in procurement that Carter's 1982 budget called for, Reagan wanted $19.7 billion more.

In August, Reagan signed into law the largest tax cut in U.S. history—known as the Economic Recovery Tax Act of 1981 or the Kemp-Roth Tax Cut—delivering on one of his campaign promises. There was broad consensus at the time that some order of tax relief was appropriate; Kemp-Roth went beyond the consensus figures, though. Free market advocates contended that and any decrease in tax revenue would more than be made up for by the growth the tax cut would trigger. Many in Washington remained skeptical. Just four months later, Stockman himself admitted in a magazine interview that the administration lied to American public:

> I mean, "Kemp-Roth" was always a Trojan horse to bring down the top [tax] rate. . . . It's kind of hard to sell "trickle down." So the supply-side formula was the only way to get a tax policy that was really "trickle down." Supply-side is "trickle-down" theory.

What sounded logical in the boardrooms of GE did not correspond with economic realities, though. By almost every measure, the economy worsened and soon thereafter the U.S. was undeniably in recession. By October the following year, the budget deficit was revealed to be $110 billion, more than twice the prediction and a new record for the federal government. The next month, unemployment hit a post-Depression high of 10.8 percent, meaning more than 12 million Americans were out of work. The state of California faced insolvency. The after-tax income of the wealthy increased considerably, furthering the income gap between the rich and poor.

Over the next few years, the economy stagnated as interest rates spiked, the cost of debt swelled, and housing construction stalled. Social welfare programs across the board—employment training, food stamps, school lunches—were cut. The national deficit ballooned with the combination of decreased tax revenue and increased military spending.

After the president's State of the Union address in 1984, Brooks issued a rare public statement:

> *[Reagan] took credit for fostering a great national economic recovery without mentioning that recovery was launched from the lowest economic depths this nation has seen since the Great Depression as a result of his policies.*

Brooks added that the president's domestic policies were "grossly unfair to large segments of the American public" and urged both Congress and voters to "evaluate very carefully his simplistic proposals that may look good in the package, but smell bad when you open the lid."

By late 1985, the deficit had tripled since 1981, going from a fringe issue to a major concern. Spending outside of defense grew too, 11 percent during the same period. The small government promises had never materialized. Options that were politically palatable for reducing the deficit were few. Spending cuts were not fought for, and raising taxes had become anathema to the GOP's platform. In the following months, Reagan would vocally support a pledge from the recently launched Americans for Tax Reform that bound Republican candidates to never support a tax increase, regardless of the amount or reason. In the decades that followed, signing "the Pledge" would become a prerequisite for any politician hoping to run as a Republican.

Back home in the Ninth District, the economic pain was real. Unemployment was as high as 21 percent in parts of the district. Thousands of residents had to decide whether or not to leave southeast Texas to find work.

STRATEGIC PETROLEUM RESERVE: In response to the oil embargoes in 1973 and 1974, Congress had established the U.S.'s Strategic Petroleum Reserve, a collection of four massive underground petroleum storage facilities along the Gulf Coast in Texas and Louisiana. The thinking was that by carefully releasing stores of oil from the reserve, Americans would be protected from future supply shocks and the federal government could bear more influence on the price of oil globally.

Just thirty miles outside of Beaumont was the Big Hill oil reserve project site. Though the land itself was nondescript, below ground were fourteen excavated salt dome cavities, each one two thousand feet high and two hundred feet wide, sufficient space to store 170 million barrels of crude oil, enough to fuel the entire country for weeks.

The project site had now been under construction for almost ten years and promised to be an economic boon to the district for decades to come. Although increasing levels of automation in the petrochemical industry had affected refinery workers since the early 1960s, petroleum remained the district's bread and butter, as it had been ever since the Spindletop gusher in 1901. The Mobil Oil refinery was still the largest employer in Beaumont, and almost every other major oil player had a large factory in the area. Big Hill promised to bring hundreds of good jobs to the district.

Brooks had fought to secure funding in Congress to build the $155 million site and was proud to have won it. Like widening the Sabine-Neches shipping channel and building the Gulfgate Bridge and the Port Arthur Seawall, it was another major win for the region. Though these types of accomplishments did not garner much attention in Washington, they represented what Brooks loved about being a congressman—looking after the interests of constituents.

While the national deficit was still compounding, the follow-on legislation to make it disappear was just as bad. Crafted by the same authors who wrote the original law, the Balanced Budget and Emergency Deficit Control Reaffirmation Act of 1987 relied on accounting shenanigans that Brooks publicly called out as "gimmickry of the worse kind." They included the sale of federal assets, "bookkeeping maneuvers," and broad and blind cuts of $1 billion, half of which would come from defense spending. Passage of the administration's second big tax law, the Tax Reform Act of 1986, had been contingent on keeping it "revenue neutral." Any reductions in the deficit had come at the expense of existing projects or programs.

The repercussions hit home in the Beaumont-Port Arthur region. Seeking new ways to reduce the deficit, the proposed budgets for 1986 and 1987 called for a moratorium on the Strategic Petroleum Reserve project and on filling of the reserves, a move that would save the federal government up to $2 billion per year. The first action among these would be to cease construction on the Big Hill site, the only one of the four sites that remained unfinished.

Stalling the project would deal a major blow to the district. Brooks had always fought for labor unions, and this loss would be felt terribly. When the new budget proposal was released in January, work on Big Hill ground to a halt. The specter of running out of public funds ceased all work at the site.

So Brooks began to speak out publicly against the president on the deficit. He hosted House Energy and Commerce Committee Chairman John Dingell at a conference and fundraiser in Beaumont. The two of them held Reagan responsible for not protecting American jobs from unfair trade practices from other countries, saying that enforcement of current trade laws would reduce the national budget deficit by $80 billion. Brooks saw serious effects on steel manufacturers and petroleum refiners in his district. "We need those jobs and we're ready to get them going again," Brooks said.

There would be another election in 1986, and the loss of jobs would be used against Brooks, who faced a challenge from thirty-year-old Lisa Duperier. This would be the fourth time in the last five elections that Republicans had run a candidate against Brooks. None had managed to make it close, but the growing frequency showed that the opposition party thought his seat was in play. In Brooks's first fourteen elections, he had faced off in a general election with a Republican candidate only four times. Since the 1978 election, it seemed that he could count on having a challenger every time.

Vice President Bush even came to Beaumont to stump for Duperier in front of the City Hall building. Bush, a fellow Texan steeped in experience with oil, said the only way to "cure the energy business's ills" was to deregulate and "to get the government off its back."

Duperier ran an advertisement in the Galveston newspaper with a cartoon riffing off the fabled wizard of Oz. Over an image of Brooks's floating bald head, a voice boomed, "I AM THE GREAT AND POWERFUL BROOKS! I HAVE FRIENDS IN WASHINGTON!" Meanwhile, a young woman tugged the curtain aside to reveal a small man working a smoke machine. Underneath the cartoon, the ad posed a handful of questions to potential voters about Brooks's record, ending with this one: "Why was Big Hill the last of the Strategic Oil Reserves to be built and the first to be cut? Maybe Jack doesn't have as many friends as he thinks."

Messages like these landed on fertile ground. The district had double-digit unemployment and with the decline in oil prices, drilling had fallen off, hurting even those people with jobs. Shipyards that had sprouted up in Orange and Beaumont after World War II to serve the Navy and private sector were all but empty now. Even Houston was in full recession from the collapse of petroleum prices.

The future operation of the Johnson Space Center in Houston was even in doubt following the explosion of the space shuttle *Challenger* in January 1986. A subsequent internal study had led to the recommendation that the most important programs be transferred to NASA's headquarters in Washington. The Space Center was outside Brooks's district, south of Houston, but Brooks, who kept a model space shuttle mounted above the television in his office, understood what it meant for the local economy, Texas, and Johnson's legacy. Brooks made a phone call to his friend and Speaker of the House Jim Wright, who then called NASA administrator James Fletcher, intimating that if NASA persisted in plans to relocate, "no future NASA funding legislation would ever be enacted." That call did the trick. In this particular instance, southeast Texas owed enormous thanks to the fact that Brooks had powerful friends in Washington.

In April, Brooks made a statement addressed directly to Reagan. One of the congressman's more convincing points was that it would be cheaper to continue purchasing oil for the reserve at its current price than to delay the project and risk paying double or more in the future.

Brooks's pressure both in the headlines and behind the scenes worked. In May, after five months of uncertainty, work at Big Hill resumed. Brooks was elated. He told a local newspaper: "I'm delighted that this project, which is of such vital importance to our nation's security, is going to be continued and that it will soon be back on schedule."

A few days later, U.S. Steel's Baytown mill was awarded two contracts by the U.S. Department of Energy for nearly $50 million to build the pipelines from the Big Hill facility to local distribution centers. The Big Hill deal was having a multiplier effect on the local economy.

SPONSORSHIP ROLE IN HOUSE: Brooks had, through his love of a good fight and mastery of the congressional process, become something of a brand himself. If other legislators needed a bill passed through the House, persuading the senior member of the Texas delegation to sponsor it ensured that it would have every opportunity available for passage, especially if it were referred to a committee or subcommittee he chaired. In the four Congresses between 1981 and 1988, Brooks introduced and sponsored no fewer than 140 bills, amendments, and joint resolutions to the House. This was multiples of what even the most outspoken and high-profile members in Congress could claim. Brooks sponsored bills in crime and law enforcement, commerce, government operations and politics, foreign trade and international finance, finance and financial sector, transportation and public works, and economics and public finance among other areas.

There was almost no area of government in which he did not bear influence. His bills included:

- National Archives and Records Administration Act of 1984
- Federal Telecommunications Privacy Act
- Major League Sports Community Protection Act
- In the wake of the space shuttle Challenger's destruction, the establishment of a Children's Challenge Center for Space Science
- Land Remote Sensing Satellite Authorization Act of 1983
- Civilian Travel Expense Amendments Act
- Federal Telecommunications Privacy Act
- Federal Polygraph Limitation and Anti-Censorship Act
- Single Audit Act
- Anti-Fraudulent Adoption Practices Act

- Creation of an Office of Drug Enforcement Coordination within the Executive Branch
- Law Enforcement Officers Protection Act
- A bill to recognize the cabinet status of the Director of the Office of Management and Budget
- A bill to amend section 218 of the Social Security Act
- Reorganization Act Amendments of 1984 (signed into law)
- A bill for the relief of the heirs of Master Sergeant Nathaniel Scott, United States Army, retired, deceased (signed into law)
- A bill to extend the authorization of appropriations of the National Historical Publications and Records Commission for five years (signed into law)
- Malt Beverage Interbrand Competition Act
- Office of Federal Procurement Policy Act Amendments of 1983 (signed into law)
- A bill to transfer from the director of the Office of Management and Budget to the administrator of General Services the responsibility for publication of the catalog of federal domestic assistance programs (signed into law)
- Paperwork Reduction Act Amendments
- National Academy of Public Administration (signed into law)
- Inspector General Act Amendments
- Forfeited Conveyance Disposal Improvements Act
- A bill to increase the effectiveness of domestic fire fighting forces and to ensure prompt and effective control of wildfires on federal lands
- A joint resolution proposing an amendment to the Constitution to provide for the direct popular election of the president and vice president
- A joint resolution proposing an amendment to the Constitution of the United States to provide for single six-year terms for the President and Vice President, and to repeal the twenty-second article of amendment to the Constitution
- And most importantly, the Competition in Contracting Act

During this time, the alumni magazine for the University of Texas published a piece on former students who had risen to positions of power. The author wrote that Brooks, described as combative and the scourge of southeast Texas, was "fearless, contentious, rough, and fair," one of the most respected legislators in Washington. "Forty-nine percent of the people in Beaumont and Port Arthur will shrivel and turn green at the mention of his name, but 51 percent will go to the well with him any time." The article went on:

> Brooks says what he thinks in the best Texas tradition, not caring what either the American Manufacturers Association or the AFL-CIO thinks about his stances. He is impossible to classify as liberal, moderate, or conservative, for he votes his conscience and instinct. . . . he has become one of the most influential men in the Washington circus.

Procurement was still Brooks's primary preoccupation. Through dozens of proposed bills and amendments over the years, Brooks remained determined to fix the ways in which the federal government bought goods and services. The field of procurement, which usually lost out to other government affairs for headline space, had recently become an ideological issue because of the so-called free-marketers that had swept into Washington. While free-market apostles expounded on exciting ideas like slashing government and tossing out long-held understandings of economics, Brooks soldiered on with putting the government's money where its mouth was, maximizing tax dollars and minimizing chances for waste. In 1983, he introduced the Office of Federal Procurement Policy Act Amendments, which further refined his vision for the role of that office, which he had created with previous legislation, and then extended it for another four years. As Reagan signed that into law, he acknowledged Brooks, along with three other sponsors, saying: "This legislation will help to strengthen the fundamental characteristics of wise and economical procurement—including the increased use of full and open competition—in the marketplace."

Simplifying processes and establishing standardization meant saving time and money. Excessive bureaucratic steps were a silent killer of taxpayer dollars. Though unimpressive on an individual level, once rolled up in the aggregate, which meant multiple agencies with tens of thousands of employees each, vast amounts of resources were being dedicated to tasks that added no value, like those that the Paperwork Reduction Act had aimed to curtail, or to completing identical tasks without any central guidance, as the Brooks Automatic Data Processing Act had aimed to eliminate with federal IT management in 1965.

To ensure that the recipient programs of federal assistance were spending their appropriated funds as intended, Brooks introduced the Single Audit Act. State and local governments received almost $100 billion in grants from the federal government annually. Urged on by hearings before Brooks's subcommittee, the OMB had been attempting for years to reduce duplicative work that grant recipients were responsible for completing. The bill, which Reagan signed into law in October 1984, sought to "establish uniform audit requirements" for everyone.

An even more egregious waste of money than duplicating work, however, was the lack of competition among vendors vying for federal contracts. Increasing value for the government and citizens through increased competition had been the bedrock concept for the ADP Act of 1965 and the Architects & Engineers Act of 1972.

The Competition in Contracting Act expanded this concept to all of federal procurement, seeking "to revise the procedures for soliciting and evaluating bids and proposals for government contracts and awarding such contracts using full and open competition." Through the use of sealed bids and competitive negotiation, Brooks's legislation proposed a more dynamic marketplace for what the government bought, which, given the quantities of the contracts, would have an effect on the American economy overall. Jim Lewin served as Brooks's chief investigator on the Government Operations Committee. One of the primary architects of the legislation, Lewin explained the rationale behind it:

> *The whole concept to full and open competition is they'll do the job of monitoring their competitors because it's in their economic interest to do so. So as long as you force competition, you don't have to have loads of regulations or hordes of auditors. The guy that's actually going to make money out of catching the other*

guy with his pants down is what's going to be the best auditor, the competitor.
And he'll say, "Wait a minute. I can do that much better, and by the way, I
heard that this guy was taking money" or whatever. But you can't do that when
it's a closed system of favoritism and old boy network.

Unfortunately, there were few members of Congress interested in procurement issues, and of those most seemed to be committed to the status quo.
Brooks warned, "There will come a time when competitive procurements
become as rare as a balanced federal budget," making a less-than-subtle
jab at the Reagan administration, which he noted had "added more to our
federal debt than the entire debt accumulated under all previous postwar
administrations during a period of thirty-six years." By mid-1984, there were
signs of some economic recovery, but Brooks warned that rising interest
rates and voracious federal spending could wipe it out entirely.

During initial hearings on the Competition in Contracting Act, Brooks
reported that between 1981 and 1983 the Defense Department had awarded
$201 billion in procurements without a competitive process for awarding
contracts. Further, the department was paying more than $140 million each
year to reimburse vendors for "public relations activities," including advertising giveaways, foreign air shows, and entertainment expenses. He said:

This is the kind of impermissible activity the country cannot afford and we
cannot tolerate. There is a huge loophole in Pentagon cost allowance practices
whereby blatant advertising and public relations expenses are charged to the
taxpayers in the price of DOD contracts. The result has been simple and dev-
astating.

In a news release following the hearings, Brooks stated that his bill would:
"open up the government marketplace . . . remove bias and favoritism
which is currently plaguing the government's procurement system . . . ensure
that the government receives innovative and cost effective products and
services . . . [and] support the American free enterprise system by requiring
competition as the driving force by which the federal procurement system
will be governed."

Predictably, the Pentagon vocally opposed what officials saw as more bureaucratic hoops to jump through. According to a deputy secretary, the bill would "wipe out almost forty years of legal precedents and business practices . . . question exactly what portions of [previous] laws would still be effective . . . [and instigate] years of court challenges."

$435 HAMMERS: Unfortunately for the Pentagon, there was actually some public interest in procurement, and the potential for waste with sole sourcing had entered the country's consciousness by 1983. In addition to the increased scrutiny that the deficit brought to public spending, the previous months had seen another scandal brewing amid revelations and horror stories about the amounts of money the Pentagon had been spending on spare parts.

One in particular was spurred on by a chief petty officer at a naval air station in Pensacola, Florida, after reviewing a contractor's invoice. It was from an electronics vendor that had won a contract to develop a flight instrument trainer for an aircraft. Among the costs listed was a charge of $435 for a single hammer. Shortly after the officer began asking questions, *Newsday* ran an article titled "Would You Pay $435 for This?" with a picture of the now infamous hammer.

Ernest Fitzgerald was the whistleblower who had alerted Congress to the cost overruns of the C-5 Galaxy transport plane program. He had been fired in 1969 for his testimony, only to have the federal courts side with him and reinstate him in his former job. The Pentagon reluctantly took him back, but effectively sidelined him by not giving him much work to do.

The C-5 episode, however, had made Fitzgerald something of a hero for people who were trying to do the right thing. He had earned the nickname "godfather of whistleblowers," and as a result, he helped establish an informal network of people throughout the Department of Defense who would report cost overruns.

Once the hammer story broke, other individuals within this whistleblower network came forward with more instances of overspending in what became known as the spare parts scandal. Among the various absurdities that came to light through were receipts for:

$37 screw,

$171 flashlight,

$640 toilet seat,

$659 ashtray,

$7,622 coffee pot,

$74,000 ladder

To be fair, the coffee pot was designed to continue working if the plane it was attached to was destroyed. Pentagon apologists maintained that it was "overspecification" for military versions of common civilian items and burdensome regulations that caused expenses like this. The *Washington Post* reported that to produce whistles for the military, a defense contractor would need to follow sixteen single-spaced pages of instructions. Other defenders argued that it was an accounting issue, a question of how the total costs of a project were distributed.

Nevertheless, the scandal stuck, and the hammer became a symbol of government dysfunction and mismanagement. The media stayed with it, running hundreds of articles, features, and editorials. This was not one contract or even one weapons system; it pervaded the entire defense procurement system. Soon the department cover-ups became the story, making it even bigger.

The Carter administration had overseen an average of 12 percent annual growth in the defense budget during Carter's final two years. Once in office, the Reagan administration oversaw an average increase of 51 percent, or $100 billion, on top of that every year.

Excess charges for spare parts and household goods did not constitute the $100 billion difference in the new Reagan defense budgets, but they were emblematic of defense contractors attempting to hide costs by spreading them out where they could. This spoke to a much larger issue: the military and its suppliers had more money than they knew what to do with.

DEFENSE SPENDING: Reagan-era defense budgets included some incremental modernization but little or no improvement in the military's capability, while costing taxpayers an additional $100 billion per year. When testifying before Congress, one defense consultant refused to talk about the military buildup "because virtually no buildup had occurred." Instead, he suggested it be called a "spendup." An *Atlantic* article titled "The Spend-Up" reported, "After years of the largest military budgets in our peacetime history, it is hard to find an objective measure by which American forces have significantly improved."

The average costs of planes, helicopters, and tactical missiles rose by 35 percent to 100 percent, in some cases within a few years. This belied the principle that the marginal costs of weapons decline as more weapons are made. Of fifteen major weapons whose costs could be tracked from 1977 to 1985, thirteen of the weapons actually became more expensive as the budget increased, and often much more expensive.

Another congressional study, this one released by two Republican senators and two Republican representatives, described a similar pattern:

> *The Reagan Administration bought 23 percent more ships in its first four years than the Carter Administration did, but it spent 48 percent more to buy them. Under Reagan the Army has bought 40 percent more helicopters—but paid over 150 percent more for them. Spending for Air Force and Navy airplanes rose by 75 percent, but the number of planes purchased fell by 12 percent.*

Even the president's OMB director, Stockman, admitted before leaving the administration there was up to $30 billion worth of waste in the military budget.

Theories abounded about the spending. Some argued that billions were being spent to increase missile stockpiles and fancy delivery systems, only so they could then be used as bargaining chips to be abandoned later as talks with the USSR progressed.

Though profitability in the manufacturing sector sank to new lows, those businesses involved in defense contracts were making remarkably high profits. Historically, for most major defense firms, selling to the government had been somewhat less profitable than their commercial sales. After 1981, this situation flipped dramatically.

With this enormous influx of money and without much central guidance on purchasing or strategic planning, the overflow of defense funds created an environment rife with waste, fraud, and abuse.

Soon forty-five of the top contractors were being investigated for overcharging, bribery, or bid-rigging, according to the Pentagon's own inspector general. Brooks, during his hearings for the Competition in Contracting Act, cited that CEOs at the top aerospace defense contractors were paid 51 percent more than their executive peers in the general economy, a chasm that had grown from zero difference in 1978. He said:

> *Since the taxpayers pay the bill, the compensation for defense contractors' executives ought to be reasonable. It is just as outrageous to allow reimbursement for these salaries as it is for DoD to pay unconscionable prices for spare parts, which we discovered they were doing. These are the same people who charged such prices as $1,118 for a plastic cap for a chair leg which costs less than $1 to make.*

The executive compensation revelation came after Brooks requested that the GAO conduct a study of "bloated" compensation in the defense industry. Contractors had been reluctant to open their books for the study, forcing the GAO to issue subpoenas for executive pay records in some cases. Brooks also initiated a study of the military's use of "expensive and sophisticated missiles during training" and evaluation exercises, leading to the discovery that as much as $450 million in live ammunition was used annually, usually just to ensure that individuals remained familiar with the ordnance. Again, since there were no guiding criteria for use, each of the armed services branches had developed its own.

According to a 1985 Congressional Budget Office report, the "rate of expansion in defense budget authority [during Reagan's first four years] was higher than in any other comparable peacetime period since World War II. That report, "Defense Spending: What Has Been Accomplished," determined that in peacetime and with a far smaller operational force, during Reagan's first four years, "Congress provided about $1,100 billion in budget authority for national defense. Even after adjustment for inflation, this amount is about 36 percent greater than was spent in the previous four years."

Accounting for inflation was actually one of the significant differences in the new budgets. Rather than asking Congress for the amount needed and then requesting bumps depending on how high inflation had risen, the administration's proposed defense budgets now incorporated a "generous expected inflation rate" to cover any overages, even though inflation rates had decreased significantly since the 1970s.

At the end of the fiscal year, the Pentagon would not return any excess monies but instead folded them into their total projected baseline budget for the following year. This compounded on itself and quickly, from 1982 to 1986, the overestimation for inflation alone—not increased weapons costs, overestimated fuel prices, or even inflation itself—just the overestimation for inflation amounted to a cost of $39.5 billion, representing a cost of $165 to each American.

These practices diverged from previous military excesses. It was not akin to the cost overruns of the C-5 Galaxy program, which were the responsibility of one single vendor. This was a broad system of waste and fraud in which government officials and private business were complicit. In addition to the congressional inquiries, the scandal also triggered an investigation by the Justice Department.

There was little doubt that this massive spending increase was one of the major drivers of the ballooning national deficit. To this charge, though, Reagan responded by saying: "Our attack on waste and fraud in procurement—like discovering that $436 hammer—is going to continue, but we must have adequate military appropriations."

To the commander-in-chief, defense spending rested outside the bounds of the country's fiscal discussion. He maintained a stance that "defense is not a budget issue . . . you spend what you need." His budget director, Stockman, even claimed that it was rather the overstuffed pension system that represented the real outrage and spending scandal.

The Pentagon had officially responded to the spare parts scandal in December 1984 and shortly thereafter Reagan established a Blue Ribbon Commission on Defense Management. The investigation of Pentagon procurement took over a year, but finally the commission filed its report. It declared, "The Department of Defense's acquisition system continues to take longer, cost more and deliver fewer quantities and capabilities than originally planned." It also rebuked Reagan's claim that defense funding was above normal budget considerations.

> *Today there is no rational system whereby the Executive Branch and the Congress reach coherent and enduring agreement on national military strategy, the forces to carry it out, and the funding that should be provided—in light of the overall economy and competing claims on national resources.*

Among the findings, it determined that "there's been no effective long-range planning in the [procurement] system." Paradoxically, among the causes listed were "stifling burdens of regulation, reporting and oversight." The report recommended:

> *Congress should work to recodify all federal statutes governing procurement into a single government-wide procurement statute . . . aim[ed] not only at consolidation, but more importantly at simplification and consistency."*

Within the previous three years Congress had passed and Reagan had signed into law two of Brooks's bills written to establish that same overarching guidance for the entirety of the federal government. Military strategist Edward Luttwak wrote in his 1985 book, *The Pentagon and Art of War*: "The real waste in the Pentagon is not the cost overruns or fraud, it is the billions appropriated to weapon systems for which there is no thought-out rationale."

Brooks and the Government Operations Committee would spend much of the next four years hauling officials in before the panel. Years later, Brooks proudly stated that because of those various scandals, he had "spearheaded a complete rewrite of the government's procurement laws." Some of those gains were short-lived, however, as certain measures were whittled away.

Brooks suffered a rare legislative loss when a challenge to his Competition in Contracting Act went all the way to the Supreme Court. Several in the executive branch, especially the attorney general, Edwin Meese, claimed that one provision on "costs and fees" represented Congress overstepping its constitutional authority. Congress passes laws, but it cannot dictate how laws are enacted, so the question remained whether the comptroller general, as head of an executive agency, was really a part of the legislative branch, since he was accountable, and dismissible without impeachment, to the Congress for his actions. The attorney general wrote letters to Vice President Bush, as president of the Senate, and Speaker Tip O'Neill, arguing that certain provisions of the act were unconstitutional and should not be implemented. While the courts were hearing the cases, the House Judiciary Committee took a new approach to force the Justice Department's hand, approving a ban on funding the attorney general's office in the fiscal year 1986. That got the attorney general's attention. A few days later, Edwin Meese advised all federal agencies to comply. Eventually, though, in the case of *Bowsher v. Synar*, the Supreme Court agreed with the challenge, stating that:

> *By placing the responsibility for execution of the Balanced Budget and Emergency Deficit Control Act in the hands of an officer who is subject to removal only by itself, Congress in effect has retained control over the execution of the Act and has intruded into the executive function.*

Brooks was troubled by the Reagan administration's approach. He said: "Can the president of the United States unilaterally declare a portion of a public law to be unconstitutional and then refuse to enforce it?"

FTS-2000: Government spending outside the military had grown, too, 11 percent annually from 1981 to 1985. Though the Supreme Court case was a loss, the fundamental tenets of the Competition in Contracting Act remained sound.

Implementation of the law met one of its first big tests three years later in early 1987, when the government began the bidding process for the Federal Telecommunications System 2000, or FTS-2000, a proposed $4.5 billion telecommunications network that would replace the country's costly and outdated existing network and deliver voice, data, and video services to all federal agencies by the 1990s. Officials at the General Services Administration, the agency handling the new system, wanted a winner-take-all approach with a single vendor responsible for delivering the new network

to cut down on potential delays or waste. There were very few candidates
for such a job and only three consortiums of companies, one led by AT&T,
another by Sprint, and another by Martin Marietta Corp., even placed bids.

The contract to build this network—the largest telephone system in the
world—would be one of the biggest single procurements in government
history. Initial estimates came in around $40 billion. AT&T and Sprint,
with their teams of lobbyists in Washington, were excited about closing
the deal. Terence Golden, the new administrator of the GSA, was eager
to get started. With almost zero input from the Government Operations
Committee in designing the contract, the contract called for entering into
a decade-long arrangement with one single company, meaning virtually all
government communications, even those of the Defense Department, could
be impacted by that single relationship.

Brooks had seen how this would likely play out. He wanted the terms
restructured to allow for a multi-vendor award with "continuing competition
throughout the life of the contract." While Golden thought that, given the
technical elements of the work, the job would be done in four years, Brooks
predicted that once the ink had dried on the contract with the single supplier, it would be more like ten years. Private companies, especially industry
behemoths like AT&T, IBM, and General Electric, with which Brooks had
sparred for more than twenty years, did not have the same responsibilities
as Congress. However well-meaning they might have been, Congress could
not cede that level of power to a private business. It fell to Brooks and his
staff to pump the brakes on the procurement.

Brooks had significant experience in the area. The first federal telecommunications system had been established in 1963, connecting government
officials in forty-two major U.S. cities through dedicated switched lines
that would not falter in emergency situations and would also reduce the
government's cost. When the first phase of this new nationwide system
was complete, Jack Brooks had been asked to make the first call. He gave a
perfunctory summary of the landmark occasion at the time:

*At three minutes to 11 o'clock on the morning of February 14, 1963, I
picked up the phone in General Services Administration's building in Washing-*

ton D.C., and in 37 seconds I was talking on official government business to the man I wanted to reach, the Federal Aviation Administration's Assistant Administrator for FAA's Western Region in his office in Los Angeles, Calif. He supplied me with the information I need and we completed the call. The call marked a highly significant turning point in government communications. It was the first call made on the new Federal Telecommunications System. I dialed an FTS operator, was given an access line to the correct area, and I dialed directly the man with whom I wished to talk. The service was fast and the cost was about one-half the former commercial rate.

It surprised no one in Washington that now a full quarter century later, Brooks's top priorities for the vast project remained operational effectiveness and cost reductions to the government.

Golden publicly assured Congress that he, with a background in nuclear engineering and business, would personally select the winning vendor. Brooks countered that it would not matter. With a multi-billion dollar reward looming in the balance, the verbal sparring began to elevate. At first, few people outside of the local trade and government press took notice of the growing dispute between Brooks and Golden. In the wake of the recent defense spending scandal, though, procurement had earned a place in the public conversation. With the bidding deadline looming, various officials ratcheting up their rhetoric, and some of the competing vendors threatening to pull out, major news outlets began to cover the story.

Brooks steadfastly maintained that splitting up the contract and ensuring competition throughout the project would reduce the risks and ensure costs were held down. It would also guard against the project becoming derailed by other interests. Golden, whose staff had spent two years working on this project, knew the technical details inside and out, and felt that bureaucrats on Capitol Hill did not understand the project as well as they should. The two men took jabs back and forth at each other in the press, which cast them as powerbrokers locked in a standoff over the biggest government procurement in U.S. history. Each man had "drawn a line in the sand," and the future of the contract and even the proposed network were now in question. The *Washington Post* kept attention on the saga, publishing detailed regular updates on the developing drama for months.

Brooks stood fast. Golden may have understood the telecom industry, but he did not yet know Washington. Outside consultants were brought in to meet with the vendors and gauge possible reactions to the idea of the contract being split. The OMB supposedly backed Golden's approach, but the White House did not.

Then, in September, Brooks finally won out. Work on FTS-2000 was halted and Golden agreed with Brooks and his Republican counterpart and friend, Representative Frank Horton of New York, to split and redesign the contract. There would be two awards—one for 60 percent of the revenues and one for 40 percent—and price levels would be revisited throughout the life of the contract.

As had happened with Golden's two predecessors at the GSA, he and Brooks ended up getting along. When Golden retired in 1988, Brooks took the time to issue a statement to the media and called him an "outstanding administrator." A few years later, the ongoing FTS-2000 project which had become known as a "model Brooks Act procurement" had proven to be a major success. The GSA reported that it would save taxpayers $3 billion annually over its ten-year period.

NEARLY TWO DECADES LATER, the American Council of Engineering Companies bestowed onto Brooks its Distinguished Award of Merit for his work fixing and systematizing federal procurement laws. Upon receiving the award, Brooks told the members that after roughly ten years of successful implementation of the legislation:

> *Some government agencies, aided by their favorite contractors, eventually convinced Congress to greatly water down or eliminate the competitive requirements of Competition in Contract Act. It is therefore no surprise to me that we see an increasing number of procurement scandals resurfacing at government agencies.*

David Stockman left Washington in 1985 and released a tell-all memoir called *The Triumph of Politics: Why the Reagan Revolution Failed,* lampooning the administration's fiscal management, in which he had been a central figure. His primary grievance was that administration officials were not ideologically firm enough; they were only concerned with the tax cut policy, not understanding or even caring to understand what offsetting measures were necessary. The administration never enacted the spending cuts promised after the tax cuts passed. Tax cuts were political winners. Spending cuts were political losers.

According to William Niskanen, who served on Reagan's Council of Economic Advisers until 1985:

> *The major failure of the Reagan administration was the failure to discipline spending. We have a bigger government, with higher spending. We've slowed regulation down, but we haven't reversed it. In other words, there was no Reagan revolution.*

The struggle to prevent waste, fraud, and abuse in government contracting continues to the present day, and part of Brooks's legislative legacy is the constant attention paid to controlling fiscal irresponsibility both in the private sector and in mammoth government procurement programs.

22

Mindless Cannibalism

Brooks's pursuit of fairer procurement practices did not stop at the country's shores. Foreign governments were protecting their own businesses at the expense of American ones. The country's trade balance, which had remained even or in the U.S.'s favor in the decades since World War II, was tilting steeply in the other direction. The economy was growing, but by 1985, government spending at 24 percent of the GNP outstripped tax receipts of 18.6 percent, leaving a huge deficit.

Republicans blamed this imbalance on growing financial responsibilities for federal programs like Social Security, Medicare, Medicaid, unemployment, and welfare assistance. Democrats pointed to Reagan's corporate tax cuts and ballooning defense spending. Either way, U.S. manufacturing had paid the price. Because of the increased rate of government spending, an overvalued dollar made U.S. goods less competitive internationally.

Exacerbating this were protectionist trade policies by major partner countries that often lacked the regulations of U.S. industries and could therefore compete at cheaper prices. If sweetheart deals had rigged the federal government's process in favor of a few select vendors, then anachronistic trade policies from major allies and trading partners were rigging it against all American vendors.

Economic pain hit hard in the district. Beaumont was an early victim of the savings and loan crisis when the city manager lost $20 million in municipal funds to a shifty investment scheme. The oil industry had all but collapsed. Producers had shut down wells and were laying off employees while foreign oil dependence rose as high as 38 percent. Brooks told reporters that Texas congressmen from both parties had asked the administration to impose quotas on foreign oil imports. "We've got it under advisement," is how the administration responded. Brooks proposed legislation placing limits on oil imports, an oil import fee, and expanding incentives for domestic production only to have it killed by opposition in the administration.

At a joint press conference in Beaumont in October 1985, Brooks and Representative John Dingell, chairman of the House Energy and Commerce Committee, placed the blame for the trade deficit squarely at the feet of Reagan, who had not taken "steps to protect American industry from unfair trade practices of other nations." Dingell, another one of O'Neill's "old oaks" in the House, said, "This country sells nothing to Japan except raw materials. The Japanese sell us finished products. . . . We have given the president immense powers which he has not chosen to use, and millions of American jobs have gone down the tubes because the president has not done this." Brooks, cognizant of the free-market mood running through the country, assured:

> I'm a free trader—always have been—but I want it to be just as fair for us as it is for them. . . . They say you can't do anything to restrict fair trade because they'll take action against us. Well, they're already taking action against us, and it's high time that we take some action against them. . . . The International Trade Commission has just not used the remedies that are available to protect either the auto industries or the steel industries and certainly not the petroleum industry.

Brooks introduced the "Buy American Act" in March 1987 to ensure that no federal agencies would award a contract "for the procurement of materials mined or produced in a foreign country whose government discriminates in awarding such contracts against U.S. products or services." The *New York Times* devoted an entire feature [January 1988] to Brooks titled "A 'Fighting Marine' Battles Japan on Trade." The piece read:

> Jack Brooks is a Congressman who loves a good fight, and sometimes he goes looking for one. Such is the case now as he takes the lead in bashing Japan on its trade policy with the United States.
>
> For the sometimes irascible, fiercely independent Democrat from the Gulf Coast of Texas, it is an unusual venture into international trade policy. But the new role suits him just fine.

The 65-year-old Texan nurtures his image as a combative politician on Capitol Hill, where he has served almost half his life. On his desk, is a silver paperweight with the inscription "fighting marine." He saw action in the Marine Corps on Guadalcanal and Guam in World War II.

His weapon now is legislation that bans Japanese construction companies from participating in American public works projects for the next year.

The measure, which reflects widespread unhappiness in Congress with the obstacles Japan has placed before American construction companies seeking work in that country, was signed into law last month as part of the $604 billion catch-all spending bill. . . .

Mr. Brooks said that while he had heard from constituents on trade matters, the impetus for his unlikely involvement in trade policy was a persistent indication from the Japanese Government that it "intended to blatantly discriminate against U.S. firms in awarding public works contracts."

"I'm interested in a competitive economic situation in this country," he said, peering over his reading glasses in his Capitol Hill office. "I'm interested in a fair and equitable playing field for Americans. That's all it's about."

. . . The Texan's response to Japan's latest offer, presented last week in Washington by Prime Minister Noboru Takeshita, to open some of its public works projects to foreign construction companies, was cold. "This offer is not any good," he said. "They're going to have to come across with some real reform; nothing else is going to do."

Brooks had company on both sides of the aisle. There was great animus among liberals and conservatives alike against Japanese protectionist policies, which many saw as unnecessary and a direct cause of the current domestic hardship. George Will, a conservative columnist, wrote that Japan would still be "a formidable commercial competitor even if it did respect the rules of free trade."

By the late 1980s, anti-Japanese sentiment swept through Washington and the country at large. Books and films with sinister Japanese bosses and dire futuristic predictions abounded in the media. Congress passed resolutions calling for bans on products from Toshiba Corporation in the summer of 1987 after it came to light that one of its subsidiaries had conspired with a Norwegian entity to sell technology to the Soviets which could be used to make their submarines quieter. Several representatives in the House symbolically took a sledgehammer to a Toshiba radio recorder on the grounds outside the Capitol after one of the resolutions passed.

A-BOMB GAFFE: Back in the district, Brooks spoke to a luncheon group at the Port Arthur Kiwanis Club in October 1986 about the economic malaise affecting the district and country overall. After his speech, someone asked Brooks why the U.S. allowed Japan and other countries to dump products on the American market. With characteristic plain talk, Brooks replied, "God bless Harry Truman. He dropped two of 'em. He should have dropped four."

Brooks's staffers nearly fell out of their seats. Local television was present at the event, but aides were relieved when they learned the camera crew only recorded the speech and not the question-and-answer session. Still, the remark made headlines. Despite the anti-Japanese fervor around trade, the political zeitgeist of the moment, at least regarding treatment of the Japanese during World War II, was of contrition and reconciliation. Congress would soon pass the Japanese Reparations Bill, providing $20,000 payments to the survivors of internment camps and offering a formal apology to all survivors and their families.

Brooks had made the comment flippantly, and though it likely drew some laughs from those in the room, it was a rare political gaffe for him and caused a stir. His Republican opponent, Duperier, jumped. She said, "That's the kind of typical Jack Brooks statement that southeast Texans have gotten used to but people in the rest of the country can't stomach." Brooks issued a public statement the next day but did not exactly apologize. Instead, he emphasized that the government needed to act more strongly to protect its workers.

> *I regret that my over-graphic illustration may have been misinterpreted by some. . . . It is very frustrating to look into the thousands of faces of non-working men and women in this country who have lost their jobs as a result of the dumping of foreign products from Saudi Arabia, Japan, Korea, and elsewhere into our markets.*

Brooks likely felt no misgivings about his comment; the dropping of the bombs was an intensely personal moment for the former marine. As a twenty-two-year-old in 1945, he had been aboard a warship, waiting to be part of the Allied force that was expected to take 50 percent casualties once ordered to invade the Japanese mainland. He had personally seen the marines' requisition order for body bags.

Brooks's legislation was eventually folded into and passed into law under the Omnibus Trade and Competitiveness Act of 1988, which was cobbled together by Dan Rostenkowski, a powerful Democrat from Illinois who chaired the House Ways and Means Committee. It also explicitly called for an "end to predatory pricing activities of Japanese companies in the United States" and import limitations on Toshiba.

Japanese trade practices could not be blamed for all of the country's budget woes. There remained fundamental imbalances in federal spending and taxation. The newly inaugurated President Bush had boxed himself in unnecessarily during a debate in the 1988 presidential campaign by pledging to never raise taxes as president. Even before he took office, people in Washington wondered how he would manage to halt the growing deficit without that lever in his toolbox.

Even Reagan had raised taxes numerous times. In early 1989, Bush projected the annual deficit at $91 billion. The following year, the overall deficit stood at $3 trillion, and it would continue to grow by $291 billion and then by $352 billion the following two years.

Brooks was on better terms with the more moderate Bush than he had been with Reagan, though. Bush had been a member of the Texas delegation himself. "We were friends," said Brooks, "He was a better guy [than Reagan]."

When signing the Hate Crime Statistics Act into law in 1990 amid a gaggle of press and onlookers, the president introduced a group of senators and representatives who had played "instrumental" parts in seeing the legislation passed. The president called out Brooks by name and then quickly corrected himself. "Chairman Brooks, I should say, respectfully, to a fellow Texan."

GOVERNMENT OPERATIONS PORTRAIT: From his earliest investigations into government inefficiencies and transgressions, like the Cuba nickel contract, to more recent achievements like establishing inspector generals and the office of federal procurement policy, Brooks had reimagined the manner in which the federal government oversaw itself. His legacy with the Government Operations Committee, which he had chaired since 1975, was all but written in stone. Regarding his various pieces of legislation like the Paperwork Reduction Act and the Competition in Contracting Act, Larry Allen, a longtime president of the Coalition for Government Procurement, said: "It is almost impossible today to imagine a congressman having as much impact on federal procurement as Jack Brooks did in the 1980s."

In 1987, Congress commissioned a portrait of Brooks to hang in the anteroom of the committee hearing room. The portrait, a nearly five-foot-tall oil painting, shows Brooks standing relaxed in a dark suit and red tie, one hand in his pocket and the other holding up a cigar. A warm expression, not quite a smile, rests on his face.

It is not quite clear why leadership chose to have the painting commissioned and painted in 1987. Brooks had not left office and Rodino still chaired the Judiciary Committee. Perhaps the tightness of Brooks's 1986 election had caused a scare, or maybe Rodino showed signs of winding down. Regardless, they wanted Brooks's legacy documented. At the portrait's official unveiling on November 19, 1987, Brooks's longtime friend and fellow Texan Jim Wright composed a poem to commemorate the occasion:

> All hail our chairman named Brooks,
> Scourge of wrongdoers and crooks.
> With withering stare and cigar chomping glare,
> This guy is just as mean as he looks.

That, no doubt, drew laughter from the crowd. Wright himself knew about legacy. The representative from Fort Worth had just been elected Speaker of the House months earlier when O'Neill announced his retirement. Wright fondly remembered that he had been born four days after Brooks and said with a laugh, "And I've been trying to catch up with him ever since . . . and I've never caught him!"

When Wright's father passed away in 1962, Brooks gave some consolation.

Wright replied with a thank-you note, which Brooks kept in his records for decades.

> *Dear Jack, Words cannot adequately tell you how deeply my family and I appreciated your gracious expression at the time of my father's death. He was a truly good man who loved his family dearly and gave generously of his time and his substance. I think he was the greatest man I've ever known. You may enjoy having the enclosed, a little story I wrote about him several years ago. Please express my sincere thanks to all members of the Texas Delegation. Thank you for your kindness. It meant much to us.*

Brooks described Wright as his "bosom buddy," and he was glad to have him in the House leadership. Once elected Speaker, Wright became the most powerful Democrat in Washington, and he increasingly found himself the target of Republican ire.

GOP TACTICS RADICALIZE: The GOP had doubled down on the fiscal policies that had led the country to record spending deficits. Regardless of the economic ramifications of the Reagan tax cuts, the political victory had been won.

As the country struggled to recover from its economic doldrums, Bush sought to maneuver through even more fraught events abroad, including overseeing the first Gulf War against Saddam Hussein, the dramatic tearing down of the Berlin Wall and unification of Germany, and the collapse of America's chief adversary, the Soviet Union.

By this time, after gaining momentum in the Congress and having one of their own in the White House for the last seven years, the GOP had come to embrace a new type of political engagement. As the ideological base drifted further right, the party leaders went all out against the Democrats. Whether it was the effect of voters on Washington or of Washington on voters is up for debate, but the changes were almost instantaneous. The atmosphere on Capitol Hill turned from icily collegial to unabashedly cold. More important than specific positions or effective governance became the concept of us vs. them. On an individual level, the voters would come to support the candidate or position not because it was right or consistent with a shared ideology but because it was a Republican position, or, more precisely, because it was the opposite of the Democrats' position. Support for the GOP became almost familial; right or wrong, arguments were fought with the same ferocity.

Charlotte Brooks enjoyed a modest place in Washington's social and philanthropic circles for decades, and she came to lament "how partisan it became [in those] few years, and how much more partisan it's become since we left." She remembered herself and Brooks having "good friends in both parties, and at six o'clock at night you weren't enemies any more. You never were really enemies, just on opposite sides of issues sometimes."

Gene Peters, Brooks's longtime aide, recalled that it was during these years that GOP staffers began receiving orders not to even speak with Democrat staffers after meetings.

Some attribute part of the toxicity to the nasty, winner-take-all tactics of Lee Atwater, a political strategist from South Carolina who worked with Reagan during the 1980 campaign. While speaking anonymously with a political scientist from Case Western Reserve University in 1981, Atwater, who was then working in the Reagan White House, gave this explanation for how the language of conservative Southern politics was changing:

> You start out in 1954 by saying, "Nigger, nigger, nigger." By 1968 you can't say "nigger"—that hurts you, backfires. So you say stuff like, uh, forced busing, states' rights, and all that stuff, and you're getting so abstract. Now, you're talking about cutting taxes, and all these things you're talking about are totally economic things, and a byproduct of them is, blacks get hurt worse than whites. . . . 'We want to cut this,' is much more abstract than even the busing thing, uh, and a hell of a lot more abstract than "Nigger, nigger."

Atwater spearheaded Bush's bid for the White House in 1988, a campaign considered one of most negative in recent history, replete with whisper campaigns about Democratic nominee Michael Dukakis's wife and the infamous Willie Horton ad, which linked the former Massachusetts governor to a convicted murderer who committed rape and torture while out of prison on a weekend furlough. Dukakis had tried in earnest to run on a primarily positive race, only to reflect years later that it likely cost him the election. After Bush won, Atwater became chairman of the Republican National Committee.

HOUSE SENIORITY RULES LOOSEN: Within Congress, power was a zero-sum game, and it ebbed and flowed among the parties' leadership, the rank-and-file members, and the committee chairmen. Since even before Rayburn, there remained continual tension between the centralization and decentralization of authority. Rayburn had been a classic parliamentarian, neither bullying nor retreating in fulfillment of his duties as Speaker and letting committees control their jurisdictions without much meddling. If anyone in the rank-and-file wanted any sway, the best way to get it was to entreat leadership for a strong committee assignment. Maintaining this power equilibrium was likely one of the reasons Rayburn managed to serve as speaker for twenty-one years, still the longest tenure in history by far. His successor, John McCormack, had fostered this system, instructing freshmen members of Congress to "bow low from the waist" when they passed a chairman in the hall. Tip O'Neill had loosened the reins, letting the legislative process play out without much meddling. Wright, however, was intent on keeping an iron grip on the chamber. Tension among the factions remained constant. Wright's future successor, Tom Foley from Washington State, would say of his own challenges as Speaker:

> One of the problems of the speakership is to deal with very strong and power-ful voices within one's own party. I came to the speakership of the House as a for-mer committee chairman, but not the most senior of them. Dan Rostenkowski, John Dingell, Jack Brooks, and others had been powerful and wonderfully effec-tive legislators and committee chairmen.

From his earliest days in the House, Brooks was a product of the institution and its processes. He appreciated and abided by the House's rules, hierarchy, and traditions. Brooks had always been close to the Speaker. Rayburn had been his mentor. Brooks said McCormack had been a "wonderful friend, who always called me 'John.'" Carl Albert and Tip O'Neill had been allies, and Wright was a dear friend. While Brooks chaired his own committees with a zealous hand, in those in which he was just another committee member, he always showed deference to the chairmen, respecting their position and responsibility over his own.

Since the 1960s, there had been a growing trend among members toward egalitarianism in the House, which grew stronger during Albert's tenure in the 1970s. The "Watergate Babies" were the largest class of freshman Democrats ever elected to the U.S. House—seventy-five members—and they arrived in 1974 after explicitly campaigning against the existing seniority system. This cohort of mostly young, liberal Democrats demanded procedural reforms that eroded the authority of the powerful committee chairmen. One of their first actions in January 1975, to the leadership's dismay, was to expel two powerful incumbent Democrats from chairmanships they would have been automatically assured under the old rules.

Using secret ballots, all chair positions were now up for general votes. Fortunately for Brooks, all 261 Democrats had voted to keep him at the head of the Government Operations Committee.

Brooks recounted: "It was a different world then [under Rayburn]. Members were more responsive to the chairmen, chairmen were more responsive to the leadership, and the leadership worked with the president."

MOFFETT'S COUP: Representative Leo Ryan of California had been chairman of a subcommittee of the Government Operations Committee. In 1978, he traveled to Guyana, a former British colony on the northeastern shoulder of South America, at the behest of two constituents whose daughter had run off with Jim Jones and other members of his cult to live off the land in the equatorial jungle. As Ryan and others attempted to take off from a small landing strip in the jungle, gunmen from the cult opened fire on the plane carrying the congressman, his staff, and several reporters. Ryan was killed, the first member of the House to be assassinated in office, along with three journalists and a female member of the cult who was trying to flee. Declaring that soldiers were coming to torture and kill them, Jones and his lieutenants then forced more than nine hundred of his followers to drink poison.

When the full committee reconvened, one of the first actions was to place somebody else at the head of Ryan's subcommittee. Several of the "Watergate Babies" conspired to grab the seat from the hands of three senior members. Toby Moffett, a young congressman from Connecticut, led the cabal. He recalled:

> It would be a secret ballot vote by just the Democrats on the committee. We couldn't tell Jack what we were doing. If he knew, he would have easily shut the whole thing down, just by lobbying Democrats on the committee to support the next in line. . . .
>
> Brooks, not sensing anything out of the ordinary, said "The question comes on the gentleman from Oklahoma to be chairman taking the place of our late and dear friend, Mr. Ryan." Members scribbled and the clerk collected the ballots and went to his seat at the table facing the committee—and its powerful chairman.

Once the ballots were in, Brooks promptly moved on to the next order of business, but objections rose from across the room. The ballots should be fully counted aloud as a regular point of order. Brooks looked stunned. The votes were read, revealing that the committee's senior-most member had failed to win the subcommittee chairmanship by one vote. Representative Toby Moffett recalled that Brooks then began blowing out cigar smoke so fast that the junior members "could barely see him from [their] distant perches."

The clerk, who knew of the rebellion and was visibly sweating, handed out new ballots, and the next member in seniority was considered. Again, he lost by one vote. The third member in line was then considered and also rejected. Then Moffett, who had been fourth in line for the seat, had a vote. He won by a count of eleven to ten. Moffett recalled what happened next as he tried to escape the committee room unnoticed:

> Brooks slammed his gavel down and said, "The committee does now stand adjourned." Members headed for the doors. I recall how [Henry] Waxman was sprinting and purposely not looking back at the chairman. The press was gathering outside the committee room with news that the "Watergate Babies" had pulled off another bit of insurrection.

I gathered my stuff and headed for the door, and Brooks bellowed "Moffett!
Moffett! Would you mind coming up here?" I was shaking. I went up to the top
step to face the chairman. He blew some more smoke, this time pretty much
swallowing up both of us.

"Moffett," he said.

"Yes, Mr. Chairman," I replied, my voice cracking with fear.

"You are one tough Syrian SOB," he said, only slightly distorting my Leba-
nese heritage.

"Thank you, Mr. Chairman," I replied.

"Moffett," Brooks went on. "How old were you when you got here?"

"Twenty-nine, Mr. Chairman."

Jack leaned across the dais, his face now very close to mine. In a much lower
voice, he said, "So was I, Moffett. So was I. So I understand what you and your
gang were up to, and I can relate to it. Now come see me in my office tomorrow
so we can help make you a really good chairman."

Brooks took that incident in stride, but as time went on, he felt the
balance that had long sustained the cordiality and reciprocity in Congress
coming undone.

This gradual erosion of the traditional system may have had further
repercussions, too. Those in the congressional leadership who had long
been held with a certain reverence became subject to partisan witch-hunts.
Nowhere was the new paradigm shift more manifest than in an incident
that lacked precedent in over two hundred years of congressional operations, spurred on by a junior representative seeking to topple the highest
level of House leadership.

NEWT: Representative Newt Gingrich of Georgia was a rising star in the
GOP by 1987, either despite or because of his aggressive political tactics
toward other members. Almost as soon as the Georgian had entered the
House in 1979, he began making ethics charges against colleagues for alleged improprieties, notably against Barney Frank and Charles C. Diggs. In
addition to personally spearheading these investigations, he transformed the
speech of the political right from pointed rhetoric to sheer vitriol, referring

to past and present Democratic speakers of the House as "crooks," "traitors," and "thugs." This kind of personal attack against the opposition and even fellow Republicans would be seen again and again in the rise of other ambitious politicians in the years ahead.

But Gingrich was an early adopter. The junior representative campaigned across the country for a new type of fight against Democrats—referring to Democrats as not just rivals but enemies and regaling crowds with talk such as: "The values of the left cripple human beings, weaken cities, make it difficult for us to in fact survive as a country . . . The left in America is to blame for most of the current, major diseases which have struck this society."

He spoke of waging a civil war against liberals. He told supporters at the Heritage Foundation, a right-wing Washington think tank: "This war has to be fought with a scale and a duration and a savagery that is only true of civil wars."

This was a new kind of slash-and-burn politics that left even Republicans aghast. Senator Bob Dole refused to shake Gingrich's hand on stage. "Newt was willing to tear up the system to get the majority," Trent Lott, the Republican whip from Mississippi said. "It got to be a really negative pit over there, but that was probably the beginnings of the Republicans being able to take control."

Gingrich took the reins of a political action committee (PAC) dedicated to helping Republicans win elections. Soon thereafter, the PAC issued materials advising others to "speak like Newt," using words like "decay, traitors, radical, sick, destroy, pathetic, corruption, and shame" when referring to Democrats.

When the Democrats took back control of the Senate in the mid-term elections of 1986 and Wright ascended to Speaker, Wright tried to consolidate power. Early signs showed that his efforts were working. After Wright led the passage of a budget without a single Republican vote in April 1987, Gingrich told a congressional reporter, "If Wright ever consolidates his power, it's clear he'll be a very formidable man. We have to take him on early to prevent that."

Gingrich began his one-man ethics investigation against the Speaker; it would last for two years. He argued for the appointment of an outside ethics counsel that would investigate instances of individual breaches in conduct. Gingrich had a flare for the dramatic. He and a few other like-minded Republicans had begun a practice of waiting until the House's business had finished and the chamber had mostly cleared. It was in this period of proceedings called Special Orders when members could make one-minute speeches on any issue they liked, unconstrained by the normal strictures of procedural debate when the House considered bills and resolutions. The one-minute commentaries would be included in the *Congressional Record*, and viewers at home could watch, although since the cameras stayed fixed on whoever stood at the dais speaking, those at home had no idea there were often no members in the audience.

Gingrich and the others would approach the dais and deliver fiery speeches against the sins of liberalism. As a measure of courtesy, other members were supposed to receive notification about any continued talks on the floor, but many suspected that these notices did not always arrive in time. In one particularly egregious instance, in 1984 Gingrich accused several (absent) Democrats of being "blind to Communism" and challenged them to step forward and defend their positions or their Speaker if they could. No one did, because the room was empty, save a few teenaged congressional pages.

Because of this abuse of the cameras, Brooks had O'Neill institute a change to the programming. Every so often the cameras would now scan across the seats of the floor, revealing that some of the grandstanders were often preaching to an empty chamber. Republicans accused Democrats of playing dirty and arrogantly abusing their power. The conflict became known as "Camscam."

After Republicans caused a stir over it, O'Neill, who was still Speaker at the time, confronted Gingrich on the House floor before a full chamber: "You deliberately stood in that well before an empty House and challenged these people [when you knew they would not be there] and you challenged their Americanism. And it is the lowest thing that I have ever seen in my thirty-two years in Congress."

The thunder of applause showed that many in the House agreed. However, Trent Lott took issue with O'Neill's language, seeing it as a personal attack, which was forbidden by House rules. He asked that the House parliamentarian take the Speaker's words down from the record, which he did, in a rare rebuke to a sitting Speaker. Footage of the incident ran on all three networks that night, giving a significant boost in visibility to the fledgling C-SPAN network.

Three years later, Gingrich continued to use theatrics in his crusade against Speaker Wright. He refused to formally request an ethics investigation into the speaker's financial dealings himself, but in May 1988 the citizens' lobbying group Common Cause, compelled by the constant charges, made the request for him. The alleged violations centered around income from bulk sales of the Speaker's 1984 book, *Reflections of a Public Man*, which consisted of his speeches and essays. Gingrich then followed up with his own request. Among the charges were that Wright used his staff to help compile the book and that he had circumvented House limits on speaking honorariums by having trade associations purchase copies in lieu of paying him speaking fees.

It was clear to many that this was the effort of one man to destroy another. Some saw it as a personal vendetta because Wright had orchestrated Democratic opposition to providing military aid to the Contras in Nicaragua. Nevertheless, the House Ethics Committee conducted a six-month investigation, the majority of which was held in private, but a steady stream of leaks found their way into the press. The drumbeat of accusations against Wright, and soon his wife Betty as well, went on and on, clogging up congressional operations. Soon accusations and subsequent investigations flew against House Majority Whip Tony Coelho and chair of the House Budget Committee, Bill Gray.

Brooks, speaking to a crowd in Washington on May 18, 1989, fielded a question about the investigation. He did not hold back:

> *I think it's a disaster for Congress; if we don't win this fight, it's going to ruin Congress. That will suit Gingrich well; he wants to destroy Congress. Then he thinks they can rebuild it. Now that's the way I look at it.*
>
> *I have never seen Congress at a lower level of back-biting, knifing each other, partisanship, never in thirty-seven years. And I've dealt with what, eight Speakers. Joe Martin was Speaker when I came to Congress, Republican from Massachu-*

setts. Honest as could be. Straight as a string, nice old boy, courteous, pleasant, his word was good. I liked him. I respected him. Never said one word against him.

Charlie Halleck came up not as Speaker but as [minority] leader. Halleck was mean and devilsome. Liked to drink and party. But Halleck was honest. He was a good partisan fighter. We got along with Charlie Halleck fine. Liked him. There wasn't any feeling of acrimony. I remember sitting many times, well most every night, with Sam Rayburn in the Board of Education, drinking a little coffee in the evening. We started drinking coffee about 5:30 p.m. I didn't take cream. Many a time Charlie Halleck would come down there and visit, raise hell with me, raise hell with everybody, just argue and talk and visit about our issues. But there was never any hard feeling. We didn't go out to the press and say, "Halleck had a real load on last night." None of that business. Course not. Course not. Had nothing to do with his thought processes.

I've never seen, I've seen all kinds of problems and tough ones, but nothing ever like this. Nothing like this. And it's destroying Congress. It may destroy it if they let it. But if they do this to Jim Wright, they've already started on Coelho, they'll start . . .

The FBI, last year, went and got a copy of the financial disclosure forms of every chairman in the Congress. Now I don't know why they got it for. They didn't say they were going to investigate. They just got it because they like to read? Or they just collecting numbers on paper? I don't know what their collection is. But you and I can understand what they're trying to do. They're trying to put the pressure on every chairman. And they just got a list. They'll go through the list.

What they're mad at Jim Wright about on the program is his effectiveness, not his ethics. That's what they're going to be mad at all the Democrats about. If you elected anybody as Speaker, they would start finding fault with him because they're not for him. I don't mind them being against him, but I think when they hide partisan attacks like this, it doesn't look good. It's not good for Congress. It's not healthy. It's not conducive to encouraging decent people to run for Congress.

I feel sorry for people who've got a couple years in Congress. If they think they can enjoy the next twenty years in Congress, they're crazy, the way it's going now.

WRIGHT'S RESIGNATION: Less than two weeks later, on May 30, 1989, Wright announced that he would address the entire House the next day. He then spoke in private with Brooks and attended a friendly luncheon with other members of the delegation. Brooks said the speaker seemed "cheerful and happy" and had not explicitly told his friend what he was about to do, though Brooks had an inkling. The next day Wright stood at the dais on the House floor in front of a full chamber:

> *It is intolerably hurtful to our government that qualified members of the executive and legislative branches are resigning because of the ambiguities and the confusion surrounding the ethics laws and because of their own consequent vulnerability to personal attack. That's a shame. It's happening. And it is grievously hurtful to our society when vilification becomes an accepted form of political debate. And negative campaigning becomes a full-time occupation. When members of each party become self-appointed vigilantes carrying out personal vendettas against members of the other party. In God's name, that's not what this institution is supposed to be all about. When vengeance becomes more desirable than vindication. Harsh personal attacks upon one another's motives and one another's character drown out the quiet logic of serious debate on important issues . . .*
>
> *Surely that's unworthy of our institution, unworthy of our American political process. All of us, both political parties, must resolve to bring this period of mindless cannibalism to an end! There's been enough of it!*

Those remarks brought the entire House to its feet. Gingrich, to whom much of the criticism was directly pointed, hunkered down throughout the address. Wright continued:

> *Well, I tell you what, I'm going to make you a proposition, let me give you back this job you gave to me as a propitiation for all of this season of bad will that is going around. Give it back to you. I will resign as Speaker of the House effective upon the election of my successor.*

He finished by imploring both parties for restraint. He asked that they not try "to get" somebody from the other side as payback, even for his own sake. The institution ought to be more mature than that, he said.

The Speaker, fighting to control his emotions as he closed, left the podium and took a seat next to Brooks. No other Speaker had resigned from the position because of a scandal. This ignominious end to a long and productive career in Congress had come about not through a conviction or because of overwhelming evidence but because of an unrelenting two-year political campaign.

Brooks leaped up to the dais once Wright sat down. Brooks asked and was given permission to address the House for one minute.

Mr. Speaker, I have known Jim Wright for about fifty years. I know his wife and his children. He has been a good father, a good husband, a good congressman, a great speaker, and a superb friend.

I remember at nineteen years of age, he left the University of Texas for the Army Air Corps. Commissioned at twenty, when the Japanese controlled Guadalcanal and threatened Australia, Jim Wright was on the north coast of Australia flying long B-24 bomber runs, flying down the Crocodile River trying to locate a base one hundred miles out in the bush. Often returning with his tanks almost empty, he was among the many heroes of World War II who literally risked their lives to preserve the freedom we enjoy today.

I remember his election to the state legislature at twenty-three years of age, and his election to Congress in 1954. He never sought fame and fortune, but was always dedicated to reading and studying the issues vital to his district and to our country. He has spent his life representing the people of his district, his state, and his country.

There is an evil wind blowing in the Halls of Congress today that is reminiscent of the Spanish Inquisition. It is replacing comity and compassion with hatred and malice. Jim has not been convicted in court or in Congress, but his political opponents have pronounced him guilty, and the media has engaged in a feeding frenzy. Fleet Street never had so much competition for the most sensational headline, no matter how unfounded.

Conviction without a trial is a new and dangerous rule for this Congress and for this country. This scenario can destroy Congress and with that the strongest defense of our American people against an insidious dictatorship.

Jim Wright's decision to relinquish the office of Speaker of the House is the

clearest possible demonstration of his love for this institution and our country.
It is testament to his character that, despite his deep belief in his innocence—a
belief that I share completely—Jim is unwilling to let his personal situation
impede the work of the House.

I believe I speak for the Texas delegation and for a majority of our members
when I say history will commend Jim Wright as a good man and a great Speaker
with a magnificent, unparalleled record of accomplishments in this Congress for
our people and for peace. We thank you, Jim Wright, for your leadership, for
your friendship, and we wish for you and Betty, all of your family, the very best
for many years to come.

Brooks then spoke to reporters a few minutes later outside the chamber.
When asked about what this portended for Wright and Congress, Brooks said:

He's been lynched by leaks. He is guilty without trial. And if that's going to
be the new rule, it's to have sad consequences for both this Congress and for these
United States . . .

I know him well and I love him and I like him and respect him. But I
wonder if he wanted to stay and dangle for another six months while the com-
mittee evaluated things and while there were leaks every day. Just little leaks, not
big leaks, just little leaks. And escalation of the investigation. They could start
investigating his children, I guess, next.

Brooks later admitted that Wright's wife Betty "was embarrassed by the
publicity and she didn't like the pressure," which Brooks thought made the
decision to resign easier for Wright.

Other members' statements to the press that day varied to a degree but
many Democrats and Republicans alike ominously foretold that this would
change the nature of the House of Representatives. This was one of the most
dramatic examples of the breakdown of comity in Congress. Rancor had
grown louder and more extreme, and Rayburn's old maxim, "To get along,
go along," no longer carried the weight it once did.

Shortly after Wright's resignation, Brooks sponsored a celebratory
barbecue in Texas to honor his good friend, and the week following the

resignation, the 259-member Democratic Caucus unanimously selected Tom Foley, a mild-mannered Democrat from Washington State, to succeed Wright as Speaker. Before Foley could even assume the Speakership, there quickly spread around Capitol Hill a rumor that Foley was a child molester. After a brief scandal, the rumor was traced to a leaked memo from Atwater's RNC titled, "Tom Foley: Out of the Liberal Closet," which compared Foley to the openly gay Representative Barney Frank, a Democrat from Massachusetts. Frank responded, "This is George Bush's national committee we're seeing now. He invented Lee Atwater." Atwater acknowledged the memo but denied approving it. The communiqué had actually been crafted in part by Gingrich, and then an aide in Gingrich's office followed up by telling reporters, "We hear it's little boys." Though the rumors about Foley were entirely baseless, nearly thirty years later a Republican former House Speaker, Dennis Hastert would admit in court to sexually abusing several high school wrestlers during his time as a coach, a scandal that would culminate in a 15-month prison sentence for illegally structuring bank transactions to hide money he was using to pay off one of his former victims.

The new type of virulent partisanship that ensnared Wright and Foley was anathema to Brooks. For all the enemies he had made in Congress, even his opponents did not question his integrity. He thought Gingrich was "a scum," and that resorting to baseless personal attacks for political gain was ruining the institution of Congress and the national discourse.

As one story goes, shortly after Wright's resignation, Gingrich and a staffer were waiting for an elevator inside the Capitol building when the congressman began telling his aide of the apparent lack of blowback against him since Wright's resignation, saying, "It really hasn't been too bad. I think it'll be ok." The elevator doors opened; Gingrich walked in, and then realized he was not alone. The aide recounted the horrified look on Gingrich's face as he turned and saw Jack Brooks standing next to him. The last thing the aide could hear as the doors closed was Brooks exclaiming, "You son of a bitch!"

23

House Judiciary

The House Judiciary Committee stands apart from even the other major committees because it has jurisdiction over all amendments to the U.S. Constitution as well as the power to impeach. As one Brooks aide put it, the committee was "the heartland for legal and constitutional law." Brooks had served on the Judiciary since 1955 and had been second in seniority to Chairman Rodino since 1975, when the more senior Harold Donohue retired. Nevertheless, as the One Hundredth Congress drew to a close in late 1988, Brooks was not assured the position. The traditional rules of seniority in the House had been turned on their head, and the next member in line behind Brooks, Robert Kastenmeier of Wisconsin, had already publicly expressed his interest. Kastenmeier chaired the subcommittee on courts, intellectual property, and the administration of justice. Though Brooks was heavily favored for the chair, and most assumed he would be selected if he wanted it, he did not take anything for granted. One day after Rodino announced his retirement in March 1988, Brooks issued a brief statement to the media: "Chairing that committee would be an honor and a privilege should my colleagues extend me that opportunity next year."

That was all he said. But it turned out that he did not have to wait a full year. On December 6, 1988, Democrats selected Brooks to assume the chairmanship once Rodino retired at the end of the year. Brooks left the Government Operations Committee in the hands of John Conyers, the liberal firebrand who had joined Brooks on the Judiciary before the Watergate ordeal. Conyers promised to stay faithful to Brooks's tradition

441

and decided to keep many of Brooks's staffers on the committee in place.

Brooks began the 101st Congress by holding a formal breakfast for new members, as he had come to do every cycle, and then began his transition into the new role. He was stepping down from the chairmanship of a minor committee that dealt with the nitty-gritty details of congressional operations and stepping up into the chairmanship of a major one that wrestled with the nature of the government itself.

According to some close to the congressman, ever since Rayburn had helped put Brooks onto the Judiciary Committee as a freshman in the 1950s, reaching the chairmanship was what Brooks had been hoping and working for. It was the pinnacle and culmination of his entire career, continuing in the great tradition of Manny Celler.

Jon Yarowsky worked for Brooks when he moved chairmanships. The staffer, who served as general counsel on the Judiciary and then later as one of President Bill Clinton's chief advisers, remembered:

> *It was a new era. It was a brand new era. And he moved like lightning. The Judiciary was a legislative committee in the highest sense of the word. I mean, we were on the floor, at least in the years I was there, more than any other committee. In fact, every—at the end of every Congress, we actually had to publish a report called "Summary of Activities." Under Mr. Brooks's leadership, our summary of activities was awesome! I mean, it was so much more expansive than any other committee, because that's the way he did it.*
>
> *People talk about Mr. Brooks in many different ways, but his work ethic was astounding to me. I mean, his discipline, his work ethic. Every day he came to work—literally—to work. And he expected, all the way down the chain, that people were working. He respected anybody who worked. Could be his top staff people or the secretary. If they were productive, they rated with him. If they were not productive, they weren't going to have a very good day.†*

Including the main committee, all the subcommittees, and Brooks's office aides, more than eighty people now reported to Brooks, most of them

---

† This quotation is taken verbatim from a video interview that can be viewed at www.jackbrooksfoundation.org.

lawyers. Members of Congress can be particular when it comes to staffing, but Brooks did not want to upend everything that Rodino had put in place. Brooks and his general counsel, Bill Jones, moved into the Judiciary office and, Yarowsky recalled, "integrated everybody in that wanted to get with the program, and if they didn't want to get with the program, they weren't with the program."

The committee moved fast, and as chairman, Brooks worked hand in hand with the leadership in both houses to see that priority legislation received its due consideration. The committee held hearings in October on the Americans with Disabilities Act, a marquee bill protecting individuals with disabilities from discrimination. Bush would sign that bill into law the following year.

PANCREATITIS: That winter Brooks suffered a rare personal challenge that threatened to sidetrack, if not end, his career. Flying back to Washington from Houston, Brooks was doubled over with pain. He ruled out a heart attack because, he thought, "they don't hurt much. Just kill you."

Brooks went to the airport restroom to wash his face. He stumbled down some steps and asked a young man if he would help him walk. Charlotte was waiting to pick him up. The two went home and called the doctor at the Capitol, who told Brooks to get to a hospital in Bethesda immediately. Brooks remembered:

> *The doctors there are excellent doctors, but they kept poking at me, and they didn't want to give me anything for the pain. They wanted to know where it hurt. They kept hoping it was heart or lungs, or anything. They didn't want it to be a pancreas. And it was. They decided that had to be, and they couldn't do much about that. And so, they gave me some pain medicine, and very shortly, I was in complete care, and all hooked up and wired up.*

The doctors diagnosed Brooks with idiopathic pancreatitis, which meant that he had a severe inflation of the pancreas, and they did not know what had caused it. Brooks had drunk scotch ever since his days in the Board of Education, but he never overindulged, according to friends.

The doctors did not suspect alcohol as the culprit. Brooks remained in the intensive care unit for over a month, and doctors placed him in a medically induced coma for weeks to keep him from moving and disturbing his pancreas further. They also kept trying to warn Charlotte and Brooks's staff member Sharon Matts that the congressman was almost surely going to die. Though other staff members within Brooks's inner circle were sure the doctors were right, Charlotte and Matts, both of whom came to see him every day, did not buy it.

The legislative office needed to keep functioning, regardless. People understood that Brooks's health was in bad shape—President Bush even made the effort to extend his best wishes for the congressman's convalescence—but the coma was kept secret. Matts said:

> *I didn't tell anyone. I had to run the office in the meantime. Every morning I was in the office, and I'd gather up all the letters because we kept them, the constituent letters, going. Everybody in his constituency knew that he was in the hospital, but I never even really told the staff exactly how horribly bad it was during that time. We kept it running, and we kept it upbeat.*

Somehow, after thirty days of intensive care and then ten more in rehabilitation, Brooks did survive, and, again, the doctors did not know why. He recalled with a laugh:

> *When I started re-organizing the hospital and explaining to them they got to turn some of the lights off at night, cut out those bells, quit talking loud, let people sleep that were sick. That's when they decided I needed to go.*

His last conversation with the primary doctor who directed his care stuck out in his memory too:

> *The doctor said, "And remember now, no more whiskey."*
> *I said, "Scotch? Bourbon? Gin?"*
> *He said, "No."*
> *"Wine? Red? White? Rosé?"*

"No."

"How 'bout beer? Sam Adams?"

"No. And not cough syrup with a high alcoholic content." He said, *"Now, you might do that and get away with it and never bother you, but it might cause that pancreatic system to rebel again."*

When Brooks arrived home, all ten of his direct staffers were waiting to greet him. Each one of them was smiling and had one of Brooks's cigars. Decades later, the congressman still got choked up looking at the photo of the group of them, smiling with cigars hanging out of their mouths.

The business of the Judiciary Committee continued immediately. Brooks oversaw hearings on all manner of priority legislation, from immigration to antitrust, from hate crimes to ethics in government. The Civil Rights Act, which Brooks and Chairman Celler had drafted and seen passed in 1964, had not been updated in decades. Brooks's committee saw to the modernization of that historic bill, which passed both chambers and was signed into law in 1991.

JUDICIARY: Comprehensive, or omnibus, crime bills aggregated many smaller bills concerning law enforcement, due process, judicial review, and firearm manufacturing and sales, among many other things. These behemoth pieces of legislation required input and sponsorship from an incredible number of legislators, public officials, and even the president.

The 1990 version of the House's crime bill, which Brooks introduced in July, contained many of the provisions that Bush had entered the White House promoting but quickly met "a wall of opposition" from the president, who called it tougher on law enforcement than on criminals. The revised bill was more severe, expanding the application of the death penalty, placing limitations on the manufacture and sale of cheap handguns known as "Saturday night specials" and on assault weapons, and increasing the severity of punishments for offenses such as certain white-collar crimes and possession of child pornography.

Though many colleagues sought to include additional gun control measures, the pragmatic Brooks fought to keep those amendments out because it "just makes it a lot more difficult to pass and get [an anti-crime package] through conference with the Senate before the November election."

Crime bills historically became tougher during election years. "Nobody wants to have a thirty-second commercial running against you that you're soft on crime," said Senator Paul Simon from Illinois. In crafting the House version of the bill, Brooks had achieved a delicate balance, and the bill became law in November, though Bush expressed his disappointment at the signing.

After Brooks introduced the 1991 crime bill, known as the Violent Crime Control and Law Enforcement Act, it encountered the same partisan bickering, especially over the inclusion of the Brady Bill provision, which stipulated a five-day waiting period for the purchase of handguns. Any measure to impinge gun ownership, however sensible or discreet, was politically toxic. The bill passed the House, and the Senate passed its version as well, but the political divide led to a failure to resolve the two versions. No compromise was forged the following year either.

DURING THESE FIRST FOUR years at the helm of the Judiciary, Brooks introduced no fewer than forty-four pieces of legislation that were then referred to his Judiciary Committee; these bills included legislation regarding price-fixing, foreign anticompetitive practices, antitrust laws, and increasing competition in the insurance and malt beverage industries. Every bill had its detractors, those who either disagreed on principle or who would be negatively impacted by the changes. With Brooks's visibility, sway, and seniority, he had racked up plenty of opponents over the years. Ultimately, his efforts to close loopholes and spur on competition would spark a series of events that would define the end of his career in Congress in a most bizarre way.

MAIL-ORDER SALES TAX: All businesses are required to collect a sales tax from customers purchasing their goods or services, though the amounts were left to the states' discretion. An exception to this was mail order or direct marketing businesses that solicited by sending catalogs and other promotional materials to households and potential customers through the postal system. Because of the wording of a Supreme Court decision, sending material like that did not constitute doing business in the state where the material was received, even if it resulted in a retail sale.

In 1967, the distinction may not have mattered. The volume of mail-order sales paled in comparison to regular retail sales. By 1989, however, mail-order business represented 15 percent of the overall U.S. retail market with a reported 12.5 billion catalogs flooding mailboxes across the country, resulting in billions in annual sales. The sales tax loophole meant as much as $3 billion in lost revenue each year. State budgets lay in shambles. California alone, which had been teetering on the edge of bankruptcy in 1986, was losing an estimated $389 million a year.

Brooks proposed a bill that would require out-of-state mail catalogs to collect state-specific sales tax from their customers.

The Judiciary held jurisdiction over state tax issues, so when Brooks introduced the Equity and Interstate Sales Tax Collection Act to the House in May 1989, the bill was referred to the Judiciary and then to its subcommittee on monopolies and commercial law. A Senate version had bipartisan sponsorship from Thad Cochran, a Republican from Mississippi, and Byron Dorgan, a Democrat from North Dakota. Retail trade associations supported the legislation, as did most local governments. Brooks explained to municipal officials in March 1989: "The issue is one that is not only costing them revenue but also costing main street merchants their livelihood by giving mail-order companies an unfair price advantage."

The bill's opponents were adamant, though, and particularly well-positioned to express their views. The Direct Marketing Association was an advocacy group for mail-order retailers across the country. Members included the giant, Wisconsin-based retailer Land's End, which sent a tax alert flyer to customers in one million of its clothing catalogs, encouraging people to contact their representatives in Congress to oppose the bill. Another was the Suarez Corp., run by Ohio businessman Benjamin Suarez. Suarez Corp.'s product offerings included diamond-growing kits and miracle weight-loss pills. Instead of beseeching customers to act, Suarez Corp. went straight at Congress. The company had a history of filing lawsuits and buying political attack ads throughout the country in states like California, West Virginia, and Washington against politicians who challenged their business model or the validity of their products.

In a 1989 letter to numerous representatives, Benjamin Suarez disparaged Brooks by name and argued that imposition of any sales tax would put many direct marketing companies out of business and decimate the profits of any that remained standing. In language both rambling and repetitive, Suarez touted his company's expertise in campaigning and fundraising and said he had created a nonprofit citizen's group called the United States Citizens Association (USCA), which would take action against those who sponsored this bill. He claimed to have defeated incumbents, "even ones who were considered invincible."

Actions were already underway to defeat Representative Brooks in the upcoming 1990 election, he wrote. The USCA was funding an effort to recruit candidates by phone, newspaper, TV, and radio to oppose Brooks in his district. Suarez warned that USCA sought to find other incumbents to take on as well, closing with a direct threat: "members of Congress [like him] who support this irresponsible bill will face consequences."

The threat may have been effective. When the Equity and Interstate Sales Tax Collection Act was introduced in 1987, it had fifty-three cosponsors, seventeen of whom were Republican. When Brooks reintroduced it two years later, it had twelve cosponsors, only two of whom were Republicans.

DESPITE SPEAKER WRIGHT'S PARTING words to the House, relations between the parties and the tone of the political discourse would get worse, much worse. With Brooks's steady rise through Congress came increasingly motivated opposition. The Texas House delegation not only lacked the cohesiveness it once had, it now comprised two opposing factions: nineteen Democrats and eight Republicans.

Brooks, dean of the Texas delegation for some years, now also ranked as the third most senior member of Congress, two away from being dean of the entire House of Representatives. In other times, that would have been a source of pride for all Texans. By 1990, however, incumbency and experience in Washington appeared as more of a detriment to candidates than an asset.

In the preceding seven elections, Brooks had run unopposed in three and won handily with more than 60 percent of the vote in the other four. He had sometimes received significant opposition, such as when sitting Vice President Bush campaigned for Lisa Duperier in 1986, but had always won in the end.

In advance of the upcoming 1990 election, Suarez's group ran an advertisement, under the name of the USCA, in Beaumont-area newspapers that promised to "help finance and provide expert campaign help to public-minded candidates who will run against Jack Brooks." One person who saw and responded to the ad was a computer salesman in Friendswood, a small municipality on the outskirts of the Houston suburbs.

Steve Stockman was an unusual candidate for public office. He had no previous policy or public service experience, no law degree, and had only recently found regular work. After some troubled years of what Stockman himself described to reporters as time spent suffering from "partying syndrome," including various stints in jail for traffic violations and felony drug possession charges, Stockman's brother kicked him out of his Wisconsin home and Stockman took a bus south to Texas, seeking a warmer climate. There he lived his first six months in Water Gardens, a downtown public park in Fort Worth. Stockman told reporters that he "found Jesus" in 1984 and became interested in conservative activism. During the Iran-Contra scandal, Stockman said he was angered by "Brooks's mistreatment of [Colonel] North during televised congressional hearings."

Once Stockman connected with Suarez after seeing the advertisement, the Suarez Corp., this time operating under a subsidiary named Pol-Serv Corp., provided the new candidate with its political expertise and more than $80,000 in advertising and campaign services. In addition, Benjamin Suarez, his wife Nancy (then president of Suarez Corp.), and two other employees made personal donations to Stockman for Congress.

In a tight Republican primary, Stockman lost, but finished close enough to run in the runoff. He lost that as well, and Suarez Corp. demanded its $80,000 back, contending that it had been a loan. After an investigation by the Federal Election Commission (FEC) several years later to determine whether the monies had constituted an illegal campaign contribution,

Stockman argued that it could not have been a loan because both parties had understood that he never had a chance at winning.

The victorious Republican candidate was Maury Meyers, a popular and influential local Republican who was coming off eight years as the mayor of Beaumont. With the collapse of the oil industry, jobs fleeing the district and state, and with local financial mismanagement rampant, the district was primed for a change. Republicans saw Democratic seats as vulnerable. Even Oliver North, who had been convicted of several felonies since the Iran-Contra hearings, was sweeping through the state to speak at fundraisers.

As Brooks was quite literally lying on his deathbed during his pancreatitis scare in December 1989, Meyers announced his candidacy and formally filed against Brooks, figuring it would be an easy win. As the story goes, when Brooks heard the news, he called his son Jeb into his hospital room and said, "Jeb, I want you to promise me that you're going to get that son of a bitch."

As fate would have it, Brooks was able to beat Meyers himself. Once recuperated, Brooks ran an active campaign against the challenger. In several debates, the two agreed on most major issues like environmental protections, public education reform, and President Bush's military actions in the Persian Gulf, but disagreed vehemently on the deficit.

As Duperier had done four years earlier, Meyers sought to make Brooks's time and stature in Washington his greatest liability. Brooks refused to appear complacent in his role, reminding voters that he still had a lot of fight in him. Of his health ordeal just months earlier, he said, "The doctors gave me less than a 20 percent chance of recovery. I won that battle with the help of thousands of your prayers."

Meyers was ten years younger than Brooks, but a fifty-eight-year-old freshman in Congress would not "have much stroke" in the chamber. Bubba Pate, a Republican who had run against Brooks in 1980 and 1982, actually came out and endorsed his former foe. When Brooks asked Pate in private why he had done it, Pate exclaimed, "Why would we wanna elect somebody in the minority party that's nearly as old as you are?"

Meyers gave Brooks his closest election finish yet, only the second time since entering Congress that Brooks had garnered less than 60 percent of the vote. Nevertheless, Brooks succeeded in corralling what the *New York Times* called his "coalition of minority members, labor unions, abortion rights activists, and loyal Democrats" to win reelection with 57 percent of the vote.

1992 ELECTION: Stockman ran again in 1992. This time Stockman won the Republican primary and soon was gaining name recognition and popularity, perhaps because his promotional tactics became more flagrant. According to the *Beaumont Enterprise* and the *Houston Chronicle*, Stockman had:

> . . . *lied on his resume in '92 about being an accountant, lied about having worked for IBM, lied about being a graduate of the University of Houston-Clear Lake (he did later graduate), and lied about being a computer consultant at the school.*

To court prospective donors, Stockman also organized a "congressional cruise" in the Houston Ship Channel. He claimed that donors would have an opportunity to rub elbows with Republican members of the Texas delegation, except no members came. The *Houston Chronicle* reported that they had boycotted the event and that Stockman had "concealed the fact" that profits from the cruise would go solely to his campaign fund.

With the continued help of Suarez Corp., Stockman continued his direct mail approach, with aides running a pro-Stockman newspaper called the *Southeast Texas Times* out of his house in Friendswood, which also served as his campaign headquarters. The shady publication would later be the focus of yet another FEC investigation, for which the Stockman campaign would acknowledge wrongdoing and pay a $40,000 fine.

Voter turnout in that election surprised everyone. In a district were total votes typically hovered around 130,000, more than 214,000 people came out to cast a ballot in 1992. Brooks won reelection again, but this time with only 55 percent of the vote. More than 96,000 constituents voted against him.

24

Crime Bill

T he 103rd Congress entered Washington firmly Democratic, with nearly 60 percent majorities in each chamber, but parity between the two parties had gradually emerged. Texas Republicans maintained the inroads they had first made into the states' delegation ten years earlier. They had one of two seats in the Senate, and when Clinton appointed Democratic Texas Senator Lloyd Bentsen to be his secretary of the treasury, a special election gave Republicans that seat as well, the start of what would become a decades-long GOP grip on that chamber. Texas representation in the House included nine Republicans, a solid third of the delegation, but the House still stood firmly in Democratic control, and among pundits and prognosticators at the time there was little worry that the Democrats would loosen their thirty-eight-year grip on the chamber.

Republicans could not compete with Bill Clinton, the charming former governor of Arkansas. The Clinton-Gore ticket came into office with optimistic proposals to reform the welfare system and health care and stem the scourge of violent crime that had gripped the nation since the crack cocaine epidemic of the mid-1980s. The Clinton campaign had also made the preceding twelve years of Republican fiscal policy and enormous budget deficits a key issue.

Brooks made sure that the Beaumont area was a welcome place; both Hillary Clinton and Al Gore campaigned there with Brooks leading up to the election. Gore, appearing at Lamar University just days before the election, got crowds of cheering students to their feet with oft-repeated lines like:

Now it's our turn in the United States of America to have change. Young people in the United States are saying: "Trickle-down economics is really stupid! Let's get rid of it!"

The Clinton administration immediately took to Brooks, who would accompany the president, vice president, and first lady on trips to Texas. When Clinton made a phone call from the Johnson Space Center in Houston to astronauts aboard the space shuttle *Discovery* as it orbited the Earth, he handed the call over to Brooks to say hello. The president had Brooks join him at various bill signings, consultations in the Oval Office, and luncheons around Washington throughout the first two years of his presidency. Brooks liked both Bill and Hillary. Of the two, Brooks thought Hillary was smarter and "put up with him, which is a real chore."

Clinton soon came to rely on Brooks for his deep knowledge of the federal government. As Congress approved the creation of new federal judgeships and Clinton searched for qualified candidates, he came to Brooks for suggestions. Brooks immediately gave him two: Thad Heartfield of southeast Texas and David Folsom of Arkansas.

When Brooks had run against Joe Tonahill for the Democratic primary in 1952, both candidates had asked Heartfield's grandfather for his support. The elder Heartfield was a respected local judge at the time and his opinion mattered. He decided to support Brooks, and the young man never forgot it. Four decades later, Brooks was back in the district and passing some leisure time with the younger Heartfield, who would later recall this moment:

I'm out fishing with Brooks and we come home, and as I'm walking down the driveway he says, "Thad, come back here." Of course, I can't mimic exactly the way he talks—he says, "Thad, come on back here."

I said, "Yes, sir, Mr. Chairman."

He says, "I'm getting on a plane with Bill Clinton tomorrow afternoon, and I'm going to recommend you to be a new federal judge," and I said, "My God, can I have some time to think about it?"

He says, "Take all the time you want until 5:30 tomorrow morning." I was at his front door at five o'clock the next morning with a paper in hand, and I agreed to do it.

Clinton—reflecting later in his memoir, *My Life*—spoke fondly of Brooks, going so far as to say the grouchy old Texan was "one of my favorite congressmen." All the while, as he called out other officials by name and title—Senator Kennedy, Congresswoman Morella, General Reno—Clinton always referred to Brooks as "Chairman," just as every other president had. Clinton was the tenth president Brooks had worked with. Truman, who had remained a lame duck in office until March 1953, was the first.

SENIOR MEMBER: As the "Chairman" had been President Carter's entrée to the House, the House leadership was happy to have him continue his biennial breakfasts every new Congress to introduce freshman congressmen and women to the institution. Brooks had participated and then hosted this customary congressional event ever since his first in 1953, when he had the gall (or just permission from Rayburn) to invite President Truman to the breakfast.

Now, forty years later, Brooks reveled in the role that his experience and accomplishments had provided. Gene Green, a twenty-nine-year-old who had just been elected to represent a district in Houston, fondly recalled his first meeting with the chairman in Washington:

> *I remember sitting down with him when I first came to the House of Repre-sentatives. When he asked me what committee I wanted to serve on, I thought, well, I'll get what I need.*
>
> *I told him I wanted Energy and Commerce. He chewed on his cigar and said, "You'll get Ed[ucation] and Labor. And you'll like it."*

Representative Lamar Smith from San Antonio was assigned a seat on Brooks's Judiciary Committee. Even though Smith was a Republican, Brooks reached out to mentor him, "because I was from Texas," Smith said. When the young lawmaker drafted a noncontroversial bill that had no opposi-tion, Brooks called him into his office to say that his legislation had a high chance of passing through the committee. Smith said: "He let me swallow that hook, line, and sinker. Then he said 'I just want to change one word.' The next week we passed the 'Brooks bill,' not the 'Smith bill.'"

Smith would later wield the chairman's gavel in that committee and recall, "I learned two lessons there: the power of the majority and the power of the chairman."

Fellow Democrat Charlie Rangel joined Brooks on the Judiciary in 1974 right before the impeachment proceedings began. Rangel said Brooks was "one of the most cantankerous damned people I have ever met in my life" but then added that he was also "one of the greatest guys I ever met."

When Rangel, an African American from New York, would disagree with the chairman, he said Brooks used to threaten that he was "going to come to Harlem and campaign for me. He was going to get on the street in front of Adam Clayton Powell's church and tell folks about what a great congressman I was. Of course, that wouldn't have gone over at all—and he never carried out his threat."

ACROSS THE AISLE: Despite the general decline of civility in Congress between the parties, Republican members had also come to understand what made Brooks tick and respected him for it. Brooks recalled how he got along with both Senators Orrin Hatch of Utah and Bob Dole of Kansas:

> *You know, they both needed help, too. And I needed their support from time to time. Or their lack of animosity. You know, they might not endorse what I'm doing on the floor, but they might not organize against it. And there are several degrees of support and non-support in a legislative body. If they don't organize against you and they just say, "We're not helping, we're not in that fight," well, that means it's much easier for you to gather your forces and to win. And I had that kind of relationship with a lot of those Republican leaders. That helps.*

Brooks more than got along with some members of the Republican leadership. They trusted him, or at the very least believed he would follow through when he said something. Staffers later recalled several incidents in which Republicans demonstrated that trust.

Once during the previous decade, there was a time when Brooks, Speaker O'Neill, and Majority Leader Wright were discussing a piece of legislation and the particular path it would need to take through the House and the Senate. In the Senate, the congressmen knew they required the help of Senator Dole to personally shepherd the bill. As it turned out, Dole also had some legislation he wanted to see passed in the House, so he proposed the classic horse trade: "I'll help your bill if you'll help mine."

Speaker O'Neill demurred; the legislative calendar was already full for that year and they could not accommodate Dole in this term. O'Neill and the two other senior Democrats did, however, promise to take up Dole's legislation in next year's calendar. For Dole, it was a gamble, and the senator was a cautious man. If he agreed, his legislation would be at the mercy of these men from the opposition party until the following year. In Washington, a lot could happen in a year.

But finally he agreed and said, "I need a letter from your office and from your office," pointing to O'Neill and then to Wright.

"What about Brooks?" Wright asked.

"Naw, Brooks's word is good," Dole quipped, without missing a beat.

After the group disbanded, Brooks returned to his office and got Dole on the phone.

"You've got to stop praising me in front of my leadership," Brooks chided his friend. "You're making me look bad!"

Among those in Congress who had weathered the tumult of the preceding decades, there existed an understanding of how the institution of the House could function effectively for the betterment of the American people.

BY ABIDING BY THE procurement good practices outlined in his namesake ADP legislation, Brooks had shepherded the FTS-2000 telecommunications contract through award and successful execution. A Republican staffer on Brooks's committee called the project the "poster child of how the government can use its buying power to facilitate innovation and price competitiveness."

Brooks also ensured the contract's success by requiring that all federal agencies participate through congressional mandating. By official accounts, one major result was a government telecommunication cost that plummeted from thirty-five cents per minute all the way down to seven cents. Through that and other massive purchases throughout the government, the Brooks Act had already saved many billions of dollars. There were detractors, though. By February 1994, there were many people in Washington working on the FTS-2000 project who felt Brooks's procurement law no longer applied to current circumstances and could be disregarded with little to no effect. To them, complying with the law had led to the current delays the project faced.

Appearing before a House Appropriations subcommittee considering a reversal of the law, Brooks submitted to Chairman Steny Hoyer:

> *The contention that the Brooks Act plays a major role in those delays, however, is based largely on unsupported anecdotes. . . .*
>
> *There is an inscription in one of John F. Kennedy's notebooks, "Don't ever take down a fence, until you know the reason why it was put up." The Brooks Act for many years has served the taxpayers well as a fence against waste and abuse in federal [ADP] procurements.*

AMONG THOSE WHO UNDERSTOOD fences were Brooks's fellow chairmen John Dingell, Billy Ford—both from Michigan—and Dante Fascell of Florida. These three respectively chaired the committees for Energy and Commerce, Education and Labor, and Foreign Affairs, which Brooks described as "big, important committees." All four of them had served in World War II, accrued a collective 124 years in Congress since the war, and would soon have their official portraits hanging in the halls of Congress. Brooks said:

> *They were powerful members, and when I had a problem with a bill coming to the floor or something, and I called them to help, call them on the phone to help them, or see them on the floor and tell them, "I need your help on that." They were already helping. Boy, that's the kind of support that you cannot replace.*

Brooks's legislative productivity was without parallel. Whereas many senior members might settle into an easy rhythm of championing only bills that could be passed without much fuss, Brooks took on bigger and bigger legislative fights, going directly after lobbies that had successfully stalled reform in Congress for decades. During the 103rd Congress, Brooks introduced no fewer than thirty pieces of legislation, seven of which eventually passed in the House, including:

> *International Antitrust Enforcement Assistance Act of 1994*
> *Bankruptcy Reform Act of 1994*
> *Antitrust and Communications Reform Act of 1994*
> *Independent Counsel Reauthorization Act of 1994*
> *National Cooperative Production Amendments of 1993*
> *Aircraft Equipment Settlement Leases Act of 1993*

Each eventually passed the Senate as well and were quickly signed into law by Clinton. Among these were several landmark bills that reversed decades of status quo. For example, the domestic insurance industry had enjoyed an exemption from many federal antitrust regulations ever since the 1945 McCarran-Ferguson Act, which aimed to foster the industry in the aftermath of World War II by temporarily allowing insurers to pool their historical loss data to determine rates and create projections. Brooks's aide Jon Yarowsky said that the McCarran-Ferguson Act had given insurance essentially the only exemption from standard competition statutes.

> *It'd been passed in the dead of night at the end of World War II in an unrelated conference. Nobody knew what was going on. Someone slid it in, and guess what? They were exempted from the antitrust laws. No one ever thought they could take on the insurance industry. Mr. Brooks did.†*

By the late 1980s, the act had run its useful course, according to Brooks, and needed to be quashed. Insurers now "abused their privileges to fix prices and thwart competition." For years, Brooks had wanted to change the law, which served no purpose but to guard the industry against basic antitrust

---

† This quotation is taken verbatim from a video interview that can be viewed at www.jackbrooksfoundation.org.

protections. He had seen firsthand the insurance headquarter buildings in Hartford, Connecticut, which he noted were built with industry cash, not financed over many years like most companies had to do. He said, "They didn't build them on credit. They built them on profits, out of people like you and me."

Nearly every year since 1989, Brooks had ushered a similar repeal bill through his committee only to have it fail to reach the House floor in time for consideration, almost always because of strident opposition from the insurance lobby. The *Washington Post* characterized the fight as "one of the epic legislative battles of the past twenty years."

Brooks began working on two of the largest industry groups—American Insurance Association and the Independent Insurance Agents of America— and finally, after two years of negotiation, won their endorsement for the repeal bill he introduced in late 1993, much to the dismay of others in the industry and most House Republicans. In garnering their support, Brooks said the achievement marked "a turning point in the drive for reform be- cause it represents the first breach in the wall of strident opposition from an industry that, understandably, has tried to protect its unique antitrust status." Once his Judiciary Committee passed the amendment, Brooks at- tached it to Clinton's Health Security Act.

Perhaps the Clintons had learned from the last Democratic president's mistakes. When Bill and Hillary came to the White House, Hillary's role focused on moving health care reform legislation through Congress, and private memos unveiled years later showed the care the administration's team took in courting individual members of the House.

Hillary, who took the lead on plying Congress to embrace the health care agenda, received specific instructions on how to approach Brooks. "What he wants to hear is that you are aware of his legislation and that you and the president would like nothing less than to undercut his efforts in any way," the memo read.

The Clintons took heed of the advice and Brooks's repeal bill stayed intact, but once the Clinton's signature health care bill died in Congress, it took Brooks's with it, ending more than five years of his efforts to see it pass. No further serious effort to repeal the exemption would be mounted for years to come. The failed repeal bill calls to mind a statement Brooks made to a reporter years later: "Constructive change doesn't come just because you think something isn't right . . . it is tough, tedious work . . . I've tried to change a thousand things in government and only managed a few."

"A few" was an understatement almost to the point of hyperbole because, that same year, Brooks managed to bring about more change through a landmark telecommunications bill that restructured the industry for the first time in decades, something few legislators in memory had attempted to do.

The telecommunications industry had been steeped in monopoly and lawsuits ever since Alexander Graham Bell first fought off Western Union's advances on his telephone patent in 1879 and then his American Bell Company and its chief subsidiary-cum-parent company AT&T started gobbling up competitors. Since its inception in 1885, AT&T lorded over the industry, which consisted almost entirely of smaller, independent operators that had been swallowed up by the "Bell system." This consolidation created a "natural monopoly" that made sense for a fledgling utility service in which much of the infrastructure had yet to be built, but by the 1990s, things had changed dramatically.

The last major communications legislation had passed in 1934, when individuals had no television sets, wireless phones, or computers. By the 1990s, information technology and the transmission of voice and data services were among the largest industries in the country.

Industry players, notably AT&T and MCI, objected to any measures that would change the landscape—for instance, requiring them to lay fiber optic cables in place of the copper cables that had been installed decades earlier.

Brooks sent his staff to meet with companies and gather their input. Brooks's aide Jim Lewin approached attorneys at AT&T and the other Bell companies that had been sliced off in the 1980s. The reactions were mixed though universally laden with suspicion. AT&T, still the dominant player, respected Brooks for the fair and transparent procurement process for the FTS-2000 but asked Lewin point-blank, "How are you going to fuck us on this?" At MCI, officials responded, "We don't trust anybody."

Brooks and his staff wrote an outline and sent it off to the Office of Legislative Council, which then drafted the bill for Brooks. He introduced it as the Antitrust and Communications Reform Act of 1994. The bill had broad bipartisan support in both chambers. As Lewin remarked, "Quite frankly, most of the world was shocked at how rational that was." Once AT&T and other companies saw the legislation and how much sense it made, they came onboard, even though some of the measures could hurt their business.

Brooks had sparred with his fellow Democratic chairman Dingell for several years over jurisdiction on the bill. Dingell's Energy and Commerce Committee oversaw vast swaths of government and private activity. Commerce was another major committee like Judiciary, and Dingell was not someone to pick a fight with. The Michigander would go on to serve fifty-nine years in the House, the longest tenure in U.S. history.

Dingell entered Congress two years after Brooks, and both were known as "mean S.O.B.s." Dingell had also served in World War II and received orders to be part of the initial invasion of Japan in 1945. Ten years later, he entered the House, also at the age of twenty-nine.

At one point, Dingell sent Brooks a photograph with the words: "To Jack Brooks, the meanest man in Congress, from his student, friend, and admirer, with affection and high esteem, John Dingell."

After pitched battles over the jurisdiction of the bill, the two men reached an accord and it was referred to both committees. Staff from both met more than one hundred times to hammer out the details of the landmark bill, which ended up with near-unanimous support in the House, where it passed by a vote of 430 to 5. Its companion bill stalled in the Senate that year but would be taken up again in the following Congress by both Democrats and Republicans, marking the first major overhaul of telecommunications law in almost sixty-two years.

ADP ACT: Just as telecommunications required some revisiting decades after legislation that shaped the industry's landscape, so did the original Brooks Act of 1965, the Automatic Data Processing Act which helped shape that global industry when it was not yet really an industry. Technology and computer literacy had advanced so drastically in the interim that the centralized management measures enacted by the act no longer added much value.

By 1994, IBM competed among an enormous field of innovative players like Intel, Oracle, Microsoft, and Apple, companies that had not existed thirty years earlier, but were now established leaders, thanks in large part to the level playing field created by the implementation of the Brooks Act.

Brooks's ideas had been absolutely right regarding what the government would require as data became more integral to governing—interoperability and an IT management system—and then what the private market needed to grow—standardized federal policies and transparent competition. The ADP Act, as intended, had created the framework for a competitive market.

The guiding principles of the act had been so right, in fact, that they would be easy to take for granted. In the modern information age, the idea of one computer user not being able to open or view a picture or basic text file because it had been sent by a different model of computer would seem absurd. In 1965, many industry experts and government officials, including the National Bureau of Standards, did not think so. They thought computer software companies guarding their proprietary methods of operating represented the height of innovation.

One cannot overstate the impact that Brooks's ADP legislation and the GSA's dogged enforcement had on the growth and efficiency of the IT industry, which by the 1990s had revolutionized the way Americans worked, communicated with one another, and lived out their everyday lives. Brooks's ADP Act was not born from a eureka moment. The congressman had not dreamed up the provisions of the bill by himself one day. Many federal officials knew the deficiencies in data processing. Rather, in his characteristic style, Brooks was the legislator who paid special attention to the mundane details of how the government operated, read over six years of critical audit reports from the comptroller general, realized what had to be done, and then had the guts and gumption, not to mention the subcommittee chairmanship, to see it through.

THE GROUNDBREAKING CIVIL RIGHTS legislation that Brooks had contributed to in the 1960s also warranted modernization. The Civil Rights Act of 1964, which Brooks later described as "an ice breaker," needed to be broadened.

Brooks shepherded a piece of updated legislation through his Judiciary and then it moved through the entire House "in good shape," he said. However, Republican senators then began "dallying" and delaying the bill in their own chamber. Brooks recalled:

> *I didn't think that was very appropriate. I didn't like that. And so I told the senators, some of them, quietly, and happily, that if they kill that bill for some reason, delayed and delayed it and delayed it, amended it and so forth, and kept and don't get it passed and so forth.*
>
> *I said, "We'll whip you good in every big city in the United States in the next election. So, you go on and do that. Politically it would be just wonderful for me. Let the Republican Party be against civil rights. They are, so let them be. Give them credit for it!" . . . And they decided, pretty quickly, that they'd be for the bill.*

VIOLENT CRIME BILL: The Violent Crime Control and Law Enforcement Act of 1994 was the omnibus crime bill that represented Clinton's moonshot to address the skyrocketing rates of gun violence, gang activity, and murder across the United States. Homicides by firearms had peaked in 1993, when guns were used to kill 18,253 people, according to the Centers for Disease Control and Prevention.

In the wake of the crack cocaine epidemic of the 1980s, large swaths of inner-city America took on dystopian features, and a violent social order portrayed in movies like *New Jack City* and the music of gangsta rap musicians like Public Enemy, N.W.A., and myriad others celebrated this new, Wild West-like lifestyle replete with drugs, shootings, and killing.

Inner-city street gangs had undergone a transformation from fringe social groups to highly profitable and rigidly structured organizations with a primary purpose of distributing illicit narcotics. Meanwhile, the average age of most violent offenders had fallen in only two decades from eighteen years old to fifteen years old.

Combatting crime had been a lynchpin in Clinton's campaign. Once in office, the president and his allies in the congressional leadership asked Brooks and Senator Joe Biden to champion the cause. Both men had already sponsored the Crime Bill of 1991, which passed both chambers only to die in the Senate after conference. At a rare legislation introduction ceremony in August 1993, Brooks and Biden stood with Al Gore, Attorney General Janet Reno, and a handful of other public officials in the White House Rose Garden as Clinton announced his administration's proposals before the assembled cameras and reporters. Clinton noted that in the previous four years, ninety thousand murders had been committed. The month before, in Washington alone, twenty-four people were murdered in a single week.

Others then offered their own remarks. Gore bragged, "When Bill Clinton, Janet Reno, Jack Brooks, Joe Biden, and their colleagues stand together on these issues you can bet we'll be back here in the Rose Garden very soon to sign this legislation into law." Reno spoke and gave kind acknowledgment to Brooks and Biden for their influence on her. Biden gave some powerful, and at times rambling, remarks.

Brooks followed and led off by saying, "Well, let me just say thank you for those very brief remarks, Mr. Biden." Everyone, including Clinton, Gore, and Biden, laughed. Brooks continued:

> I want to praise the president for keeping his own deep commitment to fighting the scourge of crime that has threatened our streets and our homes and our very lives for far too long. It's time to fight crime with actions, not slogans. It may be hard, very hard, for some groups to let go of what they've perceived to be a wonderful issue, but our streets are flowing with blood. The American public doesn't want any more words that fly ever so lightly into the air signifying nothing. They're tired of politicians vying with each other to prove just who's tougher on crime. They're especially tired of the purists among us who want 100 percent or nothing.
>
> Now, last Congress the crime bill report was historic both in scope and approach. Without question, it was the toughest crime bill to emerge since the federal government was forced to take drastic action in the '20s and '30s. This bill did not stop. It contained a host of programs to prevent new crimes against persons and property, the type of prevention sorely lacking in past efforts in the '80s. Yet, for all its unyielding refusal to coddle criminals, it did not trample on the basic constitutional protections that make this country a nation ruled by laws and not by mob passions.

The House passed the crime bill on October 21st of '91. The Senate did it November 21st, about a month later, of '91. We went to conference November 24th of '91. We passed the conference report in the House of Representatives November 27th of '91. And when the conference moved over to the Senate, a group of obstructionist Republicans decided it was somehow better to deny the American public a victory on crime than to acknowledge the fundamental soundness of this Democratic crime bill. They bottled up the bill for almost eleven months.

Now, this Congress, the president has unmistakably extended a hand to Republicans not to delay, to join in our efforts together to fight crime. We'll see how they respond. We'll know their actions by their votes.

Then Brooks took his seat and, clad in a light suit and tie, donned a white baseball cap to shield his bald head from the summertime sun. Several others then spoke briefly and the ceremony ended. The president and others assembled broke up and mingled together in front of the gathered media.

Brooks made his way down to the end of an impromptu receiving line for the president and waited for a moment with Clinton. In archived video news footage of the event, Brooks can be seen approaching Clinton, holding him by the elbow, and telling him something. Clinton, expressionless, makes no sign of hearing him, then looks down at his elbow being held before turning away without a comment. Brooks then stood apprehensively to the side for a moment as the president scanned the crowd for others to talk to. Whatever Brooks told Clinton, whether it concerned the substance of the legislation or something else entirely, the president showed no interest in engaging him on it.

Shortly thereafter, Biden and Brooks both introduced bills to their respective chambers based on the White House's goals. Brooks introduced the House version on October 26, 1993. His 450-page bill blew away expectations. His bill created twenty-one new capital offenses, where before there had been two. In addition to the one hundred thousand additional police officers that Clinton had promised, the $30.07 billion piece of legislation called for grants to fund innovative methods to "reduce violence and crimes, enhance law enforcement, [and] provide education and activity programs for youth." According to Yarowsky, the chief counsel of the House Judiciary,

"They hadn't seen a crime bill like that in probably fifty years." Simultaneously, Brooks also introduced amendments to the standing crime bill—the Gun Control Act of 1968—that proposed measures including proposals to develop residential substance abuse treatment programs within state correctional institutions and federal prisons, develop more effective programs to reduce juvenile gang participation and drug trafficking, and develop alternative methods of punishment for young offenders.

Prevention mattered as much to Brooks in the overall fight against violent crime as punishment did, which was where many of the attached social programs came in, including the contentious midnight basketball youth program that established safe zones for kids to keep busy at night. Detractors derided the concept as the federal government paying for people to have fun. The bill also proposed drug-abuse treatment programs for released prisoners.

Even some Democrats balked at the scope of social programs in the package, fearing that without easy metrics to determine results, funds would be wasted on ineffectual programs. Brooks fervently felt the opposite was true. Just as he had supported Johnson's Great Society legislation with the full force of his seat in Congress, Brooks believed in the power of well-crafted, broad government support to improve American lives.

As Brooks hustled around Capitol Hill, crafting the language and persuading legislators, he appeared before the House Rules Committee and told the chairman and several skeptical committee members:

> *I think we have found that the utilization of tax monies in prevention is the most effective use of our tax monies. We have spent one hundred years in this country throwing everybody in jail we could catch and convict. Indict them, convict them, and throw them in "the can." Then they get out and do the same thing.*
>
> *Now this is the first time we've tried a really innovative program that has money to help prevent people from getting into this rut, from staying in it. We've got first- and second-generation criminals. We don't want third- and fourth-generation criminals. We're trying to break that cycle. It's critical.*

Brooks then leapt forward in his seat.

It may not work!

He paused to let those words sink in with the committee.

I don't guarantee it. But it is a change from what we've been doing and by God what we've been doing hadn't worked very well. And this allocates some resources to do that. Make that effort to change it. I think it's critical. I have little children just like you. I want them to have a better life. I want to try this and see if it'll improve.

THE THIRD PART OF the legislation was constitutional, concerning due process and individual protections. *Habeas corpus* is a legal concept dating back to medieval Anglo-Saxon common law, stipulating that a person cannot be indefinitely detained without appearing before a judge or court. The detained also has the right to petition a court to state why he or she is being held. The idea stands as a bedrock principle of the American judicial system. Partially because of the appeals process facing inmates on death row, *habeas* reform had become a political issue again. Yarowsky said:

In 1994, it was totally under siege, and Mr. Brooks basically drew a line, because no one could ever doubt how tough he was on crime, ever. I mean . . . he created twenty-one new capital offenses, okay. But, he said that where the Supreme Court was going on habeas corpus was to eviscerate that fundamental freedom. And so, he stood behind Don Edwards, who was on the constitutional law subcommittee, very liberal. But, on this issue, Mr. Brooks said, "he's right." And he put that [defense of habeas corpus] in the Crime Bill.

Each one of these individual provisions—defense of *habeas corpus*, drug treatment for prisoners, prevention methods for juveniles, and many others—had been the subject of debate on both sides of the aisle for decades. No clear lines divided politicians who felt adamantly one way or another about each issue. For principles both ideological and practical, slivers of viewpoints throughout the political spectrum agreed and disagreed on many of the provisions in unusual combinations. Having all of these matters together in one omnibus package resulted in a piece of legislation so far-reaching and unwieldy that some thought it was dead in the water. Brooks found a clever solution, though.

Yarowsky explained:

> *What you had was a situation where we had some very liberal members on our side that didn't like the capital punishment provisions and would probably vote against the bill, even against Mr. Brooks. It was almost a religious belief.*
>
> *You then had the Republicans, that if they could just pick off two or three people, and vote as a bloc and pick off two or three of our Dems, against habeas corpus, that could kill the bill. So, there were problems on both the left and right, Democrat and Republican.*
>
> *What were we going to do? How were you going to pass this crime bill that had all of these different types of provisions?*
>
> *Brooks had an idea. We just won't pass it in one lump. We will simply divide it up into eight or nine smaller bills.*

Instead of staging one epic legislative battle that he could not assure the president they would win, Brooks staged lots of little battles he felt certain of winning. He sliced up the bill into palatable chunks that enough Democrats would vote for or enough Republicans would join to pass them individually. Forty years of debating and vote counting in the House meant Brooks understood which politicians could be corralled together and on which issues.

Brooks possessed, just as Johnson and Rayburn had, deep institutional knowledge of the chamber and its parliamentary ways. He passed eight separate crime bills over a period of three weeks, and then took those bills to the Rules Committee, which established guidelines for the consideration of each bill before it could reach the House floor, and had the committee tie them back together into a single bill.

Yarowsky remembered:

Well, let me tell you, he was so far ahead of the president then, President Clinton, whom I later worked for after Mr. Brooks left. They were mind-boggled, 'cause, you know, they thought they were so far ahead of everybody, and they didn't even know where this was coming from. It was coming from Mr. Brooks.

Brooks's recollection was more modest:

Well, we passed them all in the subcommittee, and passed them as separate legislation, separate bills, all roughly at the same time. We didn't have a lot of trouble with any of them, and they all went to the Rules Committee, and I had the Rules Committee combine them. You didn't want to have eight bills on the floor on the same, relatively the same subject.

Through the procedure, the combined bill had essentially passed a House floor vote just eight days after Brooks first introduced it.

Unlike the president, Brooks had experience crafting legislation that multiple cohorts could get behind. In fact, he sponsored the only crime bill to ever receive the support of both the gun control and the gun enthusiast lobbies.

The ultra-conservative Republican senator Strom Thurmond of South Carolina and Brooks made strange bedfellows, but their mutual sponsorship of a crime bill in 1984 brought them together. The Law Enforcement Officers Protection Act sought to outlaw the manufacturing or importation of armor-piercing bullets—known as "cop killers" on the street—for anything other than police, military, or export purposes. It also instituted mandatory sentencing for those caught in possession of those bullets while committing a felony.

In his statement introducing the House version of the bill, Brooks said, "Soft body armor is credited with saving the lives of over four hundred law enforcement officers. My bill is to deter the availability and use of armor-piercing ammunition that can penetrate these lifesaving vests." The so-called Thurmond-Brooks Bill had wide bipartisan support, including ninety cosponsors in the Senate and endorsements from President Reagan, numerous law enforcement agencies, and the gun rights organizations.

Further complicating the crime bill was the controversial Brady Bill—first introduced by Representative Chuck Schumer of New York in 1991—a standalone measure seeking to implement a five-day waiting period and background check for purchasers of firearms. This marked an impediment to the purchase of firearms, and however commonsense and innocuous it would be in reality, to gun proponents it represented the proverbial camel's nose under the tent. For months, Democrats argued whether to include such a politically charged provision in the package. It could either be a perfect opportunity for its passage or it could sink the entire bill. Eventually, it was reintroduced by Schumer and passed through the House separately, and the Brady Bill became law in November 1993.

ASSAULT WEAPONS BAN: Another proposed measure promised just as much discord, if not more. In the wake of several mass shootings where gunmen used assault weapons to fire into school playgrounds and office buildings, the political will to limit these types of firearms had reached a crescendo, and Senator Diane Feinstein of California crafted an amendment to ban them outright from civilian purchase. Specifically, the ban referred to nineteen military-style guns that had little sporting or self-defense use.

Clinton accepted the initiative wholeheartedly. In his mind, the provision stood part and parcel with his new comprehensive crime package. When announcing the legislation in the Rose Garden ceremony, he said, "This effort against crime will not be complete if we do not eliminate assault weapons."

The Senate version of the bill had included the ban; Brooks's version in the House had not.

As someone who had taken his new bride hunting during their honeymoon decades earlier, Brooks felt no personal uneasiness around firearms. He also understood the ban to be a terrible political play, and he would advise Clinton repeatedly to drop it from his rhetoric and the bill. It is likely that when he approached Clinton in the Rose Garden ceremony, he was again advising the president to drop the amendment from the bill. Judging by Clinton's non-response, he was clearly not open to discussing the matter any further. His mind was set, and he had reasons for the certainty. Polls showed that a reported 80 percent of Americans agreed that military-grade weapons had no place in the hands of civilians. In early May, former Presidents Ford, Carter, and Reagan wrote a letter to members of the House, urging them to support the ban, pointing to overwhelming public opinion numbers as well as the stated support of "every major law enforcement organization in America and dozens of leading labor, medical, religious, civil rights, and civic groups."

Nevertheless, Brooks felt the upshot would be that single-issue voters who owned guns would be convinced this was an attack on their individual freedoms. Banning any weapons at all, regardless of the type, reason, or potential benefits to society, struck some as the first step toward the government taking away individual firearms. The vote, which many House Democrats representing rural and contested districts would need to defend, would serve as a catalyst for Republicans seeking to foment outrage within their political base at those in Washington who would take away their guns. The *New York Times* quoted Brooks saying that the crime bill was supposed to bring Americans together, but the ban divided them.

NRA: The primary stoker and embodiment of that outrage was the National Rifle Association (NRA). The association was founded in 1871 to improve marksmanship in the military and among civilian "sportsmen." It operated as such for a century until the 1970s and 1980s, when, spurred on by two pieces of legislation that curbed interstate sales of guns and the proliferation of "Saturday night specials," small handguns predominantly used for crime rather than sport, the group morphed from a loose association of firearm enthusiasts into a hardline, grassroots lobbying institution for the gun industry.

Like several other grassroots-turned-political groups, the NRA's positions became absolute. No half measures would do and no room existed for interpretation or compromise. As one executive vice president of the group said at the group's annual convention, "We must declare that there are no shades of gray in American freedom. It's black and white, all or nothing. You're with us or against us."

Some moderates lamented the changes. One former president said, "We were akin to the Boy Scouts of America . . . and now we're cast with the Nazis, the skinheads, and the Ku Klux Klan." Senator Dole complained about the lockstep position required of Republicans: "You have to have a litmus test every five minutes or you're considered wavering."

But even more celebrated the absolutist perspective and newfound power it brought. According to the NRA's own count, when Clinton came to office, more than 600,000 new members joined.

The NRA's membership rolls had the paradoxical quality of swelling not only whenever a legislative threat to gun ownership arose but also when guns were used in the commission of mass murder. One such incident occurred in 1989, when Patrick Purdy, a drifter with a lengthy rap sheet of felony arrests, purchased an AK-47 assault rifle legally in Oregon, converted it to fire fully automatic, and then attacked an elementary school in Stockton, California, shooting thirty-seven schoolchildren.

Just one month after Clinton took office, the federal Bureau of Alcohol, Tobacco and Firearms (ATF) lead a raid against a compound in Waco, Texas, that sheltered the Branch Davidian cult, which had been stockpiling firearms. After a firefight, the federal agents withdrew, and the members inside initiated a fifty-one-day standoff. Finally, the compound was set ablaze from inside and all seventy-six compound residents perished. The incident represented many gun owners' greatest fear: "jackbooted" government agents coming to confiscate their guns.

When the director of the ATF called the NRA's leaders to discuss issues concerning guns, he said, "They would not answer. They would ignore us." Realizing the depth of their members' commitment to the issue, uniformity of opinion that could be crafted, and the political clout that this then carried, the tax-exempt group expanded its activity, spending more than $1.7 million on congressional candidates in 1992, which was, according to the *Baltimore Sun*, "more than any other ideological or single-issue political action committee." Within years, they would soon spend tens of millions of dollars each federal election cycle to fund candidates sympathetic to their cause.

Brooks had joined the National Rifle Association in his youth and maintained membership all his life. In southeast Texas, hunting, military service, and gun ownership had been a way of life ever since European-descended settlers had first moved through the forested wetlands. Brooks had hunted or fished with most of his dear friends and colleagues, including Rayburn, Johnson, and Briscoe.

Brooks had also supported gun ownership rights while in Congress, so much so that in 1991, the NRA invited Brooks to address its members as the keynote speaker at its annual convention. Brooks praised the NRA for defending the Second Amendment, and, regarding the Brady Bill being considered that year, the congressmen said no evidence suggested that waiting periods deterred criminals from purchasing firearms. Brooks also stated that it would be "naive to think tampering with the Second Amendment will change society." NRA members gave Brooks a standing ovation.

Around the same time, another pro-gun group with heavy lobbying activity, the American Shooting Sports Council (ASSC), held a game-hunting banquet to honor Brooks and his work on behalf of gun rights. The ASSC named Brooks its inaugural congressional leader of the year.

As he left the fete, Brooks took one of the organizers aside and joshed, "Feldman, that was delicious. I expect to have the recipe for that venison on my desk in the morning. Otherwise, you're gonna see some pretty serious gun control coming down the pike. You hear me!"

These groups, including the more radical Virginia-based Gun Owners of America, viewed the assault weapon ban as a direct threat to their newfound political influence in Washington. If it passed, legislators would realize that despite the lobby's bluster, the public support for gun control legislation mattered more to their survival in office.

Legislators still feared the NRA, but the passage of the Brady Bill in November showed that the sentiment had waned. Clinton, for one, felt certain he was on the right side of the public sentiment. In his memoirs, the president wrote about the appeals that Brooks, Speaker Foley, and Majority Leader Gephardt made to him to remove the assault weapons ban from the bill:

> *They argued that many Democrats who represented closely divided districts had already cast a very difficult vote for the economic program, and had already defied the NRA once on the Brady bill vote. They said if we made them walk*

the plank again on the assault weapons ban, the overall bill might not pass, and that if it did, many Democrats who voted for it would not survive the election in November.

Brooks had been in the House for more than forty years and . . . represented a district full of NRA members and had led the effort to defeat the assault weapons ban when it first came to a vote. Jack was convinced that if we didn't drop the ban, the NRA would beat a lot of Democrats by terrifying gun owners.

I was troubled by what Foley, Gephardt, and Brooks had said, but I was convinced that our members could win a debate with the NRA over the issue in their backyards.

Brooks said his advice to the president that the ban would cost Democratic seats "didn't worry [Clinton] a lick." Clinton wanted it done, and if ever there was an opportunity to pass an assault weapons ban, then attaching it to the momentous crime bill was it. Clinton understood the risks. According to a memo staffers had compiled for him, there were fifty-four progressive Democrats who might oppose the bill because of the ban, but there were also forty-nine Republicans who might be persuaded to vote with Democrats. The memo also listed twenty-six Democratic representatives who risked losing reelection if they supported the ban. Brooks said:

[The crime bill] was critical and important to the country. And, it was good as I said it was. And I should vote for it. And the gun bill should not have been in it. It wasn't that important, but the people thought it was. [Clinton] had some people pressuring him for that, the more liberal element was against guns, and he kind of wanted to get along with them. And the NRA was never his piece of cake.

This was nothing new for Brooks. He had helped out sitting presidents before—such as with Carter's reorganization efforts and Department of Education bill and elements of Johnson's Great Society legislation—even when he disagreed with aspects of their agendas. He later reflected on Clinton's hubris:

You can't do everything yourself. Nobody can. Carter proved that when he was president. He's smarter than all those people that worked for him. He was, but he tried to do everything, and he couldn't.

Throughout the winter and spring, while memos within the Clinton Administration strategized on how to overcome Brooks's opposition, the chairman succeeded in keeping the ban separate from his bill, still spread into pieces in committee. In early May, amidst daily press events and behind-the-scenes wrangling by the president, the assault weapons ban passed in the House as an individual bill. Though he voted against it himself, the vote suited Brooks fine; it allowed moderate Democrats in rural districts to show their constituencies where they stood, and by not polluting the crime bill, it did not endanger their reelection chances.

The Judiciary Committee then packaged up the individual bills that had passed, except for the ban, and sent them to the Rules Committee, which tied them together into a single bill, as per Brooks's plan. But after obtaining a rule and being primed for a vote, the bill hit a wall. Liberal Democrats, protesting the capital punishment provisions, joined a newly energized Republican bloc that disliked the social programs. Together they squashed any chance for debate by voting against the rule itself. It was a procedural coup.

Clinton called Brooks to come meet with him in the Oval Office. The only way to win back the support of those liberal Democrats was to include the assault weapons ban, he felt. There was an urgency in Clinton's tone, almost as if his presidency was at stake. He had suffered several recent losses, most dramatically on his health care agenda. This crime bill would be his sole victory going into the midterms. Staffer Jon Yarowsky, who accompanied Brooks to the White House meeting, recalled the conversation:

The president said, "Well, I know what you did was amazing in the House, but now we have this situation with how the conference report has gone down." He says, "I think the only hope we have is to put in this assault weapon ban and some other gun control provisions."

And Mr. Brooks very respectfully said, "Well, Mr. President, I know that

was an issue even when I was doing it earlier, but I'm afraid, if you do that,
you could create tremendous difficulties for thirty or forty of our conservative
Democrats. And that's why I've tried to keep it separate."

The president said, "Well, this is my last option. I have to really ask you if
you'll consider it." Well, of course, here's the Democratic president asking Mr.
Brooks, and that was it. Once he got that request from the president of the
United States, Mr. Brooks—he had given his best advice, but he—you know, he
was going to be respectful of the president.

Brooks went back to his office and, with help from his staff, put the
assault weapons ban into the bill.

Clinton's gambit worked; liberal Democrats were swayed by the ban.
The crime bill came back for a vote, passed and went to conference to be
reconciled with the Senate's. Biden and eight other senators represented the
Senate, and Brooks and nine other representatives spoke for the House. As
the conference committee proceeded over the course of months, seeking
common ground, individual lawmakers nailed down specifics on how the
money would actually be spent, which always aroused dissent.

LAMAR: To prepare for the additional corrections work brought on by the
new crime bill, Brooks had earmarked $10 million for the construction of
a proposed National Center for Criminal Justice Research and Education
at Lamar University. The idea came years earlier during Bush's administration when a local Texas sheriff asked the university chancellor for more
and better training for police and corrections officers. When Brooks first
heard about the concept, he had been enthusiastic about finding a way to
finance the project. At that point, Lamar had grown its enrollment figures
to fifteen thousand students spread over five campuses, a far cry from its
days as a two-year commuter college. The local prison population, including a federal correctional complex outside Beaumont and facilities under
construction in southeast Texas and Louisiana, exceeded that by nearly six
thousand individuals.

The political dust-up over the high cost of the overall crime bill had
House Republicans searching for line items to single out. The proposed

center at Lamar was one of them, and Republicans cried foul. The *Washington Post* even ran an article on the Lamar controversy that summer. In a characteristic reply, Brooks was quoted as saying, "If it's pork, it'll be tasty."

But committee members eventually dropped the proposed center at Lamar from the bill before finally passing their conference report, a reconciled version of the House and Senate bills, on July 28. And, to Brooks's dismay, the others had thwarted, by a vote of six to four, his attempt to remove the assault weapons ban yet another time. One news outlet reported: "Brooks, though disappointed by his defeat on the weapons ban, joined Clinton at the Justice Department and praised the compromise."

Others, including Clinton, Reno, and Biden, spoke at the Justice Department news conference in support of the legislation as well. Bentsen, the Democratic senator from Texas turned treasury secretary, proudly announced:

> *This bill starts with the premise that Americans are good and decent people. Sure we have some bad apples among us. You bet we do. And all the money in the world won't totally stop them. I've never met a law enforcement official who didn't need more money and more manpower. . . .*
>
> *This is a good bill because we're spending the money in an appropriate balance between law enforcement and prevention.*

Bentsen went on to extoll the bill's most exciting programs, one-by-one.

> *One last thing I want to say. I like this bill because there's a partnership here between state and local officials and federal officials. Treasury sure can't fight this crime alone and certainly the Justice Department can't do it alone either. . . . But we can do it working together, and that's how we're going to make America a safer place for good and decent people.*
>
> *Now [chuckling] I want to introduce the Chairman "El Supremo"—friend of a lifetime, my great friend Jack Brooks.*

Biden, sitting on stage next to Brooks, took that as his queue and stood up. Everyone started laughing, Brooks, too, and Biden sat back down.

Amidst applause, Brooks playfully knocked Biden on the shoulder,

approached the podium, and gave very brief remarks. To those who had
been following the bill's journey and were aware of Brooks's position, the
restraint in his remarks spoke volumes.

> *This legislation is good legislation. It's strong. Going to put violent criminals
> in the clink where they belong. It's going to have a lot of innovative operations in
> it that give us a chance to save people so we don't have to put them jail.*

Biden spoke next, lauding the president for pushing this agenda even
before he entered office and regaling the crowd with a story of midnight
phone calls from the president-elect even before Congress was back in session.

> *Everyone should make no mistake about this. Jack Brooks and I and Lloyd
> Bentsen when he was Senator Bentsen and others tried to pass a crime bill for
> five years. It was blocked for five years. The reason there is a crime bill is this
> fellow right here, the president of the United States of America . . .*
>
> *Let me conclude, Mr. President, by thanking you for one other thing: I really
> have had a tutorial the last six months working with Jack Brooks. And I know
> I joke about him and kid about him, but I have had a tutorial in how to get
> things done.*
>
> *This man is the guy who shepherded through this legislation.*

Clinton took to the podium last and, though the bill was not yet law,
gave some thanks:

> *I cannot say enough about Chairman Brooks and Senator Biden. I like
> them both very much. It's not hard to figure out why when you hear them both
> up here talking. I ran completely out of my stash of donated cigars trying to get
> Jack Brooks to keep pushing ahead with every aspect of the Crime Bill. People
> always want to know, you know, what did the President give away to get this,
> that, or the other thing. All I gave away were mountains of crocodile tears and
> donated cigars because Jack Brooks wanted this country to have a crime bill.*

By then the omnibus bill had swelled to nine hundred pages. Though there had been bipartisan agreement on the conference version, some, including the House Republican leadership, intended to kill the bill through procedural tactics and the addition of unattractive amendments while under consideration on the House floor. For that reason, Brooks dug in and worked further on the language, resulting in what he called "a horrendous weekend for the staff," in which they pored over the bill for "twenty-seven hours in two days and nights."

Then Clinton called Brooks into the Oval Office. Yarowsky, who accompanied Brooks, remembered the conversation:

> *The president said, "Well, I know what you did was amazing in the House, but now we have this situation with the conference report has gone down." He says, "I think the only hope we have is to put in this assault weapon ban and some other gun control provisions."*
>
> *And Mr. Brooks very respectfully said, "Well, Mr. President, I know that was an issue even when I was doing it earlier, but I'm afraid, if you do that, you could create tremendous difficulties for thirty or forty of our conservative Democrats. And that's why I've tried to keep it separate."*
>
> *The president said, "Well, this is my last option. I have to really ask you if you'll consider it." Well, of course, here's the Democratic president asking Mr. Brooks, and that was it. Once he got that request from the president of the United States, Mr. Brooks—he had given his best advice, but he—you know, he was going to be respectful of the president.*

Brooks went back to his office and, with help from his staff, put the provisions back into the bill.

He then appeared before the Rules Committee on August 2, bringing all of the Judiciary subcommittee chairmen with him. After some introductory remarks about the conference report and the scope of the legislation as it currently stood, he asked the Rules Committee to establish a rule for the bill's consideration, without delay or possibility of amendments, on the floor.

Afterward, the committee chairman and various members of both parties thanked Brooks for his work and commended his good work and recognized that he in particular "has a very difficult assignment" with championing this legislation, one even calling the work tortuous. One Democrat called it the largest, most comprehensive and ambitious piece of crime legislation ever produced by Congress.

Some from both parties raised objections to several of the bill's provisions, notably the social programs, especially the residential drug treatment programs for prisoners. Brooks, almost exasperated, removed his glasses, sat back in his chair, and said:

> *The bill has some things in it that you don't want, maybe I don't want, that we don't care for. I'll give you the example candidly. The gun control ban, I'm dead set against it. You're dead set for it. It's in the bill. I think that I should not be a sorehead, and that, well, I am, [laughter]. I think I'm going to vote for the rule, and I'm going to vote for the bill. I think the significance of the bill and its importance to the American people overrides any one critical issue like that. While I might not like it, I mean it's not nearly so important as the whole crime bill and its effect on the nation.*

Once the bill obtained a rule, uncertainty still abounded. Many Democrats could not commit to supporting it. Foley and Gephardt also wanted the ban stripped from the bill, but others in the leadership, including David Bonior, the House Democratic whip, supported it. Some said it was the one of the fiercest lobbying campaigns in recent memory, with Clinton and his staff making last-minute entreaties to persuade congressmen.

Then on August 11, Republicans narrowly blocked a vote on the bill by passing a technical rule to preclude debate and a vote, with the stated logic of using the time to make the bill tougher on crime. Minority Leader Robert Michel of Illinois voted for the bill the first time around but called this compromise version an "unholy trinity of pork, posturing, and partisanship." Democrats saw it as a flagrant stall tactic to sink the bill.

The GOP's public message was that the bill contained too many wasteful social programs, but even one Republican who supported the bill said, "The NRA and the assault weapons ban—that was the stealth issue here and it had nothing to do with pork." Another said the NRA and RNC's intense lobbying had sent his colleagues "running for their lives." Immediately after the vote, the RNC distributed letters to the thirty-eight Republican members who sided with Democrats, alerting them that their reelection campaigns would be contested.

Clinton spoke to reporters that day in the White House briefing room:

> *Under any circumstance I would be disappointed if the House of Represen-*
> *tatives turned its back on the largest and toughest attack on crime in the history*
> *of our country at a time when the American people say it is the most important*
> *issue to them. But it is especially disheartening to see 225 members of the House*
> *participate in a "procedural trick" orchestrated by the National Rifle Association*
> *then heavily, heavily pushed by the Republican leadership in the House.*

Many assumed that the crime bill effort had essentially failed, and the Democrats looked to be in disarray for failing to support their president on such a high-profile proposal. Among those who had sided with the Republicans were fifty-eight Democrats, many from conservative rural districts, a desertion that even some Republicans found shocking.

Charles Schumer, a cosponsor of Brooks's version of the bill, said, "Anyone who thinks we can produce a new crime bill in the month remaining is smoking something."

Yet after ten days of negotiations and minor modifications, the bill was brought up again before the House for a final vote. It was August 21, a Sunday. Representatives and their staff worked throughout the day, and the deliberations stretched into the evening. Foley and Gephardt approached Clinton again, pleading with him to drop the assault weapons ban because of the harm it could do to the Democratic caucus.

Brooks met with his colleague John Dingell of the Commerce Committee to see if any more options existed. Dingell himself sat on the board of the NRA. He would send a letter that same day to the NRA president to say he was quitting the organization, finding an "irreconcilable conflict" between his "responsibilities as a member of Congress and my duties as a board member."

Leon Panetta, a former representative who now ran the president's affairs as his chief of staff, worked the Capitol building, making last minute appeals to individual members. NRA officials did the same. The vote was to be a nail-biter. Normally a majority party would not call a vote on a bill it was not confident would pass. No one knew what would happen with this crime bill. Panetta recalled:

> We're now approaching the moment when the bill has to be wrapped up and it has to go to the floor. I'm sitting in Dick Gephardt's office, and I can't find Jack Brooks. . . . We found out that Jack Brooks and John Dingell were meeting together to try to see if they could just stall this thing and not bring it forward.
>
> The president called up and said, "What's going on? We've got to get this done. We've got to get it happen." It was the first time I really heard him as angry as he was. I said, "Mr. President, we happen to have two chairmen here of committees who are a problem and they don't want to move it."
>
> We finally locate these chairmen in Jack Brooks's office. I said, "Mr. Chairmen, I know the political problems that are here. I dealt with them when I was on Capitol Hill. I know this is politically tough, but we think we have the votes to pass this, and the president really respectfully asks that you release this bill so that we can get it voted on.' And finally Jack Brooks, to his credit, was willing to do that.

Brooks could have caused a problem for the president but chose not to. He knew, just as he had for a year, what this vote meant, it meant "falling on his sword for the president."

Staff member Jon Yarowsky remembered walking with Brooks to the House floor.

> We were walking in the basement in the Rayburn building, couple buildings over. We were walking in the basement and you go down an escalator, then you get on the subway and you take the subway to the Capitol. No one was around. I mean, members were all there, but we were going over early, and we were almost to the point where we were going to go down to the subway, and I said, "Mr. Brooks, those gun provisions are in there. You have led the charge against those gun provisions. What are you going do?"
>
> I said—then, I even said to him, I said, "You know, you did all of this.

You're going to create a bill that they're going to pass, do you really have to vote for it yourself?" 'Cause I was learning what the constituency was, and I knew with a yes vote, people might like everything else, having those gun provisions, was not something that was going to be easy. And Mr. Brooks just looked at me and smiled and said, "It's my bill. I have everything I wanted, but it's my bill, and the president asked that I do it. How can I not vote for it now?" I mean, he never thought twice about it. †

The hold on the bill was released, and the voting began after 5 p.m. The voting took nearly three hours. Forty-six Republicans joined the majority to support it. Sixty-four Democrats, six from Texas, broke off and voted against it. After an exasperating day and an exasperating months-long effort by the Congress and the executive branch, the bill finally passed the House by a vote of 235 to 195.

Some steps remained. The bill still had to pass in the Senate, but four days later it did easily, with a vote of sixty-one to thirty-eight.

Brooks, through his parliamentary wisdom and sweat, had drafted and personally finessed the largest comprehensive crime bill in decades through the lower chamber during a Herculean effort over the last ten months. Yarowsky had been there through all of it and felt burned out. Years later, he still remembered vividly his boss's words to him the next morning:

So, the next morning I come into work, feeling good, but exhausted. Mr. Brooks is in his office, of course, brought him there. Plops down and says, "Can you come up?" I say, "OK." Came up, sat down in the chair next to his desk, and he just looked up and said, "OK, so what are we doing with today?"

The Crime Bill had passed the night before. This is maybe 9:45 or 10:00 a.m. in the morning, and he wanted to know, what are we doing today?

IT DID NOT HAPPEN as quickly as Gore had predicted one year earlier, but on September 13, the same group that had convened in the Rose Garden met back on the White House lawn to watch the crime bill be signed into

---

† This quotation is taken verbatim from a video interview that can be viewed at www.jackbrooksfoundation.org.

law. Biden, Speaker Foley, Gephardt, Hillary Clinton, and dozens of law enforcement officers stood resolute behind the president as he put his name to the bill. And just behind the president's left shoulder stood a beaming Jack Brooks, topped off with a bright red Marine Corps baseball cap.

25

1994 Election

After climbing continually for three decades, violent crime rates in the U.S. peaked in the early- to mid-1990s. In New York City, the murder rate had risen steadily since the race riots of 1968 until the years between 1990 to 1993, when an average of almost 2,100 people were murdered annually just within the city limits. Chicago, with half the population of New York City, had roughly nine hundred murders during each of those years. The crack epidemic ravaged inner-city populations unabated.

Voters continued to rate violence as a primary priority for the nation. Clinton had come to office and put his political capital behind combatting what he later termed a "genuine national crisis." In the legislation that Brooks had crafted, Clinton got nearly every tool that he had wanted to fight back. The social programs targeting recidivist criminals and at-risk youth went into effect. The community policing monies injected cash to pay for more officers. Though the eventual figures amounted to a drop in the bucket once spread throughout the budgets of municipal police departments across the nation, there was a positive effect. In New York City in particular, with a new mayor and police chief and after a quick spending spree to put more officers on the streets, crime rates began to fall almost overnight to their lowest levels in decades. They continued to decrease for eight consecutive years, the longest sustained drop in crime on record.

Debate continues over the contribution of the crime bill to that decline and how much other forces played a part. One renowned economist posited that the legalization of abortion in 1973, exactly one generation earlier, played a significant role in the reduction in crime. Other sociologists and criminologists point toward "increased employment, better policing methods, an aging of the population, [and] growth in income and inflation." Incarceration rates were already climbing by 1995, driven largely by state-level policies and practices. With the new federal offenses, stricter sentencing terms like the "three strikes" rule, which mandated life imprisonment for those convicted of three violent felonies, and "truth-in-sentencing" provisions that stipulated convicts must serve 85 percent of their stated terms, incarceration rates continued to rise as thousands more criminals were locked up each year and kept in prison for longer sentences.

The law has its detractors. One criticism charged that the stiffer federal offenses and incarcerations for minor, nonviolent offenses like drug possession resulted in the swelling of prison populations, particularly with lower-income minorities. Clinton, in the midst of his wife's second presidential campaign twenty-two years later, expressed some regret over these unplanned consequences. While citing the "extraordinary national achievement" of violence and crime reduction, Clinton nevertheless admitted that Washington had "overshot the mark," locking up far too many people who had not committed serious crimes.

The bill, several years after its passage, would go on to help the president's reelection bid, quieting critics who wanted to argue that Clinton was soft on crime. Brooks and the other Southern Democrats who supported the bill had a far tougher race to run, one that would be decided just eight weeks to the day after the crime bill's signing. Ultimately, the legislation would be most remembered for its political impact, which would reverberate beyond that first election cycle to represent a shift in American politics of historic proportions.

MIDTERMS: Political rancor in Washington had reached a fever pitch in the lead-up to the mid-term elections that summer and fall. Republican leadership fought rapaciously against the president on both his legislative agenda and whatever else they could drag into the public's consciousness. Their Whitewater investigation, an examination of a failed financial investment the Clintons made while in Arkansas, dragged on for years. Over the course of the summer, twenty-nine officials from the Clinton administration would be subpoenaed or would testify before Senate and House banking committees on the controversy. All twenty-nine would be found clear of any wrongdoing. Eventually, after almost a decade of follow-up investigations and Republican reports, findings would show that the Clintons had done nothing wrong.

At the congressional level, the anti-incumbent sentiment that had manifested in 1990 had only grown in intensity during the four years since. Right or wrong, Brooks stuck out among the pack of senior legislators. He had made more headlines during the previous six years than at any other time during his career and had beaten up on Republicans pretty badly while doing it. His opposition was ready. As one journalist put it, "Brooks is a prime target for anti-incumbent fallout this year, especially after he was caught larding President Clinton's crime bill with pork for Lamar University in his hometown of Beaumont." The anti-incumbent rhetoric was not just a local phenomenon. The entire House was up for grabs. Gingrich touted his Contract with America, which listed accomplishments the Republicans would achieve if voters placed them back in the majority, a role they had not had since 1955. Gingrich had become the GOP figurehead and chief sower of discontent against Clinton and the Democrats. Adding to this brewing maelstrom, Democrats were ill-prepared for the change in mood and doubted how much the electorate was willing to buy into GOP promises. Brooks would later characterize 1994 as "a bad year for Democrats when Democrats had a tendency to take it easy and Republicans worked hard."

Republicans, with a generally older voting base that turned out more reliably during mid-term election years, sensed opportunity all over. Oliver North, who had been paid $25,000 for appearing at two fund-raisers in 1990, decided to foray deeper into the political scene and ran for Senate, raising over $20 million from donors in an attempt to unseat Virginia Senator Chuck Robb.

THE NORTH AMERICAN FREE Trade Agreement went into effect earlier in the year, dramatically lowering tariffs between the U.S., Canada, and Mexico. More diverse ethnic demographics, including significant numbers of undocumented Mexican immigrants, were developing in the southern border states and elsewhere in America's industrial hubs.

Texas was shifting rapidly, perhaps too rapidly for some. New workers and immigrants poured into the state, supporting an economic boom that would continue for years. According to a 2005 article from the Federal Reserve Bank of Dallas, during the 1990s, the state's population grew at a rate several multiples of the national average, "adding almost 3.9 million residents and surpassing New York as the second most populous state." Starting in 1990, immigrants would go from comprising 9 percent of the state to over 16 percent in just two decades.

That was not the case in Beaumont, though. Southeast Texas in general was being left behind. People did not move into the district, choosing instead to settle in the metro areas of Austin, Dallas-Fort Worth, and Houston. The district's sole economic driver—petroleum refining—continued to stagnate as well. As other areas diversified their industries and expanded their markets, the district risked becoming a one-trick pony. The district had remained one of the most dutifully Democratic areas of Texas, not voting for a Republican presidential candidate in more than twenty years. The combination of economic malaise, new immigration patterns, and the gun control measures within the crime bill meant that the political phenomenon of the "angry white man" might rear its head once more.

Gun advocacy groups had kept true to their threats. Millions of dollars poured into opposition candidates' races across the country. The association took advantage of campaign finance loopholes to spend $70 million on political activities in that election cycle, including $7 million through its PAC, the Political Victory Fund, which focused almost exclusively on unseating Democrats who had supported the crime bill and its assault weapons ban. The group dropped its endorsements of many Democrats and targeted fifty to seventy open seats in conservative districts. On top of the NRA's hit list were Speaker Tom Foley, Chairman Dingell, Lee Hamilton of Indiana, candidates for governor in Florida and Virginia, and Jack Brooks.

NRA: As the assault weapons ban was popular with the overall public, the NRA did not make that issue the fight itself. Instead, the group coordinated with Republican Party officials to fight each individual race however they could and provide the funding needed, according to former NRA officials.

They did not restrict themselves to guns, writing constituents instead about taxes, health care, and the budget, among other things. In 1992, the NRA had spent a quarter of a million dollars in a highly visible attack against Democratic incumbent Mike Synar of Oklahoma, only to see him win reelection. In the 1994 primary, the NRA instead sponsored phone banks and home mailings but bought no newspaper or television ads. By remaining somewhat invisible, the NRA evaded any counterattack. Synar lost that primary, giving the NRA what their political director called the "first scalp" of the election cycle.

Skirting FEC regulations on campaign finance and courting money from a new donor class enabled the association to spend more money on elections in 1994 than any other organization. Despite a cultivated image as a members-driven organization fighting for the freedoms of ordinary Americans, it was around this time that the NRA discovered that deep corporate pockets abound. When polled, even NRA members reported moderate views on the use of background checks and other gun control measures.

However, the domestic gun industry produced billions in revenue annually during the early 1990s. On the supply side, more than five million firearms were manufactured in the U.S. in 1994, more than any other year prior and more than any of the fifteen years following, according to the ATF. During the following twelve months, there was only a proportional rise in the number of firearm exports, meaning that most of those guns were intended for American customers, not foreign markets.

While banning the sale of selected assault weapons may not have affected individuals and their sporting lifestyles significantly, it represented a massive loss of revenue to the industry. Modern assault weapons could be modified and accessorized in ways that traditional firearms could not. Shooters could purchase scopes, silencers, modular grips, and other accoutrements to regularly update and upgrade their basic "shooting platform," i.e. the gun itself. According to one former NRA director, "most of the money is in accessories."

Within a few short years, the NRA would be almost inextricably linked with the largest business interests in the industry. Major manufacturers would offer NRA memberships with firearm purchases and gun dealers would establish donation programs to benefit the NRA. This marriage would soon see tens of millions of dollars in corporate donations, grants, and advertising given each year to the NRA, and in return the NRA would conduct the political bidding of the industry.

Though specific figures on gun ownership are intentionally difficult to ascertain, the rates in Texas exceeded the national average. In general, roughly one of every three Texans owned a firearm. The since-instituted National Instant Criminal Background Check System conducts roughly 10 to 20 million background checks annually, any time an individual attempts to purchase a firearm from a licensed dealer. More of those checks come from Texas than from any other state, including California, which has 40 percent more residents. If the rates for Texas held true for Brooks's district, with its population of approximately 700,000, it would suggest that 250,000 residents were gun owners. However, given that almost half of Texas's residents now resided in large metropolitan urban centers, areas in which gun ownership rates plummet, the reality is that gun ownership rates in Brooks's district likely dwarfed state figures.

Voter turnout for congressional elections in the Ninth District was always around 130,000, which is why it was such a surprise when that figure spiked by 65 percent in 1992. It would spike again in 1994. If gun groups could stoke enough fear in just one-third of the voters who owned guns, the election would be a close one.

With Brooks a lifelong NRA member, recent keynote speaker at their annual convention, and chief architect of the crime bill, the association was in an awkward position. Brooks had even attempted to give the NRA a chance to participate in the crime bill process by working in a provision that would have limited the magazine capacity for the selected assault weapons rather than banning them outright, a provision that even Reagan had supported publicly. One contemporary news account stated:

> That deal, worked out by NRA lobbyist James Jay Baker, a relative moderate in NRA circles, was torpedoed by [NRA leaders Tanya] Metaksa and [Neal] Knox. According to an insider, Metaksa at that point wanted to use the assault weapon ban to mobilize the NRA's hard-core activist base and deliberately

wrecked chances of a compromise to go into the November election guns ablaze. Brooks, embittered, voted for the final crime bill and was abandoned by the NRA.

IN THE 1994 ELECTION, Brooks's Republican opponent would be Steve Stockman, the candidate who had lost to the eventual Republican challenger in 1990 and then lost to Brooks in the general election in 1992. The NRA and the Gun Owners of America came to Stockman's aid, each group donating roughly $30,000 to his campaign. Stockman admitted he had never owned a gun. "But I am interested in personal freedom," he said when asked by a reporter. Stockman also bashed Brooks for his support of the ATF's 1993 raid on the Branch Davidian compound in Waco, going so far as to pen an op-ed in which he compared the cult members, favorably, to the citizens of the Ninth District because of their shared love for the Second Amendment.

Stockman also questioned the value of the chairman's seniority to the district. If Brooks had become complacent after twenty-one terms in office, it was difficult to believe that his constituents would disregard those years of attention to personal services and bringing jobs to the area. Brooks, in television attack ads, reminded voters that Stockman lied about his experience on his résumé and had zero public service experience. While those messages may have resonated with some voters, the ads themselves also inadvertently increased Stockman's name recognition with the general public.

Stockman responded to Brooks by indulging in one of his previous campaign tactics. The *Southeast Texas Times*, a seemingly independent local newspaper geared toward conservative voters, only ran for nine brief issues in 1994. It made an impression on national journalists, though, with headlines like "Servicemen Don't Want Sodomites in the Military" and "HUD Appointee is a 'Mean Lesbian.'"

The publication purported to be independent; however, it was produced in the garage headquarters of Stockman's Friendswood home and the contact information for advertising inquiries was Stockman's home phone number. Disguising campaign literature as a community newspaper is illegal, and the Federal Election Commission launched an investigation into both it and a side business run by Stockman's campaign manager.

The *Houston Chronicle* later detailed that the Stockman campaign would admit in a conciliation agreement less than four years later that it had violated election laws "by failing to report expenses for producing the *Southeast Texas Times* and another similar publication as in-kind contributions to the campaign; by failing to correctly label the 'newspapers' as campaign materials; and by not reporting details on how the $470,000 paid to Political Won Stop, a consulting firm run by [Stockman's campaign managers], was spent." As part of the agreement, Stockman's campaign committee agreed to pay a $40,000 civil penalty.

ELECTION NIGHT: On November 8, Brooks and his supporters gathered at the Hilton to wait for the numbers to trickle in. The mood was dour. Recent polls had Brooks winning by only 2 percent, and as Sharon Matts said, "there was just a funny feeling out there."

By 6 p.m. it already appeared that the Democratic governor, Ann Richards, would lose to neophyte George W. Bush, and soon word began trickling in that Democrats might lose their majorities in the Senate and House. Supporters felt confident about Brooks's race, but the congressman kept reminding folks that it would be tough. And it was tough. His friend Cleveland Nisby recounted:

> *We were all together, down at the hotel, and he used some choice words when the Montgomery County ballots came in, and he—I'm telling you, he went in a rage. And everybody just had to follow him and calm him down, and talk with him.*

As the situation developed, though, Brooks was soon the one "boosting everybody [else] up." Heartfield remembered going upstairs to the suite the campaign had arranged for the celebration:

> *Well, everybody went upstairs, but everybody but Brooks is crying and depressed, and he's walking around handing out cigars and slapping everybody on the back and laughing. I never forgot that image of the man.*

Matts was downstairs in the hotel ballroom, meant to be the site of the victory party, when she called Brooks. She remembers hearing him saying:

"How are you doing, darling?"'

I said, "I don't know," and began to cry. I said, "I don't feel very good about this."

And he said, "I don't either," but he said, "You know what? We've worked hard together. We've done the best we could. You just come right over and you just smile to everybody, and just be the same, and we'll get through this."†

He never minded a good fight. By 11:30 p.m., with local aides giving him updated county results from all over the district, Brooks was first to see the writing on the wall. "That's it," he said, according to one staffer who was there. "I'm not going to make it." Brooks knew the district, its counties, and its people like the back of his hand. Once he had assessed the situation for himself, and against the advice of almost everyone in his inner circle, Brooks knew he had to concede defeat.

By then Matts had arrived at the hotel and was still working the phones. At one point she turned to Brooks and said, "I've got Mr. Stockman on the telephone," and she handed him the phone. Brooks picked up the receiver and said "Hello, Mr. Stockman." After a few moments, Brooks face slackened. He turned back to Matts, handed the phone to her, and said, "They hung up on me."

Brooks then approached the microphone that had been set up earlier for his victory speech and made a very brief statement before the assembled media. He was upbeat and stood surrounded by smiling supporters, including Charlotte and his daughter Kimberly. He thanked those who had supported him in this election and all of his previous ones. "I appreciate the challenge, and with gratitude the work and the help you all gave me all these years of serving you as your congressman." He closed with a characteristically simple yet acerbic quip: "I appreciate your judgment now, in electing somebody else, and I know that you'll get everything you so richly deserve."

---

† This quotation is taken verbatim from a video interview that can be viewed at www.jackbrooksfoundation.org.

He turned from the crowds and responded to questions from several reporters, one of whom asked him what he would do now outside of Congress: "Go fishing, work in the yard. Life will be pleasant. I look forward to it. I'll see y'all around."

The final numbers confirmed the outcome: 81,353 constituents voted for Stockman and 71,643 voted for Brooks. Brooks had lost by a margin of 52 to 46 percent. Only 22 percent of eligible voters had turned out.

Brooks recounted years later:

> The Democrats thought Brooks had been in for forty-two years, he's gonna be there forever. They went a fishin'. And the difficult thing was, I knew it was a tough race. I knew this, all these things, you know . . .
>
> I'd talk to my friends and tell them I hope they can support me this year, and work for me. And they'd just be, "Well, of course, we're gonna vote for you, Jack. Of course, I'm gonna vote for you." But what I needed them to say is, "We're going to support you. We're gonna get all our friends and relatives and cohorts and everybody, in-laws, to vote for you." But they didn't do that. They didn't feel that urgency. So, they didn't vote much. They took it easy. And I got beat.

No one believed this was about his opponent. As one Texas judge put it, the Republicans "could have put a monkey up there" and the outcome would have been the same. It was the crime bill and the opposition to the assault weapons ban that had done it. Though incredibly personal, Brooks's defeat and many others that year were also historic. No other U.S. representative with Brooks's years of seniority in the House had ever lost a general election. In Washington state, Tom Foley became the first Speaker of the House since 1862 to be defeated in a reelection campaign.

In all, Democrats lost fifty-four seats in the House that night. They had gone from having an eighty-two-seat majority to a twenty-six-seat minority, and the House was now in Republican control for the first time since 1955. The fifty-four-seat swing shocked even Washington insiders. It was the largest defeat for the Democrats since 1946. All the Democratic chairmen suddenly became ranking members of their own committees.

Democrats say the NRA cost them no fewer than twenty seats in the

House, and President Clinton told one reporter, "the NRA is the reason the Republicans control the House."

Just as had happened with Carter when he had come into the White House with ambitious plans to shake things up without much thought for the details of government operations or political realities, Brooks would again be proven right. Though Clinton was the consummate politician, it was Brooks who better understood voters and the weight that subjects like gun ownership and states' rights placed on individual congressmen.

The lesson was not lost on Clinton, who reflected on his presidency years later in his epic memoir and admitted:

> *Foley, Gephardt, and Brooks were right and I was wrong . . .*
>
> *Ironically, I had hurt the Democrats by both my victories and my defeats. . . . The NRA had a great night. They beat both Speaker Tom Foley and Jack Brooks, two of the ablest members of Congress, who had warned me this would happen. Foley was the first speaker to be defeated in more than a century.*
>
> *Jack Brooks had supported the NRA for years and had led the fight against the assault weapons ban in the House, but as chairman of the Judiciary Committee he had voted for the overall crime bill even after the ban was put into it. The NRA was an unforgiving master: one strike and you're out. The gun lobby claimed to have defeated nineteen of the twenty-four members on its hit list. They did at least that much damage. . . .*
>
> *I was profoundly distressed by the election, far more than I ever let on in public. We probably would not have lost the House or the Senate if I had not included the gas tax and the tax on upper-income Social Security recipients in the economic plan, and if I had listened to Tom Foley, Jack Brooks, and Dick Gephardt about the assault weapons ban.*

Republicans picked up eight Senate seats in the 1994 midterms, gaining control of that chamber too. In Texas, the popular Ann Richards, who had enjoyed a 60 percent approval rating just before the election, lost the governor's house to Bush, and elsewhere Republicans seized Democratic-held governorships in New York, Pennsylvania, Rhode Island, Tennessee, Oklahoma, Kansas, New Mexico, and Wyoming.

GOING HOME: The joke among Brooks and his staff was that this might be "divine intervention" or a "hidden blessing." Brooks would have lost his chairmanship and control of the committee, and he would have had to then live in a Republican-controlled world, one that Gingrich would direct once he was selected by his party to be Speaker. Despite the sting of the defeat, Brooks later said:

> Not a huge disappointment. I was going to quit in a couple of years, regardless. Yeah, I'd had about enough. Forty-two years is a long time. Well, my family is down here. And my farm is down here. My mama's old house is still here.

If Brooks had won, he would have become dean of the House, the body's most senior member. The position, mostly honorary, has one significant role: swearing in the Speaker of the House. Brooks added:

> I may have had to quit. I don't think I could have called Gingrich "Speaker Gingrich." I would have had to swear him in, and I don't know if I could have done it.
> . . . That would have been no atmosphere for me to live in. I didn't want to be a minority member. I wouldn't be chairman. Have Gingrich as speaker. That'd be awful! I would have had the choice of going every day to the floor and giving him hell, which meant I'd have to work hard and debrief myself and be available for press interviews and television interviews and the whole works. Be a spokesman, in effect, against him, which I was, and would have done, but it would have been an awful lot of work, which I would not have enjoyed, really.

Once the dust had settled, Brooks and Charlotte decided to move back home to the district, where he and Charlotte bought a larger house in Beaumont to fit all of Brooks's things from Congress and so that Charlotte's mother could live with them.

They also frequently visited their little farm outside Jasper, sixty miles north of Beaumont and close to the banks of the Sam Rayburn Reservoir. Charlotte commented, "We just didn't feel that strongly about Washington."

Brooks sold his ownership interests in several regional banks but still went to his office every day.

Before moving on from Washington, Brooks decided it was his "top responsibility" to find jobs for all of his staff members who were suddenly without work. He helped place Yarowsky as President Clinton's chief legal counsel. By calling friends and working his connections, Brooks placed everyone on his team into a new role in Washington. The only staffer he could not place was Matts, his longtime administrative assistant. Matts, who had accumulated enough savings, told the congressman that if she could not work for him she would not work for anybody else.

Now that the Republicans controlled the Senate as well, Clinton's judicial nominees, including those that Brooks had proposed, also hung in the limbo of the nomination process. Many candidacies would stagnate for months without ever being heard before the Senate Judiciary Committee. But Brooks did not forget. Just as he had done with his staff, Brooks followed up. He rang Biden's office. Biden, now ranking member on that committee, had a reputation for being just as loyal as Brooks to those he had worked with. But instead of asking for the senator, Brooks wanted to speak with his secretary. She explained that she clearly could not do anything about the hearings, but Brooks cajoled her into speaking with the other committee members' staffers. He told her he understood she had no official power but assured her she could do it if she tried. "You know where the bodies are buried," he wittily reminded her.

She called Brooks back a week later to report that the jurists would receive their days. Clinton renominated Thad Heartfield and David Folsom for federal judgeships in January 1995. Both received their hearings the following month and both were appointed to benches the month after that.

26

Epilogue

Brooks continued to support the Clintons, not just for the remainder of Bill's two terms but also when both Bill and Hillary came to Beaumont in February 2008 to campaign for Hillary's first presidential run. That time Brooks wore a white cowboy hat to cover his head. He remembered:

> *Well, it was a good party. Clinton made a good speech. Deviled me a little bit. They had a bunch of pictures made with all the people there. All the honorees. Then he came out and worked the crowd. Clinton was a good mixer and charismatic sort of a president.*

Brooks also continued working to improve the district, even if he no longer had an official title. He knew how government functioned and still had a certain sway. When his former constituents had issues they needed help with, they often sought him out.

Steve Stockman, the Ninth District's official representative, enjoyed an immediate spate of media attention after the 1994 election as the political upstart who had defeated a congressional giant. His term lacked much else of note. Among the bills and resolutions Stockman sponsored during his first term were just a few boilerplate, socially conservative causes, including proposals to block the U.S.-born children of illegal immigrants from being granted automatic citizenship; define human life as beginning at conception; eliminate background checks, waiting periods, and registration requirements for firearms; investigate the Kinsey Reports from 1953 on male sexual behavior; and make private school costs tax deductible.

The only successful legislation he sponsored was a resolution authorizing use of the Capitol grounds for a 1996 prayer rally called "Washington for Jesus."

Brooks, though he never considered another run himself, remained intent on seeing Stockman removed from his House seat, and the 1996 election was the first opportunity.

Nick Lampson from Beaumont had interned for Brooks years earlier. The young man had pestered Brooks with so many referral letters and job requests that when he finally ran into the congressman on the sidewalk and introduced himself, Brooks stopped and scowled at him: "Send me one more [expletive] [expletive] letter of recommendation and I'll throw your whole [expletive] file in the garbage can."

Brooks pushed past the young man and carried on down the street, but he respected Lampson's doggedness and gave him the internship. Now in his fifties, Lampson had prepared himself sufficiently for the big stage, and Brooks threw his full weight behind the man. Brooks said:

> *I worked hard in that campaign, just as hard as I had in my own, and we beat him within an inch of his life. . . .*
>
> *Oh, people didn't realize what he was. He just was a no—he did nothing in Congress. The Democrats didn't like him, and the Republicans didn't like him. He was just not an effective member. And I knew he wouldn't be, and he wasn't. But that's the way things go. . . .*

Lampson defeated Stockman by 5.5 percent in a runoff, but to the chagrin of Democrats, and notably even some Republicans, Stockman persisted in seeking public office and in 2012 ran for his old seat in the Ninth District. Most of that district had since been redistricted again into the Thirty-Sixth District, one of four new districts in Texas since the 2010 census. Before the Republican primary, a *Houston Chronicle* editorial urged citizens to vote for Stockman's opponent:

> *Stockman came from nowhere in 1994 to unseat the erstwhile Democratic*

lion Brooks after two unsuccessful tries. He was dispatched two years later by the Democrat Nick Lampson following a term marked by eccentric behavior and a clear feeling that he was not ready for prime time. . . .

Stockman's most visible backer is former U.S. Rep. Tom Tancredo, R-Colo., whose out-of-the-mainstream views on immigration are his dubious claim to fame.

Despite the notoriety, or perhaps because of it, the people of southeast Texas reelected Stockman. In fact, he won the general election with over 70 percent of the vote. Stockman had positioned himself as a vessel for far right-wing causes and seemed to relish going even further on partisan issues than his fellow Republicans. Asked how he had won a second time, Stockman replied: "There is a very conservative evangelical community here, a strong 'tea party group' that backed me, and early support from national conservative groups—Gun Owners of America and Citizens United."

But Stockman admitted that the largest factor in his landslide win was the demographic makeup of the new Thirty-Sixth District. The area included almost the entirety of the southeast corner of Texas, from the far east suburbs of Houston to the border with Louisiana. The new Thirty-Sixth District did not include Jefferson County, with the city of Beaumont at its center.

Once the new Congress convened, a story ran in *Mother Jones* titled "Steve Stockman is the Nuttiest Freshman in Congress—Again." *Texas Monthly* ran a lengthy profile on Stockman titled "Congressman Clueless."

In 2014, much to the surprise of even his fellow Texas Republicans, Stockman announced a bid to run against incumbent Republican John Cornyn for his Senate seat. He filed the candidacy paperwork fifteen minutes before the deadline. Even among those in Congress who knew Stockman well, not many risked endorsing the man. Stockman proudly boasted that the NRA and Ted Nugent had endorsed him, even though neither did. The NRA publicly endorsed Cornyn. One of the few organizations that did back Stockman was Gun Owners of America.

As amazed as people were at Stockman's last-minute entrance into the race, they were shocked further by what he did next. Stockman did not show up at any campaign events, nor for weeks of voting on the House floor. He later wrote a reporter for *Breitbart News* that he had missed the votes, seventeen in all, because he had been on an international trip with four other congressmen. Those representatives had not missed the same votes, though. His campaign for Senate did not field any questions from many other media outlets. It appeared that he had not even assembled a campaign staff.

Brooks himself had long suspected that Stockman used campaign contributions to live on. With the FEC investigations and Stockman's own stories of "eating out of a trash can" before entering public service, the charge had some weight. At the start of his quixotic Senate bid, Stockman had $32,000 in the bank and $160,000 in debt. Many assumed that his bid against Cornyn, which not even his friends considered a viable one, was essentially a "debt retirement operation." His campaign accepted donations from individuals and groups but never purchased any advertising, hired any staff, or held any events. Several Texas political insiders and journalists reported not being aware of a single event that the man attended during his three-month ghost campaign. Unsurprisingly, Stockman lost to Cornyn in the primary, but 19 percent of voters still cast ballots for him.

Then, in early 2017, Stockman was arrested in a Houston airport while trying to board a plane for the Middle East. He was indicted on federal charges of attempting to divert charitable contributions for personal use. The charges alleged that, on behalf of a charity he represented, he accepted a $350,000 donation from a Chicago businessman and then swiftly transferred the money to his own bank account, which had an existing balance of $33.

After three days of deliberation, a jury found Stockman guilty of twenty-three felony counts including wire fraud, conspiracy, and money laundering in a massive scheme in which he directed a total of $1.25 million in charitable contributions from wealthy conservative donors to pay for his personal expenses, debt, and political activities.

Ben Suarez, Stockman's first campaign benefactor, had an ignominious final act as well, as he continued to mingle political activism with his business interests. In 2014, after an investigation uncovered a scheme in which he, his wife, and multiple employees of Suarez Corp. channeled over $200,000 to two Ohio Republicans, Suarez was convicted and sentenced to fifteen months in federal prison after being charged with conspiracy, campaign finance law violations, causing false statements to be made to federal election officials, and obstruction of justice.

NEWT GINGRICH: Republicans owed the NRA a great debt following the 1994 elections. Gingrich, for one, appreciated their contribution, writing an NRA official, "As long as I am Speaker of this House, no gun control legislation is going to move."

As Speaker, Gingrich soon proved to be as willful as Jim Wright had been, and even more ruthless. Gingrich changed the way Congress operated. He took substantial power away from the committee chairmen and placed it with the Speaker. Chairmen would no longer enjoy the discretion to direct their committees as they saw fit. They would receive their marching orders from the leadership, orders that would typically serve the party's national agenda. Chairmen like Brooks, who had been able to investigate what he deemed worthy and then draft legislation on what he saw as priorities, would soon be a thing of the past.

Brooks remembered the comity that had often existed with his Republican colleagues, especially working in coordination with Frank Horton, the ranking Republican member on the Government Operations Committee, who cosponsored forty-six pieces of legislation with Brooks during the 1980s and 1990s, more than three times as many as the next Democrat. Brooks recalled the common sense of purpose between them:

> *[Frank]'s staff sometimes worked with my staff on developing and program strategy and developing and implementing a bill. That's how much we trusted him. And that's how decent they were. And they were smart. It was another world, and now those people, they just don't they don't have that kind of relationship. And Congress, and the legislative process, depends on cooperation and really on friendship, a lot.*

Gingrich continued the slash-and-burn tactics that had propelled him through the House during the 1980s, hurling invective at his opponents as he always had, yet now from the leadership position. Colleagues took note and soon followed suit. According to Brooks, Gingrich's lasting legacy would be a burgeoning of the Georgian's particular brand of the politics of division. Republican members now felt uncomfortable even being friendly with Democrats.

The breakdown in political discourse did not limit itself to the norms of civility within the House chambers; it soon pervaded Washington and beyond. Mickey Edwards, a former Republican congressman from Oklahoma who served in leadership alongside Gingrich, said, "Government is dysfunctional because the presidency and Congress no longer have the ability to compromise, and I put Newt at the heart of that."

Brooks said:

> I thought Newt was scum. And he couldn't stand me. He worked hard to get me beat. He was a crumb. He got into trouble finally. Got into trouble, serious trouble, and he's through, but it took a while. And he created an atmosphere of animosity between the Democrats and Republicans in Congress. When I left, I had a lot of Republican friends. And I don't mean I went and double-crossed the Democratic Party and voted with them. I voted Democratic and they voted Republican, but we cooperated, and we'd tell them when we could. We understood each other. And that's the way legislation is passed, with compromises and agreements between opposing parties. And now, they just don't get along at all.

Eventually, Gingrich's exit from the Speakership would come to bear a resemblance to the one he had orchestrated for Jim Wright. After a lengthy investigation, the House Ethics Committee found that Gingrich "had used tax-exempt money to promote Republican goals, and given the panel inaccurate information for its inquiry." Gingrich formally apologized, conceding he had brought discredit on the House. In January 1997, in a near-unanimous bipartisan vote, the House reprimanded him and fined him $300,000, making him the first Speaker ever disciplined for unethical conduct. Gingrich left the Speakership shortly thereafter.

THE GOP: Whereas Nixon had won his victories by shrewdly identifying and seizing upon a latent discontent within the Republican base, Brooks believed that in the 1994 election Republicans had found success by fomenting an anger within voters that had not really existed before. As one television pundit remarked, this was a historic political shift in the absence of any historically significant reason, namely a war, scandal, or recession.

In late November, Brooks met with Clinton at the White House to discuss the election season's outcomes. Afterward—along with Representative William Ford of Michigan, the retiring chairman of the Education and Labor Committee—Brooks spoke to television and print reporters outside in the driveway. When asked about the conversation, Brooks, cigar in hand, said:

> The gist of it was, our program was good. The deficit is down for the third year in a row. The country is doing pretty well. We have just let, I believe, Rush Limbaugh and the talk show, talk radio pundits, just outmaneuver us. They just talk to people day and night about what a bad deal it is when, really, things are going pretty well. The program is good. The Crime Bill was a good bill. The effort on healthcare, just the discussion, has improved the delivery of health service in this country more than it's been done in twenty years. Just talking about it. Now doctors work together. Hospitals work together.

Brooks was not alone in his perception of Limbaugh and the role his long hours of daily commentary, reaching into millions of households across the country through hundreds of radio and television stations, played in the outcome. Even before the election, Clinton had called Limbaugh's show "just a constant, unremitting drumbeat of negativism and cynicism."

When the freshman Republican class met for orientation at the Heritage Foundation in December, Limbaugh was invited as a keynote speaker, made an honorary member of the class, and introduced to the stage with these words: "Thank you, Rush, for giving us the courage to take back our country."

BROOKS'S LEGACY: Brooks's life after Congress was just as he had predicted on election night in 1994: pleasant. Once he returned to the district, Brooks managed to work some in the yard, though his advanced age kept him from pulling down too many trees on his own. He went fishing often in the Sam

Rayburn Reservoir, a perennial space of peace for him where he had relaxed with friends like Johnson and Briscoe. He and Charlotte enjoyed their lives together on the farm and welcomed guests from near and far, reliving old stories and walking guests through their framed pictures around the house, a veritable gallery of American history.

As the years rolled by, the palpable imprint Brooks had left on Congress slowly diminished. The Brooks ADP Act from 1965 was repealed two years after he left public office with the passage of the 1996 Clinger-Cohen Act, or Information Technology Management Reform Act. Though sponsored by Republicans, the new legislation dovetailed into Al Gore's "reinventing government" movement toward decentralization during Clinton's second term. With a more computer-literate workforce and sophisticated technology industry, the central management that the GSA had provided under the old law was no longer efficient. With the federal government spending $60 billion annually on information technology by 2003, much smaller, task-focused purchases for individual government agency units and sub-units made more sense. Individual pieces of equipment were affordable and prevalent enough. Each executive agency was now required to establish a chief information officer and develop individual plans for IT management under the general guidance of the director of the OMB. The GSA, perceived as a monopoly within the government at that point, was happy to hand over its responsibility in this area.

The Government Operations Committee continued to ferret out inefficiencies and abuse in the executive branch, but lost the tenacity and singularity of purpose it had exhibited under Brooks.

A second congressional portrait of Brooks was commissioned, this time in recognition of his years chairing the House Judiciary Committee. The new portrait showed Brooks standing with his hand resting on a desk. Near his hand lay a gavel resting on its side, representing the chairmanship. His eyes penetrate, revealing a congressman who tolerated no fools and was not to be trifled with. Incidentally, the artist was the son of the artist who painted Brooks's first portrait for the Government Operations Committee. Brooks must have appreciated the familial continuity.

Though his time in public service had ended, the impact of his work and his legacy remained vivid in the minds of many who understood how significant a role he had played in shaping the federal government.

On April 23, 2001, NASA honored Brooks at a ceremony at Lamar University and presented him with the agency's highest honor, the Distinguished Service Medal, for his years of contributions. NASA Administrator Daniel Goldin thanked Brooks for his long-standing support of the space program and for his integral role in "strengthening the agency during its formative years." Goldin said, "Congressman Brooks took it upon himself to personally deliver support to one of the agency's key programs: the design, development, and on-orbit assembly of the International Space Station."

More than fifteen years later, Goldin said he could think of no one who did more for the space program than Jack Brooks. After the Cold War, there was a big push for a peace dividend, putting tremendous pressure on the budget, especially for big science projects such as the Superconducting Super Collider and the Space Station. To the chagrin of America's scientists, Congress withdrew support for the Super Collider, which was later built in Switzerland and heralded for its discoveries in particle physics, leading to a Noble Prize.

A week after Congress killed support for the Super Collider, Goldin recalled "there was blood in the water and more than half the House was ready to kill the Space Station." Brooks asked House leaders to extend the voting time another fifteen minutes so he could muscle some reluctant colleagues into becoming supporters. "It was a cliffhanger," recalled Goldin. "At the last minute, Representative John Lewis walked into the chamber and voted against defunding the Space Station." The vote was 216 to 215. "Brooks saved it and reinvigorated the program," said Goldin. "It was breathtaking."

Back in 1984, *Government Computer News* magazine had recognized Brooks for outstanding contributions in the field of public sector IT. Instead of selecting new awardees in 2002, the magazine chose instead to select the top two executives from all those who had been honored during the previous twenty years. They selected an Army lieutenant general as the military honoree, and they selected Brooks as the top civilian honoree. The organization praised the 1965 Brooks Act for playing "a large role in building up the IT industry and spurring innovative technologies at agencies." Brooks traveled back to Washington to receive the award at the *Post-Newsweek* Tech Media gala and gave brief appreciative remarks that cracked up the audience of IT execs and guests: "I feel proud to see all these people making more money than I ever imagined, and their success is my reward. . . . I wanted the government to be on the leading edge of technology, and it is."

Brooks's fellow honoree, Army Lieutenant General Emmett Paige Jr., made the audience laugh as well: "[Brooks] was good for us, although none of us felt that way at the time."

In 2010, local residents stood shoulder-to-shoulder in a crowded Jefferson County Commissioners Court and cheered as county leaders voted unanimously to rename Southeast Texas Regional Airport the Jack Brooks Regional Airport. This marked the second major local landmark dedicated to Brooks after Jimmy Carter had come down in 1978 to commemorate the Beaumont Federal Courthouse as the Jack Brooks Federal Building. A public park in Galveston County was also later named in Brooks's honor.

At his alma mater, Lamar University, the honors came in droves. In 1997, the Jack Brooks Chair in Government and Public Service was established within the department of political science to recognize his accomplishments in government service and his contributions to the university. In 2008, the Jack Brooks Scholarship Program was established to allow both undergraduate and graduate students "the opportunity to study, research, and publish in the areas of public service, community leadership, and public policy." University leaders then began holding an annual Jack Brooks Conference on Government and Public Service to bring "together a broad spectrum of community and political leaders from across Southeast Texas . . . to promote the sharing of information, ideas, and discussion of important issues facing our region."

All of this was in addition to the iconic bronze statue of Brooks that the university had erected in 1989 in the quadrangle outside the student center building. Since then, students have begun a pre-game tradition of dressing the statue in school T-shirts and oversized foam hands before big games. Brooks would appreciate that, of course; he never stood on ceremony. During the campus event unveiling the statue, the tarp became hung up on the bronze so Brooks, despite pushing seventy years old, impulsive as ever to get things done, had one leg up and started climbing the base to free the sheet even as his family tried mightily to restrain him. In fact, Charlotte recalled that Brooks never showed much reverence for any statuary; she doubted whether he ever toured around the statues and monuments of the Mall during his forty-two years in Congress.

Another tradition students began was unfurling a condom on the signature cigar in the statue's right hand. When Charlotte would suggest that visitors to their home should also pay a visit to the school and see the statue, Brooks would dryly add that the visitors should not do as the students did.

To further mark his contribution, Lamar also erected a full-size reproduction of his wood-paneled congressional office on a top floor of the Mary and John Gray Library in the center of the campus. His old hunt-and-peck typewriter is at the desk, the well-used spittoon within range on the floor behind the desk, and his children's grade-school drawings are on the wall.

PASSING: In late 2012, Brooks suffered a sudden illness and was rushed to Beaumont Baptist Hospital. There, on December 4, he passed away surrounded by his family. He was two weeks shy of his ninetieth birthday. Five days later, friends and family paid their respects to Brooks at a memorial service inside the Lamar University basketball arena, large enough to seat ten thousand people, a feature that leaders at the former two-year college could have only dreamed about before Brooks's lifetime of service to the school. Up front near the stage on a short table lay Brooks's white cowboy hat and a cigar.

In the following days and weeks, dozens of publications, from major metropolitan daily newspapers to obscure quarterly technical magazines, ran lengthy profiles and obituaries of the man and his impact on the federal government.

Charlotte passed away sixteen months later after a short bout with lung cancer. She was seventy-eight years old. The couple had been married for fifty-two years and were survived by their three children—Kate, Jeb, and Kimberly—and two grandchildren.

In 2008, Brooks had donated his papers from all forty-two years in Congress to the Dolph Briscoe Center for American History at the University of

Texas at Austin. His dear friend Briscoe had established the center within the university's School for Public Affairs, a stone's throw away from Johnson's towering Presidential Library building next to the school's football stadium.

Perhaps Brooks donated the papers to the Briscoe Center because he understood the importance of what he, Johnson, and others had been trying to accomplish for the citizens of Texas, or perhaps it was simply because Briscoe had sold some of his goats back in 1952 to contribute $6,000 to Brooks's first campaign for Congress.

The collected papers, roughly 1.5 million of them divided into 625 archival boxes, were too enormous to fit in the center's main reading room archives and had to be stored off-site in the center's warehouse. Anyone can make an appointment to view the documents. Sifting through the congressman's decades of letters, photographs, mementos, and handwritten notes— some of them to and from major figures in twentieth-century American history—one feels intensely just what the man had hoped to accomplish for his country, and especially for his little corner of it down by the Gulf.

In 2017, the once and future Speaker Nancy Pelosi hosted a tree-planting ceremony in Brooks's honor on the Capitol grounds just across Independence Avenue from the entrance to the Rayburn House Congressional Office building. She had served with Brooks briefly as a junior congresswoman and the two had been fond of one another. Beside the memorial oak tree and before an audience that included Brooks's family, friends, and admirers, Pelosi gave brief and poignant remarks:

"He wielded a formidable arsenal of charm, intellect, and bare-knuckled politics. More often than not with smoldering cigar in hand."

Appendix

Key Accomplishments

Brooks did not write every word of every piece of legislation he sponsored. As with almost all laws, the language in the documents themselves is mined from the contributions of many technical experts, and junior members of Brooks's committees remember how the chairman sometimes absconded with their good ideas and slapped his own name on them. Brooks's contribution was knowing what ideas to put his weight behind, knowing what the American people wanted and needed, and what their representatives in Congress would get behind.

Among Brooks's many contributions to his district, the state of Texas, and the United States were:

- Lamar Junior College declared a four-year university
- Chairman of subcommittee on Government Activities
- Expansion and financing of the Sam Rayburn Reservoir, the largest freshwater reservoir in Texas
- Civil Rights Act of 1964
- Voting Rights Act of 1965
- Automatic Data Processing Act of 1965
- Architects and Engineers Act of 1972
- Chairman of Government Operations Committee, 1975–1989
- Secured funding for the deepening and widening of the Sabine-Neches Waterway
- Authorized the Neches River Saltwater Barrier project in 1974
- President, NATO Parliamentary Assembly, 1978
- Secured funding for the Galveston Bay Study and the development of the Wallisville Reservoir
- Secured funding for the Port of Galveston and Texas City Port improvements

- Authored legislation to provide flood insurance to businesses and individuals
- Paperwork Reduction Act
- Secured funding for the completion of the Big Hill Strategic Petroleum Reserve
- Americans with Disabilities Act
- Chairman of House Judiciary Committee, 1989–1995
- Civil Rights Act of 1991
- Credited for saving the space program, Brooks was instrumental in obtaining funding to help NASA with the International Space Station
- Competition in Contracting Act of 1994, establishing a Federal Procurement Office
- Violent Crime and Law Enforcement Act of 1994
- Approved plans for the Public Health Service Hospital in Galveston and its affiliation with the University of Texas Medical Branch
- Obtained funding for the wastewater treatment facilities in Nederland, Cheek, China, Nome, Lumberton, Port Neches, and Groves
- Obtained millions of dollars in funding for development in the city of Port Arthur
- Obtained funding to build the hurricane levee system in Jefferson County
- Obtained funding for the Taylor's Bayou Flood Protection Project

Sources

DALLAS 1963

Anthony, Beryl. Video interview.

Badger, Tony. "Southerners Who Refused to Sign the Southern Manifesto." *The Historical Journal* 42, no. 2 (1999).

Busby, Scott. "What Happened Next?" *Prospect,* December 2003.

Brooks, Jack. In discussion with the authors.

Brooks, Jack interview by Joe B. Frantz. February 1, 1971, transcript. Oral History Interview I, LBJ Presidential Library, Austin, TX.

Bugliosi, Vincent. *Reclaiming History: The Assassination of President John F. Kennedy.* New York: W. W. Norton & Company, 2007

Caro, Robert. *The Years of Lyndon Johnson: The Passage of Power.* New York: Vintage Books, 2012.

Champagne, Anthony. *The Austin-Boston Connection: Five Decades of House Democratic Leadership (1937–1989).* College Station, TX: Texas A&M University Press, 2009.

Cunningham, Sean P. *Cowboy Conservatism: Texas and the Rise of the Modern Right.* Lexington, KY: University of Kentucky Press, 2010.

Cox, Patrick. "John Nance Garner on the Vice Presidency—In Search of the Proverbial Bucket." The Center for American History, University of Texas at Austin.

Dallek, Robert. *An Unfinished Life: John F. Kennedy 1917–1963.* New York: Little, Brown and Company, 2003.

Dethloff, Henry C. *Suddenly, Tomorrow Came: The NASA History of the Johnson Space Center.* Dover Publications, 2012.

Dobbs, Ricky F. *Yellow Dogs and Republicans: Allan Shivers and Texas Two-Party Politics.* College Station, TX: Texas A&M University Press, 2005.

Fehmar, Marie. President's Daily Diary: Dictation from Congressman Jack Brooks aboard Air Force One en route to Washington. November 22, 1963. LBJ Presidential Library, Austin, TX.

Gillon, Steven M. *The Kennedy Assassination—24 Hours After: Lyndon B. Johnson's Pivotal First Day as President.* New York, Basic Books, 2009.

Hardesty, Von. *Air Force One: The Aircraft That Shaped the Modern Presidency.* NorthWood Press, 2003.

Hill, Clint. *Five Days in November.* With Lisa McCubbin. New York: Gallery Books, 2013.

Holland, Max. *The Kennedy Assassination Tapes: The White House Conversations of Lyndon B. Johnson Regarding the Assassination, the Warren Commission and the Aftermath;* New York: Alfred A. Knopf, 2004.

Holley, Joe. "Obituary: Barefoot Sanders; Tex. Political Figure and Federal Judge." *Washington Post,* September 29, 2008.

Hughes, Sarah T. interview by Joe B. Frantz. October 7, 1968, transcript, Oral History Interview I. LBJ Presidential Library, Austin, TX

Johnson, Lyndon Baines. *The Kennedy Assassination Tapes.* New York: Alfred A. Knopf, 2004.

Johnson, Robert David and David Shreve,

eds. *The Presidential Recordings: Lyndon B. Johnson: The Kennedy Assassination and the Transfer of Power, November 1963–January 1964.* Vol. 2. New York, W.W. Norton and Company, 2005.

Jones, Chris. "The Flight from Dallas." *Esquire*, October 2013.

Knaggs, John R. *Two-Party Texas: The John Tower Era, 1961–1984.* Fort Worth, TX: Eakin Press, 1985.

Manchester, William. *The Death of a President.* New York: Harper and Row, 1963.

McClendon, Sarah. Notes from Andrews Air Force Base. November 22, 1963. The Sarah McClendon Papers, The University Archives and Special Collections Department, Robert R. Muntz Library, The University of Texas at Tyler.

Miller, Merle. *Lyndon: An Oral Biography.* New York: Putnam, 1980.

Onassis, Jacqueline Kennedy. *Jacqueline Kennedy: Historic Conversations on Life with John F. Kennedy.* New York: Hyperion, 2011.

Pruitt, Francelle. "Congressman Albert Thomas and NASA's Coming to Houston: A Study in Legislative Effectiveness, 1936–1966." *The Southwestern Historical Quarterly* 105, no. 4 (2002).

Report of the President's Commission on the Assassination of President John F. Kennedy. Washington, D.C.: U.S. Government Printing Office, 1964.

Rowley, James. "Report of the United States Secret Service on the Assassination of John F. Kennedy." 1963.

Santa Cruz, Paul H. *Making JFK Matter: Popular Memory and the Thirty-fifth President.* Denton, TX: University of North Texas Press, 2015.

Semple, Robert B., ed. *Four Days in November: The Original Coverage of the John F. Kennedy Assassination.* New York: St. Martin's Press, 2003.

Thomas Jr., Robert McG. "Homer Thornberry, Appeals Judge, Dies at 86." *New York Times*, December 13, 1995.

Wright, Jim. In discussion with the author.

Wright, Jim interview by Wes Wise and Bob Porter. February 22, 1996, transcript, Oral History Interview. Oral History Collection, The Sixth Floor Museum at Dealey Plaza, Dallas, TX.

THE EARLY YEARS

Block, W.T. *A History of Jefferson County, Texas: From Wilderness to Reconstruction;* Nederland Publishing Company, 1976.

Briscoe, Dolph. Video interview.

Brooks, Jack. Video interview.

Buran, James A. "Violence in an 'Arsenal of Democracy,' The Beaumont Race Riot, 1943." *East Texas Historical Journal* 14, no. 1 (1976).

Cooke, Alistair. *The American Home Front: 1941–1942.* New York: Grove Press, 2007.

Cox, Patrick. *Ralph W. Yarborough, the People's Senator.* Austin, TX: University of Texas Press, 2001.

Dolph Briscoe Center for American History (website). "Dolph Briscoe, Texan-Biography." https://www.cah.utexas.edu/about/briscoe/bio.php

Halbouty, Michel T. and James A. Clark. *Spindletop: The True Story of the Oil Discovery that Changed the World.* Houston: Gulf Publishing Company, 2000.

Kleiner, Diana J. "Jefferson County." *Handbook of Texas.* Texas State Historical Association (2010) https://tshaonline.org/handbook/online/articles/hcj05.

Landry, Wanda A. and Laura C. O'Toole. *Betting, Booze, and Brothels: Vice, Corruption, and Justice in Jefferson County, Texas, from Spindletop to the 1960s.* Fort Worth, TX: Eakin Press, 2006.

Manry, Marie Brooks. In discussion with the author.

Schudel, Matt. "Jack Brooks, Powerful Congressman from Texas, Dies at 89." *Washington Post,* December 5, 2012.

Wells, Bruce A. "Spindletop Launches Modern Petroleum Industry." American Oil and Gas Historical Society (2017).

___

WAR!

Action Reports, various. Historical Branch, G-3 Division, Headquarters, U.S. Marine Corps.

Alexievich, Svetlana. *The Unwomanly Face of War: An Oral History of Women in World War II.* New York: Random House, 2017.

Associated Press. "Rep. Jack Brooks, co-author of 1964 Civil Rights Act, dead at 89." December 5, 2012.

Brooks, Jack. Jack Brooks to friends and family, 1944–1945. Personal correspondence, Private collection.

Clemens, Martin. *Alone on Guadalcanal: A Coastwatcher's Story.* Naval Institute Press, 2013.

Condit, Kenneth W., Gerald Diamond, and Edwin T. Turnbladh. *Marine Corps Ground Training in World War II.* Historical Branch, G-3 Division, Headquarters, U.S. Marine Corps, 1956.

Edwards, Lt. Col. Harry W. USMC (ret). *A Different War: Marines in Europe and North Africa*; Marines in World War II Commemorative Series, Historical Branch, G-3 Division, Headquarters, U.S. Marine Corps, 1994.

Goodman, David. "Pittsburgh 1941: War, Race, Biography, and History." *Pennsylvania Magazine of History and Biography* CXXXII, no. 4 (2008).

History of U.S. Marine Corps Operations in World War II. Historical Branch, G-3

Division, Headquarters, U.S. Marine Corps, 1966.

Hough, Lt. Col. Frank O., et al. *Pearl Harbor to Guadalcanal: History of U.S. Marine Corps Operations in World War II, Vol. I.* Historical Branch, G-3 Division, Headquarters, U.S. Marine Corps, 1966.

Lodge, Major O. R. *The Recapture of Guam.* Historical Branch, G-3 Division, Headquarters, U.S. Marine Corps, 1954.

Nash Jr., Douglas E. *Battle of Okinawa: III MEF Staff Ride: Battle Book.* History Division, Quantico, Virginia: U.S. Marine Corps, 2015.

Nichols Jr., Major Chas. S. and Henry I. Shaw Jr. *Okinawa: Victory in the Pacific.* Historical Branch, G-3 Division, Headquarters, U.S. Marine Corps, 1955.

O'Brien, Cyril J. *Liberation: Marines in the Recapture of Guam.* Marines in World War II Commemorative Series, Historical Branch, G-3 Division, Headquarters, U.S. Marine Corps, 1994.

Oxford, Hubert Oxford. In discussion with the author.

Pate, W.L. "Bubba." In discussion with the author.

Roosevelt, Eleanor. Transcript of Radio Address on the Attack on Pearl Harbor on December 7, 1941, 1941.

Shaw Jr., Henry I. *The United States Marines in North China: 1945–1949.* Historical Branch, G-3 Division, Headquarters, U.S. Marine Corps, 1960.

Sledge, E.B. *With the Old Breed: At Peleliu and Okinawa.* New York: Ballantine Books, 1981.

Dictionary of American Naval Fighting Ships; U.S. Naval Historical Center, 1959–1991.

___

LEGISLATURE AND LAMAR

Biographical Note: A Guide to Jack B. Brooks

Papers. Dolph Briscoe Center for American History at the University of Texas.

Briscoe, Dolph. Video interview.

Briscoe, Dolph and Don E. Carleton. *Dolph Briscoe: My Life in Texas Ranching and Politics.* Austin, TX: Center for American History, University of Texas at Austin, 2008.

Brooks, Jack. In discussion with the author.

Texas House Bill regarding Lamar State College of Technology. H.B. 52, C.H. 403.

Wright, Jim. In discussion with the author.

FIRST RACE FOR CONGRESS

Bartley, Ernest R. *The Tidelands Oil Controversy: A Legal and Historical Analysis.* Austin, TX: The University of Texas Press, 1953.

Brooks, Jack. In discussion with the author.

Green, George Norris. *The Establishment in Texas Politics: The Primitive Years, 1938–1957.* Westport, CT: Greenwood Press, 1979.

Key, V.O. *Southern Politics in State and Nation.* Knoxville, TN: University of Tennessee Press, 1949.

Matthews, Chris. *Hardball: How Politics Is Played Told By One Who Knows the Game.* New York: Simon & Schuster, 1999.

Reaud, Wayne. In discussion with the author.

Robertson, Robert J. *Fair Ways: How Six Black Golfers Won Civil Rights in Beaumont, Texas.* College Station, TX: Texas A&M University Press, 2015.

FIRST TERM

Caro, Robert. *The Years of Lyndon Johnson: The Master of the Senate.* New York: Vintage Books, 2002.

Guttery, Ben R. *Representing Texas: A Comprehensive History of U.S. and Confederate Senators and Representatives from Texas.* BookSurge Publishing, 2008.

Hendrickson Jr., Kenneth E., Michael L. Collins, and Patrick Cox. *Profiles in Power: Twentieth-Century Texans in Washington.* Austin, TX: University of Texas Press, 1993.

The Leadership of Speaker Sam Rayburn: Collected Tributes of His Congressional Colleagues. U.S. Government Printing Office, 1961.

Peters, Ronald M. "The Speaker: Leadership in the U.S. House of Representatives." *Congressional Quarterly,* March 1, 1995.

Remini, Robert V. *The House: The History of the House of Representatives.* New York: HarperCollins, 2007.

Shannon, James. "Our Man Jack: Rep. Jack Brooks, 1922–2012." *The Examiner,* December 5, 2012.

LATE 1950S

Badger, Tony. "Southerners Who Refused to Sign the Southern Manifesto." *The Historical Journal* 42, no. 2 (1999).

Brooks, Jack. In discussion with the author.

Frost, Martin. In discussion with the author.

Lassiter, Matthew. *The Silent Majority: Suburban Politics in the Sunbelt South.* Princeton: Princeton University Press, 2006.

Public Works Appropriations for 1958: Hearings Before the Subcommittee of the Committee on Appropriations, House of Representatives. Eighth-Fifth Congress, First Session, Vol. 4–5. U.S. Government Printing Office. United States Congress, 1962.

Russell, Richard, William Fulbright, Strom Thurmond, et al. "Declaration of Constitutional Principles, a.k.a. Southern

Manifesto." U.S. House of Representatives, March 1956.

RISING TEXAS TIDE

Beschloss, Michael. *Reaching for Glory: The Johnson White House Tapes 1964–1965*; New York: Simon & Schuster, 2007.

Beschloss, Michael. *Taking Charge: The Johnson White House Tapes 1963–1964*. New York: Simon & Schuster, 1997.

Caro, Robert. *The Years of Lyndon Johnson: The Master of the Senate*. New York: Vintage Books, 2002.

Carpenter, Leslie. "Washington Beat: Brooks Becomes Key LBJ Confidant." *Washington Post*, April 4, 1964.

Cullen, David O'Donald and Kyle G. Wilkison, eds. *The Texas Left: The Radical Roots of Lone Star Liberalism*. College Station, TX: Texas A&M University Press.

Germany, Kent B., et al, ed. *The Presidential Recordings: Lyndon B. Johnson: Toward the Great Society, February 1, 1964-May 31, 1964*. New York: W.W. Norton and Company, 2007.

Goldstein, Gordon M. *Lessons in Disaster: McGeorge Bundy and the Path to War in Vietnam*. New York: Henry Holt, 2008.

Johnson, Robert David and David Shreve, eds. *The Presidential Recordings: Lyndon B. Johnson: The Kennedy Assassination and the Transfer of Power, November 1963– January 1964*. Vol. 2. New York, W.W. Norton and Company, 2005.

Kilpatrick, Carroll. "Texas Crowd's Taken Over: The 'Continuity' Has Ended with Departure of Kennedy Brain Trusters and a Little Band of Lone Stars Is Filling Gaps." *Washington Post*, March 15, 1964.

Valenti, Jack. *This Place, This Time; My Life in War, in the White House, in Hollywood*. New York: Three Rivers Press, 2007.

Yoon, Robert. "State of the Union Firsts." CNN.com, February 11, 2013. Accessed April 15, 2013.

LEGISLATION: 1961–1965

ADP Act of 1965 (Brooks Act), Public Law 89–306. U. (1965).

Anderson, Jack. "Light Bulb Brooks." *Daytona Beach Sunday News-Journal*, May 28, 1966.

Brock, Gerald. *The U.S. Computer Industry: A Study of Market Power*. Cambridge, MA: Ballinger Publishing Company, 1975.

Brooks, Jack B. Papers. Government Activities Subcommittee Press Release, September 18, 1962. Box 125. Dolph Briscoe Center for American History, University of Texas.

Brooks, Jack B. Papers. Box 125, Box 161. Dolph Briscoe Center for American History, University of Texas.

Cargill, Carl. "Congressman Jack Brooks's Legacy to the World of Standards." blogs.adobe.com. December 7, 2012.

Chandler Jr, Al. *Inventing the Electronic Century: The Epic Story of the Consumer Electronics and Computer Industries*. New York: Free Press, 2001.

Davis, Bob. "Texan Wants Last Word on U.S. Contract." *The Wall Street Journal*, September 4, 1987.

Flamm, Kenneth. *Creating the Computer*. Washington, D.C.: Brookings Institution Press, 1988.

Gilchrist, Bruce and Milton Wessel. *Government Regulation of the Computer Industry*. Montvale, NJ: AFIPS Press, 1972.

Johnson, George. *The Abominable Airlines*. New York: The Macmillan Company, 1964.

Kettl, Donald F. *Sharing Power: Public Governance and Private Markets*.

Washington, D.C.: Brookings Institution Press, 1993.

Mowery, David C. *The international computer software industry: a comparative study of industry evolution and structure.* Oxford: Oxford University Press, 1996.

Senate Report (Government Operations Committee) No. 92–1219. Sept. 25, 1972 [To accompany H.R. 12807].

Swedin, Eric Gottfried and David Ferro. *Computers: The Life Story of a Technology.* Westport, CT: Greenwood Publishing Group, 2005.

Thompson, Scott A. *Flight Check!: The Story of FAA Flight Inspection.* U.S. Department of Transportation, Federal Aviation Administration, 1990.

Willis, Charles. "The Brooks Act, Is It Relevant Today?" MA thesis, Naval Postgraduate School, 1994.

Alic, John, et al. *Beyond Spinoff: Military and Commercial Technologies in a Changing World.* Cambridge, MA: Harvard Business School Press, 1992.

POWER IN THE PRESIDENCY

Baker, Robert E. "Johnson Has Close Ties to Rights Groups: Personal Influence." *Washington Post and Times Herald,* November 24, 1963.

Brooks, Jack. Video interview, November 22, 2002. LBJ Library.

Brooks, Jack B. Papers. Box 115. Dolph Briscoe Center for American History, University of Texas.

Caro, Robert. *The Years of Lyndon Johnson: Master of the Senate.* New York: Vintage Books, 2003.

Dallek, Robert. *Flawed Giant: Lyndon Johnson and His Times 1961–1973.* Oxford: Oxford University Press, 1998.

Dallek, Robert. *Lone Star Rising: Lyndon Johnson and His Times: 1908–1960.* Oxford: Oxford University Press, 1991.

Kotz, Nick. *Judgment Days: Lyndon Baines Johnson, Martin Luther King, Jr., and the Laws That Changed America.* New York: Houghton Mifflin Harcourt, 2005.

Kraft, Joseph. *Profiles in Power: A Washington Insight.* New York: New American Library, 1966.

Pfiffner, James P. *The Managerial Presidency.* College Station, TX: Texas A&M University Press, 1999.

Sundquist, James. *Politics and Policy: The Eisenhower, Kennedy, and Johnson Years.* Washington, D.C.: The Brookings Institution, 1968.

Suri, Jeremi. *The Impossible Presidency: The Rise and Fall of America's Highest Office.* New York: Basic Books, 2017.

"Timeline of 1964 Civil Rights Bill." Dirksen Congressional Center.

Updegrove, Mark K. *Indomitable Will: LBJ in the Presidency.* New York: Crown, 2012.

Whalen, Charles and Barbara Whalen. *The Longest Debate: A Legislative History of the 1964 Civil Rights Act.* Seven Locks Press, 1989.

LEGISLATION: 1965–1968

Brooks, Jack. "The Federal Government and Computer Compatibility," *Signal* March 1967.

Brooks, Jack. "The Growing Use of Electronic Data Processing in Government." *Armed Forces Comptroller,* April 1966.

Brooks, Jack B. Papers. Press releases and speeches. Dolph Briscoe Center for American History, University of Texas.

de Grazia, Alfred, ed. *Congress, the first branch of government: Twelve studies of the organization of Congress conducted under the auspices of the American Enterprise*

Institute for Public Policy Research. American Enterprise Institute for Public Policy Research, 1966.

Kirchner, Jake. "Brooks Unrelenting in Fight for Better U.S. DP." *Computer World,* December 18, 1978.

Sherrill, Robert and James David Barber. *Why They Call it Politics: A Guide to America's Government.* New York: Harcourt Brace Jovanovich, 1979.

Traaen, Timothy. "The Brooks Act: An 8-Bit Act in a 64-Bit World? An Investigation of the Brooks Act and Its Implications to the Department of Defense Information Technology Acquisition Process." Washington, D.C.: The Industrial College of the Armed Forces, 1995.

U.S. Congress. Hearing, 89–1, Aug. 25, 1965. Lyndon Baines Johnson Presidential Archival Depository.

All the Way with LBJ

Beschloss, Michael. *In His Final Days, LBJ Agonized Over His Legacy.* PBS NewsHour, December 4, 2012.

Briscoe, Dolph. Video interview.

Brooks, Charlotte. In discussion with the author.

Brooks, Jack. In discussion with the author.

Brooks, Jack interview by Joe B. Frantz. February 1, 1971, transcript. Oral History Interview I, LBJ Presidential Library, Austin, TX.

Brooks, Jack B. Papers. Personal Correspondence with Johnson. Dolph Briscoe Center for America History, University of Texas.

Brooks, Jack. Reelection brochure. 1968.

Brooks, Jack. Video interview, November 22, 2002. LBJ Library.

Burka, Paul. "The Truth about John Connally: Does this Man Belong on a White Horse." *Texas Monthly,* November 1979.

Califano Jr., Joseph A. *The Triumph and Tragedy of Lyndon Johnson: The White House Years.* New York: Touchstone, 1991.

Caro, Robert. "LBJ's 'Passage of Power': The Transformation of a 'Legislative Genius.'" PBS NewsHour, 2012.

Caro, Robert. *The Years of Lyndon Johnson: Means of Ascent.* New York: Vintage Books, 1990.

Caro, Robert. *The Years of Lyndon Johnson: The Path to Power.* New York: Vintage Books, 1982.

Connally, John and Mickey Herskowitz. *In History's Shadow: An American Odyssey.* New York: Hyperion, 1994.

Dallek, Robert. *Lone Star Rising: Lyndon Johnson and His Times: 1908–1960.* Oxford: Oxford University Press, 1991.

Dolph Briscoe Center for American History (website). "Jack Brooks Biography." https://www.cah.utexas.edu/collections/congress_politics_brooks_bio.php

Kotz, Nick. *Judgment Days: Lyndon Baines Johnson, Martin Luther King, Jr., and the Laws That Changed America.* New York: Houghton Mifflin and Harcourt, 2005.

Johnson, Lyndon. State of the Union Address. January 8, 1964. LBJ Presidential Library.

Johnson, Robert David. *All the Way with LBJ: The 1964 Presidential Election.* Cambridge: Cambridge University Press, 2009.

LBJ Presidential Library (website). "LBJ: His Life and Times." Accessed April 16, 2013. http://www.lbjlibrary.org/lyndon-baines-johnson/timeline

Martin, Douglas. "Jack Brooks, Former Congressman, Dies at 89." *The New York Times,* December 5, 2012.

McAdams, Harry. In discussion with the author.

Ralph Nader Congress Project. *Citizens*

Look at Congress: Jack Brooks, Democratic Representative from Texas. Washington, D.C.: Grossman Publishers, 1972.

Nelson, Garrison. *John William McCormack: A Political Biography.* New York: Bloomsbury Academic, 2017.

Onassis, Jacqueline Kennedy. *Jacqueline Kennedy: Historic Conversations on Life with John F. Kennedy.* New York: Hyperion, 2011.

Pearson, Drew. "Phenomenal Record: President Johnson's Legislative Skill Tops Everybody Since Roosevelt." *Washington Post and Times Herald,* May 30, 1965.

Peters, Gene. In discussion with the author.

Richardson, Susan Smith. "Power Politics: Books about Texas, The Presidency and National Politics Remind Us That the Lone Star State Has a Long History of Influencing the Country's Agenda." *Texas Observer,* September 10, 2012.

Scates, Shelby. *War and Politics by Other Means: A Journalist's Memoir.* Seattle: University of Washington Press, 2000.

Schick, Frank Leopold, Renee Schick, and Mark S. Carroll. *The Records of the Presidency: Presidential Papers and Libraries from Washington to Reagan.* Oryx Press, 1989.

Silverleib, Alan. "8 Memorable State of the Union Moments." CNN.com, February 11, 2013

The Texas Politics Project at the University of Texas at Austin (website). "Governors of Texas." Accessed April 25, 2013. https://texaspolitics.utexas.edu/archive/html/exec/governors/index.html

Truett, Joe C. *Circling Back: Chronicle of a Texas River Valley.* Iowa City, IA: University of Iowa Press, 1996.

United Press International (website). "1963 Year in Review." accessed April 16, 2013. https://www.upi.com/Archives/Audio/Events-of-1963/Events-of-1963/

United States Senate (website). "Civil Rights Filibuster Ended." Accessed April 25, 2013. https://www.senate.gov/artandhistory/history/minute/Civil_Rights_Filibuster_Ended.htm

Winkler, Adam. *Gunfight: The Battle Over the Right to Bear Arms in America.* New York: W.W. Norton & Company, 2011.

Legislation: 1969–1974

Brooks, Jack interview by Joe B. Frantz. February 1, 1971, transcript. Oral History Interview I, LBJ Presidential Library, Austin, TX.

The Honeywell Computer Journal. "Orienting the Computer to People." 5, no. 4, (1971).

Aviation Week & Space Technology Vol. 79. McGraw-Hill, 1963.

Brooks, Jack. In discussion with the author.

Brooks, Jack. "Life and Career of Jack Brooks." C-SPAN interview, May 25, 1990.

Brooks, Jack B. Papers. Press Releases; 1966–1973. Dolph Briscoe Center for American History, University of Texas.

Brooks, Jack B. Papers. Speeches; 1972. Dolph Briscoe Center for American History, University of Texas.

Bulletin of the Atomic Scientists. 34, no. 2. Educational Foundation for Nuclear Science, Inc., 1978.

Congressional Research Support and Information Services. "A Compendium of Materials, Compiled by the Staff of the Joint Committee on Congressional Operations." May 3, 1974.

Conway, Erik. *High Speed Dreams: NASA and the Technopolitics of Supersonic Transportation, 1945–1999.* Baltimore: The Johns Hopkins University Press, 2005.

Cozine, James. *Saving the Big Thicket: From Exploration to Preservation, 1685–2003.*

Denton, TX: University of North Texas Press, 2004.

Cunningham, Sean P. *Cowboy Conservatism: Texas and the Rise of the Modern Right*. Lexington, KY: University of Kentucky Press, 2010.

Ellsberg, Daniel. *Secrets: A Memoir of Vietnam and the Pentagon Papers*. New York: Viking Penguin, 2002.

Fall, Bernard B. *Hell in a Very Small Place: The Siege of Dien Bien Phu*. New York: Da Capo Press, 1996.

Federal Aviation Administration (website). "Delegation and Designee Background." https://www.faa.gov/about/history/deldes_background/

Federal Register. "Federal Acquisition Regulation; Application of the Brooks Act to Mapping Services; Analysis of Comments." 70 FR 20329, April 19, 2005.

Glasrud, Bruce and James Smallwood. *The African American Experience in Texas: An Anthology*. Lubbock, TX: Texas Tech University Press, 2007.

Joint Committee on Congressional Operations Congress, H.R. Doc. No. 92–187 (1972).

Kampelman, Max. "Washington Week in Review." PBS, Oct 17, 1967.

Kuhn, Cpt. Dave. "The Thrust Lever." *Flying*, January 1964.

Lewin, James. In discussion with the author, 2011.

Martin, Douglas. "Jack Brooks, 89, Lawmaker Who Bucked Fellow Southerners on Civil Rights, Dies." *The New York Times*, December 8, 2012.

Martis, Kenneth C. *The Historical Atlas of Political Parties in the United States Congress, 1789–1989*. Prentice Hall, 1989.

Miyakawa, Tadao, ed. *The Science of Public Policy: Policy Process, Part III*. Routledge, 2000.

Perlstein, Rick. *Nixonland: The Rise of a President and the Fracturing of America*; New York: Scribner, 2008.

Ralph Nader Congress Project. *Citizens Look at Congress: Jack Brooks, Democratic Representative from Texas*. Washington, D.C.: Grossman Publishers, 1972.

Smith Jr., Griffin and Paul Burka. "The Best, the Worst, and the Fair-to-Middlin': Rating the Texas Congressmen From Top to Bottom." *Texas Monthly*, May 1976.

Talk of the Nation. "The Election, Gay Marriage and the GOP." December 5, 2012. https://www.npr.org/templates/transcript/transcript.php?storyId=166580520

Time. "Jumbo and the Gremlins." February 2, 1970.

University of Virginia Miller Center (website). "Richard Nixon-Key Events." Accessed July 23, 2013. https://millercenter.org/president/richard-nixon/key-events

Weber, Marc. Interview. Computer History Museum, Internet History Program.

CONGRESSIONAL OPERATIONS

Duvall, Bill and Charles Kline. Video interview, 2009. 40th Anniversary of the Net—October 29, 1969. Computer History Museum.

Newsweek Feature Service. "Capitol Hill's Own Quarterback, Frank Ryna Introduces Congress to the World of Computers." *Milwaukee Journal*, December 12, 1971.

Sheldden, David. "Today in Media History: The Internet began with a crash on October 29, 1969." The Poynter Institute, October 29, 2014. https://www.poynter.org/reporting-editing/2014/today-in-media-history-the-internet-began-with-a-crash-on-october-29–1969/

WASTE

Associated Press. "Plane Costs Suppressed, Colonel Says." April 30, 1969.

Fitzgerald, A. Ernest. *The High Priests of Waste*. New York: W.W. Norton Limited, 1972.

Fitzgerald, A. Ernest. *The Pentagonists; An Insider's View of Waste, Mismanagement and Fraud in Defense Spending*. New York: Houghton Mifflin, 1989.

Harlow v. Fitzgerald. 487 U.S. 800. 1982.

Hoover, Kurt and Wallace T. Fowler. *Studies in Ethics, Safety, and Liability for Engineers*. The University of Texas at Austin.

Nixon v. Fitzgerald.457 U.S. 731. 1982.

New York Times. "C-5A Foe Says Pentagon Stripped Him of Duties." November 18, 1969.

Rice, Berkeley. *The C-5A Scandal: An Inside Story of the Military-Industrial Complex*. New York: Houghton Mifflin, 1971.

PROCUREMENT

The Associated General Contractors of America. "Qualifications Based Selection of Contractors." August 2009. www.agc.com.

Cabral, Luis and Shane Greenstein. "Switching Costs and Bidding Parity in Government Procurement of Computer Systems." *Journal of Law, Economics and Organization* 6, no. 2 (October 1990).

Council on Federal Procurement of Architectural and Engineering Services. "COFPAES Statement on Passing of Jack Brooks, Author of 'Brooks Act.'" Dececember 5, 2012.

Davis, Hon. Tom. "Celebrating 30 Years of Quality in Federal Procurement Management." *Congressional Record* 148, pt. 17 (November 15, 2002).

Defense Acquisition University.

"Architect-Engineer Contracting Student Guide." 2003.

Didier, Kurt A. "Construction Contracting and the New Two-Phase Design-Build Selection Procedures: Balancing Efficiency with Full and Open Competition." *Public Law* (1997).

Greenstein, Shane M. "Sole-Sourcing versus Competitive Bidding: US Government Agencies' Procedural Choices for Mainframe Computer Procurement." *The Journal of Industrial Economics* 43, no. 2 (June 1995).

Greenstein, Shane M. "Going by the book: the costs and benefits of procedural rules in federal computer procurement." *Science and Public Policy* 20, no.3 (June 1993).

Loulakis, Michael. *Design-Build for the Public Sector*. Aspen Publishers, 2003.

Schneider, Judy, Christopher M. Davis, and Betsy Palmer. *Reorganization of the House of Representatives Background and History*. Nova Publishers, 2003.

U.S. General Accounting Office. *Computer Buys: Air Force Logistics Modernization Program Should Comply with the Brooks Act*. IMTEC-86–16. May 15, 1986.

FAMILY LIFE

Albert, Carl. *Little Giant: The Life and Times of Speaker Carl Albert*. Norman, OK: University of Oklahoma Press, 1999.

Brooks, Charlotte. In discussion with author.

Brooks, Jack. In discussion with author.

Chapman, William "Carl Albert: Winning with a Waiting Game." *Washington Post and Times Herald*, January 10, 1971.

Crawford, Clare. "Carl Albert Doesn't Want to be President, but He's Next in Line." *People*, November 18, 1974.

THE EXECUTIONER

Alexander, Holmes. "The 'Nixon Court' Might Save Him." *Beaumont Enterprise,* January 4, 1974.

Anthony, Carl Sferrazza. *First Ladies: The Saga of the Presidents' Wives and Their Power; 1961–1990, Vol. II.* New York: William Morrow and Co, 1991.

Associated Press. "Impeachment Articles Ready." *Ocala Star Banner,* July 18, 1974.

Berger, Raoul. *Impeachment: The Constitutional Problems.* Cambridge, MA: Harvard Univesity Press, 1974.

Bernstein, Carl. *A Woman in Charge: The Life of Hillary Rodham Clinton.* New York: Alfred A. Knopf, 2007.

Beryl, Anthony. Video interview.

Breslin, Jimmy. *How the Good Guys Finally Won: Notes from an Impeachment Summer.* New York: The Viking Press, 1975.

Brooks, Jack. In discussion with author.

Brooks, Jack. "Life and Career of Jack Brooks." C-SPAN interview, May 25, 1990.

Congressional Quarterly Inc. *Presidency, 1974.* Congressional Quarterly Inc., 1975.

Congressional Quarterly Inc. *Watergate: Chronology of a Crisis, Vol. 2.* Congressional Quarterly Inc., 1973.

Doar, John. "Q&A with John Doar." C-SPAN, January 12, 2009.

Evans, Rowland and Robert Novak. May 20, 1974; "Limiting the Impeachment Inquiry." *Washington Post,* January 12, 2009.

Farrell, John A. *Tip O'Neill and the Democratic Century.* New York: Little, Brown, 2001.

Fiss, Owen. Oral History Interview with Timothy Naftali, September 27, 2011. Richard Nixon Oral History Project, Richard Nixon Presidential Library and Museum.

Gerald R. Ford Library & Museum (website). "The Watergate Files: The Watergate Trial—Timeline." https://www.fordlibrarymuseum.gov/museum/exhibits/watergate_files/content.php?section=1&page=d

Healy, Gene. "Remembering Nixon's Wage and Price Controls." *Washington Examiner,* August 16, 2011.

Hearings of the Committee on the Judiciary, House of Representatives. U.S. Congress, 1974.

Historical Office: Office of the Secretary of Defense (website). "Melvin R. Laird." Accessed July 6, 2013. https://history.defense.gov/multimedia/biographies/article-view/article/571291/melvin-r-laird/

Holtzman, Elizabeth. Washington Journal Show. C-SPAN, February 20, 1998.

Johnson, Haynes. "President Hands Over Transcripts." *Washington Post,* May 1, 1974.

Kalb, Marvin. "Truman, Eisenhower, and the Fiscal Cliff: A Political Message from Another Era." Brookings Institute, December 7, 2012.

Kilpatrick, Carol. "President Refuses to Turn Over Tapes; Ervin Committee, Cox Issue Subpoenas." *Washington Post,* July 24, 1973.

Kilpatrick, Carol. 'Nixon Resigns." *Washington Post,* August 9, 1974.

Kilpatrick, Carol. "Nixon Forces Firing of Cox; Richardson, Ruckelshaus Quit." *Washington Post,* October 21, 1973.

Law Offices of Doar Rieck Kaley & Mack (website). "John Doar." Accessed July 10, 2013. https://web.archive.org/web/20120601084141/http://www.doarlaw.com/bios/john-doar.html

Lukas, J. Anthony. *Nightmare: The Underside of the Nixon Years.* New York: Viking Press, 1976.

Lyons, Richard. "New Faces Dominate House Group Studying Impeachment." *Washington Post,* November 14, 1973.

Lyons, Richard and William Chapman. "Judiciary Committee Approves Article to Impeach President Nixon, 27 to 11; 6 Republicans Join Democrats to Pass Obstruction Charge." *Washington Post,* July 28, 1974.

Mankiewicz, Frank. *U.S. v. Richard M. Nixon: The Final Crisis.* New York: Quadrangle/The New York Times Book Co., 1975.

McGrory, Mary. "The Committee will have to Run Just to Catch up." *Washington Star News,* May 10, 1974.

Meyer, William R. and Dale Pullen. *Ralph Nader Congress Project: Citizens Look at Congress: Jack Brooks; Democratic Representative from Texas.* New York: Grossman Publishers, 1972.

Nixon, Richard M. Joint Communiqué, Moscow. July 3, 1974.

Nixon, Richard M. "Resignation Address to the Nation." C-SPAN Video Library, August 8, 1974.

Nussbaum, Bernard. Oral History Interview with Timothy Naftali, October 1, 2011. Richard Nixon Oral History Project, Richard Nixon Presidential Library and Museum.

O'Neill, Tip. "Majority Leader Thomas P. O'Neill, Jr., says President's Surrender of Tapes Dampens Fires for Impeachment." Press Release, October 23, 1973. Richard Nixon Foundation (website). "Richard Nixon—A Timeline." Accessed July 18, 2013. https://www.nixonfoundation.org/richard-nixon-a-timeline/

Pace, Eric. "Charles Wiggins, 72, dies; Led Nixon's Defense in Hearings." *New York Times,* March 8, 2000.

Pittsburgh Post-Gazette "Editorial: Impeachment Suspense." June 1, 1974.

Rangel, Charles. In discussion with author, 2004.

Reedy, George E. *The Presidency.* New York: Arno Press, 1975.

Reeves, Richard. "The City Politic: The Impeachment Stall." *New York Magazine,* July 15, 1974.

Rodino, Peter. "Life and Career of Peter Rodino." C-SPAN interview, May 20, 1988.

Sack, Robert. C-SPAN interview, September 27, 2011.

Saxon, Wolfgang. "Obituary: Gen. William McKee, ex-F.A.A. Head, Dies." *New York Times,* March 2, 1987.

Schnapper, Morris Bartel. *Conscience of a Nation.* New York: Public Affairs Press, 1974.

Taylor, Walter. "Impeachment Work Guarded." *Washington Star News,* January 22, 1974.

Taylor, Walter. "House Unit Moving." *Washington Star News,* January 31, 1974.

University of Virginia Miller Center (website). "Richard Nixon-Key Events." Accessed July 23, 2013. https://miller-center.org/president/richard-nixon/key-events

Van Tassel, Emily Field and Paul Finkelman. "Impeachable Offenses: A Documentary History From 1787 to the Present." *Congressional Quarterly,* 1999.

Viorst, Milton. "Spotlight on Judiciary 17." *Washington Star News,* December 27, 1973.

Washington University Film & Media Archive (website). "John Doar." Accessed July 10, 2013. https://archive.li/20121215120155/http://library.wustl.edu/units/spec/filmandmedia/collections/henry-hampton-collection/eyes1/doar.htm

Weisman, Joel. "Chicago Tribune Asks

Nixon Quit or be Impeached." *Washington Post,* May 9, 1974.

Weld, William. Oral History Interview with Timothy Naftali, September 28, 2011. Richard Nixon Oral History Project, Richard Nixon Presidential Library and Museum.

West, Benjamin C. Interview with Office of History and Preservation, May 23, 2007. U.S. House of Representatives Oral History Program.

The White House, Office of the Press Secretary. "President Obama Names Presidential Medal of Freedom Recipients." Press Release, April 26, 2012.

Witcover, Jules. "Pressure for Impeachment Mounting." *Washington Post,* October 21, 1973.

Woodward, Bob and Carl Bernstein. *The Final Days: The Classic, Behind-the-scenes Account of Richard Nixon's Dramatic Final Days in the White House.* New York: Simon & Schuster, 1976.

Yergin, Daniel and Joseph Stanislaw. *The Commanding Heights: The Battle Between Government and the Marketplace.* New York: Simon & Schuster, 1997.

SNAKE KILLER

Anderson, Jack and Les Whitten. "Nixon Has Overspent Allotment by $167,000." *Utica NY Observer-Dispatch,* January 10, 1975.

Brooks, Jack B. Papers. Boxes 412, 749, et al. Dolph Briscoe Center for American History, University of Texas.

The American Presidency Project. "Gerald Ford: Remarks and a Question-and-Answer Session With Reporters Following a Meeting on General Revenue Sharing." June 3, 1976. https://www.presidency.ucsb.edu/documents/remarks-and-question-and-answer-session-with-reporters-following-meeting-general-revenue

The American Presidency Project. "Gerald Ford: Remarks at a Briefing on the Budget in Ft. Lauderdale." February 13, 1976. https://www.presidency.ucsb.edu/documents/remarks-briefing-the-budget-ft-lauderdale

The American Presidency Project (website). "Jimmy Carter: Civil Service Reform Act of 1978 Statement on Signing S. 2640 Into Law." October 13, 1978. https://www.presidency.ucsb.edu/documents/civil-service-reform-act-1978-statement-signing-s-2640-into-law

The American Presidency Project. "Jimmy Carter: Department of Education Organization Act Statement on Signing S. 210 Into Law." October 17, 1979. https://www.presidency.ucsb.edu/documents/department-education-organization-act-statement-signing-s-210-into-law

The American Presidency Project (website). "Jimmy Carter: General Accounting Office Act of 1980 Statement on Signing H.R. 24 Into Law." April 3, 1980. https://www.presidency.ucsb.edu/documents/general-accounting-office-act-1980-statement-signing-hr-24-into-law

The American Presidency Project. "Jimmy Carter: The President's News Conference." February 23, 1977. https://www.presidency.ucsb.edu/documents/the-presidents-news-conference-119

The American Presidency Project. "Jimmy Carter: Reorganization Act of 1977 Remarks at the Bill Signing Ceremony." April 6, 1977. https://www.presidency.ucsb.edu/documents/reorganization-act-1977-remarks-the-bill-signing-ceremony

Associated Press. "Ford Flays Congress For Not Passing Revenue-Sharing Bill."

Sarasota Herald-Tribune, March 16, 1976.

Associated Press. "Ford Urges Extension for Revenue Sharing"; *Spartanburg Herald-Journal,* February 24, 1976.

Biographical Directory of the United States Congress (website). "Holifield, Chester Earl, (1903–1995)." http://bioguide.congress.gov/scripts/biodisplay.pl?index=H000713

Brooks, Jack B. Papers. Copy of Gerald Ford's November 18, 1974 Speech to Congress. Dolph Briscoe Center for American History, University of Texas.

Browning, Robert X. *The C-Span Archives: An Interdisciplinary Resource for Discovery, Learning and Engagement.* West Lafayette, IN: Purdue University Press, 2014.

The Cannon Centenary Conference: The Changing Nature of the Speakership H.R. Doc. 103–204. May 1, 2004.

Cannon, James. "Federal Revenue-Sharing: Born 1972. Died 1986. R.I.P." *New York Times,* October 10, 1986.

Cannon, James. *Gerald R. Ford; An Honorable Life.* Ann Arbor, MI: University of Michigan Press, 2013.

Cannon, James. *Time and Chance: Gerald Ford's Appointment with History.* Ann Arbor, MI: University of Michigan Press, 1994.

Carter, Jimmy. The Daily Diary of President Jimmy Carter, December 19, 1980. Jimmy Carter Library.

Carter, Jimmy. *Keeping Faith: Memoirs of a President.* New York: Bantam Books, 1983.

Carter, Jimmy. Public Papers of the Presidents of the United States: 1977. National Archives and Records Service, Office of the Federal Register.

Carter, Jimmy. Public Papers of the Presidents of the United States, Book 2: June 30 to December 31, 1978. U.S. Government Printing Office.

Carter, Jimmy. Public Papers of the Presidents of the United States. Book 2: June 30 to December 31, 1978. National Archives and Records Service, Office of the Federal Register.

Carter, Jimmy. Public Papers of the Presidents of the United States. 1980–1981. National Archives and Records Service, Office of the Federal Register.

Cook, Timothy E. *Making Laws and Making News: Media Strategies in the U.S. House of Representatives.* Brookings Institution Press, 1989.

Computer Decisions, 11 (1979). "Brooks Urges Tighter Federal ADP Policies."

Craig, Barbara Hinkson. *Chadha: The Story of an Epic Constitutional Struggle.* Berkeley, CA: University of California Press, 1988.

C-SPAN (website). "Our History." Accessed March 14, 2015. https://www.c-span.org/about/history/

Cunningham, Sean P. *Cowboy Conservatism: Texas and the Rise of the Modern Right.* Lexington, KY: University of Kentucky Press, 2010.

Dyckman, Martin. "Brooks Concedes He Can't Defeat Carter Reorganization Plan." *St. Petersburg Times,* March 17, 1977.

Dyke, Richard Wayne and Francis Xavier Gannon. *Chet Holifield: Master Legislator and Nuclear Statesman.* University Press of America, 1996.

Farrell, John A. *Tip O'Neill and the Democratic Century.* New York: Little, Brown, 2001.

Fink, Gary M. New Georgia Encyclopedia (website). "Jimmy Carter (b. 1924)." September 9, 2002. https://www.georgiaencyclopedia.

org/articles/government-politics/jimmy-carter-b-1924

Ford, Gerald. Message to Congress, April 25, 1975. CQ Almanac.

Frantzich, Stephen E. *Founding Father: How C-SPAN's Brian Lamb Changed Politics in America.* Lanham, MD: Rowman & Littlefield, 2008.

Frantzich, Stephen E. and John Sullivan. *The C-SPAN Revolution.* Norman, OK: University of Oklahoma Press, 1996.

Freedom of Information Center Report, Issues 318–396. 1974. School of Journalism, University of Missouri.

Funk, William F. "The Paperwork Reduction Act: Paperwork Reduction Meets Administrative Law." *Harvard Journal on Legislation* 24, no. 1 (1987).

Hearings before the Joint Committee on Congressional Operations. Ninety-Third Congress, Second Session. U.S. Government Printing Office. U.S. Congress, 1974.

Heffernan, Robert V. *Cabinetmakers: Story of the Three-Year Battle to Establish the U.S. Department of Education.* iUniverse: 2001.

Heilemann, John. "Congress's Watch Dog: The General Accounting Office." *Washington Monthly,* November 1989.

History, Art & Archives: United States House of Representatives (website). "Historical Highlights: The introduction of televised House proceedings: March 15, 1977." https://history.house.gov/Historical-Highlights/1951–2000/The-introduction-of-televised-House-proceedings/

History, Art & Archives: United States House of Representatives (website). "Historical Highlights: The Resolution to Permit Live Radio Broadcasts of House Proceedings: September 19, 1944." https://history.house.gov/Historical-Highlights/1901–1950/

The-resolution-to-permit-live-radio-broadcast-of-House-proceedings/

Ingraham, Patricia W. and David H. Rosenbloom. *The Promise and Paradox of Civil Service Reform.* Pittsburgh: University of Pittsburgh Press, 1993.

Inspector General Act of 1978. Public Law 95–452, 5 U.S.C.

Kirchner, Jake. "Brooks Unrelenting in Fight for Better U.S. DP." *ComputerWorld,* December 18, 1978.

Lamb, Brian. Interview with Jim Keller, August 6, 2013. Hauser Foundation Oral and Video History Project of The Cable Center Oral History and Video History Program.

McCutcheon, Chuck. *Congress A to Z.* 6th ed. CQ Press, 2014.

Mixon, Franklin G. *Legislative Television As Political Advertising: A Public Choice Approach.* iUniverse, 2003.

Moore, Mark Harrison and Margaret Jane Gates. *Inspectors-General: Junkyard Dogs or Man's Best Friend?* Social Research Perspectives: Occasional Reports on Current Topics. Russell Sage Foundation, 1986.

Mullen, Megan. *The Rise of Cable Programming in the United States: Revolution or Evolution?* Austin, TX: University of Texas Press, 2003.

Radin, Beryl A. and Willis D. Hawley. *The Politics of Federal Reorganization: Creating the U.S. Department of Education.* New York: Pergamon Press, 1988.

Rosenthiel, Thomas B. "How an Unheralded Reporter Wrote the Quiet Beginnings to Wright Case." *The Los Angeles Times,* May 13, 1989.

Sass, Lauren R. and Debbie Sontag. "Television: The American Medium in Crisis." *Facts on File,* January 1, 1979.

Schudel, Matt. "John N. Erlenborn, 78; 10-Term GOP Congressman." *Washington Post,* November 2, 2005.

Shales, Tom. "C-SPAN, America's Town Hall; Looking Back on the Decade That Brought Government Home." *Washington Post,* April 3, 1989.

Shapiro, Ira S. *The Last Great Senate: Courage and Statesmanship in Times of Crisis.* New York: PublicAffairs, 2012.

Sherrill, Robert and James David Barber. *Why They Call it Politics: A Guide to American Government.* New York: Harcourt Brace Jovanovich, 1979.

Smith Jr., Griffin and Paul Burka. "The Best, the Worst, and the Fair-to-Middlin." *Texas Monthly,* May 1976.

Time in Partnership with CNN. "Koreagate on Capitol Hill?" November 29, 1976.

Toavs, Dwight V. *Pixelating Policy: Visualizing Issue Transformation In Real and Virtual Worlds—4.1.2 Fingering Paperwork As The Problem: Policy Environment 1975–1980.* Virginia Polytechnic Institute and State University, 2004.

Weil, Martin. "Abraham Ribicoff, 87, Dies." *Washington Post,* February 23, 1998.

West, Richard. Texas Monthly Reporter. *Texas Monthly,* January 1977.

Zelizer, Julian E. *Jimmy Carter.* New York: Henry Holt and Company, 2010.

IRAN-CONTRA

Ahern, Tim. "Congressmen Dispute Reagan View." Associated Press, May 18, 1987.

Anthony, Beryl. Video interview.

Associated Press. "Panel grants North platform for Contra pitch." July 14, 1987.

Associated Press. "USIA admits 84-name blacklist and error." February 10, 1984.

Brooks, Jack. In discussion with the author.

Cawley, Janet and Christopher Drew. "Probers Ask North About Crisis Plan." *Chicago Tribune,* July 14, 1987.

Gay, Lance. "Iran-Contra hearings populated by many stars, shiny and tarnished." Scripps Howard News Service, June 13, 1987.

Hamilton, Lee H. and Daniel K. Inouye. *Report of the Congressional Committees Investigating the Iran/Contra Affair.* DIANE Publishing, 1995.

Howell, William G. *Power Without Persuasion: The Politics of Direct Presidential Action.* Princeton, NJ: Princeton University Press, 2003.

Johnson, Haynes. "Elliot Abrams' Painful Lesson." *Washington Post,* June 4, 1987.

LaFeber, Walter. *Inevitable Revolutions: The United States in Central America.* New York: W. W. Norton & Company, 1993.

Margasak, Larry. "Iran-Contra committees call hearings successful . . . " Associated Press, August 9, 1987.

Martin, Douglas. "Charlie Wilson, Texas Congressman Linked to Foreign Intrigue, Dies at 76." *New York Times,* February 10, 2010.

McManus, Doyle. "The Iran-Contra Hearings: Sparring Abrams Balances Apology With Belligerence." *Los Angeles Times,* June 3, 1987.

New York Times News Service. "Tower Criticizes Congressional Iran-Contra Probe." August 11, 1987.

Prados, John. 1991; *Keepers of the Keys: A History of the National Security Council from Truman to Bush.* New York: Morrow, 1991.

Report of the Congressional Committees Investigating the Iran-Contra Affair: with Supplemental, Minority, and Additional Views. November 13, 1987. U.S. Government Printing Office.

Royko, Mike. "Ollie image blinds starstruck public." *Chicago Tribune,* July 14, 1987.

Rowan, Carl. "The Courageous at

Iran-Contra Hearings." *Chicago Sun-Times,* August 5, 1987.

Sklar, Holly. *Washington's War on Nicaragua.* Boston: South End Press, 1988.

Spong, John. "The Rehabilitation of Charlie Wilson." *Texas Monthly,* June 2004.

Thelen, David. *Becoming Citizens in the Age of Television: How Americans Challenged the Media and Seized Political Initiative During the Iran-Contra Debate.* Chicago: University of Chicago Press, 1996.

United Press International. "129 House Democrats Urge Ouster of Abrams in Letter." June 13, 1987.

Wroe, Ann. *Lives, Lies and the Iran-Contra Affair.* I. B. Tauris, 1992.

REAGANOMICS & RUNAWAY SPENDING

1980 Presidential General Election Data—National.

Associated Press. "Bias played role in list, Wick says." March 21, 1984.

Associated Press. "Bush Calls For Help for Oil Industry." *Victoria Advocate,* July 16, 1986.

Associated Press. "Military pensions blasted: Stockman calls system a 'scandal.'" February 6, 1984.

Attlesey, Sam. "Iran-contra figure North appears at Hance fund-raisers." *Dallas Morning News,* February 3, 1990.

Barry, John M. *The Ambition and the Power: The Fall of Jim Wright: A True Washington Story.* New York: Penguin Books, 1989.

Bennington, Bernard J. *Beyond FTS2000: A Program for Change.* National Academies, 1989.

Broder, David S. "Reaganomics at 10." *Washington Post,* Aug. 11, 1991.

Brooks, Jack. Testimony before the House Appropriations Committee: Hearings on Treasury, Postal Service, and General

Government Appropriations for 1995. February 22, 1994. U.S. Government Printing Office.

Bunch, Will. *Tear Down This Myth: How the Reagan Legacy Has Distorted Our Politics and Haunts Our Future.* New York: Simon & Schuster, 2009.

The Cannon Centenary Conference: The Changing Nature of the Speakership H.R. Doc. 103–204. May 1, 2004.

Cannon, Lou. "Ronald Reagan: Campaigns and Elections." University of Virginia Miller Center (website). Accessed February 17, 2016. https://millercenter.org/president/reagan/campaigns-and-elections

Carlisle, Rodney P., ed. *The Encyclopedia of Politics: The Left and the Right.* Sage Publications, Inc., 2005.

Carter, Jimmy Papers. October 22, 1980. Jimmy Carter Library and Museum.

Cheit, Earl F. "Scandal / Buying flap shows weakness in system." *Los Angeles Times,* July 21, 1985.

Coll, Steve. "Federal Phone Contract May be Split in Two." *Washington Post,* September 24, 1987.

Coll, Steve and Judith Havemann. "Rift Imperils New U.S. Telecommunications Network." *Washington Post,* August 6, 1987.

Congressional Budget Office. "Defense Spending: What Has Been Accomplished." April 1985.

Coy, Curtis Lee. "The Competition in Contracting Act." MA thesis, Naval Postgraduate School, 1986.

Dabla-Norris, Era, Kalpana Kochhar, Nujin Suphaphiphat, Frantisek Ricka, and Evridiki Tsounta. "Causes and Consequences of Income Inequality: A Global Perspective." *International Monetary Fund Staff Discussion Note,* June 2015.

Dethloff, Henry C. *Suddenly, Tomorrow*

Came: The NASA History of the Johnson Space Center. Dover Publications, 2012.

Eder, Richard. Review of *The Pentagon and the Art of War,* by Edward N. Luttwak. *Los Angeles Times,* February 17, 1985.

Evans, Diana. *Greasing the Wheels: Using Pork Barrel Projects to Build Majority Coalitions in Congress.* Cambridge: Cambridge University Press, 2004.

Evans, Thomas W. *The Education of Ronald Reagan: The General Electric Years and the Untold Story of His Conversion to Conservatism.* New York: Columbia University Press, 2006.

Fairhall, James. "The Case for the $435 Hammer." *Washington Monthly,* 1987.

Fallows, James. "The Spend Up." *The Atlantic Magazine,* July 1986.

Farrier, Jasmine. *Passing the Buck: Congress, the Budget, and Deficits.* Lexington, KY: University of Kentucky Press, 2004.

Frances, Joe. "One-of-a-kind Alumni." *The Alcalde,* January 1984 .

Fuerbringer, Jonathan. "House, 309 to 106, Votes Plan to Cut Deficit $155 Billion." *New York Times,* September 25, 1986.

Fund, John. "Ronald Reagan's Free-Market Mentors." *National Review,* February 2, 2015.

Galveston Daily News. Letters from Readers. October 29, 1986.

Greider, William. "The Education of David Stockman." *The Atlantic Monthly,* December 1981.

Havemann, Judith. "Battle over Phone Contract Escalates." *Washington Post,* August 5, 1987.

Havemann, Judith. "For Phone Contractors, A Busy Signal." *Washington Post,* August 26, 1987.

Havemann, Judith. "GSA says it will Split Federal Phone Contract." *Washington Post,* September 26, 1987.

Havemann, Judith. "General Services Administrator Golden to Resign." *Washington Post,* March 4, 1988.

Havemann, Judith. "Marietta Don't Split Phone Work." *Washington Post,* August 6, 1987.

Jacob, John E. "The Ravages of Reaganomics: Depression hits blacks, poor the hardest." *St. Petersburg Independent,* June 30, 1982.

Kyle, Jim. "Award likely U.S. Steel may get oil reserve pipe contract." *The Baytown Sun,* May 4, 1986.

Kyle, Jim. "Texas Works plant to reap benefits from Big Hill deal." *Baytown Sun,* May 4, 1986.

Light, Paul. *The Tides of Reform: Making Government 1945–1995.* New Haven, CT: Yale University Press, 1997.

Longley, Kyle, Jeremy Mayer, Michael Schaller, and John W. Sloan. *Deconstructing Reagan: Conservative Mythology and America's Fortieth President.* M.E. Sharpe, 2007.

Luttwak, Edward N. *The Pentagon and the Art of War.* New York: Simon & Schuster, 1985.

Manning, David. "Congressmen address area's business woes." *University Press* (Beaumont, Texas) 62, no. 7, ed. 1 (October 4, 1985).

McCartney, James, Molly Sinclair McCartney. *America's War Machine: Vested Interests, Endless Conflicts.* New York: Thomas Dunne Books, 2015.

McDonough, Frank A. "The Brooks Legacy: Remembering the man who changed federal IT; FCW." *The Business of Federal Technology,* December 6, 2012.

Meyer, David S. *A Winter of Discontent: The Nuclear Freeze and American Politics.* Westport, CT: Greenwood Publishing Group, 1990.

Milwaukee Sentinel. "Proxmire takes aim at Defense." December 21, 1988.

New York Times. "A Big Push for Pentagon Reform." July 22, 1986.

Oklahoman. "Congressmen Opposing Halt to Oil Reserve Fill." March 7, 1985.

Picketty, Thomas. *Capital in the Twenty-First Century.* Cambridge, MA: The Belknap Press of Harvard University Press, 2014.

Pincus, Walter. "Defense procurement problems won't go away." *Washington Post,* May 2, 2012.

Polygraph 14 (1985). American Polygraph Association.

Rauch, Jonathan. "Gramm-Rudman—a Bad Idea Whose Time Has Come Again." *The Atlantic,* February 2005.

Risjord, Norman K. *Giants in Their Time: Representative Americans from the Jazz Age to the Cold War.* New York: Rowman and Littlefield Publishers, Inc., 2006.

Roberts, Steven V. "Washington Talk; Did the Reagan Style of Management Fail Him?" *New York Times,* March 5, 1987.

Robertson, Robert J. "Congressman Jack Brooks—'Taking Care of Business.'" *East Texas Historical Journal* 51, Issue 2, Article 7 (2013).

Rogers, Mary Beth. *Barbara Jordan, American Hero.* New York, Bantam Books, 1998.

Scott, Karyl. "GSA to divvy up FTS 2000: Two vendors to split work." *IDG Network World Inc.* 4, no. 45, (November 9, 1987).

Shapiro, Ira S. *The Last Great Senate: Courage and Statesmanship in Times of Crisis;* New York: PublicAffairs, 2012.

Shin, Annys. "Think Mogully, Act Locally." *Washington City Paper,* February 14, 2003.

Smith, Hedrick. *Power Game: How Washington Works.* New York: Random House Publishing Group, 2012.

Stockman, David. *The Triumph of Politics:*

Why the Reagan Revolution Failed. New York: Harper & Row, 1986.

Thelen, David. *Becoming Citizens in the Age of Television: How Americans Challenged the Media and Seized Political Initiative During the Iran-Contra Debate.* Chicago: University of Chicago Press, 1996.

Thornburg, Dick. Speech by Attorney General Thornburgh to Senate. June 20, 1991. Department of Justice archives.

United Press International. "He Ordered Agencies Not to Comply With '84 Law: Panel Calls Reagan's Action Unconstitutional." May 25, 1985.

White, Joseph and Aaron B. Wildavsky. *The Deficit and the Public Interest: The Search for Responsible Budgeting in the 1980s.* Berkeley, CA: University of California Press, 1989.

Wildavsky, Aaron Bernard and Michael J. Boskin, eds. *The Federal Budget: Economics and Politics.* Institute for Contemporary Studies, 1982.

MINDLESS CANNIBALISM

Associated Press. "Brooks's A-bomb remark causes stir." October 24, 1986.

Associated Press. "Brooks issues statement." October 24, 1986.

Associated Press. "Complaint on Wright is Filed." May 27, 1988.

Barry, John M. *The Ambition and the Power: The Fall of Jim Wright: A True Washington Story.* New York: Penguin Books, 1989.

Beers, David. "Newt Gingrich: Master of Disaster." *Mother Jones,* September 1, 1989.

Bernhardt, Gene. "Democrats 'ousting' committee chairmen." Associated Press, January 17, 1975.

Bernhardt, Gene. "Democrats Stun House Leaders, Vote to Dump Hays, Patman." Associated Press, January 16, 1975.

Bovard, James. *The Fair Trade Fraud: How Congress Pillages the Consumer and Decimates American Competitiveness.* New York: St. Martin's Press, 1991.

Buy American Act of 1987. H.R. 1750, 100th Congress.

The Cannon Centenary Conference: The Changing Nature of the Speakership H.R. Doc. 103–204. May 1, 2004.

Champagne, Anthony. *The Austin-Boston Connection: Five Decades of House Democratic Leadership (1937–1989).* College Station, TX: Texas A&M University Press, August 31, 2009.

Choate, Pat. *Agents of Influence; How Japan Manipulates America's Political and Economic System.* New York: Simon and Schuster, 1990.

Cohen, Richard. "The King of Oversight." *Government Executive* 20: 16–18 (September 1988).

Cook, Timothy E. *Making Laws and Making News: Media Strategies in the U.S. House of Representatives.* Brookings Institution Press, 1989.

Daley, Steve. "Foley Takes Gavel, Calls For End To Rancor." *Chicago Tribune,* June 7, 1989.

Deseret News. "Will Political Bickering Rage On?" June 1, 1989.

Diffie, Whitfield and Susan Eva Landau. *Privacy on the Line: The Politics of Wiretapping and Encryption.* Cambridge, MA: MIT Press, 2007.

Fritz, Sara. "Wright Inquiry May Undermine 'Sleaze Factor.'" *Los Angeles Times,* June 9, 1988.

Frost, Martin. "Remembering Jack Brooks." *The Hill,* December 5, 2012.

Galveston Daily News. cartoon: Lisa Duperier for Congress Committee. October 12, 1986

Gingrich, Newt, et al. House Session: debate on creation of external ethics

counsel and panning of installed cameras in chamber. June 29, 1987. C-SPAN Video Archives.

Gingrich, Newt, et al. House Session: various remarks. October 28, 1987. C-SPAN Video Archives.

Heale, M. J. "Anatomy of a Scare: Yellow Peril Politics in America, 1980–1993." *Journal of American Studies,* 43, no. 1: 19–47 (April 2009).

Jackson, Robert L. "The Resignation Of Jim Wright: Speaker's Downfall." *The Los Angeles Times,* June 1, 1989.

Johnson, Julie. "Washington Talk: Congress; A 'Fighting Marine' Battles Japan on Trade." *New York Times,* Jan. 18, 1988.

Lamis, Alexander. *The Two-Party South.* Oxford: Oxford University Press, 1990.

Los Angeles Times. "The Ethics Charges Against Jim Wright: Excerpts: 'Wright Did Not Show Reasonable Care on Gifts.'" April 18, 1989.

Mace, Scott. "White House Repeals Directive Protecting 'Sensitive' Data." *InfoWorld* 9, no. 12 (March 23, 1987).

Moffett, Toby. "An appreciation: One of Congress' rambunctious 'Watergate Babies' remembers Jack Brooks." *The Hill,* December 13, 2012.

Molotsky, Irvin. "Senate Votes to Compensate Japanese-American Internees." *New York Times,* April 21, 1988.

The New Republic. "TRB From Washington: Atwatergate." July 3, 1989.

Norquist, Grover. *Leave Me Alone: Getting the Government's Hands off Our Money, Our Gun, Our Lives.* New York: Harper Collins, 2008.

O'Neill, Tip, et al. House Session: various remarks. May 15, 1984. C-SPAN Video Archives.

Recio, Maria. "20 years later, former House Speaker Jim Wright reflects." McClatchy Newspapers, June 5, 2009.

Rosenstiel, Thomas B. "How an Unheralded Reporter Wrote the Quiet Beginnings to Wright Case." *Los Angeles Times,* May 13, 1989.

Segrave, Kerry. *Lie Detectors: A Social History.* Jefferson, NC: McFarland, 2004.

Smith, Steven S. "O'Neill's Legacy for the House." *The Brookings Review,* 1987.

Steely, Mel. *The Gentleman From Georgia: The Biography of Newt Gingrich.* Macon, GA: Mercer University Press, 2000.

Stolberg, Sheryl Gay. "Gingrich Stuck to Caustic Path in Ethics Battles." *New York Times,* January 26, 2012.

Times Wire Services. "$20,000, Apology Voted for WWII Japanese Internees: Bill Ready for Reagan Signature." August 4, 1988.

Tolchin, Martin. "Congressman Jack Brooks's Lament for the System." *New York Times,* March 14, 1977.

Wright, Jim. *Reflections of a Public Man.* Madison Publishing, 1984.

Wright, Jim. "Statement of Resignation from the House of Representatives." C-SPAN Video Archive. May 31, 1989.

THE JUDICIARY

Associated Press. "House Democrats pick new committee chiefs." December 7, 1988.

Attlesey, Sam. "Iran-contra figure North appears at Hance fund-raisers." *Dallas Morning News,* February 3, 1990.

Aukofer, Frank. "Kastenmeier has a chance for chairmanship." *Milwaukee Journal,* March 15, 1988.

Austin American-Statesman. "Brooks back from the brink and ready for any challenge." January 28, 1990.

Beaumont Enterprise. "Former Beaumont mayor Maury Meyers dies." June 16, 2014.

Bush, George H.W. Remarks on Signing the Hate Crime Statistics Act, April 23, 1990. Public Papers of the Presidents of the United States.

City-Data.com. "Canton, Ohio (OH) Political Contributions by Individuals." http://www.city-data.com/elec2/elec-CANTON-OH.html

Clark, Craig. *Brooks vs. Meyers: Debate presents candidates' views. University Press* (Beaumont Texas) 67, no. 16, ed. 1 (October 24, 1990).

Clinton, William J. *My Life.* New York: Random House, 2010.

Conciliation Agreement: Suarez Corp. v Friends of Steve Stockman. June 2, 1998. Federal Election Commission.

Eaton, Sabrina. "Canton-area businessman Benjamin Suarez fights back against federal charges that he made illegal campaign contributions." Northeast Ohio Media Group, Cleveland.com, October 11, 2013.

Equity in Interstate Competition Act of 1989. H.R. 2230, 101st Congress.

FCW, The Business of Federal Technology. "Jack Brooks: Titan of IT procurement." June 8, 2012.

Galveston Daily News. "Brooks ignored us when it counted most." October 21, 1990.

Guttery, Ben R. *Representing Texas: A Comprehensive History of U.S. and Confederate Senators and Representatives from Texas.* BookSurge Publishing, 2008.

Hayward, Steven F. *The Age of Reagan: The Conservative Counterrevolution, 1980–1989.* Three Rivers Press, 2010.

Hooks, Christopher. "Steve Stockman Can't Lose: The political genius of the wackiest firebrand in Texas." *Politico,* December 20, 2013.

Houston, Paul. "House Adopts Tough

Crime Bill." *Los Angeles Times*, October 23, 1991.

Ivins, Molly. Molly Ivins October 10. *Fort Worth Star-Telegram*, October 10, 1996

Johnson, Julie. "Washington Talk: Congress; A 'Fighting Marine' Battles Japan on Trade." *New York Times*, January 18, 1988.

Knight, Jerry. "Mail Order Merchants add Politics to their Packages in effort to Block Sales Tax." *Washington Post*, March 14, 1989.

Luque, Sulipsa. "Beaumont mayor to challenge Brooks for House." *Galveston Daily News*, December 7, 1989.

McDougal, Dennis. *The Last Mogul: Lew Wasserman, MCA, and the Hidden History of Hollywood*. Boston: Da Capo Press, 2001

Oberg, Alcestis R. "A few comments on politics, the election and NASA." *Galveston Daily News*, November 2, 1986.

Orlando Sentinel. "Bush Signs A Crime Bill But With Disappointment." November 30, 1990.

New York Times. "House Adds Tough Provisions On Death Penalty To Crime Bill." October 5, 1990.

New York Times. "Submarined by Japan and Norway," editorial. June 22, 1987.

Packer, George. *The Unwinding: An Inner History of the New America*. New York: Farrar, Straus and Giroux, 2013.

Peirce, Neal. "Should Sales Taxes Apply To Mail Orders?" Philly.com, June 26, 1989. http://articles.philly.com/1989–06-26/news/26106390_1_sales-taxes-direct-mail-mail-order-houses

Philadelphia Inquirer. "House Crime Bill Omits Gun Controls." July 20, 1990.

Rangel, Charles. In discussion with the author, 2004.

Reppert, Barton. "Japan's powerful lobby faces new trade challenges." Associated Press, July 15, 1987.

Runkel, David R., ed. *Campaign for President: The Managers Look at '88*. New York: Auburn House, 1989.

Stewart, Richard. "Primaries '90 – Rep. Brooks wins Dem contest; Meyers leads GOP opponent." *Houston Chronicle*, March 15, 1990.

Summary Report, 1993. Federal Election Commission.

Tolchin, Martin. "Foreigners Criticize Venture Bill." *The New York Times*, June 5, 1990.

Uslaner, Eric M. *The Decline of Comity in Congress*. Ann Arbor, MI: University of Michigan Press, 1993.

Will, George. "Japan Does Many Things Very Well." *Washington Post* Writers Group, April 8, 1985.

Weiner, Rachel. "C-SPAN denied cameras in the House of Representatives, again." *Washington Post*, February 5, 2011.

Yarowsky, Jonathan. In discussion with the author, 2004.

CRIME BILL

Achenbach, Joel, Scott Higham, and Sari Horwitz. "How NRA's true believers converted a marksmanship group into a mighty gun lobby." *Washington Post*, January 12, 2013.

Alic, John, et al. *Beyond Spinoff: Military and Commercial Technologies in a Changing World*. Cambridge, MA: Harvard Business School Press, 1992.

The American Presidency Project (website). "William J. Clinton: Telephone Conversation With the Space Shuttle *Discovery* Astronauts From Houston." February 7, 1994. https://www.presidency.ucsb.edu/documents/

telephone-conversation-with-the-space-shuttle-discovery-astronauts-from-houston

Aufderheide, Patricia. *Communications Policy and the Public Interest: The Telecommunications Act of 1996.* New York: Guilford Press, 1999.

Bailey, Chuck and Patrick Cox. *Picturing Texas Politics: A Photographic History from Sam Houston to Rick Perry.* Austin, TX: University of Texas Press, 2015.

Basken, Paul. "Conferees approve crime bill." UPI, July 28, 1994.

Beller, Margo D. "Lawmaker Bows to Group on Insurance Antitrust Bill Lawmaker." *Los Angeles Times,* May 24, 1994.

Black, Sharon K. *Telecommunications Law in the Internet Age.* Morgan Kaufmann, 2001.

Branch, Taylor. *The Clinton Tapes: Wrestling History with the President.* New York: Simon and Schuster, 2009.

Broder, John M. "GOP's Rising Tide Spills Over to Statehouses: Politics: Party takes control of majority of governorships for the first time since 1970. Democrats lose New York, Texas and Pennsylvania." *Los Angeles Times,* November 9, 1994.

Brooks, Jack. Letter to Chairman Steny Hoyer of the House Appropriations Committee: Hearings on Treasury, Postal Service, and General Government Appropriations for 1995. February 28, 1994.

Brooks, Jack. Remarks before the House Rules Committee. August 2, 1994. C-SPAN video archive.

Brooks, Jack. Testimony before the House Appropriations Committee: Hearings on Treasury, Postal Service, and General Government Appropriations for 1995. February 22, 1994.

Congressional Quarterly. "Insurance Antitrust Exemption Stalls With Health Care Bill." CQ Almanac, 50th ed., 183–84 (1994).

Congressional Quarterly. "Insurance Industry Kept Exemptions." CQ Almanac, 47th ed., 176–77 (1991).

Cooper, Cynthia A. *Violence on Television: Congressional Inquiry, Public Criticism, and Industry Response: A Policy Analysis.* University Press of America, 1996.

Corn, David. "The Clinton Memos: Advice on How Hillary Should Talk to a Single-Payer Advocate." *Mother Jones,* February 28, 2014.

Crenshaw, Albert B. "Insurers' Antitrust Exemption May End." *Washington Post,* May 27, 1994.

Dizard, Jan E., Robert M. Muth, and Stephen P. Andrews. *Guns in America: A Reader.* Chicago: NYU Press, 1999.

Dunham, Richard and David Wallach. "Texas political legend 'never afraid to fight.'" MySanAntonio.com, December 6, 2012.

Eaton, William. "Ford, Carter, Reagan Push for Gun Ban." *Los Angeles Times,* May 5, 1994.

Eaton, William. "House Approves Crime Bill, 285–141: Congress: $28-billion measure would add more police, build more prisons, expand death penalty. The vote sends the legislation to be reconciled with Senate version." *Los Angeles Times,* April 22, 1994.

FCW, The Business of Federal Technology. "Jack Brooks: Titan of IT procurement." June 8, 2012.

Feldman, Richard. *Ricochet: Confessions of a Gun Lobbyist.* John Wiley & Sons, Inc., 2011.

Gerst, Eric D. *Vulture Culture: Dirty Deals, Unpaid Claims, and the Coming Collapse of the Insurance Industry.* AMACOM, 2008.

Gest, Ted. *Crime & Politics: Big Government's*

Erratic Campaign for Law and Order. Oxford: Oxford University Press, 2001.

Green, Gene. Tribute to Congressman Jack Brooks. Remarks on floor of House;, December 5, 2012. Congressional Record.

Higham, Scott and Sari Horwitz. "NRA tactics: take no prisoners." *Washington Post,* May 18, 2013.

Houston Chronicle. "Jack Brooks Obituary." December 8, 2012.

Houston, James and William W. Parsons. *Criminal Justice and the Policy Process.* Chicago: Nelson-Hall Publishers, January 1, 1998.

Houston Press. "Turkeys (and Other Creatures) On the Ballot." November 3, 1994.

Johnson, Dennis W. *Political Consultants and American Elections: Hired to Fight, Hired to Win.* Routledge, 2016.

Kelman, Steve. "What to make of OMB's crackdown on 'rogue' laptop and desktop purchases." *FCW, The Business of Federal Technology,* October 19, 2015.

Kettl, Donald F. *Sharing Power: Public Governance and Private Markets.* The Brookings Institution, 1993.

Lewis, Chuck. "Charlie Rangel: Jack Brooks was 'one of the most cantankerous damned people I have ever met in my life.'" *Houston Chronicle,* December 5, 2012.

Los Angeles Times. "NRA vows to retaliate over assault weapon ban." May 8, 1994.

Martin, Douglas. "Jack Brooks, Former Texas Congressman, Dies at 89." *New York Times,* December 5, 2012.

Merry, George B. "Bullet bill unites pro- and anti-gun lobbies." *Christian Science Monitor,* July 9, 1984.

Messmer, Ellen. "'Politics as Usual' stalling House Anti-Trust Reform Act." IDG Network World Inc. 9, no. 29 (July 20, 1992).

Panetta, Leon. Interview with Chris Bury. Frontline PBS, June 2000.

Pressley, Sue Anne. "A Symbol of 'Academic Pork,' Lamar U. Feels Aggrieved." *Washington Post,* August 20, 1994.

Reuters. "Dingell Quits NRA Board, Votes for Crime Bill," August 22, 1994.

Rosenblatt, Robert A. "Insurers Group Agrees to Back Reform Bill: Legislation: Reduction in antitrust protection could mean lower prices. AIA hopes action will defuse consumer anger." *Los Angeles Times,* May 27, 1994.

Ross, Michael. "Vote on Crime Bill Is Blocked; Major Setback for Clinton: Legislation: Narrow 225–210 defeat on procedural rule in House may kill $33.2-billion measure for year. President denounces GOP and gun-control opponents." *Los Angeles Times,* August 12, 1994.

Schuster, Fred J. "Letters in the Editor's Mailbag: Recheck gun facts." *Eugene Register-Guard,* August 28, 1985.

Seelye, Katharine Q. "Assault Weapons Ban Allowed to Stay in Anti-crime Measure." *New York Times,* July 28, 1994.

Shannon, James. "Our man Jack: Rep. Jack Brooks, 1922–2012." *The Examiner: The Independent Voice of Southeast Texas,* December 5, 2012.

Shannon, Kelley. "Gun Control Bills Dominate National Rifle Association Meeting." Associated Press, April 15, 1991.

Stein, Mark A. and Peter H. King. "Rifleman Kills Five at Stockton School: 29 Other Pupils Hurt; Assailant Takes Own Life." *Los Angeles Times,* January 18, 1989.

Suro, Roberto. "The 1992 Campaign: The Youth Vote; Democrats Court Youngest Voters." *New York Times,* October 30, 1992.

Trumbull, Charles P., ed. Britannica Book of the Year: 1995.

United States House of Representatives (website). "The Honorable John D. Dingell." Archived Biography. Internet Archive, the Way Back Machine.

UPI. "Schoolyard gunman called a troubled drifter." *Deseret News,* January 18, 1989.

Wakeman, Nick. "Jack Brooks, father of modern procurement, dies at 89." WashingtonTechnology.com, December 5, 2012.

Willis, Charles I. The Brooks Act: Is it Relevant Today? MA thesis, Naval Postgraduate School, 1994.

Yarowsky, Jonathan. In discussion with author, 2004.

1994 ELECTION

Brooks, Jack. In discussion with the author.

Clinton, William J. *My Life.* New York: Vintage Books, 2005.

Evans, Diana. *Greasing the Wheels: Using Pork Barrel Projects to Build Majority Coalitions in Congress.* Cambridge: Cambridge University Press, 2004.

Ivins, Molly and Lou Dubose. *Shrub: The Short but Happy Political Life of George W. Bush.* New York: Knopf Doubleday Publishing Group, 2002.

Lichtman, Allan J. *White Protestant Nation: The Rise of the American Conservative Movement.* New York: Grove Press, 2009.

Matts, Sharon. In discussion with the author.

The *New York Times* Biographical Service, Vol. 25. *New York Times* & Arno Press, 1994.

Woodward, Bob. *The Agenda: Inside the Clinton White House.* New York: Simon & Schuster, 1994.

EPILOGUE

Andrues, Wes. "The Clinger-Cohen Act, 10 Years Later: Becoming Enterprise Architects." *Government Executive,* July 25, 2006.

Armey, Dick and Matt Kibbe. *Give Us Liberty: A Tea Party Manifesto.* New York: HarperLuxe, 2010.

Austin American-Statesman. "Rep. Brooks's long tenure in danger – The crime bill, his incumbency may sink the Democrat's bid for a 22nd term." October 22, 1994.

Aych, Joshua. "Council aims to grow LU spirit, tradition." *University Press: The Newspaper of Lamar University,* October 1, 2015.

Balz, Dan. "GOP 'Contract' Pledges 10 Tough Acts to Follow." *Washington Post,* November 20, 1994.

Balz, Dan. Interview on *Storming the Gates: Protest Politics and the Republican Revival.* C-SPAN Booknotes, February 18, 1996.

Banks, Gabrielle. "Ex-Congressman Steve Stockman gets 10 years in fraud case." *The Houston Chronicle,* November 8, 2018.

Berman, Russell. "Gallup: Tea Party's top concerns are debt, size of government." *The Hill,* July 5, 2010.

Biden, Joseph. *The Importance of Community Policing—Solutions: American Leaders Speak Out on Criminal Justice.* Brennan Center for Justice, 2015.

Chettiar, Inimai M. and Lauren-Brooke Eisen. *The Complex History of the Controversial 1994 Crime Bill.* Brennan Center for Justice, April 14, 2016.

Clinton, William J. *Foreword—Solutions: American Leaders Speak Out on Criminal Justice.* Brennan Center for Justice, 2015.

Cobb, Joshua. "Charlotte Collins Brooks: widow of late congressman, Dies at 78." *The Examiner, The Independent Voice of Southeast Texas,* April 22, 2014.

Correctional Populations in the United

States: 1990—2014. U.S. Department of Justice, Office of Justice Programs, Bureau of Justice Statistics, 2016.

Dallas Morning News. "Stockman traveled from aimless youth to halls of Congress; Texas Republican says religion saved him from 'colorful' past." June 11, 1995

Diaz, Kevin. "Cigars and civil rights: Remembering Texas congressional legend Jack Brooks." *Houston Chronicle,* September 12, 2017.

Dickinson, Tim. "The NRA vs. America: How the country's biggest gun-rights group thwarts regulation and helps put military-grade weapons in the Hands of Killers." *Rolling Stone,* February 14th, 2013.

Dreyfuss, Robert. "Political Snipers." *The American Prospect,* Fall 1995.

Dunham, Richard and Dan Wallach, et al. "Texas Political Legend 'never afraid to fight.'" MySanAntonio.com, December 6, 2012.

Eckholm, Erik. "Prison Rate Was Rising Years Before 1994 Law." *New York Times,* April 10, 2016.

The Fact. "Democratic chairman files EEG complaint against Stockman." June 6, 1996.

Firearms Commerce in the United States Annual Statistical Update, 2014. United States Department of Justice, Bureau of Alcohol, Tobacco, Firearms and Explosives.

Fuller, Jaime. "It's been 20 years since the Brady bill passed. Here are 11 ways gun politics have changed." *Washington Post,* February 28, 2014.

Gerth, Heff. "Hillary Clinton's Email Scandal Looks a Lot Like the Whitewater Investigation of 20 Years Ago." *Pacific Standard,* March 16, 2015.

Gillman, Todd J. "In 1995, Stockman admitted jail time, felony charge. Today

he denies that, accusing Cornyn allies of lying." *Dallas Morning News,* January 31, 2014.

Gillman, Todd J and Nick Swartsell. "Lawmakers on right aren't flocking to help Stockman unseat Cornyn." *Dallas Morning News,* December 11, 2013.

Gizzi, John. "Steve Stockman vies for 36th Texas District seat." *Human Events: Powerful Conservative Voices,* July 7, 2012.

Goldin, Daniel. In discussion with the author, 2017.

Good, Chris. "The Tea Party Movement: Who's in Charge?" *The Atlantic,* April 13, 2009.

Government Computer News. "GCN's top executives of the past 22 years." October 4, 2005.

Graham, David A. "From Whitewater to Benghazi: A Clinton-Scandal Primer." *The Atlantic,* November 6, 2016.

Heath, David, Elise Hansen, and AJ Willingham. "How an 'ugly,' unwanted weapon became the most popular rifle in America." CNN.com, December 14, 2017.

Hooks, Christopher. "Good Riddance to Steve Stockman: Fake candidates are ruining American politics. It's time to start ignoring them." *Politico,* March 7, 2014.

Houston Chronicle. "Stephen Takach for District 36," editorial. July 12, 2012.

Houston Chronicle. "Stockman knows about jail, homelessness" July 23, 1995.

Jordan, Jerry. "Move to honor former U.S. Rep Jack Brooks." *The Examiner: The Independent Voice of Southeast Texas,* March 26, 2010.

Joseph, Cameron and Molly K. Hooper. "Lawmakers: Cornyn will easily defeat Stockman." *The Hill,* December 10, 2013.

Keneally, Meghan. "What's Inside the Controversial 1994 Crime Bill That's

Plaguing Hillary Clinton on the Campaign Trail." ABC News, April 11, 2016.

Klinkner, Philip A. *Midterm: the elections of 1994 in context.* Westview, 1996.

Kopan, Tal. "Stockman rips press over MIA claim." *Politico,* January 27, 2014.

Ladd, Chris. "The Myth of the Southern Strategy." *Houston Chronicle,* February 10, 2015.

Levin, Matt. "Despite all the rhetoric, Texas gun ownership rates just above national average." *Houston Chronicle,* June 30, 2015.

Lieberman, Samuel. "The Murder Rate in Chicago Is Up 84 Percent This Year." *New York Magazine,* March 29, 2016.

Limbaugh, Rush. "Remarks at the Heritage Foundation Congressional Freshman Orientation." C-SPAN, 1994.

Merida, Kevin. "Rush Limbaugh Saluted as a 'Majority Maker.'" *Washington Post,* December 11, 1994.

McCabe, David. "Bill Clinton renounces his 1994 crime bill." *The Hill,* May 6, 2015.

McCarty, James. Ben Suarez sentenced to 15 months in federal prison for witness-tampering, fined $15,000." *Plain Dealer,* November 14, 2014.

Miller, Jason. "Brooks honored as father of modern procurement." *Government Computer News,* November 1, 2002.

Mitchell, Chris. "The Killing of Murder: As the homicide rate continues to drop, the impossible beckons: What would it take to go all the way to zero?" *New York Magazine,* January 7, 2008.

Murphy, Tim. "Steve Stockman Is the Nuttiest Freshman in Congress—Again." *Mother Jones,* January 23, 2013.

Narula, Svati Kirsten, Ryan Jacobs, and Judith Ohikuare. "32 Republicans Who Caused the Government Shutdown: Meet the House conservative hardliners." *The Atlantic,* October 4, 2013.

New Americans in Texas: The Political and Economic Power of Immigrants, Latinos, and Asians in the Lone Star State. American Immigration Council. January 2015.

NICS Firearm Background Checks: Year by State/Type. Federal Bureau of Investigation, 2016.

Nolan, Heather. "Attorney wants airport re-named for Jack Brooks." *Beaumont Enterprise,* March 26, 2010.

Onley, Dawn S. "Paige shares the praise with his staff." *Government Computer News,* November 15, 2002.

Orrenius, Pia M., Madeline Zavodny, and Melissa LoPalo. "Gone to Texas: Immigration and the Transformation of the Texas Economy." Federal Reserve Bank of Dallas, November 2013.

Peterson, D'Ann and Laila Assanie. "The Changing Face of Texas: Population Projections and Implications." Federal Reserve Bank of Dallas, October 2005.

Population Estimates of Texas Cities, 1990–99. Population Estimates Program, Population Division, U.S. Bureau of the Census.

Posner, Sarah. "How Steve Stockman is Challenging John Cornyn without Religion." Religion Dispatches, University of Southern California, Annenberg, December 10, 2013.

Puzzanchera, C. and W. Kang. *Easy Access to FBI Arrest Statistics 1994–2012.* National Center for Juvenile Justice, 2017.

Rogers, Brian and Margaret Kadifa. "Former U.S. Rep. Steve Stockman blames 'deep state' conspiracy for arrest: Federal charge unsealed Friday says he lied on campaign reports." *Houston Chronicle,* March 17, 2017.

Rutkus, Denis Steven. Judicial Nominations by President Clinton During the

103rd and 104th Congresses. Congressional Research Service, The Library of Congress. January 24, 1997.

Sanchez, Humberto. "113th Congress: Steve Stockman, R-Texas (36th District)." *Congressional Quarterly,* November 6, 2012.

Scarborough, Rick. "Enough is Enough." *FrontLine,* 2008.

Skocpol, Theda. "Why the Tea Party Isn't Going Anywhere: The movement's structure means it can withstand low popularity and continue to exert a huge pull on the GOP." *The Atlantic,* December 26, 2013.

Theda Skocpol and Vanessa Williamson. *The Tea Party and the Remaking of Republican Conservatism.* Oxford: Oxford University Press, 2012.

Sattler, Brian. "Memorial service for Hon. Jack Brooks to be held 2 p.m. Sunday." *Lamar University News & Events,* December 6, 2012.

Seelye, Katharine Q. "The 104th Congress: The Pension Plan; Gingrich on Tightrope Over Congress's Pensions." *New York Times,* January 18, 1995.

Snyder, Howard N. Arrest in the United States, 1990–2010. U.S. Department of Justice, Office of Justice Programs, Bureau of Justice Statistics. October 2012.

Stevens, John Paul. *Six Amendments: How and Why We Should Change the Constitution.* Little, Brown and Company, 2014.

Stolberg, Sheryl Gay. "Gingrich Stuck to Caustic Path in Ethics Battles." *New York Times,* January 26, 2012.

Swartsell, Nick. "NRA backs Cornyn; another gun group supports Stockman in Senate race." *Dallas Morning News,* December 18, 2013.

Swartz, Mimi. "Congressman Clueless: A year after East Texas voters elected political novice Steve Stockman to fight in Newt Gingrich's Republican revolution, Stockman's harebrained ideas and headline-making gaffes have made him the laughingstock of his own party." *Texas Monthly,* February 1996.

Vindicator. "Meet the candidates for U.S. Senate and U. S. Congress, District 36." October 11, 2012.

Wallach, Dan. "Memorial service set for Charlotte Brooks, wife of former congressman." *Beaumont Enterprise,* April 22, 2014.

Wallach, Dan and Richard Dunham. "Brooks remembered as a 'legend.'" *Beaumont Enterprise,* December 6, 2012.

Washington Post. "The Whitewater Timeline." 1998.

Weisman, Jonathan and Chris Cillizza. "DeLay to Resign from Congress." *Washington Post,* April 4, 2006.

Index